FINDING THE COLLEGE THAT'S RIGHT FOR YOU

John Palladino, Ed.D.

McGraw-Hill

New York   Chicago   San Francisco
Lisbon   London   Madrid   Mexico City
Milan   New Delhi   San Juan   Seoul
Singapore   Sydney   Toronto

This book is dedicated to all my children—Adam, John Matthew, Jackie, and Jessica—for their silence, their pain, their laughter, and their joy, and the promise of an everlasting life together.

A special dedication is for my twin brother, Anthony, whose generous, enduring heart—similar to all great colleges and universities—brings out the best in those who have the pleasure of his company.

The McGraw-Hill Companies

Copyright ©2004 by John Palladino, Ed.D. All rights reserved. Printed in the United States of America. Except as permitted under the United States Copyright Act of 1976, no part of this publication may be reproduced or distributed in any form or by any means, or stored in a data base or retrieval system, without the prior written permission of the publisher.

Library of Congress Cataloguing-in-Publication Data

Palladino, John.
   Finding the college that's right for you / John Palladino.
     p. cm.
   Includes bibliographical references and indexes.
   ISBN 0-07-142306-0 (alk. paper)
   1. College choice—United States. 2. Universities and colleges—United States—Directories.   I. Title.
   LB2350.5.P36 2005
   378.73—dc22

                        2004012719

1 2 3 4 5 6 7 8 9 0   DOC/DOC   0 9 8 7 6 5 4

ISBN 0-07-142306-0

This publication is designed to provide accurate and authoritative information in regard to the subject matter covered. It is sold with the understanding that neither the author nor the publisher is engaged in rendering legal, accounting, or other professional service. If legal advice or other expert assistance is required, the services of a competent professional person should be sought.
        —From a declaration of principles jointly adopted by a committee of the American Bar Association and a committee of publishers.

 This book is printed on recycled, acid-free paper containing a minimum of 50% recycled de-inked fiber.

McGraw-Hill books are available at special quantity discounts to use as premiums and sales promotions, or for use in corporate training programs. For more information, please write to the Director of Special Sales, Professional Publishing, McGraw-Hill, Two Penn Plaza, New York, NY 10121-2298. Or contact your local bookstore.

CONTENTS

INTRODUCTION

There is a funny line, very much relevant to this book's focus, and it goes something like this: "College is great! Where else can you get your parents to pay $100,000 so that you can live on your own and party for four years!" For many college students in this country, this is a very apt description of the essence of their four years devoted to a college "education." Considering the significant truth of this situation, why then do approximately 30 percent of freshmen at American colleges not return for their sophomore years? This appears to be quite a paradox, deserving greater analysis.

The overwhelming number of students graduating from high school can be termed "midrange" students. These are not students who studied advanced placement college-level courses, nor are they students who were enrolled in honors-level courses. The typical high school graduate studied an academic program leading to a high school diploma. Upon completion of their studies, they were either C or B students with SAT 1 scores in the range of 900 to 1,050. This midrange academic profile fits the entrance criteria for the largest segment of American colleges and universities. These colleges and universities are rated either "competitive" or "moderately difficult." In fact, there are about 600 of these four-year institutions, which will gladly accept the tuition of these midrange students.

The problem—and the focus of this book—is that only about 25 percent of these colleges and universities would be "best" choices for these midrange students. That's right. After examining the main and typically accepted criteria that help to create a quality college experience, there are only 150 schools that I would confidently recommend to students.

In a nutshell, what is happening year after year is that students and families are making poor decisions regarding college selection. And, for the most part, who can blame them? Inundated with marketing materials from college admissions offices and seduced by the ease of getting information via the internet, students and parents mistakenly confuse information with the wisdom that comes from experience. Let's face it: For the midrange student, college selection decisions are made based upon tuition, campus location, campus facilities, and the availability of certain areas of study. These are the very factors that admissions offices highlight in their slick marketing materials and internet web sites. Once the decision is made and students are dropped off at their dorms each fall, the joke line is quite true: You are paying a lot of money to educate your children, many of whom will be living independent of you (finally!) and partying three days a week.

But as the semester rolls by, multiple problems emerge for the student. He or she is falling behind in the work; there are harsh words and threats, and then come the considerations of transferring or dropping out. This book will help to prevent this scenario.

The first chapter helps you to identify "midrange" students. Chapter 2 considers the critical factors that should be reviewed by students, parents, and counselors in the college selection process. And the third and largest chapter identifies and describes the 150 best colleges for midrange students, based upon my study of the critical factors discussed in chapter 2.

The schools selected for this guide represent a broad diversity of private and public institutions, and even include 22 schools that accept students who have been home-schooled. The guide is comprised of 98 colleges and 52 universities.

This book is based upon my 30-plus years of experience as a teacher, professor, administrator, and college admissions specialist.

ACKNOWLEDGMENTS

It was wonderful working with Barbara Gilson, whose editorial direction included a flexibility that was crucial for the success of this project. Special thanks to my literary agent, Richard Curtis, whose talented eye saw a work that would truly benefit countless students and their families, provided a valuable mentoring, and had the wisdom to respect the unique approach a writer brings to such a work as this. Pattie Amoroso was superb in supervising the editing of the book. I also appreciated the "human face" Mary Loebig Giles gave the project when I needed it most.

For my inspiration and self-discipline, thanks be to God, always.

WHO ARE MIDRANGE STUDENTS?

Midrange high school seniors can be defined in terms of their high school grade point average, SAT or ACT scores, and rank in their graduating class.

In terms of grade point average, the midrange student typically achieves from a C through a low B, or numerically on a four-point scale, a 2.0–3.4 grade point average.

Scholastic Aptitude Test (SAT I) scores typically total in the 900–1050 range, often with either a math score considerably higher than the verbal score, or vice versa. American College Testing (ACT) scores usually range from 19–22.

The midrange student's rank in class is typically the middle of the graduating class: part of the middle 50 percent of the class, with 25 percent of the class graduating with a higher rank and 25 percent with a lower rank.

Both the higher ranked and lower ranked students typically receive a great deal of a school's attention and resources. The lowest ranked students have often failed many subjects, and as a result receive counseling, remedial instruction, and attend summer school. These are students who often enter the workforce upon graduation from high school, enter the military, attend a community college, or postpone decisions about their immediate futures.

The highest ranked students, those who have achieved grade point averages of B+ and above and SAT I scores above 1050 or ACT scores above 22, often receive the most attention from a high school staff. This is the population of students who will provide the greatest public relations for the school, so their college selection efforts are monitored very carefully, with hopes that several will gain acceptance to an Ivy League or other prestigious college.

The largest portion of midrange students are students who have worked to the best of their abilities. Also, midrange students usually have excellent attendance, good behavior, many friends, and are well liked by teachers.

Midrange students are in good—and very large—company. When you consider the thousands of high schools across the country and the fact that at the overwhelming majority of these schools midrange students represent 50 percent of the graduating class, we can easily conclude that the midrange student is the typical college applicant.

That's quite a sizable college freshman population! Fortunately, there are about 600 colleges and universities that typically accept midrange students. These colleges and universities are usually rated "competitive" or "moderately difficult." That number represents more than one-third of all the four-year regionally accredited colleges and universities in America! So there are obviously plenty of choices. That's the good news.

The bad news is that within this huge grouping of competitive colleges there are incredible differences in quality. How do you select the colleges to which you will apply? That is, which of these schools are the best ones? Fortunately, there are traditional, time-tested criteria that we can examine in order to determine an answer to this question. The next chapter will explain each of these critical criteria.

WHAT ARE THE MAJOR CHARACTERISTICS OF GREAT COLLEGES FOR MIDRANGE STUDENTS?

As was mentioned in the introduction, there are over 600 colleges that will accept students who have midrange high school academic performances, with grade point averages of C to B, and total SAT I scores that range from 900 to 1050. But just as there is a wide range of differences in the quality of high schools, there is a wide range—possibly wider—in the quality of these more than 600 colleges and universities. To help students, parents, and counselors with selection of the best of these schools, this chapter will identify and explain the most important characteristics that should be considered when selecting schools for application.

GRADUATION RATES

By far, the most significant indicator of a great college for midrange students is the graduation rates of the institution. These rates are usually stated in terms of four years, five years, and six years. The rates are typically stated as a statistic. For example: four years: 45 percent; five years: 55 percent; six years: 65 percent. What this means is that a freshman class that entered in the fall of 1996 had 55 percent of those freshmen graduate by 2001.

This is an incredibly revealing statistic that tells the most about the quality of the institution. If the statistic is high—above 50 percent for five years at a "competitive" or "moderately difficult" rated school—this says that the school is doing most things right. This would include the quality of instruction, advisement, counseling, food services, social

and athletic opportunities, and safety provisions.

I would discourage the consideration of the six-year statistic for several reasons. First, it is simply too long a period of time. You don't want to send a student to a college where students need to take six years to complete a bachelor's degree. In fact, there are many public state systems that are currently proposing legislation to reduce the amount of time that students take to earn a bachelor's degree. Also, some colleges will tell you of the great virtues of having students take a year off from school for travel or work and then return to complete their degrees. Nonsense! You would ideally want your student at a college that is not a "revolving door" atmosphere, but rather a learning community that is as stable as possible, with your student moving from his or her freshman year with the same cohort of students.

I advise my clients to consider only the four- and five-year graduation statistics. Colleges and universities that have a high percentage of students with declared majors early on in their four years, as well as schools that have students studying in programs with clear, direct career paths, such as education, will usually have a higher four-year graduation rate. Although those populations may also appear at colleges with high five-year graduation rates, often these schools have programs of study that require five years, such as architecture, or have students who are majoring in two areas of study and simply can't graduate in the four-year period. Some students may need to retake courses because of low or failing grades or decide to switch their major area of study.

All of the great colleges that have been chosen for this book have five-year graduation rates of at least 50 percent.

FIRST-YEAR RETENTION RATES

In many respects it is difficult to imagine a more challenging time for teenagers than going away to college, taking courses, studying, living independently, living with roommates, making new friends, establishing a social life, and, for some, playing a varsity sport. Yikes! Yet this is what is expected in that first year of college. Many don't make it through the first year, and about 30 percent don't return to the college for the second year. There are many reasons for this, including the challenge, the finances, illness, the social dimension, the academics, etc. However, in my college counseling practice, I have found that the major reason that students leave, either during or after the completion of the first year, is that they simply made the wrong choice of college.

The first-year retention rate is very important for you to consider. The midrange student will thrive in the most stable atmosphere offered by a college. If 30 percent of the students who are part of your student's freshman class—perhaps his or her roommate—leave and don't return, that means the college has to recruit that many more students to fill those empty slots. Numerically, if a college has 2,400 total students, with 600 students in its freshman class, and 30 percent of that freshman class doesn't return the second year, the college has lost 180 students from its freshman class. This results in a "revolving door" atmosphere, where friendships and a school community become compromised.

I recommend to my clients who have midrange students that they should consider colleges and universities with a freshman year drop-out rate that is 25 percent or lower. All of the colleges and universities in this guide meet this important criterion.

TOTAL NUMBER OF STUDENTS

Midrange students appear to have greater success at institutions that have an average total school population of between 900 and 7,500 students. This population range comprises about 85 percent of American four-year colleges. Larger student populations tend to reduce the intimacy of a college campus, making college life more impersonal and often unwieldy and overwhelming for the midrange student. Dormitories and cafeterias are overcrowded, classes are too large, course registration is a horror, and professors are difficult to find when they are out of the classroom.

At the other extreme, schools with fewer than 900 students hardly seem like colleges, with many students coming from high schools of the same population or larger. At these colleges, it is often difficult to register for courses in semesters when students prefer taking them. Also, academic departments are too small, so that in some major areas of study students will have the same professor for the majority of courses in that major. At these colleges, the small size of the student population also limits most aspects of campus life outside of the classroom.

The college or university that has a student population ranging from 900 to 7,500 students provides the midrange student with few hurdles and constraints. The size is ideal for creating a genuine learning community of accessible professors and motivated students. All of the great colleges I have selected have this population range.

PERCENTAGE OF FULL-TIME FACULTY

A typical professor at a college or university that admits midrange students has the following workload: teaches four courses each fall and spring semester; conducts research that will hopefully lead to the publishing of an article or book; attends professional conferences either to deliver a presentation or just to stay abreast of the latest developments in his or her field; advises students; keeps office hours in order to meet with students; and is required to be on campus three to four days each week. The typical professor receives a yearly salary according to his or her rank, along with pension and health benefits. There are also opportunities to conduct special research or projects for which the professor is assigned fewer courses to teach. Also, every few years, a professor can request and receive a sabbatical leave of absence from the institution in order to study, travel, or conduct research related to his or her field of study. The professor receives a significant percentage of his or her full-time salary during this sabbatical leave.

If all faculty at an institution were full-time faculty receiving the above mentioned benefits, the overwhelming percentage of institutions would have difficulty paying their bills and would have to significantly increase tuition so that few families would entertain making application to these schools. Instead, the compromise position has been to hire "adjunct" faculty, who are typically employed to teach one or two courses. These professors receive payment for the courses taught, but do not receive any of the other benefits that full-time faculty receive, thereby saving the college great sums of money.

However, the downside for students is that these adjunct professors typically don't provide any of the other services provided by full-time faculty, such as student advisement, service on committees, and keeping office hours to help students. These faculty are essentially "phantom" professors who are on campus to teach a course or two and then leave. They provide nothing to the ongoing living–learning community of a great college.

The best use of these adjunct faculty is especially apparent when a current practitioner is hired to share expertise in an art, music, business, or education course. Most adjuncts are very happy to have this chance to teach because it is very different from what they usually do during their regular workdays. Other adjuncts are dissatisfied faculty who haven't been able to land a full-time college position. And then a small fraction of adjuncts have carved careers for themselves by teaching at many different colleges, literally using their cars as their offices.

There is a threshold that great colleges are keenly aware of and one that is often reinforced by the state education departments and accrediting associations that sanction the granting of degrees by each college and university: hire just the right number of adjuncts and you add great relevancy and vibrancy to your programs; hire too many adjuncts and you undermine the living–learning community that you are working so hard to create and maintain.

The great colleges for midrange students that I have selected all have a full-time faculty that make up more than 40 percent of the total faculty, with most schools having a much higher percentage.

PERCENTAGE OF FACULTY WITH DOCTORATES

A key indicator of the quality of faculty employed by a college or university is the number of faculty who have earned a doctorate, either a Ph. D. or an Ed. D. This is considered the highest degree in most fields of study. Importantly, in order to earn this degree, the professor had to conduct a research project, was supervised by a faculty mentor knowledgeable in that field of study, prepared a written report called a dissertation, and defended this report before a group of faculty. The effort exerted by the professor is a great one, typically requiring several years of work. The fruits of this labor are significant: learning how to conduct research, perform the role of mentor to students, offer constructive criticism, and conduct oneself professionally. Indeed, outside of the visual and performing arts, where professors often earn an M.F.A. (Master of Fine Arts) as a terminal degree, it is difficult to consider a faculty member a "professor" if he or she hasn't earned the doctorate.

Although the highest degree is not a guarantee of great faculty performance, I believe that it increases the chances that students will have more opportunities to learn about their professors' research as well as be supported in their own; that professors will have learned some of the key aspects of mentoring and provide this for their own students; that professors will offer even-handed criticism of student writing, speaking, reports, and performance providing intelligent insights for student growth and learning; and that the long academic journey to the doctorate has made such an indelible mark that the professor acts with integrity and professionalism, reflecting a commitment to this noble vocation.

At least 65 percent of the faculty at all of the great colleges that I have chosen hold a doctorate or other terminal degree.

ACCREDITATIONS

All colleges require the approval of a regional accrediting association in order to grant degrees to their students. In essence, these associations provide a "seal of approval" for the public, indicating that the institution has met a minimum set of established criteria that allow the institution to call itself a college or university. Without this institutional accreditation, degrees could not be granted, and without incoming tuition, the institution would cease to exist.

More important for you to consider are the program accreditations. If a college or university offers degrees in education, nursing, business, engineering, etc., you would want to know if the programs are accredited. If they are, this means that a specific professional association responsible for accrediting a specific program received an application from the college or university to review its program. This application typically requires the particular program faculty and administrator to work as a team and devote considerable time to the application. Once the application has been reviewed by the relevant accrediting association, a team of faculty and administrators from other, noncompeting institutions will visit the applicant college and attend classes; speak with students, faculty, and administrators; and request additional supportive documents. When the team gives a favorable review, the program becomes an accredited one. This accreditation has met high and specific standards set by the accrediting association. Therefore, you can expect that a college or university having an accredited program in an area of your interest will in all probability be offering an excellent program.

The only caveat is that, while the accreditation is a symbol of program quality because it has satisfied significant criteria, such as having state-of-the-art curriculum, sufficient full-time faculty, appropriate faculty credentials, suitable facilities, etc., the accreditation should never be interpreted to indicate anything about the quality of teaching. Therefore, at some colleges and universities, your specific program of interest may not be an accredited one, but involves motivated, talented, accessible professors. Although this can be the situation at an accredited program as well, the accreditation should not be construed to guarantee this kind of teaching excellence.

Nevertheless, on the whole, accreditation provides you with a strong indication of program quality. As a result, in this guide I have highlighted those college programs that have received program accreditation.

PERCENTAGE OF TRANSFER STUDENTS

As mentioned earlier, there is typically a very high percentage of first-year students who don't return for their second year, as well as a smaller percentage of students who don't complete their full undergraduate program. Many of these students are simply at the wrong institution and decide to transfer to a more suitable school, either after their first semester or, more typically, at the end of their first year.

A second large group of transfer students are those students who have attended and graduated from a two-year community college and now transfer to a four-year school for two or more years in order to complete their bachelor's degrees. It is more likely that these students had less money available for tuition, were weaker academically and needed the remedial courses offered at community colleges, or were not ready for all the challenges of living and learning at a residential school and preferred the reassuring routines and comforts of home. Many four-year colleges have developed articulation agreements with community colleges, virtually assuring an easy transfer of the community college graduate's credits to a four-year program of study. In addition, in many states four-year colleges are mandated to accept all community college graduates from their home state.

High numbers of community college transfer students, while an economic boon for private four-year colleges, unfortunately function to erode the strength of a stable, living–learning academic community and increase the sense of a "revolving door" atmosphere. Further, many of these students arrive on campus ill prepared to work at the same level achieved by traditionally admitted students. This functions to lower the academic standards at these schools.

Because of the negative impact of transfer students on four-year colleges, the great colleges admit a small number of them. The colleges I have chosen as great colleges for midrange students admit 10 percent or fewer each year, with most of the schools admitting a much lower percentage.

STUDENT–FACULTY RATIO AND AVERAGE CLASS SIZE

Midrange students function best academically when they are in classes that are not overwhelming in size. When professors are assigned to large classes, having 50 or more students, their usual teaching strategy is lecture. In a lecture the professor prepares a lengthy verbal presentation, sometimes trying to anticipate student questions, sometimes using visual aids. In smaller classes the professor typically invites student participation, whether student questions, opinions, writing, or performance. The student is simply more actively engaged in the instruction, and research shows how important this engagement is for student learning.

The student–faculty ratio gives you a sense of the intimacy of the living–learning community. The higher the ratio, the less intimate and supportive the community. The lower the ratio, the more intimate and supportive the community. Ratios such as 30 students to 1 faculty member are reflective of institutions that are more concerned with the bottom line than the creation of a living–learning academic community that would allow midrange students to succeed. On the other hand, ratios such as 20 students to 1 faculty member reflect the institution's understanding of and commitment to the importance of smaller class sizes and greater interaction between faculty and students.

The great colleges I have chosen all have a student–faculty ratio of 20 to 1 and an average class size below 30 students, with the majority of institutions having smaller ratios and class sizes.

TRANSITION TO COLLEGE PROGRAMS

For most academically advanced students attending highly competitive colleges, the traditional freshman orientation program is sufficient to help students make a successful transition from high school to college. However, for the midrange student, colleges are finding they can better help this population make the transition by offering not only the traditional freshman orientation, but also at least one other well-designed component to the students' programs.

Some colleges offer either a first semester or full-year course, for credit or no credit, that introduces the new student to other freshmen within the context of an "Introduction to College" course. Here they will meet other new students, make friends, and discuss topics relevant to achieving success at the college, ranging from the location of important offices to library resources and study skills. The classes are typically small, so that there is much student interaction. Also, very importantly, the professor who teaches this course is interested in helping the students and recognizes the importance of this program to freshmen's success.

Another example of a transition program is a course or several courses that focus on general themes. For example, "Modern Man and the Future" could be a course that integrates knowledge and study from several different subject areas. Each week students would meet a different professor, with the objectives of the course being the same as the "Introduction to College" course, but presented in a more academic, intellectual context. An added objective, especially for students who haven't declared a major, is that students are exposed to learning from several areas of study, thereby providing students with an opportunity to collect information that might be helpful in determining a major.

While some of the colleges typically viewed as "very competitive" still offer only traditional summer orientation programs, the majority of the great colleges selected for this guide provide freshmen with additional courses or programs that facilitate the transition from high school to college.

COUNSELING, ACADEMIC SUPPORT, ACCOMMODATIVE SERVICES

Each of the selected great colleges has free psychological counseling services available to students experiencing difficulty in their personal lives. Family problems, relationships, loneliness, depression, substance abuse, and grief resolution are some issues addressed in counseling. Support groups may also be offered on such topics as assertiveness training, eating disorders, shyness, and use of alcohol. Typically, these psychological services are supervised by a licensed clinical practitioner. At times, students may be referred to a mental health service within the neighboring community, and a fee for services may be charged.

Academic support services are typically provided by a center staffed by professionals and students. Peer tutoring is provided as well as special help with writing and math skills. Study groups are often established. The professional staff also offers assistance with time management, exam preparation, effective reading techniques, note taking, and study skills.

Students with special learning needs requiring specific accommodations can also find these at the great colleges in this book. Only a few of these schools offer formal, structured programs for learning disabled students. These schools would have special admissions procedures for learning disabled students, trained professionals, additional fees, and compulsory participation. Students admitted to these structured programs receive services such as note takers, oral exams, tape recording in class, books on tape, and services provided by learning disabilities specialists.

Some of these great colleges offer coordinated services. They require voluntary participation by the student and offer more than just those services mandated by section 504 of the Rehabilitation Act of 1973, but not the comprehensive services of formal, structured programs. These services may entail small or no fees, and do not provide specialized and licensed professional staff. Accommodations may include advanced registration for courses, sign language interpreters, note takers, and extended test time.

Most of the colleges offer the basic services that put them in compliance with section 504 of the Rehabilitation Act of 1973. These schools will not have specialized or licensed professional staff, nor will they monitor student academic performance. However, the student does receive accommodative services as a result of the student's request and, often, documentation of disability. These services are typically provided through the academic support center.

All of the great colleges cited in this guide offer counseling and academic support services for all students, as well as accommodative services for students with disabilities. These student services, often thought of as peripheral to the college experience, are much more central to the success of the midrange student.

ATHLETICS, INTRAMURALS, CLUB OPPORTUNITIES

Many midrange students were athletes in high school. While a portion of high school athletes make one of their first critical college decisions and end their formal athletic careers in order to focus on academics and the rest of college life, most students in this category are eager to continue their athletic careers at the college level by playing a varsity sport.

For those students who either don't want to make the time commitment required by varsity sports or simply don't have the exceptional ability level, colleges offer intramural and/or club sports. The intramural programs are the most informal, with students from the same college playing against each other on a regular basis. It is expected that students may not always be able to attend. The focus is on working out and friendship. The club programs are more formal than the intramural ones and more competitive. Students try out for a club team, which follows a schedule to play against teams from other colleges.

In addition to athletic programs, colleges offer a multitude of nonathletic activities to provide students with meaningful activities outside the classroom. From student government, to jazz band, social service, film, and religious clubs, there's something for every student. And in that rare case when there isn't, students can propose a new club to the student council and receive monies to begin it.

All of the best colleges in this guide—with one exception—have vibrant athletic and club programs. Although the specific club programs are too numerous to cite specifically in each college's description, I have cited the NCAA Division in which each school participates, as well as listing the varsity sports for both men and women.

JOB PLACEMENT STATISTICS

Each four-year college campus has a career services center, which functions to help students secure jobs upon completion of the bachelor's degree, or provide guidance about pursuing graduate study. These centers may have as few as one full-time employee or as many as nine or more, depending on the size of the student population and the nature of the specific programs of study. The center's staff provides workshops for résumé writing, conducting job searches, and training in interviewing. Additionally they publish a timely newsletter, secure periodicals and directories helpful in the job and graduate school search,

and maintain student placement folders, which typically contain a transcript of courses, grades, and letters of recommendation. This file is typically sent to prospective employers at the student's request. The center also arranges for corporate recruiters to visit campus and interview students.

Over the last decade, much more attention and resources have been given to this component of the college. One reason is that an employed graduate makes for a happy alumnus or alumna, who will make yearly contributions to fund-raising conducted by his or her alma mater. A second reason is that many for-profit schools, both degree and non-degree granting, actually promise employment upon graduation. These schools represent a potential drain on a certain part of the midrange population who may be interested in studying business, computer programming, computer graphics, etc.

Colleges report their placement statistics in two areas: students employed and students in graduate school. These statistics are typically reported for the six-month period following graduation. When colleges for midrange students have a high percentage of students attending graduate school, for example 20 percent and above, good job placement numbers are usually 70 percent and above. When there are fewer students attending graduate school, good job placement numbers—excluding times of economic recession—should be over 80 percent, as is the case with the great schools chosen for this guide.

CORE AND PROGRAM DISTRIBUTION REQUIREMENTS

A typical college academic program is comprised of about 40 three-credit courses, totaling about 120 credits for graduation.

Historically, these courses of study were rigidly determined by the colleges. In the 1960s and 1970s, however, there was a shift toward flexibility that bordered on laxity: Students could study whatever they wanted, the only proviso being that they study a certain number of courses in a major subject area and complete about 120 credits in order to earn a bachelor's degree. Some colleges have never moved from this position, with students graduating with a smorgasbord curriculum of study.

Most colleges have evolved to the important position of requiring students to take courses in each of several general academic areas (for example, the humanities, social sciences, natural sciences, and mathematics) in addition to taking about 36 credits in their major area of study. The intent here is that students, through their course distribution requirements, will be exposed to a broad range of knowledge and skills, thereby assuring to the faculty and administration that their graduates will be intellectually well-rounded.

An even smaller number of colleges subscribe to an even more purposeful agenda in order to achieve this intellectually well-rounded graduate. These colleges, with great faculty effort and creativity, have designed a core group of courses—perhaps three or four—that are taken by all students. These courses are typically designed to integrate key learnings in several academic areas. These learnings are viewed as being critical and consistent with the values of the institution to the degree that faculty want the courses to function as sort of an institutional stamp or imprimatur. The faculty attempts to produce graduates who closely represent the values and beliefs of the college, as well as cultivating critical thinking and developing excellent writing and speaking skills.

All of the colleges and universities selected for this guide have either course distribution requirements or core requirements.

RESIDENTIAL AND COMMUTER COLLEGES

The great colleges I have chosen for midrange students, while represented by both residential and commuter schools, are primarily residential colleges. This means that a significant number of students who attend these schools live either on campus or in college housing nearby and do not live at home and commute to school. This is important for two reasons.

The first reason has to do with the creation of a living–learning community. When there is a high percentage of students living on or nearby campus, the opportunity to develop friendships and relationships increases. Also, the opportunity to share and discuss schoolwork and ideas in general is greatly increased. Students have greater access to one another and learn how to relate and interact more maturely.

The second reason has to do with the social life of the campus. When more students reside on the campus, the administration must provide more entertainment in the form of concerts, movies, plays, lectures, clubs, and athletics as well as constructing facilities to accommodate these. This means that students don't have to rely on bars and alcohol for entertainment.

At the same time, the guide also describes many commuter colleges that are great colleges because they have satisfied my rigorous selection criteria and will also provide excellent educations for those students who choose to live at home.

AAUP ENDORSEMENT

A very influential group in higher education is the American Association of University Professors (AAUP). Perhaps the most significant function performed by this association is that of "watchdog" for violations committed by college and university administrations and governing boards.

Typically, the working relationship between faculty and administration is spelled out either in a contract or governance policy or both. At times administrations have either taken actions or have actually placed in governance documents language that serves to undermine generally recognized principles of academic freedom and faculty tenure. Both of these represent the heart and soul of a college or university.

Academic freedom implies that faculty have the freedom to speak freely in classrooms, meetings, and conferences and pursue and publish research without constraint, even when what is said or written may be controversial or at odds with the majority opinion of the faculty or administration, or society at large. Tenure is the right to a certain set of procedures if a faculty member is not hired to stay

on after an arduous six-year probationary period has ended. Also, if charges are brought against faculty, or if departments have lost enrollment, tenure provides for a well-defined series of steps involving review, consultation, and evaluation. The tenured professor is a full-time faculty member who, by virtue of his or her outstanding probationary performance, has earned this tenured status.

The American Association of University Professors, either through its network of representatives on most college campuses or through its own investigations, discovers and determines that unsatisfactory conditions of academic freedom exist or that violations of tenure have occurred or can occur as a result of existing contractual or governance language. The AAUP then publishes a list of the names of these institutions. This list serves to censure the administrations and trustees for their wrongdoings and encourages their prompt remediation so that the names of these institutions may be removed from the censure list at the association's next annual meeting.

As of June 2003, none of the great colleges cited in this guide are on this censure list.

INDIVIDUAL PROFILES OF THE 150 GREAT COLLEGES FOR MIDRANGE STUDENTS

EXPLANATORY NOTES

This chapter will provide complete descriptions of each of the 150 great colleges for midrange students. Each description has a factual, statistical section followed by a section that attempts to provide the reader with the heart or essence of the college, the key aspects that help to distinguish it from the others. Much of the factual, statistical part is self-explanatory, with only a few sections and terms that warrant clarification.

The Tuition and cost of Room and Board are indicated by dollar ($) signs, with the number of dollar signs reflecting a cost range. It is important for families to keep in mind that colleges and universities also charge fees for activities, health, and even technology. These fees may range from $300 to $3,000 per year, affecting overall costs. The tuition range of $16,001 to $22,000 is where the reader will find most (60 percent) of the schools described in this guide, while most (40 percent) of the schools charge room and board costs in the $3,000 to 6,000 range.

TUITION	ROOM AND BOARD
$=$3,000–$10,000	$=$3,000–$6,000
$$=$10,001–$16,000	$$=$6,001–$7,000
$$$=$16,001–$22,000	$$$=$7,001–$8,000
$$$$=$22,001–$29,000	$$$$=$8,001–$10,000

The Top Programs of Study are the academic programs in which most students are enrolled. The most popular program is listed first, the second most popular program listed second, etc. The reader should keep in mind that at most institutions there is not a great difference in enrollment numbers for these top programs.

Following the Top Programs of Study are all of the programs offered by the institution and categorized as either Arts and Sciences, Business, Education, or Pre-Professional. The Pre-Professional programs are those that typically provide the students with courses that are required for entrance into a professional school leading to a degree in one of the professional areas, such as medicine, law, dentistry, and others. Often the college or university will have an adviser for students who indicate that they are interested in one of these professions.

Special Programs include cooperative (co-op) programs, which allow students to work in a career-related job while they are in college, earn a salary, and receive course credit. Also, some colleges offer 3–2 degrees, whereby students spend their first three years on their home campus, and then the next two years at a different college or university that offers a specialized program, such as engineering, that is not offered at their home campus. These are actually dual-degree programs, whereby the student earns a bachelor's degree from both institutions.

Similarly, a 3-4 program offers students a bachelor's degree after three years of study at the student's home college. If the student is then admitted to a graduate or professional program affiliated with the home college—for example, schools of dentistry and medicine—

the student receives an M.D. after four years of study at the second institution.

This is also true with 3-3 programs. For example, when colleges or universities have their own law school, students who are admitted to the law school receive both a bachelor's and doctor of law degree when they graduate from the law school.

Student Life and Housing provides important information about the number of students that the institution can accommodate in college housing and whether that housing is guaranteed for all four years. If no guarantee is indicated—and many institutions do not offer this—students usually find housing near the college campus. Perhaps most important, the section also provides the reader with the degree of student diversity on campus—both racial/ethnic diversity and geographic diversity. Students who are looking for greater diversity would look with favor at those colleges and universities that have a mix of racial and ethnic groups as well as students from many states and foreign countries. Those students who prefer a more homogeneous student population and feel more comfortable with students of the same race, ethnicity, or geographical background will find that information in this section. When the Caucasian population—or African-American population at a historically black institution—was below 90 percent, the entry provides information listing the other racial and ethnic groups.

Accommodations for Students with Disabilities provides helpful information, such as the level of services and contact details for people or offices. When institutions do not provide detailed information about their accommodations and services, the entry simply states "In compliance with section 504," indicating that they are at least in compliance with the federal law regarding the Rehabiliation Act of 1973

and do provide reasonable accommodations and services when requested, documented, and evaluated on a case-by-case basis.

The Financial Aid section offers the latest statistics provided by the institution. While some had complete numbers, others projected their percentages and awards from a recent year. Nevertheless, the statistics reflect the total of all forms of financial aid offered to students.

The Application section indicates whether the institution has an Early Decision Plan or Early Action Program, along with application deadlines for each. With the Early Decision Plan, the applicant, in effect, is telling the college/university that it is the applicant's first-choice school and, if accepted, will withdraw all applications that the applicant has sent to other institutions. Under the Early Action Plan, the applicant is simply asking the institution to evaluate his or her application early and inform the student as to whether the college/university would be accepting the student. The student is under no obligation to enroll at that institution or withdraw all applications to other institutions.

Although many of the schools provide application deadlines, some do not. Instead, these institutions use a rolling admissions policy, whereby students send applications and, once the school receives all application materials, it makes an admissions evaluation, communicating the decision within a matter of weeks.

International Students who apply to these schools are usually required to take an examination assessing English language proficiency for nonnative speakers of English. The TOEFL is the Test of English as a Foreign Language, a multiple-choice exam consisting of three sections: Listening Comprehension, Structure and Written Expression, and Reading Comprehension.

ALBRIGHT COLLEGE
Reading, Pennsylvania

Total Undergraduate Enrollment: 2,076
Men: 907 Women: 1,169
Five-Year Graduation Rate: 67%

Tuition: $$$$
Room and Board: $$$
Residential Students: 70%

History The merger of three separate colleges was completed in 1929, with the college named after the founder of the original denomination, Jacob Albright. The college's United Methodist affiliation undergirds Albright's dedication to a values-based education.

Location Albright has a 100-acre campus located in a residential section of Reading, Pennsylvania (population 80,000) at the foot of Mount Penn, about 55 miles west of Philadelphia. The historic city of Reading celebrated its 250th birthday in 1998. In addition to being named for the famous Reading Railroad, Reading is also the home of the Reading Phillies minor league baseball team, as well as the major East Coast center for outlet shopping.

Top Programs of Study Business/marketing, psychology, social sciences, history

Arts and Sciences American civilization, art, art history, biochemistry, biology, chemistry, child and family studies, communications, computer science, criminal justice, cultural anthropology, digital media, English, environmental policy, environmental science, European studies, film/video, French, history, information systems, Latin American studies, marine science, mathematics, music, music business, optics, philosophy, photography, physics, political science, psychobiology, psychology, religious studies, sociology, Spanish, textiles and design, theater, visual and apparel merchandising, women's studies

Business Accounting, administration, economics, finance, international business, management, marketing

Education Art, early childhood, elementary, secondary, special

Pre-Professional Dentistry, law, medicine, veterinary medicine

Accredited Programs Accounting, chemistry, economics, business

Special Programs Students have the opportunity to shadow medical professionals in Albright's rotation program at Reading Hospital. Students can also conduct professional-level research in Hawaii, Iceland, and Bermuda. There are cooperative programs in environmental studies, forestry, and natural resources management with Duke and the University of Michigan.

Facilities There are 36 buildings, including a center for the arts and a licensed child development center that includes preschool, kindergarten, and extended daycare programs. The campus center contains bowling lanes. There is an indoor swimming pool, a comprehensive life sports center, a radio station, and the Freedman Art Gallery. Students have access to outstanding labs in the natural sciences, including a rare immunology lab.

Transition to College Program Albright's First Year Orientation provides new students with the information, knowledge, and confidence needed for a successful transition to college life. Students are given the necessary tools to adjust to the academic life of college and to be successful as a college student and beyond.

Athletics NCAA III, Middle Atlantic Conference, Philadelphia Association of Intercollegiate Athletics for Women

Men: Baseball, basketball, cross-country, football, golf, soccer, swimming, tennis, track & field, wrestling

Women: Badminton, basketball, cheerleading, cross-country, field hockey, soccer, softball, swimming, tennis, track & field, volleyball

Student Life and Housing About 1,100 students can be accommodated in college housing, which is guaranteed for all four years. Sixty-seven percent of the students are from Pennsylvania, the remainder from 26 other states and 21 countries. Ethnicity: Caucasian—82 percent; African-American—7 percent; International—4 percent; Hispanic-American—3 percent; Asian-American—2 percent. There are three national fraternities and three national sororities. Upperclassmen may keep cars.

Accommodations for Students with Disabilities In compliance with section 504

Financial Aid About 85 percent of all freshmen receive aid. The average award was about $17,700.

Requirements for Admission SAT I or ACT scores and a college prep high school program.

Application Applications should be submitted before March 1. Students are notified of an admission decision on a rolling basis, typically two to three weeks after their application is complete.

International Students It is strongly recommended that students take both the TOEFL and SAT.

Transfer Students Students should submit an application, essay, transfer application form, at least one teacher recommendation, and official transcripts from the colleges attended. A high school transcript is required if the student has completed fewer than 24 credit hours of transferable courses at the time of application. Admission is available in both fall and spring semesters. Fall application deadline is July 15; spring deadline is December 15. Students typically receive credit for courses with a grade of C or better.

Admission Contact
Office of Admissions
Albright College
13th and Bern Streets
P.O. Box 15234
Reading, PA 19612-5234
Phone: (800) 252-1856; (610) 921-7512
FAX: (610)-921-7294
E-mail: *Albright@alb.edu*
Web: *www.albright.edu*

The Heart of the College Albright College is a place where you make connections. Academically, the focus is on helping students see the interconnectedness of all things. This is particularly motivated by the interdisciplinary foundation courses offered to students. As an example, the college's new Johnson Centers for Multidisciplinary Studies prepares students for the twenty-first century by focusing on Latin American studies, cultural ecology, and digital media.

Albright will also encourage students to make connections to foreign countries. Its alliances with colleges, universities, institutions, and organizations for foreign study provide connections with England, France, Germany, Mexico, Spain, Iceland, Korea, Poland, Israel, and others.

The college's interactive classrooms foster other kinds of connections. Students in a Spanish class might e-mail a student in Chile, or students may participate in an environmental trip to the Galapagos Islands. Professors help students cross the boundaries of a particular subject to see connections with others.

Connections between students and faculty are many as they pursue collaborative projects. One science student and her chemistry professor recently conducted research on the links between protein structures and cancer. Students are also able to present their findings at professional symposia.

Albright's Experience Program fosters more connections between classroom learning and cultural life outside the classroom. In this program students expand their sense of what it is to be human through an impressive array of nationally known guest speakers, faculty, student lectures, presentations, performances, theater productions, and art exhibits.

Finally, connections are made to the workplace via internships, practicums, field experiences, and clinicals. Internship opportunities include the Federal Reserve Board, Johnson and Johnson, National Institutes of Health, U.S. Senate, U.S. Attorney's Office, Walt Disney, and Vanity Fair Corporation.

Albright's supportive, flexible faculty and academic climate expand intellectual horizons and prepare students for careers through a multitude of interesting connections.

ALFRED UNIVERSITY
Alfred, New York

Total Undergraduate Enrollment: 2,000

Men: 1,000 Women: 1,000
Five-Year Graduation Rate: 65%

Tuition: $$$; SUNY College of Ceramics: $
Room and Board: $$$
Residential Students: 65%

History Alfred University was founded in 1836 as a private institution. It is the oldest coeducational institution in New York State and the second oldest in the country.

Location The 232-acre campus is located in Alfred, New York, a rural area 70 miles south of Rochester in western New York.

Top Programs of Study Art and design, business administration, ceramic engineering

Arts and Sciences Athletic training, biology/biological science, ceramic art and design, ceramic engineering, chemistry, communications, computer science, criminal justice, cross cultural studies, dramatic arts, economics, electrical/electronics engineering, English, environmental science, fine arts, French, geology, gerontology, glass, history, interdisciplinary studies, mathematics, mechanical engineering, performing arts, philosophy, physics, political science/government, public administration, science, sociology, Spanish

Business Accounting, administration and management, banking and finance, economics, management science, marketing/retailing/merchandising

Education Art, elementary, secondary

Pre-Professional None

Accredited Programs Art and design, business, engineering

Special Programs There are cooperative programs in engineering and business with Duke, Clarkson, Columbia, and SUNY/Brockport, and a five-year program in environmental engineering/forestry with Duke. There are opportunities for study abroad, Washington, D.C., and Albany, N.Y. Semesters, internships, student designed majors, and double majors. The SUNY College of Ceramics is located at Alfred and charges a lower SUNY tuition.

Facilities There are 54 buildings, mostly Georgian and modern brick, along with a stone castle; the new Miller Performing Arts Center; the Steinhem Museum; Olin, the new business building; the Powell Campus Center; a Glass Science Laboratory; and a radio station.

Transition to College Program The university offers a traditional orientation.

Athletics NCAA III, Empire 8 Athletic Conference

Men: Basketball, cross-country, equestrian sports, football, golf, skiing (cross-country), soccer, swimming, tennis, track & field

Women: Basketball, cross-country, equestrian sports, golf, skiing (downhill), soccer, softball, swimming, tennis, track & field, volleyball

Student Life and Housing About 1,300 students can be accommodated in college housing, which includes special interest houses, and housing is guaranteed for all four years. Sixty-nine percent of the students are from New York State, the remainder from 38 other states and 13 countries. Ethnicity: Caucasian—88 percent; African-American—4 percent; Hispanic-American—4 percent; Asian-American—2 percent; International—2 percent; There are two local and six national fraternities, and three local and one national sorority. All students may keep cars.

Accommodations for Students with Disabilities In compliance with section 504

Financial Aid About 90 percent of all freshmen receive aid. The average freshman award was about $19,000.

Requirements for Admission SAT I or ACT scores and a college prep high school program, or the GED. An interview is encouraged. Applicants to B.F.A. programs must submit a portfolio.

Application Freshmen are admitted to fall and spring semesters. Early Decision applications should be filed by December 1, with an admission decision made by December 15. Regular applications should be filed by February 1 for fall admission and December 1 for spring admission, with an admission decision made by March 15.

International Students Applicants whose native language is not English must score a minimum of 550 on the TOEFL.

Transfer Students Required are official high school and college transcripts, an overall minimum GPA of 2.5, and at least one letter of recommendation. Art students must submit a portfolio. The last 30 credits must be completed at Alfred.

Admission Contact
Office of Admissions
Alfred University
Alumni Hall
Saxon Drive
Alfred, NY 14802
Phone: (800) 541-9229; (607) 871-2115
FAX: (607)-871-2115
E-mail: *hooker@alfred.edu*
Web: *www.alfred.edu*

The Heart of the University Why would students be attracted to a university located in a tiny town, a very rural area with very cold winters, about 70 miles to the nearest metropolitan area, and a fairly sedate social scene? The answer is distinctive academic programs and a supportive campus community. At Alfred University, a strong liberal arts college, the programs that act as magnets for students are ceramic engineering, ceramics, glassworks, and business administration. The university has the unique distinction of "hosting" the State University of New York's College of Ceramics, which contains two schools: the School of Ceramic Engineering (the development and refinement of ceramics materials) and the School of Art and Design. Students interested in studying in internationally recognized programs, ironically, pay a tuition that is only one-third of the regular Alfred tuition. This is surely one of the best bargains in higher education, and about one-third of the students at Alfred study in these two schools of the university. Even the number of buildings on campus devoted to ceramics demonstrate the program's significance. There is the school's Library of Ceramics, housing the largest ceramic engineering research collection in the world; the International Museum of Ceramic Art; and the Center for Ceramic Technology. With Corning, New York, nearby, the home of Corningware, there is an important connection here.

A strong business program and engineering program complement a significant core program within the liberal arts. Students find the academics challenging. But Alfred can boast of a very supportive student and faculty community, where talented professors view their primary responsibilities to be teaching and advising. The personal attention from faculty and easily formed friendships help students achieve.

While fraternities and sororities are an important part of the social scene, the Student Activities Committee schedules movies and dances, brings comedians, musicians, and presenters to campus. Students are also noted to be health conscious and are attracted to intramurals, the fitness center, and the varsity program.

Ironically, while located in a rural area, Alfred shares the town with the State University of New York/College of Technology at Alfred and its 3,000 students, creating a "college town" dynamic. Alfred University offers 100 clubs and organizations.

In a typical year 97 percent of Alfred's graduates have either gained employment or entered graduate or professional schools within six months of graduation.

ALMA COLLEGE — Alma, Michigan

Total Undergraduate Enrollment: 1,400
Men: 590 Women: 810
Five-Year Graduation Rate: 70%

Tuition: $$$
Room and Board: $$
Residential Students: 85%

History Alma College was founded by Presbyterians in 1866 as a liberal arts and sciences college. The college was named to the Templeton Foundation's Honor Roll of Character-Building Colleges.

Location Alma is located on a 100-acre campus in a residential neighborhood of Alma, Michigan (population 10,000), 50 miles north of Lansing, the state capital, in the center of Michigan's lower peninsula. The college is two and a half hours northwest of Detroit and two hours from Michigan's beaches and ski areas.

Top Programs of Study Business, education, biology

Arts and Sciences Art and design, biochemistry, biology, chemistry, communication, computer science, dance, economics, English, exercise and health science, foreign service, French, German, history, mathematical sciences, music, philosophy/religious studies, physics, political science, psychology, sociology, anthropology, Spanish, theater

Business Administration, international business administration

Education Early childhood, elementary, secondary

Pre-Professional Dentistry, engineering graphic design, law, medical illustration, medicine, ministry and Christian education, occupational therapy, physical therapy

Accredited Programs Chemistry, music

Special Programs Alma has a nationally recognized Career Preparation Program, is a Phi Beta Kappa institution, and is a member of the Undergraduate Science Group because of its outstanding science programs. The college confers 3–2 engineering degrees with the University of Michigan, Michigan Technological University, and Washington University in St. Louis. McGregor Tutorials are mentor opportunities where faculty work with freshmen in the fall to design an independent research or performance project. There are internships, study abroad, and opportunities to spend semesters in Washington, D.C., and an Urban Life Center in Chicago, as well as a Stillman College Exchange. There are several interdisciplinary minors offered.

Facilities There are 25 buildings that surround a scenic central mall. Most of Alma's buildings have been built or renovated since the late 1950s, giving the campus a modern look. The Dow Science

Center has a greenhouse and planetarium. The newest building is McIntyre Center for Exercise and Health Science and a technology building is being proposed. Other facilities include the Heritage Center for the Performing Arts, the Beck Art Gallery, the Stone Center for Recreation, the Van Dunsen Campus Center, and the Dunning Memorial Chapel. Also, the college's ecological station is located about 12 miles west of the campus, a 185-acre tract that has been used for faculty/student research since 1889.

Transition to College Program Students are offered one-credit seminars given during Preterm Orientation when students get to know the campus and one another.

Athletics MCAA III, Michigan Intercollegiate Athletic Association

Men: Baseball, basketball, cross-country, football, golf, soccer, swimming and diving, tennis, track & field

Women: Basketball, cross-country, golf, soccer, softball, swimming and diving, tennis, track & field, volleyball

Student Life and Housing Almost all students can be accommodated in college housing, which includes a variety of options. Ninety-five percent of the students are from Michigan, the remainder from 21 other states and 13 countries. Ethnicity: Caucasian—93 percent. There are one local and four national fraternities, and one local and four national sororities. All students may keep cars.

Accommodations for Students with Disabilities Alma provides reasonable accommodations in programs, services, and classroom activities. Students need to contact the Dean of Student Development. Special services are also provided for visually- and hearing-impaired students.

Financial Aid About 98 percent of all students receive aid. The average freshman award was about $17,000.

Requirements for Admission An SAT score of about 1030 or ACT score of 22 and about a B average in a college prep high school program.

Application Freshmen are admitted fall, winter, and spring semesters. Early Action applications should be submitted by November 1; regular applications are open for fall admission. Notification of Early Admission is made by November 15; regular admission notification is made on a rolling basis.

International Students Official transcripts of most recent high school or college work translated into English, TOEFL scores of 525 or above on the paper exam, or 195 on the computer exam, as well as the affidavit of support and declaration of finance forms are required. Applications should be made by May 1.

Transfer Students Required are a B average in coursework at another institution as well as being in good standing, high school and college transcripts, a college catalogue if the school is outside of Michigan, ACT or SAT scores, and a Transfer Recommendation form completed by an official at the previous institution. Only courses with a minimum of a C grade will be considered for transfer, and a maximum of 68 credits may be transferred from a two-year institution.

Admission Contact
Office of Admissions
Alma College
614 W. Superior Street
Alma, MI 48801-1599
Phone: (800) 321-ALMA
FAX: (989) 463-7057
E-mail: *admissions@alma.edu*
Web: *www.alma.edu*

The Heart of the College The term *alma mater* is Latin for fostering mother, and Alma College certainly provides that, especially to its newest students. The McGregor Tutorials provide faculty mentors for first-year students to help students design an independent research project or performance project during the fall semester, and then complete the project during the winter semester. The tutorials have served to focus student achievement for their years at Alma. The McGregor Summer Colloquium allows students to participate in guided seminar discussions, collaborative research, and community service activities. Students are also given $2,500 to support summer research. These programs help to distinguish Alma in it efforts to bring students and faculty together in ways that help to create a supportive, nurturing community.

Alma is considered one of the best national liberal arts colleges as well as a "best buy." Its science programs, offering state-of-the-art laboratories, are considered outstanding. Biology is one of the largest majors and all science majors, including chemistry and biochemistry students, are provided with careful guidance if graduate school is on their horizons. When that is the case, students are encouraged to complete an independent research project culminating in a senior thesis. Alma graduates enroll at a very impressive list of graduate schools, including Duke, Notre Dame, Chicago, Princeton, Harvard, Georgetown, and Michigan.

With class sizes of about 20 and only professors teaching classes, students are guaranteed a quality academic as well as personal experience. In addition, special programs include a Diplomatic History Research Program, where students, supervised by faculty, travel to presidential libraries, regional, national, or international archives, or the Library of Congress to examine personal papers and public documents for research that often leads to a senior thesis or published paper. There are a number of multicultural courses that are either totally or partially devoted to diversity of the American experience. Alma also has an active service learning program, that links instruction in certain courses with community service, either in the Alma area, other communities in Michigan, or outside of the United States. The Undergraduate Research and Performance Programs teams faculty with students to conduct field, laboratory, or archival research, often leading to scholarly papers presented at conferences. Students in the performing arts share their work in a variety of forums.

Alma offers an extensive variety of study abroad programs in destinations such as Australia, New Zealand, London, France, Italy, Equador, and Ireland. During spring term, Alma faculty offer courses at international sites, such as Poland, Germany, Bolivia, and Spain.

With 120 organizations, clubs, and an athletic program in which one-third of the students participate, and individual musical, theater, or dance performances each year in which another third participate, the campus is a lively one. Alma's campus is a five-minute walk to downtown shops. Two hours from campus students can enjoy skiing and beaches.

The outcomes for Alma College are impressive, with 96 percent of the graduating class finding employment in fields related to their academic programs or entering graduate or professional schools within six months of graduation. Teacher Education students have a 100 percent passing rate on the Michigan Certification Exam. Employers of recent graduates include Allstate Insurance, CNN, Dow Corning, General Motors, Kellogg Company, Salomon Smith Barney, and WLNS TV Lansing.

ASBURY COLLEGE Wilmore, Kentucky

Total Undergraduate Enrollment: 1,200
Men: 500 Women: 700
Five-Year Graduation Rate: 69%

Tuition: $$$
Room and Board: $
Residential Students: 87%

History Asbury College was founded in 1890 and is named to honor the founder of American Methodism, Bishop Francis Asbury. A liberal arts college guided by the classical tradition of Christian thought, Asbury views scripture as God's infallible word. Asbury's mission is to prepare students, through the liberal arts in the Wesleyan tradition, for leadership and service in the vocation to which they are called. Asbury is named to the Templeton Foundation's Honor Roll of Character-Building Colleges.

Location Located in Wilmore, Kentucky, a rural area 15 miles from Lexington, Kentucky, the second largest city in the state.

Top Programs of Study Education, communication arts, Christian ministries and missions, philosophy, business

Arts and Sciences Applied communication, art, athletic training, biochemistry, biology, chemistry, classical languages, engineering, English, exercise science, French, Greek, history, information technology, journalism, Latin, mathematics, media communication, ministry (biblical languages), Christian ministries/missions, music, nursing, philosophy, psychology, recreation, social work, sociology, Spanish

Business Accounting, business management

Education Art, elementary, middle school, physical education, secondary, music

Pre-Professional Dentistry, law, medicine, ministry, seminary

Accredited Programs Music

Special Programs Asbury has joint-degree programs with the University of Kentucky in medical technology, computer science, and engineering. The Teacher Education program is being used as a model for the state of Kentucky. The co-curricular program, Lead On!, provides training for leadership.

Facilities There are 30 buildings, mostly Georgian colonial architecture, on a picturesque campus of rolling hills of Kentucky Bluegrass. The McCreless Fine Arts Center provides comprehensive facilities for the study of music. Corbett Hall and Bethel Studios house five audio/radio stations, a television station, and a cable television station. The Luce Physical Activities Center is a new comprehensive facility.

Transition to College Program Student leaders are assigned to small groups of new students to assist them in becoming more immediately connected to campus life, facilities, and activities. The groups meet throughout their first semester.

Athletics NAIA, plays independent of a conference

   Men: Baseball, basketball, cross-country, soccer, swimming, tennis

   Women: Basketball, cross-country, softball, swimming, tennis, volleyball

Student Life and Housing About 1,000 students can be accommodated in college housing, which is guaranteed for all four years. Only 21 percent of the students are from Kentucky, with the majority from 40 other states and 20 countries. Ethnicity: Caucasian—95 percent. There are no fraternities or sororities. Community standards include abstinence from alcohol, tobacco, and sexual relationships outside of marriage. Students adhere to a dress code and curfew. Upper-classmen may keep cars.

Accommodations for Students with Disabilities In compliance with section 504

Financial Aid About 83 percent of all freshmen receive aid. The average award was about $9000.

Requirements for Admission SAT I or ACT scores and a college prep high school program.

Application Applications should be submitted May 1 for the fall semester, December 1 for the spring semester, and April 15 for the summer semester. When all materials are received, admission decisions are made on a rolling basis.

International Students A minimum score of 550 on the TOEFL or a 213 on the computer-based test is required. Only those students interested in participating in intercollegiate sports must take the SAT or ACT.

Transfer Students Official transcripts from all other colleges attended are required. The applicant should be in good standing at the last college attended and have a GPA of at least 2.5. Individual courses must carry a grade of C− or above to be considered for transfer. Students should also present a high school transcript and either SAT I or ACT scores.

Admission Contact
Office of Admissions
Asbury College
One Macklem Drive
Wilmore, KY 40390-1198
Phone: (800) 888-1818; (859) 858-3511

FAX: (859)-858-3921
E-mail: *admissions@asbury.edu*
Web: *www.asbury.edu*

The Heart of the College The heart of Asbury College is its commitment to a faith-based, Christian education. In addition to being noted scholars in their fields, professors are committed Christians who often pray or lead students in a short devotional before class. Biblical principles are seen and lived out in the faculty. All classes are taught from a Bible-based viewpoint. Chapel is significant part of an Asbury education. Services are held three times a week, offering students an opportunity to hear from world-renowned ministers, evangelists, business people, politicians, faculty, and students.

Another integral aspect of the Asbury experience is the opportunity for mission and service trips—both life-changing experiences for many students. Whether it's the inner-city of Chicago or the streets of Peru, Asbury promotes service opportunities year-round. Spring break offers dozens of overseas and domestic experiences, or students can participate, as most do, in some form of local community outreach. Seventy percent of the students participate in some form of community service.

Last, the residence halls or "units" become a family away from home. The students' multitude of shared experiences foster not just friendship, but a spirit of brother and sisterhood.

And the outcomes are excellent. From 1980 to 1999, 100 percent of the graduates who applied to professional schools in dentistry, pharmacy, and clinical laboratory science were accepted.

ASSUMPTION COLLEGE — Worcester, Massachusetts

Total Undergraduate Enrollment: 2,053
Men: 797 Women: 1,256
Five-Year Graduation Rate: 76%

Tuition: $$$
Room and Board: $$$$
Residential Students: 89%

History Assumption College is a Catholic college founded in 1904 by the Augustinians. Assumption seeks to educate the student in the traditions of Christianity and liberal arts.

Location Assumption is located on a 145-acre campus in the residential Westwood Hills section of Worcester, Massachusetts, about three miles from the center of the city and an hour from Boston. There are eight other colleges in Worcester, a city offering many cultural opportunities.

Top Programs of Study Communications, English, education

Arts and Sciences Biology, biotechnology, chemistry, classics, computer science, economic issues and policy, economic theory, economics, English, environmental science, French, global studies, history, international economics, Latin American studies, mass communication, mathematics, philosophy, political science, psychology, social and rehabilitation services, sociology, Spanish, theology, visual arts, writing

Business Accounting, international business, management, marketing, organizational communication

Education Elementary, secondary

Pre-Professional Dentistry, law, medicine

Accredited Programs Social and rehabilitation services

Special Programs Students can take courses at neighboring colleges as part of the Westchester Consortium. Students interested in engineering can study three years at Assumption and two years at Worcester Polytechnic Institute. The Reach Out Center provides community service opportunities.

Facilities There are 38 buildings, including a new Science and Technology Center and a comprehensive Plourde Recreation Center, student development center, and a TV station.

Transition to College Program Assumption provides a traditional orientation program.

Athletics NCAA II, Northeast 10 Athletic Conference

Men: Baseball, basketball, crew, cross-country, football, golf, hockey, lacrosse, soccer, tennis

Women: Basketball, crew, cross-country, field hockey, lacrosse, softball, tennis, volleyball

Student Life and Housing About 1,800 students can be accommodated in college housing, which is guaranteed for all four years. Seventy percent of the students are from Massachusetts, with the remainder from 20 other states and 10 countries. Ethnicity: Caucasian—96 percent. There are no sororities or fraternities. Upperclassmen may keep cars.

Accommodations for Students with Disabilities Students with learning disabilities are encouraged to meet with the Director of the Academic Support Center for appropriate help.

Financial Aid About 90 percent of all freshmen receive aid. The average freshman award was about $14,000.

Requirements for Admission SAT I or ACT scores and a college prep high school program. However, the admissions committee is more interested in the quality of student work, general promise, and seriousness of purpose.

Application Application deadline is March 1 for the fall semester. The Early Decision application deadline is November 15, with admission decision by December 15. If not accepted for Early Decision, students are automatically reconsidered for regular admission.

International Students Required are high school transcripts and TOEFL scores, a teacher or counselor recommendation, and notarized documentation regarding financial means. All documents must be filed by March 1 for fall admission, and October 1 for spring admission.

Transfer Students A high school transcript and the results of the SAT I or ACT are required. Students need to forward a transcript for each college attended and submit a copy of the catalogue of each college attended, with the titles of the courses taken and the pages on which they are described. Courses in which the student has earned a grade of C− or better are considered for transfer.

Admission Contact
Office of Admissions
Assumption College
500 Salisbury Street
Worcester, MA 01609-1296
Phone: (888) 882-7786; (508) 767-7285
FAX: (508) 799-4412
E-mail: *admiss@assumption.edu*
Web: *www.assumption.edu*

The Heart of the College Assumption College can be characterized as an unusually caring community that resembles an extended family helping students to learn, achieve, and contribute. The college's innovative General Education Curriculum introduces students to the different aspects of personal, intellectual, cultural, and spiritual development through the liberal arts tradition. Students begin to realize how ideas in one course are related to ideas in other courses, as well as the world beyond the campus. Students learn the importance of moral and ethical decisions made daily.

Students are encouraged to achieve, especially through working with others, a common goal, whether in the classroom, playing field, musical stage, or residence hall. Students in the new Living/Learning Center, an apartment-style complex, work in teams on a range of topics, such as Cinema in Society.

By participation in study abroad programs in Argentina, France, Italy, Greece, Spain, and other countries, students learn the core values that unite peoples of our world, with students returning to campus better able to see the connections between classroom and life.

Assumption provides many opportunities to contribute to the lives of others. Over 500 students volunteer annually through the college's Reach Out Center, serving in shelters, soup kitchens, after-school programs, and nursing homes.

As a Catholic college, Assumption provides an extended family focused on faith and the liberal arts and graduates students who are successful learners, achievers, and contributors.

AUGUSTANA COLLEGE   Sioux Falls, South Dakota

Total Undergraduate Enrollment: 1,804
Men: 649 Women: 1,155
Five-Year Graduation Rate: 68%

Tuition: $$$
Room and Board: $
Residential Students: 61%

History Originally begun in 1860 by Scandinavian immigrants, the college moved from Chicago with the westward movement of pioneers, and in 1918 was established in Sioux Falls. The college is part of the Evangelical Lutheran Church in America and seeks to promote academic excellence and individual development within a Christian context. The college has been named to the Templeton Foundation's Honor Roll of Character-Building Colleges.

Location Located on 100 acres in a residential section of Sioux Falls, South Dakota (population 125,000), a retail, manufacturing, and distribution center. The city provides many cultural, educational, and vocational opportunities. The campus is 150 miles north of Omaha, Nebraska.

Top Programs of Study Business, education, biology

Arts and Sciences Art, athletic training, biology, chemistry, communication, communication/business, communication disorders, computer information systems, engineering management, French, German, government and international affairs, history, international studies, journalism, mathematics, medical technology, modrrn foreign languages, music, nursing, philosophy, physics, psychology, religion, socilogy, Spanish, theater

Business Accounting, business administration, economics, professional accountancy

Education Deaf and hard of hearing, elementary, middle, physical education, secondary, special

Pre-Professional Architecture, chiropractic, dentistry, engineering, law, medicine, occupational therapy, optometry, veterinary medicine

Accredited Programs Athletic training, chemistry, education, education of the deaf and hard of hearing, music, nursing

Special Programs The college houses the Center for Western Studies, providing access to the heritage of the Northern Plains and the American West through its archives, library, artifacts, events, speakers, and publications. The college's 15 vocal and music ensembles have toured some of the world's finest concert halls. There are opportunities for interdepartmental majors and study abroad.

Facilities There are 30 buildings, including the newly renovated Edith Mortenson Center, which includes a 280-seat, state-of-the-art theater and scene and costume shops; the Fantle Building, which houses the Center for Western Studies; and the technological "smart" Madsen Social Science Center.

Transition to College Program The New Student Seminar program meets weekly with a faculty mentor to share experiences, thoughts, challenges, and to learn more thoroughly what the college has to offer.

Athletics NCAA II, North Central Conference

Men: Baseball, basketball, cross-country, football, golf, tennis, track & field, wrestling

Women: Basketball, cross-country, golf, soccer, softball, tennis, track & field, volleyball

Student Life and Housing About 1,100 students can be accommodated in college housing, which is guaranteed for all four years. Fifty-one percent of the students are from South Dakota, the remainder from 30 other states and 12 countries. Ethnicity: Caucasian—96 percent. There are no fraternities or sororities. All students may keep cars.

Accommodations for Students with Disabilities In compliance with section 504

Financial Aid About 98 percent of all freshmen receive aid. The average award is about $14,500.

Requirements for Admission Recommended is a minimum SAT I score of 950 or ACT score of 20, and a 2.5 GPA in a college prep high school program, with a rank in the upper half of the class.

Application Freshmen are admitted fall, spring, and summer semesters. March 1 is the priority application date. Notification is sent on a rolling basis.

International Students Applications should be submitted by June 1 for the fall, and December 1 for the spring. A minimum TOEFL score of 550 is required, along with secondary and, if applicable, postsecondary school transcripts, two recommendations, and documentation of financial support.

Transfer Students Official transcripts of high school and college work and one recommendation from a professor or adviser are required. A C average is needed, with C− and above grades considered for transfer. A maximum of 65 credits may be transferred from two-year schools.

Admission Contact
Office of Admissions
Augustana College
2001 South Summit Avenue
Sioux Falls, SD 57197
Phone: (800) 727-2844; (605) 274-0770
FAX: (605) 274-5518
E-mail: *info@inst.augie.edu*
Web: *www.augie.edu*

The Heart of the College Augustana College states very clearly, "Developing faith, values, and moral principles is the heart and soul of an Augustana education." The college points to research that supports its mission. This research concludes that the integration of faith and values into the academic experience enhances the value of a college education. Available are daily community worships, outreach teams, Bible studies and prayer groups, and worship bands. In the spring of 2002, 20 students traveled to New York City to feed the homeless and served the survivors of September 11.

This focus on faith and values blends nicely with a strong liberal arts program that creates a lively learning climate. Students analyze and discuss literature, philosophy, history, and the sciences, developing creative thinking and communication skills—attributes prized by prospective employers. With small classes and a student-centered environment, faculty are dedicated to teaching and always demonstrate a passion for learning. No teaching assistants here, only professors teaching courses. Even senior faculty teach entry-level courses. Faculty chat with students over lunch and give out their phone numbers.

Augustana is proud of its outcomes. Over the last several years, an average of 95 percent of graduates have obtained positions related to their field of study within eight months of graduation. Other graduates moved on to graduate and professional schools at institutions such as MIT, Harvard, Johns Hopkins, University of Chicago, Yale, Notre Dame, and Michigan. Augustana points to several reasons for this success. First is the comprehensive services of the Career Center offered throughout the student's education. Second is the pool of 220 talented members of Augustana's Alumni Career Mentor Program, from whom students can receive a firsthand look at a specific career. Third are the Academic Associates residing in residence halls, who are only a door-knock away to provide students with the academic help they may need. Last, the college has exceptional ties to the business community, providing many opportunities for internships or part-time jobs.

Many students consider the city of Sioux Falls an asset—safe and accessible and retaining a small-town ambience. With 230 sunny days per year, a typically robust economy, the Empire Mall, museums, the Washington Pavilion of Arts and Sciences, and nearby skiing, hiking, and boating, there is much to offer.

BERRY COLLEGE
Mount Berry, Georgia

Total Undergraduate Enrollment: 1,898
Men: 698 Women: 1,200
Five-Year Graduation: 57%

Tuition: $$
Room and Board: $
Residential Students: 72%

History Berry College was founded in 1902 by Martha Berry as a high school for rural boys, when few public schools existed in Georgia. In 1909 a girls unit was added; in 1926, a junior college; in 1930, a four-year college; and in 1972, graduate programs. Martha Berry received funding from wealthy contributors, such as a member of the Ford family, Andrew Carnegie, and Vanderbilt Hammond. Berry is an independent college with an interdenominational Christian tradition.

Location The 28,000-acre campus is located in Mount Berry, Georgia, nestled in the foothills of northwest Georgia, a rural area adjacent to Rome, Georgia (population 89,000), 65 miles northeast of Atlanta, and 65 miles from Chattanooga, Tennessee.

Top Programs of Study Business administration, communication, early childhood education

Arts and Sciences Animal science, anthropology, art, art history, biology, chemistry, communication (concentrations in electronic media, journalism, public relations, speech), computer science, decision science, English, environmental sciences, family studies, French, German, government, health and physical education, history, horticulture, interdisciplinary studies, mathematics, music, music business, physics, psychology, religion and philosophy, social science, sociology, Spanish, theater

Business Administration (concentrations in accounting, finance, information systems, management, marketing), economics

Education Art, early childhood, health and physical education, middle school

Pre-Professional Dentistry, engineering, law, medicine, optometry, pharmacy, theology, veterinary medicine

Accredited Programs Education, music

Special Programs There is a Multicultural Student Affairs Office and a Writing Across-the-Curriculum Program. There are several minors, including writing, family studies, and film studies. There are dual degree programs in engineering with Georgia Institute of Technology and Mercer University, as well as nursing with Emory University. There are opportunities for cooperative education, internships, and study abroad in Spain, Cuba, Germany, Ireland, and Italy.

Facilities There are 38 buildings of Gothic and Georgian architecture. The mountain campus, located three miles north of the main campus, is the home of many campus landmarks, including the Gunby Equestrian Center. The campus includes Oak Hill, the 170-acre plantation home of Martha Berry, the college's founder, which attracts tourists from around the world. The campus includes the 500-seat Ford Auditorium, Ford Hall (modeled after the dining halls at Oxford), a new Science Center, a child development center, Krannert Student Center Blackstone Hall, which houses the Young Theater, the Berry College Elementary School, a private K–8 school,

on-campus horticultural studies, and beef and dairy operations.

Transition to College Program The Freshman Center offers a variety of services to help students adjust to college life, including a "crash course" in college success, as well as a book discussion that allows freshmen to enjoy dinner and conversation with Berry faculty, usually in their homes, and also a Service Day that gives freshmen an opportunity to get to know one another and the community through a day of service in Rome and Floyd Counties.

Athletics NAIA, Trans South Conference

   Men: Baseball, basketball, cross-country, golf, indoor–outdoor running, soccer, tennis

   Women: Basketball, cross-country, golf, indoor–outdoor running, soccer, tennis

Student Life and Housing About 1,300 students can be accommodated in air-conditioned college housing. Eighty-one percent of the students are from Georgia, the remainder from 35 other states and 23 countries. Ethnicity: Caucasian—94 percent. There are no fraternities or sororities. All students may keep cars.

Accommodations for Students with Disabilities In compliance with section 504

Financial Aid Ninety-seven percent of all freshmen receive aid. The average freshman award was about $12,000.

Requirements for Admission SAT I or ACT scores and a college prep high school program.

Application Applications are received for all semesters, and should be submitted no later than 30 days prior to the beginning of the semester for which admission is sought. Applicants for the fall semester should submit applications by February 1 in order to receive full consideration.

International Students Students must meet regular admission requirements a well as take the TOEFL if the student is not a native English speaker.

Transfer Students Required are official transcripts from previous colleges attended. The applicant must be in good standing at the previous institution, have a GPA of at least 2.5 at the previous institution, and have an overall GPA of at least 2.5 for all college work. A maximum of 67 credits are transferable from accredited colleges and universities, and 32 credits must be completed at Berry for a degree.

Admission Contact
Office of Admissions
Berry College
P.O. Box 490159
Mount Berry, GA 30149
Phone: (800) BERRY-GA; (706) 236-2215
FAX: (706)290-2178
E-mail: *admissions@berry.edu*
Web: *www.berry.edu*

The Heart of the College Berry College is considered one of the best comprehensive colleges in the South as well as a "best buy," but Berry's real claim to fame lies in it size. It is the world's largest college campus at 28,000 acres! Filled with forests, streams, mountains, lakes, and meadows, Berry College is truly one of the most beautiful settings in the world. Having come quite a distance from its one-room, log cabin beginnings, some of the world's wealthiest people have helped create a campus of architectural beauty. Outdoor enthusiasts love the hiking and biking, jogging paths, and horseback riding trails. Those students who clamor for urban recreation and culture travel to nearby Rome, Atlanta, and Chattanooga.

On campus there are many clubs, organizations, and activities, and with 70 percent of the students living on campus, there is a strong sense of community and friendship among students and faculty. Only full-time faculty teach courses, with more than 90 percent having earned the doctorate. While faculty are expected to be involved with scholarship in their respective fields, the institution's greater expectation is that teaching be their priority. In addition to excellent teaching, faculty provide advisement and devote a great deal of out-of-class time to guiding their students. The warm, friendly Berry community is aided by having a number of professors living right on campus, with many more involved in campus activities.

The college's programs represent the legacy of its founder, Martha Berry, who believed in an education of the head, the heart, and the hands. The nationally accredited education program has a long history of excellence. With two on-campus private schools—The Child Development Center for ages 3–5 and the Berry College Elementary School—teacher education students have abundant opportunities for observation, field experiences, and student teaching. Also, as with most distinguished teacher training programs, Berry College has ongoing relationships with nearby "professional development schools." The college places its trainees with those schools' best teachers.

The college is a specifically Christian institution, although not affiliated with any one denomination. Therefore, the college seeks to cultivate a spiritual life through its Religion-in-Life Program, comprised of active student organizations, church services, and an emphasis on community services.

The "hands" of a Berry education are critical, in that every student is assured of an opportunity for campus employment. In a typical year, about 75 percent of the full-time students work on campus in 100 different job classifications. Berry College budgets $3 million annually for this Work Opportunity Program. In addition, the Career Development Center places students in cooperative education positions where students earn salaries one semester and are back in classes the next. The Center has an exceptional record of matching students with companies such as Georgia Pacific, Sun Trust Bank, Redmond Regional Medical Center, and Georgia Department of Natural Resources.

BETHEL COLLEGE St. Paul, Minnesota

Total Undergraduate Enrollment: 2,500
Men: 1,000 Women: 1,500
Five-Year Graduation Rate: 73%

Tuition: $$$
Room and Board: $$
Residential Students: 74%

History Bethel College was established in 1871 and is affiliated with the Baptist General Conference.

Location The campus is situated on a 231-acre lakeside parcel of wooded, rolling hills in Arden Hills, a suburb of St. Paul, Minnesota.

Top Programs of Study Education, business, biology, nursing

Arts and Sciences Applied physics, art, athletic training, biblical and theological studies, biochemistry, biology, chemistry, communication, community health, computer science, engineering science, English literature and writing, environmental studies, French, history, international relations, mathematics, media communication, music, philosophy, physics, political science, psychology, sacred music, social work, sociocultural studies, Spanish, theater arts, third world studies, writing, youth ministry

Business Administration (emphases in accounting, finance, human resources management, international business, and marketing), business and political science, business management, economics, economics and finance, organizational leadership

Education Elementary, middle, music, physical education, secondary, teaching English as a foreign language (TEFL), teaching English as a second language (TESL), visual arts education

Pre-Professional Law, medicine

Accredited Programs Education, nursing, social work

Special Programs Students can design individualized majors. A contemporary Music Center, located on Martha's Vineyard off the coast of Cape Cod, Massachusetts, offers young musicians and aspiring music industry executives the opportunity to learn about a career in the music industry. There are Army and Air Force ROTC programs.

Facilities The buildings are modern, including an art gallery; a radio station; a theater; modern science labs; the Bethel College Library; a Community Life Center, which has an outstanding performance hall; and modern music practice rooms.

Transition to College Program Bethel offers a traditional orientation program.

Athletics NCAA III, Minnesota Intercollegiate Athletic Conference

   Men: Baseball, basketball, cross-country, football, golf, hockey, soccer, tennis, track & field

   Women: Basketball, cross-country, hockey, soccer, softball, tennis, track & field, volleyball

Student Life and Housing About 1,500 students can be accommodated in college housing. Sixty-two percent of the students are from Minnesota, the remainder from 42 other states and Canada. Ethnicity: Caucasian—94 percent. There are no fraternities or sororities. Upperclassmen may keep cars. Students are bound to the Bethel Covenant of Commitments that describes expectations regarding student behavior.

Accommodations for Students with Disabilities In compliance with section 504

Financial Aid About 92 percent of freshmen receive aid. The average award was about $14,000.

Requirements for Admission A minimum of a 21 on the ACT or 920 on the SAT I, with a class rank in the upper half of the class, in a college prep high school program.

Application Freshmen are admitted fall, winter, and spring semesters. The Early Admissions Application deadline is December 1 for fall and November 1 for spring admission.

International Students Applications should be submitted by March 1. Required are a recommendation; official transcripts from high school and, if applicable, college; TOEFL scores; a two-page writing sample; a copy of current visa; and a certification of finances form.

Transfer Students Required are an essay, two references, college and high school transcripts, and a list of courses currently in progress.

Admission Contact
Office of Admissions
Bethel College
3900 Bethel Drive
St. Paul, MN 55112-6999
Phone: (800) 255-8706; (651) 638-6242
FAX: (651)635-1490
E-mail: *bcoll-admit@bethel.edu*
Web: *www.bethel.edu*

The Heart of the College Bethel College is a Christian learning community where students and professors examine the academic disciplines with a Christian perspective.

The strong liberal arts curriculum is taught by a talented faculty who are recognized by the college as the critical element in a Bethel education. Not only are the faculty respected leaders in their fields, making ongoing contributions, they are a team of professors deeply committed to their students. The small class sizes foster closer interactions with each student.

Preparation for careers in missions, business, and government involves greater focus on having students think and work cross-culturally. Students study courses in world citizenship and have the option of living for a time in another culture. Another focus is on technology. Having evolved to a service and information society, Bethel believes that Christian leaders in all fields need to develop competencies in the sciences and technology. With the impersonal nature of these new technologies, coupled with the increasing alienation in contemporary society, Bethel focuses on the development of interpersonal relationships.

With a good many graduates heading for ministries abroad, Bethel offers a variety of international study and ministry opportunities, including Russia, England, Europe, China, Guatemala, and the Middle East. These off-campus semesters abroad do little to detract from the warm community on campus that cultivates life-long friendships at one of the best liberal arts colleges in the North.

BIOLA UNIVERSITY La Mirada, California

Total Undergraduate Enrollment: 2,824
Men: 1,071 Women: 1,753
Five-Year Graduation Rate: 54%

Tuition: $$$
Room and Board: $
Residential Students: 69%

History Originally founded as a Bible Institute in 1908 by Lyman Stewart, co-founder of the Union Oil Company, the university is an evangelical Christian institution.

Location The 95-acre campus is located in La Mirada, California, 22 miles southeast of downtown Los Angeles. La Mirada is a suburban residential community of 40,000. The campus is 12 miles from Disneyland and one hour from beaches and mountains.

Top Programs of Study Business, communications, psychology

Arts and Sciences Anthropology, art bible, bio-chemistry, biological sciences, communication, communication disorders, computer science, engineering, English, history, humanities, inter-cultural studies, mathematics, music, nursing, philosophy, physical science, psychology, radio-television-film, social science, sociology, Spanish

Business Administration accounting, computer information, management, marketing

Education Christian, elementary, physical education, secondary

Pre-Professional Chiropractic, law, physical therapy

Accredited Programs Art, business, nursing, psychology

Special Programs The Student Missionary Union provides opportunities for students to evangelize for Christ in local ministries. Students can also participate in the Au Sable Institute of Environmental Studies, located in northern Michigan. There are several unique study abroad programs: a summer program in the Holy Land; a three-week interterm field trip to Baja, California and Mexico to study the natural history of the Baja peninsula; and a fall semester living with a family in Honduras to study life in the third world. There are Army and Air Force ROTC programs.

Facilities There are 31 buildings, including a new production center for the radio-TV-film program. The newest addition is the Library Resource Center in the center of campus.

Transition to College Program Biola offers a traditional orientation program.

Athletics NAIA, Golden State Athletic Conference

  Men: Baseball, basketball, cross-country, diving, soccer, track & field

  Women: Basketball, cross-country, soccer, swimming/diving, tennis, track & field, volleyball

Student Life and Housing About 1,900 can be accommodated in campus housing. 79 percent of the students are from California, the remainder from 43 other states and 40 countries. Ethnicity: Caucasian—77 percent; Asian-American—9 percent; Hispanic-American—7 percent; International—3 percent; African-American—2 percent. There are no sororities or fraternities. All students may keep cars.

Accommodations for Students with Disabilities The Office of Disability Services provides accommodations to students with documented disabilities.

Financial Aid About 65 percent of freshmen receive aid. The average award was about $12,000.

Requirements for Admission SAT I or ACT scores and a college prep high school program. Applicants must be evangelical believers.

Application Admission deadline for the fall is May 1 (priority deadline is February 1) and January 1 for the spring semester. Admission notification is on a rolling basis.

International Students The minimum TOEFL score for admission is a total of 500 paper and 173 computer. Students may submit a SAT I score instead of the TOEFL.

Transfer Students Students must submit both high school and college transcripts. A cumulative GPA of 2.5 is required with C grades and above considered for transfer.

Admission Contact
Office of Admissions
Biola University
13800 Biola Avenue
La Mirada, CA 90639-0001
Phone: (800) OK-BIOLA; (562) 903-4752
FAX: (562) 903-4709
E-mail: *admissions@biola.edu*
Web: *www.biola.edu*

The Heart of the University The mission of Biola University is a Bible-centered education. All students are Christians and must study 30 credits of Bible in order to graduate.

Biola has a caring, intelligent faculty who both teach and mentor. While they are experts in their fields, producing many publications a year and giving presentations, they take an active interest in students and their whole lives. Students are mentored and in return learn how to mentor. One student comments: "You receive a lot of individual attention, and they're extremely willing to help you out in any way that they can."

The Student Ministries Office provides countless ministry opportunities, including Big Brothers/Big Sisters and feeding the homeless.

Biola students also have a Christian Service requirement involving a three-hour off-campus commitment.

Biola students relish their location in sunny Southern California, which affords recreational and cultural activities on the water and snow, film and television studios, concert halls, museums, and theme parks.

In addition, Biola provides a generous financial aid package, 30 majors, including pre-professional programs, and a diverse student population.

Biola provides committed Christians with a nurturing education in a wonderful location that allows students to grow in their faith.

BIRMINGHAM-SOUTHERN COLLEGE

Birmingham, Alabama

Total Undergraduate Enrollment: 1,275
Men: 525 Women: 750
Five-Year Graduation Rate: 77%

Tuition: $$$
Room and Board: $$
Residential Students: 85%

History Birmingham-Southern College is the result of a merger of Southern University, founded in Greensboro, Alabama in 1856, with Birmingham College, opened in 1898 in Birmingham, Alabama. The merger took place in 1918. The college is affiliated with the United Methodist Church. The college was named to the Templeton Foundation's Honor Roll of Character-Building Colleges.

Location The 192-acre campus is located on a rolling hilltop in an urban area 3 miles west of downtown Birmingham, the largest city in Alabama, with many cultural, educational, and recreational opportunities.

Top Programs of Study Business administration

Arts and Sciences Art, art history, Asian studies, biology, chemistry, computer science, dance, English, French, German, history, mathematics, music, philosophy, physics, political science, psychology, religion, sociology, Spanish, theater arts

Business Accounting, administration, economics

Education Art, educational services, elementary, middle, music, secondary

Pre-Professional None

Accredited Programs Business, chemistry, education, music

Special Programs There are several cooperative five-year master's degree (3–2) programs offered: engineering with the University of Alabama, environmental studies with Duke, and nursing with Vanderbilt. The college operates on a 4-1-4 academic calendar, with students taking four courses in the fall, one in the winter, and four in the spring. There are interdisciplinary majors offered and students can design individualized majors. There is a Phi Beta Kappa chapter. The college was selected as one of the most computer-wired colleges in America. There are Army and Air Force ROTC programs.

Facilities There are 35 buildings, including the Norton state-of-the-art Campus Center, the Olin Computer Science and Mathematics Center, and the Stephens Science Center, billed as one of the leading undergraduate science teaching facilities in the country. There is also a new fitness and recreation center. The Edwards Bell Tower serves as a centerpiece to the campus.

Transition to College Program The college offers a traditional orientation program.

Athletics NCAA I, Big South Conference

Men: Baseball, basketball, cross-country, golf, soccer, tennis

Women: Basketball, cross-country, golf, rifle, soccer, softball, tennis, volleyball

Student Life and Housing About 1,200 students can be accommodated in college housing, which is guaranteed for all four years. Seventy-seven percent of the students are from Alabama, with the remainder from 28 other states and 18 countries. Ethnicity: Caucasian—89 percent; African-American—7 percent; Asian-American—3 percent. There are six national fraternities and seven national sororities. All students may keep cars. An honor code is in effect.

Accommodations for Students with Disabilities Students submit a Request for Academic Accommodation form along with appropriate documentation from a certified professional in the field of learning disabilities. Students are responsible for discussing their needs with instructors. Reasonable accommodations are made, but no general education requirement can be waived.

Financial Aid Ninety-eight percent of all students receive aid. The average freshman award was about $13,500.

Requirements for Admission SAT I or ACT scores with a college prep high school program.

Application Freshmen are admitted fall, spring, and summer semesters. Applications should be filed by January 15 for fall admission, December for winter admission, January 15 for spring admission, and May 1 for summer admission.

Early Action applications should be submitted by December 1, and are notified by December 15. All other applicants are notified on a rolling basis.

International Students Students must file the same credentials as the regular applicants along with a minimum TOEFL score of 500 or computer 173, or have completed level 109 at an ESL Language Center, or achieved an English sub-score of 21 on the ACT or a verbal sub-score of 475 on the SAT. A complete set of educational credentials with English translations, if necessary, and an affidavit of financial responsibility are also required.

Transfer Students Students must have been in good standing at the previous college, and have at least a C average for a full schedule of courses attempted and acceptable at Birmingham-Southern. Not more than 64 credits will be transferred from a two-year institution.

Admission Contact
Office of Admissions
Birmingham-Southern College
Box 549008
900 Arkadelphia Road
Birmingham, AL 35254
Phone: (800) 523-5793; (205) 226-4696
FAX: (205) 226-3074
E-mail: *admission@bsc.edu*
Web: *www.bsc/admission*

The Heart of the College The heart of Birmingham-Southern College is the feel of a distinctive institution, where so many elements of a college education are of great quality that student involvement and great outcomes flow naturally. The new Foundations general education program has students working collaboratively, taking courses in the arts and sciences, performing arts, foreign languages and culture, mathematics and writing, and then presenting a Senior Conference project publicly. The Provost says that Foundations is "about small classes with innovative teaching." And this teaching comes from a talented, well-qualified faculty, distinguished for its close interaction with students. Not only are classes taught in a highly interactive manner, with dozens of students collaborating with faculty on research projects initiated by students, but there are also professors who know students by name, invite students for dinner, and hold evening study sessions.

The college also has one of the outstanding leadership studies programs in the country, where students are called to analyze leadership theory and study the relationship between leadership and community service. Unlike other leadership programs, Birmingham-Southern's is open to all students in their sophomore and junior years. The linkage between the leadership program and the service learning program is a genuine one, its popularity demonstrated by the fact that more than 65 percent of the students and faculty take part each year, working locally in projects such as men's and women's shelters; or nationally, building a playground for the Headstart Program of the Cherokee Nation in Oklahoma; or even internationally, working with Mother Teresa's Missionaries of Charity in India.

The college has an excellent record of job placement, building upon a meaningful internship program that places students in the U.S. Senate, FBI Headquarters, Mayo Clinic, the Women's Fund of Birmingham, and Urban Ministries. Graduates get jobs in NASA, Kraft Foods, Ernst & Young, and American Express, for example. Most impressively, 62 percent of a recent graduating class went to graduate school! A good percentage have been admitted to law, medical, and physical therapy programs at schools such as Vanderbilt, Yale, Cornell, and Duke.

Students also have the luxury of a thriving Birmingham, home of the Alabama Jazz Hall of Fame, Birmingham Civil Rights Institute, Birmingham Zoo, dining, and cultural opportunities. Imagine a campus in a city recently named "The Most Livable City in America" by the U.S. Conference of Governors!

BLOOMSBURG UNIVERSITY

Bloomsburg, Pennsylvania

Total Undergraduate Enrollment: 6,790

Men: 2,690 Women: 4,100
Five-Year Graduation Rate: 60%

Tuition: In-state—$;
Out-of-state—$$
Room and Board: $
Residential Students: 40%

History Originally a teachers college, Bloomsburg University was founded in 1839 and became a comprehensive public university in 1983, with emphasis on liberal arts and career education. It is part of the Pennsylvania State Higher Education System.

Location Bloomsburg University is located on 282 acres within walking distance of Bloomsburg, Pennsylvania, a town of 12,000 people located in the Susquehanna River Valley and the home of the regionally famous Bloomsburg Fair. New York is three hours away and Philadelphia two and a half.

Top Programs of Study Elementary education, marketing, accounting

Arts and Sciences Allied health preparatory programs (cytotechnology, medical imaging, medical technology, occupational therapy, pharmacy, physical therapy, respiratory therapy), anthropology, art history, art studio, audiology and speech pathology, biology, chemistry, clinical chemistry, computer and information systems, computer and information science, communication studies, criminal justice, earth science, economics, electrical and electronics engineering technology, English, exercise science, French, geography, geology, German, health physics, history, interdisciplinary studies, interpreting for the deaf/hard of hearing, mass communications, mathematics, music, nursing, office information systems, philosophy, physics, political science, psychology, Spanish, social welfare, sociology, theater arts

Business Accounting, economics, finance, management, marketing

Education Business, early childhood, elementary, music, secondary, special

Pre-Professional None

Accredited Programs Audiology and speech pathology, education, education of the deaf, social work

Special Programs There are study abroad, dual majors, and internship opportunities. Bloomsburg offers a cooperative five-year master's degree (3–2) program in engineering with Pennsylvania State University and Wilkes University.

Facilities There are 54 buildings, including a new Student Services Center, new academic facilities and student housing, and the new Harvey Andruss Library. The Haas Center for the Arts includes an art gallery. The campus has television and radio stations.

Transition to College The university offers a traditional orientation program.

Athletics NCAA II, Penn State Athletic Conference

   Men: Baseball, basketball, cross-country, field hockey, football, lacrosse, soccer, softball, swimming, tennis, track, wrestling (Div. I)

   Women: Basketball, cross-country, soccer, swimming, tennis, track

Student Life and Housing About 3,000 students can be accommodated in college housing. Ninety-one percent of the students are from Pennsylvania, with the remainder from 22 other states and 27 countries. Ethnicity: Caucasian— 94 percent. There are 13 sororities and 14 fraternities. Upperclassmen may keep cars.

Accommodations for Students with Disabilities Students are encouraged to contact the accommodative services office prior to their orientation, in order to discuss anticipated needs.

Financial Aid About 70 percent of all students receive aid. The average award was about $4,500.

Requirements for Admission SAT I and a college prep high school program.

Application The Early Decision application deadline is November 15. Students are notified on a rolling basis, within two weeks of receiving a completed application.

International Students Application for the fall semester should be submitted by March 1 and for the spring semester by September 1. Students must submit a certified bank statement verifying the student's ability to meet all expenses. Non-English speaking students must earn a 500 or better on the paper-based TOEFL or 173 on the computer-based test.

Transfer Students Students must submit a high school transcript and SAT I scores or a GED and official transcripts from each college attended. Applications for the fall and summer semesters should be submitted by March 15, and for the spring semester by October 15. The student must be in good standing at the college last attended and have a 2.0 GPA or better. Grades of C or higher will be considered for transfer. Those students who have earned an associate's degree at a community college which is part of the state system are guaranteed admission.

Admission Contact
Office of Admissions
Bloomsburg University
400 E. Second Street
Bloomsburg, PA 17815
Phone: (570) 389-4316
FAX: (570) 389-4741
E-mail: *buadmiss@bloomu.edu*
Web: *www.bloomu.edu*

The Heart of the University Bloomsburg University is mostly about people—its students, professors, and staff. Students come from varied home towns and form a community where people support one another, lend a helping hand, and form friendships that last a lifetime. While every ethnic and cultural group is represented, in Bloomsburg's close-knit community students are expected to bring and share their values, perspectives, and heritage.

Faculty and staff are very approachable and help develop and sustain the strong feeling of community at Bloomsburg. Professors do more than teach; they act as mentors and advisers. They are active in classroom discussion, assist with student lab work, and meet with students outside of class to help overcome hurdles. Professors get to know their students personally and work with them on a one-to-one basis, making communication so much easier and developing meaningful professor–student ties.

There are many fine programs, with education and business garnering most students. This interest is well deserved, considering the excellence of these programs as attested to by their national accreditation.

The campus is an attractive one close to the small town of Bloomsburg, where students can enjoy movies, restaurants, and a friendly small town ambience.

Bloomsburg students believe that the university sincerely cares about them and that this caring community will help students function as graduates in the larger global society.

BLUFTON COLLEGE   **Blufton, Ohio**

Total Undergraduate Enrollment: 1,053
Men: 434 Women: 619
Five-Year Graduation Rate: 58%

Tuition: $$$
Room and Board: $$
Residential Students: 71%

History Blufton College was founded in 1899 by regional leaders of the Mennonite Church. The college has been named to the Templeton Foundation's Honor Roll of Character-Building Colleges.

Location The 65-acre campus, partially covered by more than 100 different varieties of trees, is in the small town of Blufton, Ohio, 60 miles south of Toledo in northwestern Ohio, only a few hours from Columbus, Cleveland, and Indianapolis.

Top Programs of Study Elementary education, recreation management, business

Arts and Sciences Apparel/textile merchandising and design, art, biology, chemistry, child development, communication, computer science, criminal justice, dietetics, English, family and consumer services, food and nutrition, health and recreation, history, mathematics, music, physics, psychology, recreation management, religion, social work, sociology, Spanish, youth ministries and recreation

Business Accounting, administration, information systems, Spanish/economics, sports management

Education Early childhood, intervention specialist for special education, middle, multi-age preK–12, physical education, secondary, vocational

Pre-Professional Law, medicine, seminary

Accredited Programs Dietetics, music, social work

Special Programs Blufton is cited as one of the most computer-wired colleges in America. Students are able to design their own majors. There are opportunities for study abroad, internships, and a Washington, D.C., semester.

Facilities There are 25 buildings, including Centennial Hall, a state-of-the-art building featuring technology classrooms where students can use presentation equipment and computer labs with internet access. There is an arts center, art gallery, and radio station. Adjacent to the college is a 130-acre nature preserve with an eight-acre lake, which serves as an outdoor education site.

Transition to College Program Students are required to do summer reading.

Athletics NCAA III, Heartland Athletic Conference

Men: Baseball, basketball, cross-country, football, golf, soccer, tennis, track & field

Women: Basketball, cross-country, golf, soccer, softball, tennis, track & field, volleyball

Student Life and Housing About 750 students can be accommodated in college housing, which is guaranteed for all four years. Eighty-nine percent of the students are from Ohio, the remainder are from 15 other states and 15 countries. Ethnicity: Caucasian—88 percent; Asian-American—2 percent; International—2 percent; Hispanic-American—1 percent. There are no fraternities or sororities. All students may keep cars. Students abide by an honor system.

Accommodations for Students with Disabilities A counselor for disability services interviews students with documented disabilities in order to determine appropriate accommodations.

Financial Aid All students receive some aid. The average freshman award was about $16,500.

Requirements for Admission Students must achieve two of the following three: obtain a minimum ACT of 19 or SAT I of 920; achieve a minimum of a 2.3 GPA in a college prep high school program; rank in the top half of the graduating class.

Application Freshmen are admitted to all semesters. Applications should be submitted by May 31 for fall admission, with admission notification provided within two weeks.

International Students Students whose primary language is not English must take the TOEFL and score a minimum of 500 on the paper-based or 180 on the computer version. Also required are official secondary school transcripts and, if applicable, postsecondary transcripts, as well as a Declaration of Finances.

Transfer Students Required are official high school and college transcripts, a transfer recommendation, a minimum of a C GPA in all college work, and good standing at the previous institution. Course credit is given for courses that have a minimum grade of C− and which are comparable in content to courses at Blufton. Students with an associate's degree are admitted with junior year standing.

Admission Contact
Office of Admissions
Blufton College
280 W. College Avenue, Ste. 1
Blufton, OH 45817-1196
Phone: (800) 488-3257; (419) 358-3257
FAX: (419) 358-3232
E-mail: *admissions@blufton.edu*
Web: *www.blufton.edu*

The Heart of the College Imagine a college that offers a "satisfaction guarantee" to new first-year residential students entering fall term. That's right. If students are dissatisfied to the extent that they withdraw after the fall term, they will be refunded the part of the tuition paid by their parents. Now that's confidence!

The Blufton experience is rooted in what it terms "a Community of Respect," where students, faculty, and staff are held in mutual high regard. As a Mennonite college, the most powerful aspect of this learning community is the shared belief that every human being is created in the image of God. This caring, Christian community provides students with many opportunities to develop a richer spiritual life through organizations such as

Brothers and Sisters in Christ, an interdenominational group for students, faculty, and staff that provides support, fellowship, and growth. Chapel services are held each Thursday, with Sunday worship on alternating Sundays. Students enjoy the special celebrations and Christian concerts.

Many service opportunities take students to soup kitchens to feed the homeless, play a game with a resident at a retirement home, build a house with Habitat for Humanity, or teach underprivileged kids to read. Students grow as a result of this giving of service. Many students also elect to complete a cross-cultural experience in locations such as Central America, Europe, Jamaica, Canada, Trinidad, and Vietnam.

Students comment about the "down to earth" professors who are authentic in their care for students. Faculty are asked not only to share their subject area expertise and develop critical and creative thinkers in their courses, but also to develop character and encourage faith. As a result of such commitment and engagement on the part of the faculty, students strive to live up to faculty expectations.

Courses are made interesting and important because professors incorporate industry standards, technological advances, and student needs, making classes more personalized and relevant. From the first-year interdisciplinary seminar in "Identity" to the senior capstone course, "Christian Values in a Global Community," students learn to ask important questions about themselves and the roles they may play as Christians in a contemporary world.

BRADLEY UNIVERSITY   Peoria, Illinois

Total Undergraduate Enrollment: 5,000
Men: 2,300 Women: 2,700
Five-Year Graduation Rate: 68%

Tuition: $$$
Room and Board: $
Residential Students: 86%

History Bradley University was founded in 1897 as the first coeducational college in the nation without a specific religious affiliation. The founder, Lydia Moss Bradley, was one of the most influential and wealthiest businesswomen in the nation and has been inducted into the National Women's Hall of Fame.

Location Bradley is located in Peoria, Illinois, cited by *Money Magazine* as one of the "300 Best Places" to live in America, with a metropolitan area population of 350,000. The 75-acre campus is three hours from Chicago and St. Louis.

Top Programs of Study Psychology, communications, education

Arts and Sciences Administration of criminal justice, actuarial science, art, art history, biology, biochemistry, cell and molecular biology, chemistry, civil engineering, civil engineering with environ-mental option, communications, computer science, computer information systems, construction, economics, electrical engineering, electrical engineering with computer option, engineering physics, English, environmental science, family and consumer sciences—dietetics/foods and nutrition, family and consumer sciences—general, family and consumer sciences—retail merchandising, French, geology, German, health science (leads to a master's degree in Physical Therapy), history, industrial engineering, manufacturing engineering, manufacturing technology, mathematics, mechanical engineering, medical technology, multimedia, music, music business, music education, music performance, nursing, philosophy, physics, political science, psychology, religious studies, social service, social work, sociology, Spanish, studio art, theater arts, theater performance, theater production

Business Accounting, actuarial science—business, business computer systems, business management (management and administration, entrepreneurship, human resource management, legal studies in business), economics, finance, international business, marketing, risk management and insurance

Education Early childhood, elementary, family and consumer sciences, secondary, special art

Pre-Professional Law, medicine

Accredited Programs Art and design, business, chemistry, construction, dietetics, engineering, music, nursing, physical therapy

Special Programs Bradley offers a five-year master's program that includes a three-year bachelor's and then a two-year option in accounting. Bradley's Small Business Institute, NAFTA Opportunity Center, Center for Executive and Professional Development, and Center for Economic Development provide additional opportunities to translate business theory into action. Nursing students earn a salary as they participate in a cooperative education program. "Medical Buddies" pairs pre-med students with medical students at the University of Illinois College of Medicine at Peoria.

Facilities There are 41 buildings, including the new Caterpillar Global Communications Center, a greenhouse research laboratory, and a PBS television studio, art gallery, and radio station.

Transition to College Program Orientation programs assist new students and their parents in adjusting to the university and the parents' adjustment to being parents of a college student. Academic, career, and personal skills are assessed and enhanced. The Academic Exploration Program is an award–winning program designed to help students explore different courses in which advisers represent different academic interests to help students determine a major area of study.

Athletics NCAA I, Missouri Valley Conference

Men: Baseball, basketball, cross-country, golf, soccer, tennis

Women: Basketball, cross-country, golf, indoor and outdoor track, softball, tennis, volleyball

Student Life and Housing About 3,000 students can be accommodated in college housing, which is guaranteed for all four years. Eighty percent of the students are from Illinois, with the remainder from 41 other states and 60 countries. Ethnicity: Caucasian—83 percent; African-American—5 percent; International—2 percent; Asian-American—2 percent. There are 10 sororities and 19 fraternities. Upperclassmen may keep cars.

Accommodations for Students with Disabilities The Center for Learning Assistance provides a contact person, support services, peer tutors, and student referral service for off-campus testing resources. Students must provide current documentation of disabilities.

Financial Aid About 80 percent of all freshmen receive aid. The average freshman award was about $11,000.

Requirements for Admission SAT I or ACT scores and a college prep high school program, with a minimum 2.5 GPA.

Application There are no application deadlines. Notification of admission is made on a rolling basis.

International Students Students whose native language is not English must submit a paper-based TOEFL score of 500 or a 173 computer-based score. A financial certification form must be submitted to confirm that all expenses are covered for each year. The application deadline is June 1 for the fall semester and November 1 for the spring semester.

Transfer Students Official transcripts of all college work are required. It is strongly recommended that application be made several months prior to the beginning of the semester.

Admission Contact
Office of Undergraduate Admissions
Bradley University

100 Swords Hall
1501 West Bradley Avenue
Peoria, IL 61625-0002
Phone: (800) 447-6460; (309) 677-1000
FAX: (309) 677-2797
E-mail: *admissions@bradley.edu*
Web: *www.bradley.edu*

The Heart of the University Bradley is unique in that it is one of 36 private, medium-sized, independent colleges in America. This uniqueness is best demonstrated by the balance afforded to students in myriad ways. For example, take Bradley's location. While Peoria, Illinois represents the best of a Midwestern small city in terms of safety, friendliness, work ethic, and family orientation, Peoria will also surprise students in terms of "big city" opportunities. The metro area is the cultural, medical, and retail center for downstate Illinois, with a symphony orchestra, professional theater companies, a civic center, and Riverfront—the entertainment center of the town.

Academically, Bradley offers a balance of breadth and depth. With 90 undergraduate and 26 graduate programs, Bradley, unlike small colleges, includes faculty members whose specializations cover the full range of an academic discipline. At a larger university offering such a breadth of programs, students may be taught by graduate assistants. At Bradley, all courses are taught by professors who help students pursue their interests.

Also, faculty are both teachers and researchers who bring their research results into the classroom to enrich their instruction. Faculty also mentor student research and creative productions. While many faculty have won either prestigious awards or recognition, or performed as professionals in the subjects they teach, students always find them in their offices during office hours, ready to welcome students.

Bradley also offers a balance between classroom learning and career preparation, always teaching with an eye toward career preparation. With early and ongoing field experiences, teacher education and health science graduates have nearly a 100 percent job and graduate school placement rate.

BRIDGEWATER COLLEGE

Bridgewater, Virginia

Total Undergraduate Enrollment: 1,363
Men: 614 Women: 749
Five-Year Graduation Rate: 64%

Tuition: $$$
Room and Board: $$$
Residential Students: 84%

History Bridgewater College was established in 1880 and soon became the first coeducational liberal arts college in Virginia.

Location Bridgewater College's 190-acre campus is located in Bridgewater, Virginia (population 5,000), in the heart of the beautiful and historic Shenandoah Valley, eight miles south of Harrisonburg, Virginia. The college is situated between the Allegheny and Blue Ridge Mountains, and is commuting distance to cultural centers in Washington, D.C.; Richmond, Virginia; and Lexington, Kentucky.

Top Programs of Study Business administration, biology, psychology

Arts and Sciences Allied health science, art, athletic training, biology, chemistry, communication studies, computer science, economics, English, family and consumer sciences, French, health and exercise science, history, history and political science, information systems management, international studies, liberal studies, mathematics, medical technology, music, nutrition and wellness, philosophy and religion, physical science, physics, physics and mathematics, political science, psychology, sociology, Spanish

Business Administration (concentrations in accounting, finance, international commerce, managerial economics, organizational management)

Education Elementary, ESL, secondary, special

Pre-Professional Dentistry, engineering, law, medicine, pharmacy, physical therapy, veterinary medicine

Accredited Programs Business

Special Programs The college offers several dual degree programs: biology and environmental science with Duke; physical therapy at Shenandoah University; and veterinary science at Virginia Tech. Students can spend part or all of their junior year at one of 11 campuses in Europe, India, Japan, Ecquador, or China.

Facilities There are 25 buildings, including the newly renovated Carter Center for Worship and Music and the Funkhouser Center for Health and Wellness. There is also a radio station and an art gallery.

Transition to College Program In the Personal Development Program at freshman orientation, students are assigned to a faculty mentor who works with a small group of students throughout the fall semester in a credit-bearing course. Students set personal and academic goals and participate in a variety of experiences to achieve these. Benchmarks are set for the remaining college years, leading to a portfolio of accomplishments at graduation.

Athletics NCAA III, Old Dominion Athletic Conference

  Men: Baseball, basketball, cross-country, football, golf, soccer, tennis, track

  Women: Basketball, cross-country, field hockey, lacrosse, soccer, softball, tennis, track, volleyball

  Coed: Cheerleading, equestrian

Student Life and Housing About 1,000 students can be accommodated in college housing, which is guaranteed for all four years. Seventy-five per-

cent of the students are from Virginia, with the remainder from 20 other states and 12 countries. Ethnicity: Caucasian—92 percent. There are no sororities or fraternities. All students may keep cars. The students adhere to an honor code.

Accommodations for Students with Disabilities Students must contact the Director of Counseling.

Financial Aid All freshmen receive aid. The average award was about $15,700.

Requirements for Admission SAT I or ACT scores and a college prep high school program. An on-campus interview and good character are required.

Application Applications are due no later than August 1 for the fall semester, and 30 days prior to the spring semester.

International Students Students must score a minimum of 500 on the paper TOEFL or 173 on the electronic version, and also take the SAT I or ACT.

Transfer Students Required are transcripts from each college attended, SAT I or ACT scores, and good standing at the previous college. If students have an associate's degree from an accredited college, 68 credits may be transferred. Only courses with a grade C or better will be considered for transfer. Students must have a minimum GPA of 2.0.

Admission Contact
Office of Admissions
Bridgewater College
402 East College Street
Bridgewater, VA 22812-1599
Phone: (800) 759-8328; (540) 828-5375
FAX: (540) 828-5481
E-mail: *admission@bridgewater.edu*
Web: *www.bridgewater.edu*

The Heart of the College The mission of Bridgewater College is to educate and develop the whole person, graduating students who will "become leaders, living ethical, healthy, useful, and fulfilling lives with a strong sense of personal accountability and civic responsibility." This mission is fulfilled within a Christian learning community where students are encouraged to develop a personal faith and to find a meaningful place in the world.

Bridgewater's innovative approach to educating the whole person is through a Personal Development Portfolio Program, where students are encouraged to seek personal growth in several aspects of a rewarding life: ethical development, social proficiency, cultural awareness, physical wellness, aesthetic appreciation, leadership, and academic accomplishment. The PDP Program begins at freshman orientation and continues through all four years to graduation. Students are assigned a faculty mentor who helps students set goals for achieving skills and experiences that will benefit the student's personal and academic development, always with an eye toward educating the whole student.

Goals are varied and student activities to fulfill these are diverse. Students might research a moral dilemma in a career or industry for ethical development, volunteer on the rescue squad for service learning, train for a race to develop wellness, or work for a political party to develop citizenship skills.

Benchmarks are set for continuing personal development during sophomore, junior, and senior years. At graduation, students have a record of accomplishments to show prospective employers or graduate admissions committees, as well as having established a pattern for living that will bring a more meaningful life.

Bridgewater is ranked first among Southern colleges for the percentage of faculty who teach full time. This helps to establish the quality of community that is necessary to fulfill its mission of educating the whole person.

BRYANT COLLEGE Smithfield, Rhode Island

Total Undergraduate Enrollment: 2,700
Men: 1,660 Women: 1,040
Five-Year Graduation Rate: 65%

Tuition: $$$$
Room and Board: $$$$
Residential Students: 85%

History Bryant College was founded in 1863 in Providence, Rhode Island, and moved to its present location in 1971. Bryant is a private, non-denominational institution with emphasis on careers in business.

Location The 392-acre campus is located in Smithfield, Rhode Island, a suburban area 12 miles northwest of Providence.

Top Programs of Study Finance, management, marketing

Arts and Sciences Communications, economics, English, history, information technology, international studies, psychology

Business Accounting, accounting information systems, applied actuarial, computer informa-

tion systems, finance, financial services, management, marketing, mathematics

Education None

Pre-Professional None

Accredited Programs Business

Special Programs There are several minors, including International Business, Biotechnology, Legal Studies, and Women's Studies. There are opportunities for study abroad and internships. There is an Intercultural Center to provide programs, counseling, and support services for Bryant's international and multiethnic community. There is an Army ROTC program.

Facilities There are 45 buildings, including the Bryant Student Center, which has a hair salon and dry-cleaning service; a new Wellness Center with a six-lane pool and an outstanding fitness facility; the Athletic and Recreation Center; Bulldog Stadium; the new Bello Center for Information and Technology, which houses a trading room and a cyber café; the Koffler Technology Center; an FM radio station; a new television studio; and a video conference center.

Transition to College Program The Faculty Mentoring Program assists first-year students with the transition. Also, the Academic Center for Excellence provides instruction in taking better notes, forming effective study groups, test-taking strategies, and more.

Athletics NCAA II, Northeast 10 Conference

Men: Baseball, basketball, cross-country, football, golf, lacrosse, soccer, tennis, track & field (indoor and outdoor)

Women: Basketball, cross-country, field hockey, golf, lacrosse, soccer, softball, tennis, track & field (indoor and outdoor), volleyball

Student Life and Housing About 2,500 students can be accommodated in college housing, which is guaranteed for all four years. Only 17 percent of the students are from Rhode Island, with the majority from 32 states (mostly the Northeast) and 40 countries. Ethnicity: Caucasian—83 percent; International—5 percent; African-American—3 percent; Hispanic-American—3 percent; Asian-American—2 percent. There are seven national fraternities and three national sororities. All students may keep cars.

Accommodations for Students with Disabilities In compliance with section 504

Financial Aid About 87 percent of all freshmen receive aid. The average freshman award was about $13,000.

Requirements for Admission SAT I or ACT scores and a college prep high school program. A personal, on-campus interview is recommended.

Application The Early Decision deadline is November 1, with admission notification sent December 15. The regular application deadline is March 15, with decision notification sent on a rolling basis, usually 4–6 weeks after the application file is complete.

International Students Required are official school transcripts or statement of marks for all years completed, a progress report for all courses not yet completed, standard exam results, SAT I or ACT scores, a minimum TOEFL score of 550, at least one recommendation from a counselor or teacher, and completion of a certification of finances form with supporting bank statements.

Transfer Students Required are official secondary and all college transcripts, as well as a list of courses (not included on transcripts) that the student expects to complete before the proposed date of transfer. Course descriptions or syllabi will be needed for credit evaluation. Students must be in good standing at the college of transfer.

Admission Contact
Office of Admissions
Bryant College
1150 Douglas Pike
Smithfield, RI 02917-1284
Phone: (800) 622-7001; (401) 232-6100
FAX: (401) 232-6741
E-mail: *admissions@bryant.edu*
Web: *www.bryant.edu*

The Heart of the College Bryant College is unique for its emphasis on business. If students want to prepare for careers in the business world, Bryant provides a high-caliber, student-centered education. Not only does Bryant teach skills and knowledge to get that first position—working in and leading groups, communicating effectively, problem solving in a rapidly changing marketplace, and technological proficiency—but also those qualities that provide a long-term perspective that will prepare the student for a second and third career.

The resources for an education in business are exceptional. The campus is home to the World

Trade Center Rhode Island; the Chafee Center for International Business, whose Export Assistance Center has received the U.S. Department of Commerce's highest award; the Verizon-Bryant College Telecommunications Center, which prepares businesses, community organizations, and schools to use evolving telecommunications for e-business and e-education; a partnership with the Rhode Island School of Design, which assists entrepreneurs in the development or improvement of products through creative design as well as helping artists and designers to develop effective business practices; the Institute for Family Enterprise, which researches the oldest family businesses in the world in order to learn the practices of operating and sustaining a successful family business. Also, technology is given premium status, with each instructional computer on campus upgraded or replaced every two years.

Study abroad programs give students opportunities to study Asian business practices in Japan, business in France, a proficiency in a second language, and the critical importance of gaining a global perspective. Other travel sites include Spain, Ireland, Italy, Austria, Germany, Greece, and others.

The faculty are scholars and business professionals with a focus on teaching. While they gain recognition and expertise through their research and consulting for business, government, and industry, they work at Bryant because of its student-centered approach, which places professors in roles as mentors. While Bryant's classes are not very small, the average class size is small enough for professors to know students by name as well as their strengths and weaknesses. One student commented: "Bryant's professors are exceptional. They make the time to meet with you and really get to know you on a personal level."

Bryant has an active Career Services staff which brings more than 300 corporations to campus yearly, provides Shadow programs and individual career counseling, and places students in internships with more than 300 companies. These services, along with an extensive alumni network that works as a strong advocate for Bryant students result in significant outcomes: Within six months of graduation, 98 percent of Bryant' graduates are employed or enrolled full time in graduate school; 52 percent are employed at Fortune 1000 firms.

Although Bryant is noted for its education for the world of business, an enterprise typically associated with competition, the same can't be said of its students, who demonstrate a genuine cooperative spirit. In addition to their work in groups, their lives on campus may help to develop this cooperative spirit. With plenty of clubs and groups, a strong athletic program—including club and intramural, excellent outdoor and indoor facilities, as well as residence facilities that move students from dorms to townhouses by senior year, students develop close friendships quickly.

Off campus, Providence is just 15 minutes away, beckoning students with its malls, sporting events, theater, Performing Arts Center, and the East Side eclectic mix of cultures. Also, nearby are Newport's beaches and coastal city, with the big city mecca of Boston an hour away.

CALIFORNIA BAPTIST UNIVERSITY

Riverside, California

Total Undergraduate Enrollment: 1,400
Men: 475 Women: 925
Five-Year Graduation Rate: 53%

Tuition: $$
Room and Board: $$$
Residential Students: 43%

History California Baptist was founded in 1950 and is the only Southern Baptist college or university on the West Coast. The university offers a liberal arts education in a Christian environment.

Location California Baptist is located in Riverside, California (population 240,000), one hour east of Los Angeles, on a beautiful 80-acre campus, complete with palm trees and views of the San Bernardino Mountains.

Top Programs of Study Behavioral sciences, education

Arts and Sciences Art, behavioral science, biology, Christian studies, communication arts, criminal justice administration, English, fine arts, fine arts ministry, history, information systems, liberal studies, mathematics, music, philosophy, political science, psychology, social science, visual arts

Business Administration, organizational management

Education Elementary, physical education, secondary

Pre-Professional Law, medicine

Accredited Programs Business, music

Special Programs Students have the opportunity to participate in the university's partnership with the Los Angeles Film Institute. There is also an affiliation with the Focus on the Family Institute in Colorado. Students have many opportunities for Christian mission and ministry. The university has one of the best speech and debate teams in the nation. The university participates in the Au Sable Institute of Environmental Studies in Michigan and a Latin American studies program in Costa Rica. Master's degrees are offered in business administration, education, and counseling psychology.

Facilities There are 25 mission-style buildings with distinctive red brick, including the newly constructed Lancer Sports Center, an aquatic center, the Wallace Theater, the Metcalf Gallery, a Mac lab for graphic artists, and the Gabriel Library.

Transition to College Program New students participate in FOCUS, consisting of two parts: an orientation and a university success course. The course consists of a semester-long series of small group seminars, activities, and discussions to help students succeed academically, socially, emotionally, and spiritually.

Athletics NAIA, Golden State Athletic Conference

Men: Baseball, basketball, cross-country, soccer, swimming, volleyball, water polo

Women: Basketball, cross-country, soccer, softball, swimming, track & field, volleyball, water polo

Student Life and Housing About 750 students can be accommodated in college housing, which is comprised of single-sex dorms and three apartment complexes. Seventy percent of the students are from California, with the remainder from 40 other states and 14 countries. Ethnicity: Caucasian—86 percent; International—10 percent. There are no sororities or fraternities. All students may keep cars.

Accommodations for Students with Disabilities In compliance with section 504

Financial Aid About 89 percent of all freshmen receive aid. The average freshman award was about $8,500.

Requirements for Admission SAT I or ACT scores and a college prep high school program.

Application There are no application deadlines. When all required documents are submitted, an admission decision is made on a rolling basis.

International Students The application for the fall semester is July 15, and for the spring semester is November 15. Students must submit secondary school and college transcripts, with a certified English translation for students applying from non-English speaking countries, and have a 520 TOEFL score, or 430 on the verbal SAT I, or 17 in the English section of the ACT, or a 2.0 minimum GPA in a college where English is the primary language. A certified bank statement indicating that the student has sufficient funds for a college education is also required.

Transfer Students Official transcripts from previous institutions are required. If students have more than 30 transferable credits from an accredited institution, they need not submit high school transcripts or SAT I or ACT scores.

Admission Contact
Office of Admissions
California Baptist University
8432 Magnolia Avenue
Riverside, CA 92504-3297
Phone: (877) 228-8866; (909) 689-5771
FAX: (909) 343-4525
E-mail: *admission@calbaptist*
Web: *www.calbaptist.edu*

The Heart of the University As a Christian university, the heart of California Baptist is an education that focuses on understanding the world through a Christ-centered lens.

In Cal Baptist's liberal arts foundation there is much reading, writing, thinking, and saying as students develop the ability to communicate effectively, think critically, and work as part of a team. These foundational skills help students succeed in several outstanding programs. The teacher education program focuses both on teaching and learning and the skills and knowledge to make a difference in the life of a student. The fine arts program offers visual artists the latest equipment for graphic artists, an excellent gallery, and a partnership with the Los Angeles Film Institute. The nationally accredited music program offers many opportunities for students to demonstrate their developing expertise. The major in Christian studies provides many concentrations for students to select from. The popular and well regarded psychology program prepares students to serve as counselors, therapists, and social service workers. Students have the luxury of having a master's degree program on campus, as well as many internship opportunities right in the Riverside area.

Cal Baptist students build their faith through weekly chapel services, youth ministry, and peer mentoring. Then through volunteer work, missions, and ministry, students put their faith, knowledge, and skills to work in a wide variety of outreach activities, including giving up their dining hall lunches and delivering them to homeless people, ministries to the elderly in local nursing homes, serving in a home for runaway teens, and helping operate a safe house for victims of domestic violence. In addition, each May, small groups of students and faculty set out for more distant destinations to serve as teachers and builders in countries such as Australia, China, Kenya, Russia, Vietnam, and Italy. An administrator of campus ministries captures the powerful effect of such work when she says: "Nothing compares to the lessons of humility and gratitude we learn through service to those suffering in poverty or oppression."

The faculty—85 percent of whom hold terminal degrees—teach small classes, which help them provide personal attention and function as mentors and friends as well. One professor describes the faculty this way: "We are Christians who teach." Students say that professors provide plenty of support and make them feel welcome.

The campus is a lively one, with many clubs and organizations, music ensembles, drama and forensics teams, active ministries programs, and top-notch athletics teams in water polo, swimming and diving, volleyball, and track & field. The Office of Job Development and Placement helps place students in valuable internships with high-tech firms and Fortune 500 companies, as well as with schools, social agencies, and churches. Students get plenty of counseling, workshops, and excellent graduate school counseling.

Cal Baptist's Southern California location offers students much as well: sunny days, Malibu beaches, ski slopes, Disneyland, professional sports, Los Angeles, and cultural, dining, and entertainment opportunities.

CALIFORNIA LUTHERAN UNIVERSITY

Thousand Oaks, California

Total Undergraduate Enrollment: 1,518
Men: 698 Women: 820
Five-Year Graduation Rate: 60%

Tuition: $$$
Room and Board: $$$
Residential Students: 83%

History Richard Pederson, the son of Norwegian immigrants, donated his scenic ranch that was to become the heart of the campus of California Lutheran, founded in 1959 by the American Lutheran Church and the Lutheran Church in America.

Location California Lutheran is located on a beautiful 290 acres, 12 miles from the Pacific Ocean, in Thousand Oaks, California (population 100,000), a city rated as one of the safest in America. The campus is situated midway between Los Angeles and Santa Barbara, a one hour drive from each. The campus is bordered by the Santa Monica Mountains and Mount Cliff Ridge, with many cultural and outdoor activities available.

Top Programs of Study Business, education, sciences

Art and Sciences Art, biochemistry and molecular biology, biology, chemistry, communication arts, computer information systems, computer science, criminal justice, drama, economics, English, exercise science and sports medicine, French, geology, German, interdisciplinary studies, international studies, liberal studies, marketing communication, mathematics, multimedia, music, philosophy, physics, political science, psychology, religion, social science, sociology, Spanish, youth ministry

Business Accounting, administration (concentrations in finance, information technology, international business, management, marketing, small business/entrepreneurship)

Education Elementary, physical education, secondary

Pre-Professional Dentistry, medicine, physical therapy, seminary

Accredited Programs None

Special Programs Students have the luxury of many professional internship opportunities in the biotech-laden Thousand Oaks area. Drama students participate in a summer Shakespeare Festival at the university's Kingsmen Park. Geology students visit the Grand Canyon and other significant sites. Political science majors have access to the Ronald Reagan Presidential Library, only 10 minutes from campus. A Washington, D.C., semester is also available. There are Army and Air Force ROTC programs.

Facilities There are 40 buildings, including the 600-seat Samuelson Chapel, the state-of-the-art Ahmansen Science Center, the Pearson Library, a new humanities center, a refurbished Forum used for music and drama productions, an art gallery, and a radio station. A master plan includes the construction of an athletics complex and a new student union building.

Transition to College Program Freshman Seminar is comprised of classes with 20 students who have similar academic interests, led by an academic adviser and a peer student adviser, meeting weekly to plan the students' college years.

Athletics NCAA III, Southern California Intercollegiate Conference

Men: Baseball, basketball, cross-country, football, golf, soccer, tennis, track & field

Women: Basketball, cross-country, softball, soccer, tennis, track & field, volleyball

Student Life and Housing About 900 students can be accommodated in college housing, which is guaranteed for all four years. Eighty-four percent of the students are from California, and the remainder from 30 other states and 19 countries. Ethnicity: Caucasian—80 percent; Hispanic-American—12 percent; Asian-American—3 percent; International—3 percent; African-American—2 percent. There are no sororities or fraternities. All students may keep cars.

Accommodations for Students with Disabilities Reasonable efforts will be made to accommodate students with special learning needs who self-identify and have documentation. Students should discuss their needs for accommodation with the Academic Advising and Learning Center.

Financial Aid About 87 percent of all freshmen receive aid. The average freshman award was about $17,000.

Requirements for Admission SAT I or ACT scores, a college prep high school program, and the quality and scope of extracurricular activities.

Application There are no deadlines. A rolling admissions plan is used to notify students of an admissions decision as soon as all application materials have been received.

International Students Official detailed transcripts are required. Students whose primary language is not English are required to have a minimum TOEFL score of 530. Students must provide proof that sufficient funds will be available to meet their educational expenses.

Transfer Students Transcripts from all previous colleges are required. If fewer than 28 credits have been earned, a high school transcript and SAT or ACT scores are required. The student must be in good standing at the previous college.

Admission Contact
Office of Admissions
California Lutheran University
60 West Olsen Road
Thousand Oaks, CA 91360-2787
Phone: (877) CLU-FOR-U; (805) 493-3135
FAX: (805) 493-3114
E-mail: *cluadm@clunet.edu*
Web: *www.clunet.edu*

The Heart of the University There's no question that California Lutheran views students as its first priority and is designed to meet their needs in a multitude of attractive ways. These ways are planned to graduate students as "world-citizens"—leaders for our global society, strong in character, and committed to service and justice.

The university offers students an integrated core curriculum—Core 21—which helps students comprehend issues from a variety of perspectives, helping each student to answer three major questions: Who am I? Why am I here? What shall I do? The courses are offered in small classes with plenty of student involvement. The academic program is set in an open-minded community where students feel free to speak their minds and explore new ideas. There is no one type of student, so everyone values diversity of thought, background, and faiths. Faculty help nurture this open-minded climate, caring more about mentoring, teaching, encouraging, and doing research with their students than about themselves.

Location, location, location. The beautiful campus is located in Thousand Oaks, halfway between Santa Barbara and Los Angeles, with vast cultural, entertainment, and sporting opportunities nearby. Students are nine miles from Malibu beaches and an hour from ski slopes!

The university has a great appreciation for an education that prepares students for careers and graduate school. In addition to career counseling and development, students are encouraged to do internships. Agilent, CNN, Unisys, Warner Brothers, the Los Angeles Dodgers, and Baxter Pharmaceuticals are some of the internship opportunities. In a typical year, 96 percent of the graduates are placed in graduate school or jobs within three months of graduation. The university reports nearly a perfect acceptance rate into medical, dental, and veterinary schools. Students say its like having a headhunter on campus, with students landing jobs with Disney, Sony, Rockwell Science Center, and Baxter Biotech.

California Lutheran is all about a successful student-centered education.

CALVIN COLLEGE   Grand Rapids, Michigan

Total Undergraduate Enrollment: 4,300   Tuition: $$$
Men: 1,940 Women: 2,360   Room and Board: $$
Five-Year Graduation Rate: 71%   Residential Students: 65%

History Calvin College, established in 1876, is a private institution affiliated with the Christian Reformed Church, which bases its whole faith on the Bible as God's infallible word. The college has been named to the Templeton Foundation's Honor Roll of Character-Building Colleges.

Location The 370-acre wooded campus is located in suburban Grand Rapids, Michigan (population 650,000).

Top Programs of Study Education, business, engineering

Arts and Sciences Art, art history, biochemistry, biology, biotechnology, chemistry, classical civilization, classical languages, communication arts and sciences, computer science, criminal justice, Dutch, economics, engineering, English, environmental science, environmental studies, film studies, French, geology, German, Greek, history, Latin, mathematics, music, nursing, philosophy, physics, political science, psychology, recreation, religion, religion and theology, social work, sociology, Spanish, telecommunications, theater

Business Accounting, administration, management

Education Early childhood, physical education, special

Pre-Professional Architecture, dentistry, engineering, law, medicine, pharmacy, physical therapy, seminary, social work

Accredited Programs Chemistry, education, engineering, music, nursing, social work

Special Programs The college uses a 4-1-4 calendar with two four-month semesters and a three-week January term. Opportunities exist for study abroad internships, double majors, and student designed majors. Domestic programs include a Chicago semester and an American studies semester in Washington, D.C., a film studies program in Hollywood, and an environmental program in Michigan's lower peninsula. There are minors in several subjects, including dance, ESL, journalism, and third world development studies. There is an Army ROTC program.

Facilities There are 40 buildings including Knollcrest Fieldhouse, which seats 4,500; a new Engineering Building that contains space for student–faculty research and design; the new DeVries Hall of Science with medical research laboratories and classrooms; the Hekman Library-Hiemanza Hall, an excellent research facility accommodating 1,500 students and housing a television studio; centers for Christian Scholarship and Calvinism Studies; a teacher education curriculum center; the Spoelhof College Center, which houses an art gallery and studios; a 340-seat auditorium; a Fine Arts Center with a 1,000-seat auditorium; a Science Complex with an electron microscope and an observatory; and a new Communications Building and Conference Center. The campus is the home of the Calvin Theological Seminary.

Transition to College Program The Gateway Program is comprised of two linked courses required of all first-year students. The first, "Prelude," is a progressive orientation to Calvin as an academic community in the Reformed tradition and is offered in the fall. The second, "Developing a Christian Mind," is a first-year course designed to introduce students to a Reformed Christian worldview and its relevance for contemporary issues.

Athletics NCAA III, Michigan Intercollegiate Athletic Conference

Men: Baseball, basketball, cross-country, golf, soccer, swimming, tennis, track

Women: Basketball, cross-country, golf, soccer, softball, swimming, tennis, track

Student Life and Housing About 2,500 students can be accommodated in college housing, which includes single-sex dorms, on-campus apartments, a multicultural residence hall wing, and three houses with an urban focus. Fifty-four percent of the students are from Michigan. The remainder are from 46 other states and 35 countries. Ethnicity: Caucasian—84 percent; International—8 percent; Asian-American—3 percent; African-American—1 percent; Hispanic-American—1 percent. There are no fraternities or sororities. All students may keep cars.

Accommodations for Students with Disabilities Inquiries regarding reasonable accommodations should be directed to the Vice President for Administration and Finance.

Financial Aid About 91 percent of all freshmen receive aid. The average freshman award was about $11,000.

Requirements for Admission ACT or SAT I scores, a 2.5 GPA, and evidence of Christian commitment and the capacity to learn.

Application Applications should be filed by August 15 for the fall semester, December 15 for the winter semester, and January 15 for the spring semester.

International Students Those students whose first language is not English must score a minimum of 550 on the TOEFL, or take the MELAB if the score is below that minimum. Required are essays, official high school and, if applicable, college transcripts, a recommendation, ACT or SAT I scores, a declaration of finances, and a profile of educational background form.

Transfer Students Required are official high school and college transcripts of all institutions attended, a minimum GPA of 2.0 for students from four-year institutions and a 2.5 GPA for those from two-year institutions. Thirty-one credits must be completed at Calvin. A minimum course grade of C is required to transfer credit. No more than 70 credits can be transferred.

Admission Contact
Office of Admissions
Calvin College
3201 Burton Street, SE
Grand Rapids, MI 49546
Phone: (800) 688-0122; (616) 957-8551
FAX: (616) 957-6777
E-mail: *admissions@calvin.edu*
Web: *www.calvin.edu*

The Heart of the College The heart of Calvin College, considered one of the top evangelical colleges in America, flows from its mission statement: "We pledge fidelity to Jesus Christ, offering our hearts and lives to do God's work in God's world." Calvin is a Christian academic community in the pursuit of a liberal arts education. The core curriculum is really a group of general education requirements from which students select courses that provide the knowledge, skills, and virtues to prepare them to live an informed life of Christian service. Students learn about God, the world, and themselves; develop speaking and writing skills; and cultivate the virtues of honesty, patience, charity, and love. The 4-1-4 calendar allows for the January Series, a month-long lecture–cultural enrichment series that has several times won the prestigious Silver Bowl Award for the best college/university lecture series in America.

Calvin has a strong athletic program and over 50 student organizations. The Director of Student Activities, along with a student board, plan a calendar of movies, concerts, comedy, and theater. In addition to varsity, club, intramural sports participation, and club and organization activities, many students participate in music programs comprised of bands, choral groups, and chamber ensembles, as well as art workshops, and working with visiting artists. The English Department nurtures Calvin's long tradition of creative writing for publication and private reading. Students participate in service opportunities that are integrated within the context of their courses. They are also encouraged to participate in chapel services held Sunday evening and weekday mornings, as well as Bible study groups, prayer groups, and Campus Crusade.

Calvin viewed God's plan for His kingdom on earth to be comprised of diverse people; therefore, the college, once a very homogeneous population, is ardently reaching out to expand its multicultural population. An Office of Multicultural Student Development helps promote the effort as well as providing support services to students of other ethnicities. Mosaic House is a residence hall for students from a variety of backgrounds who choose to learn about one another by living together.

Students enjoy the excellent academic programs in education, engineering, business, communication arts, and sciences, as well as the varied residence halls, the "best buy" tuition, and the numerous scholarship opportunities. Classes are small, making relationships with a Christian faculty that focuses on teaching and advisement much easier to establish and very rewarding. These relationships help shape collaborative research projects for professors and students, especially funded summer research.

Grand Rapids offers malls, cultural opportunities, and professional sports. Lake Michigan beaches are only an hour away.

CANISIUS COLLEGE   Buffalo, New York

Total Undergraduate Enrollment: 3,440
Men: 1,618 Women: 1,822
Five-Year Graduation Rate: 64%

Tuition: $$$
Room and Board: $$$
Residential Students: 41%

History Canisius was founded in 1870 by the Jesuits and is conducted in the Catholic and Jesuit tradition. The College is named for St. Peter Canisius, a sixteenth-century Dutch scholar who was an early member of the Jesuits.

Location Canisius is located on a 32-acre campus in a residential area of Buffalo, in northwest New York. The Metro Rail rapid transit system connects the college directly with many cultural and entertainment opportunities in Buffalo, home of the Buffalo Bills football team. The campus is 30 minutes from beautiful Niagara Falls.

Top Programs of Study Education, social sciences, marketing

Arts and Sciences Art history, biochemistry, bioinformatics, biology, chemistry, clinical laboratory science, communication studies, computer sciences, criminal justice, digital media arts, economics, English, environmental science, European studies, French, German, history, international relations, mathematics and statistics, philosophy, physics, political science, psychology, religious studies, sociology/anthropology, Spanish, urban studies/public administration

Business Accounting, accounting information systems, economics, entrepreneurship, finance, management, management computer information systems, marketing

Education Athletic training/sports medicine, early childhood, physical education, secondary, special

Pre-Professional Dentistry, engineering, environmental science and forestry, law, medicine, pharmacy, veterinary medicine

Accredited Programs Athletic training, business, chemistry

Special Programs There are several joint degree programs: dentistry, optometry, podiatry, and early assurance admission programs in medicine with Buffalo and Syracuse's Medical Schools; fashion merchandising with the Fashion Institute of Technology, New York City. The university offers a major in the innovative field of bioinformatics. There is an Army ROTC program.

Facilities There are 40 buildings, including a planetarium and radio and television studios. Digital media arts students use state-of-the-art facilities in the recently renovated Lyons Hall. The college has spent over $80 million over the past several years in order to provide state-of-the-art classrooms, recreational facilities, and residence halls.

Transition to College Program Canisius offers a First-Year Experience involving a series of weekly programs to help students in everything from stress management to writing a biology lab.

Athletics NCAA I, Metro Atlantic Athletic Conference

Men: Baseball, basketball, cross-country, football, golf, ice hockey, lacrosse, rifle, soccer, tennis, track

Women: Basketball, cross-country, lacrosse, soccer, softball, swimming and diving, synchronized swimming, tennis, track, volleyball

Student Life and Housing About 1,000 students can be accommodated in college housing, which is guaranteed for all four years. Ninety-one percent of the students are from New York, with the remainder from 35 states and 32 countries. Ethnicity: Caucasian—78 percent; African-American—8 percent; International—3 percent; Hispanic-American—2 percent; Asian-American—1 percent. There is one fraternity and one sorority. All students may keep cars.

Accommodations for Students with Disabilities Intracampus shuttle service, interpreters, specially adapted equipment, note takers and lecture taping are some of the many accommodations available. Testing facilities, proctors, and readers are also available.

Financial Aid About 80 percent of freshmen receive aid. The average freshman award was about $16,500.

Requirements for Admission SAT I or ACT scores and a college prep high school program is recommended.

Application Once all application materials have been received, the college notifies students of admission decisions on a rolling basis. Freshmen are admitted fall and spring semesters and application deadlines are open.

International Students Students whose native language is not English must submit a TOEFL minimum score of 500, all secondary school records and grades, all college transcripts, if applicable, and a certification of finances form accompanied by supporting official bank statements.

Transfer Students High school and college transcripts are required. A 2.0 GPA is required. Canisius has transfer agreements with many colleges in New York. Students who are earning an associate's degree from another institution are encouraged to speak with their advisers in order to facilitate appropriate transfer credit.

Admission Contact
Office of Admissions
Canisius College
2001 Main Street
Buffalo, NY 14208-1098
Phone: (800) 843-1517; (716) 883-7000

FAX: (716) 888-3230
E-mail: *inquiry@canisius.edu*
Web: *www.canisius.edu*

The Heart of the College Canisius College is a Catholic college sharing the Jesuit heritage "care for the individual" with 27 other Jesuit colleges and universities in America. The combined emphasis at Canisius provides an education that seeks to develop leaders—graduates who will lead in their chosen professions, communities, and in service to humanity.

Canisius College's mission is experienced by students through both the college' core academic program and internship focus. No matter what major a student chooses, he or she graduates with a solid foundation in a diverse group of courses known as a core curriculum. These courses focus on critical thinking, written and oral communication, and global understanding of people and history. Students study the core curriculum as well as the required courses in their major field of study. Students are taught by a knowledgeable, caring faculty, who enjoy working closely with students.

Two of the college's newest and most innovative programs are digital media arts and bioinformatics. The digital media art major focuses on digital design and interactive media, and is offered in state-of-the-art facilities. The biology and computer science departments collaborated to offer a bioinformatics major that involves the understanding, generation, processing, and propagation of biological information.

Canisius offers its students wonderful internship opportunities. Students are encouraged to begin discussing internship possibilities with their professors or academic advisers as early as freshman year. Students are impressed with the ease and quality of these internships, including those at the Buffalo Sabres National Hockey Team, The Children's Hospital of Buffalo, CBS Hollywood, Forensic Mental Health Services of Western New York, HSBC Bank USA, and PricewaterhouseCoopers. In a recent year, 100 percent of the students who applied to law school were accepted, as well as 93 percent to medical or other health science professional schools.

CARROLL COLLEGE   **Helena, Montana**

Total Undergraduate Enrollment: 1,200
Men: 480 Women: 720
Five-Year Graduation Rate: 63%

Tuition: $$
Room and Board: $
Residential Students: 70%

History Carroll is a Catholic liberal arts college founded by Bishop John Patrick Carroll, second Bishop of the Diocese of Helena, who desired to build a college in western Montana. Originally called Mount Saint Charles College, its doors opened in 1910. Later, the school's name was changed in honor of Bishop Carroll.

Location The 64-acre campus is located in the state capital, Helena, Montana—a small town 110 miles east of Missoula and 100 miles west of Bozeman.

Top Programs of Study Biology/pre-med, business, education, nursing

Arts and Sciences Biology, chemistry, civil engineering, classical studies, communication studies, computer science, English, English writing, environmental studies, ethics and values studies, French, history, international relations, mathematics, nursing, philosophy, psychology, public administration, public relations (concentrations in business and journalism), social science, sociology, Spanish, theater, theology

Business Accounting, administration (concentrations in economics, finance, management), concentration in sports management

Education Elementary, health and physical education, secondary, TESOL

Pre-Professional Clinical laboratory science, dentistry, law, medicine, optometry, pharmacy, veterinary medicine

Accredited Programs Civil engineering, nursing

Special Programs Carroll offers a cooperative (3-2) engineering program with Columbia University, Notre Dame, Montana State University, and other schools. The college has an excellent forensics (debate) team, an Intensive Language Institute for international and cross-cultural students, and an Army ROTC program. Students have internships, cooperative education, and study abroad opportunities.

Facilities There are 12 buildings, including the state-of-the-art Fortin Science Center, outfitted with new, high-tech research equipment; the renovated Carroll Campus Center; the recently renovated Simperman Hall classroom building; the new Nelson Stadium; the Waterbarn Theatre; a network television station, NBC affiliate, KTVH Channel 12; an observatory; and a 12-piano music lab.

Transition to College Program Carroll offers a traditional orientation program.

Athletics NAIA, Frontier Conference

    Men: Basketball, football, golf

    Women: Basketball, golf, soccer, volleyball

Student Life and Housing About 800 students can be accommodated in college housing, which is guaranteed for all four years. Sixty-eight percent of the students are from Montana, the remainder are from 21 other states and 10 countries. Ethnicity: Caucasian—94 percent. There are no fraternities or sororities. All students may keep cars.

Accommodations for Students with Disabilities Recent documentation of disability or an IEP on file at the high school within the last three school years is acceptable. The Academic Resource Center, in cooperation with the campus departments, coordinates accommodations. Students need to disclose disability to admission and ARC staff.

Financial Aid About 96 percent of all freshmen receive aid. The average freshman award was about $11,500.

Requirements for Admission ACT (preferred) or SAT I scores and a college prep high school program.

Application Rolling admission policy, with a priority admission deadline of June 1 for fall admission and November 1 for spring admission. An admission decision is made three weeks after a completed application is submitted.

International Students Certified copies of transcripts, diplomas, certificates, and degrees received are required, as well as certified copies of all subjects for which the applicant was enrolled. If records are not in English, an official certified translation is required. Regular application deadlines apply. English-speaking students must submit ACT or SAT I results, while non-English-speaking students are required to have a minimum score of 550 on the TOEFL.

Transfer Students A GPA of 2.5 is required along with official transcripts from previous colleges. An official high school transcript is required if fewer than 30 credits have been earned, along with a letter of recommendation, and ACT or SAT I scores. These students need a C or 2.0 GPA. Courses with C grades or better are considered for transfer.

Admission Contact
Office of Admissions
Carroll College
1601 N. Benton Avenue
Helena, MT 59625
Phone: (800) 992-3648; (406) 447-4300
FAX: (406) 447-4533
E-mail: *enroll@carroll.edu*
Web: *www.carroll.eddu*

The Heart of the College Although Carroll is a Catholic college, religion is not the most prominent feature of the college. Forty percent of the students are not Catholic.

The heart of Carroll College is the quality of its academic programs and nurturing faculty. Many of Carroll's biology students choose the program because of its success in preparing students to move on to medical and veterinary school, or graduate studies in molecular biology and biotechnologies. Also, state-of-the-art laboratories and faculty–student research projects helped a recent class of Carroll students applying to medical school with 90 percent being accepted. In mathematics and engineering, almost half of the graduates go on to do graduate work at schools such as Columbia, Purdue, Notre Dame, and MIT. Performing arts students are offered a high level of personalized attention and the opportunity even as freshmen and sophomores to have choice roles in performances. Students often spend their summers performing and interning with repertory theaters across the country. The excellent nursing program offers sophomores clinical experience in a variety of environments, including hospitals, retirement homes, long-term care, psychiatric and school settings. It is no surprise that in a recent class 67 percent had accepted positions before graduation!

Many of the faculty are involved in research projects with their students. With small classes and no teaching assistants teaching courses, Carroll has a dedicated faculty, each of whom advises a maximum of 20 students, helping to foster a mentor relationship—the kind of caring, supportive relationship that realizes that students stay up all night studying for finals, so professors serve students a Midnight Breakfast.

The college is situated in Helena, the state capital, a place filled with history, theater, movies, hockey and baseball teams. The capital offers Carroll's students popular internships with elected officials. Helena also offers the great outdoors: hiking, skiing, whitewater rafting, snowboarding, fishing, rock climbing, and more.

CARROLL COLLEGE
Waukesha, Wisconsin

Total Undergraduate Enrollment: 2,718
Men: 920 Women: 1,798
Five-Year Graduation Rate: 56%

Tuition: $$$
Room and Board: $
Residential Students: 56%

History In 1841 settlers living in the Wisconsin Territory community of Prairieville established an academy that would in 1846 become Carroll College. Affiliated with the Presbyterian Church, the early patrons believed that higher education would civilize the wilderness, spread the Gospel, and plant the roots of democracy. Carroll, Wisconsin's oldest college, is known as the "Pioneer College."

Location The college is located on a 52-acre campus in Waukesha, Wisconsin (population 62,000), west of Milwaukee, and minutes from state forests and parks, with Chicago 100 miles south.

Top Programs of Study Education, business, nursing

Arts and Sciences Actuarial science, art, athletic training, biochemistry, biology, chemistry, communication, computer science, criminal justice, English, environmental science, exercise science, forensic science, geography, graphic communication, history, international relations, journalism, marine biology, mathematics, music, nursing, photography, physical therapy, politics, psychology, public relations, religious studies, social work, sociology, Spanish, theater arts

Business Accounting, administration (concentrations in finance, management, marketing, small business ownership/entrepreneurship), human resources, organizational leadership

Education Adaptive, early childhood, elementary, physical education, secondary

Pre-Professional Clinical lab sciences, dentistry, engineering, law, medicine, occupational therapy, pharmacy, veterinary medicine

Accredited Programs Accounting, chemistry, medical technology, social work

Special Programs Available are self-designed majors, a Washington semester at American University, and a United Nations semester. Students also have the opportunity for international travel to destinations that are culturally different from their own, such as Latin America, Africa, Asia, Western and Eastern Europe. There is an Air Force ROTC program.

Facilities There are 31 buildings, including the recently renovated Wehr Library, Van Male Fieldhouse, and Main Hall, Carroll's signature classroom building. There is also a radio station.

Transition to College Program The First-Year Seminar introduces students to ideas at the heart of liberal studies, seeks to strengthen a range of skills needed for academic achievement, and introduces students to Carroll life. Also, students take a writing seminar to improve their writing abilities.

Athletics NCAA III, Midwest Conference

Men: Baseball, basketball, cross-country, football, golf, soccer, swimming, tennis, track & field

Women: Basketball, cross-country, golf, soccer, softball, swimming, tennis, track & field, volleyball

Student Life and Housing About 1,200 students can be accommodated in college housing, which is guaranteed for all four years. Seventy-eight percent of the students are from Wisconsin, the remainder from 30 other states and 27 countries. Ethnicity: Caucasian—92 percent. There are three local fraternities and four national sororities. All students may keep cars.

Accommodations for Students with Disabilities Requests should be made through the Walter Young Center. Students must provide recent, relevant, and comprehensive documentation to be eligible for reasonable accommodations.

Financial Aid About 98 percent of all students receive aid. The average freshman award was about $14,000.

Requirements for Admission SAT I or ACT scores and a college prep high school program.

Application Freshmen are admitted fall and spring semesters, with a March 15 deadline for fall and November 1 for spring.

International Students Students whose primary language is not English must take the TOEFL and score a minimum of 550 on the paper-based or 213 on the computer version. Students should submit official secondary school and, if applicable, postsecondary transcripts, as well as a declaration of finances.

Admission Contact
Office of Admissions
Carroll College
100 N. East Avenue
Waukesha, WI 53186
Phone: (800) 277-7655; (262) 524-7220
FAX: (262) 524-7139
E-mail: *cc.info@ccadmin.cc.edu*
Web: *www.cc.edu*

The Heart of the College Carroll College has historically offered a strong liberal arts program, beginning with a Freshman Year Seminar program, then a core general education program and a major area of study, concluding with a capstone project, in which students integrate the skills and knowledge they have learned by presenting a project in their major. This is a very thoughtful program, with great student support and appreciation. But the heart of Carroll has more to do with its ability and willingness to create evolving and diversified programs to meet the demands and expectations of students, parents, and the workplace. As a result, the college has added a significant number of new programs that increase the value of their strong liberal arts program. Some of these new programs include athletic training, forensic science, organizational leadership, and pre-pharmacy.

Carroll is a place where students receive the careful, individualized attention that they need to grow and learn. Students have easy access to their professors, who provide academic and career counseling, in addition to offering excellent teaching.

The campus is located in Waukesha, not only a beautiful area, but also one of the state's fastest growing communities. With proximity to Milwaukee as well, Carroll students have opportunities for internships with a variety of organizations, including Fortune 500 companies.

CARSON-NEWMAN COLLEGE

Jefferson City, Tennessee

Total Undergraduate Enrollment: 1,942
Men: 866 Women: 1,076
Five-Year Graduation Rate: 56%

Tuition: $$
Room and Board: $
Residential Students: 51%

History Carson-Newman College began as Mossy Creek Missionary Baptist Seminary in 1851, holding classes in a local Baptist Church. Soon after, the institution became Mossy Creek Baptist College and occupied its own buildings on the site of the present campus. In 1880 the college was renamed Carson College and for several years existed alongside Newman College, a separate institution for women. In 1889 the two colleges united as one of the first coeducational institutions in the South. Later, the college became affiliated with the Tennessee Baptist Convention. The college has been named to the Templeton Foundation's Honor Roll of Character-Building Colleges.

Location The 100-acre campus is located in Jefferson City, Tennessee, a small town 27 miles northeast of Knoxville that is set in the foothills of the Great Smoky Mountains.

Top Programs of Study Education, biology, business

Arts and Sciences Art, athletic training, biology, broadcasting, chemistry, computer science, child and family studies, consumer services, drama, family and consumer sciences education, foods and nutrition, French, general communication, general studies, history, human services, journalism/speech, mathematics, nursing, philosophy/religion, political science, psychology, religion, sociology, Spanish

Business Accounting, administration, computer information systems, financial economics, international economics, long-term health care management, management

Education Physical education, special, elementary

Pre-Professional Dentistry, engineering, health information management, law, medical technology, medicine, optometry, pharmacy, physical therapy, physician assistant

Accredited Programs Biology, education, psychology

Special Programs There are individualized majors and concentrations in Appalachian Studies, China Studies (a cross-cultural program with Chinese universities), gerontology, and film studies. The college has one of the few nationally accredited long-term health care management programs in America.

Facilities There are 27 buildings, many of neo-Georgian architecture, including two art galleries, a recital hall and theater, television studio, and one of the top student centers in the nation.

Transition to College Program The college offers a traditional orientation program.

Athletics NCAA II, South Atlantic Conference

Men: Baseball, basketball, cross-country, football, golf, soccer, tennis, wrestling

Women: Basketball, cross-country, soccer, tennis, track, volleyball

Student Life and Housing About 1,500 students can be accommodated in college housing, which includes separate dorms for men and women, and is guaranteed for all four years. Sixty-five percent of the students are from Tennessee, the remainder are from 38 other states and 17 countries. Ethnicity: Caucasian—88 percent; African-American—8 percent; International—3 percent. There are two local fraternities and one national fraternity, and two local sororities and one national sorority. All students may keep cars.

Accommodations for Students with Disabilities In compliance with section 504

Financial Aid About 92% of all freshmen receive aid. The average freshman award was about $4,300.

Requirements for Admission A minimum ACT score of 19 and verbal SAT of 480 and math 440, a 2.25 GPA or higher in a college prep high school program, and a rank in the upper half of the graduating class.

Application The priority deadline for the fall semester is April 1. The college uses a rolling admissions policy.

International Students The application deadlines are June 1 for the fall semester and November 1 for the spring semester. Students must meet the same requirements as the domestic applicants. For students whose native language is not English, a minimum TOEFL score of 550 or 213 computer-based or an APIEL score of 4 with a compulsory placement exam is required. Official transcripts in both the native language and English from secondary and, if applicable, post-secondary schools attended, with professional course-by-course evaluation of the completed studies is required. Also, confirmation of financial support, an essay, and letter of recommendation from a teacher or administrator.

Transfer Students Required are transcripts from all previous colleges and a minimum GPA of 2.0 or higher. Applicants who have completed fewer than 32 credits must also submit official high school transcripts.

Home-Schooled Students Required are an official transcript of all high school coursework completed and SAT or ACT score reports. If unable to submit an official transcript, then the applicant must submit GED scores. Regular admission requirements apply.

Admission Contact
Office of Admissions
Carson-Newman College
P.O. Box 72025
Jefferson City, TN 37760-9990
Phone: (800) 678-9061; (865) 471-3223
FAX: (865) 471-3502
E-mail: *sgray@cnadmit.cn.edu*
Web: *www.cn.edu*

The Heart of the College The heart of Carson-Newman College resides in its people: students, faculty, administrators, and staff. Because of this, students are offered a very personalized Christian, liberal arts education, with several nationally accredited programs. The faculty and staff are caring, mentoring, and an inspiration for students to use their talents for a lifetime of service. Students comment about the impact that their professors have had on them. This faculty enjoys meeting in professional development activities to explore different styles of teaching and learning and ways to adapt to student learning styles. Their dedication is typified by the student anecdote about a professor who phoned the student's dorm room to tell the student that he had found information that might be helpful for a project that the student was struggling with.

Students come to Carson-Newman ready to be friendly and are immediately impressed with the welcoming community. These are students who give to one another and to the larger community. Considered a national leader in student mission work, more than half of the students participate in community service or missions-related projects, such as Appalachian Outreach, a home repair ministry, and Samaritan House, which provides family shelters. Many of these students choose careers that are oriented toward serving. The nursing program at Carson-New-

man has a 100 percent passing rate on the first attempt at the state boards. The music and education programs are held in high regard, with the education program preparing the second largest number of teachers in the state.

In addition, Career Services attracts notable companies to campus, such a American Express, AT&T, Coca-Cola, the FBI, Hilliard-Lyons Investments, Lockheed-Martin, and Roche Laboratories.

Students looking for a college with a commitment to teaching and developing a sense of values, opportunities to serve, excellent programs, and a friendly community on a campus surrounded by natural beauty will be very happy at Carson-Newman College.

CARTHAGE COLLEGE
Kenosha, Wisconsin

Total Undergraduate Enrollment: 1,850
Men: 832 Women: 1,018
Five-Year Graduation Rate: 55%

Tuition: $$$
Room and Board: $
Residential Students: 75%

History Carthage College was founded in 1847 in Hillsboro, Illinois, and later moved to Springfield and then to Carthage, Illinois, where the college acquired its present name. In 1962 the college relocated to Kenosha, Wisconsin. Carthage is affiliated with the Evangelical Lutheran Church and welcomes students of all faiths.

Location The 83-acre campus is located on the Lake Michigan shore in the northeast corner of Kenosha, Wisconsin (population 80,000), in a suburban community midway between Milwaukee and Chicago, about one hour away. The campus was once a city park and is adorned by oak trees and sandy beaches. There are many cultural and entertainment opportunities in neighboring Chicago.

Top Programs of Study Business administration, education, math and science

Arts and Sciences Art (studio and graphic design), athletic training, biology, chemistry, classics, communications, computer science, criminal justice,

economics, English, French, geography, German, history, information systems, international political economy, mathematics, music, music theater, neuroscience, philosophy, physics, political science, psychology, religion, social science, social work, sociology, Spanish, theater

Business Accounting, administration, marketing

Education Elementary, middle, physical education, secondary, special, sport and fitness instruction

Pre-Professional None

Accredited Programs Business, chemistry, music, social work

Special Programs Carthage offers two dual degree programs: engineering with the University of Wisconsin—Madison College of Engineering and occupational therapy with Washington University in St. Louis. There are special internship opportunities to work in Tokyo or Osaka, Japan. There are Army and Air Force ROTC programs.

Facilities There are 13 buildings, including the new Hedberg Library, the new Tarble Athletic and Recreation Center, and the Clausen Center for World Business. Also, recent renovations were made in residence halls and the Straz Center for the Natural and Social Sciences. There are plans for a new theater and apartment–style residence halls. There is also an art gallery and a radio station.

Transition to College Program In addition to an orientation program, new students take three seminar courses called "The Heritage Studies," taught by faculty from departments across the college, with students learning within a community of learners.

Athletics NCAA III, College Conference of Illinois and Wisconsin

   Men: Baseball, basketball, cross-country, football, golf, soccer, swimming, tennis, track & field

   Women: Basketball, cross-country, golf, soccer, softball, swimming, tennis, track & field, volleyball

Student Life and Housing About 1,100 students can be accommodated in campus housing, which is guaranteed for all four years. Forty percent of the students are from Wisconsin, the remainder from 22 other states and 12 countries. Ethnicity: Caucasian—91 percent. There are four local and two national sororities, and five local and two national fraternities. All students may keep cars.

Accommodations for Students with Disabilities In compliance with section 504

Financial Aid About 90 percent of all freshmen receive aid. The average award was about $13,500.

Requirements for Admission SAT I or ACT and a college prep high school program.

Application Applications for the fall semester are strongly encouraged before December, with admission decisions made as soon as all application materials are received.

International Students Required are an official high school transcript and, if applicable, college transcript, TOEFL scores of 500 or above, and documentation of how the student's education will be financed.

Transfer Students A high school transcript is required if fewer than 12 college credits have been completed. Official transcripts are required from each college attended. Students need to be in good standing at their previous college, have a minimum 2.0 GPA, and can expect courses with C grades and higher to transfer to Carthage. A personal statement explaining why the student is considering transferring to Carthage is also required.

Admission Contact
Office of Admissions
Carthage College
2001 Alford Park Drive
Kenosha, WI 53140-1994
Phone: (800) 351-4058
FAX: (262) 55-5762
E-mail: *admissions@carthage.edu*
Web: *www.carthage.edu*

The Heart of the College With a healthy graduation rate and a typically high employment rate, Carthage College students experience an education that appears seamless in its design quality. Students are provided a quality liberal arts education within a supportive Christian environment. Taught by a dedicated, accessible, talented faculty in small classes, students learn to be critical thinkers, to analyze information, and to form and communicate an opinion. The curriculum is "challenging, but not brutal," with many courses offering team projects. A senior thesis taking the form of a research project, music recital, or other original, creative work is required to demonstrate mastery of the student's chosen area of study.

   As part of the curriculum, Carthage offers both an excellent Humanities Semester Abroad and a Study Abroad program. In the humanities semester, students take study trips, guided by professors, to Ireland, Thailand, Greece, Italy, and other countries. The Study Abroad program includes Argentina, Canada, France, Germany, and Spain. A strong proficiency in the Japanese language and an interest in business provides students with internships with Mizuno Sports in Tokyo.

As a Lutheran college within a Christian tradition, Carthage seeks to be an inclusive community with part of its mission to provide opportunities "to serve others in the world and the church." There are many campus religious organizations that give graduates a sense of meaning and purpose.

Students love Carthage's beautiful location on the Lake Michigan shore. Once a city park, the campus retains its natural beauty, adorned by stately oak trees and sandy beaches. Only one hour from Chicago, Carthage students have a multitude of cultural, entertainment, and internship opportunities in one of the great metropolitan areas of America. Also, the Carthage campus has several state-of-the-art facilities. The Hedberg Library features electronic classrooms, a media and technology AV production/presentation site, and a 24-hour cyber-café. The Tarble Athletic and Recreation Center features a 40-meter, 16-lane swimming pool, climbing wall, and a 5,000 square foot fitness center. There are 10 tennis courts, 6 of them lighted.

CENTRAL COLLEGE   Pella, Iowa

Total Undergraduate Enrollment: 1,700
Men: 800 Women: 900
Five-Year Graduation Rate: 70%

Tuition: $$$
Room and Board: $$
Residential Students: 99%

History Central College was founded in 1853 as a Baptist institution by pioneer settlers who emigrated to Iowa to escape religious tyranny in the Netherlands. In 1916 Central became affiliated with the Reformed Church in America.

Location The 130-acre Central College campus is located in Pella, Iowa (population 10,000), 40 miles southeast of Des Moines, Iowa. Pella features flower-lined streets and attracts visitors because of the annual tulip festival and other aspects of its distinctive Dutch heritage.

Top Programs of Study Elementary education, business management, natural sciences

Arts and Sciences Art, biology, chemistry, communication studies, computer science, economics, English, environmental studies, exercise science, French, general studies, German, history, information systems, international studies, linguistics, mathematics, mathematics/computer science, music, natural science, philosophy, physics, political science, psychology, religion, social science, sociology, Spanish, theater

Business Accounting, international management, management

Education Elementary, music

Pre-Professional Dentistry, law, medicine, ministry, physical therapy

Accredited Programs Chemistry, education, music

Special Programs Central offers dual programs in architecture with Washington University in St. Louis and engineering with Iowa State University, the University of Iowa, and Washington University in St. Louis. Students have the opportunity to create their own major area of study. Central has international study campuses in London and Colchester, England; France; Austria; Spain; Mexico; Wales; and the Netherlands, where almost half of Central's students study during their college years. There is a not-for-profit management program. Special internships are available with the state government, Washington, D.C. Center, and the Chicago Metropolitan Center.

Facilities There are 45 buildings, including the Weller Center for Business and International Studies, the Kruidener Center for the Performing Arts, a radio station, the new Schipper Fitness Center, and a renovated Vermeer Science Center.

Transition to College Program Students take a college success course. Also available is an Exploring Experience Program in the first two years at Central, in which students learn about various majors, about themselves, and about career development.

Athletics NCAA III, Iowa Intercollegiate Conference

Men: Baseball, basketball, cross-country, football, golf, soccer, tennis, track, wrestling

Women: Basketball, cross-country, golf, soccer, softball, tennis, track, volleyball

Student Life and Housing About 1,300 students can be accommodated in college housing, which is guaranteed for all four years. Eighty-two percent of the students are from Iowa, with the remainder from 40 other states and 20 countries. Ethnicity: Caucasian—90 percent. There are two local sororities and five local fraternities. All students may keep cars.

Accommodations for Students with Disabilities In compliance with section 504

Financial Aid About 95 percent of all freshmen receive aid. The average award was about $13,000.

Requirements for Admission SAT I or ACT scores and a college prep high school program.

Application Applications should be filed by March 1 for fall admission, November 1 for spring admission, and May 1 for summer admission. Students are notified of an admissions decision as soon as all application materials have been received.

International Students Required are transcripts of all work completed in secondary school and, if applicable, college, as well as financial aid statements indicating that sufficient funds are available to cover the applicant's expenses. All documentation must be in English. If English is not the student's native language, students must submit a paper TOEFL minimum score of 530 or at least a 197 computer version. A teacher or faculty recommendation is also required.

Transfer Students Official transcripts from each college are required. Students with fewer than 24 credits must submit a high school transcript. Students must be in good standing at the previous college. C— grades and above are considered for transfer.

Admission Contact
Office of Admissions
Central College
Campus Box 5100
812 University Street
Pella, IA 50219
Phone: (641) 628-5285
FAX: (641) 628-5316
E-mail: *admission@central.edu*
Web: *www.central.edu*

The Heart of the College Central College is a liberal arts college in the Christian tradition, offering students a holistic education with a balanced emphasis on the development of mind, body, and spirit. Students are offered a well-designed core curriculum that teaches students to be critical thinkers, effective communicators, and to see the interconnected nature of knowledge. No matter what the student's major, graduates will have this important foundation for success in life and career.

Central's fine arts program is one of the best in the nation, having one of the region's finest collegiate theaters. Students direct many shows throughout the year, and guest directors from all over the world are also invited. Many students pursue a musical career at Central in one of the many outstanding music performance or education programs. Music students have the opportunity to participate in internships with groups like the London Philharmonic and Central's music ensembles perform internationally.

Few colleges can match the athletic success achieved by the Central Dutch teams, who have placed in the top 10 nationally 56 times, more than any other Division III college in Iowa. Athletes also earn honors for their scholastic achievement. One of the coaches writes about her holistic approach where athletes are challenged "to improve each day, and about learning to work hard, sacrifice and serve others."

With campuses in Mexico, England, Wales, the Netherlands, France, Spain, and Austria, nearly 50 percent of Central's students travel abroad for a semester of study. Valuable internship opportunities are also offered, with recent

Central students working at Warner Brothers International, the Philadelphia Eagles, Pella Corporation, Nike, the Republican Party of Iowa, and WGN-TV.

In a typical year, one year after graduation 99 percent of Central's graduates have jobs or are in graduate schools. Employment has been at the Arizona State Legislature, Deere and Company, Des Moines Public Schools, Exxon Exploration Company, Ford Motor Company, and Gannett Communications. Graduates also head to some of the top graduate schools, including Princeton, UCLA, University of Iowa, and the University of Missouri-Columbia Law School.

A dedicated faculty helps Central students "be good at everything they do, and to enjoy everything they do." Central gets high marks for its holistic emphasis seeking to "cultivate the life of the mind, nurture depth of character, and foster habits of the heart that prepare students for a lifelong adventure in learning, growth, and service."

THE CITADEL **Charleston, South Carolina**

Total Undergraduate Enrollment: 1,906

Men: 1,816 Women: 90
Five-Year Graduation Rate: 75%

Tuition: In-state–$;
  Out-of-state–$$
Room and Board: $
Residential Students: 100%

History The Citadel, the Military College of South Carolina, is a state-supported college. In 1822 the South Carolina legislature established an arsenal to protect the city of Charleston. Later in 1842 the arsenal was converted into the South Carolina Military Academy to provide an education for the young men serving there. Burned during the Civil War, the academy reopened in 1882 and became The Citadel in 1910. In 1922 the college moved to its Charleston location. The college has been coed since 1996. One-third of the graduates enter the armed forces, an equal number enter graduate or professional studies, and another third enter directly into the workforce.

Location The Citadel is located on 40 acres in suburban Charleston, South Carolina, both a historic and contemporary city, with many cultural and entertainment opportunities.

Top Programs of Study Business administration

Arts and Sciences Biology, chemistry, civil and environmental engineering, computer science, criminal justice, electrical and computer engineering, English, French, German, health and physical education (concentrations in health and wellness, sports management), history, mathematics, physics, political science (concentrations in law and legal studies, American government and politics, and international politics and military affairs), psychology, Spanish

Business Business administration

Education Physical education, secondary

Pre-Professional None

Accredited Programs Business administration, chemistry, civil and electrical engineering, education

Special Programs Students have opportunities for social service in the Charleston community. There is a Phi Beta Kappa chapter. There are Air Force, Army, Navy/Marine ROTC programs.

Facilities The college has 40 buildings, including residence halls, a military museum and archives, a library, two engineering buildings; the entire campus is linked to a fiber-optic network.

Transition to College Program Transition classes for incoming students are offered through the College Success Institute. The First Year Seminar provides the academic and life skills to help students make a successful transition to college. Also, attention is given to lifestyle and relationship issues.

Athletics NCAA I, Southern Conference

Men: Baseball, basketball, cross-country, football, golf, indoor and outdoor track & field, soccer, tennis, wrestling

Women: Cross-country, golf, indoor and outdoor track & field, soccer, tennis, volleyball

Student Life and Housing All students live on campus, including coed barracks, and remain on campus on weekends. Fifty-one percent of the students are from South Carolina, with the remainder from 45 other states and 22 countries. Ethnicity: Caucasian—82 percent; African-American—8 percent; Hispanic-American—5 percent; International—3 percent; Asian—2 percent. There are no sororities or fraternities. Upperclassmen may keep cars. Students are bound by an honor code.

Accommodations for Students with Disabilities The Office of Access Services, Instruction, and Support (OASIS) provides individualized help with accommodations.

Financial Aid About 54 percent of all freshmen receive aid. The average award was $3,000.

Requirements for Admission SAT I or ACT scores and a college prep high school program. Great emphasis is placed on maturity and motivation. Students must be between 17 and 23 years old, may not be married or have a dependent biological child, or have a record of conviction of a criminal offense.

Application Students are encouraged to apply in the fall semester. Final admission is contingent upon the results of a physical exam.

International Students Students from a foreign country whose native language is not English must submit a TOEFL score off 550 and above.

Transfer Students Official high school and college transcripts must be submitted. Students must have completed a minimum of two semesters of full-time study (24 credits) and maintain a minimum 2.0 GPA. Students with fewer than 24 credits will be viewed on a case-by-case basis.

Admission Contact
Office of Admissions
The Citadel
171 Moultrie Street
Charleston, SC 29409
Phone: (800) 868-1842
FAX: (843)-953-7630
E-mail: *admissions@citadel.edu*
Web: *www.citadel.edu*

The Heart of the College President George W. Bush, in a speech at The Citadel, described the heart of the college. "The Citadel is a place of pride and tradition. A place where standards are high, the discipline is strong, and leaders are born." In everything that The Citadel does, from its focus on undergraduate education in liberal arts and sciences—because leaders need to know how to think critically and solve problems—to the regimented barracks residence, to the honor code, the heart of The Citadel is its focus on developing qualities of leadership.

Camaraderie is an easy outcome of such a disciplined education, especially when students go through the rigorous first year, living a regimented schedule, "learning followership"—a necessary first step to leadership. That camaraderie and leadership skills are also learned on the playing fields, where teamwork, discipline, and exerting a 100 percent effort are important reasons why all students (cadets) study physical education and compete in intramural competition.

It is not surprising that with an education that develops thoughtful, respectful, disciplined leaders who can work under pressure, Citadel graduates are very successful upon graduation. About 55 percent enter careers in business, including positions at Coopers and Lybrand Consulting, DuPont, IBM, and Bank of America. Those who head to graduate school find places at Duke, Georgetown, Johns Hopkins, Clemson, and the University of Virginia.

As each cadet's "free time" increases each year, the charming city of Charleston is there to offer historic cobblestone streets, beaches, museums, arts festivals, restaurants, and parks.

CLAFLIN UNIVERSITY

Orangeburg, South Carolina

Total Undergraduate Enrollment: 1,350
Men: 475 Women: 875
Five-Year Graduation Rate: 75%

Tuition: $
Room and Board: $
Residential Students: 80%

History Claflin University was established in 1869 and is named for Lee Claflin, a Boston philanthropist, and his son, Massachusetts Governor William Claflin, who provided initial financing for the university. Claflin is a historically black institution, affiliated with the United Methodist Church. Claflin is listed on the Templeton Foundation's Honor Roll of Character-Building Colleges.

Location Claflin's 38-acre campus is located in Orangeburg, South Carolina (population 18,000), 40 miles south of Columbia, the state capital.

Top Programs of Study Sociology, business, biology, education

Arts and Sciences American studies, art, biochemistry, bioinformatics, biology, biotechnology, black studies, chemistry, child development, computer science, environmental science, English, history, mass communications (concentrations in broadcast journalism, print journal-

ism, public relations, radio production, television/video production), mathematics, music, sociology, sports management

Business Administration (concentrations in accounting, management, marketing), management information science

Education Art, early childhood, elementary, music, physical, secondary, special

Pre-Professional None

Accredited Programs Business, education

Special Programs The following dual degree programs are offered: cytotechnology, medical technology, occupational therapy, and physical therapy with the Medical University of South Carolina and Clemson University; and a chiropractic program with Sherman College of Straight Chiropractic. The Center for Excellence in Science and Mathematics trains students who plan careers in science, engineering, mathematics, and technology. A Leadership Studies minor is offered. Student Performance Portfolios are required of all students beginning with the class of 2005. The portfolios will document course-work, academic achievement, co-curricula and extra-curricula activities.

Facilities There are 24 buildings, including the new Kennedy Business and Communications Building, a new student center, the new Leadership Development Center, a television studio, radio station, and an art gallery.

Transition to College Program Freshmen take a year-long course that introduces them to tools necessary for academic and personal success in college and implements diagnostic evaluations that will result in proper placement and provide accommodations, programs, and services, monitor the progress of students, and provide enhancement activities that are tailored to the specific needs of the student.

Athletics NAIA, Eastern Collegiate Athletic Conference

   Men: Baseball, basketball, track & field

   Women: Basketball, softball, track & field, volleyball

Student Life and Housing About 1,200 students can be accommodated in college housing. Eighty-three percent of the students are from South Carolina, the remainder from 24 other states and 14 countries. Ethnicity: African-American—94%. There are four national fraternities and four national sororities. Upperclassmen may keep cars.

Accommodations for Students with Disabilities In compliance with section 504

Financial Aid About 96 percent of freshmen receive aid. The average freshman award was about $8,000.

Requirements for Admission SAT I or ACT scores and a minimum GPA of C in a college prep high school program.

Application Freshmen are admitted for fall and spring semesters, with application deadlines open.

International Students Deadlines for applications are March 1 for the fall semester, August 1 for the spring semester, and February 1 for the summer semester. Students whose native language is not English must take the TOEFL. Also required are evidence of adequate financial resources, official certificates and/or final secondary school records, university transcripts, mark sheets, official translations and syllabi, and results from the SAT or ACT for regular degree students.

Transfer Students Required are official transcripts from each college attended, good standing from previously attended colleges, a minimum GPA of C, and submission of catalogues of previously attended colleges. No transfer grade below C is accepted. If fewer than 30 college credits have been earned, students must submit official high school transcript, GPA, SAT or ACT scores, and rank in class.

Admission Contact
Office of Admissions
Claflin University
400 Magnolia Street, N.E.
Orangeburg, SC 29115-9970
Phone: (800) 922-1276; (803) 535-5346
FAX: (803) 531-3860
E-mail: *kboyd@claflin.edu*
Web: *www.claflin.edu*

The Heart of the University It's easy to identify the heart of Claflin University because it is so powerfully evident on its campus. While many colleges have established wonderful learning communities, Claflin, a historically black institution, has created a "family." You can witness this at the very top of the institution, when Claflin's president, Dr. Henry Tisdale, routinely schedules Thursday open-door sessions for students to share with him their interests and concerns. The president also attends most student activities and welcomes students to his home for formal and informal visits. Dr. Tisdale symbolizes the thrust of Claflin's mission of "providing a Christian, caring, open, nurturing, concerned, and supportive" environment. Students find that this quality, caring community fosters friendship, camaraderie, and a sense of belonging—all factors that create a strong scaffolding for studying in some excellent programs, as well as the liberal arts at Claflin.

Of particular note is Claflin's attempt to address the problem of underrepresentation of African-Americans in the sciences. Its generously funded Center for Excellence in Science and Mathematics recruits and provides quality instruction and facilities for those students interested in pursuing careers in science, mathemat-

ics, medicine, engineering, or technology. Also, a mentoring program pairs first-year students with mentors from the campus and surrounding communities to guide freshmen during their critical first year. Professional internships allow students to spend quality time in the workplace.

With small classes and a "family" community, it's easy to get to know faculty members in and outside the classroom. Many become favorite professors because they teach "with love, skill, and high expectations"—a formula that makes for exceptional teaching.

Although the oldest historically black university in South Carolina, Claflin has proven in so many ways its forward-looking vision and its ability to inspire its students.

COE COLLEGE   Cedar Rapids, Iowa

Total Undergraduate Enrollment: 1,300
Men: 559 Women: 741
Five-Year Graduation Rate: 66%

Tuition: $$$
Room and Board: $
Residential Students: 85%

History Coe College was founded in 1851 and is affiliated with the Presbyterian Church.

Location The attractive 75-acre campus is located in Cedar Rapids, Iowa (population 175,000), the second largest city in Iowa, and 225 miles west of Chicago.

Top Programs of Study Business/economics, biology, psychology

Arts and Sciences African-American studies, American studies, art, Asian studies, athletic training, biochemistry, biology, chemistry, classical studies, computer science, English, environmental science, French, French studies, gender studies, German, German studies, history, literature, mathematics, molecular biology, music, nursing, philosophy, physics, political science, psychology, public relations, religion, sociology, Spanish, Spanish studies, speech, theater arts

Business Accounting, administration, economics

Education Art, elementary, music, physical education, secondary

Pre-Professional Architecture, dentistry, engineering, law, medicine

Accredited Programs Chemistry, music, nursing

Special Programs Coe offers an Urban Education program with student teaching in Chicago. The college was selected as one of the most "wired" in America. There is a Writing Across the Curriculum program. There is a cooperative program in architecture with Washington University in St. Louis and a clinical laboratory scientist/medical technologist program with St. Luke's Methodist Medical Laboratories in Cedar Rapids. Coe offers a New York semester, "Fine Arts in New York City," as well as a Washington, D.C., semester. There is an Army ROTC program.

Facilities There are 19 buildings, which include a radio station; art gallery; planetarium; the Stewart Memorial Library, which displays a $4 million art collection; the Peterson Hall of Science, which contains state-of-the-art equipment; and the Dows Hall of Fine Art Center, with spacious art studios and a computer graphics lab with animation capabilities; and a 300-seat theater.

Transition to College Program Coe offers a first-year seminar with a writing emphasis, taught by a professor who acts as mentor and adviser throughout the students' college years.

Athletics NCAA III, Iowa Conference

Men: Baseball, basketball, cross-country, diving, football, golf, soccer, swimming, tennis, track, wrestling

Women: Basketball, cross-country, diving, golf, soccer, softball, swimming, tennis, track, volleyball

Student Life and Housing About 1,000 students can be accommodated in college housing, which is guaranteed all four years. Sixty-two percent of all students are from Iowa, the remainder are from 40 other states and 20 countries. Ethnicity: Caucasian—89 percent; International—5 percent; African-American—2 percent; Asian-American 1 percent; Hispanic-American—1 percent. There are four national fraternities and three national sororities. All students may keep cars.

Accommodations for Students with Disabilities In compliance with section 504

Financial Aid About 90 percent of all freshmen receive aid. The average award was about $20,000.

Requirements for Admission A minimum ACT score of 20 or SAT I score of 1,000, a 3.0 GPA in a college prep high school program, and rank in the top 40 percent of the class. An interview is recommended.

Application The Early Application deadline is December 15, with students notified of an admissions decision by January 15. Regular applica-tions should be submitted by March 1, with students notified by March 15.

International Students Required are official certified translated copies of all secondary school work, certified copy of all national exam results, results from the TOEFL (if English is not first language), SAT I results, a letter of recommendation from a school official, high school and, if applicable, college transcripts. A minimum grade of C is needed for courses to transfer. Graduates of accredited associate degree programs will receive junior year status at Coe if applicants have a minimum GPA of 2.5.

Transfer Students New students may enroll at the beginning of any of the four regular terms. Students must be in good standing at their former institution and submit official high school and college transcripts. A minimum grade of C is needed for courses to transfer. Graduates of accredited associate degree programs will receive junior year status at Coe if applicants have a GPA of 2.5 or higher.

Admission Contact
Office of Admissions
Coe College
1220 First Avenue, NE
Cedar Rapids, Iowa 52402
(800) CALL-COE
FAX: (319) 399-8816
E-mail: *admission@coe.edu*
Web: *www.admission.coe.edu*

The Heart of the College Coe College is enthusiastic about the benefits of a liberal arts program as the best preparation for life and career. But in addition to a major and 12 general education courses, Coe requires all students to complete a sequence of activities designed to lead students through the process of finding their life's work. This four-year plan begins in freshman year with students taking a first-year seminar, which has a writing emphasis, along with general education courses. During the second year students devote additional time to community service, issue dinners, and career planning seminars on résumé writing, interviewing, and networking. Part of the third year is spent satisfying Coe's hands-on requirement through an interesting internship, research, practicum, or participation in a wonderful study abroad program, which includes Spain, Germany, Thailand, and Northern Ireland, as well as other travel destinations to Italy, Russia, India, and Japan. In the senior year students spend time preparing a senior project and put finishing touches on plans for graduate school or work. The success of Coe's four-step plan is demonstrated by the fact that 98 percent of their graduates are either employed or in graduate school within six months of graduation.

Students, professors, and graduates all agree that Coe "people" really make the college special.

The faculty really know and care about their students and act as mentors, starting with the first-year seminar required of all students. A professor is assigned as a faculty adviser who advises the student throughout a Coe education. Coe students also have a College Adjustment Peer, an upperclassman chosen for his or her involvement on campus and interest in helping new students. Then there are the Coe upperclassmen who, for example, direct the research efforts of small groups of younger students. As younger students rise through the ranks, they in turn direct their own research groups.

Cedar Rapids also offers cultural and entertainment opportunities, as well as a Czech Village, which houses a new National Czech and Slovak Museum and Library.

COLLEGE OF MOUNT ST. JOSEPH

Cincinnati, Ohio

Total Undergraduate Enrollment: 1,856
Men: 578 Women: 1,278
Five-Year Graduation Rate: 68%

Tuition: $$
Room and Board: $
Residential Students: 32%

History The College of Mount St. Joseph is a Catholic college founded by the Sisters of Charity in 1920 as a college for women, which later became coed. The college is listed on the Templeton Foundation's Honor Roll of Character-Building Colleges

Location The 75-acre campus is nestled in suburban hills overlooking the Ohio River, 15 minutes from downtown Cincinnati, Ohio, which offers many cultural and entertainment opportunities.

Top Programs of Study Business administration, nursing, education

Arts and Sciences Art, athletic training, biology, chemistry, chemistry/mathematics, communication arts, computer information systems, computer science, English, fine arts, gerontological studies, graphic design, history, humanities, inte-

rior design, liberal arts and sciences, mathematics, medical technology, music, natural history, natural science, nursing, paralegal studies for nurses, parish/nurse/health ministries, physical therapy, psychology, recreational therapy, religious pastoral ministry, religious studies, school nurse, social work, sociology

Business Accounting, administration

Education Art, early childhood, medical technology, middle school, physical education, religious, secondary, special

Pre-Professional None

Accredited Programs Music, nursing, physical therapy, social work

Special Programs In addition to many cooperative learning programs, students can participate in the Plus-One option, whereby students can integrate a community service project into their coursework and receive course credit, tuition free. There are Air Force and Army ROTC programs.

Facilities There are 12 buildings on campus, including a Center for Innovative Teaching, a state-of-the-art Health Science Instructional Suite, the new Harrington Student Center, an art gallery, and a Children's Center providing child-care for children of Mount students.

Transition to College Program The college uses a traditional orientation program.

Athletics NCAA III, Heartland Collegiate Athletic Conference

Men: Baseball, basketball, football, tennis, wrestling

Women: Basketball, cross-country, soccer, softball, tennis, volleyball

Student Life and Housing All freshmen and sophomore students under the age of 21 who are not living with their parents or where the home address is beyond a 35-mile radius from the college are expected to live on campus, where housing is guaranteed for all four years. Eighty-five percent of the students are from Ohio, with the remainder from 24 other states and 27 countries. Ethnicity: Caucasian—85 percent; African-American—8 percent; International—2 percent; Asian-American—1 percent. There are no fraternities or sororities. All students may keep cars.

Accommodations for Students with Disabilities Project Excel is a structured program of support, providing a full range of accommodative services.

Financial Aid About 99 percent of all freshmen receive aid. The average award was about $9,000.

Requirements for Admission SAT I or ACT scores and a college prep high school program.

Application Applications are reviewed on a rolling basis, and admission decisions are generally made within two weeks of the date that admission materials have been completed. Freshmen are admitted to all semesters, with an August 15 fall application deadline.

International Students Students must submit a certified copy of the secondary school or university record, a notarized statement of financial support, and a TOEFL paper score of at least 450 or a computer-based score of at least 133.

Transfer Students Required are high school and college transcripts, a college GPA of 2.0 or better, with a minimum of 12 credits.

Admission Contact
Office of Admissions
College of Mount St. Joseph
5701 Delhi Road
Cincinnati, OH 45233-1672
Phone: (800) 654-9314; (513) 244-4531
FAX: (513) 244-4851
E-mail: *admissions@mail.msj.edu*
Web: *www.msj.edu*

The Heart of the College Mount St. Joseph has crafted a wonderful Catholic academic community in which students experience the teaching and support of a caring, encouraging faculty who are dedicated to the development of the whole student—intellectually, morally, and spiritually. The college combines the liberal arts, with its focus on critical and creative thinking, problem solving, and communication, with a career orientation. Students have the option to co-op in all the liberal arts majors and career preparation programs, starting with the freshman year. In addition to cooperative education programs that give students credits while gaining paid work experience, students are offered an opportunity for "service learning." Through the College's Plus-One option, students can integrate a community service project with a course they are taking at the college.

Students are pleased with the amount of attention Mount St. Joseph has given to technology. The college was one of America's first wireless campuses with the introduction of Merlin, a wireless computer network, allowing students to use laptops in classrooms, lounges, and all around campus. Students use Merlin to access course notes, library resources, and faculty/staff discussions. Even the Center for Innovative Teaching provides for faculty to develop and use new technologies in teaching.

The college campus is just seven miles west of downtown Cincinnati, where students can enjoy the arts, entertainment, professional sports, and shopping in a major metropolitan city. The city has a zoo, ice-skating, and the world's second oldest Oktoberfest.

Also, as a major city, Cincinnati is home to a number of Fortune 500 companies that offer many career and co-op opportunities. Headquartered here are Procter & Gamble, Federated Department Stores, American Financial Group, Cinergy, and Ashland. The Office of Career Development works with more than 120 companies, health care facilities, schools, and nonprofits in order to place graduating seniors.

The College of Mount St. Joseph provides a quality liberal arts education, never losing sight of the fact that students will be looking for jobs at the end of their college experience.

COLLEGE OF SAINT BENEDICT AND SAINT JOHN'S UNIVERSITY   St. Joseph and Collegeville, Minnesota

Total Undergraduate Enrollment: 3,969
Men: 2,072 Women: 1,897
Five-Year Graduation Rate: 78%

Tuition: $$$
Room and Board: $
Residential Students: 85%

History The College of Saint Benedict and Saint John's University function as coordinate institutions, the first a women's college founded by the Benedictine Order in 1887 and the second founded by Benedictine monks in 1857 as a men's college. Students share a common education, as well as coeducational social, cultural, and spiritual programs. Both share a common curriculum, identical degree requirements, and a single academic calendar. All academic departments are joint and classes are offered throughout the day on both campuses. The two campuses are linked by free bus service throughout the day and night. CSB and SJU are listed on the Templeton Foundation's Honor Roll of Character-Building Colleges.

Location Saint Benedict's campus is located on 315 acres adjacent to the town of St. Joseph (pop. 4,000). The Saint John's University 2,400-acre campus is located in Collegeville, a rural area 15 miles west of St. Cloud (population 185,000), and 70 miles northwest of Minneapolis and St.

Paul, located on the shores of Lake Sagaton in central Minnesota.

Top Programs of Study College of Saint Benedict—Elementary education, occupational therapy, nursing, Saint John's University—Management, biology; communications

Arts and Sciences Art, biology, biochemistry, chemistry, classics, communication, computer science, computer science/mathematics, dietetics, economics, English, French, German, history, humanities, liberal studies, mathematics, medieval studies, music, natural science, nursing, nutrition science, peace studies, physics, political science, psychology, social science, social work, sociology, Spanish, theater, theology (pastoral ministry, theological studies)

Business Accounting, management

Education Elementary, secondary

Pre-Professional Dentistry, divinity, engineering, forestry, law, medicine, occupational therapy, pharmacy, veterinary medicine

Accredited Programs Chemistry, dietetics, education, music, nursing, social work, theology

Special Programs A dual degree program is offered in engineering with the University of Minnesota and Washington University. Students can design their own majors. There are several minors, including women's studies, writing, Asian studies, and environmental studies. CB/SJ is rated as one of the most computer-wired-institutions in America. There is an Army ROTC program.

Facilities The College of Saint Benedict has 33 buildings—an impressive combination of contemporary and restored and maintained turn-of-the century buildings. The campus is centered around the Clemens Library. There is the new Ardoff Science Center; new Haehn Campus Center; the Benedictine Arts Center, one of the region's most highly regarded arts facilities; and the restored Sacred Heart Chapel.

Saint John's University has 35 buildings, with several listed in the National Register of Historic Places, and many renovated buildings, including Simons Hall, which houses the social sciences; the Humphrey Theater, music classrooms, and practice rooms; Engel Science Center; the Art Center; the Warner Palaestra, which houses the gym and swimming pool; the home of the Minnesota Public Radio Station; the Pottery Studio; the largest wood-burning kiln in America; and a library and art collection focused on the interplay of religion and artistic expression.

Transition to College Program The First Year Symposium is a required two-semester course designed to help students in thinking, speaking, and writing. Professors from many disciplines offer a variety of themes, allowing students to choose an area of personal interest. The class stays together for the whole year, developing a sense of community. The professor functions as the students' adviser.

Athletics NCAA III, Minnesota Intercollegiate Athletic Conference

Men: Baseball, basketball, cross-country, football, golf, ice hockey, Nordic skiing, soccer, tennis track & field, wrestling

Women: Basketball, cross-country, ice hockey, Nordic skiing, soccer, softball, swimming and diving, tennis, track & field, volleyball

Student Life and Housing At each of the campuses about 1,500 students can be accommodated in college housing. Eighty-three percent of the students are from Minnesota, the remainder are from 31 other states and 25 countries. Ethnicity: Caucasian—92 percent. There are no fraternities or sororities. All students may keep cars.

Accommodations for Students with Disabilities In compliance with section 504

Financial Aid About 93 percent of all freshmen receive aid. The average freshman award is about $15,000 at both of the institutions.

Requirements for Admission SAT I or ACT scores, a college prep high school program, rank in class, and personal qualifications that give promise of success. A campus visit and interview are strongly recommended.

Application Application deadlines are open. The institutions review applications on a rolling basis beginning October 1, with an admission decision provided within three weeks.

International Students Students must fulfill regular admission requirements, as well as demonstrate English proficiency in a number of ways, including providing TOEFL scores.

Transfer Students Students are admitted on the combined basis of high school and college achievement. Applicants are required to have a minimum college GPA of 2.75. Required are official transcripts of all high school and college work, a transfer student evaluation form, and official ACT or SAT I scores, if fewer than 28 college credits have been completed. Preferred deadline for fall entrance is March 15 and for spring entrance, November 15.

Home-Schooled Students Students should provide appropriate documentation of a college prep curriculum and college entrance exams. Nontraditional indicators that are considered but not required for admissions include GED scores, study of a second language, community service, travel, art shows, work, or published writing.

Admission Contact

Office of Admissions	Office of Admissions
College of Saint Benedict	Saint John's University
37 South College Avenue	P.O Box 7155
St. Joseph, MN 56374-2099	Collegeville, MN 56321-7155
Phone: (800) 544-1489; (320) 363-5308	(800) 245-6467; (320) 363-2196
FAX:(320) 363-5010	(320) 363-3206
E-mail: *admissions@ csbsju.edu*	*admissions@csbsju. edu*
Web: *www.csbju.edu*	*www.csbsju.edu*

The Heart of the Colleges The College of Saint Benedict, a women's college, and Saint John's University, a men's college, only four miles apart, function as coordinated institutions as if they were one school. Typically, this would be a difficult institutional relationship, but because these are Catholic, Benedictine schools, the coordination is a smooth and easy one, offering its "Bennies and Johnnies" almost one acre each, excellent programs, outstanding facilities, and a talented faculty. Here is one case where more is better. The institutions, in fact, are considered two of the best national liberal arts colleges in America as well as a "best buy."

The science programs receive top billing. Professors teach all classes, provide a great deal of support for student learning, and are considered excellent teachers, even though they have significant publication records. There is a great emphasis on student research, with 10-week summer research with faculty mentors and individual student research required for graduation in several programs. Of course, the 3,200-acre campus is a living laboratory, offering a variety of ecosys-

tems—lakes, oak savanna, wetlands, and prairies—for exploration and study. In addition, the combined campuses provide new facilities and millions of dollars in instrumentation, including a nuclear magnetic resonance spectometer and UNIX workstations. The nursing program also has three state-of-the-art facilities, including a critical care laboratory. The dietetics program is the only private college program in Minnesota that integrates classroom learning with clinical experiences required for licensure. The nutrition science major is considered an excellent preparation for medical school. All programs are supported by leading-edge technology, and the College of Saint Benedict has distinguished fine arts programs and is highly regarded for its Literary Arts Institute.

Half of all CSB/SJU students study abroad at least once, with opportunities in 12 countries; faculty members serve as on-site directors. Other interesting travel programs include community internships in Latin America, a Scandinavian urban studies term, and the city arts of Minneapolis and St. Paul. Also, with several social justice organizations available to them, many students, passionate about social justice, have opportunities to become involved.

The new and combined athletic facilities provide students with enormous opportunities, rivaling many Division I schools. Consider two fieldhouses, two fitness centers, two indoor tracks, an indoor climbing gym, a great football stadium, and much more. The strong athletic programs attract many athletes, and health and wellness are prominent considerations. Just as the campus provides a natural laboratory, it also offers an incredible array of outdoor activities, from running and hiking to skiing and sledding to canoeing and swimming.

The outcomes are exceptional: Over 80 percent of students graduate in four years; one year after graduation 96 percent of graduates were either working full-time, volunteering, or furthering their education; 20 percent go right to graduate school. Much of this success is attributed to comprehensive career services, which include a mentor program, career and education fairs, a career exploration series, and opportunities to develop networking skills. Also a significant factor is that 87 percent of students participate in an internship, practicum, or other career-related experience. "Bennies" and "John-nies" have an excellent reputation with employers, prompting comments such as the one from an Ernst and Young consulting manager: "We find that CSB/SJU graduates perform exceptionally compared to their peers from other schools. . . ."

THE COLLEGE OF WOOSTER   Wooster, Ohio

Total Undergraduate Enrollment: 1,856
Men: 868 Women: 988
Five-Year Graduation Rate: 67%

Tuition: $$$
Room and Board: $$
Residential Students: 97%

History The College of Wooster was founded in 1866 by Presbyterians on land donated by Wooster citizen Ephraim Quinby. A bitter fight in 1915 determined the liberal arts and science orientation the college would follow. From its inception there was a commitment to offer an education for all regardless of sex or race, a vital role for religion, an international dimension, and a strong commitment to the physical sciences. Though fully independent, the college maintains a relationship with the Presbyterian Church of America.

Location The 240-acre campus is located in Wooster, Ohio (population 26,000), a residential area in north central Ohio, 55 miles southeast of Cleveland and 90 minutes to Columbus, the state capital.

Top Programs of Study Communications, English, history

Arts and Sciences Anthropology, archaelology, art history, art studio, biochemistry and molecular biology, biology, black studies, chemical physics, chemistry, Chinese, classical studies, communication sciences and disorders, communication studies, comparative literature, computer science, cultural area studies (concentrations in East Asia, South Asia, Latin America, Russia and Eastern Europe, Modern Western Europe), economics, English, French, geology, German, history, international relations, mathematics, music, philoso-phy, physics, political science, psychology, religious studies, sociology, Spanish, theater-dance, urban studies, women's studies.

Business Economics

Education Art, early childhood, foreign languages, middle school, music, secondary

Pre-Professional Business, law, medicine, physical therapy, seminary, social work, veterinary medicine

Accredited Programs Art and design, chemistry, music

Special Programs There are several cooperative degree programs: architecture with Washington University in St. Louis; dentistry, social work, and nursing with Case Western Reserve and Washington University. There are opportunities for study abroad and internships. There are also self-designed majors. There are several minors, including International Business Economics. There is also an Upward Bound program.

Facilities There are 39 buildings, many of them the English collegiate Gothic type of architecture. The Andrews and Gault Libraries seat more than 800 students and house the McCreight Learning Laboratory for foreign language instruction. The Freelander Theatre seats 400. There are the Schneider Music Center and the Severance Art Building. Master Hall houses the biology department and a greenhouse and Kauke Hall, the central building of the Quadrangle, contains the liberal arts departments. Wishart Hall contains a speech and hearing clinic and dance studio. There is also a nursery school and the Wooster Inn, which provides overnight accommodations for 33 guests.

Transition to College Program The First Year Seminar, usually taken in the fall semester, provides an intellectual opportunity for students and faculty to participate in a small discussion disciplinary course that introduces students to the kinds of critical thinking and academic skills needed for college success.

Athletics NCAA III, North Coast Atlantic Conference

Men: Baseball, basketball, cross-country, football, golf, indoor track & field, lacrosse, soccer, swimming, tennis, track & field

Women: Basketball, cross-country, field hockey, indoor track and field, lacrosse, soccer, softball, swimming, tennis, track & field, volleyball

Student Life and Housing About 1,860 students can be accommodated in college housing, which includes single-sex and coed dorms and is guaranteed all four years. Fifty percent of the students are from Ohio, the remainder are from 44 other states and 36 countries. Ethnicity: Caucasian—84 percent; International—7 percent; African-American—5 percent; Asian-American-1 percent; Hispanic-American—1 percent. There are three local fraternities and three local sororities. All students may keep cars.

Accommodations for Students with Disabilities In compliance with section 504

Financial Aid About 97 percent of all freshmen receive aid. The average freshman award was about $16,000.

Requirements for Admission SAT I or ACT scores and a college prep high school program. A campus visit and interview are strongly recommended.

Application Freshmen are admitted in fall and spring semesters. There are two Early Decision deadlines: December 1 with admission decision by December 15; January 15 with admission decision by February 1. Regular decision applications are due by February 15 with admission decisions by April 1.

International Students Some foreign diplomas may receive up to one year credit. A minimum TOEFL score of 550 paper or 213 computer, or a 4 on the APIEL, will demonstrate English language proficiency. A declaration of finances is required.

Transfer Students The college will accept a maximum of 16 Wooster course equivalents completed elsewhere, and students must complete at least 16 courses at Wooster, including the Independent Study Thesis. Required are official transcripts from each institution attended, an overall GPA of at least 2.5, and graded courses of C or better, if they are the equivalent of Wooster courses. The application deadline is June 1 for the fall semester and December 1 for the spring semester, with announced decision within two weeks of completed applications.

Home-Schooled Students In addition to the standard application requirements, home-schooled students are also required to interview with a Wooster admissions counselor. Students should also submit detailed course descriptions and/or syllabi for academic work completed through the home-schooling program and three letters of recommendation, including one from a person who has provided academic instruction to the student and at least two from outside the student's school instruction. Required also are a copy of a recent academic paper and an essay or a statement describing why the student and/or family chose the home-schooling option.

Admission Contact
Office of Admissions
The College of Wooster

Wooster, OH 44691-2363
Phone: (800) 877-9905
FAX: (330) 263-2621; (330) 262-2270
E-mail: *admissions@wooster.edu*
Web: *www.wooster.edu*

The Heart of the College What would make so many students journey from other states and countries to the small town of Wooster, Ohio, to receive a college education? It certainly isn't the unabashed attitude toward the virtues of a liberal arts education, because that attitude is maintained by many institutions in this guide. The answer is offered by one of Wooster's students: "Wooster's location is inconsequential. I'd come here if it was in Antarctica. The education has just been amazing." That education consists of a logical progression through a four-year curriculum, beginning with developing a broad base of academic skills in the First Year Seminars of Critical Inquiry, where in classes of 15, students study public art, which results in their designing functional sculpture for selected gateways and walkways on campus, or students study the myths, reality, and consequences of bad weather. These seminars are focused, and cross-disciplinary in nature, helping students see the connections between disciplines. In their sophomore year students choose a major, or double majors or minors, and focus on a particular area of study. In junior year students begin to prepare for their senior year independent study project (I.S.) by studying the nature of research in their major and the research techniques they will need to complete the I.S.

The I.S. is the linchpin of a Wooster education. Much of the premise of this I.S. is based on Emerson's words: "Do your work, and I will know you." Wooster understands this to mean that a student's truest self emerges when he or she is passionately involved in work he or she has chosen, a unique work close to the heart that is entirely of the student's own making. To accomplish this, students have a faculty adviser to collaborate with them and enter into the intellectual conversation that they have been preparing for during their first three years at Wooster. Students then complete a significant project, present it to a department, and in doing so are changed forever by the experience. Some examples of I.S. projects have been: "Conveying Corporate Images Through Advertising: A Case Study on Polo/Ralph Lauren," "Nazi Germany on Trial: An Historical and Philosophical Analysis of the Nuremberg Trials," "Factors Influencing Airfares in the Deregulated U.S. Airline Industry."

The I.S is supported by a separate Gault Library for Independent Study and a progressive Wooster policy that allows faculty to take a leave every fifth year to embark on research or artistic work that will allow them to return to share their work and experiences with their students. The whole campus appreciates I.S. in terms of securing a job or applying to graduate school. It has been positively recognized by admission deans and Fortune 500 executives and results in three significant outcomes: 90 percent of the graduating class find jobs within six months; twenty to twenty-five percent go directly to graduate school; after five years, about half of the graduating class have earned an advanced degree or are in graduate school.

Wooster has a great faculty that uses novel teaching methods and loves the personal contact it has with its students, who are motivated, intelligent, take risks, and are unpretentious. Wooster is a place for passionate work and fun, where 40 percent of the students are engaged in volunteer activities, 25 percent in a varsity sport, and 35 percent in some musical activity. Wooster's open, flexible environment has also been a beacon for international students.

CORNELL COLLEGE   Mount Vernon, Iowa

Total Undergraduate Enrollment: 1,001
Men: 396 Women: 605
Five-Year Graduation Rate: 68%

Tuition: $$$
Room and Board: $$
Residential Students: 92%

History First established in 1853 as a Methodist Seminary, in 1855 the institution became Cornell College, named for New York iron merchant William Wesley Cornell.

Location Located on a wooded crest, the 129-acre campus is in Mount Vernon, Iowa, 15 miles east of Cedar Rapids. Cornell is one of only two campuses listed entirely on the National Register of Historic Places. It is 200 miles west of Chicago.

Top Programs of Study Education, psychology, English

Arts and Sciences Art, biochemistry and molecular biology, biology, chemistry, classical studies, computer science, English, environmental studies, ethnic studies, French, geology, German, history, international relations, Latin American studies, mathematics, medieval and early modern studies, philosophy, physics, politics, psychology, religion, Russian, Russian studies, sociology, sociology and anthropology, Spanish, women's studies

Business Economics and business, international business

Education Elementary, physical education, secondary

Pre-Professional Law, medicine, social work/human services, theology

Accredited Programs Chemistry, music

Special Programs Cornell offers an early acceptance program in dentistry with the College of Dentistry of the University of Iowa. Combined degree programs are offered in engineering with Washington University in St. Louis, a forestry program with Duke, nursing and allied health sciences with Rush University in Chicago, and medical technology with St. Luke's Hospital in Cedar Rapids. There is a Phi Beta Kappa chapter. Several interdisciplinary programs are offered.

Facilities There are 41 buildings including the refurbished Armstrong Hall of Fine Arts and Law Hall Technology Center. The college has a radio station and a natural history museum.

Transition to College Program Cornell offers a traditional orientation program.

Athletics NCAA III, Iowa Conference

   Men: Baseball, basketball, cross-country, football, golf, indoor and outdoor track, soccer, tennis, wrestling

   Women: Basketball, cross-country, golf, indoor and outdoor track, soccer, softball, tennis, volleyball

Student Life and Housing About 1,000 students can be accommodated in college housing, which is guaranteed for all four years. Only 30 percent of the students are from Iowa with the majority from 38 other states, mostly the Midwest, and 7 countries. Ethnicity: Caucasian—90 percent. There are seven local fraternities and seven local sororities. All students may keep cars.

Accommodations for Students with Disabilities A student qualifies for accommodation when appropriate documentation is submitted to the Registrar.

Financial Aid About 83 percent of all freshmen receive aid. The average freshman award was about $16,000.

Requirements for Admission Required are SAT I or ACT scores, a recommended 2.8 GPA in a college prep high school program, and a rank in the upper half of the class. An interview is strongly recommended.

Application Freshmen are admitted for fall and spring semesters. Application deadlines are open, with decision notification sent on a rolling basis.

International Students Applicants will need to provide evidence of English language proficiency, satisfactory completion of secondary schooling, sufficient financial support, and either a TOEFL, SAT I, or ACT score.

Transfer Students Application deadline is March 1. Required is a statement of good standing from the college last attended, with official transcripts. Grades of C or better are considered for transfer. A maximum of 64 credits are transferable from a two-year college.

Admission Contact
Office of Admissions
Cornell College
600 First Street West
Mount Vernon, IA 52314-9988
Phone: (800) 747-1112; (319) 895-4477
FAX: (319) 895-4451
E-mail: *admission@cornellcollege.edu*
Web: *www.Cornellcollege.edu*

The Heart of the College Cornell College is considered one of the top liberal arts colleges in America. Consider these facts: the average class size is 14 and all classes are capped at 25; over one-third of the students study abroad; in a recent year two-thirds of the students received scholarships and grant support totaling more than $11 million; 75 percent of Cornell students participate in service projects; almost 50 percent of Cornell students double major; over two-thirds did one or more independent study courses with a professor; almost two-thirds of Cornell students have at least one career-related or pre-professional internship.

The heart of Cornell College lies in its OCAAT calendar—"one course at a time," extended over nine blocks, each of which is three-and-a-half weeks in length for each academic year. So students are studying one course by itself, immersing themselves in the subject, allowing professors great flexibility, with no distractions from other courses. For example, classes can watch full-length films without interruption, go off campus for daylong fieldtrips, or become involved in experiments, projects, and discussions, without worrying about the class abruptly ending after an hour. There are courses taught by talented, involved faculty, who teach students who are curious and love to learn. One student comments, "Your favorite class may have nothing to do with your major, but it broadens your mind."

In addition, students may spend semesters abroad studying the arts in England and Italy, archaelogy in Greece, or international studies in Switzerland, to name just a few. There are also semesters in France, Spain, Mexico, and Bolivia, to study language and culture, studying environmental and ecological issues in Australia, Kenya, Nepal, and New Zealand, or studying political change and social justice in Brazil, Mexico, or Central Europe.

Cornell College offers close faculty–student interaction, intellectual challenge, and intensive one-course-at-a-time scheduling on a historic campus.

CREIGHTON UNIVERSITY Omaha, Nebraska

Total Undergraduate Enrollment: 3,607
Men: 1,451 Women: 2,156
Five-Year Graduation Rate: 68%

Tuition: $$$
Room and Board: $$
Residential Students: 53%

History Creighton University, founded in 1878, is a Catholic university in the Jesuit tradition.

John and Edward Creighton, builders of the transcontinental telegraph that linked pioneer

America, provided funding for the establishment of the university.

Location The 92-acre campus is located in Omaha, Nebraska (metropolitan population 700,000), affording students many cultural and recreational activities.

Top Programs of Study Biology, journalism, psychology

Arts and Sciences American studies, anthropology, art, atmospheric sciences, biology, chemistry, classical and Near Eastern civilizations, communications, computer science, emergency medical services, English, environmental science, exercise science (athletic training), French, German, graphic design, health administration and policy, history, international studies, journalism and mass communication, justice and society, mathematics, music, Native American studies, nursing, philosophy, physics, political science, psychology, social work, sociology, Spanish, theater, theology

Business Accounting, economics, entrepreneurship, finance, international business, management information systems, marketing

Education Elementary, secondary, special

Pre-Professional Dentistry, law, medicine, occupational therapy, pharmacy, physical therapy

Accredited Programs Accounting, business, education, emergency medical services, nursing, social work

Special Programs Creighton has been selected as one of the most "wired" school in America. The Creighton Preference gives CU graduates preference to all Creighton graduate and professional programs. There are dual programs in engineering with Mercy College in Detroit, and a 3-3 Business Administration and Law Degree with Creighton's School of Law. There is a Freshman Leadership Program and many study abroad and student exchange programs. Creighton was selected as having one of the top 100 campuses in the nation. There is an Army ROTC program.

Facilities There are 56 buildings, each of which now has a computer lab. There are a new student center, a Center for the Arts, a new fitness center, and a new state-of-the-art science complex. After a great deal of expansion, the university is now focusing on beautification of the central campus, including a pedestrian mall, to add green space to the heart of the undergraduate living area.

Transition to College Program Students take a "Master Student" course, which is designed to help reinforce study and thinking skills and ensure a smooth start for freshmen.

Athletics NCAA I, Missouri Valley Conference

   Men: Basketball, baseball, cross-country, golf, soccer, tennis

   Women: Basketball, crew, cross-country, golf, soccer, softball, tennis, volleyball

Student Life and Housing All full-time students can be accommodated in college housing, which is guaranteed all four years. Forty-nine percent of the students are from Nebraska, with the remainder from every state and 65 countries. Ethnicity: Caucasian—78 percent; Asian-American—10 percent; African-American—3 percent; Hispanic-American—3 percent; International—3 percent. There are seven national fraternities and six national sororities. All students may keep cars.

Accommodations for Students with Disabilities Students need to make requests for reasonable accommodations as soon as possible after acceptance, as well as submit appropriate documentation of disability. Students should contact the Coordinator of Services for Students with Disabilities.

Financial Aid About 90 percent of freshmen receive aid. The average freshman award was about $14,000.

Requirements for Admission ACT or SAT I scores and a college prep high school program.

Application Freshmen are admitted to all semesters. Applications should be submitted by August 1

for fall admission and January 1 for spring admission. Admission notification is on a rolling basis.

International Students Required are official high school and, if applicable, postsecondary transcripts with certified English translations, a minimum TOEFL score of 550 (if English is not the student's native language), counselor evaluation, teacher recommendation, ACT or SAT scores, and proof of financial support.

Transfer Students Students have to be in good standing at an accredited college and submit official college and high school transcripts. Students must earn at least 48 credits at Creighton. Courses with C or better are considered for transfer.

Admission Contact
Office of Undergraduate Admissions
Creighton University
2500 California Plaza
Omaha, Nebraska 68178
Phone: (800) 282-5835
FAX: (402) 280-2685
E-mail: *admissions@creighton.edu*
Web: *www.admissions.creighton.edu*

The Heart of the University The heart of Creighton University is its career orientation taught within a Jesuit tradition of education. As a Creighton undergraduate, students will find themselves on a campus shared by a sizable number of graduate students. This is a positive trait of Creighton's because the school has a policy called the "Creighton Preference," which gives its own students preference for admission to its own nationally recognized professional schools in dentistry, law, medicine, pharmacy, and physical and occupational therapy. Besides this "preference" edge, undergraduates are taught within a 400-year-old Jesuit tradition of education and service, the worth of the individual, and appreciation of ethnic and cultural diversity.

Because this is a medium-sized institution and a university, Creighton has the appeal to attract students from every state in the United States, as well as 65 other countries. Creighton is the most diverse institution of its size in the United States and, as a result, diversity is certainly a core value here. Also the Creighton Center for Service and Justice encourages and supports students to experience a variety of service opportunities, including weekly service trips, Habitat for Humanity, spring and fall break service trips, and student service groups. Creighton's success is reflected by the fact that 95 percent of its graduates are employed, involved in volunteer work, or are attending graduate or professional school within six months of graduation. The career advising, internships, and strong alumni program are all instrumental in this success.

The academic programs are cutting-edge. For example, in business, students can study a Portfolio Practicum course in which students invest $300,000 in university endowment funds; the Semestre Domenicano, a semester abroad business program in a third world country; an e-commerce program; and a leadership program. The nursing program has a one-year option for those students who possess a non-nursing degree.

The faculty is an accomplished one, both excellent teachers and experts in their fields, some having gained national recognition. Yet, with an average class size of 24, student–faculty relationships are one of the greatest strengths of a Creighton education.

Omaha offers a Midwestern friendliness to Creighton students, as well as museums, shopping, a zoo, and sporting events. Also, a new Convention Center Arena has opened, along with miles of walking and biking paths and two riverfront parks. All of this is within walking distance to campus.

DE SALES UNIVERSITY

Center Valley, Pennsylvania

Total Undergraduate Enrollment: 1,150
Men: 506 Women: 644
Five-Year Graduation Rate: 70%

Tuition: $$$
Room and Board: $$$
Residential Students: 71%

History De Sales University is a Catholic college originally founded in 1964 as Allentown College of Saint Francis De Sales by the Oblates of St. Francis de Sales. In 2001 the college was renamed De Sales University in order to reflect its growing programs.

Location De Sales is located on 400 acres in suburban Center Valley, Pennsylvania, in scenic Lehigh Valley, one hour from Philadelphia and the Pocono Mountains and 90 minutes from New York City.

Top Programs of Study Business, theater, natural sciences

Arts and Sciences Biology, chemistry, communications, computer science, dance, English, environmental science, environmental studies, history, law and society, liberal studies, management of information and technology, marriage and family studies, mathematics, nursing, philosophy, physician assistant, political science, psychology, social work, Spanish, sports management, theater, theology, TV/film

Business Accounting, finance, management

Education Elementary, secondary

Pre-Professional Dentistry, law, medicine, optometry, pharmacology, podiatry, technical theater, veterinary medicine

Accredited Programs Nursing, physician's assistant

Special Programs De Sales has one of the best performing and fine arts departments in America. The university offers a five-year physician's assistant program. There is cross-registration with Lehigh, Cedar Crest, Moravian, Lafayette, and Muhlenbeg Colleges. There is an Army ROTC program.

Facilities There are 18 buildings, including the Labuda Center for the Performing Arts (home of the acclaimed Pennsylvania Shakespeare Festival), the newly renovated Billera Hall Sports and Recreation Center, the Iacocca Television and Film Studios, and the newly constructed Campbell Hall classroom building.

Transition to College Program The university offers a traditional orientation program.

Athletics NCAA III, Middle Atlantic States Collegiate Athletic Conference and the Eastern Collegiate Athletic Conference

Men: Baseball, basketball, cross-country, golf, lacrosse, soccer, tennis, track

Women: Basketball, cross-country, soccer, softball, tennis, track, volleyball

Student Life and Housing About 800 students can be accommodated in college housing, which is guaranteed for all four years. Seventy-four percent of the students are from Pennsylvania, with the remainder from 10 other states and 8 countries. Ethnicity: Caucasian—95 percent. There are no fraternities or sororities. All students may keep cars.

Accommodations for Students with Disabilities The Learning Center provides services for students with documented disabilities.

Financial Aid About 94 percent of all freshmen receive aid. The average freshman award was about $11,000.

Requirements for Admission SAT I or ACT scores and a college prep high school program. An on-campus interview is strongly recommended.

Application The university uses a rolling admissions policy; however, maximum consideration is given to students who apply by December 1. Physician's assistant candidates must apply by January 15 for the fall semester.

International Students Fall deadline for application is April 1. Demonstration of financial arrangements to cover expenses must be provided. A minimum TOEFL score of 550 is required.

Transfer Students A minimum 2.0 GPA is required (3.0 for physician's assistant program, with high science and/or health care related courses). Official high school and college transcripts are required, as well as a course catalogue from each college attended. Courses with a minimum grade of C− will be considered for transfer.

Admission Contact
Office of Admissions
De Sales University
2755 Station Avenue
Center Valley, PA 18034-9568
Phone: (877) 4DE-SALES; (610) 282-1100
FAX: (610) 282-0131
E-mail: *admiss@desales.edu*
Web: *www.desales.edu*

The Heart of the University De Sales University seeks to "discover the good in each student and to draw it out." The university is very successful with this mission because it attracts students who enjoy the unpretentious quality of De Sales and its Catholic community flavor. De Sales is a friendly campus, with 70 percent of its students living on the spacious campus, away from the hustle and bustle of big-city life. Students remark on the quality of sincere, genuine friendships they make at De Sales. With a dedicated, friendly, accessible faculty who see their work more as a "calling" than a career, students experience a very personal, supportive approach to their education. The education consists of a broad-based liberal arts program with career-focused specializations. One administrator remarked: "Learning isn't a spectator sport here." That's good news for students as they learn, in small classes, how to think critically and creatively and communicate effectively. Notable among career specializations are the programs in nursing—one of the finest in Pennsylvania—and the five-year physician's assistant program. Both programs offer clinical experience in area hospitals and other health care institutions. Also, while not big-city based, De Sales is surrounded by smaller settings for valuable internship opportunities in accounting firms, corporate finance departments, sports news, law firms, and computer firms. De Sales points with pride at its 97 percent rate of full-time employment or enrollment in graduate or professional school within six months of graduation.

The most renowned program at De Sales is performing arts, which leads to degrees in theater, dance, and TV/film, and ranks as one of the finest in America. Students are taught by outstanding teachers in world-class facilities and participate in first-rate productions. The much acclaimed Pennsylvania Shakespeare Festival is held each summer at De Sales, offering additional opportunities for internships.

DORDT COLLEGE Sioux Center, Iowa

Total Undergraduate Enrollment: 1,350
Men: 607 Women: 743
Five-Year Graduation Rate: 69%

Tuition: $$
Room and Board: $
Residential Students: 90%

History Dordt College was founded in 1953 as the Midwest Christian Junior College. In 1956 the name was changed to Dordt, and it became a four-year college in 1961. Dordt is a Christian college with a belief in the Bible as the infallible word of God.

Location Dordt is located on a 50-acre campus in Sioux Center, Iowa—an attractive, prosperous community in northwest Iowa, an hour's drive from Sioux City, Iowa, and Sioux Falls, South Dakota.

Top Programs of Study Education, business administration, engineering

Arts and Sciences Agriculture, art (studio, history), biology, chemistry, communications, computer science, Dutch, engineering, engineering science, English (literature and writing), environmental studies, general science, German, health and recreation, history, individual studies, mathematics, music, philosophy, physics, political science, psychology, radio/TV, social studies, social work, Spanish, theater arts, theology (general, youth ministry)

Business Accounting, administration (general and information systems)

Education Art, business, elementary, physical education, secondary, special

Pre-Professional Dentistry, law, medical, nursing, occupational therapy, optometry, pharmacy, physical therapy, seminary, veterinary medicine

Accredited Programs Engineering, social work

Special Programs There are many opportunities for mission work. Dordt offers a bachelor's degree in medical technology that includes three years at Dordt and one year at an approved school of medical technology. Students can design their own majors. Students can participate in the Chicago Metropolitan Center Program, study problems and issues of metropolitan life, and intern in an area related to their major or career interest. Students can also participate in the Los Angeles Film Studies Program, which explores the film industry within a Christian context. They can study at several international sites.

Facilities There are 22 buildings, including an observatory, a remodeled and expanded science and technology center, an art gallery, radio sta-

tion, and the Agricultural Stewardship Center, which is two miles north of campus, and includes a dairy and 160 acres of farmland used for production, crop testing, and research.

Transition to College Program Orientation includes learning experiences in goal-setting, self-assessment, advising, campus life, learning skills and abilities, available resources, and building community. Also, during the first semester, there is a focus on personal counseling and targeted academic skills.

Athletics NAIA, Great Plains Athletic Conference

Men: Baseball, basketball, cross-country, golf, soccer, tennis, track

Women: Basketball, cross-country, soccer, softball, tennis, track, volleyball

Student Life and Housing About 1,300 students can be accommodated in college housing, which is guaranteed for all four years. Thirty-six percent of the students are from Iowa, the remaining students coming from 30 other states and 13 countries. Ethnicity: Caucasian—95 percent. Each school year begins with a religious retreat. Chapel services are held twice each week. There are no fraternities or sororities. All students may keep cars.

Accommodations for Students with Disabilities Students should contact the Coordinator of Services for Students with Disabilities as early as possible to develop and implement a plan of services and accommodations. Documentation of disability is required.

Financial Aid About 98 percent of all freshmen receive aid. The average award was about $14,000.

Requirements for Admission SAT I or ACT scores and a college prep high school program. Also required is a signed statement of faith, which is included in the application, regarding the college's expectation that the student adhere to the Christian principles of the Dordt College community.

Application A rolling admissions policy is used, with admission decisions made when all application materials have been received.

International Students A TOEFL score of 500 or higher is required, as well as an entrance interview (except for Canadians) in order to determine whether students will need to take English as a Second Language courses during their first year.

Transfer Students A maximum of 30 credits can be transferred, but 61 credits can be transferred by graduates from community colleges. A minimum course grade of C− is required for transfer. Official high school and college transcripts are required, as well as a GPA of 2.0 or above.

Admission Contact
Office of Admissions
Dordt College
498 Fourth Avenue, NE
Sioux Center, IA 51250-1697
Phone: (800) 343-DORDT; (712) 722-6080
FAX: (712) 722-1967
E-mail: *admissions@dordt.edu*
Web: *www.dordt.edu*

The Heart of the College Dordt College is a Christian college in the Reformed faith, committed to promoting student learning for life-long Christian service. Members of the Dordt College community are not just "Sunday Christians"; they learn through a core curriculum and their major field of study to develop analytical, communication, artistic, and physical skills that will prepare students for the Christian life. One student writes: "If you want to learn how to use your Christian faith in practically everything you do—your job, your family life—this is where you want to attend college."

The Dordt facilities are modern. The students are drawn from many geographical regions, allowing for 90 percent to live on campus. The wonderful facilities and the high percentage of resident students develop an exceptional community, with students feeling a sense of belonging, caring, and family.

During Spring Break 250 students travel across the country to provide teaching and childcare, do home repair projects, and renovate ministry centers. Internationally, students share agricultural knowledge with Ukraine farmers and help construct irrigation systems in Honduras. Locally, students provide tutoring assistance for children and help people with developmental disabilities.

Dordt offers internship opportunities in nearby Sioux Falls and throughout the world. This plus an active alumni association have provided for 98 percent of Dordt graduates to find employment or go on to graduate study within six months—and 85 percent of those employed are placed in jobs within their immediate fields of study. The range of employment is interesting, from writing for the television show, "Touched by an Angel," to being a heart surgeon, news anchor, the owner of a candy company, to fighting world hunger through agricultural missions work.

DRURY UNIVERSITY   **Springfield, Missouri**

Total Undergraduate Enrollment: 1,494
Men: 653 Women: 841
Five-Year Graduation Rate: 62%

Tuition: $$
Room and Board: $
Residential Students: 52%

History Drury University was founded in 1873 to prepare students for successful careers through a New England liberal arts tradition. The university is affiliated with both the United Church of Christ and the Disciples of Christ.

Location The 80-acre tree-lined campus, surrounded by a historic midtown neighborhood, is located in Springfield, Missouri (metro population 330,000), 200 miles southwest of St. Louis and 150 miles southwest of Kansas City.

Top Programs of Study Business administration, biology/pre-med, education

Arts and Sciences American political studies, art history, arts administration, biology, broadcasting, chemistry, computer science, criminology, design art, English, environmental science, environmental studies, exercise and sport science, fine arts, French, German, history, international political studies, journalism, mathematics, music, music therapy, philosophy, philosophy/religion, physics, politics and government, psychology, public relations, religion, sociology, Spanish, speech communication, theater, writing

Business Accounting, administration, advertising, computer information systems/e-commerce, economics, international business

Education Elementary, physical education, secondary

Pre-Professional Dentistry, law, medical, medical technology, optometry, sports management, veterinary medicine

Accredited Programs Architecture, business, education

Special Programs The Hammonds School of Architecture is the first one on a small university campus to be accredited in the United States. There are dual degree programs in engineering and occupational therapy with Washington University in St Louis. Drury also has early admission partnerships in medicine and law. There are many study abroad opportunities, including a Drury campus in Greece. Drury has been selected as one of the most computer-wired campuses in America. There is an Army ROTC program.

Facilities There are 19 buildings, including a new science center, the Hammonds School of Architecture, the new Olin Library, an art gallery, and a radio station.

Transition to College Program The First-Year Experience Program includes academic and personal counseling, mentor classes and group activ-ities, and special programming. The Director of the First-Year Experience Program serves as a resource for all students who may seek additional assistance with transition.

Athletics NCAA II, Heartland Conference

    Men: Basketball, cross-country, golf, soccer (Div. I), swimming and diving, tennis

    Women: Basketball, cross-country, golf, soccer (Div. I), swimming and diving, tennis, volleyball

Student Life and Housing About 800 students can be accommodated in college housing, which is guaranteed for all four years. Seventy-five percent of the students are from Missouri; the remainder are from 37 other states and 51 countries. Ethnicity: Caucasian—90 percent. There are four national fraternities and four national sororities. All students may keep cars.

Accommodations for Students with Disabilities Appropriate documentation of disability must be submitted, along with requests for accommodations, to the Director of Student Development.

Financial Aid About 80 percent of freshmen receive aid. The average freshman award was about $7,000.

Requirements for Admission SAT I or ACT scores and a college prep high school program.

Application Freshmen are admitted to all sessions. Deadlines are August 1 for fall admission and December 1 for spring admission. Admissions decisions are sent on a rolling basis.

International Students Deadlines are April 1 for fall semester and November 1 for spring semester. Required are a writing sample or application essay, official secondary or, if applicable, post-secondary transcripts with English translations as applicable, documentation of graduation and of financial support, minimum TOEFL score of 530, and scores of 980 on the SAT I or 21 on the ACT. Letters of recommendation are encouraged.

Transfer Students Students must be in good standing with a previous accredited college. Official high school and college transcripts and ACT or SAT scores are required if the student has completed fewer than 30 credits, as well as a recommendation from an official at the previous college. C grades or higher are considered for transfer students with an associate's degree from an accredited college who will enter with junior status.

Admission Contact

Office of Admissions
Drury University
900 North Benton Avenue
Springfield, MO 65802
Phone: (800) 922-2274; (417) 873-7205
FAX: (417) 866-3873
E-mail: *druryad@drury.edu*
Web: *www.drury.edu*

The Heart of the University The heart of a Drury education is the well-designed core curriculum known as Global Perspectives 21, a four-year integrated core that helps students find personal meaning and career success by providing skills and knowledge needed in a rapidly changing global society. The program has two dimensions. The scientific perspective focuses on mathematical literacy, technology, and the social sciences. The second dimension is Global Studies, which focuses on critical thinking, writing, language skills, diverse cultural heritages, and the values raised by the challenges and opportunities of a global future. There's a great deal of discussion and writing in small classes, with science taught by teams of professors who use more of a discovery process of teaching than lots of student memorization. Along with this distinctive program, students study a major. Every major ends with a research project. Labs in every science department are available for student–faculty research projects.

The small classes and talented faculty provide for a welcoming community at Drury, with professors taking a personal interest in student progress. There's much student–faculty collaboration on projects and research, with all classes taught by professors.

Drury's outstanding academic programs and quality faculty open the door for many special opportunities in terms of early acceptance programs at medical schools and dual degree programs, as well as participation in Biosphere in Arizona. The success of the program is demonstrated by the fact that one year after graduation 93 percent of the graduates are working and 33 percent are attending a graduate or professional school. A strong Career Center aids in this success, as well as the fact that 75 percent of the students complete at least one internship.

Drury has a special relationship with its city home of Springfield and surrounding communities. For example, students in the Hammonds School of Architecture worked with city leaders to revitalize the downtown area and develop a marketing plan for the area. Also, the Drury Office of Student Outreach coordinates more than 1,000 student volunteers in dozens of projects. The education program has joined with Yale University and three neighborhood public schools in the nationally acclaimed School Development Project, helping to transform troubled schools into successful ones.

Springfield is a perfect blend of Midwestern friendliness and big city culture. There are many cultural and entertainment opportunities, as well as water-skiing, fishing, camping, boating, and, only a few minutes away, are the Ozark Mountains and lakes.

EASTERN MENNONITE UNIVERSITY

Harrisonburg, Virginia

Total Undergraduate Enrollment: 926
Men: 388 Women: 538
Five-Year Graduation Rate: 57%

Tuition: $$$
Room and Board: $
Residential Students: 60%

History Eastern Mennonite first began as a Bible academy. In 1930 it became a junior college and in 1947 a four-year college. Affiliated with the Mennonite Church, the university believes that the Bible is the inspired word of God.

Location Eastern Mennonite is located on a 90-acre campus in Harrisonburg, Virginia (population 40,000), in the heart of the scenic and historic Shenandoah Mountains. The university is 115 miles from Richmond, the state capital, and 125 miles southwest of Washington, D.C.

Top Programs of Study Business, education, biology

Arts and Sciences Art, biblical studies and theology, biochemistry, biology, camping, recreation and outdoor ministries, chemistry, coaching, communication, computer information systems, computer science, congregational and youth ministries, culture, economic development, economics, English, environmental science, exercise science, family studies, French, German, history, history and social science, international agriculture, journalism, justice, peace and conflict studies, liberal arts, mathematics, medical technology, missions, music, nursing, physics, political science, psychology, recreation and sport leadership, religion and mission, religion and philosophy, social work, socio-economic development, sociology, Spanish, theater, youth ministry

Business Accounting, administration, finance, international management and organizational development, marketing

Education Early childhood, elementary, health and physical education, secondary, special, TESOL

Pre-Professional Dentistry, engineering, exercise physiology, law, medicine, optometry, physical therapy, podiatry, veterinary medicine

Accredited Programs Education, nursing, social work

Special Programs The Global Village Curriculum is designed to educate students to be world citizens. Students have opportunities to study in Central America, the Middle East, Europe, China, Japan, Russia, and Africa. In the United States, students can choose to study New Orleans, and Native American reservations. There are many opportunities for social outreach efforts. University chapel provides national and international Christian leaders, social and political activists, mission and service workers.

Facilities There are 38 buildings, including the Brackbill Planetarium, an arboretum, an art gallery, an observatory, a radio station, a new art building, and the new University Commons.

Transition to College Program All students enroll in a fall orientation course. Also, a First-Year Experience orients students to the university environment by teaching academic skills, life management skills, and information pertinent to the university and community.

Athletics NCAA III, Old Dominion Athletic Conference

   Men: Baseball, basketball, cross-country, soccer, tennis, track & field, volleyball

   Women: Basketball, cross-country, field hockey, soccer, softball, tennis, track & field, volleyball

Student Life and Housing About 700 students can be accommodated in college housing, which is guaranteed for all four years. Thirty-eight percent of the students are from Virginia, with the majority from 36 other states and 15 countries. Ethnicity: Caucasian—87 percent; African-American—6 percent; International—5 percent; Hispanic-American—2 percent. There are no sororities or fraternities. All students may keep cars. Chapel attendance is required.

Accommodations for Students with Disabilities The Academic Support Center serves as advocate for students with learning disabilities, attention deficit disorders, and physical disabilities. Students with documented disabilities must register for services with the Coordinator of Student Disability Support Services.

Financial Aid About 92 percent of all students receive aid. The average freshman award was about $13,000.

Requirements for Admission SAT I or ACT scores and a college prep high school program. An interview is recommended. As part of the application, students must sign a community lifestyle agreement, indicating willingness to cooperate with the standards and purpose of a Christian university.

Application Application deadlines are 30 days prior to either the beginning of the fall or spring semesters. For maximum financial aid, students should submit their applications six months prior to the semester in which they plan to enroll. An admission decision is made approximately 10 days after all application materials have been received.

International Students Students complete the International Student Application Form. Students whose native language is other than English must receive a TOEFL score of 550 or higher, or an English Language Proficiency Test score of at least 965. Students must provide evidence of financial ability to pay for education.

Transfer Students Transfer students from two-year colleges may transfer up to 65 credits. Students should contact the admissions staff as early as possible. Grades of C or better will be reviewed for transfer.

Admission Contact
Eastern Mennonite University
1200 Park Road
Harrisonburg, VA 22802-2462
Phone: (800) EMU-COOL; (540) 432-4000
FAX: (540) 432-4444
E-mail: *admiss@emu.edu*
Web: *www.emu.edu*

The Heart of the University Eastern Mennonite is a university rooted in the Christian faith, which "challenges students to answer Christ's call to a life of nonviolence, witness, service, and peace building." Eastern Mennonite accomplishes this by having students study a broad based liberal arts curriculum and a specific major area of study, as well as having a significant experience in a cross-cultural setting. The heart of the university can be found in its Global Village curriculum—designed to educate "world citizens." Students study the humanities, the Bible, the Christian heritage, "village skills" of communication, problem solving, scientific investigations, and learning how to stay fit, as well as participating in the Cross-Cultural Program. In this program students study in a wide range of locations, such as Central America, the Middle East, Europe, China, Japan, Russia, New Orleans, and Native American reservations. Students typically find these to be life-changing experiences, that broaden their world view and expand possibilities after graduation.

Small classes are taught by professors who challenge and inspire their students. When graduates talk about their most important influences on campus, they choose their professors. This is easy to understand, because these professors serve as role models of scholarly achievement, faith, and commitment to service, with about 75 percent having lived and worked abroad.

Almost a quarter of the students are actively involved in outreach efforts. Students assist at a half-way house for ex-offenders, tutor Spanish-speaking migrant workers, befriend the elderly, "adopt" needy children, and help build homes for low-income families. During spring break, some students travel with work teams and gospel teams.

At the center of the campus community is university chapel, where students, faculty, and staff gather three times a week for workshops and a variety of faith-related presentations. Chapel speakers include national and international Christian leaders, social and political activists, mission and service workers.

ELIZABETHTOWN COLLEGE

Elizabethtown, Pennsylvania

Total Undergraduate Enrollment: 1,800
Men: 700 Women: 1,100
Five-Year Graduation Rate: 70%

Tuition: $$$$
Room and Board: $$
Residential Students: 85%

History Elizabethtown College was founded in 1899 and is affiliated with the Church of the Brethren, one of three historic peace churches, along with the Quakers and the Mennonites. The college's early mission was to train teachers and educated students in the ways of commerce. The college affirms the values of human dignity and social justice and believes that the pursuit of knowledge is most noble when used to benefit others.

Location The 185-acre campus is located in Elizabethtown, Pennsylvania (population 20,000), in historic southeastern Pennsylvania. There are many cultural and entertainment activities in the area. Harrisburg, the state capital, is 25 minutes away and Philadelphia, Baltimore, and Washington, D.C. are 90 minutes away.

Top Programs of Study Business administration, early and elementary education, biology, communications

Arts and Sciences Art, biochemistry, biology, biotechnology, chemical physics, chemistry, chemistry management, clinical laboratory science, communications, computer engineering, computer science, engineering, English, environmental science, French, German, history, industrial engineering, mathematics, music, music therapy, occupational therapy, philosophy, physics, political science, psychology, religious studies, social work, sociology–anthropology, Spanish

Business Accounting, administration, computer science/business information systems, economics, international business

Education Early childhood, elementary, music, secondary

Pre-Professional Dentistry, law, medicine, ministry, veterinary medicine

Accredited Programs Business, music, social work

Special Programs There are several joint programs offered in allied health sciences in cooperation with Thomas Jefferson University in Philadelphia: biotechnology, diagnostic imaging, laboratory sciences, nursing, occupational therapy, and physical therapy. There is a five-year forestry and environmental science degree offered in cooperation with Duke, as well as a five-year degree in engineering offered with Penn State. There are internship opportunities in Philadelphia, Washington, D.C., New York City, and Harrisburg.

Facilities There are 24 buildings, including the new Leffler Chapel and Performance Center, the new High Library, the renovated Zug Memorial Hall, the Schreiber Senior Townhouse Quadrangle, and a new all-weather track

Transition to College Program Students can participate in the Freshmen Interest Group, where students share common courses as well as living space, and the Faculty Mentor Program, which brings faculty into the residence halls for both academic and social interaction. Also there is a Special Advising Program designed for the freshmen who need an "academic boost" in terms of specific academic course work, advising, and tutoring.

Athletics NCAA III, Middle Atlantic Conference

Men: Baseball, basketball, cross-country, golf, lacrosse, soccer, swimming, tennis, track & field, wrestling

Women: Basketball, cross-country, field hockey, lacrosse, soccer, softball, swimming, tennis, track & field, volleyball

Student Life and Housing About 1,400 students can be accommodated in college housing, which is guaranteed for all four years. Sixty-eight percent of the students are from Pennsylvania, with the remainder from 30 other states and 30 countries. Ethnicity: Caucasian—94 percent. There are no sororities or fraternities. All students may keep cars. Students voluntarily sign a pledge of honesty and integrity.

Accommodations for Students with Disabilities Students should contact the Director of Counseling Services or the Dean of Admissions for information regarding services.

Financial Aid About 90 percent of all freshmen receive aid. The average award was about $12,000.

Requirements for Admission SAT I or ACT scores and college prep high school program. An interview is strongly recommended.

Application Admission decisions are made on a rolling basis, beginning in November, as soon as application materials are complete. Applications for specialized programs have specific deadlines.

International Students Official copies of secondary school and college records are required, as well as TOEFL scores and/or SAT I results, an autobiographical statement, and two letters of reference. Students must also provide financial certification.

Transfer Students Transfer students are accepted for both fall and spring semesters. Students must be in good social and academic standing, present two letters of recommendation from professors, a final high school transcript, and transcripts for all college work. An interview is recommended. Up to 64 credits can be transferred. A 2.5 GPA is typically required for admission.

Admission Contact
Office of Admissions
Elizabethtown College
One Alpha Drive
Elizabethtown, PA 17022-2298
Phone: (717) 361-1400
FAX: (717) 361-1365
E-mail: *admissions@etown.edu*
Web: *www.etown.edu*

The Heart of the College Elizabethtown College's affiliation with the Church of the Brethren places it with similar colleges affiliated with the Quakers and Mennonites and their heritage of affirming values of peace, nonviolence, human dignity, and social justice—all in the global community. Students are offered a thematic core curriculum that integrates with academic majors. The typical liberal arts goals of developing independent, critical, creative thinkers with excellent communication skills are prized.

Elizabethtown is a place of warm, caring community. Students remark on how easy it is to make lasting friendships. Also, the talented faculty are the key to the heart of Elizabethtown's "hand-crafted" education. With small classes and a student-centered orientation that mentors and encourages students' learning and aspirations, faculty help to personalize each student's education. Ninety percent of the faculty serve as advisers, and many collaborate with students in research projects that culminate in presentations at professional conferences.

Students find historic Elizabethtown an ideal location. The town serves as a residential community for many who work in Hershey, Harrisburg, and Lancaster. There is much to do within 30 minutes of the campus, in addition to a very active campus life. Students have completed internships with Hershey Medical Center, *New Yorker Magazine,* the Pennsylvania Department of Environmental Protection, National Public Radio, Hershey Foods, and Merrill Lynch. Elizabethtown graduates are employed or pursue advanced degrees within eight months of graduation at an average rate of 95 percent. More than 90 percent of pre-law graduates are admitted to law school and more than 80 percent of medical school applicants are accepted.

ELMIRA COLLEGE

Elmira, New York

Total Undergraduate Enrollment: 1,200
Men: 400 Women: 800
Five-Year Graduation Rate: 67%

Tuition: $$$$
Room and Board: $$$$
Residential Students: 96%

History Elmira College is a product of a reform movement in the pre-Civil War decades when a group, whose benefactor was Simeon Benjamin, founded Elmira in 1855 as a women's college. The college became coeducational in 1969 and is private with no denominational association.

Location The 42-acre suburban campus is located in Elmira, New York (population 36,000), 90 miles west of Syracuse, and dominates the south-central region of New York, which is the trade, industrial, financial, medical, and transportation hub of the Finger Lakes Region.

Top Programs of Study Education, management, psychology

Arts and Sciences American studies, anthropology and sociology, art, biology, biology-chemistry, chemical engineering, chemistry, classical studies, computer information systems, criminal justice, economics, English literature, environmental studies, French, history, human services, international studies, mathematics, medical technology, music, nursing, philosophy and religion, political science, psychology, public affairs, social studies, Spanish, speech and hearing, theater

Business Accounting, administration (concentrations in finance, international business, management, marketing)

Education Childhood, adolescent

Pre-Professional Law, medicine

Accredited Programs Nursing

Special Programs The college is the home of the Center for Mark Twain Studies. There is a Phi Beta Kappa chapter. A cooperative program is offered in chemical engineering with Clarkson University. Also, 4+1 M.B.A. programs are offered in cooperation with Alfred, Clarkson, and Union College. The college has an affiliation with the Bahamian Field Station on the island of San Salvador in the Bahamas, where students study marine and island habitats. Students also study at off-campus sites during spring term in several international destinations. There are individualized majors. There are Air Force and Army ROTC programs.

Facilities There are 25 buildings representing a blend of the contemporary and traditional designs, with eight buildings on the National Register of Historic Places. Cowles Hall is the original college building. Carnegie Hall houses the nursing program and science labs. Hamilton Hall houses the Great Hall, which is used for concerts. The renovated Emerson Hall houses the Gibson Theater. Kolker Science Hall houses a greenhouse and an animal room. In addition, there are the Watson Fine Arts Building and Art Gallery, a regulation NCAA hockey rink, the Mark Twain Study and Quarry Farm, and the new Speidel Gymnasium.

Transition to College Program Freshmen are given the opportunity to attend a Saturday morning class during the fall term. The goal is to get the weekend off to a productive academic start, meet with fellow freshmen, and improve writing and analytical tools that students need for academic success. Also, an Encore Program gives students the opportunity to experience a variety of cultural events for which credit is earned. Attendance is required for eight performances in terms I and II of the freshman and sophomore years, including concerts in theater, dance, and music.

Athletics NCAA III, Eastern College Athletic Conference, New York State Women's Collegiate Athletic Conference, Empire 8 Conference

Men: Basketball, ice hockey, lacrosse, soccer, tennis

Women: Basketball, cheerleading, field hockey, ice hockey, lacrosse, soccer, softball, tennis, volleyball

Student Life and Housing About 1,200 students can be accommodated in college housing, which includes single-sex and coed dorms, and is guaranteed for all four years. Fifty-five percent of the students are from New York; the remainder are from 35 other states and 23 countries. Ethnicity: Caucasian—87 percent; International—6 percent; African-American—2 percent; Hispanic-American—2 percent; Asian-American—1 percent. There are no fraternities or sororities. All students may keep cars. Freshmen are required to live on campus and have a roommate.

Accommodations for Students with Disabilities In compliance with section 504

Financial Aid About 80 percent of all freshmen receive aid. The average freshman award is about $21,000.

Requirements for Admission SAT I or ACT scores and a college prep high school program.

Application There are two Early Decision Plans. Early Decision I applications are due by November 15 with decision notification by December 15. Early Decision II applications are due by January 15 with notification by January 31. Students not accepted under these plans are typically placed in the regular admission group of students. Regular admissions uses a rolling admissions policy.

International Students The application deadline is March 1. Students whose native language is other than English must take the TOEFL no later than May of the year in which they wish to enter. Students must submit an official financial statement.

Transfer Students The student must be in good standing at the previous institution. There are no deadlines, and applications will be considered so long as openings exist for the terms beginning in September, January, and April. Required are official transcripts of all college work, a letter of recommendation from the most recently attended college, and a copy or catalogue of course descriptions if the college attended is outside of New York. An official high school transcript is required if fewer than 12 credits have been completed. Only courses with a minimum grade of C− are considered for transfer from an accredited institution.

Admission Contact
Office of Admissions
Elmira College
One Park Place
Elmira, NY 14901-9968
Phone: (800) 935-6472; (607) 735-1724
FAX: (607) 735-1718
E-mail: *admissions@elmira.edu*
Web: *www.elmira.edu*

The Heart of the College Elmira College is the quintessential small liberal arts college. It has no religious affiliation and a rich living–learning community. With 96 percent of the students residing on campus, a true community is created, characterized by a spirit of caring, openness, and support. Students are able to participate in an abundance of organizations and activities. Three-quarters of the students engage in intramural athletics. When students reflect on their years at Elmira, perhaps their most vivid memories are of Elmira's traditions, including the "Candlelight Ceremony," the "Octagon Fair," Alumni Reunion Weekend, "Mountain Day," and several others that remind students of the wonderful community of Elmira College.

The education program includes a writing program that involves a one-on-one writing tutorial with an experienced lecturer. The core curriculum consists of three courses that bring students into the wonderful world of literature, philosophy, and scientific achievement. Community service and an internship, along with study in a major, complete the program, which is taught in small classes by faculty who really know their students. The internship is a required 240-hour experience at an agency or company in a student's chosen field.

One of the distinctive aspects of an Elmira education is "Term III," a six-week term beginning at the end of April, which allows students special study options, including travel. On-campus, students study "The Golden Age of Television," participate in a Model United Nations, volunteer in a Habitat for Humanity Program, or stage a musical production.

The great American writer, Mark Twain, looms very large at Elmira. Twain married Olivia Langdon, an Elmira alumna, whose family gave the college the Quarry Farm, a historic site where Twain wrote his great novels. The house at the farm attracts Twain scholars from around the world. On campus is the Mark Twain Study, where he wrote his *Adventures of Huckleberry Finn*. Also, there is a Twain Exhibit, which contains photographs and other memorabilia.

Close to the campus are movie theaters, restaurants, and a hockey facility for a professional team. Elmira boasts a performing arts center, the Arnot Art Museum, and a historic district. Off-campus recreation includes biking, canoeing, fishing, golfing, hiking, horseback riding, skiing, and NASCAR auto racing.

The college is often cited for its generous merit-based scholarship program, which rewards academic excellence, leadership, and community service. The educational outcomes are superb, with 97 percent of the graduates employed or in graduate school within four months. About 30 percent gain employment before graduation.

ELON UNIVERSITY

Burlington, North Carolina

Total Undergraduate Enrollment: 4,270
Men: 1,651 Women: 2,619
Five-Year Graduation Rate: 69%

Tuition: $$$
Room and Board: $
Residential Students: 63%

History Elon College was founded by the Christian Church (now the United Church of Christ) in 1889. Elon is named for the Hebrew word for *oak* because the university is located in what was once an oak forest, and many of the majestic trees still grace Elon's campus. On June 1, 2001, Elon became a university.

Location Elon has a beautiful campus located on 500 acres in the picturesque Piedmont section of North Carolina in a suburb of Burlington (population 52,000). Twenty minutes to the west is Greensboro (population 200,000). Elon is centrally located between mountains and beach resorts, as well as a host of other colleges and universities.

Top Programs of Study Business, communications, education

Arts and Sciences Art, biology, chemistry, communications, computer science, computer science/

engineering, economics, engineering (engineering chemistry, engineering physics, engineering mathematics, environmental engineering), English, environmental studies, French, health education, history, human services, independent major, international studies, journalism, leisure/sport management, mathematics, medical technology, music, music performance, philosophy, physics, political science, psychology, public administration, religious studies, sociology, Spanish, sports medicine, theater arts

Business Accounting, administration (finance, international business, management, management information systems, marketing)

Education Elementary, middle, music, physical education, secondary, special

Pre-Professional Dentistry, law, medicine, ministry

Accredited Programs Allied health education programs, education

Special Programs Elon's Model U.N. team competes against other schools at national conferences in Washington, D.C., and New York City. Music theater majors work in summer stock in theaters across the country. The study abroad program is ranked Number 1 among comprehensive colleges and universities. Elon has a leadership program and many opportunities to provide social service and conduct research with a faculty member. Seventy-six percent of students complete an internship or co-op work experience before they graduate. The Teaching Fellows Program awards 400 fellowships to North Carolina students interested in studying education at Elon. There is an Army ROTC program.

Facilities There are 104 buildings, including the new Danieley Center residence with flats and apartments, the new Rhodes Stadium, and the new Belk Library. The Rockefeller Center for the Arts has a 600-seat theater and houses dance, drama, music, and art facilities. There is also a new communications facility that houses a student-run cable channel.

Transition to College Program Elon 101 is a specially designed academic advising course/program that introduces first semester students to life at Elon. Students explore academic expectations and how to become involved in campus activities. The weekly course is co-taught by the students' academic advisers and student teaching assistants, with class size limited to 16.

Athletics NCAA I, South Atlantic Conference

Men: Baseball, basketball, cross-country, football, golf, soccer, tennis

Women: Basketball, cross-country, golf, indoor track & field, outdoor track & field, soccer, tennis, volleyball

Student Life and Housing About 2,600 students can be accommodated in college housing. Only 26 percent of the students are from North Carolina, with the majority from 44 other states and 37 countries. Ethnicity: Caucasian—89 percent; African-American—6 percent; Hispanic-American—1 percent; International—1 percent. There are nine sororities and nine fraternities. All students may keep cars.

Accommodations for Students with Disabilities Accommodations are made for students who provide documentation of disability and specific accommodations needed. Contact the Disabilities Service Coordinator in the Academic Advising Center.

Financial Aid About 37 percent of all freshmen receive aid. The average award was $10,000.

Requirements for Admission SAT I or ACT scores and a college prep high school program.

Application Early Decision applications are due November 15, with decision notification within three weeks. Regular admission is on a rolling basis, with the priority application deadline February 1. After that date students are admitted on a space-available basis.

International Students Required are translated transcripts from all secondary and postsecondary schools, certification of financial responsibility, and TOEFL results if the student's native language or the language of instruction is not English.

Transfer Students Students need to have completed at least 24 credits with a minimum GPA of 2.5 from two-year institutions and 2.3 from four-year colleges. Official high school and college transcripts are required, and the student must be in good standing at the previous college. The priority application deadline is June 1 for the fall and December 1 for the spring semester. After these dates, applications will be considered on a space-available basis. No more than 65 credits will be tranferred from a two-year college, and no grade lower than a C− is transferable.

Admission Contact
Office of Admissions
Elon University
2700 Campus Drive
Elon, NC 27244-2010
Phone: (800) 334-8448
FAX: (336) 278-7699
E-mail: *admissions@elon.edu*
Web: *www.elon.edu*

The Heart of the University The heart of Elon University is its distinctive academic programs and innovative faculty. The curriculum is dynamic and challenging, grounded in the liberal arts and sciences along with excellent professional programs. There are many colleges and universities that can make the same claim, but Elon is one of the few that has an exciting hands-on focus. For example, in the freshman Global Experience course, students not only read aloud a United Nations debate, they also become members of Elon's Model U.N. team, taking on the roles of delegates and debating such critical issues as international terrorism. Business administration majors become entrepreneurs by launching a production company to produce and market a jazz CD. Computer science majors work with computer-generated holograms. Communication majors write scripts for MTV or produce a news show for Elon student television. And on and on.

Students report that it is the faculty that they like best about Elon. These professors are dedicated scholars with real-world experience who love to teach. Caring and supportive, many will offer their home phone number in case students need help with an academic problem. These are the professors who create the quality of classrooms that earned Elon a ranking as one of the top four schools in America in terms of "student engagement." Elon students put Elon at the top in five categories: level of academic challenge, active learning, interaction with faculty, educational opportunities outside of the classroom, and supportive campus environment.

The educational opportunities outside of the classroom are called "Elon Experiences" and include a four-year leadership training program. There are also hundreds of ways to get involved with service at Elon through the university's Elon Volunteers, which matches students' talents with the needs of nearly 50 organizations in the community. Typically 75 percent of seniors participate in such service. The Student Undergraduate Research Forum provides students with a forum to present the results of student–faculty collaborative research. Normally, 200 students take advantage of this forum. Also, with more than 50 percent of its students studying abroad, Elon is ranked Number 1 in the nation among comprehensive colleges and universities for the percentage of students who study abroad. At Elon, 76 percent of students complete an internship or co-op work experience at such sites as British Broadcasting Corporation, IBM, Merrill Lynch, the White House, NBC News, and Duke University Medical Center. Elon is also rated as one of the most computer-wired colleges in the nation.

EMMANUEL COLLEGE   Boston, Massachusetts

Total Undergraduate Enrollment: 1,080
Men: 295 Women: 785
Five-Year Graduation Rate: 62%

Tuition: $$$
Room and Board: $$$$
Residential Students: 82%

History Emmanuel College, founded in 1919 by the Sisters of Notre Dame de Namur, provides an education shaped by ethical values, reflecting a Catholic academic tradition. The college was originally founded as the first Catholic college for women in New England.

Location The 16-acre tree-lined campus is in Boston, Massachusetts, providing a broad range of cultural and entertainment activities within a major American city comprised of numerous colleges and universities.

Top Programs of Study Management/economics, education, psychology

Arts and Sciences American studies, art (graphic design, studio), biology, chemistry (biochemistry and medical technology), English, global studies, history, mathematics, nursing, political science, psychology (counseling and health, developmental, and general/experimental), religious studies, Spanish, sociology

Business Management (concentrations in economics, global management, marketing, media, and design)

Education Art, elementary, secondary

Pre-Professional Dentistry, law, medicine, veterinary medicine

Accredited Programs Nursing

Special Programs Emmanuel is a member of the Colleges of the Fenway, a collaboration that offers cross-registration, common social events, and access to the academic resources and services of six institutions. Directed Studies gives students an opportunity to work with a faculty member on a topic of interest that is not in the general curriculum. Individualized majors are available. There is a dual degree program in engineering technology with Wentworth Institute of Technology. There are student exchange programs with sister colleges in California and Japan, a Washinton, D.C., semester, and study abroad opportunities.

Facilities There are eight buildings: a new state-of-the-art Student Center that features an atrium and a new gymnasium, a new fitness center, a dance studio, art and music studios, state-of-the-art computer classrooms, the Cardinal Cushing Library, an art gallery, a state-of-the-art lecture hall with satellite technology, and a language laboratory. Marion Hall houses the science facilities.

Transition to College Program The Director of First Year Programs coordinates all programs designed to assist new students in their transition, including a 10-week first-year seminar course, "Surviving and Thriving: Transitioning to College."

Athletics NCAA III, ECAC, GNAC

Men: Basketball, cross-country, indoor track & field, outdoor track & field, soccer, volleyball

Women: Basketball, cross-country, indoor track & field, outdoor track & field, soccer, tennis, volleyball

Student Life and Housing About 850 students can be accommodated in college housing, which is guaranteed for all four years. Seventy-eight percent of the students are from Massachusetts, the remainder are from 23 other states and 30 countries. Ethnicity: Caucasian—60 percent; African-American—10 percent; International—6 percent; Hispanic-American—5 percent; Asian-American—3 percent. There are no fraternities or sororities. Upperclassmen may keep cars.

Accommodations for Students with Disabilities In compliance with section 504

Financial Aid About 83 percent of freshmen receive aid. The average award is about $14,000.

Requirements for Admission SAT I or ACT scores and a college prep high school program. An interview is recommended.

Application The Early Decision is November 1 with an admission decision by December 1. Regular admission is handled on a rolling basis and provides an admission decision within two weeks of receiving completed application materials.

International Students Required is a sample of written work; an official secondary school transcript accompanied by an English translation, validated by a certified public translator (mid-year or first semester grades from senior year should be submitted also); two recommendations, one by a teacher and another by an adviser, either written in English or accompanied by an English translation validated by a certified public translator; a TOEFL minimum score of 500 paper-based or 173 computer-based. Students whose first language is English should submit SAT I scores. Also, a certification of finances form must be submitted with supporting bank documentation. An interview is recommended. Admission decisions are made after December 1.

Transfer Students Required are official high school and college transcripts; SAT or ACT results; two letters of reference, with at least one from a recent professor or adviser; course description catalogues for each college attended. A minimum GPA of 2.0 is required.

Admission Contact
Office of Admissions
Emmanuel College
400 The Fenway
Boston, MA 02115-9911
Phone: (617) 735-9715
FAX: (617) 735-9801
E-mail: *enroll@emmanuel.edu*
Web: *www.emmanuel.edu*

The Heart of the College Emmanuel College offers a small campus set in Boston, one of the most vibrant, youthful American cities. Although Emmanuel offers a very personalized education with small classes, an interactive environment, and close contact with faculty, there is no doubt that the heart of an Emmanuel education is its Boston location. Students often comment on how Boston offers so much culture, history, and activities. With the Quincy Marketplace, Fenway Park, the Celtics and the Bruins, the Freedom Trail, the Gardner Museum, the Museum of Science, the Longwood Medical and Academic Area, and shopping, cafes, and restaurants, Emmanuel students have a city as a classroom.

In fact, as part of the Freshman Core of studies, the Cityscapes program introduces the liberal arts by focusing on Boston to examine several themes common in the liberal arts. Through readings, short papers, and field experiences, students develop skills of careful observation, critical thinking, and thoughtful expression, with Boston as their focus. The city provides Emmanuel students with many wonderful internship opportunities, giving students hands-on experience. More than 80 percent of Emmanuel's students do at least one internship in a corporation, scientific research facility, school, not-for-profit community service organization, a local affiliate of a major TV network, or a publishing house, with many internships turning into full-time jobs after graduation. Assisting the successful career search is Emmanuel's Career Development Network, comprised of more than 300 Emmanuel graduates, who work in a wide range of professions and enthusiastically volunteer to serve as models and mentors to Emmanuel students.

As a Catholic college, Emmanuel has a long tradition of service and commitment to the Boston community, with students serving as dedicated volunteers in many service organizations and activities throughout the greater Boston area. Also, Emmanuel provides students with several campus ministry programs, including prayer groups, Bible study, Eucharistic and music ministry, and liturgical celebrations.

EMORY & HENRY COLLEGE

Emory, Virginia

Total Undergraduate Enrollment: 960
Men: 480 Women: 480
Five-Year Graduation Rate: 83%

Tuition: $$
Room and Board: $
Residential Students: 67%

History Emory & Henry was founded in 1836 and is affiliated with the United Methodist Church. Its name was derived from two influential men: John Emory, an eminent Methodist Bishop of the era when the college was founded, and Patrick Henry, a renowned patriot of the American revolution and Virginia's first governor. The names were chosen to represent the guiding principles of the college: Christian leadership and distinctive statesmanship.

Location The college is located on 168 acres of beautiful campus in rural southwest Emory, Virginia. The campus is within view of Virginia's two highest peaks, Mount Rogers and White Top Mountain, and near Abingdon, Virginia, the home of the renowned Barter Theater. There are many recreational opportunities.

Top Programs of Study Business, education, mass communications

Arts and Sciences American political studies, anthropology, Appalachian studies, art, biology, chemistry, comparative and international studies, computer information management, computer science, earth science, East Asian studies, economics, engineering, English, (creative writing, literature), environmental policy, environmental science, European community studies, forestry, French, geography, graphic design, history, human services, land usage and analysis planning, mass communications, mathematics, medical technology, Middle Eastern and Islamic studies, music, philosophy, physics, physics and business, political science, sociology, Spanish, speech and theater, sports medicine, women's studies

Business Accounting, management

Education Early childhood, elementary, middle, physical education, secondary

Pre-Professional Dentistry, law, medicine, ministry, pharmacy, veterinary medicine

Accredited Programs None

Special Programs There are cooperative programs in forestry with Duke, engineering with Tulane, North Carolina State, and the University of Tennessee, and medical technology with Roanoke Memorial Hospital. An Emerging Leaders Program enables students to interact with popular political, educational, and business leaders. A Friends of the Sciences Program provides stipends and site placements for students to conduct research and practicums at well-known labs and hospitals. There are many opportunities for social service, internships, study abroad, and exchange programs.

Facilities There are 20 buildings, including an art gallery, the newly renovated and expanded King Health and Physical Education Center, a radio station, and the Fulton Observatory.

Transition to College Program The college offers a traditional orientation program.

Athletics NCAA III, Old Dominion Athletic Conference

Men: Baseball, basketball, cross-country, football, golf, soccer, tennis

Women: Basketball, cross-country, softball, soccer, tennis, volleyball

Student Life and Housing About 700 students live in college housing, which includes single-sex dorms and is guaranteed for all four years. Seventy-four percent of the students are from Virginia, with the remainder from 19 other states and 7 countries. Ethnicity: Caucasian—92%. There are seven local fraternities and six local sororities. All students may keep cars.

Accommodations for Students with Disabilities Recent documentation (within 12 months before beginning college) must be submitted to the Director of Academic Support Services. Reasonable accommodations will be permitted depending upon the specific disability and the recommendations of the consulting doctor. It is the student's responsibility to speak to professors and to the Director to arrange for accommodations.

Financial Aid About 64 percent of all freshmen receive aid. The average freshman award was about $13,000.

Requirements for Admission SAT I or ACT scores and a college prep high school program.

Application The college offers an Early Decision Program, with applications due by December 1 with an admission decision within three weeks. Otherwise, the college has a rolling admissions policy, accepting applications beginning in October with an admission decision made within two weeks of receiving all material.

International Students Students are required to submit certified, translated copies of all academic records, as well as documentation of financial ability to pay all expenses. A minimum TOEFL score of 550 is required for students from non-English-speaking countries.

Transfer Students A personal essay is required along with official transcripts from colleges attended. Grades of C or better are transferable. Graduates from any member of the Virginia Community College System with an associate's degree in business administration, education, general studies, liberal arts, or sciences are automatically accepted for admission. A maximum of 62 credits may be transferred.

Admission Contact
Office of Admissions
Emory & Henry College
30479 Armbrister Drive
P.O. Box 10
Emory, VA 24327-0947
(800) 848-5493; (540) 944-6133
FAX: (276) 944-6935
E-mail: *ehadmiss@ehc.edu*
Web: *www.ehc.edu*

The Heart of the College Its mission statement says that the college seeks to develop in its students "lives of service, productive careers and global citizenship." The college's comprehensive liberal arts core curriculum is special because it spans all four years, in which students study "Western Traditions," "Great Books," "Values Inquiry," "Global Studies," and "Religion." Courses in English, composition, speech, math, computer literacy, and interdisciplinary studies round out the core.

This is a thoughtful curriculum. Carefully designed by a talented faculty who take a holistic approach to education whereby faculty members seek not only to teach but also to advise, mentor, challenge, be respectful, and invite students to attend dinner at their own homes. "We encourage them (students) to be free thinkers and to explore all their options."

In seeking to develop lives of service, Emory & Henry offers a major in Public Policy and Community Service. This major assists one of the major missions of the college by having students understand social change and civic responsibility and become agents of change. Students have tutored migrant workers, helped the disabled, assisted welfare recipients, and worked with the elderly.

Productive careers are facilitated by a diversity of internship opportunities, including investment companies, law firms, detention centers, and professional theaters. And talk about theaters—the neighboring historic town of Abingdon is the home of the world-renowned Barter Theater, which provides instruction for theater students.

The mission of "global citizenship" is aided by the wonderful study abroad and exchange programs in Europe, South America, the Far and Near East, Adventures have included digging in Etruscan and biblical archeological sites, teaching English to Brazilian students, and studying Roman art and architecture in Italy.

About 94 percent of Emory & Henry recent graduates have been placed in jobs or graduate schools. Alumni have ranked in the top 1 percent of American colleges and universities for their contributions to their alma mater. Seventy percent of the students participate in some organized athletic activity.

FRANKLIN COLLEGE   Franklin, Indiana

Total Undergraduate Enrollment: 1,048
Men: 466 Women: 582
Five-Year Graduation Rate: 52%

Tuition: $$$
Room and Board: $
Residential Students: 91%

History Founded in 1834, Franklin College is the 102nd oldest institution of higher education in America and the first in Indiana to admit women. Franklin is affiliated with the American Baptist Church.

Location The beautiful 74-acre tree lined campus is in Franklin, Indiana (population 15,000), a small town 20 miles west of Indianapolis.

Top Programs of Study Education, journalism, business, biology/chemistry

Arts and Sciences American studies, athletic training, biology, Canadian studies, chemistry, computer science, English, French, history, journalism (concentrations in advertising/public relations, broadcasting, news/editorial), mathematics, philosophy, political science, psychology, recreation, religious studies, sociology (concentrations in criminal justice, social work), Spanish, theater

Business Accounting, business (concentrations in finance, general business, international business, management, marketing), computer information systems, economics

Education Elementary, physical education, secondary

Pre-Professional Dentistry, engineering, law, medicine, ministry, nursing, optometry, physical therapy, veterinary medicine

Accredited Programs Education

Special Programs Cooperative programs are available in environmental studies and forestry with Duke, medical technology with the Methodist Hospital in Indianapolis and St. Francis Hospital in Beech Grove, and nursing with Rush University in Chicago. There are many study abroad opportunities, including Franklin's own college in Switzerland. All students study Leadership Development. Each student must prepare a Professional Development Portfolio. Franklin has a highly respected School of Journalism. There is an Army ROTC program.

Facilities There are 20 buildings, both historic and new, including the Johnson Center for the Arts, the First Year Experience Center, the Dietz Center for Professional Development, renovated Faught Football Stadium, and both new and renovated residence halls.

Transition to College Program Through New Step each first-year student is assigned to a mentor group consisting of approximately 14 students, one upperclass student who serves as a mentor, and one faculty/staff adviser. The student mentor's role is to provide peer leadership, one-on-one contact with new students, and first-hand recommendations about how to make a successful transition to college life. The faculty/staff adviser assists with curricular and class scheduling matters and develops a personal relationship with each student. Mentor groups meet weekly during the first semester.

Athletics NCAA III, Heartland Collegiate Athletic Conference

Men: Baseball, basketball, cross-country, football, golf, soccer, tennis, track

Women: Basketball, cross-country, golf, tennis, track, soccer, softball, volleyball

Student Life and Housing About 700 students can be accommodated in college housing. Ninety-three percent of the students are from Indiana, with the remainder from 19 other states and five countries. Ethnicity: Caucasian—94 percent. There are five national fraternities and four national sororities. All students may keep cars.

Accommodations for Students with Disabilities In compliance with section 504

Financial Aid About 96 percent of all freshmen receive aid. The average freshman award was about $15,000.

Requirements for Admission SAT I or ACT results and a college prep high school program.

Application Freshmen are admitted to all semesters. Application deadlines are open, with admission decisions sent on a rolling basis.

International Students Required is an international application, all educational transcripts and evidence of all test results for various governmental examinations, TOEFL results or successful completion of 109 in an English Language Service Center.

Transfer Students Required are official high school and college transcripts and SAT I or ACT results. Admission decisions are based upon the academic records of both secondary and postsecondary transcripts.

Admission Contact
Office of Admissions
Franklin College
501 East Monroe Street

Franklin, IN 46131-2598
Phone: (800) 852-0232; (317) 738-8062
FAX: (317) 738-7274
E-mail: *admissions@franklincoll.edu*
Web: *www.franklincollege.edu*

The Heart of the College Franklin College is considered among the top schools for leadership and professional development. Every student on campus receives leadership education as an integral part of their college experience. Franklin is one of the few schools that has artfully woven leadership theory and practice right into the curriculum. The program begins with a month-long introduction to leadership issues for all first-year students. In almost every major, students will be taught by professors who have spent at least two years studying leadership theory and exploring ways to incorporate it into their classrooms. Upper division students may participate in a winter term internship with a leader in the students' chosen career field. Students who complete the leadership program are recognized with certificates in leadership along with their diplomas.

Franklin, while a liberal arts college with several career programs, is very "career sensitive." In addition to completing an internship—almost 90 percent of the students complete at least one—in order to graduate each student must prepare a professional development portfolio designed to help students make a confident and successful transition from college to the workplace. Professional development activities include résumé writing, interviewing skills, networking and decisionmaking skills, and also conflict resolution skills.

The Pulliam School of Journalism has an excellent reputation, with faculty who are accomplished journalists and mentors for students. Students enjoy quality internship experiences ranging from *Reader's Digest* to *Mademoiselle* to television shows, as well as campus-based opportunities. Alumni have careers at the *Chicago Sun-Times*, the *St. Petersburg Times*, and other newspapers, and television networks across America. Also, Franklin's nationally accredited education program has partnered with an Indianapolis public school in secondary education and offers over 1,000 hours of field experience for elementary education students. Job placement rates are in the 90 to 100 percent range for teacher education graduates. The School of Business has graduated former presidents of Chase Manhattan Bank, Standard Oil of California, and Washington National Insurance.

Franklin College students enjoy its suburban location, as well as the convenience of a 30-minute ride into Indianapolis, with its professional sports, museums, shopping, zoo, and internship sites.

GENEVA COLLEGE

Beaver Falls, Pennsylvania

Total Undergraduate Enrollment: 1,563
Men: 648 Women: 915
Five-Year Graduation Rate: 59%

Tuition: $$
Room and Board: $$
Residential Students: 74%

History Geneva College was founded in 1848 by Reverend John Johnston as Geneva Hall in honor of Geneva, Switzerland, early center of the Reformed Presbyterian Church. Geneva College later became the official name and moved to Beaver Falls in 1880. Geneva College is founded upon a biblical view of life. The college is listed on the Templeton Foundation's Honor Roll of Character-Building Colleges.

Location The 50-acre campus is located on College Hill overlooking the Beaver River, in a residential area of Beaver Falls, Pennsylvania (population 14,000). The campus is located 30 miles northwest of Pittsburgh, a city offering many cultural and entertainment opportunities.

Top Programs of Study Business, engineering, education

Arts and Sciences Applied math, biblical studies, biology, chemical engineering, chemistry, Christian ministries, communications, communication disorders, computer science, engineering (civil, electrical, mechanical), English, history, human services, independent major, music, music business, philosophy, physics, political science, psychology, sociology, student ministries, writing

Business Accounting, administration (concentrations in aviation, finance/economics, human

resource management, management, management information systems, marketing)

Education Elementary, elementary/special, music, secondary, secondary/special, special

Pre-Professional Law, medicine, ministry, nursing

Accredited Programs Business, cardiovascular technology, chemistry, engineering

Special Programs Art programs, including fashion merchandising, photography, industrial design technology, interior design, and fashion illustration, are offered at the Art Institute of Pittsburgh. A dual degree program in business administration and aviation is offered with the Community College of Beaver County. A dual degree program is offered in cardiovascular technology with Inova Fairfax Hospital in Falls Church, Virginia. The College has a Center for Law and Public Policy, which brings Christian thought to issues of law, government, and public policy. Many mission and service opportunities are available. There is an ROTC program.

Facilities There are 30 buildings, including the newly constructed Northwood Hall academic and human services building, a new fitness center, a renovated dining area, and a radio station.

Transition to College Program A Learning and Transition Class is a one-credit course required for all students during the fall semester of freshman year and an option for transfer students. Each class of 15 students is taught by a faculty adviser and two upper-class mentors. The class meets weekly and focuses on college policies, study skills, time management, spiritual development, community services, and vocational development. The class is supplemented with social gatherings.

Athletics National Christian College Athletic Association and NAIA I

Men: Baseball, basketball, cross-country, football, soccer, track & field

Women: Basketball, cheerleading, cross-country, soccer, softball, tennis, track & field, volleyball

Student Life and Housing About 1,000 students can be accommodated in college housing, which includes single-sex dorms, and is guaranteed for all four years. Seventy-seven percent of the students are from Pennsylvania, with the remainder from 37 states and 25 countries. Ethnicity: Caucasian—91 percent. There are no fraternities or sororities. Upperclassmen may keep cars, and freshmen may request to do so. Students are expected to abide by the Christian standards of the Geneva College community.

Accommodations for Students with Disabilities Students must submit documentation of the disability to the Director of Student Support Services. The type of accommodation provided will depend on the needs of the student, the circumstances of the student's classes, and the current resources of the college.

Financial Aid About 95 percent of all freshmen receive aid. The average freshman award is about $15,000.

Requirements for Admission SAT I or ACT scores and a college prep high school program.

Application Students should apply by March 1 for the fall semester and November 1 for the spring semester. Admission decisions are made two weeks after completed materials are submitted. Upon acceptance, students are asked to reply within three weeks, either confirming a decision to enroll or requesting an extension of time.

International Students Official high school and college transcripts, if applicable, certification of ability to meet educational expenses, an academic reference, and TOEFL results are required.

Transfer Students Students from four-year colleges must complete at least 48 credits at Geneva, including at least 15 in their chosen major. All transfer courses are evaluated, and some courses in a major may have to be repeated if the age or performance is not sufficient.

Admission Contact
Office of Admissions
Geneva College
3200 College Avenue
Beaver Falls, PA 15010-3599
Phone: (800) 847-8255; (724) 847-6500
FAX: (724) 847-6776
E-mail: *admissions@geneva.edu*
Web: *www.geneva.edu*

The Heart of the College Geneva College is part of the Reformed Presbyterian Church of North America and believes that the Bible is the inerrant, authoritative word of God. The mission of the college is "to glorify God by educating and ministering to a diverse community of students for the purpose of developing servant–leaders . . ." The college is the home of the Center for Higher Education and Faith, founded to revitalize open discussion about the relationship between faith and learning.

Academics are grounded in a liberal arts core of classes in the sciences, humanities, arts, and biblical studies, where students look at the courses from many perspectives, especially a Christian worldview. The academic program integrates Christian faith with higher learning.

Students speak of the special support system comprised of a community of seekers, made up of administrators, faculty, and staff. Students also love the many opportunities for service and ministry. Geneva has 15 student-led ministry programs on campus, and each semester more than half of the student population participates in a community service project. Students also enjoy weekly chapel and convocation, which often feature interesting guest speakers.

Geneva students are offered valuable off-campus and study abroad programs at sites such as the Art Institute of Pittsburgh, the China Stud-ies Program, the Latin American Studies Program in Costa Rica, the Los Angeles Film Studies Center, and the Summer Institute of Journalism in Washington, D.C.

Geneva has graduated leaders in a variety of fields, including attorneys, chairmen of foundations, college presidents, missionary doctors, opera singers, professors, CEOs, and scientists.

The campus location affords students both serenity and the cultural and recreational attraction of a major city.

GEORGETOWN COLLEGE

Georgetown, Kentucky

Total Undergraduate Enrollment: 1,290
Men: 561 Women: 729
Five-Year Graduation Rate: 56%

Tuition: $$
Room and Board: $
Residential Students: 92%

History Georgetown College was established in 1829 as the first Baptist college west of the Allegheny Mountains. Georgetown was always a blend of Northwestern influence and Southern tradition, and international students first arrived in 1852.

Location The beautiful 104-acre campus is located in Georgetown, Kentucky (population 20,000), in the heart of the Kentucky bluegrass.

Top Programs of Study Business, psychology, communication arts

Arts and Sciences American studies, art, biology, chemistry, church music, communication arts, computer science, English, environmental science, European studies, French, German, history, kinesiology, mathematics, music, philosophy, physics, political science, psychology, religion, sociology, Spanish

Business Accounting, business administration/computer science, business administration and ethics, business administration (concentrations in finance, management, marketing), commerce, information systems, international business management, language and culture, management information systems

Education Elementary, music

Pre-Professional Dentistry, law, medicine, ministry, nursing, pharmacy, physical therapy, veterinary medicine

Accredited Programs None

Special Programs The college offers several dual degree programs: engineering arts (agricultural chemical, civil, material, mechanical) with the University of Kentucky; medical technology with any AMA approved school; nursing with the University of Kentucky; theology with Regent's Park College at Oxford University in England. There is a Center for Leadership and Ethics and The Marshall Center for Christian Ministry. There are many study abroad programs and opportunities to create individualized majors. There is an Air Force ROTC program.

Facilities There are 40 buildings, both historic and new, including the new Ensor Learning Resource Center, a planetarium and greenhouse, an art gallery, a radio station, arboretum, a new fitness and recreation center, and a state-of-the-art conference and leadership training center where the Cincinnati Bengals football team trains.

Transition to College Programs The college has a traditional orientation.

Athletics NAIA, Mid-South Conference

Men: Baseball, basketball, cross-country, football, golf, soccer, tennis

Women: Basketball, cross-country, golf, soccer, softball, tennis, volleyball

Student Life and Housing About 1,300 students can be accommodated in college housing, which is guaranteed for all four years. Eighty-three percent of the students are from Kentucky, the remainder from 26 other states and 16 countries. Ethnicity: Caucasian—96 percent. There are one local and four national fraternities, and four national sororities. All students may keep cars.

Accommodations for Students with Disabilities In compliance with section 504

Financial Aid About 96 percent of all freshmen receive aid. The average freshman award was about $16,000.

Requirements for Admission SAT I or ACT scores, a B grade point average in a college prep high school program, and a rank in the upper half of the class.

Application Early Decision application deadline is November 15, with admission decisions by December 20. Regular admission deadline is April 15. Decisions are made about three weeks after a completed application is received.

International Students Required are one or more letters of recommendation, a minimum TOEFL score of 520 paper or 190 computer, all secondary school transcripts, and documentation of student financial support.

Transfer Students Applicants need to be in good standing at their most recent colleges. Official high school and college transcripts are required, plus a completed application for admission. Courses taken at an accredited institution, with a minimum of a C grade, and similar in content to Georgetown courses will be considered for credit. Graduates from two-year institutions may transfer up to 66 semester hours of credit.

Home-Schooled Students ACT or SAT I scores, a transcript documenting performance in secondary-level coursework, and other pertinent curriculum information are required.

Admission Contact
Office of Admissions
Georgetown College
400 East College Street
Georgetown, KY 40324
Phone: (800) 788-9985
FAX: (502) 868-7733
E-mail: *admissions@georgetowncollege.edu*
Web: *www.georgetowncollege.edu*

The Heart of the College Georgetown College, an outstanding liberal arts college, provides a rigorous academic program with a commitment to Christian values. The college can boast of 34 college presidents, 5 Rhodes scholars, and 12 Fulbright Scholars among its alumni. A recent medical school acceptance rate was 100 percent. But what distinguishes Georgetown is its commitment to community. When students first arrive they see how people reach out to them and later develop lifelong friendships.

The talented faculty is the heart and soul of this community. Professors share with students their labs, their studios, their offices, and their homes. They offer outstanding instruction in small classes, as well as the opportunity to conduct individual research or creative projects chosen by students.

What best symbolizes the heart of Georgetown is the "Presidential Chauffeurs Program." Every Georgetown college student has the opportunity to serve as the college president's driver for the day. Students have the opportunity to ask questions, attend meetings, and get to know the president one-to-one.

Georgetown takes technology literacy seriously so that students will become sophisticated knowledge gatherers. New students take a technology assessment test to determine whether additional computer training is necessary. Technology is also integrated into many courses.

The college also has a tradition of excellence in the performing arts. Maskcrafters is the oldest theater troupe in Kentucky, and there are also nine student music groups. The Center for Leadership and Ethics allows students to participate in

intense leadership and values training. The Marshall Center for Christian Ministry is the center for Baptist thought on campus.

Students enjoy the beautiful campus, friendly, quaint town, and Georgetown's location near Lexington, Louisville, and Cincinnati, and the cultural and recreational opportunities they offer to Georgetown students.

GRACE COLLEGE   Winnona Lake, Indiana

Total Undergraduate Enrollment: 900
Men: 360 Women: 540
Five-Year Graduation Rate: 53%

Tuition: $$
Room and Board: $
Residential Students: 91%

History Grace College was founded in 1948 under the leadership of Dr. Ava McClain and Dr. Herman Hoyt. Grace is the only undergraduate institution of arts and sciences affiliated with the Fellowship of Grace Brethren Churches. The college is evangelically conservative and is active in its evangelistic and missionary outreach missions. The college believes that the Bible is the written word of God.

Location The 165-acre campus is in Winnona Lake, Indiana, a rural area 40 miles west of Fort Wayne and 50 miles south of South Bend, centrally located between Detroit, Indianapolis, and Chicago. The many diversified industries of the area make it a fast-growing community and offer students employment opportunities.

Top Programs of Study Elementary education, behavioral sciences, business

Arts and Sciences Biblical studies, biology, Christian ministries, communication, counseling, criminal justice, drawing and painting, English, French, general science, German, graphic design, illustration, information processing, international languages, management information technology, mathematics, music, psychology, social work, sociology, Spanish, youth ministries

Business Accounting, administration, international business, organizational management

Education Art, business, elementary, music, physical education, secondary

Pre-Professional Chiropractic, dentistry, law, medicine, optometry, pharmacy, physical therapy, seminary, veterinary science

Accredited Programs Education, music

Special Programs Study abroad opportunities as well as double majors are available.

Facilities There are 15 buildings, including a seminary; a new student center; an air-conditioned women's residence; an art gallery; the Cooley Science Center; Mount Memorial Hall, which houses a state-of-the-art computer graphic design laboratory; and an auditorium that seats 1,400.

Transition to College Program The Freshman Seminar is the first course in the core curriculum taken by all freshmen. This course is intended to make the four years at Grace College the best experience possible. Probing questions are considered. For example: What gives life meaning? Where does knowledge come from? There are small group discussions led by select faculty members.

Athletics NAIA, National Christian Athletic Association and Mid-Central Conference

    Men: Baseball, basketball, cross-country, golf, soccer, tennis, track & field

Women: Basketball, cheerleading, cross-country, soccer, softball, tennis, track & field, volleyball

Student Life and Housing About 800 students can be accommodated in college housing, which includes single-sex dorms. Forty-seven percent of the students are from Indiana, with the remainder from 37 other states—mostly Midwestern—and 8 countries. Ethnicity: Caucasian—94 percent. There are no fraternities or sororities. All students may keep cars. Students are expected to adhere to the college's lifestyle commitment.

Accommodations for Students with Disabilities Services are provided through the Student Academic Counseling Center.

Financial Aid About 90 percent of all freshmen receive aid. The average freshman award was about $11,000.

Requirements for Admission ACT scores of at least 20 or SAT I scores of at least 950, a minimum 2.3 GPA in a college prep high school program, and a class rank in the upper half. Applicants must be in harmony with the evangelical Christian viewpoint of the college.

Application Freshmen are admitted to all semesters. Applications should be filed by August 1 for fall semester. Decision notification is sent on a rolling basis.

International Students Students whose primary language is not English must take the TOEFL and score a minimum of 500 on the paper version and also score a minimum of 950 on the SAT I. Students should submit secondary school transcripts and, if applicable, postsecondary transcripts, as well as a declaration of finances.

Transfer Students Official transcripts are required of all postsecondary work. Credit is awarded for coursework in which a minimum of a C grade was earned. A maximum of 30 credits are transferable from a Bible college and another 30 credits in non-Bible courses. All transfer students must complete a minimum of 30 credit hours at Grace.

Admission Contact
Office of Admissions
Grace College
20 Seminary Drive
Winnona Lake, IN 46590
Phone: (800) 54-GRACE; (574) 372-5100
FAX: (574) 372-5120
E-mail: *enroll@grace.edu*
Web: *www.grace.edu*

The Heart of the College The heart of Grace College is reflected in the words of a student who visited and subsequently enrolled: "I haven't been at any other college where everyone is so great and has such a love for the Lord." As a Christian college, Grace makes a concerted effort to integrate Christ into every part of a student's college experience. Students and graduates applaud the faculty for their care, guidance, and influence.

Grace College believes that the Bible is God's authentic written revelation; as a result, the Bible is central to all areas of study. Chapel meets three times a week and is required. Students are informed, entertained, and challenged with a variety of speakers, musicians, and topics. Weekly Growth Groups provide dorm students opportunities for discipleship and devotion. In addition there are Bible studies, prayer groups, and prayer in class. Ministries abound at Grace, including an Inner-City Ministry, short-term mission trips, community service projects, a clown and puppet ministry, and many others.

Winnona Lake, the home of Grace College, is a picturesque, historic town, with artisan shops, newly redone streets and sidewalks, and attractive places to walk or bike. Adjacent to Winnona Lake is the city of Warsaw, which offers a variety of shopping and entertainment, beautiful parks and lakes, as well as part-time job opportunities for Grace students.

GUILFORD COLLEGE   Greensboro, North Carolina

Total Undergraduate Enrollment: 1,200   Tuition: $$$
Men: 550 Women: 650   Room and Board: $
Five-Year Graduation Rate: 65%   Residential Students: 73%

History Guilford College was founded in 1834 by members of the Religious Society of Friends (Quakers), and is the third oldest coeducational college in the nation. The college is listed on Templeton Foundation's Honor Roll of Character-Building Colleges.

Location The 340-acre campus is located in a suburb of Greensboro, North Carolina, the third largest city (population 210,000) in North Carolina. The campus is listed as a National Historic District.

Top Programs of Study Management, English, psychology

Arts and Sciences African-American studies, art, athletic training, biology, chemistry, community and justice studies, computer information systems, computing and information technology, earth studies, economics, education studies, English, environmental sciences, German, German studies, health sciences, history, integrative studies, international studies, life sciences, mathematics, music, peace and conflict studies, sports management, theater studies, women's studies

Business Accounting, management

Education Elementary, K-12 French and Spanish, secondary (9–12 English and social studies)

Pre-Professional Dentistry, law, medicine, ministry, veterinary

Accredited Programs Education

Special Programs The Friends Center provides opportunities for education and information about Quakerism. There are study abroad programs, internships, a Washington, D.C., semester, and off-campus seminars held in different parts of the United States. The college is a member of the seven-college Greater Greensboro Consortium, providing students with cross-registration opportunities. There are cooperative degree programs in the following: engineering; environmental science and engineering with Duke; and physician's assistant with Wake Forest. Students can double major and design their own majors. Guilford is rated as one of the most computer-wired colleges in the nation.

Facilities There are 31 buildings of predominantly Georgian architecture, including Hege Library, which houses the Friends Historical Collection; a new Frank Family Science Center uniquely designed to facilitate interactions among disciplines; an observatory; a greenhouse; a language laboratory; a physical education center; Dana Auditorium, a proscenium theater seating 1,100; Hege-Cox Hall, which houses art facilities; and the Guilford College art library.

Transition to College Program A First Year Program includes several elements: a pre-orientation consisting of 3–4 days in August of rafting, rock climbing, mountain biking, service projects, and writing. Just prior to the opening of school is CHAOS (Community, health, advisement, orientation, and services) where students meet weekly in groups of 4–6 with a mentor to discuss the transition to college, time management, study skills, and campus resources. Athletes are also matched with a sophomore mentor.

Athletics NCAA III, Old Dominion Conference

Men: Baseball, basketball, football, golf, lacrosse, soccer

Women: Basketball, lacrosse, soccer, softball, tennis, volleyball

Student Life and Housing About 850 students can be accommodated in college housing, which is guaranteed for all four years. Forty-eight percent of the students are from North Carolina, with the majority coming from 43 other states and 25 countries. Ethnicity: Caucasian—84 percent; African-American—10 percent; Asian-American—2 percent; International—3 percent; Hispanic-American—1 percent. There are no fraternities or sororities. All students may keep cars.

Accommodations for Students with Disabilities There is a Learning Disabilities Association that offers peer support and programs for the college's large population of disabled students.

Financial Aid About 99 percent of all freshmen receive aid. The average freshman award is about $12,000.

Requirements for Admission SAT I or ACT scores and a college prep high school program. An on-campus interview is required. Students may substitute a comprehensive portfolio for the SAT or ACT. The portfolio should reflect the student's academic, creative, and personal interests and accomplishments . . . Guilford actively seeks a diverse student population whose backgrounds and talents will enrich the college community.

Application The Early Decision deadline is November 15, with admissions decisions by December 15. The Early Action deadline is January 15, with admission decisions by February 15. Regular applications are processed on a rolling basis, with February 15 as a deadline.

International Students Required are official transcripts of secondary and postsecondary schools, if applicable; a TOEFL minimum score of 550; and a completed financial statement. Students can be admitted provisionally if they rank in the upper 40 percent of the graduating class, have maintained at least a C GPA, and agree to continue studying in an intensive English language program until a TOEFL score of 550 is achieved.

Transfer Students Transfer applications are evaluated according to the same criteria as freshman applications, In addition, required are a minimum of a C average for all college work taken, a transcript from all high schools and colleges attended, either ACT or SAT I results while in high school, and a recommendation from the dean of students of each college attended.

Admission Contact
Office of Admissions
Guilford College
5800 W. Friendly Avenue
Greensboro, NC 27410
Phone: (800) 992-7759; (336) 316-2100
FAX: (336) 378-0154
E-mail: *admission@guilford*
Web: *www.guilford.edu/admission*

The Heart of the College Although Guilford has many of the characteristics of the other schools described in this guide, what distinguishes Guilford from the other schools is its Quaker heritage. This dramatically shapes its policies, programs, and, most importantly, its students. Guilford's mission has much to do with "bettering the world." The guiding question at Guilford is: "Who will you become?" The college captures this mission when it quotes Gandhi: "Be the change that you wish to see in the world." As a result, service learning gets lots of attention at Guilford, with students volunteering in local, national, and international service projects every semester.

The campus community is also shaped by Quaker values. For Guilford this implies bringing to campus a diverse student population and addressing multicultural issues and perspectives in courses such as "Many Voices," where students read the works of Native Americans and Americans of African, Jewish, Arab, and Hispanic descent. It also implies the offering of an interdisciplinary major, "Peace and Conflict Studies," that draws on the Quaker heritage of seeking the roots of situations of injustice and oppression then seeking nonviolent solutions. The Quaker heritage also implies a nurturing, student-centered instruction, where students are taught by talented scholars who view themselves as partners with students. This results in tremendous respect offered to students' views, backgrounds, and beliefs along with collaborative research that is shaped more by the students than by the professors, as well as the time-honored Quaker tradition of using first names rather than formal titles with faculty.

Another implication is that students take a great deal of responsibility for designing their own educations at Guilford. There is no "cookie-cutter" approach here. Students are characterized as independent thinkers, designing their own majors, double majoring, doing volunteer service, or studying abroad, all to the purpose of "becoming the change." Students can journey to Ghana and intern at a health post or local development project or study the history, culture, language, and art of Munich, Germany. A global perspective resounds here, as does a hands-on learning theme that brings students internship opportunities in each major.

With seven colleges in Greensboro, weekend dances, theater performances, bonfires by the lake, and athletics, there's much to do on this temperate-climate campus.

Guilford has garnered a reputation for impacting students' lives. Speaking for many, one student commented: "What I got at Guilford becomes more precious as time passes. Funny, but true. How did it change me . . . it made me what I am today."

HAMLINE UNIVERSITY Saint Paul, Minnesota

Total Undergraduate Enrollment: 1,800
Men: 700 Women: 1,100
Five-Year Graduation Rate: 64%

Tuition: $$$
Room and Board: $$
Residential Students: 52%

History Hamline University, founded in 1854, was Minnesota's first university. It was founded by a group of Methodist ministers and educators to provide education, leadership, and service to the frontier people of the Minnesota territory. Its affiliation with the United Methodist Church encourages the exploration of spiritual values within a social context.

Location Hamline's 50-acre campus is located in a residential area midway between the downtowns of Minneapolis and Saint Paul. This metropolitan area provides many cultural and entertainment opportunities.

Top Programs of Study Psychology, biology, English

Arts and Sciences American law and legal systems, anthropology, art, art history, biology, chemistry, communication studies, criminal justice, East Asian studies, economics, English, environmental studies, exercise and sports science, French, German, history, international management, international studies, Latin American studies, legal studies, mathematics, musical performance, musical studies, philosophy, physics, political science, psychology, religion, Russian, Central, and East European studies, social justice, social studies, sociology, Spanish, theater arts, urban studies, women's studies

Business Management

Education Elementary, physical education, secondary

Pre-Professional Dentistry, engineering, international journalism, medicine, occupational therapy, physical therapy, veterinary medicine

Accredited Programs Chemistry, education, music

Special Programs There are many internship opportunities with multinational corporations. The university offers the nationally recognized Hamline Plan, a set of goal-oriented graduation objectives specifically designed to prepare students for success. A dual degree 3/3 B.A./J.D program is offered with the Hamline University School of Law; other dual degree programs are offered with other universities as well. Hamline has a Center for Multicultural and International Affairs and takes pride in its racially/ethnically diverse student population. There is an Air Force ROTC program.

Facilities There are 27 buildings, including a renovated Bush Library, the new Walker Fieldhouse athletic and sports medicine facility, and a Center for Excellence in Urban Teaching.

Transition to College Program The First-Year Seminar introduces students to the liberal arts, where students develop skills in careful reading, critical analysis, group discussion, and writing, with a focus on interdisciplinary topics.

Athletics NCAA III, Minnesota Intercollegiate Athletic Conference

   Men: Baseball, basketball, cross-country, football, ice hockey, soccer, swimming and diving, tennis, track & field

   Women: Basketball, cross-country, softball, gymnastics, soccer, ice hockey, swimming and diving, tennis, track & field, volleyball

Student Life and Housing About 800 students can be accommodated in college housing, which is guaranteed for all four years. Seventy-one percent of the students are from Minnesota, with the remainder coming from 37 other states and 34 countries. Ethnicity: Caucasian—86 percent; African-American—4 percent; Asian-American—4 percent; International—3 percent; Hispanic-American—1 percent. There is one local sorority and one local fraternity. All students may keep cars.

Accommodations for Students with Disabilities To be eligible for disability-related services,

students must have a disability documented by a licensed practitioner or medical doctor, and documentation must be no more than three years old.

Financial Aid About 80 percent of all freshmen receive aid. The average award was about $15,000.

Requirements for Admission SAT I or ACT scores and a college prep high school program.

Application The Early Action deadline is December 1. After December 1, students are considered for admission on a rolling basis, with the first admission decisions mailed January 15.

International Students Students need to complete a college prep program, provide a paper-based TOEFL score of at least 550 and 213 on the computer-based exam. Some financial assistance is available.

Transfer Students The priority admission deadline is April 1, and regular deadline is August 1. The deadline for the spring semester is December 11. A maximum of 64 credits will be accepted from two-year colleges. Students must be in good standing at their previous colleges. Courses with grades of C or higher are considered for transfer.

Admission Contact
Office of Admissions
Hamline University
1536 Hewitt Avenue
Saint Paul, MN 55104-1284
Phone: (800) 753-9753; (651) 523-2207
FAX: (651) 523-2458
E-mail: *clas-admis@gw.hamline.edu*
Web: *www.hamline.edu*

The Heart of the University Hamline University has all the essentials of a fine liberal arts community, including a multicultural population, talented professors, small classes, a friendly campus, service and study abroad opportunities, and student research. But the heart of the university is the very focused connections it has made with the world of the workplace. Faculty have been able to keep their "finger on the pulse" of the workplace by inviting representatives from the Twin Cities—Minneapolis and St. Paul—to campus to discuss how Hamline's academic programs can more closely connect with career skills and expectations of employers. The result of these discussions led faculty to develop Hamline's distinctive curriculum, "The Hamline Plan," which has received national attention and imitation by liberal arts colleges across the nation.

"The Hamline Plan" establishes educational goals tied directly to graduation requirements. The plan helps students to understand and appreciate the liberal arts; communicte effectively; use computers; reason logically; become aware of culture, gender, minority, and age issues; work independently; understand the world of work; establish depth in one area; and examine personal values and recognize other value systems. These goals are woven throughout the overall curriculum and co-curricular activities.

As a result of this plan, employers readily seek out Hamline students to fill positions as interns or employees. Hamline's location certainly adds to these opportunities. Only a 10-minute commute to either St. Paul, the state capital, or Minneapolis, students have as neighbors Fortune 100 corporations, as well as the political world of the state capital. Internships are available at the state capital for students especially interested in law or political science. Pace Laboratories and 3M are examples of corporations offering internships.

In their first year, Hamline students are paired with a campus staff adviser, who, with an academic adviser, helps students to think about a career path. An extensive alumni network also serves as a resource, offering valuable advice and job connections.

The Twin Cities offers lakes, parks, art galleries, night and comedy clubs, the Mall of America, concerts, sunny skies (220 days of the year), and a young person's town (44 percent of the metro area's 2.5 million residents are under age 35).

HAMPDEN-SYDNEY COLLEGE

Hampden-Sydney, Virginia

Total Undergraduate Enrollment: 1,038
Men: 1,036 Women: 2
Five-Year Graduation Rate: 61%

Tuition: $$$
Room and Board: $$$
Residential Students: 95%

History Hampden-Sydney College, founded in 1775 as a liberal arts college for men, is one of the oldest colleges in America. Associated with the Presbyterian Church, the college is named after two Revolutionary War heroes.

Location Hampden-Sydney's 660-acre campus is in a rural area, five miles from Farmville, Virginia (population 6,500), and one hour from Richmond and Charlottesville, with several women's colleges within a short driving distance.

Top Programs of Study Economics, history, political science

Arts and Sciences Biology, chemistry, classical studies, economics, economics with mathematics, English, fine arts, French, German, Greek, Greek and Latin, history, humanities, interscience, Latin, mathematics, applied mathematics, mathematics and computer science, philosophy, physics, political science, psychology, religion, religion and philosophy, Spanish

Business Management economics

Education None

Pre-Professional Dentistry, law, medicine

Accredited Programs Chemistry

Special Programs Students have the opportunity to customize an area of study. There are many opportunities for foreign study in 20 countries, as well as language immersion programs abroad for language majors. Students interested in marine science may take courses at Duke University's Marine Laboratory in Beaufort, North Carolina. There are internship opportunities and a Washington, D.C., semester. Students may study education, studio art, or Army ROTC at neighboring Longwood College. A dual degree program in engineering is offered with the University of Virginia. Hampden-Sydney is also the home of the Wilson Center for Leadership in the Public Interest.

Facilities There are 60 buildings, including an observatory; radio and TV stations; International Communications Center, which receives satellite broadcasts from around the world; Eggleston Library; and a Computing Center.

Transition to College Program The college uses a traditional orientation.

Athletics NCAA III, Old Dominion Athletic Conference

Men: Baseball, basketball, cross-country, football, golf, lacrosse, soccer, tennis

Student Life and Housing About 1,000 students can be accommodated in college housing, which is guaranteed for all four years. Sixty percent of the students are from Virginia, the remainder are from 34 other states and 3 countries. Ethnicity: Caucasian—94 percent. There are 11 national fraternities. All students may keep cars. The college has an honor code.

Accommodations for Students with Disabilities Students should contact the Associate Dean for Academic Support and provide documentation of disability. The Dean and the student's adviser will design, with the student, an appropriate program.

Financial Aid About 79 percent of all freshmen receive aid. The average award was about $14,600.

Requirements for Admission SAT I or ACT scores and a college prep high school program. While not required, SAT I exams in writing, mathematics, and a third subject are recommended. An interview is strongly recommended.

Application Early Decision application deadline is November 15; the Early Action deadline is January 15; and the regular application deadline is March 1.

International Students Applications and completed supporting materials are due by March 1 for fall admission. Secondary school records with English translations as well as TOEFL scores are required.

Transfer Students Official high school and college transcripts and letters of recommendation from a dean or other official are required. A total of 60 credits may be transferred. A 3.0 grade point average is required for two-year college transfer students seeking junior standing. An interview is recommended.

Admission Contact
Office of Admissions
Hampden-Sydney College
Graham Hall, Box 667
Hampden-Sydney, VA 23943-0667
Phone: (800) 755-0733; (434) 223-6120
FAX: (434) 223-6346
E-mail: *hsapp@hsc.edu*
Web: *www.hsc.edu*

The Heart of the College Hampden-Sydney is one of only three men's colleges in America. For over 200 years the college has remained so because it has heeded the need of certain students who learn better when members of the opposite sex are not around. Without social pressures, a real brotherhood binds students together, as it would an athletic team. Of course, with several women's and coed colleges nearby, Hampden-Sydney students have plenty of opportunities to be with women—but not in the classroom.

The heart of the college is the great sense of

community experienced by students. Students are able to chat with professors in the classrooms and in their backyards. Students are also active contributors to this tightly knit community by serving in the fire department, working on the local bike track, or building a Habitat house. Students marvel at the friendships and camaraderie at Hampden-Sydney.

Critical to the development of this community is the college's honor code, which is entirely student-run and enforced. The code is something to live by, making students feel they are being treated as mature adults, responsible for their actions. Students enjoy the freedom it provides. For example, students feel at ease keeping car and dorm doors unlocked.

Students often dress up for football games and oral class presentations. These "gentlemen" are reported to be appreciated not only by the women they meet but also by prospective employers.

The liberal arts education at the college is set within a core curriculum and aims to develop a well-rounded student educated in world cultures, literate, articulate, and a critical thinker. Of special note is the college's rhetoric program, focusing on student writing ability and practicing presenting and defending ideas in class. The results are amazing with 1 in 10 graduates acting as president or CEO of a business and another third doctors, lawyers, or similar professionals. Hampden-Sydney graduates consistently rank among the top five schools in the nation regarding percentage of alumni in *Who's Who*.

HAMPTON UNIVERSITY   Hampton, Virginia

Total Undergraduate Enrollment: 4,979
Men: 2,000 Women: 2,979
Five-Year Graduation Rate: 50%

Tuition: $$
Room and Board: $$
Residential Students: 54%

History Hampton University was founded in 1868 as Hampton Normal and Agricultural Institute with a mission to prepare African-American men and women to lead and teach their newly freed people. A private, nonsectarian institution, the school was later renamed Hampton Institute and in 1984 became a university. The university is listed on the Templeton Foundation's Honor Roll of Character-Building Colleges.

Location The 204-acre campus is located in Hampton, Virginia, on the banks of the Hampton River, near the Chesapeake Bay, 15 miles west of Norfolk and 15 minutes to Williamsburg.

Top Programs of Study Psychology, biology, business management

Arts and Sciences Advertising, architecture, art (including graphic design), aviation, biology, broadcast journalism, chemical engineering, chemistry, computer engineering, computer information systems, electrical engineering, English, history, leadership, marine science, mass media arts (broadcast journalism, media management, print journalism, public relations/advertising), mathematics, music, music engineering technology, nursing, physics, political science, print journalism, psychology, public relations, recreation (recreation leadership, therapeutic recreation), religion, sociology (including criminology), Spanish, theater arts

Business Accounting, economics, entrepreneurship, finance, management, marketing (including professional tennis management), sports management

Education Elementary, middle, music, physical education, secondary, special

Pre-Professional Pharmacy

Accredited Programs There are several master's programs, including a 5-year M.B.A., and also doctoral degrees awarded in pharmacy, physical therapy, physics, and nursing.

Special Programs There are opportunities for study abroad, internships, community service, and co-op placements. The university has been cited as one of the most computer-wired campuses in America. There are Army and Navy ROTC programs.

Facilities There are 125 buildings, including historic landmarks. The Harvey Library includes a new Academic Technology Mall and the Peabody collection of 33,000 catalogued items by and about black people. The new School of Journalism is a state-of-the-art facility, as are the athletic facilities. The university has a new Student Center with a movie theater and bowling alley and owns Hampton Harbor, a housing and shopping development that borders the campus and offers attractive apartment living.

Transition to College Program "University 101" is a credit-bearing course with activities ranging from exploring the University Museum to learning stress management skills.

Athletics NCAA I, Mid-Eastern Athletic Conference

Men: Basketball, cross-country, football (Div.I-AA), golf, sailing, tennis, track & field

Women: Basketball, bowling, cross-country, golf, sailing, softball, tennis, track & field, volleyball

Student Life and Housing About 3,000 students can be accommodated in college housing, which includes single-sex dorms. Thirty percent of the students are from Virginia, the majority from 43 other states, mostly Mid-Atlantic, and 34 countries. Ethnicity: African-American—96 percent. There are five fraternities and four national sororities. Upperclassmen may keep cars. Students must adhere to a standards of conduct pledge as well as a student dress code.

Accommodations for Students with Disabilities In compliance with section 504

Financial Aid About 56 percent of all freshmen receive aid. The average freshman award was about $4,116.

Requirements for Admission SAT I or ACT scores and a college prep high school program.

Application The Early Action deadline is December 1, and admission decision letters are mailed December 15. The regular admission deadline is March 1, with decision letters mailed April 1. The recommended application deadline is December 1.

International Students Required are TOEFL scores and a copy of the national examination results.

Transfer Students Transfer students are students who have successfully completed at least 15 credits at another college or university with a minimum GPA of 2.3. Required are SAT I or ACT scores (for students with fewer than 60 credits), a personal statement, and college transcripts from each school.

Admission Contact
Office of Admissions
Hampton University
Hampton, VA 23668
Phone: (800) 624-3328; (757) 727-5000
FAX: (757) 727-5095
E-mail: *admissions@hampton.edu*
Web: *www.hampton.edu*

The Heart of the University Hampton University, affectionately referred to by the Hampton education community as their "Home by the Sea," is one of the most beautiful campuses in America. Consistently rated as one of the best of the 117 historically African-American institutions, Hampton seeks to provide an "education for life," one that has an impact on the whole student. Steeped in great history and tradition, the huge Emancipation Oak spreads its strong arms across the lawn as a reminder of powerful words spoken in an 1863 reading of the Proclamation of Emancipation to a gathering of the Virginia Peninsula's black community. Although 94 percent of its students are African-American, Hampton still refers to itself as multicultural because it serves students from many states and countries with diverse cultural and economic backgrounds.

The heart of Hampton University is the special community it has created and sustained. Better characterized as a "family," the faculty, support staff, and policies provide students with a strong sense of family to ease the transition to college, as well as to motivate and support students in their preparation for life. Faculty are distinguished scholars and accomplished professionals, dedicated teachers who lead by example. With small class sizes, students get lots of personal attention, which also enables the university to track and support individual student progress through several exemplary and nationally accredited programs. Many students comment about the encouragement provided by professors as well as the important collaborative research that is developing breakthrough surgical devices and exploring particle physics. Faculty take great pride in this collaborative research. Peer counselors provide great support for students, and the career counseling professionals bring more than 500 corporations

to the campus annually, matching students with valuable internships, co-ops, and permanent positions with corporations, nonprofit organizations, and government. As a Templeton Foundation's Character-Building College, Hampton enforces high standards for students in terms of a dress code and a code of conduct. The prevailing philosophy here is that it is an honor to be a member of the Hampton "family," and students must demonstrate behavior and values of integrity, honesty, and respect for oneself and others.

The Hampton campus offers much to do, including a strong athletics program that includes the nation's first intercollegiate sailing program at a historically black institution. Recent visitors to the campus have included President George Bush, Reverend Jesse Jackson, author Toni Morrison, poet Maya Angelou, and 2003 commencement speaker, Bill Cosby.

One student's comment reinforces the dynamic impact of Hampton's education: "You will leave Hampton with an attitude that you can compete with anybody from anywhere— because, in fact, you can." Hampton's outstanding outcomes support this contention: nearly 100% of Hampton's students are placed in jobs or enrolled in graduate school within six months of graduation.

HANOVER COLLEGE   Hanover, Indiana

Total Undergraduate Enrollment: 1,000   Tuition: $$
Men: 500 Women: 500   Room and Board: $
Five-Year Graduation Rate: 68%   Residential Students: 99%

History Hanover College was founded as a small school by Reverend John Finley Crowe in 1827. The school grew and was taken under care by the Presbyterian Church as Hanover Academy in 1828. In 1833 the school became Hanover College, and it maintains an affiliation with the Presbyterian Church. Hanover is the oldest college in Indiana.

Location The 650-acre campus is located in Hanover, Indiana, a rural area 45 miles north of

Louisville, Kentucky, 70 miles from Cincinnati, and 95 miles from Indianapolis.

Top Programs of Study Business administration, sciences/pre-med, education

Arts and Sciences Art, biology, chemistry, classical studies, communication, computer science, cultural anthropology, English, French, geology, German, history, international studies, Latin American studies, mathematics, medieval-renaissance studies, music, philosophy, physical education, physics, political science, psychology, sociology, Spanish, theater, theological studies

Business Administration (with minors in accounting, banking, finance, management), economics

Education Childhood (K-6), early, early adolescence and young adult (grades 5–12), middle

Pre-Professional Dentistry, law, medicine, veterinary medicine

Accredited Programs Education

Special Programs Hanover uses a 4-4-1 academic calendar. The college offers study abroad opportunities in Australia, Belgium, France, Germany, Mexico, Nepal, Spain, and Turkey. There is a Philadelphia semester and many spring-term study opportunities in other cities and abroad. Students are also able to study at any of seven other colleges that form the Spring Term Consortium.

Facilities There are 35 buildings, including a new Science Center; the Duggan Library; the Horner Health and Recreation Center, which includes a state-of-the-art fitness center, an art gallery; planetarium; TV station; and a geology museum.

Transition to College Program Hanover uses a traditional orientation.

Athletics NCAA III, Heartland Collegiate Athletic Conference

  Men: Baseball, basketball, cross-country, football, golf, soccer, tennis, track

  Women: Basketball, cross-country, field hockey, golf, soccer, softball, tennis, track, volleyball

Student Life and Housing All students can be accommodated in college housing, which is guaranteed for all four years. Sixty-four percent of the students are from Indiana, the remainder are from 36 other states and 19 countries. Ethnicity: Caucasian—91 percent. There are four national fraternities and four national sororities. Upperclassmen may keep cars.

Accommodations for Students with Disabilities In compliance with section 504

Financial Aid About 51 percent of all freshmen receive aid. The average freshman award was about $9,000.

Requirements SAT I or ACT scores, a B average in a college prep high school program, and a recommended rank in the top third of the class.

Application The Early Admission date is December 1, with admission notification by December 20. Students who apply after December 1 will be notified on a rolling basis beginning February 1. Applications received after March 1 will be considered on a "space available basis" only.

International Students Required are official secondary, and, if applicable, college transcripts, official SAT I and/or TOEFL scores, a writing sample, a recommendation, and a financial guarantee.

Transfer Students Required are official high school and college transcripts, official SAT I or ACT scores, a recommendation, and a writing sample. Only courses taken at regionally accredited institutions with a minimum grade of C− are considered for transfer.

Admission Contact
Office of Admissions
Hanover College
P.O. Box 108
Hanover, IN 47243
Phone (800) 313-2178; (812) 866-7022
FAX: (812) 866-7098
E-mail: *admission@hanover.edu*
Web: *www.hanover.edu*

The Heart of the College You may recall the actor Woody Harrelson when he played Sam's assistant bartender in the hit television program, "Cheers." His role was one of a "country bumpkin" who moved to the big city of Boston, and often recounted funny stories about his growing up in Hanover, Indiana. What Mr. Harrelson omitted from his stories was that he attended Hanover College, a top liberal arts college and a "best buy."

The actor was excellent at his craft, because Hanover offers a challenging program of studies, and "country bumpkins" are not the outcomes of a Hanover education.

The liberal arts core requires study of philosophy and theology, fine arts and literature, natural sciences, social sciences, and Western and non-Western cultures. In addition there is a focus on public communication, analytical writing, foreign language proficiency, and health and physical fitness. Also, as one of the graduation requirements, all students must pass a comprehensive examination in their major. The 4-4-1 yearly calendar provides time for Spring Term Study Opportunities. Students have much to choose from: modern language field study in France, Germany, and Mexico; English and history field study in Italy; theater and English study of Shakespeare in England; French theater in Canada; geology of national parks and monuments; tropical biology in Central America; and American government in Washington, D.C., and New York City.

Students may also use the OmniBus, Hanover College's cultural program on wheels. Eight times each semester, student surveys and recommendations point the charter bus, for Louisville, Cincin-nati, and Indianapolis for events and programs that include the Actors Theater of Louisville, an Indianapolis ice hockey game, a bluegrass band, whitewater rafting, snow skiing, and a Cincinnati Reds baseball game.

The heart of a Hanover education is the close relationships between faculty and students. This is another instance of a college with small class sizes, an outstanding faculty who focus on teaching and mentoring, and senior faculty teaching freshman courses. What distinguishes Hanover is that not only do 92 percent of the students live on campus, but almost half of the faculty do as well—families and all! This campus presence of both faculty and students creates a most caring community where there are friendships between faculty and students, with a total commitment to helping one another grow. Ask any graduate and this special community is what they will recall as most meaningful.

The Career Center's counselors and programs are successful with meaningful internships, job placement, and, especially, with graduate and professional schools where 60 percent of Hanover's graduates continue their education.

All this, and a beautiful, park-like campus, that sits on a bluff overlooking the Ohio River.

HARTWICK COLLEGE   Oneonta, New York

Total Undergraduate Enrollment: 1,400
Men: 650 Women: 750
Five-Year Graduation Rate: 59%

Tuition: $$$$
Room and Board: $$$
Residential Students: 85%

History Hartwick College was founded in 1797 as a seminary through the will of John Christopher Hartwick, a Lutheran minister who led several missions of early settlers in the Mohawk and Hudson River Valleys. The college was chartered in 1928 as a four-year college. Today Hartwick is a nondenominational college.

Location The 425-acre campus is located on Oyaron Hill in Oneonta, New York, a college town (population 14,000). Located in the northern foothills of New York's Catskill Mountains, the college is halfway between Albany and Binghamton. There are many recreational opportunities.

Top Programs of Study Psychology, management, biology

Arts and Sciences Anthropology, art, art history, biochemistry, biology, chemistry, computer science, economics, English, environmental science and policy, French, geology, German, history, information science, mathematics, medical technology, music, nursing, philosophy, physics, political science, psychology, religious studies, sociology, Spanish, theater arts

Business Accounting, management

Education Elementary, middle, music, secondary

Pre-Professional Engineering, health professions, law

Accredited Programs Art, art history, chemistry, music, music education, nursing

Special Programs Students may design their own majors. The U.S. Pluralism Program is committed to helping students explore cultural and racial diversity in America as well as celebrate that diversity at Hartwick. The Hartwick Small Business Resource Center places students in area business organizations as consultants. There are many internship and study abroad opportunities. There are cooperative engineering programs with Clarkson and Columbia, law programs with Albany Law School, and an M.B.A. with Clarkson.

Facilities There are 28 buildings on campus, including an art gallery, observatory, radio and TV stations, and, adjacent to the campus, the 914-acre Pine Lake Environmental Campus, as well as new residence halls and an addition to the campus center.

Transition to College Program During a fall orientation, first-year students receive a new computer and training, social activities, rafting, and other social and learning opportunities. Students also meet with their Foundations groups and continue to meet with the same group in the first semester. Foundations helps students to adjust better to college life, improves college survival skills, and connects with Hartwick's "Community of Learners." Also, first-year students take a First-Year Seminar in which a small group of students meet with a faculty member to study a subject in a format especially adapted to help introduce students to college-level academic work.

Athletics NCAA III, Eastern Collegiate Athletic Conference

Men: Baseball, basketball, cross-country, football, golf, lacrosse, soccer (Div. I), swimming and diving, tennis, track & field (indoor and outdoor)

Women: Basketball, cross-country, equestrian, field hockey, golf, lacrosse, soccer, softball, swimming and diving, tennis, track & field (indoor and outdoor), volleyball, water polo (Div. I)

Student Life and Housing About 1,200 students can be accommodated in college housing, which is guaranteed all four years. Sixty-two percent of the students are from New York, the remainder from 36 other states and 37 countries. Ethnicity: Caucasian—72 percent; African-American—4 percent; International—4 percent; Hispanic-American—2 percent. There are four sororities and five fraternities. All students may keep cars. All students are provided a notebook computer system that is theirs to keep.

Accommodations for Students with Disabilities In compliance with section 504

Financial Aid About 98 percent of all freshmen receive aid. The average award was about $20,000.

Requirements for Admission Sat I or ACT scores and a college prep high school program.

Application An Early Decision Option is available, with two fall deadlines: December 1 and January 15. An admissions decision is made two weeks after receiving all admissions materials. The regular application deadline is February 15.

International Students Applicants are required to demonstrate adequate proficiency in English by achieving a minimum TOEFL score of 500, or 80 on the Michigan Test of Language Proficiency.

Transfer Students A minimum of a C average is required. Transfer credit is usually given for courses similar to those offered at Hartwick and completed with a grade of C− or higher. Transfer students must attend Hartwick for at least two academic years. Official high school and college transcripts are required, along with a letter from a dean indicating that the student is in good standing at the previous college.

Admission Contact
Office of Admissions
Hartwick College
One Hartwick Drive
Oneonta, NY 13820
Phone: (888) HARTWICK
FAX: (607) 431-4154
E-mail: *admissions@hartwick.edu*
Web: *www.hartwick.edu*

The Heart of the College Hartwick College offers a very special education, tailored to the individual student. Not every student is expected to be the same or learn the same things. Students are helped by very innovative, involved faculty to "figure out their own way." The emphasis on individuality is seen in the number of students who elect to create their own majors. One student, for example, designed a major in Medical Illustration, with courses in studio art, photography, and computer graphics, combined with biology courses emphasizing human anatomy and physiology.

There is a feeling of excitement about learning, which is seen as a partnership between dedicated teachers and motivated students. Students and faculty collaborate on many research projects, from studying the effects of earthquakes on the Adirondack Mountains in New York, to why more women don't run for political office. All students complete a senior thesis, which students often cite as the highlight of their academic experience.

Hartwick is ranked fourth among liberal arts colleges in the nation for the percentage of students who engage in study abroad programs. More than 71 percent of Hartwick's students either pursue an internship or learn about another culture.

Technology is an integral part of learning at Hartwick, with management majors and science students using computers extensively in their coursework and research. As a result, all students are provided with a notebook computer system that students use and keep upon graduation.

The MetroLink Program offers 45 Hartwick students the opportunity to spend a week learning firsthand about various professions in three major cities. Students have shadowed professionals in Boston at the Museum of Art, Brigham Women's Hospital, and the Red Sox; in New York at the Museum of Natural History, the Bronx Zoo, and Saatchi and Saatchi Advertising; and in Washington, D.C., at the FBI, the Smithsonian, the U.S. Department of State, and Gannet Corporation.

Ninety percent of students get jobs or go on to graduate school within six months of graduation, and if students don't accomplish this, they are given a paid internship!

HASTINGS COLLEGE   Hastings, Nebraska

Total Undergraduate Enrollment: 1,033
Men: 499 Women: 534
Five-Year Graduation Rate: 65%

Tuition: $$
Room and Board: $
Residential Students: 53%

History Hastings College was founded in 1882 by a group of men and women who wanted a Presbyterian-related liberal arts college to provide Christian educational leadership.

Location Hastings College is located on 88 acres in Hastings, Nebraska, America's heartland, in the south-central part of the state. The campus is a two-and-a-half hour ride to Omaha.

Top Programs of Study Education, business/marketing, social science/history

Arts and Sciences Art, biology, chemistry, history, human resource management, human services administration, communication production, computer science, economics, English, German, health promotion management, leisure studies, mathematics, music, philosophy, physics, political science, psychology, religion, sociology (including criminal justice), speech, Spanish, theater arts.

Business Accounting, administration, international economics, marketing

Education Art, elementary, physical education, secondary, special

Pre-Professional Dentistry, engineering, law, library science, medical assistant, medical technology, medicine, occupational therapy, pharmacy, physical therapy, theology, veterinary medicine

Accredited Programs Education, music

Special Programs Students can design their own majors. Several study abroad programs are available, as well as internships. There is a 3-2 cooperative engineering program with Columbia, Washington University, and the University of Nebraska. Hastings has an excellent forensics (debate) team.

Facilities There are 31 buildings that include a glassblowing studio for art students, the Wilson Center for Mathematics and Computer Science, and radio and TV stations.

Transition to College Program Hastings offers a comprehensive student development program, providing orientation and assistance in personal and college adjustment and aid to improving study skills. Also, each new student is assigned an advocate who assists in planning the student's course of study and counsels on general college programs and future plans.

Athletics NAIA, Nebraska Intercollegiate Athletic Conference; Nebraska-Iowa Athletic Conference

Men: Baseball, basketball, cross-country, football, golf, soccer, tennis, track

Women: Basketball, cross-country, golf, soccer, softball, tennis, track, volleyball

Student Life and Housing About 600 students can be accommodated in college housing. Seventy-seven percent of the students are from Nebraska, the remainder are from 30 other states and 10 foreign countries. Ethnicity: Caucasian—95 percent. There are five local sororities and five local fraternities. All students may keep cars.

Accommodations for Students with Disabilities Students should contact the Learning Center or the Dean of Students Office. Hastings College will attempt to make appropriate and reasonable academic adjustments.

Financial Aid About 97 percent of all freshmen receive aid. The average award was about $11,500.

Requirements for Admission SAT I or ACT scores and a college prep high school program.

Application Applications for the fall semester are due by July 1 and January 1 for admission to the spring semester.

International Students Students whose primary language is not English must score a minimum of 500 on the paper version of the TOEFL, submit official copies of secondary and, if applicable, postsecondary school transcripts, as well as a declaration of finances.

Transfer Students Required are official high school and college transcripts, a report completed by the Academic Dean of the student's previous institution, and SAT I or ACT scores.

Admission Contact
Office of Admissions
Hastings College
800 N. Turner Avenue
Hastings, NE 68901
Phone: (800) LEARN HC

FAX: (402) 461-7490
E-mail: *admissions@hastings.edu*
Web: *www.hastings.edu*

The Heart of the College As a Midwestern college with an Ivy League appearance, students find Hastings to be a friendly, congenial community, in a sense mirroring the positive stereotype Americans have about the Midwest. Part of the comfortable feeling that students have about the college is a result of the two options for completing their education programs. Students can elect to study in Hastings' highly regarded liberal arts program, which includes a major and core requirements in a broad range of subjects. Also, Hastings offers a unique opportunity for the creative, resourceful student who elects a personalized program, where students can tailor their studies to fit individual academic or professional goals.

A Hastings education is offered within a caring, family atmosphere, where highly regarded faculty teach every class. Students are offered small classes, personal attention, and supportive faculty. Students comment about the ease with which they can talk with their professors whenever they want, as well as the encouragement they receive from faculty.

Hastings has made program changes that better serve their students in the workplace. For example, recognizing the growing importance in the world of business for communication, teamwork, and analytical and problem solving skills, Hastings has combined its programs in communication arts and business administration/economics.

In addition, Hastings has garnered an excellent reputation among medical schools and graduate health professional programs because of its strong liberal arts and science education. Hastings was one of the first colleges to make the internship part of its pre-professional training. Although many internships are served at medical centers, others are available with local dentists, veterinarians, physical therapists, pharmacies, and professional sports clinics with the Denver Broncos and the Dallas Cowboys. Graduates have gone on to professional and medical schools, including Washington University, University of Wisconsin, Johns Hopkins, Baylor, and the University of Nebraska Medical Center.

A quality faculty and strong academic program in a friendly setting make Hastings an outstanding educational value.

HIGH POINT UNIVERSITY

High Point, North Carolina

Total Undergraduate Enrollment: 2,900
Men: 1,200 Women: 1,700
Five-Year Graduation Rate: 58%

Tuition: $$
Room and Board: $$
Residential Students: 64%

History High Point University was founded in 1924 by the predecessors of the United Methodist Church. High Point is one of the youngest and fastest growing universities in the United States. The teaching of ethics is emphasized across the curriculum and, although a nonsectarian institution, the university actively seeks to encourage spiritual formation among its very diverse student religious traditions. The university is listed on the Templeton Foundation's Honor Roll of Character-Building Colleges.

Location The university is located on 78 acres in the city of High Point, North Carolina (population 85,000), the furniture capital of the world. The cities of High Point, Greensboro, and Winston-Salem form the Piedmont Triad, North Carolina's largest metropolitan area with a population of 1.4 million and many cultural, recreational, and social opportunities.

Top Programs of Study Business administration, education, psychology

Arts and Sciences Athletic science, art, biology, chemistry, computer information systems, computer science, criminal justice, English (literature, media/communications, writing), exercise science, French, history, home/furnishings management, home furnishings marketing, human relations, industrial/organizational psychology, interior design, international studies, mathematics, medical technology, modern languages, North American studies, philosophy, political science, psychology, recreation, religion, sociology, Spanish, sports management, sports medicine, theater arts

Business Accounting, administration, chemistry-business, international

Education Art, elementary, middle, physical education, special

Pre-Professional Dentistry, law, medicine, pharmacy, physical therapy, physician's assistant, theology

Accredited Programs Allied health programs, education

Special Programs High Point offers the nation's only majors in home furnishings management and marketing. Students have the opportunity to create their own majors. There are many opportunities for internships and study abroad. There is a dual degree program in environmental management and forestry with Duke. The university offers a cocurricular program, "American Humanics," designed for students seeking careers in human services. The university competes in the Harvard Model United Nations Competition.

Facilities There are 25 buildings, including a new fine arts center, air-conditioned residence halls, a newly renovated chapel, a TV studio and radio station, two theaters, an Olympic pool, and an art gallery. The International Center for Home Furnishings will soon be constructed on campus.

Transition to College Program The Freshman Success Program consists of a three-credit course, "Foundations for Academic Success," and partici-

pation in other supportive services and instructional conferences, as well as learning time management and interpersonal skills.

Athletics NCAA I, Big South Conference

Men: Baseball, basketball, cross-country, soccer, tennis, track

Women: Basketball, cross-country, indoor track, soccer, tennis, track, volleyball

Student Life and Housing About 1,800 students can be accommodated in college housing, which is guaranteed for all four years. Thirty-three percent of the students are from North Carolina, with the majority from 39 other states and 41 countries. Ethnicity: Caucasian—85 percent; African-American—11 percent. There are one local and four national sororities, and five national fraternities. All students may keep cars on campus. High Point uses an honor code.

Accommodations for Students with Disabilities In compliance with section 504

Financial Aid About 70 percent of all freshmen receive aid. The average award was about $5,000.

Requirements for Admission SAT I or ACT scores and a college prep high school program. Students must submit a recent photograph.

Application High Point University uses a rolling admissions policy. When all application materials have been received, an admissions decision is made.

International Students TOEFL scores, certification of financial support, and official school transcripts are required, as well as a recent photograph.

Transfer Students SAT I or ACT scores should be submitted only if students haven't completed 12 credits of college work. Official high school and college transcripts are required, as well as a statement of good standing at the previous college.

Admission Contact
Office of Admissions
High Point University

University Station 3188
833 Montlieu Avenue
High Point, NC 27262-3598
Phone: (800) 345-6993
FAX: (336) 888-6382
E-mail: *admiss@highpoint.edu*
Web: *www.highpoint.edu*

The Heart of the University High Point University has a beautiful campus within a 60-minute radius of 19 other colleges and universities. It offers students a wealth of activities, events, and nightlife especially designed for young adults. But what makes High Point truly distinctive is its diverse student population. In a typical year, the student body includes students from 39 states and 41 countries! The campus becomes a microcosm for the world, where students learn to live and work in the larger global society. This diversity includes differences in family incomes, races, ethnicities, and religious backgrounds. Yet students view this incredible diversity as a real plus in their educations and report how easy it is to make meaningful friendships with people from different geographical regions and cultures. It is an advantage for the university community that two-thirds of the students are not from North Carolina, because this creates a large residential community that stays on campus on the weekends. Students comment on the friendliness of their classmates, their openness to new ideas, and willingness to learn from one another.

In addition, the university has designed curricula options to prepare students to live and work internationally. The major in North American studies is an interdisciplinary program that examines the cultures and societies of Canada, Mexico, and the United States, and prepares students to work in a NAFTA environment. The Phillips School of Business offers a major in international business and a major in business administration with a concentration in international management. Students can also major or minor in international studies or modern languages.

Students speak highly of their professors and in recent surveys identify the faculty as what students liked best about High Point. These are faculty who are easily accessible in addition to being excellent teachers.

The development of character is important at High Point. Every student takes a course in ethics; faculty are expected to address ethical issues in their courses; and students are required to adhere to a university code of conduct. Although a nonsectarian university that enrolls students from a variety of religious traditions, the university seeks to encourage spiritual formation as well. Students study at least one course in religion, and many attend chapel service.

High Point offers a very progressive education, indicative of its position as one of the youngest universities, and is growing in size, programs, endowment, and stature. Its location, faculty, global focus, and student diversity provide for a rich education.

HIRAM COLLEGE   Hiram, Ohio

Total Undergraduate Enrollment: 941
Men: 409 Women: 532
Five-Year Graduation Rate: 69%

Tuition: $$$
Room and Board: $$$
Residential Students: 93%

History Hiram College was founded in 1850 and is a private, residential liberal arts and sciences college.

Location The 110-acre campus is located in the center of the village of Hiram, Ohio, a rural area 35 miles southeast of Cleveland in northeast Ohio.

Top Programs of Study Biology, business, education, psychology

Arts and Sciences Art, art history, biochemistry, biology, biomedical humanities, chemistry, classical studies, communication, computer science, English (emphasis in creative writing), environmental studies, French, German, history, philosophy, political science, psychobiology, religious studies, science, sociology/anthropology, Spanish, theater arts

Business Economics, management

Education Elementary, secondary

Pre-Professional Business, dentistry, law, medicine, optometry, podiatry, seminary, veterinary medicine

Accredited Programs Music

Special Programs Students can minor in all major areas as well as in exercise and sport science, gender studies, Greek international studies, Latin, and urban studies. The Center for the Study of Ethical Issues helps students develop the resources to assess the ethical significance of historical and contemporary events. The college has a Phi Beta Kappa chapter. Hiram offers a cooperative, dual degree program in engineering with Case Western Reserve and Washington University in St. Louis. The Hiram academic calendar is composed of of a semester divided into a 12-week period and a 3-week period. There is a Model U.N. Program. Students can design their own majors and double majors. There are opportunities for study abroad, internships, and volunteer service. The college also offers a Washington, D.C., semester.

Facilities There are 28 buildings, a blend of restored and new. The new buildings include a new library with a video production room; Gerstacker Science Hall, with state-of-the-art facilities and instrumentation; an observatory; the Northwoods Field Station in upper Michigan; the 260-acre Barrow Field Station, three miles from campus, which provides study of aquatic and terrestrial ecosystems; Price Gum and Fleming Fieldhouse. Hiram is also constructing a new sports, recreation, and fitness center.

Transition to College Program The New Student Institute is a one-week orientation program conducted by faculty for groups of 10 freshmen. This is followed by a semester-long seminar in which the first-year students continue to meet and discuss the liberal arts tradition.

Athletics NCAA III, North Coast Athletic Conference

    Men: Baseball, basketball, cross-country, football, golf, soccer, swimming and diving, tennis, track & field

    Women: Basketball, cross-country, soccer, softball, swimming and diving, tennis, track & field, volleyball

Student Life and Housing About 1,000 students can be accommodated in college housing, that includes single-sex and coed dorms, and is guaranteed for all four years. Seventy-nine percent of the students are from Ohio, the remainder are from 23 other states and 13 countries. Ethnicity: Caucasian—84 percent; African-American—8 percent; International—3 percent; Asian-American—1 percent; Hispanic-American—1 percent. There are no fraternities or sororities. All students may keep cars.

Accommodations for Students with Disabilities In compliance with section 504

Financial Aid About 83 percent of freshmen receive aid. The average freshman award was about $17,500.

Requirements for Admission SAT I or ACT scores and a college prep high school program. A campus interview is highly recommended, while a parent recommendation is optional.

Application Freshmen are admitted fall and spring semesters. The Early Decision deadline is December 1 and regular admission February 1 Decision notification is made on a rolling basis.

International Students Students for whom English is not their first language must submit TOEFL results.

Transfer Students The transfer application deadlines are July 1 for fall semester and December 1 for spring semester. Applicants should submit official copies of all college work, be in good standing, provide a teacher/faculty recommendation, have a minimum overall GPA of 2.5, and submit an essay. Students who have less than one year of full-time college credit must also submit a Secondary School Report Form, a high school transcript, and SAT I or ACT scores.

Admission Contact

Office of Admissions
Hiram College
P.O. Box 96
Hiram, OH 44234
Phone: (800) 362-5280
FAX: (330) 569-5944
E-mail: *admission@hiram.edu*
Web: *www.hiram.edu*

The Heart of the College Hiram College offers a unique academic calendar that distinguishes Hiram's liberal arts program from most others in this guide. Each semester students study three courses over 12 weeks, then study one course for 3 weeks. This one-course format allows professors and students the luxury of immersing themselves in a concentrated field, motivates greater faculty creativity, and permits time for fieldtrips, spending time at the Northwoods Field Station, pursuing a research project, or an internship. Some examples of three-week field experiences include visiting state and federal penitentiaries for a history course, "Prisons and Public History"; studying Shakespeare at the Northwoods Field Station with theater arts and English professors; and traveling to Malaysia to study an interdisciplinary course, "Cultures and Peoples of Malaysia." Interdisciplinary courses are held in high esteem at Hiram because both faculty and students are required to look at knowledge from different viewpoints.

Although the calendar is unique, the heart of the college is in its hands-on orientation to learning. Students are still offered traditional classroom instruction by excellent faculty, of whom one alumnus said; "At Hiram, I had professors who cared about teaching as much as I cared about learning." This motivation to teach and learn is most evident in research experiences, lab and field work, and other experiential learning activities that professors tailor to the specific interests of students. These experiences are often cited by students as one-on-one opportunities for great learning. Examples include ongoing research of indigenous amphibian and reptile populations at the Barrow Field Station; the investment club, which manages a portfolio initially valued at $50,000 that has consistently outperformed the S&P 500; or reviewing, revising, and submitting student writing to literary journals.

This care in tailoring and personalizing learning opportunities can be seen in Hiram's extensive off-campus study programs. It is no wonder that over 50 percent of all Hiram students study off campus when faculty and staff customize domestic and travel abroad study with specific coursework. Students benefit in so many ways from having their professors travel with them to sites on six continents, including Spain, Germany, the Galapagos Islands, Russia, and the Arizona desert, as well as marine science opportunities in the Gulf of Mexico, the Long Island Sound, and the Gulf of Maine.

Hiram is also fond of referring to its community as an "academic village." This helps to capture the importance the college places on the diverse student population that it serves and its firm belief in the intellectual and personal growth that diversity produces. The Center for International Studies hosts cultural events and encourages greater international content in the curriculum. The "academic village" also includes more than 70 clubs and organizations and an athletic program that involves 80 percent of the students!

Considered a "best buy" with strong science programs, 30 percent of Hiram graduates go on to outstanding professional and graduate schools and land positions at the U.S. Office of Management and Budget, Microsoft, Bureau of Labor and Statistics, Hewlett-Packard, General Electric, and the Cleveland Indians.

HOBART AND WILLIAM SMITH COLLEGES

Geneva,
New York

Total Undergraduate Enrollment: 1,866
Men: 831 Women: 1,035
Five-Year Graduation Rate: 78%

Tuition: $$$$
Room and Board: $$$
Residential Students: 90%

History Hobart College for Men, founded in 1822, and William Smith College for Women, founded in 1908, are coordinate, liberal arts colleges that share faculty, facilities, and curriculum, but maintain separate dean's offices, athletic programs, student governments, and traditions. Hobart is named for its founder, John Henry Hobart, Bishop of the Episcopal Diocese of New York. William Smith College is named for a local benefactor who wanted to establish a college for women.

Location The colleges share a 170-acre campus in Geneva, New York, a small town 50 miles west of Syracuse and 50 miles east of Rochester, on the north shore of Seneca Lake in the heart of the Finger Lakes Region.

Top Programs of Study English, economics, psychology

Arts and Sciences African studies, American studies, anthropology, architectural studies, art (history and studio), Asian languages and cultures, biology, biochemistry, chemistry, classics, comparative literature, critical social studies, dance, economics, English, environmental studies, European studies, French, geoscience, Greek, history, international relations, Latin American studies, lesbian, gay, and bisexual studies, mathematics, media and society, modern languages, music, philosophy, physics, political science, psychology, public policy studies, religious studies, Russian area studies, sociology, Spanish, urban studies, women's studies, writing and rhetoric

Business None

Education Childhood, childhood and special, secondary

Pre-Professional Law, medicine

Accredited Programs None

Special Programs There are joint degree programs in engineering with Columbia, Rensselaer, Dartmouth, and Washington University in St. Louis; a 4+1 M.B.A. program with Clarkson and Rochester Institute of Technology; and a 3+4 architecture program with Washington University in St. Louis. Students can design their own majors. There are many study abroad opportunities. The colleges have had a distinguished national record in lacrosse.

Facilities There are 92 buildings, including a 108-acre wildlife preserve used especially for ecological studies; the HWS Explorer, a 65-foot research vessel operated on the Finger Lakes and used for research activities; and several new and renovated buildings. There are modern science facilities, the Smith Library, and the Houghton House Arts Center.

Transition to College Program The colleges use a traditional orientation.

Athletics Upstate Collegiate Athletic Conference

　Hobart: Basketball, cross-country, football, golf, ice hockey, lacrosse (Div. I), soccer, tennis

　William Smith: Basketball, crew, cross-country, diving and swimming, field hockey, lacrosse, soccer, sailing, squash, tennis

Student Life and Housing About 1,500 students can be accommodated in college housing, which is guaranteed for all four years. Forty-nine percent of the students are from New York, the remainder from 37 other states, (mostly in the Northeast), and

17 countries. Ethnicity: Caucasian—86 percent; African-American—4 percent; Hispanic-American—4 percent; Asian-American—2 percent; International—1 percent. There are five national fraternities and no sororities. All students may keep cars.

Accommodations for Students with Disabilities Students must voluntarily disclose their disability and provide recent documentation. Students must contact, each semester, the Director of the Center for Academic Support Services and provide information regarding specific courses for which accommodations are being requested.

Financial Aid About 72 percent of all students receive aid. The average freshman award was about $26,000.

Requirements for Admission ACT I or ACT scores and a college prep high school program. Also, two recommendations are required from both eleventh and twelfth grade teachers, one of whom must be an English teacher. An interview is recommended along with evidence of special talents via portfolio, written work, projects, or tapes.

Application There are two Early Decision Plans: a November 15 deadline, with notification December 15; or January 1, with notification February 1. The regular admission deadline is January 1.

International Students Applications are due March 1. Students whose native language is not English may take either the TOEFL or the SAT I.

Transfer Students Acceptance decisions are made on a rolling basis. Students should offer at least a full year of undergraduate work. Required are official high school and college transcripts, along with a catalogue from the previous institution, recommendations from the Academic Dean and a professor, and SAT I or ACT scores. An interview is recommended. A maximum of two years' work is accepted for transfer, and students must spend a minimum of two years at Hobart and William Smith. Only courses with C grades or higher are considered for transfer.

Admission Contact
Office of Admissions
Hobart and William Smith Colleges
629 Main Street
Geneva, NY 14456
Phone: H (800) 852-2256; WS (800) 245-0100
FAX: H (315) 781-3471; WS (315) 781-3914
E-mail: *admissions@hws.edu*
Web: *www.hws.edu/admissions*

The Heart of the Colleges Hobart and William Smith Colleges provide a unique structure of separate-but-together institutions and all the wonderful things that flow from borrowing from single-sex colleges and coeducational colleges and then putting them together to create a "best of both worlds" education. This is a place where students come to know many things through the college's distinguished liberal arts and sciences program. If students don't want to stretch their intellectual boundaries and come to know more about ideas, their world, and themselves, Hobart and William Smith is not the college for them. Students achieve this modality with double majors or a major and minors, or the creation of a major, active participation in research and campus organizations, as well as clubs, service opportunities, and domestic and international internships.

The faculty are distinctive because they have academic interests that span many fields, allowing them to teach the more interesting interdisciplinary courses. They are scholars/teachers who engage in teaching while actively involved in writing and scholarship. The faculty also encourage close interaction with students and actively provide them with ideas.

More than half of the students spend a semester studying abroad. The college is very proud of its extensive off-campus study abroad program, offering programs on six continents.

This is a high-energy college, where students work very hard. One student comments that "your friends are interesting people— . . . excited about learning. . . . That's what makes this college the perfect place for me."

HOPE COLLEGE Holland, Michigan

Total Undergraduate Enrollment: 3,035
Men: 1,187 Women: 1,848
Five-Year Graduation Rate: 74%

Tuition: $$$
Room and Board: $
Residential Students: 81%

History Hope College's origins date back to 1851, when a group of Dutch pioneers, led by the Reverend Albertus C. Van Raalte, came to America to seek religious freedom and economic advantage. A love of liberty and a devotion to God set the guidelines for the academy they opened to meet the educational needs of the young colony they founded in Holland, on the eastern shore of Lake Michigan. In 1866 the school was chartered as Hope College and is affiliated with the Reformed Church.

Location The 45-acre campus is located in Holland, Michigan (population 60,000), 26 miles southwest of Grand Rapids and 5 miles east of Lake Michigan.

Top Programs of Study Business, English, psychology

Arts and Sciences Art, athletic training, biology, chemistry, communication, computer science, dance, engineering, English, exercise science, French, geology, German, history, kinesiology, Latin, mathematics, music, nursing, philosophy, physics, political science, psychology, religion, social work, sociology, Spanish, theater

Business Accounting, administration, economics

Education Elementary, secondary, special

Pre-Professional Dentistry, engineering, law, medical technology, medicine, physical therapy, seminary, veterinary science

Accredited Programs Art, athletic training, chemistry, dance, education, engineering, music, nursing, social work, theater

Special Programs A Campus Community Hour is set aside each week to provide for the examination of significant issues by notable speakers or developing symposia along department lines. The Phelps Scholars Program provides a multicultural program for freshmen. There are student exchange programs with Japanese colleges; an Arts Program in New York; an Oak Ridge, Tennessee, Science Semester; and Philadelphia, Chicago, and Washington, D.C., semesters. There is a Phi Beta Kappa chapter. There are many study abroad programs.

Facilities There are 105 buildings, with several original buildings surrounding Pine Grove, the center of the campus. Many of the buildings were renovated in the 1980s, including Peale Science Center, one of the nation's finest facilities for undergraduate education. There are radio and TV stations, a planetarium, and an art gallery.

Transition to College Program The First-Year Seminar, worth two credits, is intended to provide an intellectual transition into Hope College by introducing students to college-level ways of learning. The interdisciplinary course is taught topically, and the instructor will be the students' academic adviser. Conversations about courses, grades, adjustment, personal interests, career goals, and campus involvement occur more naturally in this setting. Students discuss primary texts in a seminar format, do expository writing, present their ideas, and attend out-of-class events.

Athletics NCAA III, Michigan Intercollegiate Athletic Association

Men: Baseball, basketball, cross-country, football, golf, soccer, swimming, tennis, track

Women: Basketball, cross-country, golf, soccer, softball, swimming, tennis, track, volleyball

Student Life and Housing About 2,200 students can be accommodated in college housing, which is guaranteed for all four years. Seventy-seven percent of the students are from Michigan, the remainder from 42 states, mostly Midwestern, and 36 countries. Ethnicity: Caucasian—93 percent. There are six local fraternities and six local sororities. All students may keep cars.

Accommodations for Students with Disabilities In compliance with section 504

Financial Aid About 66 percent of all students receive aid. The average freshman award was about $16,000.

Requirements for Admission SAT I or ACT scores with a college prep high school program. An interview is recommended.

Application Freshmen are admitted to all semesters. Application deadlines are open. Students are notified of an admission decision shortly after all application materials are submitted.

International Students Required are an official copy of the secondary school record, a minimum TOEFL score of 550 for non-English native speaking students, and evidence of financial responsibility.

Transfer Students Students must be in good standing at previous accredited institutions. Required are official high school and college transcripts and ACT or SAT I scores. A maximum of 65 credits may be transferred from a two-year institution. Students must complete their last 30 credits at Hope College to receive a degree.

Admission Contact
Office of Admissions
Hope College
69 E. 10th Street
P.O. Box 9000
Holland, MI 49422-9000
Phone: (800) 968-7850; (616) 395-7850
FAX: (616) 395-7130
E-mail: *admissions@hope.edu*
Web: *www.hope.edu*

The Heart of the College Hope College is recognized as one of the nation's outstanding liberal arts colleges. A typical Hope student is one who is looking for close contact with faculty as well as with fellow students, wants a solid program in the liberal arts, is a serious student, and considers religion to be a prominent part of his or her life. The college president has said: "The combination of exceptional academics and a genuine faith dimension is what makes Hope special."

There is abundant evidence for viewing Hope as a leading educational institution. For example, the college has received government and foundation grants of almost $4 million the past several years. Hope is also the only private four-year liberal arts college in America with accreditation for its programs in art, dance, music, and theater! The college's program in sciences and mathematics was recognized as a model for other institutions to consider. Five departments in science have been awarded more grants than all but a handful of any institutions in America—including research universities! The nationally accredited education program received one of only six "Distinguished Achievement Awards" nationwide for effectively blending technology into its course offerings. Also, Hope is ranked as one of the outstanding producers of future Ph. D. holders. Hope has very high admission rates to law, dental, and medical schools. Approximately one-third of Hope's graduates enter graduate or professional schools to pursue advanced training.

The faculty is a distinguished one and has a deep concern for the growth and development of students. It serves not only as teachers, but also as counselors, advisers, and friends to students. Outside the classroom, the faculty members contribute to the intellectual vitality of the campus by inviting students to their homes; participating in "bull sessions" in residence halls, colloquia, and performances; and many other informal contacts. Hope's finest professors teach introductory courses as well as advanced ones.

Hope strives to be an active Christian community. There is a comprehensive campus ministry team; voluntary chapel services three times a week, as well as Sunday service; more than 20 mission trips for students to reach out to urban, rural, national, and international settings suffering from poverty, drug abuse, and spiritual hunger; and many opportunities for interpersonal Christian growth through prayer groups, Bible studies, and retreats.

The town of Holland has been honored as an All-American city, where people show intense pride in their town and in Hope College. Well-kept parks and residential areas, the yearly Tulip Festival, and proximity to the Lake Michigan beaches make this an ideal location.

IONA COLLEGE   New Rochelle, New York

Total Undergraduate Enrollment: 2,985
Men: 1,507 Women: 1,478
Five-Year Graduation Rate: 62%

Tuition: $$$
Room and Board: $$$$
Residential Students: 37%

History Iona College was founded in 1940 by the Congregation of Christian Brothers and is a Catholic college. Iona is named for the island of Iona, off the coast of Scotland, where a great monastery was founded in 563 A.D.

Location Iona's 35-acre campus is in suburban New Rochelle, New York (population 72,000), a 25-minute train ride into New York City with its many cultural, recreational, and social opportunities.

Top Programs of Study Business, communication arts, education

Arts and Sciences Applied mathematics, biochemistry, biology, chemistry, computer science, criminal justice, ecology, economics, English, French, history, information and decision technology management, interdisciplinary science, international studies, Italian, mass communications, mathematics, medical technology, philosophy, physics, political science, psychology, religious studies, social work, sociology, Spanish, speech communication studies

Business Accounting, administration, finance, international business, management, marketing

Education Early childhood, elementary, secondary

Pre-Professional Chiropractic, dentistry, medicine, physical therapy

Accredited Programs Business, social work

Special Programs Iona offers the following joint programs: a B.S./M.S. program in physical therapy with New York Medical College and a six-year program in speech/language pathology and audiology with New York Medical College. The college also offers five-year bachelor's/master's programs in accounting, computer science, history, and psychology. The Service Learning Program allows students to earn credit through community service. There are many internship opportunities in the New York Metropolitan Area, study abroad, and mission opportunities.

Facilities There are 60 buildings, including a new arts center with gallery, renovated science education and research facilities, an Olympic pool, two radio stations, and a TV studio.

Transition to College Program Incoming students enroll in a First-Year Seminar that focuses on strategies for transition from high school to college, academic advising and mentoring, and enrichment programs.

Athletics NCAA I, Metro Atlantic Athletic Conference

Men: Baseball, basketball, crew, cross-country, football, golf, ice hockey, indoor track, outdoor track, soccer, swimming and diving, tennis, water polo

Women: Basketball, crew, cross-country, indoor track, outdoor track, soccer, softball, swimming and diving, tennis, volleyball, water polo

Student Life and Housing About 450 students can be accommodated in campus housing. Eighty-seven percent of the students are from New York, the remainder from 35 states and 40 countries. Ethnicity: Caucasian—72 percent; Hispanic-American—13 percent; African-American—13 percent. There are seven local and two national sororities and eight local and two national fraternities.

Accommodations for Students with Disabilities The Academic Resource Center provides comprehensive services.

Financial Aid About 92 percent of all freshmen receive aid. The average freshman award is about $14,000.

Requirements for Admission SAT I or ACT scores and a college prep high school program.

Application Iona uses a rolling admissions policy, with students given an admissions decision within four weeks of submitting a completed application. March 15 is a preferred deadline for fall applicants. The college has an Early Action deadline of December 1, with an admissions decision by December 21.

International Students Applicants must apply by March 15 for the fall semester and November 1 for the spring semester. TOEFL scores are required if English is not the native language, otherwise SAT or ACT scores should be submitted. Official high school and, if applicable, college records in English or a certified translation must accompany originals, along with external exam results, such as A-Levels.

Transfer Students Students must have earned at least 12 credits. Preference is given to students who apply by August 1 for the fall semester and December 20 for the spring term. Official high school and college transcripts are required, with SAT I or ACT scores if students have taken fewer than 24 credits and recommendations from professors, advisers, employers, or community leaders.

Admission Contact
Office of Admissions
Iona College
715 North Avenue
New Rochelle, NY 10801-1890
Phone: (800) 231-IONA; (914) 633-2502
FAX: (914) 633-2096
E-mail: *admissions@iona.edu*
Web: *www.iona.edu*

The Heart of the College As a Catholic college, Iona's mission statement captures the essence of the college when it says: "We, therefore, prize the values of justice, peace, and service while we welcome persons of diverse backgrounds into our community." With students from 35 states and 40 countries, and a large commuter population, a typical community is difficult to achieve. Instead, students achieve a real sense of community by participation in Iona's volunteer and missions programs, where students apply what they have learned in the classroom to a different culture. The Center for Campus Ministries, Iona's spiritual and religious heart, organizes many opportunities for service and ministry, with most Iona students participating. Midnight runs, meal deliveries, soup kitchens, tutoring children, and building low-income housing are some of the opportunities. Students can also travel with Iona-in-Mission to explore and improve the conditions caused by the effects of violence, poverty, and racial injustice in such areas as Kenya, Central America, and rural Appalachia, and live with the Lakota Sioux, Navajo, and migrant workers. Iona students view helping to heal the world "one step at a time and two feet on the ground" as a central part of their education now and in the future.

Iona offers students a strong liberal arts foundation, supported by a core curriculum that includes study in the humanities, sciences, computing, reasoning, and problem solving and communication skills.

Iona students don't ignore the lively social and cultural scene in Manhattan, just a short train ride away with an abundance of museums, art exhibits, dance clubs, and Broadway.

This proximity to Manhattan means that Iona students receive rewarding and prestigious internships, including those at ABC, the Sundance Channel and SONY Pictures, American Express, Avon Products, MYV, Merrill Lynch, IBM, Coca-Cola, and MasterCard International.

JOHN CARROLL UNIVERSITY

University Heights, Ohio

Total Undergraduate Enrollment: 3,500
Men: 1,700 Women: 1,800
Five-Year Graduation Rate: 85%

Tuition: $$$
Room and Board: $$
Residential Students: 65%

History John Carroll University, a Catholic university, was founded as a Jesuit institution in 1886, called St. Ignatius College. In 1923 the college was renamed John Carroll University, after the first archbishop of the Catholic Church in the United States. In 1935 it was moved from its original location on the west side of Cleveland to its present site. In 1968 the university became coeducational. The university is listed on the Templeton Foundation's Honor Roll of Character-Building Colleges.

Location John Carroll is located in University Heights, a suburban area 10 miles east of Cleveland. The 60-acre campus is part of the Heights Area, a very attractive setting in northern Ohio, surrounded by the residential areas of Shaker Heights, Cleveland Heights, and University Heights.

Top Programs of Study Business, communication, psychology

Arts and Sciences Art history, biology, chemistry, communications, computer science, economics, engineering physics, (concentrations in computers and electrical engineering), English, French, German, Greek, history, humanities, Latin, mathematics, philosophy, physics, political science, psychology, religious studies, sociology, Spanish, world literature

Business Accounting, business logistics, economics, finance, management, marketing

Education Early childhood, exercise science, middle school, physical, secondary

Pre-Professional None

Accredited Programs Accounting, business, chemistry, education

Special Programs John Carroll offers a program in Italian-American Studies. The Business School uses advanced computer systems and software to create a "virtual corporation." The university has a greater than 75 percent acceptance rate into the law, medical, and dental schools. There are many opportunities for interdisciplinary study. The university's co-op program links students with positions in major corporations. There is an Army ROTC program.

Facilities There are 26 buildings, including the recently expanded Grasselli Library; the O'Malley Center for Communications and Language Arts, which houses television stations and a newsroom; Bruening Hall, which houses the business school; the Marinelli Theatre; and the new Bolan Center for Science and Technology. The university owns Thorn Acres, a 33-acre students' villa used for skiing, hiking, and swimming.

Transition to College Program All freshmen participate in a First-Year Seminar, with small classes and study built around a theme; students read the same books, thereby facilitating greater student–student connection. A First-Days Program also introduces students to the campus and Cleveland, which provides many cultural and entertainment opportunities. Also, three of the residence halls are freshmen only, giving students an opportunity to connect quickly within a group.

Athletics NCAA III, Ohio Athletic Conference

Men: Baseball, basketball, cross-country, diving, football, golf, indoor and outdoor track, swimming, tennis, wrestling

Women: Basketball, cross-country, diving, golf, soccer, softball, swimming, tennis, volleyball

Student Life and Housing About 2,000 students can be accommodated in campus housing. Seventy-five percent of the students are from Ohio, with the remainder from 34 other states and 21 countries. Ethnicity: Caucasian—89 percent; African-American—4 percent; Asian-American—3 percent; Hispanic-American—2 percent. There are six national sororities and eight national fraternities. Upperclassmen may keep cars.

Accommodations for Students with Disabilities Students should contact Services for Students with Disabilities at (216) 397-4967 and speak with the Coordinator. Information regarding disabilities is confidential and will not be used in making admissions decisions. Accommodations are arranged on an individual basis through the Coordinator of each semester. Documentation is the responsibility of the student.

Financial Aid About 95 percent of all freshmen receive aid. The average award was about $14,500.

Requirements for Admission Sat I or ACT scores and a college prep high school program.

Application There is a rolling admissions policy, with students receiving an admissions decision within four weeks of receiving a completed application.

International Students Students who officially reside in foreign countries and are not American citizens must submit official transcripts with notarized English translations. SAT I or ACT scores and TOEFL results are required. The affidavit of Support from U.S. Immigration and Naturalization service is required before any student visas will be issued.

Transfer Students Students must be in good academic and personal standing at the previous college. A 2.0 average from the most recent term is required, and a 2.5 GPA or higher is recommended.

Admission Contact
Office of Admissions
John Carroll University
20700 North Park Blvd.
University Heights, OH 44118
Phone: (216) 397-4294
FAX: (216) 397-4981
E-mail: *admission@jcu.edu*
Web: *www.jcu.edu/admiss*

The Heart of the University John Carroll offers students a stimulating climate, starting with its proximity to Cleveland, only 20 minutes away. The university mirrors the energy of this Renaissance city, home of the eleventh largest concentration of Fortune 500 companies, an entire family of major league sports teams, and more lake and shore than any metropolitan area in the world. As the only five-time winner of the All-American City Award, Cleveland is home to 80 ethnic groups, speaking 60 languages; eight museums; the Cleveland Playhouse; one of the largest zoos in America; the Flats, a 4,000- seat amphitheatre offering outdoor entertainment; and a half-mile boardwalk along the Cuyahoga River with more than 40 cafes, restaurants, and nightclubs.

Also impressive is the stimulating academic program offered by John Carroll, one of America's 28 Jesuit institutions. It is deeply rooted in the liberal arts and creates a close-knit community for learning and values development. In addition to studying an academic major, all students study an academic core of subjects aimed at developing critical thinkers, effective communicators, and students wanting to "live lives of greater service to God and to neighbor." This excellent academic program pushes and challenges students, helping them grow in a multitude of ways. Tim Russert, a John Carroll alumnus and now Senior Vice President of NBC News, writes: ". . . it is an education that says it is not enough to have a skill, not enough to have read all the books or know all the facts. It is an education that says values are what really matter."

Guiding this education is a stimulating faculty, including 24 Jesuits, who love to teach and make themselves available to students. It is a faculty that appreciates the importance of blending scholarship and teaching in order to create vibrant, stimulating courses. Some of these courses are clustered as interesting interdisciplinary concentrations, such as Aging Studies, which mixes sociology, psychology, and religious studies.

This stimulation can also be seen in its extensive study abroad opportunities, steady flow of guest speakers, and multitude of service opportunities.

JUNIATA COLLEGE Huntingdon, Pennsylvania

Total Undergraduate Enrollment: 1,345
Men: 560 Women: 785
Five-Year Graduation Rate: 74%

Tuition: $$$
Room and Board: $
Residential Students: 86%

History Juniata College was established in 1876 by members of the Church of the Brethren to prepare students "for the useful occupations of life." Juniata is a college of liberal arts and sciences. The name Juniata refers to the Juniata River that runs through the area.

Location The 1,167-acre rural campus is in Huntingdon, Pennsylvania (population 10,000), a small town 31 miles south of Penn State University, located in the scenic Central Pennsylvania mountains.

Top Programs of Study Biology, business, education

Arts and Sciences Anthropology, art, biochemistry, biology, botany, chemistry, communications, computer science, criminal justice, ecology, English, environmental science, environmental studies, exploratory studies, French, geology, German, health communication, history, information technology, interdisciplinary studies, international politics, international studies,

mathematics, microbiology, molecular and cell physiology, peace and conflict studies, physics, politics, psychology, public administration, religion, Russian, social work, sociology, Spanish, zoology

Business Accounting, business and information technology, economics, finance, human resource management, international business, management, management information systems, marketing

Education Early childhood, early childhood and special education, elementary, elementary and special education, secondary

Pre-Professional Chiropractic, dentistry, genetic counseling, health administration, law, medicine, ministry, optometry, physician's assistant, podiatry, veterinary medicine

Accredited Programs Chemistry, social work

Special Programs Juniata offers cooperative degree programs with 15 outstanding institutions in the areas of biotechnology, cardiovascular technology, cytotechnology, diagnostic imaging/radiology, medical technology, nursing, occupational therapy, physical therapy, and engineering. The college produces a high number of graduates who go on to earn doctoral degrees. It was selected as one of the most computer-wired colleges in America.

Facilities There are 42 buildings, including the new Liebeg Center for Science, a museum of art, an Olympic-size pool, an early childhood center, the 665-acre Raystown Environmental Studies Field Station, and a 316-acre nature preserve and peace chapel.

Transition to College Program The college uses a traditional orientation program.

Athletics NCAA III, Mid-Atlantic States Collegiate Athletic Conference

Men: Baseball, basketball, cross-country, football, soccer, tennis, track & field, volleyball

Women: Basketball, cheerleading, cross-country, field hockey, soccer, softball, swimming, tennis, track & field, volleyball

Student Life and Housing About 1,100 students can be accommodated in college housing, which is guaranteed for all four years. Seventy-six percent of the students are from Pennsylvania, the remainder from 36 other states and 22 countries. Ethnicity: Caucasian—92 percent. There are no fraternities or sororities. All students may keep cars.

Accommodations for Students with Disabilities Students with documented disabilities will be considered for reasonable accommodations upon request to the Dean of Students and/or the Director of Academic Support Services.

Financial Aid Almost all freshmen receive aid. The average freshman award was about $18,000.

Requirements for Admission SAT I or ACT scores and a college prep high school program. A campus visit is strongly recommended.

Application The Early Decision deadline is November 15 with notification no later than December 31. The regular admission deadline is March 15 with an admission decision within four weeks.

International Students Required are a complete set of original or notarized educational credentials with certified English translations, an affidavit of financial responsibilities, a minimum TOEFL paper score of 550 or 213 computer-based for non-English speaking students.

Transfer Students Applicants are considered transfer students if they have completed one full-time semester at a regionally accredited institution. An admission decision is given within one month upon receipt of all credentials, including official transcripts of high school and college work, a college catalogue, or course descriptions taken at the previous college. A minimum course grade of C is needed for transfer consideration. Students with an associate's degree are awarded junior status and a maximum of 60 credits.

Home-Schooled Students Students must be approved by their local district. They must submit an application for admission and include standardized test results, an application essay, one recommendation, and additional information to support their applications. Contact the Juniata Home School Coordinator in the Enrollment Center for more information.

Admission Contact
Office of Admissions
Juniata College
1700 Moore Street
Huntingdon, PA 16652
Phone: (877) JUNIATA
FAX: (814) 641-3100
E-mail: *admissions@juniata.edu*
Web: *www.juniata.edu*

The Heart of the College The heart of Juniata College is in the choices it offers that motivate students to do what liberal arts and sciences are supposed to do—encourage students to explore their interests in hopes that they may find a passion that will lead to a career, or graduate or professional school. At Juniata, students can combine interests into a degree that's all their own in the Program of Emphasis (POE). Similar to a traditional major, the POE enables students to prepare for a dream career and hone market-ready skills by graduation. The POE is what makes a Juniata education distinctive, because students are actively encouraged to design their own course of study or pair academic disciplines that interest them. About 40 percent of Juniata students follow one of the designated POEs, while the remaining 60 percent design their own. To ensure that students are on target for graduate school or a job, two advisers help students design their POEs. An example of a designated POE would be communication and conflict resolution, a pair of disciplines that have an apparent affinity for each other. An example of a student-designed POE would be social work and business management, disciplines that are paired, in this case, with a specific career path in mind.

At Juniata, students find professors who are challenging and supportive, who really care about student success, and who really love to teach. Every day they join students in shared research, in lab work, in theater rehearsals, and in front of computer screens. They are energetic and bring the best in current thinking on their subjects into the classroom. One professor, named Pennsylvania Professor of the Year, comments: "I want them [students] to know that learning is exciting."

A great emphasis is placed on internships and study abroad opportunities. About 88 percent of all students have at least one internship at sites ranging from Hershey Medical Center to state senators' offices, to Northwestern Mutual Life, to social service agencies. Another 30 percent travel overseas to study in 23 study abroad and student exchange programs, including Australia, China, France, Germany, Russia, and the United Kingdom.

Juniata's outcomes testify to the college's fine reputation. About 95 percent of Juniata applicants are accepted to dental, law, medical, optometry, and veterinary schools. Typically, 98 percent of the graduates are employed or attending graduate or professional school within six months of graduation.

As one student commented: "Anything you can dream of, you can do here."

KEENE STATE COLLEGE

Keene, New Hampshire

Total Undergraduate Enrolment: 4,114

Men: 1,710 Women: 2,404
Five-Year Graduation Rate: 51%

Tuition: In-state—$;
Out-of-state—$$
Room and Board: $
Residential Students: 56%

History Keene College was founded in 1909, became a Teachers College in 1939, and became Keene State College in 1963, part of the New Hampshire State College System.

Location Keene College is located on a 150-acre campus in Keene, New Hampshire (population 23,000), a few minutes from its lively and historic downtown. Nestled in the Ashuelot River Valley, Keene looks east toward Mount Monadnock and is two hours from Hartford, Connecticut, and Boston. There are many outdoor recreational activities.

Top Programs of Study Education, management, psychology

Arts and Sciences American studies, applied computer science, art (options in graphic design and studio art), biology, chemistry, chemistry/physics, communication, computer mathematics, economics, engineering, environmental studies, French, general science, geography, geology, health science, history, journalism, music, music performance, physical education (athletic training), physical science, psychology, safety studies, social science, sociology, Spanish, technology studies, theater, dance, and film

Business Management

Education Early childhood, elementary, elementary/special, middle school, physical education, secondary, vocational

Pre-Professional None

Accredited Programs Education, allied health education, music

Special Programs Students are able to design their own majors. There are two-year programs in applied computer science, chemical dependency, general studies, and technology studies. There are many opportunities for service learning and study abroad. The Children's Literature Festival brings to the campus distinguished authors and illustrators from around the world. Keene collaboratively operates a public elementary school, which serves as a laboratory school for Keene education students.

Facilities The 70 buildings are laid out in the style of a traditional New England college, with ivy covered buildings, grassy commons, and brick walkways. The buildings include an arboretum; the extensive facilities of the Redford Arts Center, with four theaters and two art galleries; a child development center; a mall business institute; a new sports fieldhouse; and a new residential complex. Keene also owns a 400-acre preserve.

Transition to College Program The Aspire Program provides advising, tutoring, study skills training, and career planning.

Athletics NCAA III, Little East Conference

   Men: Baseball, basketball, cross-country and track, lacrosse, swimming and diving

Women: Basketball, cross-country and track, field hockey, lacrosse, swimming and diving, volleyball

Student Life and Housing About 2,100 students live in campus housing. Fifty-eight percent of the students are from New Hampshire, the remainder are from 30 other states and 25 countries. Ethnicity: Caucasian—91 percent. There are three local and two national sororities, and two local and four national fraternities. Upperclassmen may keep cars.

Accommodations for Students with Disabilities The Office of Disability Services provides reasonable accommodations, academic adjustment, and/or auxiliary aids and services for students with appropriate documentation.

Financial Aid About 55 percent of all freshmen receive aid. The average freshman award was about $6,800.

Requirements for Admissions SAT I or ACT scores and a college prep high school program.

Application While Keene uses a rolling admissions policy, the college encourages applications by April 1 for the fall semester and December 1 for the spring semester.

International Students Official secondary and postsecondary academic records, with official English translations, a TOEFL score of at least 500, and documentation of financial support.

Transfer Students Required are official high school and college transcripts; SAT or ACT scores; a letter of recommendation from a faculty member, employer, or administrator; and the student must be in good standing. Shortly after admission, students will receive an official transfer evaluation of credits.

Admission Contact
Office of Admisions
Keene State College
229 Main Street
Keene, NH 03435-2604

Phone: (800) KSC-1909; (603) 358-2276
FAX: (603) 358-2767
E-mail: *admissions@keene.edu*
Web: *www.keene.edu/admissions*

The Heart of the College Keene State College represents an exception that constitutes the heart of the college. Often, state institutions are large, anonymous schools, with facilities in disrepair. Keene State is just the opposite. A populaton of about 4,000, students comment that the college is just the right size. With over 50 percent of the students residents, there are plenty of opportunities to develop close relationships within a caring community. The faculty represents a blend of scholarship and teaching and, in support of its mission statement, it offers time and attention to mentoring students. At Keene State the college asks students the question: "Who do you want to become?" It then helps students find their unique individual answers to the question and provides an education to realize their goals.

There are no graduate students teaching classes, only a talented faculty involved with research, writing, consulting, exhibiting, and performing. They place their greatest emphasis on every student succeeding academically. Learning, of course, isn't confined to the classroom, as campus life is rich in opportunities to be exposed to visiting novelists, poets, musicians, activists, and artists. And during the presidential campaign season, the New Hampshire Primary brings many presidential hopefuls to campus.

Unlike many state institutions, Keene is a beautiful, well-maintained campus. The campus arboretum, with its rich growth of trees, shrubs, and flowers is integrated into the natural flow of pedestrian traffic. In addition to academic and cultural state-of-the-art facilities, the athletic teams also enjoy some of the top facilities in the region. Located in the Monadnock Region, students are offered mountain climbing, skiing, canoeing, bicycling, water sports, golfing, and camping, all within a few miles of the campus.

Keene State offers a friendly New England community with excellent faculty, facilities, and a beautiful campus—a private college experience at a state school tuition.

KING'S COLLEGE   Wilkes-Barre, Pennsylvania

Total Undergraduate Enrollment: 1,800
Men: 900 Women: 900
Five-Year Graduation Rate: 71%

Tuition: $$$
Room and Board: $$$
Residential Students: 65%

History King's College is a Catholic college founded in 1946 by the Congregation of the Holy Cross and is part of a nationwide network of Holy Cross colleges and universities. King's has a philosophy of public service, of integrating research and teaching with Catholic ideals, and translating faith into action. The college has been listed on the Templeton Foundation's Honor Roll of Character-Building Colleges.

Location King's College is located on a 15-acre campus in a residential area near downtown Wilkes-Barre, Pennsylvania (population 50,000), two-and-a-half hours from New York City and two hours from Philadelphia. There are cultural and recreational opportunities, and several Pocono Mountain ski resorts within a 30-minute drive.

Top Programs of Study Elementary education, business administration, physician's assistant, criminal justice

Arts and Sciences Athletic training, biology, chemistry, computer science, computers and information systems, criminal justice, English, environmental studies, French, general science, history, human resource management, mathematics, media communications/media technologies, neurosciences, philosophy, physician's assistant, political science, psychology, sociology, Spanish, theater, theology

Business Accounting, administration, business, finance, economics, international business, marketing

Education Early childhood, elementary, secondary

Pre-Professional Dentistry, law, medical, optometry, pharmacy, veterinary medicine

Accredited Programs Athletic training, chemistry, physician's assistant

Special Programs King's has a cooperative program in special education and a B.S./M.S. physician's assistant program. There are many volunteer, study abroad, internship, and international internship programs available. King's has a four-year career advisement and placement process. Students in all majors learn how to make multimedia presentations. King's was selected as one of the nation's most computer-wired colleges. There are Air Force and Army ROTC programs.

Facilities There are 18 buildings, including an Olympic pool, a state-of-the-art sports medicine facility, the new Sheehy-Farmer Campus Center, new lab facilities for the physical and life sciences, and a sports medicine clinic.

Transition to College Program The First-Year Experience Seminar is taken in the first semester. Led by a faculty member and student assistants, students are introduced to college life and the King's college community. There is focus on intellectual development, service learning, career planning, and social issues, and students are required to attend at least four campus events during the semester.

Athletics NCAA III, Middle Atlantic Conference

Men: Baseball, basketball, cross-country, football, golf, lacrosse, rifle, soccer, swimming, tennis, wrestling

Women: Basketball, cross-country, field hockey, lacrosse, rifle, soccer, softball, swimming, tennis, volleyball

Student Life and Housing About 1,200 students can be accommodated in college housing, which is guaranteed for all four years. Seventy-two percent of the students are from Pennsylvania, the remainder are from 16 other states and 14 countries. Ethnicity: Caucasian—93 percent. There are no fraternities or sororities. All students may keep cars.

Accommodations for Students with Disabilities The First-Year Academic Studies Program enrolls students in regular core classes, but supports each class with a structured, supplementary program of course-specific learning strategies.

Financial Aid About 85 percent of all freshmen receive aid. The average award was about $13,000.

Requirements for Admission SAT I or ACT scores and a college prep high school program.

Application The college uses a rolling admissions procedure, with March 1 the preferred application deadline. Admission decisions are made two to four weeks after receiving completed applications.

International Students The SAT or TOEFL scores are required along with evidence of financial support. Official copies of secondary and/or college records are required.

Transfer Students A maximum of 60 credits can be transferred, but no more than 50 percent of major requirements. Evaluation is made on a course-by-course basis, not by degree, and a minimum C grade is required.

Admission Contact
Office of Admissions
King's College
133 North River Street
Wilkes-Barre, PA 18711
Phone: (800) KING'S PA; (570) 208-5858

FAX: (570) 208-5971
E-mail: *admissions@kings.edu*
Web: *www.kings.edu*

The Heart of the College King's College is an urban college set on only 15 acres. This size lends itself to the friendly community that attracts students and helps them succeed. Located in one of the safest cities in America, many students comment on the "family" feeling at King's, where everyone knows one another. Students succeed because everyone at King's—the librarians, the coaches, student life staff, counselors, campus ministers, as well as faculty—view themselves as part of the teaching community. This is a real student-centered approach where faculty are not only scholars, researchers, and teachers, but also mentors, nurturers, and advisers. Only faculty teach courses at King's; there are no teaching assistants. Faculty members assist in arranging internship opportunities as well as involving students in collaborative research. There is also an active Office of Multicultural and International Affairs.

Students are often surprised to find that King's has facilities and equipment found at larger schools, as well as the opportunity to do research on a higher level. Technology is incorporated into all classes, with all students learning to make multimedia presentations. King's is also rated as one of the most computer-wired colleges in America.

Students study a broad-based liberal education in the Catholic tradition, which includes a core curriculum and a major area of study. The strong academic program is complemented with many opportunities for meaningful community service as well as a very active advisement and career development program. Students intern locally, nationally, and internationally, including with IBM, BMW, Nabisco Foods Group, ABC, Calvin Klein, the Department of Energy, AIB Investment Managers, and Canadian Broadcasting Corporation.

King's College's success can be gauged by the fact that 99 percent of its graduates are employed in their fields or go on to graduate and professional schools within six months of graduation. The pre-law program, during the past several years, has placed 100 percent of its students in law schools such as Boston College, Columbia, Fordham, and the University of Notre Dame. The pre-health program has placed graduates at Albert Einstein Medical College, Georgetown, and Dartmouth Medical School.

LAKE FOREST COLLEGE   Lake Forest, Illinois

Total Undergraduate Enrollment: 1,300
Men: 545 Women: 755
Five-Year Graduation Rate: 65%

Tuition: $$$$
Room and Board: $$
Residential Students: 84%

History Lake Forest College was founded in 1857 as Lind University by a group of Presbyterians who founded the town of Lake Forest in 1861. The institution grew to include a coeducational undergraduate college as well as graduate schools of medicine and dentistry and law. Eventually the graduate schools were disassociated from the university, with full attention devoted to its undergraduate college. Accordingly, the institution was renamed Lake Forest College in 1965 and maintains an affiliation with the Presbyterian Church.

Location The 107-acre wooded campus is located in a suburb of Lake Forest, Illinois (population 18,000), about 30 miles north of Chicago.

Top Programs of Study Business/economics, education, English, psychology

Arts and Sciences African-American studies, American studies, area studies, art (history, studio), Asian studies, biology, business, chemistry, classical studies, communication, computer science, English (literature, writing), environmental studies, Chinese language and literature, French language and literature, German language and literature, Italian language and literature, Japanese language and literature, Portuguese language and literature, Russian language and literature, Spanish language and literature, history, international relations, Latin American studies, mathematics, metropolitan studies, music, philosophy, physics, politics, psychology, religion, sociology and anthropology, theater, women's and gender studies

Business Business, economics

Education Elementary, middle/junior high, primary, secondary

Pre-Professional Dentistry, law, medicine, veterinary medicine

Accredited Programs None

Special Programs There is a dual degree program in engineering with Washington University in St. Louis. Lake Forest students are able to cross-register at nearby Barat College for additional coursework in dance, ceramics, and photography. There is a Washington, D.C., semester, a Chicago Arts immersion semester, an Oak Ridge Science semester near Knoxville, Tennessee, and an Urban Education program that offers students a multicultural experience in a variety of Chicago schools. There are numerous study abroad programs. Students can design their own majors.

Facilities There are 30 buildings, including Hixon Hall, which houses the Allan Carr Theater; an indoor ice rink; the Johnson Science Center; a student commons; the Durand Art Institute; a radio station; and an electronic music studio.

Transition to College Program Students take a course in freshman studies, small classes devoted to interesting topics such as "The Nature of Mathematics," "Music in Chicago," and "Civil Disobedience and Political Obligation" that encourage discussion and interaction. The courses stress critical thinking and writing, along with the development of good work habits and academic skills.

Athletics NCAA III, Midwest Conference; Northern Collegiate Hockey Conference

Men: Basketball, cross-country, football, handball, ice hockey, soccer, swimming and diving, tennis

Women: Basketball, cross-country, handball, ice hockey, soccer, softball, swimming and diving, tennis, volleyball

Student Life and Housing About 1,200 students can be accommodated in college housing, which is guaranteed for all four years. Forty-three percent of the students are from Illinois, with the majority from 44 other states and 42 countries. Ethnicity: Caucasian—80 percent; International—8 percent; African-American—5 percent; Asian-American—4 percent; Hispanic-American—3 percent. There are two local fraternities and one national fraternity, and three local sororities and one national sorority. Upperclassmen may keep cars.

Accommodations for Students with Disabilities In compliance with section 504

Financial Aid About 88 percent of all freshmen receive aid. The average freshman award was about $19,000.

Requirements for Admission SAT I or ACT scores and a college prep high school program. A personal interview is an important part of the admission process.

Application There is an Early Notification Program whereby students who apply by December 1 receive an admission decision by December 20. The Early Decision deadline is January 1, with students receiving an admissions decision about three weeks after all required materials are received. Regular application deadlines are March 1 for the fall and December 15 for the spring semester, with review beginning January 15. Students are notified by the end of March.

International Students Applicants must adhere to the regular admission requirements for freshmen and transfer students. In addition, a minimum TOEFL paper score of 500 or 220 computer-based is required.

Transfer Students Applicants must have an overall GPA of at least 2.0 and be in good academic standing at the previous college. Grades of C− and better are accepted with a maximum of 60 credits transferable. Graduates of accredited community colleges and holders of associate degrees will be granted full junior standing. Official secondary and college transcripts are required.

Admission Contact
Office of Admissions
Lake Forest College
555 North Sheridan Road
Lake Forest, IL 60045-2399
Phone: (800) 828-4751; (847) 735-5000
FAX: (847) 735-6271
E-mail: *admissions@lfc.edu*
Web: *www.lakeforest.edu*

The Heart of the College The college is a beautiful tree-lined residential campus, a 10-minute walk to Lake Michigan and its broad beachfront, and a short train ride into Chicago, the third largest city in the nation. The typical student comment is: "There's no place I would rather be." Who can doubt this, with the beachfront inviting biking, barbeques, volleyball, jogging, sailing, and swimming during warmer months. The city of Chicago complements the weekly roster of cultural and social events on campus with professional sports, recreation, and cultural activities. This close proximity to Chicago and the abundant beauty of Lake Forest's location is certainly one of the major reasons students are attracted to Lake Forest College.

The distinguished faculty, 98 percent of whom hold doctorates, use Chicago as a second campus: business classes observe the activities of the Chicago Board of Trade and Mercantile

Exchange; political science students visit housing projects to explore the concerns of tenants; and theater classes attend the Chicago Shakespeare Company. The city is simply an extension of the student's education, with professors incorporating the many dimensions of urban metropolitan life into the curriculum. This is really important at Lake Forest because teaching quality and advisement offered to students are the most important criteria for faculty tenure! Even with this high standard, faculty still conduct scholarly research, write books, and deliver papers, with many faculty involving students in their research and attendance at conferences.

As a liberal arts college—or, as Lake Forest refers to these—"the liberating arts" provide the focal point of study. Graduates who represent the educational ideal of the college are students who have studied a broad range of ideas, are competent readers, writers, speakers; possess mathematical skills; have studied in the humanities, natural sciences, social sciences; and have studied a major in depth. For Lake Forest College, this "liberating arts" education, along with study in cultural diversity and links to internships, provides full access to sophisticated facilities and laboratories and represents the best education for life and career. Also, students clearly see the importance of experiential learning as a major asset to their education; 80 percent of Lake Forest students are involved in study abroad, internships, off-campus programs, and research.

The internship opportunities in Chicago are many, interesting, and valuable. Examples include editorial assistant, brokerage house researcher, media planner, international research and program assistant, theater crew member, public relations person, and creative design assistant. Graduates' jobs are even more interesting, from author to senior field producer at CNN, to Managing Director of Morgan Stanley & Company. David Mathis, Chairman and CEO of Kemper Insurance says: "My years at Lake Forest provided me with a foundation to succeed. I now enjoy giving back to this special community that helped shape my life."

LA SALLE UNIVERSITY

Philadelphia, Pennsylvania

Total Undergraduate Enrollment: 3,300
Men: 1,419 Women: 1,881
Five-Year Graduation Rate: 69%

Tuition: $$$
Room and Board: $$$
Residential Students: 53%

History La Salle University, established in 1863, is named for the French educator and founder of the Christian Brothers, John Baptist de La Salle. As a Catholic university, the school's focus is not only on devotion to excellence in teaching, but also on ultimate values and the individual values of it students.

Location The 100-acre park-like campus is located eight miles northwest of the center of Philadelphia, Pennsylvania, a major city offering many cultural, entertainment, and recreational opportunities.

Top Programs of Study Communication, business, elementary and special education

Arts and Sciences American studies, art history, biochemistry, biology, chemistry, classical languages, communication, computer science, criminal justice, digital arts and multimedia design, economics, economics and international studies, English, environmental science (concentrations in biology, chemistry, geology), French, German, history, information technology, integrated science, Italian, business and technology, mathematics, music history, nursing, nutrition, philosophy, political science, psychology, public administration, religion, Russian social work, sociology, Spanish speech-language-hearing science

Business Accounting, finance, management, management information systems, marketing

Education Elementary, secondary, special

Pre-Professional Dentistry, law, medicine, veterinary medicine

Accredited Programs Chemistry, education, management, nursing, social work

Special Programs The following programs are offered in affiliation with Thomas Jefferson University: medical technology, occupational therapy, and physical therapy. There is cross-registration with Chestnut Hill College. There are Air Force and Army ROTC programs.

Facilities There are 56 buildings, a blend of old and new, including the La Salle University Art Museum, with a permanent collection of Western art from the Renaissance to present times; the Connelly Library, with seating for 1,000; science equipment, which includes scanning electron microscopes; a newly renovated gymnasium; modern residence halls; an art gallery; and television and radio stations.

Transition to College Program The First-Year Odyssey, a one credit course, creates a community in which students can form bonds with fellow students and professors, introduces students to university resources and traditions, helps students feel at home in Philadelphia, and helps students enjoy the rich offerings of urban life, in terms of art, music, ethnic traditions, etc. In most cases, course instructors are faculty members, with the courses organized around a specific theme or "essential question," such as "What Is Community?"

Athletics NCAA I, Atlantic 10 Conference

Men: Baseball, basketball, crew, cross-country, football, golf, soccer, swimming and diving, tennis, track & field

Women: Basketball, crew, cross-country, field hockey, lacrosse, soccer, softball, swimming and diving, tennis, track & field, volleyball

Student Life and Housing About 2,000 students can be accommodated in college housing, which is guaranteed for all four years. Sixty-eight percent of the students are from Pennsylvania, the remainder are from 36 other states and 23 countries. Ethnicity: Caucasian—81 percent; African-American—11 percent; Hispanic-American—5 percent; Asian-American—3 percent. There are two local and six national fraternities, and one local and four national sororities. All students may keep cars.

Accommodations for Students with Disabilities
In compliance with section 504

Financial Aid
About 95 percent of all freshmen receive aid. The average freshman award was about $20,000.

Requirements for Admission
ACT or SAT I scores and a college prep high school program. A campus visit is strongly recommended.

Application
Freshmen are admitted fall and spring semesters. Regular admission deadlines are April 1 for fall admission and December 15 for spring admission. Admission notification is on a rolling basis.

International Students
Required are official transcripts from secondary school and any postsecondary institutions, scores from all applicable state examinations, minimum TOEFL scores of 500 paper-based and 173 computer-based, an academic recommendation, and financial certification.

Transfer Students
Required are official high school and college transcripts, SAT I or ACT scores, a letter of recommendation from a teacher or counselor, and indication that the student is in good academic standing. Students should have an overall 2.7 GPA, and courses with a minimum of a C grade will be considered for transfer. Normally, 70 credits is the maximum number of credits accepted for transfer.

Admission Contact
Office of Admissions
La Salle University
190 W. Olney Avenue
Philadelphia, PA 19141
Phone: (800) 328-1910; (215) 951-1500
FAX: (215) 951-1656
E-mail: *admiss@lasalle.edu*
Web: *www.lasalle.edu*

The Heart of the University The heart of this Catholic university resides in what the Christian Brothers community brings to it: an insistence on treating every single person with respect; a quest for excellence; a devotion to teaching; and the commitment to take care of the community. This all makes for a caring, supportive community where professors are really interested in students. "Late Night Breakfast" typifies the community spirit, when student affairs professionals whip up breakfast—everything from omelets to waffles—for students and players after a basketball game.

"Branch Out Day" also typifies the university's focus on service to the community. Every fall nearly 1,000 members of the La Salle community spend a day serving over 30 sites in the greater Philadelphia area, with projects ranging from planting flowers to visiting nursing homes.

Now just imagine attending college in the nation's fifth largest city! There are quality internships galore, with nearly every major at La Salle offering one to help test classroom theories in the real world while developing a more significant résumé. Interesting internships are offered with the Philadelphia District Attorney's Office, the *Philadelphia Magazine*, and the Philadelphia Eagles.

Philadelphia is a college student's dream: a lively college town, incredible sports mecca, and a cultural haven. La Salle frequently sponsors trips downtown, with public transportation only two blocks from campus. Whatever season, students have some team to cheer for: the baseball Phillies, the basketball 76ers, the football Eagles, the hockey Flyers, and college Big 5 basketball. Students more interested in culture have a city filled with museums and theaters.

La Salle's outcomes demonstrate the excellence of its education. Recently, the nursing graduates had the highest pass rate in Pennsylvania on the licensing exam. The School of Business had a 100 percent job placement rate for three consecutive years. The medical school acceptance rate is 100 percent for those applicants recommended by La Salle.

LEBANON VALLEY COLLEGE

Annville, Pennsylvania

Total Undergraduate Enrollment: 1,879
Men: 773 Women: 1,106
Five-Year Graduation Rate: 65%

Tuition: $$$
Room and Board: $$
Residential Students: 74%

History Lebanon Valley College was founded in 1866 on the site of the Annville Academy. It became a four-year institution by 1883 as the lower grades were phased out. The college has a historical relationship with the United Methodist Church.

Location The 200-acre campus is in Annville, Pennsylvania, a small town seven miles east of Hershey, in the heart of the Pennsylvania Dutch countryside two hours from Baltimore and Philadelphia.

Top Programs of Study Business, education, social sciences

Arts and Sciences Actuarial science, American studies, biochemistry, biology, chemistry, computer science, digital communications, economics, English, French, German, health care management, historical communications, history, mathematics, medical technology, music, music business, music recording technology, philosophy, physical therapy, physics, political science, psychobiology, psychology, religion, sociology, Spanish

Business Accounting, administration

Education Elementary, music, secondary, special

Pre-Professional Dentistry, law, medicine, ministry, veterinary medicine

Accredited Programs Chemistry, music

Special Programs The college has several cooperative degree programs: allied health professions with Thomas Jefferson University in Philadelphia; engineering with Penn State, Case Western Reserve, University of Pennsylvania, and Widener University; forestry and environmental studies with Duke; medical technology with a CAHEA approved hos-

pital. There are individualized majors and several study abroad programs. There is an Army ROTC.

Facilities There are 33 buildings, with almost two-thirds of the campus renovated over the past few years, including the state-of-the-art Bishop Library, part of the Arnold Sport Center, new suites and gymnasium, the Arnold Art Gallery, and greenhouses. The academic buildings cluster around a beautiful tree-lined quad.

Transition to College Program The college uses a traditional orientation program.

Athletics NCAA III, Middle Atlantic Conference

Men: Baseball, basketball, cross-country, football, golf, ice hockey, soccer, swimming, tennis, track & field

Women: Basketball, cross-country, field hockey, soccer, softball, swimming, tennis, track & field, volleyball

Student Life and Housing About 1,000 students can be accommodated in campus housing, which is guaranteed for all four years. Seventy-nine percent of the students are from Pennsylvania, the remainder are from 24 other states and 26 countries. Ethnicity: Caucasian—92 percent. There are two local and two national fraternities, and one local and three national sororities.

Accommodations for Students with Disabilities In compliance with section 504

Financial Aid About 98 percent of all freshmen receive aid. The average freshman award was about $16,000.

Requirements for Admission SAT I or ACT results and a college prep high school program. A campus visit and interview are strongly recommended.

Application Freshmen are admitted fall and spring semesters. Application deadlines are open, with a priority deadline of March 15. Admission notification is sent on a rolling basis beginning October 15.

International Students Students whose primary language is not English must score a minimum of 550 on the paper-based TOEFL. Students must also take either the SAT I or ACT.

Transfer Students Required are an official transcript of previous college work. C grades or higher are considered for transfer. Associate degree holders can transfer up to 60 credits.

Admission Contact
Office of Admissions
Lebanon Valley College
101 North College Avenue
Annville, PA 17003-1400
Phone: (866) LVC-4ADM; (717) 867-6181
FAX: (717) 857-6026
E-mail: *admission@lvc.edu*
Web: *www.lvc.edu*

The Heart of the College Lebanon Valley College is a small college that helps students to achieve great things. One only has to look at the graduation rate, which places the school in the top 3 percent in the nation, to recognize that Lebanon Valley College does many things well. The heart of the college is the "family" climate created by down-to-earth, practical, career-focused students. This is a friendly campus, where close relationships are formed. Augmenting this "family" climate is a faculty that puts students first, listens, is genuinely concerned, and takes extraordinary steps to assist students. The faculty offers an outstanding academic experience, setting high standards and teaching in small classes. Professors

make sure that a Lebanon Valley education is both interactive and unique, whether it's an English professor leading a class in a full period costume as she plays the role of a character students are reading about, or having e-marketing students develop web sites for real companies.

Humanities and social science students have an outstanding range of internships, with many having gone on to some of the country's most prestigious law schools, including Harvard, University of Chicago, Stanford, and William and Mary. The science program offers facilities and research opportunities typically afforded to graduate students. The outstanding science program graduates students to top medical, dental, or other professional schools, as well as to work in industry for Du Pont, Exxon, Pfizer, and Lockheed Martin. The music program is among the strongest offered by any small liberal arts college, with many performance opportunities offered with both small and large ensembles. Business students have excellent internship opportunities and have gone on to work with Big Five accounting firms, manufacturing companies, and small businesses. The success of the Lebanon Valley graduates is in part due to the college's on-line Career Connection Program, which allows students to network with hundreds of alumni.

The college's "family" climate is enhanced by its high level of student participation in sports, clubs, and activities. Lebanon Valley is one of the strongest schools in NCAA Division III with about 40 percent of the students participating and about 70 percent participating in intramurals on superb athletic facilities.

The college offers a simple and generous scholarship program: If students rank in the top 10 percent of their graduating classes, they receive awards worth one-half of tuition; if students rank in the top 20 percent of their classes, they receive awards worth one-third the cost of tuition.

LE MOYNE COLLEGE   Syracuse, New York

Total Undergraduate Enrollment: 2,100
Men: 850 Women: 1,250
Five-Year Graduation Rate: 76%

Tuition: $$$
Room and Board: $$$
Residential Students: 69%

History Le Moyne College was founded in 1946 and is a Catholic college in the Jesuit tradition. Le Moyne is the first Jesuit college in the world to open as a coeducational institution. The Jesuits stress academic excellence, preparation for life in the professions and workplace, education of the whole person, and service to others.

Location Le Moyne's 150-acre campus is in a suburban area on the eastern edge of Syracuse, New York, home to many colleges and many cultural, social, and recreational opportunities.

Top Programs of Study Business, psychology, English

Arts and Sciences Actuarial science, anthropology, biochemistry, biology, chemistry, communications, creative writing, criminal justice, criminology, drama, economics, English, fine arts, French, history, human resource management, human services, international studies, Japanese, Latin, Latin American studies, literature, management information systems, mathematics, multiple science, philosophy, political science, psychology, public policy, religious studies, sociology, Spanish

Business Accounting, finance, industrial relations, labor management relations, marketing, operations management, operations research, organizations and management, organizational training and development

Education Elementary, secondary, special, teaching English to speakers of other languages (TESOL)

Pre-Professional Dentistry, medicine, optometry, physical therapy, physician's assistant, podiatry

Accredited Programs None

Special Programs Le Moyne has cooperative degree programs in environmental science and forestry with the State University of New York College of Environmental Science and Forestry at Syracuse University; engineering with Clarkson; cytotechnology, medical technology, respiratory care, physical therapy, physician's assistant with the State University of New York Health Care Center at Syracuse; optometry with Pennsylvania College of Optometry; dentistry with SUNY Buffalo; and podiatry with New York College. There are Early Assurance Programs in dentistry and medicine with SUNY Buffalo. There are many internship, study abroad, and social ministry opportunities.

Facilities There are 31 buildings, including the Coyne Science Center, the beautiful Panasci Family Chapel, the Heninger Athletic Center, a new Performing Arts Center, an expanded dining facility, new labs, an art gallery, and a radio station.

Transition to College Program The First-Year Advisement Program provides specially selected faculty advisers to students and meets in a weekly "common hour" to assist students in adjusting to college and social life.

Athletics NCAA II, Northeast 10 Conference

Men: Baseball (Div. I MAAC), basketball, cross-country, golf, lacrosse, soccer, swimming and diving, tennis

Women: Basketball, cross-country, lacrosse, (Div. I MAAC), soccer, softball, swimming and diving, tennis, volleyball

Student Life and Housing About 1,400 students can be accommodated in college housing, which is guaranteed for all four years. Ninety-three percent of the students are from New York, with the remainder from 24 other states and 12 countries. Ethnicity: Caucasian—86 percent; African-American—4 percent; Hispanic-American—3 percent; Asian-American—1 percent. There are no fraternities or sororities. All students may keep cars.

Accommodations for Students with Disabilities Students must contact the Director of the Academic Support Center as soon as possible to ensure that accommodations can be made in a timely manner. Written documentation of disability is required.

Financial Aid About 80 percent of all freshmen receive aid. The average freshman award was about $9,000.

Requirements for Admission SAT I or ACT scores and a college prep high school program. An interview is encouraged.

Application The Early Decision application deadline is December 1 with an admission decision made by December 15. Regular applications are received on a rolling basis, with March 1 a priority deadline for the fall and December 1 for the spring semester.

International Students SAT I or ACT scores and a minimum TOEFL score of 550 are required, along with official school records and a statement of financial ability.

Transfer Students Official high school and college transcripts, a recommendation from a dean, academic adviser, or transfer counselor from the last college attended, and a personal statement are required. If students have taken fewer than 10 college courses, SAT I or ACT scores are required. A maximum of 60 credits from a two-year college and 90 credits from a four-year college can be accepted with grades of C− or higher. Transfer credit is based on a course-by-course evaluation.

Admission Contact
Office of Admissions
Le Moyne College
1419 Salt Springs Road
Syracuse, NY 13214-1399

Phone: (800) 333-4733 (ext. 4300); (315) 445-4300
FAX: (315) 445-4711
E-mail: *admission@lemoyne.edu*
Web: *www.lemoyne.edu*

The Heart of the College As a Catholic college with a Jesuit intellectual and religious tradition, students experience the importance placed upon academic excellence, education of the whole person, the development of a concern for others, and an emphasis on ethics and values. Jesuits believe in the lifelong benefits of a comprehensive liberal arts tradition, and at Le Moyne there are 12 courses taken by all students that form a humanities-based core curriculum. What distinguishes the Le Moyne program is that every course is infused with a values approach. This translates to a campus where society's moral and ethical issues are part of the fabric of life. The intent is to help students to clarify their own values as they relate to the discussed issues and to instill in them the courage to act on their beliefs in real-life situations

Classes are small and taught by a talented faculty who, although active scholars, are professors that love to teach and put students first. All courses are taught by Le Moyne faculty, never by graduate students. This is an enthusiastic faculty that also provides academic advisement for their students. Students get plenty of personal attention. Add all this up and you get a very strong community, strengthened by an almost 70 percent student residential population.

Students are enjoying the new Performance Arts Center as well as the more than 60 science research laboratories, which include electron microscopes and a nuclear resonance spectrometer.

Le Moyne provides many volunteer and service opportunities, as well as internship opportunities at IBM, Anheuser-Bush, Mobil Oil, Lockheed Martin, Carrier, Blue Cross-Blue Shield, and Farmers and Traders Life Insurance. The college is also part of a Communications Consortium (along with Cornell, Colgate, Ithaca, and Syracuse) that provides employers such as ESPN and CBS with access to a talented pool of communications graduates.

LENOIR-RHYNE COLLEGE
Hickory, North Carolina

Total Undergraduate Enrollment: 1,350
Men: 553 Women: 797
Five-Year Graduation Rate: 59%

Tuition: $$
Room and Board: $
Residential Students: 65%

History Lenoir-Rhyne College, established in 1891, is affiliated with the Evangelical Lutheran Church. Originally organized to train teachers, ministers, and offer a religious-oriented education to all youth, the college subsequently became a liberal arts school and then added major fields related to careers. The college is named for Captain Lenoir who donated the land and Daniel Rhyne, an industrialist who provided money for the college's endowment. The college is listed on the Templeton Foundation's Honor Roll of Character-Building Colleges.

Location The 100-acre campus is located in Hickory, North Carolina (population 36,000), nestled in the foothills of the Blue Ridge Mountains 45 miles northwest of Charlotte.

Top Programs of Study Education, business nursing

Arts and Sciences Biology, chemistry, communication, computer information systems, computer science, economics, French, German, health and exercise science, history, human and community services, medical technology, music, music performance, nursing, occupational therapy, philosophy, physician's assistant, political science, premedical service, psychology, religious studies-outdoor personal and spiritual development, religious studies-family development, sacred music, sociology, Spanish, sports management, sports medicine, theater-English, theology and philosophy

Business Accounting, finance, international business, management, management information systems, marketing

Education Art, business, deaf and hard-of-hearing, early childhood, elementary, middle, music, physical education, theater

Pre-Professional Engineering, forestry/environmental management, law, medicine

Accredited Programs Business, education, nursing, occupational therapy, sports/athletic training

Special Programs Dual degree programs are offered in the following fields: engineering with North Carolina AT&T, North Carolina State University, and the University of North Carolina at Charlotte; medical technology with an approved medical technology school; physician's assistant with an accredited program; environmental management (forestry) with Duke. There are several study abroad programs.

Facilities There are 30 buildings, including a new admissions building; a new living–learning center; and the McCrorie Center, designed to offer the most technologically advanced learning environment for students in the health sciences, including nursing, occupational therapy, and sports medicine.

Transition to College Program The college uses a traditional orientation program.

Athletics NCAA II, South Atlantic Conference

Men: Baseball, basketball, cross-country, football, golf, soccer

Women: Basketball, cross-country, golf, soccer, softball, volleyball

Student Life and Housing About 900 students can be accommodated in college housing. Seventy percent of the students are from North Carolina, the remainder are from 29 other states and 10 countries. Ethnicity: Caucasian—87 percent; African-American—8 percent, Asian-American—2 percent; Hispanic-American—1 percent. There are three national fraternities and four national sororities. All students may keep cars.

Accommodations for Students with Disabilities The college provides comprehensive services. Students must provide appropriate documentation and request disability-related modifications in courses and other college programs from the Disability Services Office.

Financial Aid About 95 percent of all freshmen receive aid. The average freshman award was about $10,500.

Requirements for Admission SAT or ACT scores and a college prep high school program. Students who plan to major in nursing must have completed a chemistry course.

Application Freshmen are admitted to all sessions. There are no application deadlines, and students are sent admission decisions on rolling basis.

International Students Required are official transcripts that have been evaluated and translated into English; TOEFL, SAT or ACT scores; and a completed certificate of finance certified by a bank official, attorney, or notary public. Students should follow guidelines for either freshman or transfer students depending on their enrollment status.

Transfer Students Students must be in good standing at previous colleges. New students are admitted fall, spring, and summer semesters. Official college transcripts are required. An official high school transcript and either an SAT or ACT score is required if the applicant has completed fewer than 30 credits. C graded courses or higher are considered for transfer from a regionally accredited college. Students may transfer a maximum of 64 credits from a two-year institution. The last 32 credits must be completed at Lenoir-Rhyne.

Home-Schooled Students Students are welcome to apply using regular freshman admission criteria.

Admission Contact
Office of Admissions
Lenoir-Rhyne College
P.O. Box 7227
Hickory, NC 28603
Phone: (800) 277-5721; (828) 328-7300
FAX: (828) 328-7378
E-mail: *admission@lrc.edu*
Web: *www.lrc.edu*

The Heart of the College Lenoir-Rhyne provides students with an edge that is supported by research findings about Lutheran colleges conducted by the national higher education consulting firm Hardwick-Day, Inc., of Minneapolis. Graduates reported that they felt much better prepared for their careers than those who attended large public universities, and graduates felt good about their abilities in speaking effectively, working as part of a team, writing effectively, and being leaders. The college's blend of liberal arts and professional studies certainly helps to provide these positive outcomes. Add a talented, supportive faculty, and Lenoir-Rhyne students are positioned for success. One faculty member comments: "I get to know all my students. I know who their friends are. I have met most of their families. I know what their career goals are and, together, we plan what courses they will take to achieve their goals." This is the heart of a Lenoir-Rhyne education, where all members of the college community attempt to teach the "whole" student, providing learning experiences for all aspects of the student's life. As a Christian community, the spiritual dimension of a student is well tended to with a variety of Christian clubs, chapel services, retreats, daily communion, and small group fellowships.

The town of Hickory is another important ingredient of a Lenoir-Rhyne education. The college and town have a warm, supportive relationship. Hickory is a lively town providing cultural centers, theaters, shops, and old-fashioned sidewalks. Hickory is an important provider of internships as well. A safe and hospitable community, many Lenoir-Rhyne graduates decide to make Hickory and its surrounding area their home.

Often cited as a "best buy" in college education, Lenoir-Rhyne's successful graduates help prove the point. Ninety-five percent of applicants to dental, optometry, physician's assistant, forestry, and medical technology schools are accepted; 85 percent of applicants to law school are admitted; 80 percent who apply to medical school are admitted. Also, nursing graduates consistently score near the top on state board licensing exams.

LINFIELD COLLEGE McMinnville, Oregon

Total Undergraduate Enrollment: 1,599
Men: 704 Women: 895
Five-Year Graduation Rate: 65%

Tuition: $$$
Room and Board: $$
Residential Students: 76%

History Linfield College, established in 1849, is one of the oldest colleges in the Pacific Northwest. Originally established by the Baptists as the Baptist College in McMinnville, it was later named for Frances Ross Linfield, who gifted property to the college.

Location The 193-acre campus is located in McMinnville, Oregon (population 25,000), a small city 40 miles west of Portland in the Willamette Valley.

Top Programs of Study Business, elementary education, communications

Arts and Sciences American studies, anthropology, applied physics, art, art history, Asian studies, athletic training, biology, chemistry, coaching, communication arts, computer science, creative writing, economics, English, environmental studies, European studies, exercise science, French, gender studies, general science, German, health sciences (Portland campus), Japanese, Latin American studies, mathematics, music, nursing (Portland campus), philosophy, physics, political science, psychology, religious studies, sociology, Spanish, theater arts

Business Accounting, finance, international business

Education Elementary, health, physical education, secondary

Pre-Professional Dentistry, engineering, law, medicine, occupational therapy, optometry, pharmacy, physical therapy, veterinary medicine

Accredited Programs Education, music

Special Programs There is a cooperative degree program in engineering (3-2) with Oregon State University, the University of Southern California, and Washington State University. There is an on-campus preschool and The Linfield Research Institute. The college has a significant study abroad program.

Facilities There are 67 buildings spanning over a century, including Graf Hall and Murdock Hall, which house the science facilities; Taylor Hall, a computer center; a Health and Physical Education/Recreation Complex; the new Miller Fine Arts Center; art galleries; dance and music studios; a theater; and a radio station. Also, there are plans for a new library, theater, and communication arts facility.

Transition to College Program Linfield offers a traditional orientation program.

Athletics NCAA III, Northwest Conference

Men: Baseball, basketball, cross-country, football, golf, soccer, swimming, tennis, track & field

Women: Basketball, cross-country, golf, lacrosse, soccer, softball, swimming, tennis, track & field, volleyball

Student Life and Housing About 1,250 students can be accommodated in college housing. Fifty-seven percent of the students are from Oregon; the remainder are from 33 other states and 25 countries. Ethnicity: Caucasian—79 percent; Asian-American—6 percent; Hispanic—3 percent; African-American—2 percent; International—2 percent. There are one local and three national sororities, and one local and three national fraternities. All students may keep cars.

Accommodations for Students with Disabilities Students with a documented disability requiring classroom accommodation must register with the Director of Learning Support Services.

Financial Aid Almost all freshmen receive aid. The average freshman award was about $17,700.

Requirements for Admission SAT I or ACT scores and a college prep high school program.

Application The Early Action deadline is November 15 with an admission decision by January 15. The deadline for regular admission applications is February 15, with admission decision decisions by April 1.

International Students The priority deadline for the fall is March 1, and December 1 for the spring semester. Required are certified copies of academic records, letters of recommendation with certified English translations. TOEFL scores of 550 paper-based or 213 computer-based, demonstrated college level writing skills on Linfield's ESL essay test, and provided evidence of financial responsibility.

Transfer Students Required are official transcripts from all colleges and universities attended and one recommendation from either a professor or a former teacher. An official high school transcript is required if the applicant has completed fewer than two years of college work, as well as SAT I or ACT scores. Students must have attended an accredited institution, taken course work corresponding to that at Linfield, and credit is given for courses in which the student has received a grade of C or better.

Admission Contact
Office of Admissions
Linfield College
900 SE Baker Street
McMinnville, OR 97128-6894
Phone: (800) 640-2287; (503) 434-2213
FAX: (503) 434-2472
E-mail: *admission@linfield.edu*
Web: *www.linfield.edu*

The Heart of the College Consider what the chairperson of a national accreditation organization said about Linfield College: "Linfield students are happier than any college student has a right to be." One can start with the very thoughtfully designed curriculum, highlighted by the Inquiry Seminar, taken by all first-year students, which certainly differentiates Linfield from other colleges. Students choose a course in an area of interest that has a strong writing, speaking, and research component and is taught by professors from many different fields of study. The Linfield faculty is a dedicated one, open to questions before, during, and after class. Linfield students rate their faculty as top-notch in terms of academic advisement, concern for the individual, and instructional effectiveness. Also significant are the number of students who are able to collaborate with professors in research across the curriculum, leading to coauthored articles and presentations at national conferences. The Linfield Research Institute gives science students outstanding opportunities for faculty–student research.

Linfield prides itself in its diverse student population. Adding to its international flavor is a quality study abroad program, where the college pays students for their air travel! Over 50 percent of Linfield's students take advantage of a January term in Sicily, studying the "Crossroads of History"; or study "Traditional and Non-Traditional Health Care in Mexico"; or spend a fall semester in Austria, Japan, France, or Ireland; or live abroad for a full year in France, Spain, Austria, or Mexico.

Students love the charming town of McMinnville, less than an hour away from the Oregon Coast and nearby skiing. The town offers a historic district, jazz and rock bands, a community theater, art galleries, and movie theaters. Only 40 minutes away are the attractions of big city Portland, with its professional sports, concerts, quality shopping, aquarium, and zoo. With all this going for them, no wonder Linfield's students are so happy.

LONGWOOD COLLEGE   Farmville, Virginia

Total Undergraduate Enrollment: 3,640

Men: 1,226 Women: 2,414
Five-Year Graduation Rate: 59%

Tuition: In-state–$;
Out-of-state–$$
Room and Board: $
Residential Students: 73%

History Longwood College was founded in 1839 as a teachers' college for men. Now a coeducational institution, Longwood is a public state-supported college.

Location Longwood College is located on a 100-acre campus in Farmville, Virginia (population 7,000), a dynamic small town about one hour west of Richmond that provides cultural, recreational, and social activities.

Top Programs of Study Business, elementary education, psychology

Arts and Sciences Anthropology, art, biology (including medical technology), chemistry, communication studies, communication disorders, computer science, English, French, German, history, liberal studies, music, physics, psychology, social work, Spanish, therapeutic recreation, visual and performing arts

Business Administration, economics

Education Elementary, middle, physical education, secondary

Pre-Professional Dental hygiene, dentistry, engineering, law, medicine, occupational therapy, pharmacy, veterinary medicine

Accredited Programs Education, music, social work, therapeutic recreation

Special Programs Longwood offers a dual B.S./M.S. degree in engineering with the University of Virginia and Old Dominion University. There are internship and study abroad opportunities. There is an Army ROTC program.

Facilities There are 53 buildings, a mix of red-brick Jeffersonian and contemporary architecture, including the Jarman Auditorium, with seating for 1,100; Hull Education Building; Hiner Hall, with student network capability; Molnar Recital Hall; a health and physical education complex; a language lab; an art gallery; a greenhouse; radio and TV stations; and the 100-acre Longwood Estate and Golf Course. The campus is fully networked.

Transition to College Program The Longwood Seminar is a required one-credit course for all freshmen. Students are assigned to a seminar section based on their academic interests and are housed in the residence halls in similar groupings.

Athletics NCAA II, Virginia Athletic Conference; Eastern College Athletic Conference

Men: Baseball, basketball, golf, soccer, tennis, wrestling

Women: Basketball, field hockey, golf, lacrosse, soccer, softball, tennis

Student Life and Housing About 2,500 students can be accommodated in college housing, which is guaranteed for all four years. Ninety percent of the students are from Virginia, the remainder coming from 22 other states and 20 countries. Ethnicity: Caucasian—87 percent; African-American—8 percent; Hispanic-American—2 percent; Asian-American—2 percent. There are 8 fraternities and 12 sororities. Upperclassmen and out-of-state students may keep cars. Longwood uses an honor system.

Accommodations for Students with Disabilities In compliance with section 504

Financial Aid About 63 percent of all freshmen receive aid. The average freshman award was about $6,000.

Requirements for Admission SAT I or ACT scores and a college prep high school program.

Application Longwood uses a rolling admissions policy, with a preferred application deadline of March 1.

International Students Required are a TOEFL minimum paper score of 550 or 213 computer-based, and SAT results.

Transfer Students March 1 is a preferred application deadline. SAT scores are required if the student has taken fewer than 30 credits. A minimum 2.2 GPA is required, as well as official high school and college transcripts.

Admission Contact
Office of Admissions
Longwood College
201 High Street
Farmville, VA 23909
Phone: (800) 281-4677; (804) 395-2060
FAX: (434) 395-2332
E-mail: *lcadmit@longwood.lwc.edu*
Web: *www.lwc.edu*

The Heart of the College Longwood students receive a strong liberal arts education with thoughtful faculty-designed majors (or self-designed ones) taught by a supportive faculty. One art student comments: "My teachers cared about me. They let me be my own artist, but care enough to push me to be better." Classes are small and inter-active, all taught by professors who are rewarded for good teaching. The campus is a close-knit community with abundant camaraderie among a diverse student population, representing a wide range of backgrounds, talents, and interests.

What distinguishes Longwood is that it makes sure that a student's education is not an "Ivory Tower" experience, but rather one that allows the student to stay connected to the real world. This means that students put their learning into action doing internships or fieldwork. In fact, Longwood is the only college in Virginia that arranges an internship for all of its majors!

Special programs include the School of Business and Economics, accredited by AACSB, which accredits only the best business programs in the nation. In Longwood's Small Business Development Center, students gain experience designing business plans and marketing strategies for regional start-ups. The center has served over 2,000 clients and helps generate more than $172 million in new business for Virginians. Also, few colleges can match Longwood's reputation for preparing teachers. Begun as a teachers college, three Longwood graduates have won the prestigious Sallie Mae First-Year Teacher Award, an exceptional number for one college. Longwood is also one of the first colleges in the nation to require freshmen to have a computer (a special purchase program offers laptops at reduced prices), and Longwood integrates technology into every area of study.

Downtown Farmville is only a block away. A thriving college town, Farmville is the business and cultural center for the entire south central Virginia heartland. The town's mix of sophistication and small-town charm is an attractive feature for students, as are the movies, restaurants, entertainment, festivals, and art center. The Blue Ridge Mountains and Appalachian Trail are only an hour away.

Longwood's successful approach to education can be measured by the fact that 95 percent of its graduates are in careers within three months of graduation or enter graduate schools for law, education, business, and health-related professions at Duke, Virginia, Chicago, and Longwood, as well.

Longwood offers students a friendly, relaxed learning environment in which to find out how their studies relate to the world around them, and, as a public institution, it does this at a very affordable tuition.

LORAS COLLEGE   Dubuque, Iowa

Total Undergraduate Enrollment: 1,525
Men: 750 Women: 775
Five-Year Graduation: 61%

Tuition: $$$
Room and Board: $
Residential Students: 62%

History Loras College is a Catholic liberal arts college and the oldest college in Iowa. It was founded in 1839 by the first bishop of Dubuque, Reverend Mathias Loras, who established a seminary and an undergraduate college program.

Location The 60-acre campus is located in Dubuque, Iowa, sitting atop the highest bluff of historic Dubuque 10 blocks from the center of the downtown area. The campus is 180 miles west of Chicago.

Top Programs of Study Accounting and business, communication arts, education

Arts and Sciences Athletic training, art, biochemistry, biology, biological research, chemistry, classical studies, computer science, criminal justice, electromechanical engineering, French, general studies, history, international studies, journalism, liberal studies, literature, media studies, medical technology, music, parish ministry, philosophy, politics, physics, psychology, public address, public relations, religious studies, sociology, social work, Spanish, sport management and administration, sport science, writing

Business Accounting, business, finance, human resource management, international business, management information systems, marketing

Education Art, elementary, music, physical education, secondary, special

Pre-Professional Dentistry, engineering, law, medicine, mortuary science

Accredited Programs Chemistry, social work

Special Programs Loras offers cooperative programs in the following areas: nursing with the University of Iowa, medical technology with any accredited school of medical technology, and engineering with several institutions. Loras also offers a teacher training program for the Catholic schools of Dubuque as well as a Catholic Studies Program. There are study abroad opportunities. All students receive an IBM computer. Loras also has a seminary program within the college for students preparing for the priesthood.

Facilities There are 18 buildings, including the state-of-the-art Academic Resource Center, art gallery, planetarium, radio and TV stations, and the $4 million Grabler Sports Complex.

Transition to College Program Loras offers a traditional orientation program.

Athletics NCAA III, Iowa Intercollegiate Athletic Conference

   Men: Baseball, basketball, cross-country, football, golf, indoor and outdoor track & field, soccer, swimming and diving, tennis, wrestling

   Women: Basketball, cross-country, golf, indoor and outdoor track & field, soccer, softball, swimming and diving, tennis, volleyball

Student Life and Housing About 1,000 students can be accommodated in college housing, which is guaranteed for all four years. Fifty-seven percent of the students are from Iowa, 31 percent from Illinois, the remainder from 26 other states and 14 countries. Ethnicity: Caucasian—91 percent. There are three national fraternities and two national sororities. All students may keep cars.

Accommodations for Students with Disabilities Loras offers a structured program of services.

Financial Aid About 87 percent of freshmen receive aid. The average freshman award is about $11,000.

Requirements for Admission SAT I or ACT results and a college prep high school program.

Application Freshmen are admitted to both fall and spring semesters. Application deadlines are open, with admission decisions made on a rolling basis.

International Students Students whose primary language is not English must score a minimum of 500 on the TOEFL paper version, submit official secondary and, if applicable, postsecondary transcripts, as well as a Declaration of Finances.

Transfer Students Students must submit official college and high school transcripts or GED certificates and official financial aid transcripts from each college attended. Only C or better courses from accredited institutions will be considered for transfer.

Home-Schooled Students Students will be considered by the admission committee on an individual basis. Applicants must present the results of the GED and either the SAT or ACT results.

Admission Contact
Office of Admissions
Loras College
P.O. Box 178
Dubuque, IA 52004-9976
Phone: (800) 245-6727
FAX: (563) 588-7119

E-mail: *adms@loras.edu*
Web: *www.loras.edu*

The Heart of the College Loras College's most notable graduate is arguably Greg Gumble, the famous sports broadcaster. Mr. Gumble appears to be a wonderful representative of a college that focuses on the total development of the student. In this attempt, Loras College strives to provide students opportunities to learn in active ways; think in reflective, critical, and creative ways; become ethical decisionmakers; and make responsible contributions to their careers and communities.

The Loras Center for Experiential Learning dramatically expands learning opportunities for students. Working with individuals and groups of students, the center helps coordinate internships, study abroad, and service learning. The center offers students the chance to complete internships for credit while taking courses at locations that include Dubuque, Chicago, Philadelphia, and Washington, D.C. Students can study abroad in Japan, Colombia, Ireland, Ukraine, South Africa, or Spain. The center also provides service opportunities at local, national, and international sites.

Loras provides each student with a laptop computer and students take them to small classes taught by professors only, to whom students have great access. The faculty is a knowledgeable one, with seven current faculty having received prestigious Fulbright Scholar Awards.

The many opportunities for participation in clubs, activities, and athletics help to create a friendly community where students have a real feeling that they belong here.

The campus has a breathtaking panoramic view of the Mississippi River and historic downtown Dubuque, which offers something for everybody. From the Victorian mansions, art galleries, restaurants, specialty shops, and music to the greyhound dog races, trolley rides, paddlewheel riverboats, hiking, and skiing at Sundown Mountain, Dubuque offers students year-round fun and adventure.

LYCOMING COLLEGE Williamsport, Pennsylvania

Total Undergraduate Enrollment: 1,420
Men: 654 Women: 766
Five-Year Graduation Rate: 69%

Tuition: $$$
Room and Board: $
Residential Students: 90%

History Lycoming College was founded in 1812, making it one of the 50 oldest colleges in America. First founded as an elementary and secondary school academy, in 1848 the Methodists purchased the school to use as a seminary. Later it became the first junior college in Pennsylvania. In 1947 Lycoming became a four-year college. Lycoming takes its name from *locomic,* an Indian word meaning great stream. Lycoming is listed on the Templeton Foundation's Honor Roll of Character-Building Colleges.

Location Lycoming is located on a 35-acre campus in the small town of Williamsport, Pennsylvania (population 35,000), the home of the Little League Baseball World Series.

Top Programs of Study Biology, psychology, business

Arts and Sciences: Actuarial mathematics, American studies, archaeology and culture of the ancient Near East, art, astronomy, biology, chemistry, communication, computer science, criminal justice, French, German, international studies, history, mathematics, music, philosophy, physics, political science, psychology, religion, sociology-anthropology, Spanish, theater

Business Accounting, administration (marketing, finance, management, international business), economics

Education Elementary, school nurse, secondary

Pre-Professional Dentistry, law, ministry, optometry, veterinary medicine

Accredited Programs Business, chemistry

Special Programs There are combined degree programs (3-2) in engineering with Penn. State, and forestry and environmental management with Duke. There are accelerated professional programs in optometry and podiatry with Pennsylvania College of Optometry and Podiatric Medicine. There is a Washington, D.C., semester and many study abroad opportunities. Close to one-third of the students complete an internship. Lycoming's student newspaper won a first place from the Columbia Scholastic Press Association. There is an Army ROTC.

Facilities There are 23 buildings, most of which have been built since 1950. The buildings include a student union; the Welch Theatre; the Fine Arts Center; the Communications Center, which houses a television studio and FM radio station; the Heim Biology and Chemistry Building; the Clarke Building and Chapel, which houses music facilities; and the Snowden Library. There are also a planetarium, art gallery, a state-of-the-art computer graphics lab, a nursing skills laboratory, and a video conference facility. A 12-acre athletic field and football stadium are a few blocks north of the campus.

Transition to College Program There is an Office of the Assistant Dean for Freshmen, which provides an easy resource to solving problems, developing solutions, and coordinating services. This counseling and support continues into the sophomore year, when students have small group retreats and individual conferences with the Assistant Dean for Sophomores.

Athletics NCAA III, Middle Atlantic Freedom League

Men: Basketball, cross-country, football, golf, lacrosse, soccer, swimming, tennis, track, wrestling

Women: Basketball, cross-country, lacrosse, soccer, softball, swimming, tennis, track & field, volleyball

Student Life and Housing About 1,200 students can be accommodated in college housing, which is guaranteed for all four years. Seventy-nine percent of the students are from Pennsylvania; the remainder are from 20 other states and 14 countries. Ethnicity: Caucasian—94 percent. There are one national and three local sororities and four national fraternities. All students may keep cars.

Accommodations for Students with Disabilities In compliance with section 504

Financial Aid About 90 percent of all freshmen receive aid. The average freshman award was about $16,000.

Requirements for Admission SAT I or ACT scores and a college prep high school program.

Application April 1 is the application deadline for the fall semester, and December 1 for the spring semester. The college reviews applications on a rolling basis, with an admission decision made within three weeks.

International Students Required are English translated official transcripts of all secondary, and, if applicable, postsecondary schools attended; TOEFL scores of 500 paper or 173 computer; an affidavit of financial support; and two letters of recommendation.

Transfer Students Required are high school and college transcripts, SAT I or ACT scores, catalogues from each college attended, and at least a C GPA. Only courses with C− and above will be considered for transfer.

Admission Contact
Office of Admissions
Lycoming College
700 College Place
Williamsport, PA 17701
Phone: (800) 345-3920; (570) 321-4000
FAX: (570) 321-4317
E-mail: *admissions@lycoming.edu*
Web: *www.lycoming.edu*

The Heart of the College Lycoming College is considered a "best buy" in college education. Students are often surprised at how a 1,500-student campus can offer such a breadth of excellent academic programs and services typically associated with more costly colleges. Students can expect the friendly personal climate of a small residential college, as well as excellent equipment and small classes, all taught by full-time faculty because Lycoming is solely an undergraduate institution. Students love the personalized education and getting to know professors and their families.

The curriculum includes a broad-based education in the liberal arts and sciences, a writing-across-the-curriculum requirement, as well as proficiency in a foreign language. Leadership opportunities abound through the many clubs, organizations, and volunteer service opportunities. Lycoming also offers a May term that allows students to earn extra credits, take a study tour abroad, or get a jump start on a summer job. The college has an accredited creative writing program, a very strong program in the physical and health sciences, with hands-on learning from basic courses to individual research. Both the chemistry and biology departments offer summer paid research projects. Lycoming is also proud of its music program, which includes a 100-member choir and 40-member Tour Choir, which goes on tour over spring break and has recorded two CDs. Lycoming's education program also initiated a new program in Urban Teaching. One of Lycoming's newest programs is the Institute for Management Studies, in which business leaders participate in seminars, classrooms, give guest lectures, and serve as "industry contacts."

Located in Williamsport, students are surrounded by the beauty of Pennsylvania's mountains, and recreational opportunities such as hiking, rafting, canoeing, skiing, and camping abound.

There is good reason why close to 100 percent of Lycoming graduates are fully employed or in graduate school within six months of graduation. Williamsport is the hub of north central Pennsylvania, affording Lycoming students excellent internship opportunities close to campus. In addition, a superb Career Devel-opment Center works closely with students to identify and satisfy career paths. The Center also offers special programs for students planning careers in law and health professions.

LYNCHBURG COLLEGE   Lynchburg, Virginia

Total Undergraduate Enrollment: 1,665
Men: 665 Women: 1,000
Five-Year Graduation Rate: 59%

Tuition: $$$
Room and Board: $
Residential Students: 75%

History Lynchburg College was founded in 1903 as Virginia Christian College by Dr. Joseph Hopwood, a minister and educator. The college is historically related to the Christian Church (Disciples of Christ).

Location Lynchburg College is located on a 214-acre suburban campus in Lynchburg, Virginia (population 220,000), recently cited as the second-best small Southern city in which to live. Nearby are the beautiful Blue Ridge Mountains. There are many recreational, social, and cultural opportunities.

Top Programs of Study Education, communication, business administration, nursing

Arts and Sciences Applied physical science, art, athletic training, biology, biomedical science, chemistry, communication studies, computer science, English, environmental science, exercise physiology, French, health movement science, health promotion, history, international relations, mathematics, music, philosophy, philosophy and political science, philosophy and religious studies, political science, psychology, religious studies, sociology, sociology and religious studies, Spanish, sports management, theater

Business Accounting, administration, economics, management, marketing

Education Elementary, human development and learning, secondary, special

Pre-Professional Art therapy, dentistry, forestry and wildlife, law, library science, medicine, ministry, occupational therapy, optometry, pharmacy, physical therapy, veterinary medicine

Accredited Programs Nursing

Special Programs There are many internship, service, travel abroad, and student–faculty research opportunities. Dual degree programs in engineering are offered with the University of Virginia and Old Dominion University.

Facilities There are 26 buildings plus the Claytor Nature Study Center, a 470-acre conservancy that serves as a field laboratory in the Blue Ridge Mountains. The buildings include the Daura Art Gallery, a newly renovated health and wellness center, a theater, and a new academic and conference center that will house a model stock exchange center.

Transition to College Program The Freshman Success Seminar, a one-credit elective taught by student leaders, addresses topics such as goal setting, academic success strategies, policies and procedures, and adjustment to college life. Also, immediately prior to the first day of classes is a four-day Welcome Week, which focuses on involvement opportunities, community service, and a new student convocation.

Athletics NCAA III, Old Dominion Athletic Conference

Men: Baseball, basketball, cross-country, golf, indoor and outdoor track lacrosse, soccer, tennis,

Women: Basketball, cross-country, field hockey, indoor and outdoor track, lacrosse, soccer, softball, tennis, volleyball

Student Life and Housing About 1,100 students can be accommodated in college housing, which is guaranteed for all four years. Fifty-five percent of the students are from Virginia, the remainder are from 37 other states and 13 countries. Ethnicity: Caucasian—84 percent; African-American—12 percent; Hispanic-American—2 percent. There are five sororities and four fraternities. Upperclassmen may keep cars.

Accommodations for Students with Disabilities In compliance with section 504

Financial Aid About 90 percent of all students receive aid. The average award was about $14,000.

Requirements for Admission SAT or ACT scores and a college prep high school program. An interview is strongly recommended.

Application Early Admission students should apply by November 15 for the fall semester. Regular applications are reviewed on a rolling admissions basis.

International Students The fall deadline is July 31, and the spring deadline is November 30. An English-translated secondary school transcript; a World Evaluation Services college transcript evaluation, if applicable; a letter of recommendation; an essay; a TOEFL score; and official certification of finances are required.

Transfer Students Students must be in good standing at their former colleges. A minimum of a C GPA is required. Lynchburg faculty and the Registrar will evaluate the suitability of transfer credits. Only C grades or above will be considered for transfer. Application deadlines are July 31 for the fall semester and November 30 for the spring semester.

Home-Schooled Students Students must submit standardized test scores and may be required to submit a bibliography of high school literature and portfolios of performance-based assessments.

Admission Contact:
Office of Admissions
Lynchburg College
1501 Lakeside Drive
Lynchburg, VA 24501-3199
Phone: (800) 426-8101
FAX: (434) 544-8653
E-mail: *admission@lynchburg.edu*
Web: *www.lynchburg.edu*

The Heart of the College Lynchburg offers a great education. In a recent survey, Lynchburg students ranked their experience well above the national average in terms of level of academic challenge, active and collaborative learning, student interactions with faculty, enriching educational experiences, and a supportive campus environment. The academic program combines the liberal arts and sciences with career development and is taught by a knowledgeable faculty who love to teach and truly care for their students. One of the administrators says, "We know every one of our students by name. We give you our home phone numbers and e-mail addresses. If you are not in class we call you." Faculty also works with students to conduct advanced research and present findings in scholarly articles or conference reports. The importance of academics and the support that students receive is further illustrated by the philosophy of the athletic programs, where coaches are committed to cultivating student–athletes.

Lynchburg enjoys having students put their skills to work. In the business school, marketing students create marketing plans for area organizations. The Integrate Business class uses grant money to actually start businesses. Most students complete at least one substantive hands-on, real-world project during their course of study. Many students complete internships during their junior or senior years at such sites as Adams Akin & Cheatham CPAs, Applied Analytical Industries,

MTV, Cove Health Systems, Johns Hopkins University and Hospital, and Schwab Capital Markets.

Students love the community feel of the campus and the diverse student population with which to form friendships. The college sets as a goal the appreciation of the diversity of other cultures by studying a foreign language, study abroad opportunities, and by students interacting with a diversity of students on campus.

Lynchburg students enjoy the campus location and climate. Tucked into the foothills of the Blue Ridge Mountains of central Virginia, the college is surrounded by spectacular beauty. In addition, the city of Lynchburg offers all the amenities of a larger city.

Lynchburg's quality education, strong faculty, diverse student community, and ideal location make the college a very attractive one.

MANCHESTER COLLEGE North Manchester, Indiana

Total Undergraduate Enrollment: 1,101
Men: 500 Women: 601
Five-Year Graduation Rate: 50%

Tuition: $$$
Room and Board: $$
Residential Students: 74%

History Manchester College was founded in 1889 after it had been an academy and a Bible school. The college is affiliated with the Church of the Brethren and has a long-standing involvement with important social issues such as justice, diversity, peace, and the environment. The college is listed on the Templeton Foundation's Honor Roll of Character-Building Colleges.

Location Manchester College is located on a 124-acre campus in North Manchester, Indiana (population 6,000), a classic Hoosier hometown 35 miles west of Fort Wayne, the second largest city in the state. It offers students many cultural, social, and recreational opportunities.

Top Programs of Study Education, accounting/business

Arts and Sciences Art, athletic training, biology, biology/chemistry, chemistry, communication studies, computer science, engineering science, English, environmental studies, exercise science, French, German, history, individualized interdisciplinary major, mathematics, media studies, medical technology, music, peace studies, philosophy, physics, political science, psychology, religion, social work, sociology, Spanish, theater arts

Business Accounting financial, accounting managerial, administration, economics, finance, non-profit management, small business administration

Education Elementary, physical education, secondary

Pre-Professional Law, medicine, nursing, occupational therapy, physical therapy

Accredited Programs Athletic training, education, social work

Special Programs There are associate degrees awarded in several academic areas, including early childhood education, gerontology, health and fitness instruction, criminal justice, and broadcast media. There are opportunities for internships, study abroad, and service. The science program has an ongoing relationship with NASA.

Facilities There are 44 buildings, including a new fitness center, a multicultural student center, some air-conditioned residence halls, Petersime Chapel, and a radio station. The college also has a 100-acre tract (Koinonia) and an environmental and retreat center 12 miles north of the campus.

Transition to College Program First-Year Colloquia are courses designed to integrate new students into college life. Taught by specially selected faculty, these interdisciplinary courses focus on an exciting range of topics. Students learn valuable skills as they study each topic, and the small classes allow students to get to know one another.

Athletics NCAA III, Heartland Collegiate Athletic Conference

Men: Baseball, basketball, cross-country, football, golf, soccer, tennis, track & field, wrestling

Women: Basketball, cross-country, golf, soccer, softball, tennis, track & field, volleyball

Student Life and Housing About 1,000 students live in college housing, which is guaranteed for all four years. Eighty-six percent of the students are from Indiana, the remainder are from 24 other states and 24 countries. Ethnicity: Caucasian—90 percent. There are no fraternities or sororities. All students may keep cars.

Accommodations for Students with Disabilities The college provides comprehensive services.

Financial Aid Almost all freshmen receive aid. The average award was about $15,000.

Requirements for Admission SAT or ACT scores and a college prep high school program.

Application The college uses a rolling admissions policy and will provide an admissions decision within three weeks.

International Students Students whose primary language is not English must score a minimum of 550 on the TOEFL paper version or 213 on the computer version. Also required are official secondary and, if applicable, postsecondary transcripts, as well as a declaration of finances.

Transfer Students SAT and ACT scores are waived for those students who have successfully completed at least one full academic year at another college. Official high school and college transcripts are required, as well as confirmation of being in good standing at the previous college. C grades and higher are considered for transfer.

Admission Contact
Office of Admissions
Manchester College
604 E. College Avenue
P.O. Box 365
North Manchester, IN 46962-0365
Phone: (800) 852-3648
FAX: (260) 982-5239
E-mail: *admitinfo@manchester.edu*
Web: *www.manchester.edu*

The Heart of the College Manchester College is an exciting blend of "a community of faith and learning" and career preparation. Studying the liberal arts and sciences and preparing for a career are in perfect balance. While the college's mission statement speaks of developing "an international consciousness, a respect for ethnic and cultural pluralism, and an appreciation for the infinite worth of every person"—lofty and important goals indeed—the college also offers an employment guarantee that provides students who take advantage of the college's services and opportunities with a year's worth of study at no cost if they are not employed within six months of graduation. Manchester College's extensive career services program has obviously been immensely successful since it can offer such a guarantee, with 96 percent of its graduates over a seven-year period working within six months of graduation.

The college's accounting program is widely recognized as one of the strongest in the Midwest, with 50 percent of Manchester's students who take the CPA exam passing on the first sitting. Ninety percent of the accounting students who completed internships were offered full-time positions by PricewaterhouseCoopers and other top firms. Also, in the biology/chemistry program, 85 percent of the graduates who apply to medical school get accepted. In addition, 94 percent of elementary and secondary education students passed the initial licensing exam.

With a diverse student community, Manchester fosters a global perspective, including study abroad programs to Japan, Costa Rica, Greece, and Mexico. The college also began a peace studies program following World War II in order to explore and create new ways to resolve conflicts peacefully, to promote responsible world citizenship, and to encourage the justice necessary for peace to prevail. In addition, Manchester offers students the opportunity to make a commitment to a greener world by providing an innovative environmental studies program. Graduates of the program follow a Manchester tradition of pinning green ribbons on their graduation gowns to demonstrate their pledge to take into account the environmental consequences of any job they consider.

Students enjoy the picturesque Victorian architecture of small town North Manchester, as well as the convenience and opportunity of a big city like Fort Wayne, a half hour's drive away.

MANHATTAN COLLEGE

New York City, New York

Total Undergraduate Enrollment: 2,600
Men: 1,350 Women: 1,250
Five-Year Graduation Rate: 61%

Tuition: $$$
Room and Board: $$$$
Residential Students: 75%

History Manhattan College was founded in 1853 by the Brothers of the Christian Schools in lower Manhattan. It was later moved to its current uptown location and became chartered as Manhattan College to give prominence to professional and technical education as well as the traditional liberal arts and sciences. From its beginnings the college focused attention on the education of first-generation college students and was an early proponent of providing access to minority students. The college became coeducational in 1973. Although it is a private, independent institution, the college maintains an affiliation with the Christian Brothers of the Catholic Church and is founded upon the Lasallian Catholic tradition of excellence in teaching.

Location The 26-acre campus is located in the residential Riverdale section of the borough of the Bronx in New York City, New York, 10 miles north of midtown Manhattan, adjacent to suburban Westchester County.

Top Programs of Study Engineering, business, arts.

Arts and Sciences Allied health (concentrations in health care administration, health counseling), biochemistry, biology, chemical engineering, chemistry, civil engineering, communications, computer engineering, computer science, economics, electrical engineering, engineering, English environmental, French, general science, government, history, international studies, mathematics, mechanical engineering, nuclear medicine, peace studies, philosophy, physical education (concentrations in exercise science/sports medicine), physics, psychology, radiation therapy, religious studies, sociology, Spanish, urban affairs

Business Accounting, computer information systems, economics, global business, finance, management, marketing

Education Elementary, physical education, secondary, special/elementary

Pre-Professional None

Accredited Programs Allied health, chemistry, engineering, radiation therapy

Special Programs The college has a Phi Beta Kappa chapter. Manhattan has an inter-institutional program with the College of Mount Saint Vincent, sharing facilities, programs of study, faculties, and sponsoring a program of joint social and cultural activities. There are opportunities for cooperative education, internships, social service, study abroad, and double majors. The Coalition for the Performing Arts is comprised of five premier performing arts ensembles (chorus, drama, band, dance, gaelic pipes and drums) that provide opportunities for students to develop their artistic talents and provide campus performances. There is an Air Force ROTC program.

Facilities There are 28 buildings, including the completely renovated Cardinal Hayes Library, with fully wired reading rooms; a sophisticated media center; an Internet café; and the Thomas Hall Student Center. In addition, there is a radio station. Most notable are the superb computer facilities, including Jasper Net, a campus-wide network, and nine microcomputer laboratories.

Transition to College Program During the beginning of each semester, workshops and activities are planned to help students gain valuable college and life skills. The college also provides personal and academic counseling, with each freshman provided a faculty adviser from his or her own academic school. Students in the School of Business take the mandatory First-Year Seminar, an eight-week course designed to assist students in acquiring the skills for academic success.

Athletics NCAA I, Eastern College Athletic Conference; Metro Atlantic Athletic Conference

Men: Baseball, basketball, cross-country, indoor and outdoor track & field, golf, lacrosse, soccer, tennis

Women: Basketball, cross-country, indoor and outdoor track & field, lacrosse, softball, soccer, swimming, tennis, volleyball

Student Life and Housing About 1,500 students can be accommodated in college housing, which is guaranteed for all four years. Seventy-five percent of the students are from New York, the remainder from 33 other states and 10 countries. Ethnicity: Caucasian—67 percent; Hispanic-American—14 percent; African-American—6 percent; Asian-American—6 percent; International—2 percent. There are one local and three national fraternities, and four local sororities. All students may keep cars.

Accommodations for Students with Disabilities The Specialized Resource Center provides comprehensive services.

Financial Aid About 82 percent of all freshmen receive aid. The average freshman award was about $10,500.

Requirements for Admission SAT I or ACT scores and a college prep high school program or a GED. A campus visit and interview are strongly recommended.

Application Freshmen are admitted fall and spring semesters. Early Decision Applications are due November 15, with an admission decision provided by December 1. Regular application deadlines are open, with decision notification made on a rolling basis.

International Students Required are official secondary school, and, if applicable, postsecondary transcripts, a minimum TOEFL score of 550 paper and 230 computer-based, as well as certification of finances.

Transfer Students Required are official high school and college transcripts, a list of courses presently taken, college catalogues from all institutions previously attended, and financial aid transcripts from all colleges previously attended.

Admission Contact
Office of Admissions
Manhattan College
4513 Manhattan College Parkway
Riverdale, NY 10471
Phone: (800) MC2-XCEL; (718) 862-7200
FAX: (718) 862-8019
E-mail: *admit@manhattan.edu*
Web: *www.manhattan.edu*

The Heart of the College Manhattan College has several major strengths, including academic programs, talented supportive faculty, a diverse student population, and a prized location. In the School of Arts (ironically, fine arts is not offered here), first-year students study courses that integrate liberal arts disciplines, such as "Classical Origins of Western Culture" and "Global Origins." The School of Engineering is one of the most respected engineering programs in the nation, with the chemical engineering program right at the top. The program in environmental engineering has world-class research facilities. Much of the school's success can be attributed to its continual re-examination of how its curriculum matches the changes in the real world of engineering. This is accomplished through consultation with distinguished engineers and industrial leaders who, with Manhattan faculty, comprise the Manhattan College Council on Engineering Affairs.

The School of Business points with pride to the Standard & Poors ranking of Manhattan College, which lists it as third among liberal arts colleges and first among Catholic colleges in the number of graduates who hold corporate leadership positions. The business programs capitalize on their proximity to New York City for internships and cooperative education experiences, as well as numerous and influential alumni connections. The teacher education program has a long history at the college, with programs offered in the 1920s for the preparation of Brothers and Sisters of the Christian Schools. Today, extensive field experience and learning to use leading-edge teaching technology are the hallmarks of the teacher education program. The School of Sci-

ence has excellent research facilities enjoyed by faculty and students for research opportunities. Manhattan College can boast of its number one ranking among New York private undergraduate colleges for the number of graduates who go on to earn doctorates in the sciences or medicine.

Add to these strong programs a top-notch faculty focused on teaching; small classes; and a geographically, ethnically, and economically diverse student population and Manhatttan College appears a real gem. The Dean of the School of Arts says with admiration: "I can't imagine students of such diverse backgrounds getting along any better than they get along here." Much of this can be attributed to the student-centered approach of the faculty.

Now add to this a campus location on the periphery of New York City, a safe tranquil location only a subway ride away from Broadway, Madison Square Garden, Greenwich Village, Fifth Avenue, Yankee Stadium, and Central Park. In addition, that train ride can take students to the corporate and financial capital of the world. Faculty make great use of these resources and students enjoy the great degree of experiential learning required for their courses. One student commented: "That's a very strong aspect of the college. The campus world and the real world are tied together, and the faculty is very good at utilizing the city as a classroom."

MARIETTA COLLEGE   **Marietta, Ohio**

Total Undergraduate Enrollment: 1,100   Tuition: $$$
Men: 550 Women: 550   Room and Board: $
Five-Year Graduation Rate: 57%   Residential Students: 91%

History Marietta was first established as the Muskingum Academy, founded by pioneer settlers in 1797. The academy became the first institute of higher education in the Northwest Territory. In 1835 Marietta was chartered to offer college degrees. It is a private, nonsectarian liberal arts college and has been listed on the Templeton Foundation's Honor Roll of Character-Building Colleges.

Location The 120-acre campus is located in the small town of Marietta, Ohio (population 15,000), a picturesque riverboat town at the confluence of the Ohio and Muskingum Rivers. The town is a frequent stopping point for passenger luxury steamboats and has trolley tours and historic residences. The town is about two hours from Columbus, Ohio, and Pittsburgh, Pennsylvania.

Top Programs of Study Business, education, psychology

Arts and Sciences Advertising and public relations, allied health, art (studio), biochemistry, biology, chemistry, communication studies, computer information systems, computer science, English, environmental science, environmental studies, geology, graphic design, history, journalism, mathematics, music, musical theater, organizational communication, petroleum engineering, philosophy, physics (applied), political science, psychology, radio/television, Spanish, sports medicine, theater

Business Accounting, economics, human service management, international business, management, marketing, public accounting

Education Early childhood, middle childhood, secondary

Pre-Professional Dentistry, law, medicine, physical therapy, veterinary medicine

Accredited Programs Chemistry, petroleum engineering, sports medicine

Special Programs Marietta is the only small, private liberal arts college that offers a degree in petroleum engineering, where students are prepared for careers in the oil and natural gas industries. The McDonough Leadership Program offers students a comprehensive minor involving community service internships and a Visiting Scholar Program that brings prominent leaders to campus. The Investigative Studies Program provides the opportunity to do independent research with faculty and also receive a $1,500 stipend. There is a study abroad program with a variety of international universities, including a China Program that offers opportunities to teach and study in China through a Teaching English as a Foreign Language Program. There is a Phi Beta Kappa chapter.

Facilities There are 41 red brick buildings, offering New England charm on a stately campus. The campus includes a new career center and the newest building, The McDonough Center for Leadership and Business. There are also radio and TV stations, a greenhouse, art gallery, observatory, and a learning resource center.

Transition to College Program In addition to a College Experience Seminar required of all freshmen in their first semester, which is designed to help students make the social and intellectual transition from high school to college, as part of the Marietta Plan, freshmen take content courses that are also designed as transition courses. Here the students are helped to understand the expectations of college-level work, produce written work on a regular basis, and receive guidance to help students complete assignments.

Athletics NCAA III, Ohio Athletic Conference

Men: Baseball, basketball, crew, cross-country, football, golf, lacrosse, soccer, tennis, track

Women: Basketball, crew, cross-country, golf, soccer, softball, tennis, track, volleyball

Student Life and Housing About 1,100 students can be accommodated in college housing, which is guaranteed for all four years. Fifty-seven percent of the students are from Ohio, with the remainder from 45 other states and 12 countries. Ethnicity: Caucasian—92 percent. There are three national fraternities and sororities. All students may keep cars.

Accommodations for Students with Disabilities Marietta complies with section 504 in striving to make reasonable accommodations to students with documented disabilities. Students should contact the Academic Resource Center.

Financial Aid About 96 percent of all freshmen receive aid. The average freshman award was about $18,000.

Requirements for Admission SAT I or ACT scores and a GPA of at least 2.0 in a college prep high school program. An interview is strongly recommended.

Application Freshmen are admitted fall and spring semesters. Applications for fall should be filed by April 15. Decision notification is sent on a rolling basis.

International Students Students must file an International Application for Admission Form, have TOEFL minimum scores of 550 on the paper test or 213 on the computer test, and provide verification of ability to pay all costs.

Transfer Students Students must file the Application for Transfer Admission, submit a high school transcript and college transcripts, transfer documentation, and a Transfer Clearance Form. Courses with C or better are eligible for transfer. Students who have graduated with an associate's degree with a 2.3 GPA may be admitted with junior class standing.

Admission Contact
Office of Admissions
Marietta College
215 Fifth Street
Marietta, OH 45750-4000
Phone: (800) 331-7896; (740) 376-4600
FAX: (740) 376-8888
E-mail: *admit@marietta.edu*
Web: *www.marietta.edu*

The Heart of the College Marietta students feel that they are very much a part of a living, dynamic community with faculty and administration. This feeling of community is a prominent goal for the faculty, who are very approachable and caring. Because they view themselves as role models, the professors are examples of honesty, kindness, and concern. This focus on community meshes nicely with the serious attention the college pays to the development of character.

In addition to building community and character, Marietta views itself as a college that develops leadership skills and abilities. One of the Nine Core Values of the college stresses that the role of citizen–leader must become a way of life in order to create a livable, sustainable, ethical future. In order to develop these leadership skills, Marietta offers a comprehensive program through its McDonough Leadership Program.

Although a small college nestled in a picturesque part of the Ohio countryside, Marietta emphasizes a view of the world as a global village where economic growth and political stability are achievable only as the result of cooperative efforts among nations. Marietta graduates— these citizen–leaders—are educated so that they will be able to thrive in a diverse global society. This is emphasized by the college's strong link with China, where students can study and teach as part of the college's China Program. Also, Marietta's excellent study abroad program extends to Spain, Germany, England, Japan, Australia, Scotland, France, Ireland, Argentina, and India.

MARQUETTE UNIVERSITY   **Milwaukee, Wisconsin**

Total Undergraduate Enrollment: 7,500
Men: 3,525 Women: 3,975
Five-Year Graduation Rate: 74%

Tuition: $$$
Room and Board: $$
Residential Students: 50%

History Marquette was established in 1881 as a Catholic university in the Jesuit tradition.

Location The 90-acre urban campus is located in Milwaukee, Wisconsin, 90 miles north of Chicago. Milwaukee offers students entertainment, cultural activities, and internships, and has recently been named as one of America's 15 best cities in which to live and work.

Top Programs of Study Nursing, psychology, mechanical engineering

Arts and Sciences Advertising, anthropology, athletic training, biochemistry and molecular biology, biological sciences, biomedical engineering, biomedical sciences, broadcast and electronic communication, chemistry, civil and environmental engineering, classical languages, classical studies, clinical laboratory science, computational mathematics, computer engineering, computer science, criminology and law studies, economics, English, electrical engineering, exercise science, French, German, history, industrial engineering, nursing, philosophy, physics, physiological sciences, physical therapy, political science, psychology, public relations, social welfare and justice, sociology, Spanish language and Spanish for the professions literature, speech pathology and audiology, theater arts, theology

Business Accounting, business economics, finance, human resources management, information technology, international business, marketing, operations and supply chain management

Education Elementary, middle, secondary

Pre-Professional Dentistry, law, medicine, optometry, pharmacy, podiatry, veterinary medicine

Accredited Programs Business, communication studies, dental hygiene, education, engineering, journalism, language, nursing, physical therapy, social work, speech

Special Programs Marquette has a cooperative art program with the Milwaukee Institute of Art. The Center for the Study of Entrepreneurship provides assistance to students seeking to start their own businesses. The Les Aspin Center in Washington, D. C., offers students an opportunity to live, study, and intern in one of the nation's leading congressional internship programs. There are Army, Navy, Marines, and Air Force ROTC programs.

Facilities There are 54 buildings, mostly modern, including the newest buildings, a theater, art museum, recreation center, and a computer center. There are an art gallery, TV and radio sta-

tions, and the St. Joan of Arc Chapel, the oldest building in the Western hemisphere, having been built in France in 1400 and then transplanted to Wisconsin.

Transition to College Program Marquette offers a traditional orientation program.

Athletics NCAA I, Conference USA

   Men: Basketball, cross-country, golf, soccer, tennis, track

   Women: Basketball, cross-country, soccer, tennis, track, volleyball

Student Life and Housing About 3,200 students can be accommodated in college housing, which is guaranteed for all four years. Forty-eight percent of the students are from Wisconsin, the remainder are from all states and 80 countries. Ethnicity: Caucasian—85 percent; African-American—4 percent; Asian-American—4 percent; International—2 percent. There are seven national fraternities and seven national sororities. All students may keep cars.

Accommodations for Students with Disabilities In compliance with section 504

Financial Aid About 90 percent of all freshmen receive aid. The average freshman award was about $14,600.

Requirements for Admission SAT I or ACT scores and a college prep high school program.

Application Freshmen are admitted to all semesters. Application deadlines are open; however, the first letters of admission are mailed November 15, and then on a rolling basis.

International Students Students whose primary language is not English must have a minimum TOEFL score of 525. Also required are official secondary school and, if applicable, postsecondary school transcripts, as well as a declaration of finances.

Transfer Students Required are official high school and college transcripts and a minimum

GPA of 2.0. SAT or ACT scores are required for those students who have completed fewer than 12 college credits. A minimum of 30 credits must be completed at Marquette.

Admission Contact
Office of Admissions
Marquette University
Marquette Hall, 106
P.O.Box 1881
Milwaukee, WI 53201-1881
Phone: (800) 222-6544; (414) 288-7302
FAX: (414) 288-3764
E-mail: *admissions@marquette.edu*
Web: *www.marquette.edu*

The Heart of the University Marquette University is one of the larger colleges recommended in this guide, having an undergraduate enrollment of about 7,500 students and a graduate enrollment of about 2,000 students. What makes Marquette unique is both its Jesuit traditions and how it is able to maintain the strengths of a smaller institution. At Marquette there is a climate of excellence that asks faculty and students to do more and achieve more, "as a reflection of our gratitude to God for our gifts and abilities." Marquette's faculty love working there because the institution provides them with opportunities to do research and scholarship and also encourages the faculty to share its expertise through teaching and collaborative research with students. So the close, supportive student–faculty relationships typically found on much smaller campuses are very much apparent at Marquette.

Marquette's academic programs are brought to students through six colleges and a school of education. At the heart of every student's program is a distinctive core curriculum comprised of liberal arts courses. On the flip side, the school's career and pre-professional programs offer students an edge because Marquette has its own schools of dentistry and law.

One of the main advantages of a Marquette education is its location in Milwaukee, a major American city that puts students within minutes of significant internships often leading to full-time positions. For example, 9 out of 10 accounting internships lead to offers of full-time employment. Employers have included American Express, Ernst & Young, and PriceWaterhouseCoopers. The major in biochemistry and molecular biology allows students to conduct research with internationally known professors. Students majoring in biomedical engineering participate in a senior-year capstone course in which they design and solve real biomedical problems. GE Medical Systems, the global leader in medical technologies, is headquartered only minutes from Marquette.

Community service is a big deal at Marquette. Although it's not required, few students leave Marquette without participating. That's the reason why Marquette students typically give more than 100,000 hours of service each year, fulfilling the Jesuit tradition of faith and justice put into action and ranking the school in the top 20 for community service.

The city of Milwaukee offers students parks and beaches; the Marcus Center for the Performing Arts; plenty of pubs, restaurants, professional sports, shopping malls, and theaters. But what is most distinctive about the city is that it mirrors the incredible campus diversity with its own special ethnic diversity of Serbian, German, Italian, Mexican, and Polish communities.

Marquette is a major university with excellent academic programs that retains the strengths of a smaller college.

MARYMOUNT MANHATTAN COLLEGE

New York City,
New York

Total Undergraduate Enrollment: 2,350
Men: 705 Women: 1,645
Five-Year Graduation Rate: 83%

Tuition: $$
Room and Board: $$$$
Residential Students: 23%

History Marymount Manhattan College is one of six colleges founded in the United States by the Religious of the Sacred Heart of Mary. The college was originally established as the city campus of Marymount College of Tarrytown, New York. In 1961 the college was chartered as a separate institution. The college is listed on the Templeton Foundation's Honor Roll of Character-Building Colleges.

Location The one-acre campus is located in an East Side residential section of Manhattan.

Top Programs of Study Communications, theater, dance, business

Arts and Sciences Acting, art, art history, biology, communication arts, dance, English, history, humanities, international studies, political science, psychology, sociology, speech pathology and audiology, theater arts

Business Accounting, management

Education Inclusive Dual Certification teaching students with disabilities in grades 1–6 or grades 7–12, secondary certification in social studies and English, theater, dance, speech and language

Pre-Professional Law, medicine

Accredited Programs None

Special Programs The college has a Community Leadership Program for students who desire to be actively involved in shaping the future of New York City. The Bridge to College Program provides students, especially foreign students, an opportunity to develop proficiency in all English language skills. There is a HEOP program for students with academic potential who are economi-cally disadvantaged and academically underprepared. The Women in Urban Leadership Program prepares students for leadership roles. There are several applied minors, such as Substance Abuse Counseling and Arts Management. There are several cooperative programs, including bachelor's and master's degrees in Publishing with Pace University, Computer Science with Polytechnic University, and Dance with the Martha Graham School of Dance. There are certificate programs in Gerontology and Non-Profit Management. The Writing Center hosts a Best-Selling Author Series and Annual Writer's Conference. There are opportunities for travel and study abroad, internships, and independent study. Students can minor in several areas, including Creative Writing.

Facilities There are three buildings and a modern high-rise residence hall. The buildings house the Shanahan Library; the new Freeman Science Center; the Lang Center for Producing with facilities for traditional video as well as television production; the Smadbeck Communication and Learning Center, for children and adults with hearing, language, and learning disorders. There are also a radio station and a TV studio, the off-Broadway Theresa Lang Theater, an Olympic-size pool, a student union, an art gallery, and a chapel.

Transition to College Program An orientation seminar termed "Common Ground" provides students with an opportunity to identify their learning styles; make informed decisions; develop time management strategies, leadership skills, the adoption of a wellness lifestyle, and an appreciation for what it means to live in a diverse community.

Athletics There are no varsity sports. There are three intramural sports for men and three for women.

Student Life and Housing About 500 students can be accommodated in college housing, most of which is suite units located in a high-rise building 16 blocks from the campus. Sixty-five percent of the students are from New York, the remainder are from 48 other states and 63 countries. Ethnicity: Caucasian—52 percent; African-American—20 percent; Hispanic-American—16 percent; International—6 percent; Asian-American—4 percent. There is one national sorority and are no fraternities. All students may keep cars.

Accommodations for Students with Disabilities Marymount's Program for Academic Access is a comprehensive program of support services for students with documented disabilities, which consists of a complete psycho-educational evaluation completed within the last year and a personal statement about interests and goals for college study and career. The cost is $3,000 annually, and students may leave after the first year, provided that they are in good academic standing and show evidence of academic independence. Students may elect not to be in the full program and receive free accommodations.

Financial Aid About 85 percent of all students receive aid. The average freshman award was about $18,500.

Requirements for Admission SAT I or ACT scores and a college prep high school program, or GED score sheet and GED diploma.

Application Freshmen are admitted to all semesters. The Early Decision application deadline is November 1, with decision notification by December 15. Regular application deadlines are open with decision notification made on a rolling basis.

International Students Application deadlines are March 1 for the fall semester and November 1 for the spring semester. The TOEFL is required for all students whose first language is not English. A minimum score of 500 paper or 173 computer-based is required. An interview is recommended.

Transfer Students Required are a complete list of every academic institution attended, including dates of entry, termination, and name of certificate or diploma received, beginning with the first year of high school; the official high school diploma and high school transcripts; official college transcripts; all official records must be translated and notarized; and financial documentation.

Admission Contact
Office of Admissions
Marymount Manhattan College
221 East 71st Street
New York, NY 10021
Phone: (800) MARYMOUNT; (212) 517-0430
FAX: (212) 517-0448
E-mail: *admissions@mmm.edu*
Web: *www.marymount.mmm.edu*

The Heart of the College If you walk too quickly down East 71st Street in Manhattan, you may pass one of the best liberal arts colleges in the Northeast. Marymount Manhattan is unique in many ways, including its campus. It consists of only three buildings and there are no landscaped greens, trees, pond, or football stadium. In fact, Marymount is the only college in this guide that doesn't have varsity sports. The college is truly a reflection of New York City. As a result it has one of the most diverse student populations in the Northeast, with over 40 percent of the students of African-American, Latino, and Asian heritage. Also, the average age of the student population is 26, with almost half of all students returning adult learners. Over 50 percent of the students are first-generation college students.

Marymount has so much to offer its students, not the least of which is a location in one of the most sought-after residential neighborhoods in Manhattan. It is within walking distance of the Metropolitan Museum of Art, Lincoln Center, and Rockefeller Center, and a bus or subway ride away from Broadway, Wall Street, and the United Nations, with proximity to the finance, communications, and entertainment centers of the world, which offer wonderful internship opportunities.

Most students come to Marymount to study the fine and performing arts, business, and communications. The college features programs in theater, dance, and art, with students receiving conservatory-style training from faculty members who are scholars as well as practitioners of their art. The 250-seat Lang Theatre, complete with orchestra pit, provides students with exposure to the professional dance, opera, and theater performances at the college. Art students have the opportunity both to show their work and to curate exhibitions in the MMC Art Gallery. The Business Management students can select a concentration and intern at one of the multinational corporations or nonprofit institutions that abound in Manhattan. The new Lang Center for Producing provides communication arts students with a video studio and cutting-edge technology that make possible a curriculum that will "define the state of the art for American undergraduate education in Communication Arts." One outstanding faculty member says: ". . . our goal is to make our Center for Producing one of the major sources of creative talent and leadership, well into the twenty-first century."

These are all exciting programs that help to nourish the heart of the college, which is comprised of an energy, a camaraderie, and personal attention that are found at few colleges. Much of this can be attributed to a truly outstanding, dedicated faculty, many of whom still feel the joy of working at a college that nurtures and supports their own scholarship and creativity. This dynamic community produces excellent outcomes: 90 percent of students who apply are accepted into professional schools; 100 percent of teacher education students pass all three categories of the New York State Certification Exam (one of only eight colleges in the state to accomplish this); and graduates of Speech-Language Pathology and Audiology are admitted with substantial scholarships into advanced study programs at Columbia, the City University of New York, and other colleges.

About 500 resident students live in a new modern high-rise with suite-style accommodations, 16 blocks from the campus on East 55th Street. The building has 24-hour doorman security, a health club, wiring for computer and Internet access, lounges, and classrooms. The resident advisers plan neighborhood tours, movie nights, and much more. There are two other residential sites for students.

MARYWOOD UNIVERSITY

Scranton, Pennsylvania

Total Undergraduate Enrollment: 1,800
Men: 600 Women: 1,200
Five-Year Graduation Rate: 63%

Tuition: $$$
Room and Board: $$$
Residential Students: 50%

History Marywood was founded in 1915 by the Congregation of the Sisters, Servants of the Immaculate Heart of Mary, as a Catholic college concerned with the needs of women in northeast Pennsylvania. Marywood became coeducational in 1970 and a university in 1997.

Location Marywood is set on 115 acres in suburban Scranton, Pennsylvania, bordering the Pocono Mountains and offering students access

to beautiful lakes, forests, and outdoor activities. Scranton, through its museums, celebrates its history as a labor center. The campus is located two-and-a-half hours from New York City and Philadelphia.

Top Programs of Study Education, visual and performing arts, psychology

Arts and Sciences: Arts administration, art therapy, advertising and public relations, athletic training, biology, church music, criminal justice, deaf studies, design, English, environmental science, French, general science, health services administration, history, industrial organizational psychology, legal studies, mathematics, media/theater, music therapy, music and theater, nursing, nutrition and dietetics, performing arts, physical activity, political science, psychology, psychology/clinical practice, religious studies, social sciences, social medical technology/clinical laboratory science, social work, Spanish, studio art, telecommunications

Business Accounting, aviation management, computer information and telecommunications systems, financial planning, hotel and restaurant management, international business, management, marketing, retail business management

Education Art, early childhood, elementary, family and consumer sciences, music, secondary, special

Pre-Professional Audiology, chiropractic, dentistry, law, medical, physician's assistant, speech-language pathology

Accredited Programs Allied health professions, art and design, business, education, law, music, nursing, nutrition and dietetics, social work

Special Programs There are opportunities for self-designed majors, volunteer social service, and internships. The early childhood students study on campus in a Montessori-based pre-school/kindergarten program. The marketing major includes e-commerce and Internet sales. Foreign language students can study in France, Italy, Mexico, Canada, and Spain. Music majors can participate in summer workshops or a music camp. There is a five-year master's degree in Criminal Justice. There are several minors, including dance and journalism. There are Air Force and Army ROTC programs.

Facilities The 30 buildings include a new studio arts center; two art galleries; the new McGowan Center for Graduate and Professional Studies, which houses the Speech-Language-Hearing Clinic; the Marywood Early Childhood Center; and the Fricchione Day Care Center.

Transition to College Program Marywood uses a traditional orientation program.

Athletics NCAA III, Pennsylvania Athletic Conference

Men: Baseball, basketball, cross-country, soccer, tennis

Women: Basketball, cross-country, field hockey, soccer, softball, tennis, volleyball

Student Life and Housing About 600 students can be accommodated in college housing, which is guaranteed for all four years. Eighty percent of the students are from Pennsylvania, with the remainder from 24 other states and 26 countries. Ethnicity: Caucasian—94 percent. There is one local sorority and one local fraternity. All students may keep cars on campus.

Accommodations for Students with Disabilities Reasonable accommodations are provided for documented disabilities, made to either admissions or the Coordinator for Students With Disabilities.

Financial Aid Almost all freshmen receive aid. The average award was about $15,000.

Requirements for Admission SAT I or ACT scores and a 2.5 GPA in a college prep high school program.

Application Freshmen are admitted to all semesters, with application deadlines open.

International Students Required are TOEFL scores of 500 on the paper test or 173 on the computer test, as well as documentation of sufficient funds to cover all costs. Students must meet the regular academic standards for admission. Marywood conducts an English as a Second Language Program to assist those whose first language is not English.

Transfer Students Official high school and college transcripts are required, along with two letters of recommendation. A C grade or higher is required for courses to be eligible for transfer.

Admission Contact
Office of Admissions
Marywood University
2300 Adams Avenue
Scranton, PA 18509-1598
Phone: (800) 346-5014; (570) 348-6234
FAX: (570) 961-4763
E-mail: *ugadm@es.marywood.edu*
Web: *www.marywood.edu*

The Heart of the University Marywood's focus is on service and academic excellence. As a Catholic university its mission is the development of the person as well as the mastery of career-related skills and knowledge. Because Marywood is essentially a commuter school, it's been very successful in implementing its mission through a carefully crafted core curriculum. The lack of cohesion that the student typically finds at a commuter school is substituted by a feeling of community where all students focus on a curricular theme: "Living Responsibly in an Interde-

pendent World." The studies are integrated by the core curriculum, which is organized into four liberal arts categories. In these studies students explore the ultimate questions of life, helping students to make ethical decisions in the promotion of justice, peace, and compassion in the contemporary world. Students learn an appreciation of nature and the interdependence of human beings. They cultivate a sensitivity to human concerns. An aesthetic appreciation is fostered, as well as the ability to communicate effectively. The academic core, therefore, helps to create a community of learners who will provide service to an increasingly interdependent world.

At the same time, students experience their college life as one that is preparing them for important careers because Marywood's excellent professional programs are carefully integrated with the core curriculum. So many of the programs have received national accreditation that students have an unmistakable feeling that they are learning in programs of great quality, ranging from art to nutrition to nursing to physician's assistant. The student experience is one that is career focused.

McDANIEL COLLEGE
Westminster, Maryland

Total Undergraduate Enrollment: 1,600
Men: 686 Women: 914
Five-Year Graduation Rate: 72%

Tuition: $$$
Room and Board: $
Residential Students: 90%

History The college was established in 1867 as Western Maryland College. It was named after the Western Maryland Railroad, the company owned by John Smith, a major benefactor and first president of the college's board of trustees. Because the name caused confusion regarding its actual location, in January 2002 the school was renamed to honor a former student, faculty member, and policy maker.

Location The 160-acre campus overlooks historic Westminster, Maryland, 30 miles north of Baltimore and 56 miles north of Washington,

D.C. Rolling countryside, a mountain forest with nature trails, and skiing are all nearby.

Top Programs of Study Biology, business, social sciences

Arts and Sciences Art, art history, biology, chemistry, communication, economics, English, exercise science, French, German, history, mathematics, music, philosophy, physics, political science, international studies, psychology, religious studies, social work, sociology, Spanish, theater arts

Business Administration

Education Elementary, physical education, secondary

Pre-Professional Deaf education, engineering, forestry, law, medical and health professions, ministry, museum studies

Accredited Programs None

Special Programs There are dual degree programs in engineering, forestry, and biomedical engineering. The college offers a Washington, D.C., semester and Drew University's Semester on the United Nations and Semester on the New Europe. There are individualized majors available as well as study abroad opportunities, including McDaniel's own campus in Budapest, Hungary. There is a Phi Beta Kappa chapter and an Army ROTC program.

Facilities There are 60 buildings, including six buildings listed on the National Register of Historic Places. New buildings include a Science Center, a renovated Fine Arts Building, and six classroom buildings on a campus that is being transformed by a $40 million capital campaign. There are also an art gallery and state-of-the-art training facilities in the Blumberg Lifetime Fitness Center. The college is the summer training camp of the National Football League's Baltimore Ravens.

Transition to College Program Each fall the college schedules special seminars for first-year students, who study a variety of topics that emphasize writing, oral presentation, study skills, critical thinking, and time management.

Athletics NCAA III, Centennial Conference

Men: Baseball, basketball, cross-country, football, golf, indoor and outdoor track, lacrosse soccer, swimming, tennis, wrestling

Women: Basketball, cross-country, field hockey, golf lacrosse, indoor and outdoor track, soccer, softball, swimming, tennis, volleyball

Student Life and Housing About 1,200 students can be accommodated in campus housing, which is guaranteed for all four years. Sixty-eight percent of the students are from Maryland, the remainder from 27 other states and 23 countries. Ethnicity: Caucasian—79 percent; African-American—8 percent; Asian-American—2 percent; Hispanic-American—2 percent; International—4 percent. There are two local and three national fraternities, and two local and two national sororities. Upperclassmen may keep cars. Students adhere to an honor code.

Accommodations for Students with Disabilities The college provides comprehensive services.

Financial Aid About 60 percent of the students receive aid. The average freshman award was about $12,000.

Requirements for Admission SAT I or ACT scores and a college prep high school program. A campus tour is encouraged.

Application Freshmen are admitted fall and spring semesters. Applications should be submitted by February 1 for fall admission. Admission notification is sent by April 1.

International Students In addition to the typical application requirements, required are official copies of diplomas and certificates translated into English; a minimum TOEFL score of 213; results from any and all secondary school, university, and national examinations; and a certificate of finances form.

Transfer Students Required are official transcripts from all secondary and postsecondary institutions attended; SAT or ACT scores, unless 30 or more credits have been earned at an accredited institution; and a statement from the Dean of Students of the previous college indicating that the student is in good standing. No grades of D will be approved for transfer. The submission deadline is June 1.

Admission Contact
Office of Admissions
McDaniel College
2 College Hill

Westminster, MD 21157-4390
Phone: (800) 638-4390
FAX: (410) 857-2757
E-mail: *admissio@mcdaniel.edu*
Web: *www.mcdaniel.edu*

The Heart of the College Comprised of inquisitive students who challenge themselves and a faculty that is student-focused, McDaniel is a perfect place for students to learn and grow. Anchored by a solid liberal arts program, the college also offers more than 100 different student activities and organizations. This gives students many out-of-class opportunities to become leaders and stars whether they are writing for the newspaper or yearbook, acting in plays and musicals, or performing with the Jazz Ensemble or percussion band. Service involvement could involve raising funds for world hunger relief to organizing rock concerts. Almost 40 percent of the students compete in a varsity sport, and 20 percent are involved in Greek life. The athletic program has been nationally ranked in several sports. The 70-member College Activities Planning Board sponsors a multitude of events that keep McDaniel students involved in campus life. This emphasis on involvement is symbolized by the fact that professors receive special funds to host extracur-

ricular activities, including pizza parties in their homes.

The faculty hardly needs these funds because its interest in the students is so authentic. Students comment: "I can talk to my professors on a very personal level if I need to." This friendly and enthusiastic faculty devotes itself to classroom, lab, and studio teaching. When faculty members conduct research, many involve students. This emphasis on teaching and student-centeredness is typified by the fact that the president and top administrators at the college spend time with students and teach courses!

An important part of McDaniel's liberal arts program also takes place outside of campus. Certainly, the opportunity to study at the Budapest, Hungary, campus is frequently cited as a highlight by students. Also, the college sponsors special programs, such as public forums to hear Pulitzer Prize–winning writers and foreign ambassadors, as well as the noted speakers brought to the campus by the Phi Beta Kappa Visiting Scholars Program. Some students use the January term for study in Belize and Cuba.

The Career Services Center's marvelous program has resulted in 98 percent of graduates beginning their careers or entering graduate school within a few months of graduation.

MERCYHURST COLLEGE   Erie, Pennsylvania

Total Undergraduate Enrollment: 3,445
Men: 1,329 Women: 2,116
Five-Year Graduation Rate: 62%

Tuition: $$$
Room and Board: $$
Residential Students: 86%

History Mercyhurst College is a Catholic liberal arts institution founded in 1926 by Mother Borgia Egan and the Sisters of Mercy.

Location Mercyhurst is located on 85 acres on a hill overlooking Erie, Pennsylvania, the fourth largest city in the state. Located on the shore of Lake Erie, the city is centrally located between Cleveland, Pittsburgh, and Buffalo.

Top Programs of Study Business, education, Archaeology

Arts and Sciences Archaeology/anthropology, art, art therapy, biochemistry, biology (concentrations in environmental science, medical technology, neuroscience), chemistry, communications, computer systems, criminal justice, dance, English, forensic science, French, geology, history, hotel, restaurant and institutional management (concentration in professional clubhouse and golf management), human ecology (concentrations in fashion merchandising and interior design), medicine, music, musical theater, philosophy, political science, psychology, religious studies, sociology, social work, Spanish, sports

Business Accounting, business (concentrations in advertising, finance, marketing, management, sports marketing), business chemistry

Education Art, dance, early childhood, elementary, music, secondary, special, religious education

Pre-Professional Dentistry, law, medicine, osteopathy, pharmacy, veterinary

Accredited Programs Dietetics, social work

Special Programs There are cooperative programs with Gannon and Edinboro Universities in dietetics. Also, Duquesne University Law School and Mercyhurst have a dual degree 3-3 program. The Research, Intelligence, and Analysis Program (R/IAP) prepares graduates for careers in the intelligence agencies. The dance program is considered one of the finest in the nation.

Facilities There are 40 buildings, including a new academic building, the new Sister Carolyn Herrmann Student Union, a new Mary D'Angelo Performing Arts Center, and an addition to the Hammerhill Library.

Transition to College Program Mercyhurst uses a traditional orientation program.

Athletics NCAA II, Eastern Collegiate Athletic Conference

   Men: Baseball, basketball, cross-country, field hockey, football, golf, ice hockey (Div. I), lacrosse, rowing, soccer, tennis, volleyball, water polo, wrestling

   Women: Basketball, cross-country, field hockey, golf, ice hockey (Div. I), rowing, soccer, softball, tennis, volleyball, water polo

Student Life and Housing About 1,500 students can be accommodated in college housing, which is guaranteed for all four years. Sixty percent of the students are from Pennsylvania, the remainder from 37 other states and 14 countries. Ethnicity: Caucasian—91 percent. There are no fraternities or sororities. Upperclassmen may keep cars.

Accommodations for Students with Disabilities A comprehensive Structured Program is offered.

Financial Aid About 92 percent of all freshmen receive aid. The average freshman award was about $7,000.

Requirements for Admission SAT I or ACT scores and a college prep high school program.

Application Application deadlines are open, with students notified of admission decisions as soon as all credentials have been received.

International Students Applications must be made at least five months prior to admission. If a student's native language is not English, a minimum TOEFL score of 555 is required. English translations of all academic documents are required. Evaluations of academic records must be made through World Education Services. Proof of sufficient financial resources is required.

Transfer Students Application deadlines should be filed well in advance of the term students expect to enter. High school and college transcripts are needed. A minimum 2.0 GPA is required in previous college work. No grade below a C is transferable.

Admission Contact
Office of Admissions
Mercyhurst College
501 East 38th Street
Erie, PA 16546-0001
Phone: (800) 825-1926, ext. 2202; (814) 824-2202
FAX: (814) 824-2071
E-mail: *rengel@mercyhurst.edu*
Web: *www.mercyhurst.edu*

The Heart of the College When students first visit the Mercyhurst campus they know immediately that it is the right college for them. Many students talk about how it has "just the right feel" while one foreign student, after a long flight, started crying because she was so taken by the beauty of the campus. Situated on a beautiful site overlooking Lake Erie, just one block from the city limits of Erie, Mercyhurst students enjoy the suburban, pastoral setting while being only minutes from downtown Erie, the fourth largest city in Pennsylvania. Erie is a friendly city with many recreational and cultural activities and, with four other colleges nearby, a lively collegiate community.

As a Catholic institution, the college integrates the liberal arts and sciences with career programs. Mercyhurst views itself as "a community of learning dedicated to the development of the whole person," with special emphasis on the qualities of excellence, compassion, creativity, and service to others. Career preparation is a pri-

ority at Mercyhurst, and students have cooperative education opportunities enabling them to work and earn salaries as they advance through their major fields of study. Internships, field studies, and practicum opportunities all lead to the significant statistic that shows that 93 percent of graduates are employed or enrolled in graduate school within six months of graduation.

One of the few programs of its kind in the nation is Mercyhurst's Research/Intelligence Analyst Program, designed for students who wish to pursue careers as research and/or intelligence analysts in government agencies and private enterprise.

Students enjoy the personal, supportive attention they receive from a talented faculty, small classes, and the many opportunities for community service. Also, sports are big at Mercyhurst, with over 20 percent of the students participating in an excellent 26-team athletic program that includes Division I teams in both men's and women's ice hockey.

MEREDITH COLLEGE

Raleigh, North Carolina

Total Undergraduate Enrollment: 2,100
Men: 0 Women: 2,100
Five-Year Graduation Rate: 66%

Tuition: $$$
Room and Board: $
Residential Students: 61%

History Meredith College is named for Thomas Meredith, who helped establish the college as Baptist Female University in 1891. Ten years later the name was changed to Meredith College. It is the largest private four-year college for women in the Southeast.

Location Meredith's 225-acre campus is located in suburban Raleigh, North Carolina, nestled in the heart of North Carolina's Research Triangle (Raleigh, Durham, Chapel Hill), rated the Number 1 place to live in America! This area is home to major universities, historic sites, cultural attractions, and beaches only two hours away.

Top Programs of Study Business, psychology, education, interior design

Arts and Sciences American civilization, art (history, studio, graphic design), biology (biological diversity, environmental science, health science, molecular biology), chemistry, child development, clothing and fashion merchandising, communication, computer information systems, computer science, dance, economics, English, exercise and sports science, family and consumer sciences, foods and nutrition, French, history, interior design, international studies, mathematics, music, music performance, musical theater, political studies, psychology, public history, religion, social work, sociology, Spanish, theater

Business Accounting, business administration (economics, finance, human resource management, management, marketing), international business

Education Dance, early childhood, elementary, middle, music, secondary

Pre-Professional Art therapy, dentistry, law, medicine, pharmacy, physical therapy, physician's assistant, veterinary medicine

Accredited Programs Dietetics, education, interior design, music, social work

Special Programs Meredith's research program provides opportunities for students to create and explore a research area with a faculty mentor in any area. LeaderShape is a leadership development experience in which students develop leadership skills, plan a project, and then implement the plan. There are opportunities for students to design their own majors, volunteer, do an internship, or engage in a cooperative education experience. Interested students may spend a semester at Marymount Manhattan College in New York City.

Facilities The 30 buildings include a new science and math building with research labs, outdoor classrooms, and a rooftop telescope platform. There are also a learning resource center; art gallery; child care lab; greenhouse; and psychology, language, and autism labs.

Transition to College Program All freshmen are expected to attend Freshman Discovery twice during the fall semester. These sessions help students cope with issues that may arise while they are at college. Also, students are encouraged to enroll in the First-Year Experience class, which helps students make a successful transition to college life.

Athletics NCAA Div. III, independent of any conference, basketball, soccer, soft ball, tennis, volleyball

Student Life and Housing About 1,200 students can be accommodated in college housing, which is guaranteed for all four years. Ninety-one per-

cent of the students are from North Carolina, with the remainder from 25 other states and 27 countries. Ethnicity: Caucasian—88 percent; African-American—6 percent; Hispanic-American—2 percent; Asian-American—1 percent; International—1 percent. There are no sororities. All students may keep cars. The college operates under an honor system.

Accommodations for Students with Disabilities In compliance with section 504

Financial Aid About 85 percent of all freshmen receive aid. The average freshman award was about $8,000.

Requirements for Admission SAT I or ACT scores and a 2.0 GPA in a college prep high school program.

Application Early Decision applications should be filed by October 15. Regular applications should be filed by February 15 for the fall semester and December 1 for the spring semester.

International Students Students must provide official transcripts in English from secondary schools and colleges, an official copy of each diploma or degree, a course equivalent evaluation, and TOEFL scores if the student is not an English native speaker or English is not the principal language of instruction. Students must provide proof of financial responsibility and a health form.

Transfer Students An overall C average is required in previous college work, and the student must be in good standing at the previous college, as well as be recommended by college officials. If the student has fewer than 30 semester hours of transferable credit, the student must also meet regular freshman admission requirements.

Admission Contact
Office of Admissions
Meredith College
3800 Hillsborough Street
Raleigh, NC 27607-5298
Phone: (800) MEREDITH; (919) 760-8581

Fax: (919) 760-2348
E-mail: *admissions@meredith.edu*
Web: *www.meredith.edu*

The Heart of the College As with all good women's colleges, the mission of Meredith is to educate women to excel. American society has provided women with more choices and opportunities than previous generations had, so Meredith takes this mission very seriously and creates a climate of excellence where students feel comfortable in taking the initiative. One example is the quality internships that are available to students as a result of Meredith's location in the Raleigh/Durham/Chapel Hill Research Triangle. IBM and state government internships provide experiences that are résumé-worthy. This location also provides opportunities to meet and learn from the 90,000 other college students who attend one of the area's nine colleges.

Meredith is one of only two private institutions among just 14 schools statewide selected to be part of the prestigious Teaching Fellows Program for North Carolina residents. Through the program, students attend special seminars, trips, and cultural activities as students become members of a close-knit community of about 100 future teachers.

At Meredith students become technology savvy, because Meredith believes that technology is often a key to career success. Part of the Meredith Technology Initiative provides for a laptop for each full-time freshman and replaces it two years later.

Students at Meredith are also encouraged to create their own paths by designing their own majors. The LeaderShape Program focuses on leadership skills and the creation and implementation of a project. Take the pulse of Meredith and it is vibrant with opportunities and excellence.

MILLERSVILLE UNIVERSITY

Millersville, Pennsylvania

Total Undergraduate Enrollment: 6,600

Men: 2,900 Women: 3,700
Five-Year Graduation Rate: 59%

Tuition: In-State–$;
Out-of-State–$$
Room and Board: $
Residential Students: 41%

History Millersville University was founded in 1854 as a three-story academy but soon became the Lancaster County Normal Institute—a result of the then Superintendent of Lancaster Schools J. P. Wickersham's interest in establishing a teacher training institute. In 1927 Millersville became a state teacher's college, and in 1983 it was authorized to become a university.

Location The 250-acre campus is located in Millersville, Pennsylvania, a small town five miles west of Lancaster, one-and-a-half hours from Baltimore and Philadelphia, and two-and-a-half hours from Washington, D.C.

Top Programs of Study Education, accounting/management, criminal justice, marketing

Arts and Sciences Anthropology, art, biology (options in botany, environmental, marine, medical technology, molecular biology/biotechnology, nuclear medicine technology, respiratory therapy), chemistry (options in biochemistry, environmental, polymer), communication and theater, computer science, earth sciences, economics, English, French, geography, geology, German, government and political affairs, history, industrial technology, international studies, mathematics, meteorology, music (option in music industry), nursing (option in public school nursing), occupational safety and environmental health, oceanography, philosophy, physics, psychology, social work, sociology (option in criminology), Spanish

Business Administration (options in accounting, finance, international business, management, marketing)

Education Art, early childhood, elementary, music, secondary, special, technology

Pre-Professional Dentistry, law, medicine, optometry, podiatry, veterinary medicine

Accredited Programs Business, chemistry, computer science, education, industrial technology, music, nursing, occupational safety and hygiene management, respiratory therapy, social work

Special Programs A PACE academic enrichment program is offered for those students who are educationally and economically disadvantaged but show academic promise to succeed at the college level. There are several associate degree programs. The university offers a cooperative program in engineering with the University of Pennsylvania and Penn State. Students may also take courses at nearby Franklin and Marshall College. The Urban Education program prepares students to teach in urban schools. Millersville is also the founder of the Marine Science Consortium, 14 colleges and universities that operate a marine station at Wallops Island, Virginia, which has several seagoing vessels and laboratories with biological and oceanographic equipment. The Harrisburg Internship Semester places students with policy-makers in governmental agencies. There are opportunities for study abroad, cooperative education, and internships. There is a Center for Politics and Public Affairs, an Artists/Scholars in Residence Program, and an Orchestral Great Artist Program. The university offers many master's degree programs and post-baccalaureate and post-master's certification programs. Millersville is rated as one of the most "computer-wired" universities in America.

Facilities There are 92 buildings, including the Student Memorial Center, where much of the campus social life is focused and which includes a café and a multipurpose room used for film series, parties, and lectures. Byerly Hall houses the foreign language media center and several satellite receivers providing both live and delayed newscasts available in foreign languages. Osburn Hall houses technology labs, and there are over a dozen general purpose and specialized computer labs located throughout the campus. There is a new Science and Technology Building that houses 26 lab spaces dedicated to student–faculty research. The university is also home to Jenkins Early Childhood Center, a radio station, and new television studios.

Transition to College Program The university uses a traditional orientation program.

Athletics NCAA II, Pennsylvania State Athletic Conference

Men: Baseball, basketball, cross-country, football, golf, soccer, tennis, track & field (indoor and outdoor), wrestling (Div. I)

Women: Basketball, cross-country, field hockey, lacrosse, soccer, softball, swimming, tennis, track & field, (indoor and outdoor), volleyball

Student Life and Housing About 2,500 students can be accommodated in college housing. Ninety-six percent of the students are from Pennsylvania, the remainder are from 21 states and 49 countries. Ethnicity: Caucasian—90 percent. There are one local and nine national fraternities, and two local and nine national sororities. Upperclassmen may keep cars.

Accommodations for Students with Disabilities Students with physical disabilities are encouraged to contact the Assistant Vice President for Student Affairs/Student Support Services immediately after admission to the university. The university complies with section 504.

Financial Aid About 75 percent of all freshmen receive aid. The average freshman award was about $5,400.

Requirements for Admission SAT I or ACT scores and a college prep high school program or GED.

Application Applicants are admitted to all semesters. There is a rolling admissions policy, with admission decisions made within a month of receiving a completed application.

International Students In addition to satisfying general admission requirements, students must show English proficiency by scoring a minimum of 500 on the TOEFL paper exam or 183 on the computer-based exam. Students from English-speaking countries may choose to take the SAT or ACT as an option to the TOEFL.

Transfer Students Required is an overall GPA of at least 2.0 at a regionally accredited institution, official college transcripts for each school attended, as well as a high school transcript. Applicants with less than a 2.0 GPA may be admitted probationally. Typically, any courses with grades of C– or better are considered for transfer. The university participates in the state Passport System, which allows students who have earned at least 12 credits to transfer from community colleges with even D graded courses considered for transfer, with every attempt made to transfer previous course work into required General Education or major program course requirements.

Admission Contact
Office of Admissions
Millersville University
P.O. Box 1002
Millersville, PA 17551-0302
Phone: (800) MUADMIT; (717) 872-3011
FAX: (717) 871-2147
E-mail: *admissions@millersville.edu*
Web: *www.millersv.edu*

The Heart of the University The university lies near the edge of the famous Pennsylvania Dutch country—an area filled with family-style restaurants, horse-drawn carriages, clothing outlets, and rich farmland. This setting and tradition are reflected in the tranquil campus, with aspects of traditional architecture. Students are very pleased with such an attractive, peaceful campus setting that is only a shuttle-ride to Lancaster

attractions, and where the size of the student population offers that perfect blend of small enough to be personal yet large enough to offer many programs and a rich campus life. Students say they like the feeling of knowing about everyone and being able to make friends so easily.

But the university's setting belies its mission to prepare its students for an increasingly pluralistic and technologically complex society, preparing students for productive careers, yet firmly grounding programs in the liberal arts. Its quality academic programs and excellent faculty have made Millersville one of the top public universities in the Middle Atlantic Region.

The faculty, while also engaged in research and scholarship, make students their first priority. With an average class size of 25, professors teach all classes and give great time and energy to preparing interesting lessons. They work closely with students, encouraging collaborative research and inspiring and helping their students.

For science majors, this small university is ideal. They receive personal attention, work closely with faculty on crucial research projects from robotics to human reproduction, and have state-of-the-art science facilities. The biology program has an excellent reputation, and, in general, Millersville's science programs are well regarded by employers and graduate schools. A second program of excellence, one that has a long history because of the origins of the university, is the teacher education program. Taught by highly regarded faculty, students are offered that perfect blend of theory and practice as they engage in supervised field experiences and tutoring in schools. Early Childhood students have the luxury of the Jenkins Early Childhood Center right on campus. The program in Urban Education is a distinctive one, requiring students to work as teaching assistants part of a semester to learn the truths, myths, and misconceptions about teaching in urban schools. The humanities and social science programs excel because of their emphasis on participation. Here students will find many occasions for art students to exhibit their work, business students to be involved in internships and co-op programs, music students to be involved in numerous performance formats, theater students to be involved in presentations, social science students to engage in field work, and communication students to work in new broadcast studios.

The outcomes are significant. In a recent class 97 percent of the graduates reported that they were employed, with 86 percent getting jobs related to their majors. Teacher education graduates are working in almost every one of Pennsylvania's 501 school districts. And about 25 percent of the grads enroll in graduate school.

MILLIKIN UNIVERSITY
Decatur, Illinois

Total Undergraduate Enrollment: 2,400
Men: 1,100 Women: 1,300
Five-Year Graduation Rate: 60%

Tuition: $$$
Room and Board: $$
Residential Students: 72%

History The university is named for James Millikin, who founded the university in 1901 as an institution that would embrace the practical side of learning as well as the literary and classical. Millikin is affiliated with the Presbyterian Church.

Location Millikin is located on 70 acres in Decatur, Illinois (population 85,000), on the historic west side. Centrally located, the university is two hours from St. Louis and three hours from Chicago.

Top Programs of Study Business administration and management, elementary education, exploratory studies

Arts and Sciences American studies, art management, art therapy, athletic training, biology, chemistry, commercial art/computer design, commercial music, communication, computer science, English (literature and writing), experimental psychology, exploratory studies, fitness and sport (sports management), French, German, history, human services, international studies, interdisciplinary studies, mathematics, modern languages, music, music performance, musical theater, nursing, philosophy, political science, psychology, religion, sociology, Spanish, theater

Business Accounting, management, finance, international business, management information systems, marketing

Education Art, elementary, music, physical education, secondary

Pre-Professional Chiropractic, dentistry, engineering, law, medicine, medical technology, occupational therapy, optometry, pharmacy, physical therapy, physician's assistant

Accredited Programs Music, nursing

Special Programs: Students have the opportunity to design their own majors. There are many internship and study abroad opportunities. Millikin has a 3-2 cooperative engineering degree program with Washington University in St. Louis.

Facilities There are 28 buildings, including the renovated Perkinson Music Center; the Kirkland Fine Arts Center; a new science center, with observatory, greenhouse, and research labs; and the new Decatur Indoor Sports Center.

Transition to College Program Freshmen are on campus a week before regular classes and begin to focus on study skills, expectations, time management, and a service component. A Freshman Seminar is combined with an English course and students choose the seminar they would like to attend based upon the seminar topic. The same group of students meet to discuss, research, and write about the topic.

Athletics NCAA III, College Conference of Illinois and Wisconsin

Men: Baseball, basketball, cross-country, football, golf, soccer, swimming, wrestling

Women: Cross-country, golf, soccer, softball, swimming, track

Student Life and Housing About 1,400 students can be accommodated in college housing. Eighty-five percent of the students are from Illinois, with the remainder from 33 other states and 13 countries. Ethnicity: Caucasian—84 percent; African-American—7 percent; Hispanic-American—2 percent; Asian-American—1 percent. There are nine national fraternities and three national sororities. Upperclassmen may keep cars.

Accommodations for Students with Disabilities In compliance with section 504

Financial Aid Almost all freshmen receive aid. The average freshman award was about $7,000.

Requirements for Admission SAT I or ACT scores and a 2.0 GPA in a college prep high school program.

Application Freshmen are admitted to all semesters. The application deadlines are open.

International Students Original transcripts of all secondary and postsecondary work are required along with certified English translations. In addition, a certification of student finances, a TOEFL minimum score of 550, a completed health information form, and health insurance are required.

Transfer Students In general, a C average is necessary, along with official records for high school and colleges attended. Associate degree transfers are generally given full credit for up to a maximum of 66 credits.

Admission Contact
Office of Admissions
Millikin University
1184 West Main Street
Decatur, IL 62522-2084
Phone: (800) 373-7733
FAX: (217) 425-4669
E-mail: *admis@mail.millikin.edu*
Web: *www.millikin.edu*

The Heart of the University The university has the educational outcomes to demonstrate the quality of its undergraduate program. Ninety-eight percent of Millikin's students garner a job or go to graduate school—89 percent in their chosen field—within six months of graduation. Millikin is also one of the leading institutions for Academic All-Americans, ranked fifteenth in the nation. This excellence has caught the eye of the American Association of Colleges and Universities, which has given a special commendation to Millikin for its Millikin Program of Student Learning.

This program offers students an integrated, flexible curriculum that is unified by the common threads of Learning Goals; Core Questions, Values, Means; and Proficiencies. For example, a Learning Goal in the area of "knowledge" is the "interaction between technology and society." An example of a Core Question is "Who am I?" An example of Core Means is the use of primary texts. Proficiencies are written and oral communication, quantitative skills, library research, information technology, with the study of a second language made optional.

The approach to learning blends thinking with doing, and there are plenty of opportunities to "do" in Millikin's nationally renowned Service Learning Program, where all freshmen go into the community and learn by doing.

The city of Decatur offers the best of both worlds: large international corporations blend with small city opportunities to offer abundant quality internships and jobs throughout the school year and summer.

With excellent faculty that is passionate about its academic fields and teaching, many students work as partners with faculty on research projects. All of the undergraduate program is characterized by learning practices that are integrated, experiential, collaborative, and engaged. Millikin is considered a "best buy" and one of the top 50 small universities in the nation for technology.

MONMOUTH COLLEGE   Monmouth, Illinois

Total Undergraduate Enrollment: 1,125
Men: 540 Women: 585
Five-Year Graduation Rate: 63%

Tuition: $$$
Room and Board: $
Residential Students: 97%

History Monmouth College is a private liberal arts college founded in 1853 by Scottish-Irish Presbyterians. The college still retains an affiliation with the Presbyterian Church.

Location Monmouth College's 50-acre campus is located in the small town of Monmouth, Illinois (population 9,500), in the western part of the state about 150 miles southwest of Chicago and north of St. Louis. The Mississippi River is 15 minutes from campus.

Top Programs of Study Business, education, sciences

Arts and Sciences Art, biology, chemistry, communication/theater arts, computer science, economics, English, environmental science, French, Greek, history, Latin, mathematics, music, philosophy and religious studies, physics, political science, psychology, public relations, sociology/anthropology, Spanish

Business Accounting, business administration

Education Elementary, middle, physical education, secondary

Pre-Professional Architecture, dentistry, engineering, journalism, law, library science, medicine, medical technology, ministry, nursing, occupational therapy, physical therapy, social service, veterinary medicine

Accredited Programs None

Special Programs The Wackerlee Career and Leadership Center promotes greater self-awareness and leadership skills by encouraging community service and involvement in campus organizations. Students may study at the American College of Thessalonika in Greece, as well as other European universities. A Washinton, D.C., semester is also offered. Monmouth offers students study at a wilderness field station in northern Minnesota.

Facilities There are 26 buildings, including the new Mellinger Teaching and Learning Center, the LeSuer Biological Field Station, and the renovated Hewes Library. There are also radio and television stations.

Transition to College Program The Freshman Seminar addresses the goals and purposes of a liberal arts education. Students read a variety of texts, write papers, make presentations, and discuss interdisciplinary themes that promote self-discovery.

Athletics NCAA III, Midwest Athletic Conference

   Men: Baseball, basketball, cross-country, football, golf, soccer, tennis, track

   Women: Basketball, cross-country, golf, soccer, softball, tennis, track

Student Life and Housing Almost all students live in college housing, which is guaranteed for all four years. Eighty-nine percent of the students are from Illinois, with the remainder from 20 other states and 22 countries. Ethnicity: Caucasian—87 percent; African-American—5 percent; International—3 percent; Hispanic-American—2 percent. There are three national sororities and three national fraternities. All students may keep cars.

Accommodations for Students with Disabilities In compliance with section 504

Financial Aid About 95 percent of all students receive aid. The average award was about $19,500.

Requirements for Admission SAT I or ACT scores and a 2.5 GPA in a college prep high school program.

Application Freshmen are admitted to both fall and spring semesters. Application deadlines are open, with admission notification sent on a rolling basis.

International Students A minimum TOEFL score of 504 on the paper test is required.

Transfer Students Previous college transcripts must be submitted. The Registrar evaluates transcripts to determine transferability of credit. A C− is a minimum grade for transferability. Students with an associate degree from a two-year college may be admitted with junior standing.

Admission Contact
Office of Admissions
Monmouth College
700 E. Broadway
Monmouth, IL 61462-9896
Phone: (800) 74 SCOTS
FAX: (309) 457-2141
E-mail: *admit@monm.edu*
Web: *www.monm.edu*

The Heart of the College Monmouth College bills itself as "what college was meant to be." And it's right about this in a multitude of ways,

including the friendly atmosphere that makes friendships so easy to develop and the overall nurturing environment. Symbolic of this climate is the college's "no-cut" policy in athletics, which allows all students the chance to play on a varsity team each year.

Monmouth has a student–faculty ratio of 14:1 and an average class size of 22. Over 90 percent of its faculty have the terminal degree in their fields. Monmouth points with special pride to this dedicated faculty who go "above and beyond the call of duty to help you attain your academic goals." These full-time faculty members act as mentors, are professionally active, constantly incorporate new knowledge and innovations into their classrooms, and never lose sight of their major function: teaching undergraduate students. And all of this is done in the luxury of many new and renovated facilities. In addition to athletics and Greek life, the array of activities allows students to learn teamwork, dedication, initiative, and leadership.

The success of Monmouth's efforts is seen in their 97 percent placement rate of seniors in jobs or graduate school within six months of graduation.

The friendly, nurturing climate and excellent placement rate confirm for students that Monmouth has done a careful job in creating a college that provides quality programs and quality results.

MORAVIAN COLLEGE   Bethlehem, Pennsylvania

Total Undergraduate Enrollment: 1,451
Men: 581 Women: 870
Five-Year Graduation Rate: 76%

Tuition: $$$
Room and Board: $$$
Residential Students: 73%

History In 1741 settlers from Germany and Moravia (now a province of the Czech Republic) founded the community of Bethlehem in Pennsylvania and in 1742 opened separate schools for boys and girls. These later became seminaries and colleges. In 1954 they merged to form Moravian College, an independent liberal arts college affili-

ated with the Moravian Church. Moravian is the sixth oldest college in America.

Location The 80-acre campus is in Bethlehem, Pennsylvania (population 75,000), 60 miles north of Philadelphia and 90 miles west of New York City, located in the greater Lehigh Valley area where the population totals more than 600,000.

Top Programs of Study Management, psychology, art

Arts and Sciences Art history and criticism, art studio, biology, chemistry, classics, clinical counseling, computer science, criminal justice, drama and theater, economics, English literature and language, experimental psychology, French, German, graphic and interactive design, history, industrial/organizational psychology, mathematics, music, nursing, philosophy, physics, political science, psychology, religion, social/developmental psychology, sociology, Spanish, writing

Business Accounting, international management, management

Education Art, elementary, music, secondary

Pre-Professional Dentistry, law, medicine, ministry, veterinary medicine

Accredited Programs Allied health education, chemistry, education, music, nursing

Special Programs Moravian offers the following cooperative degree programs: medical technology with several hospitals; natural resources management with Duke University; cytogenetic technology, diagnostic imaging, medical technology, occupational therapy, and physical therapy with Thomas Jefferson University in Philadelphia; engineering with Lehigh, the University of Pennsylvania, and Washington University in St. Louis; and geology with Lehigh University. There is also a dual degree (3-4) program with the Temple School of Dentistry. Students can take courses at any one of the five colleges that comprise the Lehigh Valley Consortium. There are interdepartmental and individually designed majors available, as well as study abroad programs, including a year-abroad at Oxford University, England. There is also a Washington, D.C., semester. There is an Army ROTC program.

Facilities There are 55 buildings, including a new academic building, a new field house, an expanded

library, and a seminary. The college's art and music programs are located eight-tenths of a mile from the main campus on the Hurd Campus in the heart of the colonial historic district, where Moravian settlers constructed buildings of renowned beauty and endurance. The Hurd Center for Music and Art includes seven buildings on Church Street, which has been identified as one of the 10 most distinctive historic streets in America.

Transition to College Program As part of the First-Year Experience, students are required to take an Introduction to College Life half-course that aims to introduce first-year students to the intellectual life of Moravian College, promote a smooth transition to college life, and help students develop a coherent plan for their education.

Athletics NCAA III, Middle Atlantic Commonwealth Conference

Men: Baseball, basketball, cross-country, football, golf, lacrosse, soccer, tennis, track & field

Women: Basketball, cross-country, field hockey, lacrosse, soccer, softball, tennis, track & field, volleyball

Student Life and Housing About 1,000 students can be accommodated in college housing, which is guaranteed all four years. Sixty-three percent of the students are from Pennsylvania, the remainder from 19 other states and 18 countries. Ethnicity: Caucasian—93 percent. There are two national fraternities and four national sororities. Upperclassmen may keep cars.

Accommodations for Students with Disabilities With appropriate documentation of need, students may register for reduced course load and/or classroom accommodations.

Financial Aid About 90 percent of all freshmen receive aid. The average freshman award was about $9,000.

Requirements for Admission SAT I or ACT scores and a college prep high school program. A college visit and interview are recommended. Music majors are required to audition, and art majors are encouraged to submit a portfolio of work with their applications.

Application Freshmen are admitted fall and spring semesters. Early Decision applications should be filed by February 1. Regular applications should be filed by March 1 for fall admission and December 1 for spring admission. Admission notification of Early Decision is made between December 15 and February 15, with regular decision by March 15.

International Students Required are official original and translated transcripts of secondary and postsecondary schooling, results of the SAT exam if instruction has been in English, and evidence of financial responsibility. TOEFL results of 550 minimum on the paper exam and 213 on the computer-based one are required if English is not the student's first language.

Transfer Students Application deadlines are May 1 for fall admission and January 1 for spring admission. A recommendation from the Dean of Students at the institution currently attended is required. Courses of C or better from an accredited institution are considered for transfer. A maximum of 64 credits will be accepted from two-year institutions and 96 credits accepted from four-year institutions.

Admission Contact
Office of Admissions
Moravian College
1200 Main Street
Bethlehem, PA 18018
Phone: (800) 441-3191; (610) 861-1320
FAX: (610) 625-7930
E-mail: *admissions@moravian.edu*
Web: *www.moravian.edu*

The Heart of the College The Moravian College experience is a unique one for several reasons, most noteworthy of which is that Moravian actually consists of two campuses less than one mile apart and complementing each other to the

degree that students are attracted to both. The North Campus, or the Main Street Campus, is the hub of daily life for most students, home of the student union, library, and athletics center. Almost all students spend part of the day here. An eight-block walk or shuttle bus will take students to the South Campus, The Priscilla Payne Hurd Campus, the home of Moravian's art and music departments. The buildings are colonial historic ones in a setting steeped in history and bursting with the creative energy of music and art. Nearly all students come to the South Campus to take an art class, attend a concert or gallery show, sing in the choir, or reside in a more historic ambiance.

These two physical settings blend to create a superb living–learning community. First is the rich diversity of student religions, ethnicity, racial mix, and socioeconomic class that form a collegial population of friendly, supportive students. Add to this a scholarly, dedicated, caring faculty that students compliment for its willingness to provide additional support and assistance outside of the classroom. Student evaluations also rate their professors highly in terms of teaching ability. Importantly, even the most senior faculty teach entry level courses. In nearly every department students have opportunities to participate or initiate scholarly projects that involve their professors. In fact, Moravian's SOAR program provides stipends, travel allowance, and research expenses to support and encourage this research collaboration.

After an eight-year study of the curriculum, the faculty has created an innovative program of general education called Learning in Common (LinC), comprised of multidisciplinary courses designed to sharpen the critical knowledge and skills of writing, computer competence, knowledge of economic and social systems, and quantitative reasoning.

The wonderful community at Moravian is assisted by the high degree of participation by students in college life. About a third play a varsity sport, while almost two-thirds are involved in intramurals. About 25 percent of the students participate in Greek life, and about half are involved in volunteer service in the local community.

In recent years, more than 90 percent of Moravian's graduates are either employed or in graduate school within six months of gradua-tion. This is testimony to the aggressive career planning and placement system that begins in freshman year and includes speakers and career panels, individual counseling by alumni, and campus interviews.

MOUNT SAINT MARY COLLEGE

Newburgh, New York

Total Undergraduate Enrollment: 2,042
Men: 583 Women: 1,459
Five-Year Graduation Rate: 72%

Tuition: $$
Room and Board: $$
Residential Students: 70%

History Mount Saint Mary is an independent institution that has maintained a firm belief in the value of a liberal arts education and a com-mitment to Judeo-Christian principles since its founding in 1960. The college is an outgrowth of Mount Saint Mary Normal School, begun by the Dominican Sisters for teacher training in 1930.

Location Mount Saint Mary's 70-acre scenic campus is located in Newburgh, New York, over-looking the Hudson River. It is 58 miles north of New York City and 12 miles north of the U.S. Mil-itary Academy at West Point.

Top Programs of Study Business, education, nursing

Arts and Sciences Biology/biological science, chemistry, communications, computer science, criminal justice, English, Hispanic American studies, history, human services, information sci-ences and systems, interdisciplinary studies, mathematics, media arts, political science/gov-ernment, psychology, public relations, social sci-ence, sociology

Business Accounting, administration, manage-ment

Education Adolescent, childhood, elementary, special

Pre-Professional Dentistry, law, medical, veteri-nary medicine

Accredited Programs Education, nursing

Special Programs The college is home to one of the oldest and largest artistic theaters in the mid-Hudson region. Drama, dance, and musical shows featuring renowned artists are offered each year for students, children, and the community at large. Also, the annual "Artists on Campus" art show focuses on the visual arts, with many local artists participating and hundreds of people attending. There are internships and cooperative education programs available. The college also has cooperative degree programs with other institutions in physical therapy, social work, and engineering. Students can design their own majors. There is a Phi Beta Kappa chapter.

Facilities There are 41 buildings, including the modern Kaplan Recreational Center; Aquinas Hall, the main college building housing state-of-the-art computer science labs; a theater; a multi-media digital production center; an art studio; music facilities; and a photography lab. The cam-pus includes the Bishop Dunn Memorial School, an elementary and junior high school used by teacher education students.

Transition to College Program The college uses a traditional orientation program.

Athletics NCAA III, Skyline Athletic Conference; Knickerbocker Baseball Conference

Men: Baseball, basketball, soccer, swimming, tennis

Women: Basketball, soccer, softball, swimming, tennis, volleyball

Student Life and Housing About 1,000 students can be accommodated in college housing, which is guaranteed for all four years. Eighty-five percent of the students are from New York, with the remainder from 16 other states and 7 countries. Ethnicity: Caucasian—80 percent; African-American—11 percent; Hispanic-American—7 percent; Asian-American—2 percent. There are no fraternities or sororities. All students may keep cars.

Accommodations for Students with Disabilities Students should report to the Coordinator of Services for Persons with Disabilities to determine policies and procedures for available assistance.

Financial Aid About 80 percent of all freshmen receive aid.

Requirements for Admission SAT I or ACT scores and a college prep high school curriculum. An interview is recommended.

Application Freshmen are admitted to all semesters. Application deadlines are open, with admission notification made on a rolling basis.

International Students A minimum score of 500 on the TOEFL is required.

Transfer Students Students are admitted in all semesters. Transcripts of previous college work are evaluated by the college Registrar for transferability of credit. Students with associate degrees are awarded full junior status and guaranteed 60 credits in transfer. C grades or better are transferable.

Admission Contact
Office of Admissions
Mount Saint Mary College
330 Powell Avenue
Newburgh, NY 12550
Phone: (888) YES-MSMC; (845) 561-0800
FAX: (845) 562-6762
E-mail: *mtstmary@msmc.edu*
Web: *www.msmc.edu*

The Heart of the College Providing a beautiful hilltop campus on the west bank of the Hudson River just down the hill from the largest historic district in New York, Mount Saint Mary College is located midway between the state capital of Albany and Manhattan. Nearby is hiking on Storm King Mountain and skiing at Hunter Mountain. This is what is available to students at Mount Saint Mary College, a Catholic liberal arts college dedicated to teaching the whole person.

Equally impressive is the family atmosphere and close-knit caring community. Students comment about the talented faculty members who provide encouragement, support, and personal attention and do all their teaching with small class sizes. What is distinctive about the faculty is the strong sense of camaraderie, which fosters close collaboration among the various academic departments. This is highly atypical for faculty, who usually focus their work within their own academic department "kingdoms."

By virtue of its location and the challenge and support of faculty, students gain internship experience in nearly all majors. In addition to a highly regarded nursing program, the excellent education program places students in a school located right on campus. One student interned with New Line Cinemas to promote a Jennifer Lopez film; a psychology major shadowed a New York City psychologist; a history and political science major worked in the New York Senate in Albany. Other students have interned at ABC Sports, IBM, International Paper, Lenox Hill Hospital, Time Inc., and the New York State Department of Health.

Also, technology is big at Mount Saint Mary. Students have access to advanced technologies that will add to their effectiveness in whichever career they choose. The college has chosen a business model that makes a commitment to replace academic computing resources every three years. So all students benefit from a wireless campus-wide network and "smart" classrooms, including a dedicated lab for nursing students that includes multimedia software that simulates a clinical setting.

MOUNT SAINT MARY'S COLLEGE

Emmitsburg, Maryland

Total Undergraduate Enrollment: 1,500
Men: 720 Women: 780
Five-Year Graduation Rate: 80%

Tuition: $$$
Room and Board: $$$
Residential Students: 92%

History Mount Saint Mary's College was founded in 1808 by Father John Dubois, who, disguised as a woman, escaped the French Revolution. The college is the second oldest Catholic institution in America and is listed on the Templeton Foundation's Honor Roll of Character-Building Colleges.

Location The college is located on 1,400 acres in the Catochkin Mountains, in Emmitsburg, Maryland, 60 miles northeast of Washington, D.C., and 50 miles west of Baltimore.

Top Programs of Study Business and finance, elementary education, biology

Arts and Sciences Biochemistry, biology, biopsychology, chemistry, communications and rhetoric, computer science, economics, fine arts (art, music, theater), French, German, history, international studies, mathematics, philosophy, political science, psychology, sociology (concentration in criminal justice), Spanish, theology (concentration in religious education)

Business Accounting, and concentrations in finance, international business and economics, management, marketing, and sports management

Education Elementary, secondary

Pre-Professional None

Accredited Programs Education

Special Programs The college offers a cooperative program in nursing with Johns Hopkins University. The Career Action Plan (CAPS) helps students begin developing their personal career paths early in their freshman year. The college offers study abroad programs, interdisciplinary and self-designed majors.

Facilities The college has 28 buildings, including one of the best sports centers in the nation, the Knott Athletics Recreation Convocation Complex, an art gallery, and radio and TV stations.

Transition to College Program Students take a year-long, six-credit, mandatory Freshman Seminar Program, with a focus on reading, writing, peer critiquing, critical thinking, and an orientation to the institution. The seminar professor also functions as the students' adviser

Athletics NCAA I, Northeast Conference

Men: Baseball, basketball, cross-country, golf, indoor and outdoor track & field, lacrosse, soccer, tennis

Women: Basketball, cross-country, golf, indoor and outdoor track & field, lacrosse, softball, tennis

Student Life and Housing About 1,200 students can be accommodated in college housing, which is guaranteed for all four years. Fifty-three percent of the students are from Maryland, with the remainder from 30 other states and 17 countries. Ethnicity: Caucasian—89 percent; African-American—5 percent; Asian-American—2 percent. There are no fraternities or sororities. All students may keep cars.

Accommodations for Students with Disabilities In compliance with section 504

Financial Aid About 84 percent of all freshmen receive aid. The average freshman award was about $16,000.

Requirements for Admission SAT I or ACT scores and a college prep high school program or GED. An interview is recommended.

Application Freshmen are admitted to fall and spring semesters. The Early Action application deadline is December 1. Regular applications should be filed by March 1 for the fall and December 1 for the spring. Admission notification is sent on a rolling basis.

International Students Students must score a minimum of 550 on the paper TOEFL and take the SAT or ACT.

Transfer Students Students require a 2.5 GPA in previous college work and must be in good academic standing. High school and college transcripts must be submitted as well as a college recommendation.

Admission Contact
Office of Admissions
Mount Saint Mary's College
16300 Old Emmitsburg Road
Emmitsburg, MD 21727
Phone: (800) 448-4347; (301) 447-5214
FAX: (301) 447-5860
E-mail: *admission@msmary.edu*
Web: *www.msmary.edu*

The Heart of the College What distinguishes Mount Saint Mary's College is the incredible spirit that pervades the campus. One factor that fosters this spirit is that 90 percent of the students live on campus, and with the broad range of clubs, organizations, and activities offered, this becomes a very lively campus. Another factor influencing this spirited college is that almost 40 percent of the students are involved in varsity athletics—and with great success! Considering that Mount Saint Mary's is one of the nation's smallest Division I schools, the Mount's spirit has helped their teams defeat much larger schools, such as Georgetown, Maryland, and Villanova. The college is pleased that student athletes have graduation rates equal to or better than the rest of the student population. The college's spirit also comes from the many service opportunities, or, as the college likes to call these, "compassionate actions." In recent years dozens of Mount students have traveled to Kentucky, South Carolina, Florida, and other states to offer their skills and time. The Mount's spirit also flows from its mission statement as a Catholic college striving to graduate students "who live by high intellectual and moral standards" and "seek to resolve the problems facing humanity."

The college's core curriculum has received national attention. Comprised of 16 courses in the humanities, social and natural sciences, and mathematics, students are required to think critically and see connections across disciplines, cultures, and centuries. It's a thoughtful, well-designed curriculum taught by its designers, a talented Mount Saint Mary's faculty who also offer study semesters abroad to England, Italy, France, Ireland, and Costa Rica.

Mount Saint Mary's offers a spirited community for living and learning, an outstanding athletic program, and a creative curriculum.

MOUNT UNION COLLEGE

Alliance, Ohio

Total Undergraduate Enrollment: 2,372
Men: 1,025 Women: 1,347
Five-Year Graduation Rate: 67%

Tuition: $$$
Room and Board: $
Residential Students: 67%

History Mount Union College was founded in 1846 by Orville Hartshorne, who represented a progressive group of citizens of the village of Mount Union. They believed there was a need for an institution where men and women could be educated with equal opportunity without regard to race, gender, or position, and where science would parallel the humanities. The college is affiliated with the United Methodist Church.

Location The 115-acre campus is located in Alliance, Ohio (population 25,000), a suburban area in northeast Ohio about 20 miles east of Canton and about 75 miles from Cleveland and Pittsburgh.

Top Programs of Study Early childhood education, business, psychology

Arts and Sciences American studies, art, athletic training, biology, chemistry, communication studies, computer science, English, environmental biology, exercise science, French, geology, German, history, information systems, international studies, Japanese, mathematics, media computing, media studies, music, music performance, non-Western studies, philosophy, physics–astronomy, political science, psychology, religion, interdisciplinary studies, sociology, Spanish, sports management, theater, writing

Business Accounting, administration, economics, international business and economics

Education Early childhood, middle school, physical education

Pre-Professional Dentistry, engineering, medicine, ministry, law

Accredited Programs Athletic training, clinical laboratory services, music

Special Programs The college has a cooperative program in engineering with the University of Pennsylvania. There are several minors, including African-American studies, classics, gender studies, adolescent to young adult education, and legal studies, as well as minors in most majors. There are opportunities for internships, study abroad, and cooperative education. There are Air Force and Army ROTC programs.

Facilities There are 26 buildings, including the Eels Art Center; Chapman Hall; a classroom building; an observatory; Cope Music Hall, which houses a complete keyboard laboratory of 13 Roland electronic pianos and connects with the Rodman Playhouse and Crandall Gallery; the Stouffer Courtyard Theater; the Dewald Chapel; the Hoover-Price Campus Center; the extra-curricular heart of the campus, which houses a radio station; the Timkin Physical Education Building, which houses the McPherson Center for Human Health and Well-Being; a movie theater; a 109-acre nature center; the Wilson Science Building; and a park with two lakes.

Transition to College Program A more traditional—though longer—orientation is offered on four weekends in June and July. In addition, new students are required to attend an orientation period preceding the beginning of classes in August, when students are introduced to campus life, traditions, expectations, and regulations.

Athletics NCAA Div. III, Ohio Athletic Conference

Men: Baseball, basketball, cross-country, football, golf, indoor and outdoor track & field, soccer, swimming

Women: Basketball, cross-country, golf, indoor and outdoor track & field, soccer, softball, swimming and diving, tennis, volleyball

Accommodations for Students with Disabilities The college provides reasonable accommodations for students with documented disabilities. All requests for accommodations should be made through the Academic Support Center as soon as possible.

Financial Aid About 84 percent of all freshmen receive aid. The average freshman award was about $13,600.

Requirements for Admission SAT I or ACT scores and a college prep high school program. An interview is strongly recommended.

Application Application deadlines are open, with fall and spring semester admission. Admission decisions are made on a rolling basis.

International Students Required are certified English translations of secondary, and, if applicable, postsecondary transcripts, including the results of any government-level examination required for completion of secondary school, a teacher reference form completed by an instructor at the latest educational level, certification of adequate financial support, and the results of either the TOEFL or the Michigan Test for all applicants whose native language is not English.

Transfer Students Required are a minimum overall 2.0 GPA from the institution previously attended, a personal statement explaining the reason for leaving that institution and selecting Mount Union College, official transcripts forwarded from all institutions previously attended, a statement of honorable dismissal, and a financial aid transcript from each institution attended. Only courses with grades of C or better, taken at regionally accredited institutions, and courses that have an equivalent offered by Mount Union will be considered for transfer.

Admission Contact
Office of Admissions
Mount Union College
1972 Clark Avenue
Alliance, OH 44601
Phone: (800) 334-6682; (330) 823-2590
FAX: (330) 823-5097
E-mail: *admission@muc.edu*
Web: *www.muc.edu*

The Heart of the College Mount Union has earned a reputation as a top liberal arts college in the Midwest, with much of its status credited to the myriad ways it has successfully brought "real world" experiences to its students' education. The college's mission includes a commitment "to prepare students for meaningful work," and students are offered numerous internships to help accomplish this, with some students taking two and three internships. One student comments: "Overall, Mount Union gives students the tools to be successful in their careers." In addition to intern-

ships, there are cooperative education opportunities and study abroad programs. Professors have a tendency to move students beyond the classroom with observation and research assignments.

The "real world" and "meaningful work" will involve technology, so Mount Union provides students with computer-generated presentations, telecasts, and Internet resources. Professors list course requirements and updates online and many have interactive web pages where students can submit questions and receive immediate feedback. Technology can be accessed anywhere, anytime on campus, with an Information Center providing 24-hour access to computer labs and research materials and a completely wired campus.

Campus organizations also help bring the "real world" to students. One of the most popular ones is the Investment Team, which provides students with opportunities to apply learning from finance classes as they make investment decisions with real money. Students appreciate Mount Union's confidence in its students.

Alumni also appreciate the hard work of the Career Services Center, including the Career Connections Dinner, which allows students to meet with prospective employers.

Classes are small, making faculty very accessible. Sunday night service and weeknight Bible studies are available. The 80 student organizations, including a very successful athletic program, provide students with plenty of leadership and recreational opportunities.

Noteworthy are the fine programs in teacher education, whose students typically meet or exceed the statewide pass rates in all areas. Also, a special Lectureship Series brings to campus such notables as Supreme Court Justice Sandra Day O'Connor and Henry Kissinger. Other speakers represent literature and the fine arts, with all programs providing additional enrichment, dialogue, and discussion.

MUSKINGUM COLLEGE   New Concord, Ohio

Total Undergraduate Enrollment: 1,600
Men: 800 Women: 800
Five-Year Graduation Rate: 61%

Tuition: $$
Room and Board: $
Residential Students: 88%

History Muskingum College, established in 1837, has a proud heritage reaching back to the early 1800s when Ohio was an infant state and covered wagons were bringing settlers westward over the newly completed National Road through New Concord. The college's Native American name is a source of pride, recognizing its frontier heritage. The community was established by farm people of Scotch-Irish descent. The college has maintained a relationship with the United Presbyterian Church.

Location The 215-acre campus is located in the village of New Concord, Ohio, 50 miles east of Columbus.

Top Programs of Study Education, business, speech communication

Arts and Science American studies, art, biology, chemistry, child and family studies, conservation science, computer science, earth science, economics, English, environmental science, French, geology, German, history, humanities, international affairs, journalism, mathematics, molecular biology, music, neuroscience, philosophy, physics, political science, psychology, public affairs, religion, religion and philosophy, sociology, Spanish, speech communication, theater

Business Accounting, business, international business

Education Art, Christian, early childhood, intervention specialist middle, music, physical education, secondary, special

Pre-Professional Christian ministry, dentistry, engineering, law, medical technology, medicine, physical therapy, veterinary medicine

Accredited Programs Chemistry, music

Special Programs The college offers an accelerated degree option whereby students can graduate in three years. There are opportunities for self-designed interdisciplinary majors.

Facilities There are 33 buildings, including a radio station and a cable TV station. There is also a small lake near the center of campus and McAllister Biology Station, a 57-acre tract of land located in nearby Otsego, is used as a biology preserve and study area.

Transition to College Program The First-Year Seminar provides students with a common academic experience during the first semester. The course offers an extended orientation to the academic environment within a context of common readings, assignments, and activities, integrated by an annual theme. The course also introduces students to academic resources on campus.

Athletics NCAA III, Ohio Athletic Conference

Men: Baseball, basketball, cross-country, football, golf, indoor and outdoor track, soccer, tennis, wrestling

Women: Basketball, cross-country, golf, indoor and outdoor track, soccer, softball, tennis, volleyball

Student Life and Housing About 1,000 students can be accommodated in college housing, which is guaranteed for all four years. Eighty-five percent of the students are from Ohio, the remainder from 26 other states and 20 countries. Ethnicity: Caucasian—94 percent. There are three local and two national fraternities, and three local and two national sororities. All students may keep cars.

Accommodations for Students with Disabilities A comprehensive structured program is offered.

Financial Aid About 90 percent of all freshmen receive aid.

Requirements for Admission SAT I or ACT scores and a college prep high school program. Prospective music majors must schedule an audition with the music department.

Application Students are admitted to all semesters. The college uses a rolling admissions plan. Students are notified of an admissions decision as soon as all credentials have been received.

International Students Applications should be directed to the Director of International Programs. A TOEFL paper score of 550 or higher is required, although an English Support Program will be provided to academically qualified students with a lower score. The international student application contains full requirements for application.

Transfer Students Required are official secondary and college transcripts. Courses with a C grade or higher are considered for transfer. The college has articulation agreements with several Ohio colleges. Associate degree holders of an accredited institution receive junior status. Typically, a maximum of 60 credits may be transferred, and 48 credits must be completed at Muskingum.

Home-Schooled Students A recognized state agency, such as the superintendent of public education, must verify that the applicant has met the academic core requirements. If this verification is not possible, applicant should submit ACT or SAT results, or in certain cases, submit a GED.

Admission Contact
Office of Admissions
Muskingum College
163 Stormont Street
New Concord, OH 43762
Phone: (800) 752-6082
FAX: (740) 826-8100
E-mail: *adminfo@muskingum.edu*
Web: *www.muskingum.edu*

The Heart of the College Muskingum College is generally considered a very good educational value among Midwest colleges. The college offers students a solid liberal arts program with several interdisciplinary majors and the opportunity to design their own interdisciplinary major. About 25 percent of the students carry a double major and 88 percent pursue a minor. The curriculum is balanced with interesting field work projects. Muskingum's unique partnership with the Wilds—a 9,000-acre natural habitat wildlife preserve for endangered species—provides students with opportunities for internships, research, and extended classroom experiences.

Muskingum is especially proud of its science division, rated among the top science programs in the nation. Among its innovative programs are neuroscience, conservation, conservation science, and environmental science. Also well respected are Muskingum's education programs, with about one-third of the students pursuing a teacher licensure program.

Students will usually comment that the two things they like best about the college are the quality of the academic programs and the people, both students and faculty. With 85 percent of the students from Ohio, the college community is comprised of Midwestern values of honesty, a strong work ethic, and friendliness. The faculty is a very supportive one, student-centered, and very accessible and visible on campus. The faculty prides itself for its vibrant interactive classes, with a strong hands-on approach to learning that keeps students interested and engaged.

The PLUS Program is Muskingum's comprehensive level of services for students with documented disabilities. Services include tutoring, coursework support, taping of texts and lectures, and extended test time. There are three learning disabilities specialists on staff. There are about 130 students receiving services.

Located in the rolling hills of central Ohio, Muskingum offers the peace and quiet of the countryside, the security and relaxed environment of a small town, and the beauty and fun of the great outdoors. For more urban activities, Zanesville, a city of 40,000, is 15 minutes away, and Columbus is about an hour away.

Among recent graduating classes, about 95 percent were employed or in graduate or profes-

sional schools within five months of graduation. Earlier notable graduates were astronaut John Glenn and Jack Hanna, host of the television program "Jack Hanna's Animal Adventures" and director emeritus of the Columbus Zoo.

NEBRASKA WESLEYAN UNIVERSITY   Lincoln, Nebraska

Total Undergraduate Enrollment: 1,563
Men: 695 Women: 868
Five-Year Graduation Rate: 63%

Tuition: $$$
Room and Board: $
Residential Students: 51%

History Nebraska Wesleyan University, founded in 1887, unified the state's three Methodist colleges. Originally chartered as a university in 1940, the school began serving as an undergraduate liberal arts college. The college maintains an affiliation with the Methodist Church. The college is listed on the Templeton Foundation's Honor Roll of Character-Building Colleges.

Location The 50-acre campus is located in the historic residential area of Lincoln, Nebraska (population 225,000), the state capital, 50 miles west of Omaha.

Top Programs of Study Biology, business, education

Arts and Sciences Applied music, art, athletic training, biochemistry and molecular biology, biology, biopsychology, business psychology, business sociology, chemistry, communication studies, communication and theater arts, computer science, economics, English, exercise science and wellness, French, German, global studies, health and physical education, history, mathematics, music, nursing, philosophy, physics, political communication, political science, psychology, religion, social work, sociology-anthropology, Spanish, theater arts, women's studies

Business Administration, e-design, information systems, international business

Education Elementary, middle, music, secondary, special

Pre-Professional Dentistry, engineering, law, medical technology, medicine, occupational therapy, optometry, osteopathic medicine, pharmacy, physical therapy, physician's assistant, podiatry, theology, veterinary medicine

Accredited Programs Business, chemistry, education, music, nursing, social work

Special Programs Interdepartmental and interdisciplinary majors are available. Education students may elect to student teach in Chicago or abroad, including Australia, Ireland, Germany, and other countries. The Urban Life Center offers students the opportunity to live and learn in Chicago. The Capitol Hill Internship Program provides students the opportunity to live, intern, and study in Washington, D.C. There are study abroad opportunities. There is a ROTC program.

Facilities There are 17 buildings, including Old Main, the original campus building listed on the National Register of Historic Places, a planetarium, greenhouse, a remodeled field house, two new residence halls and townhouse village, and a state arboretum.

Transition to College Program The Liberal Arts Seminar for first-year students introduces students to the college and allows students to talk to their advisers at least three times a week, as well as to upperclass student assistants.

Athletics NCAA III and NAIA, Great Plains Athletic Conference

Men: Baseball, basketball, cross-country, football, golf, indoor and outdoor track, soccer, tennis

Women: Basketball, cross-country, golf, indoor and outdoor track, soccer, softball, tennis, volleyball

Student Life and Housing About 1,000 students can be accommodated in college housing, which is guaranteed for all four years. Ninety-four percent of the students are from Nebraska. The remainder are from 22 other states and 8 countries. Ethnicity: Caucasian—95 percent. There are one local and three national fraternities, and two local and two national sororities. All students may keep cars.

Accommodations for Students with Disabilities Reasonable accommodations are made for students who document their disabilities following admission and request accommodations

Financial Aid About 95 percent of all freshmen receive aid. The average freshman award was about $11,000.

Requirements for Admission An ACT score of 20 or a SAT score of 950 and a rank in the top half of the graduating class in a college prep high school program.

Application Freshmen are admitted fall and spring semesters. The Early Decision deadline is November 15, with admission notification by December 15. Regular admission deadline is May 1.

International Students Required are certified copies of secondary school and university transcripts, with English translations if in a language other than English. Also, a certified copy of a secondary school diploma. For students whose native language is not English, official results of one of the following tests should be submitted: TOEFL, APIEL, or IELTS.

Transfer Students Students must be in good standing and have a 2.0 GPA. Credits from regionally accredited two-year institutions are evaluated on a course-by-course basis. A maximum of 64 credits will be transferred from two-year institutions. Only courses with grades of C− or better are considered for transfer.

Admission Contact
Office of Admissions
Nebraska Wesleyan University
500 Saint Paul Avenue
Lincoln, NE 68504
Phone: (800) 541-3818; (402) 465-2218
E-mail: *admissions@nebrwesleyan.edu*
Web: *www.nebrwesleyan.edu*

The Heart of the University As one student writes: "Without a doubt, my four years at Wesleyan have supported the idea that college is one of the best times of your life." Nebraska Wesleyan lives up to its reputation as the number one liberal arts college in Nebraska, offering a high quality liberal arts education and several nationally accredited programs. Career placement and graduate school outcomes reflect this quality, with nearly one-third of the graduates going directly to graduate and professional school and another third pursuing advanced degrees within three years of graduation.

Wesleyan's commitment to active learning finds that nearly all majors complete professional internships or senior research projects. Students are able to choose from dozens of progressive local companies, such as Northwestern Mutual Life and Pfizer Pharmaceuticals, and National Fortune 500 corporations.

Students find the university community very attractive, and they involve themselves in some of the nearly 80 student organizations, excellent athletic teams, creative student-initiated activities, and a number of housing options. Wesleyan students also enjoy the strong commitment the institution has to serving and helping others. From volunteering at local elementary schools to traveling to a foreign country to help construct a child care center, service projects are also opportunities for students to create and provide leadership for their self-designed projects.

The university boasts a faculty that cares about

teaching and is rewarded for its teaching expertise. These professors challenge student thinking in small, highly interactive classes. Student–faculty relationships are caring, supportive, and enjoyable. The heart of the university is this combination of academic rigor and faculty support.

The city of Lincoln, with more than 40,000 students, is a true college town. It not only offers shopping, sports, restaurants, and shows, but also, as the state capital, offers internship and employment opportunities. As a community of higher education, Lincoln often hosts recognized speakers and political leaders, including Elie Wiesel, Colin Powell, and Maya Angelou.

NIAGARA UNIVERSITY   Niagara, New York

Total Undergraduate Enrollment: 2,635
Men: 1,048 Women: 1,587
Five-Year Graduation Rate: 56%

Tuition: $$$
Room and Board: $$$
Residential Students: 56%

History Niagara University is a Catholic university founded in 1856 by the Vincential Order. First chartered as a seminary, in 1883 it was rechartered as a university for the "liberal and useful arts and sciences."

Location The 160-acre campus is located in Niagara, New York, in a suburban area four miles north of Niagara Falls, overlooking the Niagara River Gorge 20 miles north of Buffalo.

Top Programs of Study Education, business, criminal justice

Arts and Sciences Biochemistry, biology (concentration in biology, biotechnology, environmental studies), chemistry, communication studies, computer and information sciences, criminology and criminal justice, English, French, history, hotel and restaurant management, international studies, life sciences, mathematics, philosophy, political science, psychology, religious studies, social sciences, sociology, social work, Spanish, theater studies, tourism and recreation management

Business Accounting, commerce (concentration in economics, general business, human resources, management, marketing, transportation, and logistics)

Education Childhood and middle childhood, early childhood and childhood, elementary, middle and adolescence, secondary, special education

Pre-Professional Dentistry, health professions, law

Accredited Programs Business, education, hospitality and tourism management, social work

Special Programs There is a HEOP program for academically underprepared and financially disadvantaged New York State residents. Associate degrees are awarded in pre-engineering, liberal studies, and business. There is an Office of Multicultural and International Student Affairs. There are opportunities for study abroad, cooperative education programs, and internships. Niagara has an Academic Exploration Program for students undecided about a major. Learn and Serve Niagara provides students with service opportunities. Students can study at Niagara's partner university in Engelberg, Switzerland. There is an Army ROTC.

Facilities There are 27 buildings providing a pleasant contrast between stately ivy-covered buildings and those of more contemporary design, including the Gallagher Student Center; the Castelloni Art Museum; the Kiernan fitness and recreational facility; the Dwyer Arena, consisting of two full-sized (National Hockey League) rinks; and a-state-of-the-art teaching facility for the Institute of Travel, Hotel, and Restaurant Administration.

Transition to College Program The university has a required Freshman Symposium, a series of programs focusing on a variety of special college issues and held during the first six weeks of the fall semester.

Athletics NCAA I, Metro Atlantic Athletic Conference

Men: Baseball, basketball, cross-country, golf, ice hockey, soccer, swimming and diving, tennis

Women: Basketball, cross-country, ice hockey, lacrosse, soccer, softball, swimming and diving, tennis, volleyball

Student Life and Housing There are about 1,300 students who can be accommodated in college housing, which is guaranteed for all four years. Eighty-seven percent of the students are from New York, the remainder from 31 other states and 11 countries. Ethnicity: Caucasian—87 percent; International—6 percent; African-American—4 percent; Hispanic-American—2 percent. There are two national fraternities and no sororities. All students may keep cars.

Accommodations for Students with Disabilities Reasonable accommodations are provided for students with documented disabilities. Students must contact the Coordinator of Specialized Support Services (716) 286-8076. Documentation must be current and submitted by a qualified professional.

Financial Aid About 85 percent of all freshmen receive aid. The average freshman award was about $14,600.

Requirements for Admission SAT I or ACT results and a college prep high school program.

Application There is an Early Decision Plan. Regular admission deadlines are August 15 for the fall semester, and January 10 for the spring semester. A rolling admissions policy notifies students about an admission decision within a few weeks from the date that the completed application is received.

International Students Required are a Leaving Certificate, Diploma, or General Certificate of Education, a TOEFL score, official college transcripts in the original language, as well as English translations, and financial documentation equal to one year's expenses. Minimum TOEFL scores are as follows: 550 paper and 173 computer-based for the College of Business and the College of Hospitality and Tourism Management; 550 paper and 213 computer for the College of Arts and Science and the Academic Exploration Program; between 520 and 560 paper and 190 and 220 computer for the College of Education.

Transfer Students Required are official high school and college transcripts and, if appropriate, an official copy of the GED.

Home-Schooled Students Required are submission of SAT or ACT scores, a transcript or portfolio documenting performance in secondary school courses, and other pertinent curriculum information.

Admission Contact
Office of Admissions
Niagara University
639 Bailo Hall
Niagara, NY 14109-2011
Phone: (800) 462-2111
FAX: (716) 286-8710
E-mail: *admissions@niagara.edu*
Web: *www.niagara.edu*

The Heart of the University Niagara University is all about caring and support. What is special is that it works both ways: students not only receive but also provide these important qualities. With a faculty that is more personal than ivory-tower in approach, students are accustomed to professors' knowing their names, really knowing their professors, and collaborating with professors on research. Niagara also shows its support for students in its Academic Exploration Program, aimed at students who want to take a little time before declaring a major. Students meet monthly with an adviser to discuss the students' interests, abilities, and values. Together they choose courses that will explore student strengths. Students also comment on the support offered by the work of the Career Development Center, including the securing of valuable and interesting internships and cooperative work opportunities, ranging from accounting firms to aquariums. Even the design of the campus had support for students in mind, in that buildings are relatively close together so it is easy to get to that next class during the cold winters.

Students provide support for both the campus community and the Niagara community. Student participation in campus activities and organizations is very high, with more than half participating in intramural sports. The Learn and Serve Niagara Program gives students an opportunity to serve and support the Niagara community while earning academic credit. Education students tutor at local schools, others work in

domestic violence prevention, help build houses for Habitat for Humanity, or teach conflict resolution to high school students. There's also NUCAP, a student organization that supports the work of 50 local agencies to help the poor, the sick, the homeless, the elderly, and the mentally and physically challenged. With such a great climate of support and caring, it's no wonder that friendships made at Niagara last a lifetime.

There are several excellent programs, including a renowned theater program; nationally accredited education and business programs; and a hotel, restaurant, and tourism program that requires an 800-hour internship offering such placements as Disney World, Hilton Head, and Las Vegas.

There's also much to do in the Niagara region, which is a hub of international tourism and commerce. Not only do students have nearby Buffalo for professional sports, culture, and entertainment, but they can also cross the border into Canada for big-city life in Toronto, only 90 minutes away.

NORTHWESTERN COLLEGE

Orange City, Iowa

Total Undergraduate Enrollment: 1,313
Men: 509 Women: 804
Five-Year Graduation Rate: 59%

Tuition: $$
Room and Board: $
Residential Students: 89%

History Northwestern College was founded in 1882 as a classical academy to prepare students for college and ultimately for ministry in the Reformed Church in America. Led by Henry Hospers, part of the Dutch Reformed people who emigrated to the United States, and the Reverend Seine Bolks, the first pastor of Orange City's First Reformed Church, the academy became a junior college and then a teacher training institution. In 1970 the college received full accreditation as a Christian liberal arts college, upholding beliefs in the Bible as the sole authority in matters of life and belief. The college is listed on the Templeton Foundation's Honor Roll of Character-Building Colleges.

Location The 55-acre campus is located in Orange City, Iowa (population 5,000), a small town 40 miles northeast of Sioux City and 75 miles southeast of Sioux Falls.

Top Programs of Study Education, business, biology

Arts and Sciences Art, biology, biology health professions, chemistry, church music, communication studies, computer science, English, environmental science, exercise science, health science, history, humanities, mathematics, medical technology, music, philosophy, political science, psychology, religion, social work, sociology, Spanish, theater, theater/speech, writing and rhetoric

Business Administration (options in agri-business, finance, general business administration, information systems management, marketing), economics

Education Business, Christian, early childhood, elementary, ESL, middle, physical education secondary, special, reading

Pre-Professional Agriculture, art therapy, chiropractic, dentistry, engineering, graphic design, law, medicine, mortuary science, music performance, music therapy, nursing, occupational therapy, optometry, pharmacy, physical therapy, professional studio, veterinary medicine

Accredited Programs Education, social work

Special Programs There is an associate's degree in office management and minors in cultural studies, ESL, health, journalism, and physics, and in nearly all of the majors. Students can also design their own majors. There are opportunities for internships, study abroad, including a China Studies Program, a Latin American Studies Program in Costa Rica, a Middle Eastern Studies Program, and a Russian Studies Program, as well as programs sponsored by other colleges. There are also domestic programs in Washington, D.C., Chicago, Los Angeles, and the Great Lakes. Northwestern also offers a dual degree in engineering with Washington University in St. Louis and a coordinated transfer program with Iowa State University. The college is rated one of the most computer-wired colleges in America.

Facilities There are 25 buildings, a blend of old and new, including Zwemer Hall, which is listed in the National Register of Historic Places. Eighty percent of the classrooms have been built or renovated since 1986, including Van Peursem Hall, the main academic building; DEMCO Business/Economic Center; Kresge Education Center; and Granber Hall. The architectural award-winning Christ Chapel/Performing Arts Center and DeWitt Music Hall contains a 1,000-seat auditorium. The Bultman Center for Health, Physical Education and Inter-

collegiate Athletics has a 2,200-seat gymnasium. The Rowenhorst Student Center contains a beautiful mall surrounded by a theater, art gallery, and the DeWitt Physical Fitness Center. The Learning Resource Center serves as the technological hub of the campus, with 230 workstations. The Ramaker Library houses a Dutch Heritage Room, and the Bushmer Art Center includes eight teaching studios. The Playhouse, in downtown Orange City, contains a turntable stage and a digital sound system. There is also a radio station.

Transition to College Program A summer two-credit course focuses on the general topic of transitions and especially transition to college, taking special note of some basic aspects of identity: age, race, ethnicity, affiliation, family ties, gender, beliefs, and religion. Students explore the topic of transition through a close reading and discussion of selected texts.

Athletics NAIA, Nebraska-Iowa Athletic Conference

Men: Baseball, basketball, cross-country, football, golf, soccer, tennis, track, wrestling

Women: Basketball, cross-country, golf, soccer, softball, tennis, track, volleyball

Student Life and Housing About 1,000 students can be accommodated in college housing, which includes single-sex dormitories and married housing, and is guaranteed for all four years. Fifty-seven percent of all the students are from Iowa, the remainder from 27 other states and 14 countries. Ethnicity: Caucasian—96 percent. There are no fraternities or sororities. All students may keep cars.

Accommodations for Students with Disabilities In compliance with section 504

Financial Aid Almost all students receive aid. The average freshman award was about $12,400.

Requirements for Admission SAT I or ACT scores and a college prep high school program or a GED. Qualities of character are also considered; therefore an interview is recommended.

Application Freshmen are admitted to all semesters. Application deadlines are open and the college uses a rolling admissions policy.

International Students In addition to an International Student Application, students need to submit appropriate school transcripts and a declaration of finances. For students whose native language is not English, TOEFL scores of 550 will grant regular admission. Students scoring lower will be granted provisional admission.

Transfer Students Required are secondary school and college transcripts from accredited colleges, a recommendation, ACT or SAT scores, as well as regular freshman admission requirements. Only graded courses of C− or better will be considered for transfer. A maximum of 62 credits may be transferred from a two-year institution. Students must earn the last 30 credits at Northwestern.

Admission Contact
Office of Admissions
Northwestern College
101 College Lane
Orange City, IA 51041-1996
Phone: (800) 707-7130
FAX: (712) 707-7164
E-mail: *rondj@nwciowa.edu*
Web: *www.nwciowa.edu*

The Heart of the College Regarded as one of the best Midwestern colleges and a very affordable one, Northwestern focuses on helping students develop a career and personal focus for their lives. This is accomplished in a "loving community" comprised of students characterized by their openness and a respectfulness.

Northwestern has strong programs in the sciences, teacher education, social work, and theater. In addition, the college offers career concentrations, a cluster of courses that prepares students for entry-level employment upon graduation and generally includes an off-campus internship during the senior year. Career concentrations include Computer Science, Criminal Justice, Fitness Management, Mission Service, Recreation, and Christian Theater Ministries. In addition, the college offers a large number—19—of pre-professional programs with assigned directors for advisement. The General Education Program taken by all students is intended to develop an understanding and appreciation of biblical teaching, the relationship between the Christian faith and the academic disciplines, and a Christian worldview. Northwestern is also rated as one of the most computer-wired colleges in America.

The prevailing student comment about faculty is that they are highly qualified and choose Northwestern because of its Christian perspective of creating close supportive academic relationships with students. Students comment that professors set high standards for their students and take pride in their students' learnings and success. There are several programs that demonstrate how Christian faith is an integral part of Northwestern. Students attend 25-minute chapel services three times a week for exciting programs of contemporary music, nationally known speakers, and missionaries, as well as morning chapel and a student-led Sunday night Praise and Worship Service. A special campus ministry program is the Summer of Service projects that enable students to obey the biblical command to make disciples of all nations by participating in a cross-cultural Christian service experience with 20 to 40 students sent to project sites on every continent. A domestic service program involves more than 200 students in spring service to sites throughout the United States.

The outcomes are excellent, with 96 percent of the graduates reporting employment within six months of graduation. This should be no surprise since Northwestern students are focused on communication and writing skills, integrity, and a strong work ethic.

NORTH CENTRAL COLLEGE

Naperville, Illinois

Total Undergraduate Enrollment: 2,116
Men: 850 Women: 1,266
Five-Year Graduation Rate: 65%

Tuition: $$$
Room and Board: $$
Residential Students: 60%

History North Central College, originally known as Plainfield College and located in that town, was founded in 1861 by the Evangelical Association, a forerunner to the United Methodist Church. The college was shaped by the advanced ideas of the founders who believed that the Christian religion and intellectual attainment were compatible, while also holding to a commitment to the inclusiveness and diversity characterizing the Methodist Church.

Location The 54-acre campus is located in Naperville, Illinois (population 130,000), in a suburban area 30 miles west of Chicago. Naperville is a residential neighborhood that is listed in the National Register of Historical Places.

Top Programs of Study Education, business, psychology

Arts and Sciences Actuarial science, applied mathematics, art, arts and letters, athletics, athletic training, biochemistry, biology, broadcast communication, chemistry, classical civilization, computer science, East Asian studies, economics, English (literature and writing), exercise science, French, German, history, humanities, Japanese, mathematics, music (instrumental, vocal, and jazz studies), musical theater, organizational communication, philosophy, physics, political science, print journalism, psychology, religious studies, science, social studies, sociology, sociology and anthropology, Spanish, speech communication, theater

Business Accounting (concentrations in certified management, certified public and corporate accounting), entrepreneurship and small business management, finance, international business, management, management information systems, marketing

Education Art, elementary, music, physical education, secondary

Pre-Professional Dentistry, engineering, law, medical physics, medical technology, medicine, nursing, physical therapy, veterinary medicine

Accredited Programs None

Special Programs Students may design their own interdisciplinary majors. There are several minors, including anthropology, business administration, information systems, and professional conflict resolution. There are cooperative programs in medical technology, nursing, and medical physics with Rush University. There is also a dual degree program in engineering with the University of Illinois and other schools. North Central also offers the Richter Independent Study Fellowship Program to fund student projects. The student-staffed radio station has won 20 national Marconi Awards. There are opportunities for study abroad, internships, a Washington, D.C., semester, a Model U.N. Program, and a Mock Trial Program. There are also Air Force and Army ROTC programs.

Facilities There are 24 buildings, including Oesterle Library, Cardinal Stadium, a student-run coffee house, an art center, Krochler Science Center, a radio station, and a foreign language lab.

Transition to College Program The Freshman Year Information Program (FYI) is an extended advising/orientation program that gives all freshmen a forum to discuss the transitions they are experiencing. A faculty adviser, a student development staff member, and one or two upperclass student mentors meet weekly with a group of approximately 18 freshmen, beginning Opening

Week and continuing for the first three weeks of fall semester. Topics include volunteerism, academic transitions, co-curricular involvement, diversity, campus and community resources, and decision making.

Athletics NCAA, College Conference of Illinois and Wisconsin

Men: Baseball, basketball, cross-country, football, golf, soccer, swimming, tennis, track & field, wrestling

Women: Basketball, cross-country, golf, soccer, softball, swimming, track & field, volleyball

Student Life and Housing About 1,000 students can be accommodated in college housing, which includes single-sex and coed dorms, and is guaranteed for all four years. Ninety-one percent of the students are from Illinois, the remainder from 23 other states and 18 countries. Ethnicity: Caucasian—88 percent; African-American—4 percent; Hispanic-American—3 percent; Asian-American—2 percent; International—1 percent. There are no fraternities or sororities. All students may keep cars.

Accommodations for Students with Disabilities The college offers a wide range of services, accommodations, and modifications for both learning and physically disabled students.

Financial Aid About 94 percent of all freshmen receive aid. In a recent year the average freshman award was about $14,500.

Requirements for Admission A minimum SAT I score of 930 or 20 on the ACT and a college prep high school program. An on-campus interview is highly recommended.

Application Freshmen are admitted to fall, winter, and spring semesters. Application deadlines are open, with admission decisions made on a rolling basis within three weeks of receiving completed application materials.

International Students Students should apply at least four months prior to the semester in which they would like to start, with a March 1 deadline for the fall semester. Required are official, English translated transcripts from secondary school, and, if applicable, English-translated transcripts and course syllabi for all college/university level credit, a TOEFL minimum score of 520 paper or 190 computer-based, an autobiographical essay, two letters of recommendation, and evidence of financial support.

Transfer Students A minimum GPA of 2.25 is recommended. If a student has completed fewer than 24 credits, high school transcripts and ACT/SAT scores are considered. Students must be in good standing at their last institutions. Students must submit official transcripts of all college work. The maximum number of credits accepted from a two-year school is 60. There is no maximum number of credits accepted from a four-year institution. However, students must complete either their last 30 credits or 36 of their last 42 credits at North Central College.

Home-Schooled Students Required are a review of the student's portfolio and curriculum, a writing sample, an interview with the Dean of Admissions, and an interview with a faculty member.

Admission Contact
Office of Admissions
North Central College
30 North Brainard Street
Naperville, IL 60540
Phone: (800) 411-1861; (630) 637-5819
FAX: (630) 637-5819
E-mail: *ncadm@noctrl.edu*
Web: *www.northcentralcollege.edu*

The Heart of the College An informal college with a wonderful location, North Central makes the student the "central" part of this college. Certainly the trimester academic calendar, which consists of three 10-week terms and one 6-week interim break from Thanksgiving to New Year's, allows students to really immerse themselves in each course, maximizing their learning and ability to manage their time. The trimester calendar also makes it easier to double major or take a minor, both advantageous for making oneself more marketable upon graduation. The Interim Break is used very well by students in terms of study abroad, completing an internship, conducting research with a faculty member, studying one of a select group of courses, or simply taking a break to rest.

The faculty has done a remarkable job of integrating the curriculum, helping students to appreciate how all of experience is encountered in this integrated way. It provides an education that focuses on seeing connections between disciplines, allowing students to navigate their lives more successfully. This interdisciplinary experience is provided not only in Freshman Seminars and in an Interdisciplinary requirement that mandates that students study two courses that have a linkage, but also in the sciences, where students begin to see connections between biology, chemistry, and physics, an understanding that helps to increase the quality of laboratory research.

Research is a powerful attraction to North Central students. The annual Roll Symposium provides a forum for student–faculty collaborative research that ranges from art to economics and science to education. The college is also one of a dozen American undergraduate institutions to offer $5,000 Richter Independent Study Fellowship grants to students for tackling problems of unusual merit or scope.

Innovative programs include a nationally recognized Dispute Resolution Program—created by and for students—that constitutes a minor. Students gain experience on campus, or as mediators for local businesses, churches, and civic organizations. The History of Ideas Sequence of five courses offers students study in classical art, architecture, literature, and philosophy. The Model U.N. team is one of the best in the Midwestern Conference. The students in Free Enterprise learn from investment professionals and then help local businesspeople strengthen their marketing plans.

Professors view students as "central" to the college. These are faculty who set high standards, who enjoy small-group, hands-on instruction, and give much of their time to students. Students comment about how many professors provide their home phone numbers and will work individually with students.

Students love their campus location, just two blocks from downtown Naperville, considered a "mini, mini downtown Chicago," offering an Eddie Bauer, Gap, Barnes and Noble, boutiques, and one of the safest small cities in America. Then just two blocks from campus is the train that takes students to cosmopolitan Chicago and all of its attractions. Notable is the Illinois Research and Development Corridor—the Silicone Prairie—providing students with some of the best internships in the nation.

NORWICH UNIVERSITY Northfield, Vermont

Total Undergraduate Enrollment: 1,700
Men: 1,025 Women: 675
Five-Year Graduation Rate: 65%

Tuition: $$$
Room and Board: $$
Residential Students: 82%

History Norwich University was founded in 1819 by Alden Partridge, a former Superintendent of West Point, as the first private military college in the nation. It was the first private school to offer engineering and the first school to offer military training to women. The university has two populations: students who enroll in the

Corps of Cadets and follow a disciplined military regime and civilian students who lead a traditional small college lifestyle.

Location The 1,125-acre campus is located in Northfield, Vermont, a rural area 11 miles south of Montpelier, the state capital.

Top Programs of Study Criminal justice, nursing, architecture

Arts and Sciences Architecture, biochemistry, biology, biomedical technology, chemistry, civil/environmental engineering, computer engineering, communications, criminal justice, electrical engineering, English, environmental science, geology, nursing, peace, war and diplomacy, physical education, physics, political science, psychology, sports medicine

Business Accounting, business administration (concentration in accounting and management), computer information systems, computer science, economics

Education Elementary, secondary

Pre-Professional Dentistry, medicine

Accredited Programs Architecture, business, engineering, nursing

Special Programs The university offers several master's degrees: Architecture, Information Assurance, and Diplomacy and Military Science. Students may double major. There are several minors, including art, engineering science, sports medicine, and education. There are opportunities for study abroad and student exchange programs. There are Air Force, Army, Navy, and Marines ROTC programs.

Facilities There are 34 buildings including the Kreitzberg Library; a Learning Support Center; a student-run FM radio station; an award-winning student-run cable TV station; an art gallery; a greenhouse; the Shapiro Fieldhouse; Plumley Armory, which houses a gym, wrestling facility, swimming pool, and state-of-the-art equipment; Andrews Hall, which houses the varsity basketball court, and Kreitzberg Arena, a multipurpose facility used for cultural presentations and concerts, with seating for 1,500; and a Student Center.

Transition to College Program In addition to a traditional orientation, the university offers a three-day outdoor experience, NU BOUND, which provides the opportunity to develop friendships through canoeing, hiking, white water clinic, backroad biking, community service, and fishing. After classes begin, those who seek to enter the Corps of Cadets pursue a period of Basic Training, during which "rooks" are required to observe certain rules of conduct and discipline to assist them in adapting to the military routine under which all cadets live. Also, the Norwich Advantage Program improves students' academic skills and helps students to learn more about Norwich. Students study a three-credit history course, a one-credit how to succeed in college course, physical fitness training, campus workshops, and weekend trips.

Athletics NCAA III, Eastern College Athletic Conference

Men: Baseball, basketball, cross-country, football, ice hockey, lacrosse, rifle, soccer

Women: Basketball, cross-country, soccer, softball, swimming

Student Life and Housing About 1,700 students can be accommodated in college housing, which includes single-sex and coed dorms. Only 20 percent of the students are from Vermont, with the majority from all other states and 30 countries. Ethnicity: Caucasian—94 percent. There are no fraternities or sororities. Upperclassmen may keep cars. Students pledge to abide by an honor code.

Accommodations for Students with Disabilities The university provides comprehensive services.

Financial Aid About 93 percent of all freshmen receive aid. The average freshman award was about $15,300.

Requirements for Admission A college prep high school program, evidence of character and leadership potential. SAT I or ACT scores for civilian students.

Application The Early Decision deadline is November 15, with admission notification by December 15. Regular admission deadlines are open, with March 1 a preferred date.

International Students Prospective students for whom English is a second language must have a minimum TOEFL score of 500. Official secondary, and, if applicable, postsecondary transcripts are required, as well as an affidavit of support. Application forms should be obtained from the Dean of Enrollment Management.

Transfer Students Students are expected to meet the same admission requirements and follow the same procedures as freshmen applicants. Required are official high school and college transcripts, as well as college course descriptions. Credit may be granted for courses comparable to those offered at Norwich and taken at regionally accredited institutions, provided that a minimum grade of C is earned.

Admission Contact
Office of Admissions
Norwich University
158 Harmon Drive
Northfield, VT 05663-1036
Phone: (800) 468-6679; (802) 485-2001
FAX: (802) 485-2032
E-mail: *nuadm@norwich.edu*
Web: *www.norwich.edu*

The Heart of the University Norwich University is certainly one of the most unique universities in the nation. Established as America's first private military college, Norwich not only has a cadet population selecting a lifestyle of discipline, structure, and leadership (with some pursuing ROTC as part of their studies), but a second population of "civilian" students, pursuing a traditional college experience. This unique tandem student population, coupled with a student population from every state and 30 foreign countries, truly creates a campus diversity that allows Norwich faculty, students, and staff to learn about different religions, traditions, cultures, and values.

Located in the Green Mountains of Vermont, the great outdoors becomes a playground for Norwich students, with snow boarding, mountain climbing, canoeing, biking, and more. On weekends, the university's bus takes students to the ski slopes of Stowe, Sugarbush, and Killington. Burlington, a great college town, is an hour's drive north, and Boston and Montreal provide big-city excitement, culture, and professional sports. On campus there are 80 clubs and organizations, with half the students involved in intercollegiate sports, and new-release movies, comedians, and other entertainment.

There are several nationally certified programs, including a five-year architecture degree and business and engineering programs taught by faculty members who serve as consultants to business, industry, and government. They bring real-world experience to the classroom, where, with small class sizes, students receive a great deal of individual attention. The nursing program is one of the largest on campus, providing excellent lab facilities as well as fieldwork in local hospitals. The communications major has a career-oriented focus, providing internships at news media outlets, the student radio station, and the award–winning cable television show, "Norwich Today." Also, the National Security Agency has designated Norwich as a Center of Academic Excellence in Information Assurance Education, an area focused on helping people protect their privacy and prevent damage from intruders or malicious software. This information security area is viewed as a critical aspect of national security and is one of the fastest growing areas of information technology management. Students who receive scholarships to study in this area are guaranteed jobs upon graduation within governmental agencies.

Each year about 400 new "rooks," or novice cadets, arrive as freshmen and go through "Rook-dom," a training period of great challenge that lasts until just before Thanksgiving Break, when the senior-ranking cadet, in a formal ceremony called "Recognition," officially recognizes rooks as cadets, and welcomes them into the Norwich

University Corps of Cadets. Each cadet selects an ROTC branch, which after four years will lead to a commission as an officer.

Much of Norwich's focus is on leadership development, where peers and faculty or staff evaluate students in six important leadership skill areas. When students complete the leadership program, they receive a certificate along with their degree. Students will also have completed a leadership portfolio documenting all leadership activities that can be shown to prospective employers and provides graduates with an edge that comes from confidence, competence, and poise. Ninety-six percent of graduates are either employed, in graduate school, or commissioned officers in the Armed Forces.

OHIO NORTHERN UNIVERSITY

Ada, Ohio

Total Undergraduate Enrollment: 2,900
Men: 1,500 Women: 1,400
Five-Year Graduation Rate: 66%

Tuition: $$$$
Room and Board: $$
Residential Students: 65%

History Ohio Northern University was founded by Henry Solomon Lehr in 1871 to prepare teachers for public schools. The school is affiliated with the United Methodist Church.

Location The 285-acre campus is located in Ada, Ohio (population 5,000), a small town in northwestern Ohio about 70 miles south of Toledo and 80 miles north of Columbus.

Top Programs of Study Pharmacy, engineering, biology

Arts and Sciences Art, athletic training, biochemistry, biology, civil engineering, chemistry, communication arts (concentrations in broadcasting and electronic media, musical theater, professional and organizational communication, public relations, theater), computer engineering, computer science, creative writing, criminal justice, doctor of pharmacy, electrical engineering, environmental studies, exercise physiology, French, German, history, international studies, journalism, law, literature, mathematics, mathematics/statistics, mechanical engineering, medical technology, medical chemistry, molecular biology, music, music composition, music performance, music with elective studies in business, philosophy, philosophy and religion, physics, political science, professional writing, psychology, religion, sociobiology, Spanish, sports management, technology, youth ministry

Business Accounting, international business and economics, management

Education Early childhood, health, middle childhood, music, physical education, secondary, technology

Pre-Professional Dentistry, law, medicine, occupational therapy, optometry, physical therapy, physician's assistant, seminary, veterinary medicine

Accredited Programs Allied health programs, business, chemistry, education, engineering, law, music, pharmacy

Special Programs The university uses a quarter system of 10 weeks of classes and 1 week of finals each quarter. There are dual degree programs, travel abroad opportunities, international cooperative education programs, student exchange programs, and a Washington, D.C., semester. There is an Air Force ROTC program.

Facilities There are 39 buildings, including the Freed Center for the Performing Arts, which contains state-of-the-art production support facilities, as well as radio and television production facilities; a new two-story addition to Presser

Hall; the music building; a renovated McIntosh Student Center; renovated science and engineering buildings; a new sports center; the Wilson Art Center and Elzay Gallery; a renovated law school; and a new facility for the College of Business Administration.

Transition to College Program The First-Year Experience includes a Freshman Seminar, department orientation courses, and pre-professional courses. While students select offerings most suited for themselves, each student meets the general goals of the program through a set of common experiences that help students make the transition to college; acquaint students with facilities, operations, and procedures; and encourage students to participate in the many campus activities.

Athletics NCAA III, Ohio Athletic Conference

Men: Baseball, basketball, cross-country, football, golf, indoor and outdoor track, soccer, swimming and diving, tennis, wrestling

Women: Basketball, cross-country, golf, indoor and outdoor track, soccer, softball, swimming and diving, volleyball

Student Life and Housing About 2,000 students can be accommodated in college housing, which is guaranteed for all four years. Eighty-six percent of the students are from Ohio, the remainder from 42 other states and 18 countries. Ethnicity: Caucasian—95 percent. There are eight national fraternities and four national sororities. All students may keep cars.

Accommodations for Students with Disabilities In compliance with section 504

Financial Aid About 92 percent of all freshmen receive aid. The average freshman award was about $21,000.

Requirements for Admission SAT I or ACT scores and a college prep high school program.

Application Freshmen are admitted to all sessions. Applications should be filed by August 1 for fall admission and November 1 for spring admission. Admission notification is sent on a rolling basis.

International Students Students are usually admitted for the fall quarter and should apply at least nine months before their intended date of enrollment. Required are certified school records, records of examination, and proof of financial responsibility. A minimum TOEFL score of 550 paper and 213 computer-based is required, or at least 75 percent on the Michigan Language Examination. Students are encouraged to submit either ACT or SAT scores, if available.

Transfer Students Students must be in good standing at a regionally accredited institution. Courses with grades C or better are considered for transfer. Official transcripts from both secondary school and previously attended colleges are required. Students with an associate's degree from a regionally accredited institution who have a GPA of at least 2.0 will be able to transfer their credits and graduate from the School of Arts and Sciences in two years.

Home-Schooled Students A transcript/portfolio of high school work with courses completed (or in progress) and grades, including a cumulative GPA or another acceptable standard/measurement of academic success, are required. The transcripts must be signed by the instructor(s), dated, and meet the normal requirements of a college prep curriculum. In place of an accredited high school diploma or GED results, students could submit evidence of the annual approval of their program as required within their state. ACT or SAT results, a listing of extracurricular activities, and personal references are required. A campus visit and an on-campus interview are recommended.

Admission Contact
Office of Admissions
Ohio Northern University
525 S. Main Street
Ada, OH 45810
Phone: (888) 408-4ONU

FAX: (419) 772-2313
E-mail: *admissions-ug@onu.edu*
Web: *www.onu.edu*

The Heart of the University Ohio Northern University, while a top-rated liberal arts college, artfully blends the liberal arts with outstanding professional programs, especially in pharmacy and engineering, where 50 percent of the students earn their degrees. Students are admitted directly from high school into the College of Pharmacy, which uses an innovative modular format and systems approach. The faculty models a personalized attention teaching style, so that students can pass this on to their future patients. Throughout their program, students are able to attend presentations by national and international leaders in the world of pharmacy. Students are also able to earn a six-year Doctor of Pharmacy degree. A nationally recognized Drug Information Center provides a unique experience for pharmacy students by offering advanced research opportunities and detailed information on medication.

The College of Engineering offers students a scientific and technical-based major with a liberal arts program. About one-third of the students participate in the Cooperative Education Program, where students have gained work experience at BPAmoco Chemicals, Inc., the Ohio Department of Transportation, Johnson and Johnson, Ford Motor Company, Cooper Tire and Rubber, and Honda of America Manufacturing.

The nationally accredited teacher education program has available an on-campus Child Development Center, giving early childhood students a unique opportunity to work with three-, four-, and five-year-olds.

Business students have available state-of-the art computer facilities, as well as a Small Business Institute. The institute is fully-supervised and allows students to consult with local businesses while receiving college credit.

The nine pre-professional programs have an advising committee that begins the freshman year to guide students through academic course work that will optimize opportunities for admission to professional schools.

There are 8–10 shows each year in the Freed Center for the Performing Arts, at least 40 music performances, and monthly exhibitions hosted by the art department. Also, students participate in over 150 organizations, including 25 percent in Greek life, and in nondenominational chapel activities.

OKLAHOMA BAPTIST UNIVERSITY

Shawnee, Oklahoma

Total Undergraduate Enrollment: 1,829
Men: 788 Women: 1,041
Five-Year Graduation Rate: 56%

Tuition: $$
Room and Board: $
Residential Students: 64%

History Oklahoma Baptist University was established in 1910 as a result of Baptists of the Oklahoma Territory realizing the need for a Christian emphasis in higher education. The city of Shawnee contributed the original 60-acre campus and the first building. The university is owned by the Baptist General Convention.

Location The 189-acre campus is located in Shawnee, Oklahoma (population 28,000), a small town 35 miles east of Oklahoma City and 90 miles southwest of Tulsa, near the geographical center of the state.

Top Programs of Study Education, Christian service, business

Arts and Sciences Anthropology and museum management, applied ministry, art, athletic training, biochemistry, biology, camp administration, child care administration, chemistry, children's ministry, church administration, church music, communication studies, computer science, cross-cultural ministry, English, exercise and sports science, family development, family psychology, French, German, history, journalism, mathematics, missionary nursing, multilingual communication, music, musical theater, musical theater and composition, natural science, nursing, organ performance, parish nursing, pastoral ministry, philosophy, political science, physics, piano performance, psychology, public relations, recreation, religion (Bible emphasis), religion (biblical languages), religious education, social work, sociology, sports medicine, sports ministry, studio art, telecommunications, theater, voice performance, youth ministry

Business Accounting, computer information systems, finance, international business, management, marketing

Education Art, early childhood, elementary, health and physical education, music, secondary, special, speech and drama

Pre-Professional Engineering, law, medicine, occupational therapy, pharmacy, physical therapy, theology

Accredited Programs Business, education, music, nursing

Special Programs There are several minors, including business administration and creative writing, and most majors are also available as minors. The university offers many summer and January Term travel–study programs. Offered through the Council for Christian Colleges and Universities, students may participate in a Washington, D.C., semester, a China Studies semester, a Contemporary Music semester, a Latin American Studies semester in Costa Rica, a Los Angeles Film Studies Center semester, Middle East Studies semester, and a Russian Studies semester. There is an Air Force ROTC program.

Facilities There are 25 buildings, including a newly renovated art building; the new Bailey Business Center; the Ford Music Hall, containing

sound-proof, air-conditioned studios; the Geiger Student Center; a Learning Center; the newly reconstructed Montgomery Hall that houses campus ministry and the Hammonds Biblical Research Center; the Noble Athletic Complex; the renovated Raley Chapel that also houses the Fine Arts Center; Shawnee Hall, the center of campus and main classroom building that also houses the Dorland Theater; the Sarkeys Telecommunications Center, which houses a TV studio and a theater; and the Wood Science Building.

Transition to College Program Students study "Becoming A Master Student," a course that meets twice weekly and includes an orientation, goal setting, time management, memory development, test taking, study strategies, stress management, and career planning.

Athletics NAIA, Sooner Athletic Conference

Men: Baseball, basketball, cross-country, golf, indoor and outdoor track & field, tennis

Women: Basketball, cross-country, golf, indoor and outdoor track & field, softball, tennis

Student Life and Housing About 1,400 students can be accommodated in college housing, which includes single-sex dorms and married housing. All unmarried students under 21 years old must live on campus. Housing is guaranteed for all four years. Sixty-one percent of the undergraduates are from Oklahoma, the remainder are from 41 other states and 22 countries. Ethnicity: Caucasian—86 percent. There are five local fraternities and five local sororities. All students may keep cars.

Accommodations for Students with Disabilities The Special Services Office provides services to students with documented disabilities. Students should contact the Associate Dean of Students.

Financial Aid About 89 percent of all freshmen receive aid. The average freshman award was about $9,000.

Requirements for Admission Applicants are admitted either on a regular, conditional, or probationary basis. The regular admission students require a minimum of 20 on the ACT or 950 on the SAT, and a weighted GPA of 3.0, or rank in the upper half of the class in a college prep high school program. Conditional acceptance is granted to students who score 17–19 on the ACT or 800–940 on the SAT, and have a weighted GPA of at least 3.0 or class rank in the upper half.

Application Freshmen are admitted to all semesters. There is a rolling admissions policy.

International Students Students should consult with the admissions office. Minimum TOEFL scores of 500 paper or 173 computer-based, or a score of 450 on the verbal section of an English language SAT, or scores of 18 in the English and Reading sections of an English language ACT.

Transfer Students Required are good standing at the previous college, official transcripts from all previous accredited institutions, a minimum overall GPA of 2.5, and a transcript that does not include extensive remedial work. Students with fewer than 24 completed college credits must also meet regular freshmen entrance requirements. A maximum of 64 junior college transfer credits will be accepted, while full credit will be given for work completed at an accredited senior college or university.

Home-Schooled Students Admission is based on ACT or SAT scores and a written description or transcript of the home-schooled experience, or the high school transcript.

Admission Contact

Office of Admissions
Oklahoma Baptist University
500 W. University
Shawnee, OK 74804
Phone: (800) 654-3285; (405) 878-2033
FAX: (405) 878-2046
E-mail: *admissions@mail.okbu.edu*
Web: *www.okbu.edu*

The Heart of the University Oklahoma Baptist University is considered one of the top comprehensive schools in the Southwest and is certainly a tuition bargain. The environment on Bison Hill—the name given to the campus, and affectionately used by students, faculty, and others—is captured by the phrase "a culture of caring." This is a university with a Christian faculty and staff, who perform a mentoring role for students within a context of school pride, service, and involvement. Faculty invite students to their homes, join students for late-night study sessions at a local restaurant, offer help during times of personal crisis, and know how to push students to excel academically.

It's this linkage between learning and excellent academic programs, with a supportive Christian community, that is the heart of Oklahoma Baptist University. The academic programs begin with the Unified Studies program, the core curriculum, which, as with all core programs, attempts to provide students with learnings they will have in common, with courses that stress the interrelationship of all knowledge, and a foundation of knowledge that helps to inform all their university learning. That strong core helps to provide the wonderful reputation of OBU's program in the natural sciences and pre-med studies that has led to a 95–100 percent acceptance rate into medical schools of their choice. Graduates attribute much of their success to the personal attention they received as well as the easy access to laboratory experience. A second outstanding program is teacher education, in which OBU has a reputation for producing quality teachers. With teacher education encompassing the largest number of students, OBU's wide variety of field experiences has provided graduates with licensing exam results that place OBU's program near the top in Oklahoma. The School of Business, housed in the newest academic building, offers innovative coursework, including developing international management programs that are used around the world. OBU's outstanding nursing program is driven by its students and faculty who view nursing as a ministry of providing care to others. The music program is a vital part of the campus community with seven performance groups. The School of Christian Service combines an excellent academic preparation as well as practical application, with more OBU graduates serving as International Mission Board Journeymen than any other college.

Campus ministry organizations operate a dozen ongoing ministry programs. There are prayer groups and required chapel. Also, there is a special student-led praise and worship group that attracts about 700 students each week.

For OBU, its successful brand of education consists of worship, study, and service—all components of an energized living–learning community.

OTTERBEIN COLLEGE
Westerville, Ohio

Total Undergraduate Enrollment: 2,100
Men: 800 Women: 1,300
Five-Year Graduation Rate: 88%

Tuition: $$$
Room and Board: $
Residential Students: 65%

History Otterbein College was founded in 1847 by the Church of the United Brethren in Christ, and named for Philip Williams Otterbein, a co-founder of the church. Through several church mergers, the college is now affiliated with the United Methodist Church.

Location The 137-acre campus is located in Westerville, Ohio, a suburban area 12 miles northeast of Columbus, the state capital, providing students with cultural activities, recreation, sports, and internships.

Top Programs of Study Business, education, communications

Arts and Sciences Art, athletic training, biochemistry, broadcasting, computer science, economics, English, equine science, French, health education, history, international studies, journalism, life science (concentrations in environmental science, molecular biology, plant science), mathematics, molecular biology, music, music and business, music performance, nursing, organizational communication, philosophy, physical science, physics/astronomy, political science, psychology, public relations, religion, sociology (concentration in criminology), Spanish, speech communication, sports and wellness management, theater

Business Accounting, business administration (concentrations in finance, international business, management, marketing)

Education Early childhood, middle childhood, multi-age, music, physical education secondary,

Pre-Professional Dentistry, law, medicine, optometry, physical therapy, veterinary medicine

Accredited Programs Allied health education programs, chemistry, education, music, nursing

Special Programs Otterbein offers a dual degree program in engineering with Washington University in St. Louis. There are opportunities for individualized degrees. There are also study abroad and student exchange programs, including the Colmar, France Program for students interested in teaching French.

Facilities There are 28 buildings, including a new multi-purpose academic building with two-story art gallery and extensive computer facility, theater with scene shop, a fine arts center, a planetarium and an observatory, a campus radio station and TV studio, and an equine facility.

Transition to College Program The college offers a more traditional orientation called New Student Weekend right before classes begin in the fall. For four days students eat at faculty homes participate in campus tours, attend special events and presentations, socialize with other students and their orientation group, and become oriented to their first Integrative Studies class and professor.

Athletics NCAA III, Ohio Athletic Conference

Men: Baseball, basketball, cross-country, football, golf, indoor and outdoor track, soccer, tennis

Women: Basketball, cross-country, indoor and outdoor track, golf, soccer, softball, tennis, volleyball

Student Life and Housing About 1,000 students can be accommodated in college housing. Eighty-six percent of the students are from Ohio, the remainder are from 29 other states and 28 countries. Ethnicity: Caucasian—88 percent; African-American—7 percent; Asian-American—1 percent; Hispanic-American—1 percent. There are one national and six local fraternities and six local sororities. All students may keep cars.

Accommodations for Students with Disabilities The Academic Support Center facilitates special academic accommodations for students with disabilities.

Financial Aid About 92 percent of all freshmen receive aid. The average freshman award was about $14,000.

Requirements for Admission SAT I or ACT scores and a college prep high school program. A campus visit is strongly recommended.

Application Freshmen are admitted to all semesters. Applications should be filed by March 1 for fall admission, with admission notification sent on a rolling basis.

International Students Required are official copies of their academic credentials from secondary schools and previous colleges attended, English translations of the grading system, copies of any diplomas or certificates received, or the scores from any national examination. Students whose native language is not English must send an official report of a score of at least 500 on the TOEFL. Also required is proof of financial support by sending a bank statement and a sponsor's letter.

Transfer Students Required are official transcripts from secondary school and previous regionally accredited colleges. There is no limit of credits that may be transferred from four-year colleges; however, a maximum of 90 quarter hours may be transferred from all two-year institutions combined. Only those courses graded C− or better will be considered for transfer.

Home-Schooled Students Students should submit written documentation of successful completion of the equivalency of a college prep high school curriculum. Transcripts from a cooperating school district are preferred. Ninth and twelfth grade proficiency test results are encouraged for Ohio students only.

Admission Contact
Office of Admissions
Otterbein College
One Otterbein College
Westerville, OH 43081
Phone: (800) 488-8144; (614) 823-1500
FAX: (614) 823-1200
E-mail: *uotterb@otterbein.edu*
Web: *www.otterbein.edu*

The Heart of the College While Otterbein has evolved into a comprehensive college, it remains rooted in a liberal arts education in the Christian tradition, stressing values of caring and inclusiveness. For example, from its founding Otterbein was one of the first three colleges to open its doors to people of color. Its first two graduates were female. Second, Otterbein's governance system reflects this inclusiveness by having a single College Senate, composed of faculty, students, administration, alumni, and trustees. Also, the school added three elected student trustees and three elected faculty trustees as full voting members of the board. A third, more recent example, was the creation of an innovative Integrative Studies Program, intended to provide a broad study of world culture to enable students to understand the ideas, movements, and patterns that have produced our current civilization. Both the new curriculum and governance system have received national recognition.

Otterbein likes to provide a hands-on approach to education, getting students on the air on its student-run radio station or involved in Columbus's CBS-TV affiliate, equine science students feeding and experiencing horses at Otterbein's stables, or chemistry students collaborating with faculty doing research.

Two distinctive programs are the theater programs and the equine science program. Otterbein's theater program has a national reputation, with training in acting, design technology, and musical theater being top notch. The faculty's industry connections provide students with internships in major regional theaters. The equine science program provides several tracks, including equine administration, which prepares students for equine-related professions, such as bloodstock agents, insurance adjustors, editors and writers, administrators, and those involved in marketing; equine facility management; and equine science pre-veterinary medicine.

More than 80 percent of Otterbein's premed students are accepted into medical school, with more than 1,000 medical doctors across America who received their undergraduate degrees at Otterbein. Also, 95 percent of the school's graduates over the last several years are either employed or in graduate school.

Otterbein students have the best of both worlds. It is located in a quiet village setting of restored buildings, brick streets, gift and antique shops, cafes, an ice cream shop, and just minutes from Columbus, the 29th largest metropolitan area in the nation. Here students find sport attractions, cultural events and shopping, and a city that is rated among the top five cities by the number of innovative firms and by quality of workforce.

PACIFIC UNIVERSITY   **Forest Grove, Oregon**

Total Undergraduate Enrollment: 1,200
Men: 480 Women: 720
Five-Year Graduation Rate: 57%

Tuition: $$$
Room and Board: $
Residential Students: 65%

History Pacific University was founded in 1849 as a private institution affiliated with the United Church of Christ.

Location The 55-acre campus is located in Forest Grove, Oregon, a suburban community about 25 miles west of Portland and one hour from the Pacific Ocean.

Top Programs of Study Pre-med, business administration, education

Arts and Sciences Anthropology/sociology, applied science, art, biology, bioinformatics, chemistry (emphases in biological, chemical, and environmen-

tal), Chinese, Chinese studies, computer science, creative writing, coordinate studies in humanities, economics, education and learning, environmental biology, exercise science (sports medicine, human performance), French, French studies, German, German studies, history, international studies, Japanese, Japanese studies, literature, mathematics, media arts and communications (film, journalism), Spanish, music (performance, education), philosophy (bioethics emphasis), physics, political science, psychology, social work, sociology, theater

Business Administration (concentrations in accounting, finance, marketing, management)

Education None

Pre-Professional Dentistry, law, medicine, occupational therapy, optometry, physical therapy, veterinary medicine

Accredited Programs Music

Special Programs The university uses a 4-1-4 academic calendar. There are opportunities for study abroad in 11 countries, internships, community service, research, and double majors. Pacific offers a cooperative program in engineering with Washington University in St. Louis. There is an Upward Bound Program for motivated, economically disadvantaged students. The new Berglund Center for Internet Studies provides students and faculty with opportunities for discussion, research, and debate. The Oregon Holocaust Center is designed to increase understanding of violence and racial prejudice. There is an English Language Institute for international students. The McCall Forum invites notable speakers for political debate, including Newt Gingrich and James Carville. Pacific was cited as one of America's most computer-wired colleges. The university also has six graduate schools.

Facilities There are 18 buildings, including the Pacific Athletic Center, which contains a new fitness center, the Tom Miles Theater, the Taylor-Meade Performing Arts Center, the Strain Science Center, the Carvein Art Gallery, and a radio station.

Transition to College Program Freshman Orientation has students form groups where they learn the basics of college life, watch movies, attend concerts, perform community service, and make friends. Later, the First-Year Seminar helps students develop writing skills, note taking, time management, and improved communication skills. The students in each seminar class live in the same residence hall, where they can form study groups and friendships.

Athletics NCAA III, Northeast Conference

Men: Baseball, basketball, cross-country, golf, soccer, tennis, track & field, wrestling

Women: Basketball, cross-country, golf, soccer, softball, tennis, track & field, volleyball, wrestling

Student Life and Housing About 700 students can be accommodated in college housing. Fifty percent of the students are from Oregon, with the remainder from 31 other states and 8 countries. Ethnicity: Caucasian—64 percent; Asian-American—17 percent; Native-American—2 percent; Hispanic-American—2 percent. There are three local fraternities and three local sororities. All students may keep cars.

Accommodations for Students with Disabilities In compliance with section 504

Financial Aid About 92 percent of all freshmen receive aid. The average freshman award was about $16,000.

Requirements for Admission SAT I or ACT scores and a college prep high school program. Students who score above 50 on every section of the GED are also eligible for admission. A campus visit and interview are strongly encouraged.

Application The priority application deadline is February 15, with admission decisions made on a rolling basis.

International Students Students whose native language is not English must score a minimum of 550 on the TOEFL.

Transfer Students Required are official transcripts from all postsecondary institutions attended and an overall minimum GPA of 2.75. If students have fewer than 30 college credits, they must also submit a high school transcript. The preferred application deadline is June 15.

Home-School Students Students are required to submit curriculum descriptions and grades.

Admission Contact:
Office of Admissions

Pacific University
2043 College Way
Forest Grove, OR 97116
Phone: (800) 677-6712; (503) 352-2218
FAX: (503) 359-2975
E-mail: *admissions@pacificu.edu*
Web: *www.pacificu.edu*

The Heart of the University Pacific University offers students an excellent liberal arts education at a modest cost in an ideal location. The academic program is challenging, but with small class sizes and the ability to double major or establish a major and two minors, students appreciate the impact this has on career options. That versatility is augmented by the offering of special centers and programs, such as the Oregon Holocaust Center, an ESL Institute for international students, and a Center for Internet Studies.

But the heart of the university is seen in the performance of its faculty members, who have a commitment to excellence in teaching and provide students with the personal attention that supports their learning. Professors demonstrate a liking for students and want to know them as individuals. This translates to a classroom comfort level that increases student learning. As a result of a major grant, each year 20 faculty members participate in a staff development program where they direct projects that foster hands-on learning through public service work and interdisciplinary instruction. Students become the beneficiaries of faculty's motivation to provide interesting and significant instruction.

Students have an appreciation of being able to conduct independent and collaborative research with faculty beginning in the freshman year. Most students submit senior research projects for Senior Project Day, when they are presented to a group of faculty, administrators, and students. Topics have included, "Socio-Economic Status and Preschool Children's Aggression Levels" and "Japanese and American Communication Style Differences." Students realize the benefits of this research in making them stronger candidates for graduate school and more successful once they are in graduate programs.

In addition to conducting research, most students also engage in an internship, a service learning project, or study abroad. Internships are offered in corporations such as Prudential, at nonprofit corporations such as the Red Cross, government offices such as the City of Portland Affirmative Action, and also small businesses. The on-campus Pacific Humanitarian Center places students in tutoring programs, Habitat for Humanity, and housing renovations for elderly or disabled residents. Every year about 100 students spend a semester, a year, or the January term in Europe, South America, or Asia, either living with a host family or in a residence hall.

Students consider the university's location ideal, with Forest Grove being such a safe, quiet, comfortable suburb, and then Portland, with its "big city" attractions only a 30-minute bus or train ride away. In addition, outdoor enthusiasts just love the hiking, kayaking, snowboarding, mountain biking, and white water rafting offered to them in the Pacific Northwest. The Outback Program on campus sponsors 15 trips each month for as little as $5, including "urban adventures" to Seattle, San Francisco, and Vancouver. With 60 clubs and organizations and more than half of the students involved in athletics, Pacific's student population makes it easy to participate and even become leaders.

In a typical year 70 percent of Pacific's seniors have jobs or have been accepted to graduate and professional schools by the time they graduate. The acceptance rate to medical school is 80 percent. Pacific also offers six graduate programs: optometry, education, physician's assistant, physical therapy, occupational therapy, and clinical psychology. The university is unique in having a graduate school population that almost equals its undergraduate population in size—a comfortable 1,000 students.

PRESBYTERIAN COLLEGE   Clinton, South Carolina

Total Undergraduate Enrollment: 1,217
Men: 569 Women: 648
Five-Year Graduation Rate: 70%

Tuition: $$$
Room and Board: $
Residential Students: 92%

History Presbyterian College was established in 1880 as Clinton College in order to supplement the education of students at Thornwell Orphanage. The orphanage was founded five years earlier by Reverend William Plumer Jacobs, pastor of Clinton's First Presbyterian Church, who later established the college. In 1890 the college became Presbyterian College and is affiliated with the Presbyterian Church. The college is listed on the Templeton Foundation's Honor Roll of Character-Building Colleges.

Location The 220-acre campus is located in Clinton, South Carolina, a small town 40 miles south of Greenville and about two hours from Atlanta, Georgia.

Top Programs of Study Business, biology, education

Arts and Sciences Art, biology, chemistry, computer science, English, French, geography, German, Greek, Hebrew, history, interdisciplinary studies, mathematics, music, philosophy, physical education, physics, political science, psychology, religion, sociology, Spanish, speech, statistics, theater

Business Accounting, administration, economics

Education Christian, early childhood, elementary, music, secondary, special,

Pre-Professional Allied health science, dentistry, law, medicine, pharmacy, theology, veterinary medicine

Accredited Programs Business, education

Special Programs The college has several dual degree and cooperative programs: engineering with Auburn, Clemson, Mercer, and Vanderbilt; forestry and environmental studies with Duke; Christian education with the Presbyterian School of Christian Education in Richmond, Virginia. Study abroad and student exchange programs are available, as is a Washington semester. During an optional May period (Fleximester), the college offers special study programs in locations such as the Western Plains, the Galapagos Islands, and the Caribbean. The Russell Program focuses on aspects of the media and society, bringing renowned individuals such as Bill Moyers and William Bennett to campus, and also involves a media learning center and students' internships. There is an office of multicultural services.

Facilities There are 39 buildings that blend new structures with those listed in the National Register of Historic Places. Neville Hall has been updated. There are new academic, lecture, and recital halls; Harper Center, a drama center and art gallery; a renovated campus center; two new living accommodations; and the new Lake Sports Medicine Center.

Transition to College Program In addition to a traditional orientation just prior to the fall semester, freshmen are invited to participate in optional off-campus programs during the summer, which include overnight rafting and sailing trips. Faculty and staff also participate.

Athletics NCAA II, South Atlantic Conference

  Men: Baseball, basketball, cross-country, football, golf, soccer, tennis

  Women: Basketball, cross-country, soccer, softball, tennis, volleyball

Student Life and Housing About 1,000 students can be accommodated in college housing, which is guaranteed for all four years. Fifty-seven percent of the students are from South Carolina, the remainder from 26 other states and 7 countries. Ethnicity: Caucasian—92 percent. There are seven national fraternities and three national sororities. All students may keep cars. Students adhere to an honor code.

Accommodations for Students with Disabilities
The college provides reasonable accommodations for students with documented disabilities. Students should inform, in writing, the Office of Academic Affairs regarding the disability.

Financial Aid About 80 percent of all freshmen receive aid. The average freshman award was about $18,182.

Requirements for Admission SAT I or ACT scores and a college prep high school program.

Application Early Decision candidates must apply by December 5. There is no deadline for regular decision applicants. Admission notification is made within four weeks following the receipt of a completed application.

International Students Students whose primary language is not English must score a minimum of 550 on the paper-based TOEFL. Students should also take either the ACT or SAT I. Students should submit official secondary school transcripts and, if applicable, postsecondary transcripts, as well as a declaration of finances.

Transfer Students Students must have a GPA of at least 2.5 from a regionally accredited institution, be in good standing at the previous college, or have graduated from a two-year college. Required are official transcripts from all colleges or universities attended, high school transcript, SAT or ACT scores, and two transfer clearance forms (one from the academic dean and one from the dean of students at the institution last attended). A maximum of 68 credits can be transferred from a two-year college.

Admission Contact
Office of Admissions
Presbyterian College
503 South Broad Street
Clinton, SC 29325
Phone: (800) 960-7583; (864) 833-2820
FAX: (864) 833-8481
E-mail: *admissions@presby.edu*
Web: *www.presby.edu*

The Heart of the College First, Presbyterian College is neither a Bible college nor is it comprised only of students who are Presbyterians. In fact, only about 30 percent of the students indicate that they are. Second, the college is one of the best liberal arts colleges in the Southeast, principally because of the college's concern for the whole student—body, mind, and spirit.

As an NCAA Division II school, Presbyterian is able to offer athletic scholarships and about a third of the students are varsity players. To many people outside of the college, PC means sports because of the great success of its athletic teams in many sports. However, 85 percent of the students also participate in the college's intramural program for exercise, friendship, and fun.

Presbyterian College views the liberal arts as the cornerstone of a great education, with their focus on creative and critical thinking, problem-solving, communication, and the kind of flexibility of mind that will enable its graduates to live and work in a rapidly changing world. PC graduates are encouraged to see their careers not as their lives, but rather as one aspect of one's total life. This liberal arts education is assisted by professors who put students first and are hired for their ability to think and interact with students in myriad ways.

The entire college community is very proud that it lives by an honor code. In part the code reads: "In my every act, I will seek to maintain a high standard of honesty and truthfulness for myself and in the college." The term *values* obviously has an important place here, as indicated by one professor's account of a student who actually failed a take-home test. Character and high standards are part of the wholistic education at PC.

Service is at the heart of the college. In fact, the college's motto is "While we live, we serve." Presbyterian College attracts students who want to help others and at any one time has about 475 active volunteers. The Student Volunteer Service Organization places students where they can help. For example, some of the female students developed a dance program to give dance lessons to the girls at the Thornwell Orphanage, while the CHAMPS program motivates at-risk kids. Even the Greek life at the college, so very popular

with about 40 percent of the students as members, commits itself to service with a math tutoring program for kids or arranging a Senior Prom for the seniors at the Presbyterian House.

This wholistic approach is very successful, with about 99 percent of the graduates either employed or in graduate or professional schools within six months.

QUINNIPIAC UNIVERSITY

Hamden, Connecticut

Total Undergraduate Enrollment: 5,000
Men: 2,000 Women: 3,000
Five-Year Graduation Rate: 72%

Tuition: $$$
Room and Board: $$$$
Residential Students: 73%

History Founded in 1929 as the Connecticut College of Commerce by Samuel Taylor, the small business college awarded the associate's degree. In 1951 the college's name was changed to Quinnipiac, commemorating the early Native American settlers in the New Haven harbor area. The college began by offering the bachelor's degree, and then in the 1970s expanded its offerings to master's degrees. In 1966 the college moved to its current location in Hamden.

Location The 200-acre campus is located in Hamden, Connecticut, a suburban area 10 miles north of New Haven and 35 miles south of Hartford, two hours from New York and almost three hours from Boston.

Top Programs of Study Communications, physical therapy, education

Arts and Sciences Athletic training/sports medicine, biochemistry, biology, biomedical science, chemistry, computer science, clinical laboratory science (medical technology), computer science, criminal justice, diagnostic imaging, e-media, English, gerontology, health/science studies, history, interactive digital design, legal studies (paralegal), mass communications (journalism, media, production, media studies), mathematics (actuarial studies), microbiology/biotechnology, nursing, occupa-

tional therapy ($5\frac{1}{2}$ year program), physical therapy ($5\frac{1}{2}$ year program), physician's assistant ($5\frac{1}{2}$ year program), political science, psychobiology, public relations, respiratory care, social services, sociology, Spanish, veterinary technology

Business Accounting, advertising, computer information systems, economics, entrepreneurship, finance, health administration, international business, management (concentrations in human resource management, production and operations management), marketing (concentrations in marketing management and international marketing)

Education Elementary, middle, and secondary (all five-year programs leading to a master's degree)

Pre-Professional None

Accredited Programs Business, cardiovascular perfusion, clinical laboratory science, diagnostic imaging, law, legal studies, nursing, occupational therapy, physical therapist, physician's assistant, respiratory care, veterinary technology

Special Programs Independent majors are available. The Office of the Student Center and Student Leadership Development provides a comprehensive leadership program. There is an Office of Multicultural Advancement. There are opportunities for study abroad, international internships, and a

Washington, D.C., semester. The Quinnipiac University Polling Institute surveys residents in the New York, Connecticut, and New Jersey area.

Facilities There are 35 buildings, including the new Bernhard Library; a new Health Sciences Center; a learning center; a state-of-the-art Lender School of Business Building; the Ed McMahon Mass Communication Center, which houses two cable television channels; two new classroom buildings for the liberal arts; a radio station; a new School of Law; and new residence halls.

Transition to College Program The university offers a traditional orientation program.

Athletics NCAA I, Northeast Conference, MAAC (ice hockey and men's lacrosse)

Men: Baseball, basketball, cross-country, golf, ice hockey, indoor and outdoor track, lacrosse, soccer, tennis

Women: Basketball, cross-country, field hockey, ice hockey, indoor and outdoor track, lacrosse, soccer, softball, tennis, volleyball

Student Life and Housing About 3,500 students can be accommodated in college housing. Thirty-one percent of the students are from Connecticut, with the majority from 29 other states, mostly the Northeast, and 15 countries. Ethnicity: Caucasian—89 percent; Hispanic-American—4 percent; African-American—2 percent; Asian-American—2 percent. There are one local and three national fraternities, and one local and two national sororities. Upperclassmen may keep cars.

Accommodations for Students with Disabilities The Coordinator of Learning Services of the Learning Center meets with students who disclose a disability.

Financial Aid About 68 percent of all students receive aid. The average freshman award was about $12,000.

Requirements for Admission SAT I or ACT scores and a college prep high school program. An interview is recommended.

Application Freshmen are admitted fall and spring semesters. Applications should be submitted by February 15 for fall admission and December 15 for spring admission. Admission decisions are sent on a rolling basis. Candidates for the physical therapy, occupational therapy, and physician's assistant programs should apply by December 31.

International Students Required are English language descriptions of secondary schools, colleges, and universities attended; certified translations of all prior secondary and collegiate academic records, if applicable; a minimum TOEFL score of 550 paper or 213 computer-based; and official documentation of financial support.

Transfer Students Required are official transcripts from high school and post-high school institutions attended and ACT or SAT scores. If the applicant graduated from high school more than five years ago, or has successfully completed the equivalent of 30 credits of college study, he or she is not required to submit SAT or ACT scores. A 2.0 GPA is expected for previous college work. Junior standing will be awarded to a student who transfers from a Connecticut two-year college that has an articulation agreement with Quinnipiac. Only C grades or higher will be considered for transfer. Transfer students cannot be accommodated in the physician's assistant program.

Admission Contact
Office of Admissions
Quinnipiac University
275 Mount Carmel Avenue
Hamden, CT 06518
Phone: (800) 462-1944; (203) 582-8600
FAX: (203) 582-8906
E-mail: *admissions@quinnipiac.edu*
Web: *www.quinnipiac.edu*

The Heart of the University Quinnipiac University offers more than 50 undergraduate majors and 16 graduate programs. It makes every effort to combine the advantages of a university with the person-to-person learning of a small college. Its facilities and technology are state-of-the-art and students are provided with many internship programs and clinical affiliations. Quinnipiac prepares students for careers, and health care professionals and accrediting agencies agree that the School of Health Sciences is one of the premier centers for health professionals. The university offers distinctive programs in physical and occupational therapy, nursing, physician's assistant, and respiratory care. Students are offered extensive programs of internships and fieldwork, as a result of the school's having affiliations with nearly 1,000 hospitals and health care facilities across the nation.

Technology is a major part of the success of the School of Communications and its Ed McMahon Mass Communications Center, where equipment matches or exceeds professional broadcast standards and is even accessible to freshmen. For radio production, two studios offer professional-level equipment, including all major recording formats. The television studio also houses state-of-the-art suites for digital acquisition and editing. The New Technology Center features a news desk modeled after a working newsroom. Electronic news gathering provides students with up-to-the-minute stories. Multimedia computers equipped with software bring the Internet and Associated Press wire services directly to workstations. Students have as their pro-

fessors professional journalists and filmmakers and often meet with visiting journalists, such as Dan Rather, Paula Zahn, and Charles Osgood.

The School of Business has earned the highest accreditation awarded and offers more than 150 internships with companies such as ABC, Pratt and Whitney, Ernst and Young, and the Bayer Corporation. Finance majors have an opportunity to study at the New York Stock Exchange, spending part of their day with Quinnipiac alumni and traders. Because of the truly global marketplace, business students are also able to study in France and China.

Even in the College of Liberal Arts one feels the career-focus of the university. The highly acclaimed interdisciplinary gerontology program provides students with two semester-long internships in public and private agencies directly serving the elderly.

The success of these outstanding programs is demonstrated by the fact that 85 percent of the graduates report that they are either employed or in graduate school within six months of graduation.

A setting of pine groves, a stream, a pond with swans, fields and wooded pathways, and the towering Sleeping Giant Mountain overlooking the campus provide students with a beautiful, tranquil setting, only two to three hours from the big cities of New York and Boston.

RANDOLPH-MACON COLLEGE   Ashland, Virginia

Total Undergraduate Enrollment: 1,154
Men: 574 Women: 580
Five-Year Graduation Rate: 70%

Tuition: $$$
Room and Board: $
Residential Students: 85%

History Randolph-Macon College, established in 1830, is a liberal arts college affiliated with the United Methodist Church.

Location The 115-acre campus is located in a suburban area of Ashland, Virginia (population 6,000), 15 miles north of Richmond and about 90 miles south of Washington, D.C.

Top Programs of Study Economics/business, psychology, sociology

Arts and Sciences Art history, arts management, biology, chemistry, classical studies, computer science, drama, economics, English, environmental studies, French, German, Greek, history, international relations, international studies,

Latin, mathematics, music, philosophy, physics, political science, psychology, religious studies, sociology, Spanish, studio art, women's studies

Business Accounting, economics/business

Education Elementary, secondary

Pre-Professional None

Accredited Programs None

Special Programs There is an Office of Multicultural Affairs. The college offers a summer research program called SURF. There is a Phi Beta Kappa chapter. The college offers several cooperative degree programs: engineering with Columbia University and the University of Virginia; forestry with Duke; and accounting with Virginia Commonwealth University. There is cross-registration with several area colleges. There are opportunities for study abroad, internships, double majors, and a Washington, D.C., semester.

Facilities There are 65 buildings, including a newly renovated center for the performing arts, a new field house, and townhouse apartments; an observatory; Old Chapel and Pace-Armistead Hall, both listed on the National Historic Register, with Old Chapel housing the music and drama programs and the latter housing the Flippo Gallery and the studio arts program; Washington and Franklin Hall, also listed on the National Historic Register; and Brock Sport and Recreation Center.

Transition to College Program The college offers a traditional orientation program.

Athletics NCAA III, Old Dominion Athletic Conference

Men: Baseball, basketball, football, golf, lacrosse, soccer, tennis

Women: Basketball, field hockey, lacrosse, soccer, softball, swimming, tennis, volleyball

Student Life and Housing About 1,000 students can be accommodated in college housing, which is guaranteed for all four years. Sixty percent of the students are from Virginia, the remainder from 39 other states and 15 countries. Ethnicity: Caucasian—91 percent. There are seven national fraternities and five national sororities. All students may keep cars. Students adhere to a code of academic integrity.

Accommodations for Students with Disabilities To be eligible for academic accommodations, the student must register with the Office for Disability Support Services and provide appropriate documentation of the disability, outline the nature of the disability and how it affects the student in the classroom, and detail the specific accommodations requested.

Financial Aid About 95 percent of all freshmen receive aid. The average freshman award was about $16,600.

Requirements for Admission SAT I or ACT scores and a college prep high school program. A campus visit and interview are strongly recommended.

Application Early Decision applicants must file by December 1, with admission notification by December 15. The regular application deadline is March 1, with admission notification by April 1. Students are accepted for fall and spring admission.

International Students The application deadline is March 1 for the fall semester. Required are official secondary and, if applicable, college transcripts, an essay, minimum TOEFL scores of 550 paper and 213 computer, and verification of financial responsibility.

Transfer Students Required are official college transcripts and SAT I scores. Courses with C− grades or higher are considered for transfer. A minimum GPA of 2.0 is required. Students transferring from regionally accredited two-year colleges may transfer up to 65 credits. Students must be in good standing at the previous institution. At least one-half of the semester hours of the major program taken in the major department must be taken at Randolph-Macon College.

Admission Contact
Office of Admissions
Randolph-Macon College
P.O. Box 5005
Ashland, VA 23005
Phone: (800) 888-1762
FAX: 804-752-4707
E-mail: *admissions@rmc.edu*
Web: *www.rmc.edu*

The Heart of the College Randolph-Macon is a school of great opportunity. In a recent year 50 percent of the entering class received academic scholarships ranging from $5,000 to $15,000. Ninety percent of all students receive nonrepayable scholarships or grants averaging about $8,700. Close to 50 percent of the students receive need-based financial aid packages averaging about $19,000. These facts support the college's reputation not only as a best buy but also as being committed to affordability.

The college is also unique in that its south of Washington, D.C., location attracts not only Northeasterners, but also students from many other states and foreign countries, making for a geographically diverse population.

A friendly relaxed campus environment is highlighted by the quality of one-to-one interaction between students and faculty. Students' names are remembered, faculty office doors are kept open, students are invited to collaborate in research, and faculty members treat students as distinct individuals. The faculty is passionate about teaching. Students describe their professors with such terms as, "unbounded enthusiasm." Students also have an appreciation for the mentoring role their professors play, especially in recognizing what a student's specific passion is and guiding him or her toward this.

The wonderful liberal arts program is viewed by the college as being the most important kind of education, for not only surviving, but also making valuable contributions in a lifetime. Students are immersed in language, labs, social service, philosophy, history, fine arts, mathematics, writing, and literature. The program offers 30 minors, so that students have the opportunity to follow their passions in selecting areas of study that interest them.

Qualified students are able to participate in SURF, a 10-week, summer research program paying students a healthy stipend and providing on-campus accommodations. Each project is personally administered by a professor mentor and flows from either student or professor interests. Two recent projects were: "Interaction of Violent Video Games on a Frustrated Person" and "The Politics of Supreme Court Appointments."

Other opportunities include a fine study abroad program, an athletic program that involves nearly 85 percent of the students, a sophisticated Center for Career Planning, and quality internships. Add to this the charming and safe town of Ashland, surrounded by Virginia horse country. Fifteen miles south there's Richmond, the state capital, rated as the number one mid-size city in the South. For additional opportunities, Washington, D.C., is only 90 minutes away.

RIDER COLLEGE   Lawrenceville, New Jersey

Total Undergraduate Enrollment: 3,000
Men: 1,250 Women: 1,750
Five-Year Graduation Rate: 57%

Tuition: $$$
Room and Board: $$$$
Residential Students: 70%

History Rider University was founded in 1865 as Trenton Business College. After the turn of the century, teacher education was added to its programs. In 1992 Westminster Choir College in

Princeton, New Jersey, merged with Rider. In 1994 Rider became a university.

Location The 353-acre campus is in Lawrenceville, New Jersey, a suburban location three miles north of Trenton, seven miles south of Princeton, and within a 90-minute drive to Philadelphia and a train ride to New York City.

Top Programs of Study Education, business, communications

Arts and Sciences American studies, biochemistry, biology, biopsychology, chemistry, communications (concentrations in business and professional speech, interpersonal, journalism, multimedia, public relations, radio and TV), economics, English, environmental sciences, fine arts (art, dance, music, theater), French, geosciences, German, history, journalism, marine sciences, mathematics, philosophy, physics, political science, psychology, Russian, sociology, Spanish

Westminster Choir College offers the following: choral conducting; composition; music; music education; piano accompanying and coaching; piano pedagogy and performance; voice pedagogy and performance; voice, piano, and organ performance; sacred music

Business Accounting, actuarial science, advertising, administration (concentration in entrepreneurial studies), business economics, computer information systems, finance, global business, human resource management, management and organizational behavior, marketing

Education Bilingual, business, early childhood, elementary, ESL, secondary, special

Pre-Professional Allied health, law, medicine

Accredited Programs Business, education, music

Special Programs Rider offers a three-year accelerated business degree option a well as a five-year B.A. B.S./M.B.A. Program. The TRIO Program provides comprehensive support services for first-generation college students. The university operates a Small Business Institute, has a Model United Nations Program, and a Center for the Development of Leadership Skills. Rider has an EOP Program for motivated economically and educationally disadvantaged students. The university offers both an intensive foreign language study abroad program as well as an interdisciplinary studies abroad program. There is an Army ROTC program.

Facilities There are 37 buildings, including a renovated student center, a science and technology center, the Franklin Moore Library, a fine arts center, radio and TV stations, and a holocaust/genocide center. Centennial Lake centers the campus.

Transition to College Program The University Theme Program welcomes new students through study and participation in special events focused on a common theme, such as "Ethics and Social Responsibility." Early in the fall, programs foster friendship and community through campus orientation activities and social events; a keynote lecture by a distinguished faculty member; and discussion of theme readings with faculty, administrators, and fellow students.

Athletics NCAA I, Metro Atlantic Athletic Conference

Men: Baseball, basketball, cross-country, golf, indoor track, soccer, swimming and diving, tennis, track & field, wrestling

Women: Basketball, cross-country, field hockey, indoor track, soccer, softball, swimming and diving, tennis, track & field, volleyball

Student Life and Housing About 2,200 students can be accommodated in college housing, which is guaranteed for all four years. Seventy-six percent of the students are from New Jersey, the remainder from 30 other states and 9 countries. Ethnicity: Caucasian—76 percent; African-American—8 percent; Hispanic-American—4 percent; Asian-American—3 percent; International 3 percent. There are five national fraternities and seven national sororities. All students may keep cars.

Accommodations for Students with Disabilities
The university provides comprehensive services.

Financial Aid About 70 percent of all freshmen receive aid. The average aid award was about $16,000.

Requirements for Admission SAT I or ACT scores and a college prep high school program.

Application The Early Action deadline is November 15, with a decision notification by December 15. Students may enter any semester. Admission deadlines are open.

International Students Required are official transcripts from all secondary and, if applicable, postsecondary schools attended, including an English translation, an evaluation of courses completed, and grades received. A TOEFL score is required for applicants whose native language is not English. If English is a native language, either SAT I or ACT scores should be submitted. Also required is a notarized financial resource statement or bank statement.

Transfer Students C grades or higher from an accredited institution are considered for transfer. A student transferring from an accredited two-year institution may receive up to 60 credits. Students must complete their last 30 credits at Rider.

Admission Contact
Office of Admissions
Rider University
2083 Lawrenceville Road
Lawrenceville, NJ 08648-3099
Phone: (800) 257-9026; (609) 896-5042
FAX: (609) 895-6545
E-mail: *admissions@rider.edu*
Web: *www.rider.edu*

The Heart of the University Rider University gives students an edge that makes graduates not only highly marketable but also successful applicants for graduate school. Rider's reputation is that of a premier career-preparation university in the mid-Atlantic region. This reputation is supported by such statistics as the following: Graduates report 100 percent employment in majors such as actuarial science, American studies, chemistry, economics, French, German, marine science, mathematics, physics, and Spanish. Also, 94 percent of Rider's graduates successfully find employment or pursue advanced degree programs. The medical school acceptance rate is 75 percent and law school 92 percent. Much of this success is credited to a comprehensive career services program that starts as early as freshman year and the careful work of academic advisers. But the real edge that students get at Rider is provided by accomplished faculty members who inspire, mentor, and guide their students. Students are surprised at their professors'"uncanny ability to relate to students." Because of this approach to education, the faculty works hard to connect students to internships, graduate schools, and careers. As one faculty member viewed his work: "Rider is a shirt-sleeve working institution. Students come here to get skills so that they can go to work."

The Rider edge is also provided by hands-on internships in almost every department, many with Fortune 500 companies. The campus's proximity to the Route 1 corporate corridor in New Jersey helps place students in the headquarters of companies such as Merrill Lynch, Bristol-Myers Squibb, and Bloomberg. In science, about 20 students per year publish in professional journals along with their professors. State-of-the-art facilities like one of the best college television production studios in the East train students on equipment used by professionals. And with technology a way of life at Rider, professors incorporate it into their classes as much as possible.

Many students come to Rider to study an area of business or education or an area of music "down the block," at Westminster. These are all nationally accredited programs that have been highly successful. The business program has a Small Business Institute in which students can serve as consultants to small businesses, researching and analyzing a firm's problems and then making recommendations for improvement. Rider's College of Music, Westminster Choir College, offers a broad range of majors, with numerous avenues for performing, including the large Chapel Choir, the Westminster Symphonic Choir, and several ensembles.

With more than 100 clubs and organizations, Rider is a friendly campus with much to do. Nearby are Princeton, the University of Pennsylvania, the College of New Jersey, as well as urban entertainment, culture, and professional sports of New York, Philadelphia, and the New Jersey Meadowlands.

ROANOKE COLLEGE   Salem, Virginia

Total Undergraduate Enrollment: 1,700
Men: 650 Women: 1,050
Five-Year Graduation Rate: 65%

Tuition: $$$
Room and Board: $$
Residential Students: 57%

History Roanoke College was founded in 1842 by David Bittle and Christopher Baughman, Lutheran pastors, who recognized the need to educate the young men of the rural frontier. Originally located near Staunton, Virginia, and named the Virginia Institute, it was chartered in 1845 and renamed the Virginia Collegiate Institute. The school was moved to Salem, a greater center of activity, and later renamed Roanoke College. The college is listed on the Templeton Foundation's Honor Roll of Character Building Colleges.

Location The 70-acre campus is located in Salem, Virginia (population 25,000), five miles west of Roanoke. The Roanoke Valley population is 250,000. The college is 10 miles from the Appalachian Trail and 17 miles from the Blue Ridge Parkway. The college is about 35 minutes from Washington, D.C., and Charlotte, North Carolina. The city of Salem was recognized as an All-American community.

Top Programs of Study Business administration, English, sociology, psychology

Arts and Sciences Art, athletic training, biology, biochemistry, chemistry, criminal justice, computer information systems, computer science, economics, English, environmental policy, environmental science, French, health and human

performance, history, international relations, mathematics, medical technology, music, philosophy, physics, political science, psychology, religion, sociology, Spanish, theater, theology

Business Administration (concentrations in accounting, finance, global business, health care administration, marketing)

Education Elementary, secondary

Pre-Professional Dentistry, engineering, law, medicine, ministry

Accredited Programs Business, chemistry

Special Programs The Center for Community Research assists faculty members and students in conducting research projects in the local community. The college offers 28 minors. There are opportunities for internships, independent study, and independent research. There is a Washington, D.C., semester and study abroad opportunities. Roanoke offers a dual degree program in engineering with Washington University in St. Louis, Virginia Polytechnic Institute, and the University of Tennessee-Knoxville.

Facilities There are 45 buildings, a blend of historic and modern architecture. The administration building is a registered National Historic Landmark. The Funtel Library has recently been renovated and expanded.

Transition to College Program The Co-Curricula Learning Service organizes groups of students who meet periodically throughout the academic year, exposing students to different aspects of the college. Included is an enhanced academic advisement system, in which students take a course with a professor who is also their adviser. A community service component is another feature of the program.

Athletics NCAA III, Old Dominion Athletic Conference

Men: Baseball, basketball, cross-country, lacrosse, soccer, track & field, tennis

Women: Basketball, cross-country, field hockey, golf, lacrosse, soccer, softball, track & field, tennis, volleyball

Student Life and Housing About 1,000 students can be accommodated in college housing, which is guaranteed for all four years. Fifty-eight percent of the students are from Virginia, the remainder from 40 other states and 17 countries. Ethnicity: Caucasian—91 percent. There are three national fraternities and four national sororities. All students may keep cars.

Accommodations for Students with Disabilities Students are required to send a copy of their psycho-educational testing results to the Assistant Dean for Academic Affairs. The test results should be dated no earlier than 12 months before the date of application. All requests are handled on a case-by-case basis.

Financial Aid About 96 percent of all freshmen receive aid. The average freshman award was about $16,000.

Requirements for Admission SAT I or ACT scores and a college prep high school program.

Application The Early Decision deadline is November 15, with admission notification by November 30. The regular application deadline is March 1, but students are encouraged to apply by December 15. Students may apply for admission to any semester.

International Students Required are official secondary and, if applicable, postsecondary school transcripts with English translation, a minimum TOEFL score of 520 paper or 190 computer-based, or ELS level 109. Students should also submit a formal autobiographical essay of two pages, written in English, discussing why the student wishes to study at Roanoke. Also required is an official bank statement demonstrating financial responsibility.

Transfer Students Required are official transcripts from high school and previous colleges. Students must be in good standing at the previous college and have a minimum GPA of 2.2. Only courses with C− grades or higher will be considered for transfer.

Admission Contact
Office of Admissions
Roanoke College
221 College Lane
Salem, VA 24153
Phone: (800) 388-2276; (540) 375-2270
FAX: (540) 375-2267
E-mail: *admissions@roanoke.edu*
Web: *www.roanoke.edu*

The Heart of the College Roanoke College's mission statement says that "the college is committed to an integrative approach to education that strives to balance intellectual, ethical, spiritual, and personal growth." This focus on "balance" begins with an innovative curriculum that includes one year of a foreign language; a two-term writing sequence; a course in "Values and the Responsible Life"; a "Senior Symposium," which draws together and integrates materials from the core curriculum and each student's major discipline; and an Intensive Learning Term—an in-depth study of a well defined topic that may involve international or domestic travel or on-campus seminars and local travel.

The curriculum is taught by an impressive faculty, over 90 percent holding the highest degree in their disciplines from prestigious institutions, such as Cornell, Duke, Harvard, Princeton, the University of Virginia, and Yale. With small classes, faculty really get to know their students and focus on teaching excellence.

Roanoke offers students $2,500 plus course fees and campus housing to participate in the Summer Scholars Program under the supervision of a faculty mentor. At the conclusion of the summer, a day is set aside to showcase the work of these scholars. Several students have had their research published in scholarly journals.

There's plenty of opportunity for participation in 80 clubs and organizations, with about 60 percent of the students choosing to complete a credit-bearing internship, over 50 percent regularly involved in community service, and over 70 percent participating in varsity or intramural sports, as well as weekly chapel and other opportunities to explore faith issues informally. The study abroad program offers great opportunities as a result of the college's affiliation with exchange sites with over 100 colleges and universities in 38 countries. There are also summer programs at Regents College in England as well as travel courses offered by Roanoke faculty.

The success of this "balanced" approach to education is borne out by the fact that over 90 percent of Roanoke graduates receive job offers or go on to graduate school within six months of graduation.

The beautiful campus and majestic blue mountains along with the friendly towns of Salem and nearby Roanoke offer cultural and sporting attractions and many opportunities to hike, bike, climb, and backpack in a beautiful region of America.

ROGER WILLIAMS UNIVERSITY

Bristol, Rhode Island

Total Undergraduate Enrollment: 3,000
Men: 1,500 Women: 1,500
Five-Year Graduation Rate: 50%

Tuition: $$$
Room and Board: $$$$
Residential Students: 81%

History Named after the founder of Rhode Island, Roger Williams University's origins began when the Northeastern University School of Commerce and Finance opened a branch campus in the Providence YMCA in 1919, which later offered both law and engineering programs. After separating from Northeastern in 1940, the YMCA Board of Directors established the Providence Institute of Engineering and Commerce. In 1948 it received authority to grant the associate's degree. In 1956 the Institute separated from the YMCA and received a charter to become Roger Williams Junior College, the state's first. The college obtained approval in 1967 to become a four-year college and acquired 80 acres of waterfront land in Bristol. College programs were offered in both Bristol and Providence, with all full-time programs offered at the Bristol campus. The Law School opened in 1993, and the college changed its status to a university.

Location The 140-acre campus is located in Bristol, Rhode Island, 18 miles southeast of Providence, 30 minutes from Newport, and one hour from Boston.

Top Programs of Study Architecture, biology, marine biology

Arts and Sciences American studies, anthropology/sociology, architecture, art and architectural history, biology, chemistry, communications, computer science, construction management, creative writing, criminal justice, dance performance, English literature, engineering, environmental engineering, environmental science, foreign languages, historic preservation, history, legal studies, marine biology, mathematics, philosophy, political science, psychology, theater, visual arts studies

Business Accounting, computer information systems, financial services, international business, management, marketing

Education Elementary, secondary

Pre-Professional Law, medicine, veterinary medicine

Accredited Programs Architecture, business, chemistry, construction management, education, engineering, legal studies

Special Programs The university offers master's programs in architecture, elementary teacher education, literacy teacher education, and criminal justice. There are opportunities for internships, cooperative education, travel study abroad, double majors, and community service. The School of Justice Studies hosts a Distinguished Lecturer Series and the Justice Studies Training Institute offers seminars, workshops, and in-service training programs for practitioners and lawyers. There is a credit-bearing ESL program. Roger Williams' Law School is Rhode Island's first. There is an Army ROTC.

Facilities There are 42 buildings, including the Center for Economic and Environmental Development, a modern two-story bayside complex housing the science and mathematics programs. It contains 11 labs, including an open seawater lab. The Performing Arts Center has a professionally lighted stage and dance studios; there is a University Main Library with wireless computers; and the School of Architecture provides design workspace for each student, with studios open 24 hours a day. There are also a Fine Arts building; a three-story Gabelli School of Business with Academic Computing Center; a renovated and modernized School of Engineering, Computing, and Construction Management; six academic computing centers; a new Socrates Café; and the Paolino Recreation Center with its new fitness and wellness center.

Transition to College Program The university offers a traditional orientation program.

Athletics NCAA II, Commonwealth Coast Conference

Men: Baseball, basketball, cross-country, ice hockey, lacrosse, soccer, tennis, volleyball, wrestling

Women: Basketball, cross-country, soccer, softball, tennis, volleyball

Coed: Equestrian, golf, sailing

Student Life and Housing About 2,400 students can be accommodated in college housing. Only 14 percent of the students are from Rhode Island, the majority coming from 26 other states, mostly the Northeast, and 31 countries. Ethnicity: Caucasian—93 percent. There are no fraternities or sororities. Upperclassmen may keep cars.

Accommodations for Students with Disabilities Once admitted, students are strongly encouraged to self-identify and provide documentation from a psychologist or from official secondary school special education records. The Center for Academic Development provides accommodations, tutoring, advocacy, and support for learning-disabled students.

Financial Aid In a recent year about 80 percent of all freshmen received aid. The average freshman award was about $15,000.

Requirements for Admission SAT I or ACT scores and a college prep high school program.

Application The Early Decision deadline is December 1. The architecture major deadline is February 1. Regular admission deadlines are open, with students provided an admission decision on a rolling basis.

International Students Students for whom English is not their native language must submit a minimum TOEFL paper score of 550 or 213 for the computer-based test. Students whose scores are less than required can be admitted on a probationary basis if otherwise admissible and they agree to study in an ESL program. Required are official secondary and, if applicable, postsecondary transcripts in the language of instruction, as well as certified English translations, school profiles including the school's grading system, and proof of financial support.

Transfer Students Required are official high school and college/university transcripts, a minimum course grade of C− or better, as well as a course being comparable to a Roger Williams' offering for the course to be considered for transfer. Students seeking admission from a two-year college are encouraged to complete requirements for the associate's degree prior to transfer. Students transferring from a two-year school must complete 60 credits at Roger Williams, while those students transferring from a four-year school must complete their final 30 credits at Roger Williams. Architecture students must submit a portfolio of current work, will not be considered for placement beyond the third year, and can transfer courses graded C or better.

Admission Contact

Office of Undergraduate Admissions
Roger Williams University
One Old Ferry Road
Bristol, RI 02809-2921
Phone: (800) 458-7144, ext. 3500; (401) 254-3500
FAX: 401-254-3557
E-mail: *admit@rwu.edu*
Web: *www.rwu.edu*

The Heart of the University With a beautiful campus, strong career programs, an ideal location, and a supportive faculty, Roger Williams University's popularity is ever increasing in the Northeast, as reflected in the 86 percent of out-of-state students who attend the university. With the beautifully landscaped campus overlooking Mt. Hope Bay, and views of the bay from student housing, the campus is a great magnet for students shopping for a university home for four or five years.

The School of Architecture, Art and Historic Preservation offers four 5-year and master's programs in architecture. The large enrollment is a reflection of the fact that it is only one of two accredited Bachelor of Architecture programs in America within the context of a liberal arts university, as well as the excellent facilities and state-of-the-art design software. The unique undergraduate program in historic preservation is noted for its comprehensiveness. Business students have plenty of opportunities for quality internships as well as a semester of cooperative education experience. Students have interned at ESPN, Olympia Sports, and Dean Witter Reynolds. Also, students now have the luxury of an on-campus "trading room" that simulates Wall Street. The teacher education program requires students to begin their school-based experiences during the first year. There are a minimum of 100 hours of practicum, with creative use of portfolios to organize student performance. There are interesting programs in environmental engineering, the graduates of which are in demand by federal and state agencies as well as industry and construction management where students are prepared for supervisory positions. The criminal justice program is garnering a solid reputation, with faculty experience and affiliations with law enforcement agencies, quality internships with the U.S. Secret Service, the U.S. Marshall's Office and others, an excellent forensics lab, and the opportunity for students to be involved in research. The university also offers a 3-3 program with its own law school.

The faculty members have a healthy blend of classroom and real-world experience, are very supportive of student learning, and get to know students well.

The Campus Entertainment Network offers a full schedule of concerts, comedy shows, movies, and dances. When students want more, they can sun on Newport's Beach or enjoy its nightlife. It's only 30 minutes to the Great Providence Mall with zesty Italian food and a one-hour ride to Boston's big city professional sports and cultural attractions.

233

SACRED HEART UNIVERSITY

Fairfield, Connecticut

Total Undergraduate Enrollment: 3,012
Men: 1,205 Women: 1,807
Five-Year Graduation Rate: 53%

Tuition: $$$
Room and Board: $$$$
Residential Students: 70%

History Sacred Heart University, an independent Catholic university, was founded in 1963 by the Most Reverend Walter Curtis, Bishop of the Bridgeport Diocese. The university is led and staffed by lay people and serves the needs of the diocese of southwestern Connecticut.

Location The 56-acre campus is located in the northeast corner of Fairfield, Connecticut, a suburban area in southwestern Connecticut only one hour northeast of New York City and about two hours southwest of Boston.

Top Programs of Study Psychology, business, education, health

Arts and Sciences Art (concentrations in graphic design, illustration, painting), biology, chemistry, communication technology studies, computer science, criminal justice, English, environmental science, history, human movement and sports science, information technology, mathematics, media studies, modern foreign languages, nursing, philosophy, physical therapy, political science, psychology, religious studies, social work, sociology, Spanish

Business Accounting, administration, economics, finance, international business, sports management

Education Elementary, secondary

Pre-Professional Dentistry, law, medicine, optometry, pharmacy, veterinary medicine

Accredited Programs Legal assistant, nursing, physical therapy, social work

Special Programs The Center for Christian–Jewish Understanding brings together educators, theologians, scholars, and laity to foster greater knowledge about the religious traditions of each. The Center for Mission Education and Catholic and Reflection provides opportunities for discussion and reflection on the university's mission and Catholic identity. The Center for Performing Arts, with its own resident professional theater company, complemented by university students, produces several musicals yearly and is a valuable resource for southwest Connecticut's cultural life. The Hersher Institute for Applied Ethics brings speakers to campus and provides training to faculty for integrating ethical viewpoints into the curriculum. The Institute for Religious Education and Pastoral Studies focuses on the formation of Catholic school teachers. Luxembourg is the site of the university-sponsored undergraduate study-abroad program. There are several B.S./M.B.A. programs as well as minors. There is an Academic Support Program for highly motivated, academically underprepared students.

Facilities There are 19 buildings, including the Science Center, which houses the science and health science labs; the Humanities Center, which houses the Language Laboratory; the Student Union, home of a Gallery of Contemporary Art and a Performing Arts Center; a Learning Center; the new William Pitt Health and Recreation Center; a three-level facility that also houses the Sports Medicine and Rehabilitation Center, which features state-of-the-art physical therapy equipment; a multipurpose Campus Field; the Ryan-Matura Library, which includes the Schine Auditorium; and two radio stations.

Transition to College Program All freshmen take Freshmen Seminar, a one-credit course, during their first semester. The highly interactive classroom environment is designed to promote class identity and peer support. Guided by a faculty/staff instructor, who also acts as the student's academic adviser, and supported by upperclass Junior Mentors, students improve study skills and discuss relevant social, moral, and personal issues.

Athletics NCAA I, Northeast Conference, Metro Atlantic Athletic Conference

Men: Baseball, basketball, bowling, cross-country, fencing, football, golf, ice hockey, lacrosse, soccer, track & field (indoor and outdoor), tennis, volleyball, wrestling

Women: Basketball, bowling, cross-country, equestrian, fencing, field hockey, golf, ice hockey, lacrosse, soccer, softball, swimming, track & field (indoor and outdoor), tennis, volleyball

Student Life and Housing About 1,700 students can be accommodated in college housing, which is guaranteed for all four years. Only 37 percent of the students are from Connecticut, the majority from 27 other states and 51 countries. Ethnicity: Caucasian—81 percent; African-American—7 percent; Hispanic-American—6 percent; International—2 percent. There are four local fraternities and five local sororities. Upperclassmen may keep cars.

Accommodations for Students with Disabilities The Learning Center has an Adaptive Technology Lab for students with disabilities and also provides specialized tutoring for learning-disabled students.

Financial Aid About 81 percent of all freshmen receive aid. The average freshman award was about $12,500.

Requirements for Admission SAT I or ACT scores and a college prep high school program. An interview is strongly recommended.

Application Students are admitted for fall and spring semesters. The Early Decision application deadline is October 1, with admission notification by October 15. The regular admissions deadline is December 1 for fall admission, with students notified of an admission decision on a rolling basis usually within four weeks. Students not admitted Early Decision are placed in the regular admissions process.

International Students In addition to meeting regular admission requirements for either a freshman or transfer student, students must submit a TOEFL score, education credentials with English translations, and a financial statement.

Transfer Students Students must be attending or have attended a regionally accredited institution, submit official high school and college transcripts, two letters of recommendation; an interview is strongly recommended. Credit is awarded for courses that carry grades of C or better and that parallel Sacred Heart University's offerings. Typically the university will accept a maximum of 66 credits from two-year colleges and 90 credits from four-year institutions.

Admission Contact
Office of Admissions
Sacred Heart University
5151 Park Avenue
Fairfield, CN 06432-1000
Phone: (203) 371-7880
FAX: (203) 365-7607
E-mail: *enroll@sacredheart.edu*
Web: *www.sacredheart.edu*

The Heart of the University The heart of Sacred Heart University is seen in its mission to provide a Catholic education and serve the needs of the diocese and southwestern Connecticut. It does this well. Sacred Heart is certainly a Catholic university, primarily because of its student population, which is 75 percent Catholic with half of the total population having attended nonpublic high schools. However, its faculty is a lay faculty, making this student–faculty combination a unique one in Catholic higher education. Students experience a genuine sense of community at Sacred Heart, with 70 percent of the students residing in several types of new housing accommodations, ranging from traditional high-rise residence halls, and on-campus apartments to off-campus townhouses. Students are pleased with this variety as well as the opportunity to play on one of the 33 varsity athletic teams in outstanding facilities. But what students enjoy most is having a talented faculty so focused on teaching and providing the personal attention that leads to student achievement, a caring approach that has been sustained since the university's founding.

Sacred Heart serves its wider geographic community in a variety of ways. Its Center for the Performing Arts attracts thousands of guests annually to performances that have starred Julie Harris, James Earl Jones, and James Naughton. In addition, school children are entertained and educated at special events and in summer workshops. Also, the Gallery of Contemporary Art annually showcases four exhibits by professional artists. In addition, the radio station is a member of National Public Radio, offering classical music, news, and public affairs to listeners of Fairfield County. The Community Music Center and Chamber Orchestra provide music instruction and community and student musician performances. The Sports Medicine and Rehabilitation Clinic offers physical and hand therapy to students, staff, and the public. The Hersher Institute for Applied Ethics raises and examines broad ethical issues, while the Institute for Religious Education and Pastoral Studies sponsors over 35 distinct programs at many sites throughout Connecticut, providing laity, clergy, and religious students with opportunities for professional training and personal growth.

In addition to providing for the larger community, Sacred Heart encourages students to provide service, especially to the poor. To fulfill this mission, students participate in Campus Ministry, Habitat for Humanity, Hunger Task Force, Helping Hands, School Volunteers, and other student service groups that help to make a difference.

Technology is big at SHU. It is one of the first universities to provide its students with wireless access to the university's computer network from almost anywhere on campus. Also, students enjoy the opportunities for five-year accelerated graduate degree programs leading to the master's degree in accounting, business administration, chemistry, computer information systems, economics, teacher education, finance, international business, and nursing.

SAINT ANSELM COLLEGE

Manchester, New Hampshire

Total Undergraduate Enrollment: 1,940
Men: 870 Women: 1,090
Five-Year Graduation Rate: 71 percent

Tuition: $$$
Room and Board: $$$$
Residential Students: 88%

History Saint Anselm College, the third oldest Catholic college in New England, was founded in 1889 by the Benedictine monks of St. Marks Abbey in Newark, New Jersey, in response to the invitation of Bishop Bradley, the first bishop of Manchester. The institution originally offered a six-year classical course in philosophical and theological studies. In 1895 the institution was empowered to grant standard academic degrees.

Location The 404-acre campus is located in Manchester, New Hampshire (population 100,000), south of Concord, the state capital, and one hour from Boston, Massachusetts, home to a multitude of cultural, professional sports, and recreational and social activities.

Top Programs of Study Business, nursing, criminal justice

Arts and Sciences Biochemistry, biology, chemistry, classics, computer science, computer science/math, criminal justice, economics, engineering, English, environmental science, fine arts, French, history, liberal studies, mathematics, mathematics/economics, natural science, nursing, philosophy, politics, psychology, sociology, Spanish, theology

Business Accounting, business, computer science/business, financial economics

Education Secondary

Pre-Professional Dentistry, law, medicine, theology

Accredited Programs Chemistry, nursing

Special Programs A five-year engineering program is offered in cooperation with Notre Dame University and several others institutions. Several certificate programs are offered as well as internship and study abroad opportunities. There are Air Force and Army ROTC programs.

Facilities There are 63 buildings, including the Chapel Art Center, the Abbey College Church, an abbey which houses the Benedictine monks who administer the college, two convents, the Goulet Science Center, the Geisel Library, the Izart Observatory, a theater, an Institute of Politics, and the Carr Activities Center.

Transition to College Program The college offers a traditional orientation program.

Athletics NCAA II, Eastern College Athletic Conference, Northeast-10 Conference

Men: Baseball, basketball, cross-country, football, golf, ice hockey, lacrosse, skiing, soccer, tennis

Women: Basketball, cross-country, field hockey, golf, lacrosse, skiing, soccer, softball, tennis, volleyball

Student Life and Housing About 1,700 students can be accommodated in college housing, consisting of all single-sex residential facilities. It is guaranteed for all four years. Only 26 percent of the students are from New Hampshire, with the majority from 27 other states, mostly from the Northeast, and 17 countries. Ethnicity: Caucasian—93 percent. There are no fraternities or sororities. All students may keep cars.

Accommodations for Students with Disabilities In compliance with section 504

Financial Aid About 83 percent of all freshmen receive aid. The average freshman award was about $16,000.

Requirements for Admissions SAT I or ACT scores and a college prep high school program.

Application Early Decision applications should be submitted by December 1, with admission decisions made by December 15. Regular admission deadlines are March 1 for the fall and December 1 for the spring semester.

International Students Required are certified, official transcripts of secondary and, if applicable, postsecondary schools, along with English translations, a satisfactory TOEFL score, a certification of health and accident insurance, a request for a Certification of Eligibility, and a statement of financial resources.

Transfer Students Required are official transcripts of high school and previous college work. A grade of C or higher is required for a course to be considered for transfer from an accredited institution. Generally, students will need to spend two years at St. Anselm to complete their majors. All students must spend the complete senior year at St. Anselm.

Admission Contact
Office of Admissions
Saint Anselm College
100 Saint Anselm Drive
Manchester, NH 03102-1310
Phone: (888) 4ANSELM; (603) 641-7500
FAX: (603) 641-7550
E-mail: *admissions@anselm.edu*
Web: *www.anselm.edu*

The Heart of the College Saint Anselm College is unabashedly Catholic, with the Benedictine monks living in a monastery on the campus and administering the college and with several monks teaching courses. Also on the campus is a convent, the home of the Benedictine sisters, who assist the monks in running the college. The beautiful Abbey Church is the center of Saint Anselm life, with about 80 students trained as lectors, ministers of Communion, and altar servers. Over 100 students sing at the Sunday evening liturgy. Campus Ministry sponsors an active retreat program and prayer groups. All this helps to create a campus community that is like a family rather than a school, the type of community that is characteristic of the Benedictine tradition.

What else causes Saint Anselm to be rated one of the best liberal arts colleges in New England? One explanation is the curriculum, where students explore the great ideas of people with great minds, past and present, and learn "what it means to be truly human." This Humanities Program, called "Portraits of Greatness," a nationally recognized core of studies, involves students in their first two years at the college. As freshman, students recently examined the portraits of The Warrior, The Prophet, The Philosopher, The Citizen, The Poet, and others. As sophomores, students examined the lives of individuals from the Italian Renaissance to the end of the twentieth century, including Shakespeare, Marie Curie, and Gandhi.

Professors are highly qualified and are committed to teaching. Classes are small, making professors more accessible, easy to talk with, and very supportive. Also, the faculty has a strong commitment to involving students in significant research, especially in the departments of biology and psychology, which is often funded by the Undergraduate Research Scholars Program. Professors also lead many off-campus field experiences. For example, one team-taught humanities elective, entitled "Paris and New York in the Twenties and Thirties," featured a three-day visit to New York City with an itinerary that included a jazz club, Broadway show, and several museums.

As a Benedictine College, students are encouraged to serve their community and the world. During spring break many Saint Anselm students serve others in sites such as Maine, Mississippi, New Jersey, Costa Rica, and Peru. Every varsity athletic team performs a community service as a team, for example, supervising young athletes at a local YMCA. Student organizations also receive funds to take the lead in programs at three Manchester service organizations.

The college is in a suburb of Manchester, the largest city in New Hampshire and home to the world-class Carrier Gallery of Art and New Hampshire Symphony. An up-and-coming city, Manchester was recently selected the number 1 Small City in the East for Best Places to Live in America. This also provides Saint Anselm students with quality internships. The campus also serves as the home of The New Hampshire Institute of Politics. Every four years the state's primary kicks off the presidential season, so it was only logical that a new facility should be built on campus, to serve as a center for meaningful dialogue, not only during election year but at all times of the year, so that students can explore the full meaning of citizenship.

SAINT JOHN FISHER COLLEGE

Rochester, New York

Total Undergraduate Enrollment: 2,430
Men: 1,003 Women: 1,427
Five-Year Graduation Rate: 63%

Tuition: $$$
Room and Board: $$$
Residential Students: 57%

History Saint John Fisher College was founded in 1948 as a Catholic college through the combined efforts of civic leaders, the community at large, the Basilian Fathers, and Bishop Kearney of Rochester. John Fisher was the Bishop of Rochester, England, and Chancellor of Cambridge University. He was widely respected as one of the most learned men of the sixteenth century.

Originally founded as a college for men, in 1971 the first women were admitted. The Basilian Fathers, an international teaching community, serve as members of the faculty and professional staff. The college is listed on the Templeton Foundation's Honor Roll of Character-Building Colleges.

Location The 136-acre campus is located in a suburban area 12 miles southeast of Rochester, New York.

Top Programs of Study Education, management, communications and journalism

Arts and Sciences American studies, anthropology, biology, chemistry, communication/journalism, computer science, economics, English, French, history, interdisciplinary studies, international studies, mathematics, nursing, philosophy, physics, political science, psychology, religious studies, sociology (clinical sociology, community studies, criminology and criminal justice, human service administration), Spanish, sports studies

Business Accounting, management (finance, general business, marketing)

Education Elementary, secondary, special

Pre-Professional Dentistry, engineering, environmental science and forestry, law, medicine, optometry, pharmacy, podiatry, veterinary medicine

Accredited Programs Chemistry, nursing

Special Programs The college has several cooperative degree programs: in engineering with Columbia University and several other institutions; in optometry with the Pennsylvania College of Optometry; and in environmental science and forestry with SUNY College of Environmental Science and Forestry at Syracuse University. A Service Scholars Program is offered as well as an Emerging Leaders Program. There are study abroad programs and a Washington, D.C., semester. There is a HEOP program for highly motivated students who are economically and educationally disad-

vantaged. Students may register for courses in any of the several neighboring colleges of the Rochester Area Colleges Consortium. There are Air Force and Army ROTC programs.

Facilities There are 14 buildings, including completely refurbished science labs with state-of-the-art educational technology, modernized classrooms with the latest multimedia capabilities, recently renovated residence halls, Growney Stadium with an all-weather playing field, a state-of-the-art dining hall, and a new residence hall for upperclassmen.

Transition to College Program Learning Communities for first-year students give students the opportunity to take courses in "clusters" that focus on a central theme from year to year. Students learn cooperatively and develop close working relationships with other students and faculty. Recent cluster titles have included: "Hanoi, Hollywood, and Hamburger Hall: Exploring the Vietnam Conflict," and " 'Show Me the Money!' Sports, Economics, and Society." There are field trips, class size is limited, and resident students live in the same residence hall with other members of the learning community.

Athletics NCAA III, Eastern Collegiate Athletic Conference; NYS Women's Collegiate Association; Empire 8

Men: Baseball, basketball, cross-country, football, golf, lacrosse, soccer, tennis

Women: Basketball, cheerleading, cross-country, lacrosse, soccer, softball, tennis, volleyball

Student Life and Housing About 1,700 students can be accommodated in college housing, which is guaranteed for all four years. Ninety-two percent of the students are from New York, the remainder are from 44 other states and 34 countries. Ethnicity: Caucasian—49 percent; Hispanic-American—13 percent; African-American—12 percent. Asian-American—11 percent. There are no fraternities or sororities. All students may keep cars.

Accommodations for Students with Disabilities Students with documented disabilities who may need academic accommodations are advised to make an appointment with the Coordinator of Services for Students with Disabilities.

Financial Aid About 85 percent of all freshmen receive aid. The average freshman award was about $15,500.

Requirements for Admission SAT I or ACT scores and a college prep high school program. A campus visit is encouraged.

Application Freshmen are admitted to all semesters. The Early Decision application deadline is December 1. Regular admission applications have an open deadline, with admission notification made on a rolling basis.

International Students Required are original copies of records at least four months in advance of the semester in which students expect to enroll. All documents should be accompanied by certified translations, a minimum TOEFL score of 550 paper, 213 computer-based is needed for students who do not have English as a native language. Applicants must also submit proof of financial support.

Transfer Students Required are official transcripts of all previous college work. An official high school transcript is required only if the student has completed fewer than 24 credits. Also required is an acceptable health history as well as a record of current immunizations. A GPA of 2.0 is required, and graded courses lower than a C are not transferable. Students with an associate's degree are guaranteed a transfer of at least 60 credits. There is no maximum number of credits that can be transferred from a four-year institution.

Admission Contact

Office of Admissions
Saint John Fisher College
3690 East Avenue
Rochester, NY 14618
Phone: (800) 444-4640; (585) 385-8064
FAX: (585) 385-8386

E-mail: *admissions@sjfc.edu*
Web: *www.sjfc.edu*

The Heart of the College Fisher College is best captured by the motto of the Basilian Fathers who founded the college: "Teach me goodness, discipline, and knowledge." The spirit of community and service is synonymous with Fisher. The Community Service Office partners with Campus Ministry to provide many opportunities for students to serve Rochester, the surrounding area, and internationally. This is so prized by the college that it offers a Service Scholars Program that awards 36 scholarships each year to incoming freshmen who have demonstrated a commitment to community service. The scholarships provide students with unique opportunities to continue their service activities while they develop civic leadership skills. Each award is equal to one-third of the cost of tuition, fees, and room and board for four years. The college also provides scholarships for up to 36 freshmen who are the first in their families to attend college and who exhibit a high degree of motivation and academic potential.

Fisher does a very good job in linking the liberal arts with career preparation. The academic program begins with thematically linked courses that have students looking at the world in new ways, using different perspectives. The excellent accounting program is always a strong competitor in the Andersen Tax Challenge, which pits Fisher against the top 10 colleges and universities in the nation. Internships and employment are championed by a strong career counseling center that hosts up to 100 company recruiters each year. Fisher also has a loyal group of alumni in Rochester and throughout the state and nation, representing more than 2,000 businesses. So it's not uncommon for students to find positions at Xerox, Eastman Kodak, Gannett, Bausch and Lomb, Georgia Pacific, Deloitte & Touche, and PricewaterhouseCoopers. Also, with the Buffalo Bills professional football team making Fisher their training camp, the Bills offer internships to sports studies students who study the business aspects of sports, while the team's administrative personnel serve as adjunct faculty members, guest lecturers, and visiting professors.

Athletics and leadership play an important role at Fisher. The school's quality athletic facilities help to attract nearly 400 students to its NCAA varsity teams and many others to its intramural program. Other students come to Fisher because of its Emerging Leaders Program, where students meet with faculty and staff to initiate programs and events that will teach organizing, delegating, and motivating others.

The major commitment of the faculty is excellence in teaching, with an emphasis on close interaction with students. These are professors who are concerned with each student's personal development and future success. One student commented: "It's really refreshing to work with faculty members who really want you to flourish."

Rochester offers much to students, with seven colleges in the area, the International Museum of Photography, art galleries, performing arts, and a full schedule of sports.

SAINT MARY'S COLLEGE

Notre Dame, Indiana

Total Undergraduate Enrollment: 1,600
Men: 0 Women: 1,600
Five-Year Graduation Rate: 74%

Tuition: $$$
Room and Board: $$$
Residential Students: 80%

History Saint Mary's College was established in 1844 by the Sisters of the Holy Cross, who came from Le Mans, France, in response to parents who desired a Christian education for their daughters.

Location The 275-acre campus is located in a suburb of Notre Dame, Indiana, 90 miles east of Chicago.

Top Programs of Study Business, education, nursing, communications, biology

Arts and Sciences Art (studio and art history), biology, chemistry, communication studies, computational mathematics, cytotechnology, English literature, English writing, French, history, humanistic studies, mathematics, medical technology, music, music performance, nursing, political science, psychology, religious studies, social work, sociology, Spanish, statistics and actuarial mathematics, theater

Business Administration (concentrations in management information systems accounting, finance, international business, management, marketing,

Education Art, elementary, music, secondary.

Pre-Professional Allied health programs, dentistry, law, medicine

Accredited Programs Art, chemistry, education, music, nursing, social work

Special Programs The college offers a cooperative program in seven engineering fields with Notre Dame University. Also, there are articulation agreements in occupational therapy with Midwestern University, Illinois, and one in physical therapy with Central Michigan University. There are student-designed majors and a Multicultural Affairs Office. There is an on-campus Early Childhood Development Center. The Center for Academic Innovation provides programs to nurture the academic community. The college offers 40 minors and houses a Center for Women's Intercultural Leadership. There are several study abroad programs, including "Semester Around the World." The college has a co-exchange program with Notre Dame University so that students can take courses there. There are Air Force, Army, and Navy ROTC programs.

Facilities There are 14 buildings, including the award-winning Angela Athletic Facility; a Gothic-designed library; the Haggan College Center; Havisan Hall, which houses an early childhood center; the Moreau Center for Arts; a coffeehouse; and a greenhouse.

Transition to College Program The innovative Tandem Program introduces students to college life by studying units that offer first-year students the opportunity to fulfill two general education requirements simultaneously. The course material is coordinated to help students compare and integrate ideas and approaches from different fields, such as literature and philosophy. The small classes and informed atmosphere allow for open discussion and close interaction between classmates and professors.

Athletics NCAA III, Michigan Intercollegiate Athletic Association

Women: Basketball, cross-country, golf, soccer, softball, swimming and diving, tennis, volleyball

Student Life and Housing All students can be accommodated in college housing, which is guaranteed for all four years. Only 28 percent of the students are from Indiana, the majority from 49 other states, mostly the Midwest, and 5 countries. Ethnicity: Caucasian—91 percent. There are no sororities. All students may keep cars.

Accommodations for Students with Disabilities In compliance with section 504

Financial Aid About 89 percent of all freshmen receive aid.

Requirements for Admission SAT I or ACT scores and a college prep high school program. Students are required to take SAT subject tests in writing, mathematics, and the foreign language studied in high school. These tests are used for placement purposes. A personal interview is strongly recommended.

Application The Early Admission deadline is November 15, with admission notification by December 15. Otherwise, there is a modified rolling admissions policy. Students whose applications are submitted before December 1 will be notified by mid-January. Applications submitted in December or later will be evaluated within 4–6 weeks from the date of a received completed application.

International Students Required are an official copy of school records translated to English, one recommendation from an administrator or counselor, a completed certification of finances form, and SAT I scores. Students whose native language is not English must take the TOEFL. Materials should be submitted by January 15 for fall admission.

Transfer Students Deadlines are April 15 for the fall semester and November 15 for the spring semester. Required are a catalogue of the institution from which the student is transferring, official transcripts of high school and college work, and one recommendation from a college professor or academic adviser. Students who have completed fewer than the equivalent of 30 semester hours must submit either SAT I or ACT scores. A GPA of 3.0 is required and C graded courses or higher will be considered for transfer.

Admission Contact
Office of Admissions
Saint Mary's College
Notre Dame, IN 46556-5001
Phone: (800) 551-7621; (574) 284-4587
FAX: (219) 284-4716
E-mail: *admission@saintmarys.edu*
Web: *www.saintmarys.edu*

The Heart of the College Saint Mary's is a women's college and research on an all-women's education indicates powerful outcomes: Students are more likely to take intellectual risks, more likely to express their opinions, and more likely to assume a leadership role. These positive characteristics are seen in two highly visible sectors of American life: in the significant number of female Senators who have attended women's colleges and the percentage of women who are "rising stars" in the business world. Saint Mary's is considered a star among Catholic women's colleges, rated very highly and a "best buy." It also offers many programs that have received national accreditation.

The college's location provides Saint Mary's students with a full social life. Notre Dame University is virtually across the street, and both campuses host dances, concerts, parties, plays, and sports events. The co-exchange program allows students to take courses at Notre Dame and engage in volunteer projects together. Friendships are typically made at both campuses.

The liberal arts and core classes are thoughtfully designed. The college's emphasis on communication is shown by requiring all students to "get the W," as students refer to it. The W is the writing proficiency that must be demonstrated through work collected in a semester or year-end portfolio. Also unique to the program is the senior comprehensive, which requires students to pull together what they have learned in completing their majors. Illustrative projects, such as directing a one-act play, planning a marketing campaign, or carrying out a research project, give students the opportunity to practice new skills and to work independently.

Two programs characterize the uniqueness of a Saint Mary's education. Art students have their work evaluated in a Portfolio Review twice each semester, with the entire art faculty offering suggestions and feedback. Each student displays in galleries representative works from her studio courses. In biology, students are introduced to an innovative process to teach the rigors of scientific research. Students are guided through choosing a problem for study, reviewing the literature, preparing a proposal, conducting the research, writing a report of their findings, and giving a public presentation. Potential employers and graduate schools have recognized this quality approach. In addition, members of the business faculty bring "real world" experience to the classroom, emphasize teamwork, use technology, develop an international business perspective, and help develop a framework of ethics that students can use in the workplace.

As a Catholic college, Saint Mary's nurtures the spiritual life with discussion, prayer, retreats, and service projects. Catherine Hicks, star of the hit TV series "Seventh Heaven" is a 1974 graduate.

SAINT MARY'S COLLEGE OF CALIFORNIA

Moraga, California

Total Undergraduate Enrollment: 2,572
Men: 1,050 Women: 1,522
Five-Year Graduation Rate: 67%

Tuition: $$$$
Room and Board: $$$$
Residential Students: 65%

History Saint Mary's, founded in 1863 by the Most Reverend Joseph Alemany, OP, the Archbishop of San Francisco, is a Catholic college administered by the Christian Brothers. The Christian Brothers have their roots in pre-Revolutionary France, where they founded the first schools for the training of teachers in Europe and pioneered new schools for the education of the working and middle classes. Later, they spread their system of schools and colleges to five continents, operating seven colleges and universities in the United States. They are the largest Catholic order devoted exclusively to teaching.

Location The 420-acre campus is located in Moraga, California (population 17,000), a suburban area 20 miles east of San Francisco in the rolling hills of the Moraga Valley. The campus is ranked among the top 20 most beautiful in America.

Top Programs of Study Business administration, psychology, communications

Arts and Sciences Anthropology/sociology, art, biology, chemistry, classical languages, communications, computer science, English and drama, environmental science, environmental studies,

French, German, health, health science, history, international studies, Italian, Japanese, liberal and civic studies, mathematics, modern languages, nursing, performing arts, philosophy, physical education and recreation, physics, politics, psychology, religious studies, Spanish, women's studies

Business Accounting, administration, economics

Education Elementary, secondary

Pre-Professional Dentistry, medicine, physical therapy

Accredited Programs Nursing

Special Programs The college has a cooperative program in engineering with the University of Southern California and Washington University in St. Louis, as well as a nursing program with Samuel Merritt College. A Montessori Teaching Certificate Program is available in education. There are several multicultural students' organizations, study abroad opportunities, and individualized majors can be designed. The college also has a January term.

Facilities There are 58 architecturally distinct buildings, including the new state-of-the-art Gatehouse Science Complex, which has 17 laboratories for student/faculty research and a seawater tank for marine biology research, and a new performing arts center.

Transition to College Program The Collegiate Seminar Program, which begins freshman year, brings small groups of students together to discuss "The Great Books." The seminars are supplemented by social gatherings, trips, and dramatic performances. Many students form lasting friendships with fellow students in their seminar group.

Athletics NCAA I, Northern California Athletic Conference, West Coast Conference

Men: Baseball, basketball, cross-country, football, golf, soccer, tennis

Women: Basketball, cross-country, lacrosse, rowing, soccer, softball, tennis, volleyball

Student Life and Housing About 1,600 students can be accommodated in college housing. Eighty-nine percent of the students are from California, the remainder from 29 other states and 15 countries. Ethnicity: Caucasian—65 percent; Hispanic-American—16 percent; Asian-American—6 percent; African-American—6 percent. There are no fraternities or sororities. All students may keep cars.

Accommodations for Students with Disabilities Services are available through the section 504 Coordinator at (925) 631-4358.

Financial Aid About 70 percent of all freshmen receive aid. The average freshman award was about $20,000.

Requirements for Admission SAT I or ACT scores and a college prep high school program.

Application Application deadlines are February 1 for fall admission and December 1 for spring admission. The Early Action deadline is November 30.

International Students Required are original and certified translations of secondary school records, certified copies of examination results when applicable, a letter of recommendation (from teacher, counselor, or the principal), a certification of finances, and an official TOEFL score for students whose native language is not English. Conditional acceptance can be granted to students with lower scores, but those students will be enrolled in the Intensive Program's noncredit courses.

Transfer Students Required are a minimum GPA of 2.3 and official transcripts from previous institutions with graded courses of C− and above considered for transfer. The maximum number of credits transferable from a two-year institution is 64.

Admission Contact
Saint Mary's College of California
P.O. Box 4800
Moraga, CA 94575-4800
Phone: (800) 800-4SMC
FAX: (925) 376-7193

E-mail: *smcadmit@stmarys-ca.edu*
Web: *www.stmarys-ca.edu*

The Heart of the College As a liberal arts college, Saint Mary's has developed innovative programs to cultivate students' lifelong learning skills, such as critical thinking, listening carefully to others, clearly articulating a well-formed idea, writing well, and developing self-confidence. All students participate in four semesters of the Collegiate Seminar, studying, discussing, and debating around round tables the ideas of the "Great Books" of Homer, Plato, Hegel, Tolstoy, Martin Luther King, and others. The seminar creates a common bond of knowledge that unifies the Saint Mary's community and curriculum. Because the student population is very diverse, with about 35 percent non-Caucasian students, the Collegiate Seminar brings students together so that ideas reflective of different student cultures can be brought to bear within a supportive academic format. Students refer to this program as their "defining academic experience."

Another innovative approach to the liberal arts is the Integrated Program, which is a "college within a college." The curriculum is divided into seminars and tutorials that focus on the primary writings of the greatest minds in Western Civilization. With the guidance of faculty tutors who are drawn from various departments in the college, students discuss and grapple with significant ideas.

Saint Mary's is a student-centered college. Faculty are selected and retained not only for their topnotch academic and professional credentials, but also for their teaching skill and dedication to students. Faculty members get to know students well, participating in a research project or inviting students to dinner at their homes. Faculty challenge students to ask questions and be well prepared for each class.

Saint Mary's aims to cultivate in its students a sensitivity to the consequences of economic and social injustice and a commitment to the poor. CILSA is the college's clearinghouse for community service activities. Saint Mary's proximity to San Francisco offers many opportunities for service. One student comments: "Something about Saint Mary's inspires a commitment to care for others."

Although only half of Saint Mary's students are Catholic, the college not only offers daily church services, but also works to enhance the spiritual life of all students by being inclusive of many different styles of worship and traditions. Retreats, small group discussions, and interfaith prayer help to achieve this.

Over 100 companies and organizations come to campus annually to recruit students. Eighty percent who participate in these recruitment efforts have job offers at graduation. Ten percent get involved in some form of social service and 25–30 percent go on to graduate school. Since 1980 more than 80 percent of all applicants have been admitted to medical, dental, and other health professions' schools.

The San Francisco Bay Area provides beaches, shopping, a hot nightclub scene, museums, restaurants, professional sports, and Fortune 500 companies.

SAINT MARY'S UNIVERSITY

San Antonio, Texas

Total Undergraduate Enrollment: 2,400
Men: 1,000 Women: 1,400
Five-Year Graduation Rate: 60%

Tuition: $$
Room and Board: $
Residential Students: 43%

History Saint Mary's is an independent Catholic institution first established in 1852 as Saint Mary's Institute by four Brothers of the Society of Mary. The college is listed on the Templeton Foundation's Honor Roll of Character-Building Colleges.

Location The 135-acre suburban campus is located five miles northwest of San Antonio, Texas.

Top Programs of Study Biology, business, political science

Arts and Sciences Applied physics, biochemistry, biology, chemistry, computer science, computer science/application systems, criminal justice, criminology, earth sciences/geology, economics, engineering (computer, electrical, engineering science, industrial, software engineering and computer applications), English, English/communication arts, exercise and sports science, French, history, human resources, human services, international relations, mathematics, music, philosophy, physics, political science, psychology, sociology, Spanish, speech communication, theology

Business Accounting, computer information systems, entrepreneurial studies, finance (corporate financial management, financial services/risk management, general business, information systems management, international business management, marketing, multi-organization studies, organizational administration)

Education Early childhood, middle, secondary

Pre-Professional Allied health (optometry, podiatry, physical therapy), dentistry, law, medicine, nursing, pharmacy

Accredited Programs Business, engineering, music

Special Programs There is an Upward Bound program for high school students who possess strong academic potential. The McNair Scholars program encourages and assists low-income, first-generation students and students from underrepresented groups to continue their studies in graduate school. The Service Learning Center develops and supports service learning opportunities for students. There is a Writing Across the Curriculum Program, study abroad opportunities, and a Washington, D.C., semester.

There are also Air Force and Army ROTC programs.

Facilities There are 32 buildings, including the Alkek Building for the School of Business and Administration, a law school, new residence halls, a new University Center, and the new Alumni Athletic and Convocation Center.

Transition to College Program Students participate in a traditional orientation program as well as an academic convocation.

Athletics NCAA II, Heartland Conference

Men: Baseball, basketball, cheerleading, golf, soccer, tennis

Women: Basketball, cheerleading, cross-country, golf, soccer, softball, tennis, volleyball

Student Life and Housing About 1,300 students can be accommodated in college housing. Ninety-four percent of the students are from Texas, the remainder from 30 states and 34 countries. Ethnicity: Hispanic—57 percent; Caucasian—32 percent; African-American—3 percent; International—3 percent. There are one local and four national fraternities, and one local and three national sororities. All students may keep cars.

Accommodations for Students with Disabilities Services are provided through the Dean of Students. Students should contact the Student Life Office to make arrangements for all necessary accommodations.

Financial Aid About 75 percent of all freshmen receive aid. The average freshman award was about $11,000.

Requirements for Admission SAT I or ACT scores and a college prep high school program. Students should graduate in the upper half of their class. An applicant can submit a GED in place of the transcript if the composite score is at least 45, with no area lower than 40. Science and engineering students are expected to have completed four units of math and three units of laboratory science.

Application Freshmen are admitted to fall and spring semesters. Application deadlines are open.

International Students Required are official secondary and, if applicable, college transcripts, all examination records, and certificates or diplomas no later than 45 days prior to the semester in which the student intends to enroll. A minimum TOEFL score of 550 is required for those students whose native language is not English. Those who score below 550, but who meet all other academic standards, may be given an opportunity to attend an English Language Program during the summer. The SAT I or ACT scores are required for scholarship consideration. Documentation of financial responsibility is also required.

Transfer Students Students must be in good standing at the previous college, have a minimum GPA of 2.5, and submit official transcripts from each previous college attended. Courses graded 2.0 and above are considered for transfer.

Admission Contact
Office of Admissions
Saint Mary's University
One Camino Santa Maria
San Antonio, TX 78228-8503
Phone: (800) FOR-STMU; (210) 436-3126
FAX: (210) 431-6742
E-mail: *usadm@stmarytx.edu*
Web: *www.stmarytx.edu*

The Heart of the University Saint Mary's University is unique because of its majority Hispanic population. There's a wonderful fit here between the strong Catholic faith of Hispanics, as well as family bond, and the Catholic Marianist tradition of the university, which views community as an extended family. In this community, collaboration is more important than competition, and a university's ability to personalize education is what attracts and retains students. Saint Mary's does an excellent job of this. As one student commented: "I wanted to be able to count on people knowing me and being there for me if I needed help in my classes or in adjusting to being away from home.

That's what Saint Mary's gave me, not just my first year but every year." A large part of this personal attention is given by faculty who know their students well, enjoy interacting with them, offer extended office hours to assist students, and mentor students in terms of matching students with internships, research, and service learning.

Internships are easy to come by when you consider Saint Mary's location near San Antonio, the eighth largest city in America. Not only does the city provide the students with dancing, sports, recreation, and cultural opportunities, but it also is a home to many high-tech companies, leading insurance firms, major military installations, and a thriving recreation and tourism industry. The Career Services Center receives 50–70 different internship and employment listings each week in a typical year, and students have been placed in many international sites as well. Also, Saint Mary's has a network of loyal alumni to help students.

The university values of peace, justice, and service to community become significant ones for students. The Service Learning Center provides students with involvement in social problems that help develop student skills of critical reflection and a sense of compassion. The center provides short- and long-term service placements with over 65 local agencies, coordinates extended service opportunities to engage in work, prayer, and play with host communities, offers a summer program where students live in community on campus and engage in service work during the week, and provides leadership opportunities as Project Coordinators.

Technology is big at Saint Mary's and probably has a positive impact on the university's outstanding educational outcomes. All first-year students receive an Internet-ready notebook computer, preloaded with software. There are also many "smart" classrooms with network connections, access to the Internet, and state-of-the-art audio-visual capabilities. Students in all academic majors graduate with proficiencies in information technologies relevant to their majors.

Although the heart of the academic offerings is Saint Mary's carefully designed interdisciplinary core curriculum, there is much more, as evidenced by the college's ranking as one of the best universities in the Southwest and its three nationally accredited programs. The teacher education program has been recognized as one of the top 30 in the United States. The risk management program is one of a relatively few nationwide and offers internships at such industry giants as USAA Insurance Group and New York Life. The programs in international business and international relations boast world-class faculty. Sixty percent of the students applying to dental or medical school are accepted, and more than 80 percent are accepted to law school.

SAINT MARY'S UNIVERSITY OF MINNESOTA

Winona, Minnesota

Total Undergraduate Enrollment: 1,300
Men: 600 Women: 700
Five-Year Graduation Rate: 55%

Tuition: $$
Room and Board: $
Residential Students: 85%

History Saint Mary's was founded in 1912 by Bishop Heffron of Winona to provide higher education to young men in southern Minnesota's Diocese of Winona and surrounding areas. Originally an academy and junior college, the school became a college in 1925. In 1933 the college was purchased by the Christian Brothers, an international Catholic teaching order founded in France. The college became coeducational in 1969. The school became a university in 1995. The university is listed on the Templeton Foundation's Honor Roll of Character-Building Colleges.

Location The 350-acre campus is in Winona, Minnesota (population 27,000), a small town 120 miles southeast of Minneapolis-St. Paul, 275 miles northwest of Chicago, and 220 miles northwest of Milwaukee.

Top Programs of Study Management and marketing, biology, education

Arts and Sciences Art and design, biology (including cytotechnology, medical technology, nuclear medicine technology), environmental biology, chemistry, computer science, English (including writing and publishing), French, history, mathematics, media communications, music (including music business, music technology), philosophy, physics (including biophysics, chemical physics, engineering physics, environmental engineering), political science (including public administration), psychology, sociology (including criminal justice, human services, social science), Spanish, theater arts, theology (including pastoral and youth ministry)

Business Accounting, international business, management, marketing

Education Elementary, secondary

Pre-Professional Dentistry, engineering, law, medicine, optometry, physical therapy, theology, veterinary medicine

Accredited Programs None

Special Programs The university offers an interdisciplinary studies program, double majors, and study abroad programs. The De La Salle Language Institute offers college preparatory studies in English as a Second Language and cultural immersion to international students. The Hendrickson Institute for Ethical Leadership develops leadership that has a moral, ethical focus for a global society. The university has a campus in Nairobi, Africa, as well as in Minneapolis. The Metanoia Group is a not-for-profit outreach of the university serving not-for-profit organizations throughout the United States. The group also offers a master's degree in philanthropy, the first of its kind in the United States.

Facilities There are 48 buildings, most of which have been renovated in the 1990s, including a performance center; the Adducci Science Center; a recreation and athletic center; the Gostomaki Fieldhouse; and the Hendrickson Center, which includes the Center for Ethical Leadership; the new Heights Classroom Building; a radio station; an observatory; a newly redesigned central plaza; an indoor ice arena; a beautiful chapel; and the expanded Fitzgerald Library.

Transition to College Program The university offers a traditional orientation program.

Athletics NCAA III, Minnesota Intercollegiate Athletic Conference

Men: Baseball, basketball, cross-country, golf, hockey, Nordic skiing, soccer, swimming and diving, tennis, track & field

Women: Basketball, cross-country, golf, hockey, Nordic skiing, soccer, softball, swimming and diving, tennis, track & field, volleyball

Student Life and Housing About 1,100 students can be accommodated in college housing, which is guaranteed for all four years. Sixty-two percent of the students are from Minnesota, the remainder are from 24 other states and 19 countries. Ethnicity: Caucasian—92 percent. There are two national fraternities and two national sororities. All students may keep cars.

Accommodations for Students with Disabilities Students must provide documentation and make requests for academic assistance through the Academic Skills Center.

Financial Aid About eighty-four percent of all freshmen receive aid. The average freshman award was about $13,000.

Requirements for Admission SAT I or ACT scores and a college prep high school program.

Application Freshmen are admitted fall and spring semesters. Application deadlines are May 1 for fall admission and December 1 for spring admission. Admission notification is made on a rolling basis.

International Students Required are all original academic credentials, a certified bank statement, and a TOEFL score of 520 or higher.

Transfer Students Required are a 2.0 GPA from an accredited institution, official high school and college transcripts, and indication of good standing at the previous college. Only C graded courses or higher will be considered for transfer. Transfer students are required to spend at least two years at Saint Mary's.

Admission Contact
Office of Admissions
Saint Mary's University of Minnesota
Winona Campus
700 Terrace Heights #2
Winona, MN 55987-1399
Phone: (800) 635-5987; (507) 457-1SMU
FAX: (507) 457-1722
E-mail: *admissions@smumn.edu*
Web: *www.smumn.edu*

The Heart of the University The LaSallian Christian Brothers could not have found a more perfect setting for their tradition of a values-centered education, where students are encouraged to grow spiritually as well as academically to make both a living and a life. Set high on the rocky bluffs overlooking the Mississippi River and surrounded by miles of hiking trails, one student commented: "I had no idea how beautiful the bluffs were. . . . It's so spiritual. . . . I think your surroundings really influence your learning process."

The learning process here is an active one, not only in the classroom but outside. Especially characteristic of a Christian Brothers education is a focus on service, because this both broadens a student's worldview and deepens one's spirituality. So there are plenty of opportunities to serve in community-action programs, such as working with a hospice or preschoolers, or urban retreats to Milwaukee, or mission trips to South Dakota or Jamaica.

The academic experience is one that encourages independent thinking and the acquisition of real-world experience. Students have many opportunities to get involved in research projects and have access to state-of-the-art scientific instruments and facilities. Students are encouraged to design an internship opportunity where they can live in a geographic location of their choice. An internship in City Arts takes students to the arts community of the Twin Cities, while a Metro Urban Studies internship has students explore the realities of social inequality in urban America and strategies for bringing about change. There are also community internships in Latin America where students live with local families in Bogota and Colombia. These internships add to the traditional ones in business organizations, such as AT&T, CNN, the Mayo Clinic, and IBM, in nearby Winona and metropolitan areas. This focus on real-world experience is seen by Saint Mary's as placing their university on the threshold of an educational transformation that focuses more on learning than instruction.

And the instruction is very good. Freshman class size is 22, and for upperclassmen is 13. Students get much attention from professors who always take time to help students. Professors act as role models and exhibit a love for teaching. This makes participation in Saint Mary's Interdisciplinary Program linking art, literature, science, history, and theology all the more interesting, as students have more opportunities to ask questions and offer ideas. This program also makes business graduates—and there are many—very much sought after because they develop a broader understanding of the world. Recent graduates are working at General Mills, Abercrombie & Fitch, the Minneapolis Community Development Agency, Xerox Corporation, and the Chicago Board of Trade.

For those who want to learn in a majestic, tranquil setting, in a Christian community, Saint Mary's is a wonderful selection.

SAINT MICHAEL'S COLLEGE

Colchester, Vermont

Total Undergraduate Enrollment: 1,911
Men: 870 Women: 1,041
Five-Year Graduation Rate: 76%

Tuition: $$$$
Room and Board: $$$
Residential Students: 87%

History Saint Michael's College, founded in 1904 by priests and brothers of the Society of Saint Edmund, was originally called Saint Michael's Institute. The college became coeducational in the early 1970s. The college is listed on the Templeton Foundation's Honor Roll of Character-Building Colleges.

Location The 480-acre campus is located on a plateau in Colchester, Vermont, two miles east of Burlington, and has beautiful views of both the Green Mountains and the Adirondacks across Lake Champlain.

Top Programs of Study Business, psychology, elementary education

Arts and Sciences American studies, biochemistry, biology, chemistry, classics, computer science, economics, engineering, English literature, environmental science, fine arts (art, drama, music), French, history, journalism, mathematics, philosophy, physical science, physics, political science, psychology, religious studies, sociology/anthropology, Spanish

Business Accounting, administration

Education Elementary, secondary

Pre-Professional None

Accredited Programs None

Special Programs The School of International Studies teaches English as a second language and culture studies to students from around the world. There are cooperative engineering programs with Clarkson University and the University of Vermont. There are 24 minors, study abroad opportunities, and a Washington, D.C., semester.

Facilities There are 56 buildings surrounding a center mall, anchored by the Chapel of Saint Michael the Archangel at one end and the expanded Durick Library at the other. On the south side of the mall are the academic and activity buildings, and on the north side are the residence facilities, including the renovated student center. There is the new Terrant Recreation Center, the renovated Ross Sports Center and McCarthy Arts Center, as well as the completely renovated and modernized Cheray Science Hall. There is also an art gallery, observatory, and radio station. In all, about 80 percent of the campus facilities have undergone construction or substantial renovation in recent years.

Transition to College Program In addition to traditional orientation programs, the college has a full-time director of new student programs and development, who coordinates an extensive program of workshops and activities to address the intellectual, social, emotional, physical, spiritual, and cultural development of all first-year students.

Athletics NCAA II, Northeast-10 Conference

Men: Baseball, basketball, cross-country, golf, ice hockey, lacrosse, skiing, soccer, swimming and diving, tennis

Women: Basketball, cross-country, field hockey, ice hockey, lacrosse, skiing, soccer, softball, swimming and diving, tennis, volleyball

Student Life and Housing About 1,800 students can be accommodated in college housing, which is guaranteed for all four years. Only 22 percent of the students are from Vermont, the majority from 32 other states, mostly in the Northeast, and 25 countries. Ethnicity: Caucasian—92 percent. There are no fraternities or sororities. All students may keep cars.

Accommodations for Students with Disabilities Reasonable accommodations are provided for students with documented disabilities. There is also a support group through the student resource center. Services are coordinated by the Office of the Associate Dean of the college.

Financial Aid About 64 percent of all freshmen receive aid. The average freshman award was about $15,000.

Requirements for Admission SAT I or ACT scores and a college prep high school program. SAT II scores may be submitted in foreign language to satisfy the foreign language requirement. A campus visit and interview are recommended. If the student is unable to visit the campus, an alumni interview in the hometown area may be arranged by phoning the Office of Admissions.

Application Freshmen are admitted to fall and spring semesters. The Early Action deadline is November 15, with an admission notification by February 1. The regular application deadline is February 1 for fall admission and November 1 for spring admission.

International Students Required are official academic records from all secondary and postsecondary schools, evidence of financial support, and a minimum TOEFL score of 500 paper or 213 computer, if the student does not have English as a native language. Students who have demonstrated acceptable levels of academic achievement, but whose TOEFL scores are lower than required may be admitted conditionally by studying in the college's English as a Second Language Program.

Transfer Students Students must be in good standing at the previous college attended. Credit may be transferred for work completed at accredited colleges with a grade of C− or better, provided the courses correspond to offerings at Saint Michael's. An official transcript is required. All students must be in residence at least one full year preceding their graduation and earn a minimum of 30 credits at Saint Michael's.

Home-Schooled Students Students must submit a transcript of their work and the annual testing information required by the state in which they reside. ACT or SAT I scores are also required.

Admission Contact

Office of Admissions
Saint Michael's College
One Winooski Park
Colchester, VT 05439
Phone: (800) SMC-8000; (802) 654-3000
FAX: (802) 654-3000
E-mail: *admission@smcvt.edu*
Web: *www.smcvt.edu*

The Heart of the College Saint Michael's College is one of the best Catholic liberal arts colleges in the nation and is typically regarded as one of the best comprehensive colleges in the Northeast. Its faculty is both scholarly and focused on student learning. In a recent year, the faculty published 18 books; about 100 journal articles and book chapters; presented papers at 111 conferences; contributed 10 consulting reports; received 14 external grants; had poetry appear in 42 anthologies or other publications; and directed, wrote, or otherwise contributed to 7 theater productions. At the same time, all classes are taught by faculty, and there is one professor for every 13 students, assuring small class sizes and plenty of personal attention.

The curriculum reflects the college's mission to focus on "the development of human culture and enhancement of the human person in light of the Catholic faith." The liberal arts curriculum provides a balance between study of the humanities, social and natural sciences, and concentration in a major field of study. Throughout there is focus on an ethical dimension and attention to international perspectives. In the First Year Seminar, in groups of about 15, students explore great books, groundbreaking ideas, and works of art, using interdisciplinary perspectives. Students read carefully, use reasoned discussion, and write coherently. Recent titles of seminars include "Revolutionary Ideologies in the 20th Century" and "Sustainable Development in the 21st Century." Research opportunities abound for students, with every major program offering either independent study or research projects, including collaboration with professors. History students, for example, have available an actual stop on the Underground Railroad, and then there is the Shelburne Museum for a look at eighteenth- and nineteenth-century life. Science students design lab experiments and are given lab space beginning in the freshman year. Students have 24-hour access to a bank of PC's dedicated to scientific applications.

The student population is a healthy mix of lifestyles and personalities. What they do have in common, however, is their desire to participate. More than 70 percent take part in volunteer service during the year, while nearly 65 percent participate in varsity or intramural sports. There are also 40 student organizations and the very popular Wilderness Program, which takes students on Ecuadorian mountain-climbing adventures, Yucatan kayaking trips, and nearby campus rock and ice climbing.

Then, of course, there is Burlington, recently rated as the number one city to "have it all," including more than 14,000 college students in the greater Burlington area. Students seem to enjoy the 81 inches of snowfall each year as much as they enjoy the area's music groups and outdoor pedestrian mall with more than 100 shops, restaurants, and cafes. Burlington also offers wonderful internship opportunities. With all this, no wonder Saint Michael's has such a high retention rate.

Also, the outcomes are great, with 95 percent of the graduating class reporting that they are either working or attending graduate school. In fact, 60 percent go on to graduate school, with more than 70 percent of students who applied to medical school earning admission.

SAINT NORBERT COLLEGE

De Pere, Wisconsin

Total Undergraduate Enrollment: 2,180
Men: 982 Women: 1,198
Five-Year Graduation Rate: 77%

Tuition: $$$
Room and Board: $
Residential Students: 92%

History Saint Norbert College was established in 1898 as a Catholic men's college by Abbot Bernard Pennings, a Norbertine priest and educator. Women were admitted in the 1950s. The college is named after Norbert of Xanten, the founder of the Norbertines, which has its roots in twelfth-century France. The college is listed on the Templeton Foundation's Honor Roll of Character-Building Colleges.

Location The 89-acre campus is located on the banks of the Fox River in De Pere, Wisconsin (population 20,000), 5 miles south of Green Bay, a metropolitan area of 200,000 people in northeastern Wisconsin.

Top Programs of Study Business, education, biology

Arts and Sciences American studies, anthropology, art/graphic design, biology, chemistry, classical studies, communication (including media and theater), computer science, economics, English, environmental policy, environmental science, French, geography, geology, German, history, international studies, mathematics, mathematics/computer science, medical technology, music, philosophy, physics, political science, psychology, religious studies, sociology, Spanish

Business Accounting, administration, computer information systems, international business and language area studies, international economic studies

Education Early childhood, elementary, middle, music, secondary

Pre-Professional Dentistry, engineering, law, medicine, pharmacy, veterinary medicine

Accredited Programs None

Special Programs There is a College Survey Center, which is a research facility designed to serve the college and broader community and offers internships and work–study opportunities as well. There is an Office of Cultural Diversity, a minor in Leadership Studies, and a writing-across-the-curriculum program. There is an Army ROTC program.

Facilities There are 39 buildings, including the Wehr Library, Schuldes Sports Center, the Pennings Activity Center, the Bemis International Center, the Pennings Hall of Fine Arts, the Old St. Joseph Church, the recently completed Heuoel Campus Center, and the Weidner Center for the Performing Arts.

Transition to College Program The college offers a traditional orientation program.

Athletics NCAA III, Midwest Conference; Northern Collegiate Hockey Association

Men: Baseball, basketball, cross-country, football, golf, ice hockey, indoor and outdoor track, soccer, tennis

Women: Basketball, cross-country, golf, indoor and outdoor track, soccer, softball, swimming, tennis, volleyball

Student Life and Housing About 1,600 students can be accommodated in college housing, which is guaranteed for all four years. Seventy percent of the students are from Wisconsin, the remainder from 27 other states, mostly Illinois, and 30 countries. Ethnicity: Caucasian—93 percent. There are three local and three national fraternities and three local and two national sororities. All students may keep cars.

Accommodations for Students with Disabilities
The Coordinator of Services to Students with Disabilities provides academic support and advocacy to students who present documentation of disabilities from appropriate professionals. The Coordinator determines student eligibility for specific accommodations and works with students and faculty to ensure that students' needs are met.

Financial Aid About 92 percent of all freshmen receive aid. The average award was about $14,500.

Requirements for Admission SAT I or ACT scores and a college prep high school program.

Application Freshmen are admitted to all semesters. Application deadlines are open, with admission notification on a rolling basis.

International Students Required are original academic records, including an English translation; TOEFL or SAT results, or successful completion of an on-campus English proficiency examination; one letter of recommendation; and a declaration of finances.

Transfer Students Credit for college level work is granted in all areas that correspond to courses offered at Saint Norbert, so long as students have earned at least a C for the course. Students must be in good standing at the previous college and have a GPA of 2.5. There is no maximum number of credits that are transferable, but students must take the senior year and at least 25 percent of the major at Saint Norbert. The maximum amount of credit transferred from a two-year college is 72 or the equivalent of 18 courses.

Admission Contact
Office of Admissions
Saint Norbert College
100 Grant Street
De Pere, WI 54115-2099
Phone: (800) 236-4878; (920) 403-3005
FAX: (920) 403-4072
E-mail: *admit@mail.snc.edu*
Web: *www.snc.edu*

The Heart of the College Saint Norbert College is more than just the summer home of the Green Bay Packer professional football team. As a Catholic liberal arts institution with a global focus, it's much more. Students study a core program of interdisciplinary courses, focusing on skills, knowledge, and values. The college prizes the benefits of a liberal arts education, which provides its students with excellence in the communication skills of writing, reading, and verbal communication. Writing is taken very seriously at Saint Norbert, with students exposed to a writing-across-the-curriculum emphasis.

But what truly distinguishes the academic program is its global focus. Every course attempts to infuse an international component in an attempt to make Saint Norbert's graduates global citizens. In addition to the academic program, students can take part in Amnesty International, making a difference in global issues. Students can travel with band and choral concert tours, performing for international audiences and staying with host families. Study abroad opportunities take students to Austria, Colombia, Egypt, France, Italy, Norway, and Spain.

Saint Norbert's classes are small and lively. Faculty are scholars and excellent teachers who believe in highly interactive classrooms where students learn to express their views and respect the views of others. Faculty use role-playing, multimedia presentations, class forums, and technology. Students love the personal attention from faculty, and professors love the close interaction they have with students. Acting as mentors and providing careful advisement to their students, this is all part of the college's personal touch.

Students benefit from the Norbertine focus on community, characterized by caring, support, and energy. As a college that values concern for others and social justice, students have a multitude of ways that they can provide service. Campus ministry sponsors student retreats, scripture sharing, spirituality discussion groups, and the celebration of the Eucharist each day.

The college location offers students the best

of both worlds. Located in a charming small town on the banks of the scenic Fox River, the Bay area provides a variety of water recreational activities, golf, and plenty of fishing, hiking, biking, skiing, and snowboarding in neighboring Door County. Only five miles away is the Green Bay metropoli-

tan area with shopping, dance clubs, rock concerts, the Packers, and internship opportunities.

A Saint Norbert education is a successful one. Since 1977, 95 percent of its graduates seeking employment or graduate school admission have achieved these.

SAINT VINCENT COLLEGE

Latrobe, Pennsylvania

Total Undergraduate Enrollment: 1,371
Men: 678 Women: 693
Five-Year Graduation Rate: 71%

Tuition: $$$
Room and Board: $$
Residential Students: 67%

History Saint Vincent College was founded in 1846 by Boniface Wimmer, a monk from the Benedictine Abbey of Metten in Bavaria. Wimmer intended to provide an education for the sons of German immigrants, but soon learned that his monks would also have to educate the English and Irish Catholics who settled in the area. Saint Vincent College became the first Benedictine college in the United States. It became coeducational in 1983.

Location The 200-acre campus is located in Latrobe, Pennsylvania, 35 miles east of Pittsburgh.

Top Programs of Study Biology, psychology, English

Arts and Sciences Anthropology, art history, art studio, biochemistry, biology, chemistry, communication, computers and information science, economics, engineering, English, environmental chemistry, fine arts, history, liberal arts, mathematics, music, music performance, occupational therapy, philosophy, physical therapy, physician's assistant, physics, political science, psychology, public policy analysis, religious studies—Catholic theology, sociology, Spanish

Business Accounting, environmental administration, finance, management

Education Art, early childhood, elementary music, religious, secondary

Pre-Professional Chiropractic, dentistry, law, medicine, optometry, osteopathy, veterinary medicine

Accredited Programs Business

Special Programs Saint Vincent offers a cooperative program in engineering with Penn State University and Boston University, as well as limited enrollment agreements at the University of Pittsburgh and The Catholic University of America. Also, there are programs in music education and theater offered in conjunction with Seton Hill College. Degrees in occupational therapy, physical therapy, and physician's assistant are offered in conjunction with Duquesne University. There are study abroad opportunities, including an East Asia Study Tour, internships, and a cooperative education program. There is also a cooperative degree in osteopathic medicine with Lake Erie College of Osteopathic Medicine. The college offers a program for undeclared majors. There are Air Force and Army ROTC programs.

Facilities There are 23 buildings, including a new freshman residence hall; a modern science center; swimming pool and student union; a world-class library; the Instructional Technology Center; the Archabbey Basilica; the Saint Vincent Seminary; an art gallery; a new classroom building with multimedia classrooms, laboratories, and an academic cyberlounge; and a radio station.

Transition to College Program The college provides a six-week orientation in the first six weeks of freshman year. Many upperclassmen join students at concerts, trips, information sessions, games, and various other get-acquainted events.

Athletics NAIA, American Mideast Conference

Men: Baseball, basketball, cross-country, golf, ice hockey, lacrosse (NCAA Div. II), soccer, tennis

Women: Basketball, cross-country, golf, lacrosse (NCAA Div. II), soccer, softball, volleyball

Student Life and Housing About 1,200 students can be accommodated in college housing, which is guaranteed for all four years. Eighty-six percent of the students are from Pennsylvania, the remainder are from 23 other states and 16 countries. Ethnicity: Caucasian—94 percent. There are no fraternities or sororities. All students may keep cars.

Accommodations for Students with Disabilities In compliance with section 504

Financial Aid About 93 percent of all freshmen receive aid. The average freshman award was about $12,000.

Requirements for Admission SAT I or ACT scores and a college prep high school program. Music education and theater students must audition for acceptance to their respective departments at Seton Hill College. Art education majors must submit a portfolio for review by the Seton Hill Art Department. Music and music performance students must audition for acceptance and studio arts students must submit a portfolio for acceptance to the Fine Arts Department.

Application Freshmen are admitted to fall and spring semesters. Applications should be submitted by May 1 for fall admission and January 1 for spring admission. Admission notification is sent on a rolling basis.

International Students Students whose primary language is not English must score a minimum of 525 on the paper-based TOEFL. Students should submit official secondary and, if applicable, post-secondary transcripts, as well as a declaration of finances.

Transfer Students Required are official transcripts from the high school and colleges previously attended and a catalogue describing the courses taken. A personal interview is recommended. Thirty-four credits must be taken at Saint Vincent. Courses taken at other accredited institutions must have a minimum C grade for consideration of transfer, and students must have an overall 2.0 GPA.

Admission Contact
Office of Admissions
Saint Vincent College
300 Fraser Purchase Road
Latrobe, PA 15650-2690
Phone: (800) 782-5549; (724) 537-4540
FAX: (724) 532-5069
E-mail: *admission@stvincent.edu*
Web: *www.stvincent.edu*

The Heart of the College When you visit Saint Vincent College on its peaceful setting in the foothills of the Allegheny Mountains, you will see Benedictine monks, the oldest of all Christian monastic orders, going about their daily activities of communal life centered on work and prayer. It is the Benedictine tradition of hospitality that is the heart of Saint Vincent and pervades the entire campus community. This hospitality is rooted in the belief that all people should be treated with respect for their dignity, integrity, and worth. As a result, students belong to a truly caring and close-knit community.

The wonderful community and quality academic programs rank Saint Vincent as one of the top regional liberal arts colleges in the Mid-Atlantic region, as well as a "best buy." There are several noteworthy aspects of the overall program, including the Common Texts Project, in which participating faculty meet each year in a summer session to select about six texts to integrate into courses and programs the next academic year. The result is that students examine Plato's *Republic* or Miller's *Death of a Salesman* from the perspectives of different academic disciplines. Students who participate also take part in panel discussions and other special programs. Another important feature of the curriculum is the Interdisciplinary Writing Program, which ensures that in every area of study students get to improve their writing skills, as they work on journals, essays, research papers, and other assignments. Because of the Benedictine tradition of stewardship of the land and the college's location near natural wetlands, students and faculty are tackling a number of environmental challenges. The wetlands provide an invaluable resource for research projects and first-hand learning, and the college's Environmental Education Center offers a variety of wetland, mine drainage, and nature education programs. Also, research opportunities are available in almost every arena of the curriculum, with the Palumbo Student Research Endowment often awarding funding.

When graduating seniors seek recommendations from professors for jobs or graduate school, students discover how the small class sizes translate to faculty knowledge of their character, abilities, and achievements. This is a result of 50 percent of the classes having 14 or fewer students and 90 percent having fewer than 30 students.

Although the campus is located in a tranquil area, there is much to do on campus as well as many outdoor activities in the hundreds of miles of the beautiful Laurel Highlands that surround the campus. Combine this with the cultural, recreational, and professional sports activities of nearby Pittsburgh, and students appear to have the best of both worlds. Internship opportunities include Allegheny Power System, Intel, U.S. Steel, U.S. National Bank, CNN, Mercy Hospital of Pittsburgh, the Carnegie Research Institute, and the U.S. Department of Justice.

In a recent graduating class, 71 percent were employed within six months of graduation and 28 percent entered graduate school. Of those who applied to law schools, 85 percent were accepted, 70 percent were accepted to medical schools, and 95–100 percent of applicants were accepted to dental, osteopathy, optometry, physical therapy, podiatry, pharmacy, and veterinary schools. One hundred percent of all students who applied to engineering schools were accepted. Accounting graduates passed the CPA exam on their first try—three times the state average.

SALVE REGINA UNIVERSITY

Newport, Rhode Island

Total Undergraduate Enrollment: 2,000
Men: 610 Women: 1,390
Five-Year Graduation Rate: 60%

Tuition: $$$
Room and Board: $$$$
Residential Students: 60%

History Salve Regina was established as a college in 1934 by the Religious Sisters of Mercy. The Catholic institution became a university in 1991.

Location The 70-acre campus is located in Newport, Rhode Island, on the waterfront 60 miles south of Boston, Massachusetts.

Top Programs of Study Education, business and criminal justice, administration of justice

Arts and Sciences Administration of justice, American studies, anthropology, art, biology, chemistry, communication media technology, cultural and historic preservation, English, environmental science, French, history, mathematical science, media technology, music, nursing, philosophy, politics, psychology, religious studies, social work, sociology, Spanish, theater arts

Business Accounting, administration, economics and finance, information systems science, management

Education Early childhood, elementary, secondary, special

Pre-Professional Law, medicine, veterinary medicine

Accredited Programs Business, nursing, social work, visual arts

Special Programs The Feinstein Enriching America Program provides community service opportunities and service learning courses—a requirement for graduation. There are study abroad programs, internships, a Washington, D.C., semester, and a Semester at Sea. ESL courses are available. The university offers an interdisciplinary program of study focused on constructing the Good Life. The Pell Center for International Relations and Public Policy promotes public service. There is an Army ROTC program.

Facilities There are 41 buildings, a blend of historic and modern architecture, including the new state-of-the-art Rodgers Recreation Center, the Wakehurst Student Activity Building, the new McKillop Library, and the Mansions of the Ochre Court and the Breakers.

Transition to College Program The New Student Seminar is a two-credit course to help freshmen develop the skills and attitudes crucial to college success. A key part of the seminar is an individually selected community service project in which students participate during their first year.

Athletics NCAA III, Commonwealth Conference, Eastern College Athletic Conference

Men: Baseball, basketball, football, ice hockey, lacrosse, sailing, soccer, tennis

Women: Basketball, cross-country, field hockey, ice hockey, lacrosse, sailing, soccer, softball, tennis, track & field, volleyball

Student Life and Housing About 1,000 students can be accommodated in college housing. Only 20 percent of the students are from Rhode Island, the majority from 40 other states, mostly in the Northeast, and 11 countries. Ethnicity: Cau-

casian—94 percent. There are no fraternities or sororities. Upperclassmen may keep cars.

Accommodations for Students with Disabilities Students who require special accommodations should contact the Assistant Director of the Academic Development Center.

Financial Aid About 70 percent of all freshmen receive aid. The average freshman award was about $11,000.

Requirements for Admission SAT I or ACT scores with a college prep high school program. A campus visit and interview are recommended. Prospective nursing students should take biology and chemistry. Formal admission to the nursing program is contingent upon satisfactory performance in nursing and nursing-related courses in freshman and sophomore years.

Application The university uses a rolling admissions policy but encourages candidates to apply by March 1 for the fall semester and December 15 for the spring semester.

International Students Students should submit official secondary and, if applicable, postsecondary transcripts and, in place of the SAT I or ACT test, may submit TOEFL results. Students should also submit a financial verification form.

Transfer Students Required are official high school and college transcripts. Only courses bearing a grade of C or higher may be considered for transfer. Students must complete a minimum of 36 credits at Salve Regina as well as any requirements necessary to qualify for the bachelor's or associate's degree.

Home-Schooled Students Students follow the regular application process. However, the following are also required: transcripts of all home-schooled work and details on the home schooling format (correspondence-based or parent/student-based); SAT I or ACT results; a portfolio of academic accomplishments, including a reading list, course descriptions, and a list of extracurricular activities/community involvement.

Admission Contact

Office of Admissions

Salve Regina University

100 Ochre Point Avenue

Newport, RI 02840-4192

Phone: (888) GO SALVE; (401) 341-2908

FAX: (401) 848-2823

E-mail: *sruadmis@salve.edu*

Web: *www.salve.edu*

The Heart of the University The heart of Salve Regina is its location. Just imagine a campus with sweeping lawns and elegant mansions, right on the rocky coastline of the Atlantic Ocean. Many classrooms are located in great seaside houses overlooking the ocean. A student residence could be a real house with a sunny front porch. Then, of course, there's Newport, an international city within a quaint seacoast village and packed for fun! Just read the list: jazz and folk festivals, America's Cup Sailing, the Bellevue Avenue Mansions, surfing sunsets over Newport Harbor, shopping, dining, world-class art, nightlife, and the historic Cliff Walk, named one of the 19 best walks in the world by *Travel and Leisure Magazine.*

The academic program emphasizes learning by doing, integrating theoretical learning with field experience right from the start. And some of the learning locations are among the most unique in the nation. Salve Regina's history students study in Colonial Newport; science students use Aquilneck Island and the Atlantic Ocean; art students find inspiration surrounding them in this beautiful location; cultural and historic preservation students study at archeological sites, historic graveyards, and buildings in the countryside.

The pre-professional programs also get students out of the classrooms to learn on-site with practicums providing patient education to new mothers at Rhode Island Hospital in Providence; student teaching at Newport's Rogers High School; and helping with field investigations for the New England regional office of the FBI.

There are two especially innovative programs. The Pell Center for International Relations and Public Policy promotes the primary objectives of Senator Claiborne Pell's decades of service in the U.S. Senate: enhancing international dialogue and promoting efforts for world peace. The center brings to the campus visiting scholars and top policymakers who conduct research, examine critical issues, attend conferences, and offer workshops and discussions for faculty and students. The second program, Vital Studies for Whole Life Designs, engages students in an exploration of the "Good Life," learning to create and live a life of enlightenment and achievement that students can look back on with happiness and satisfaction. Students study seven interdisciplinary courses, one each term, working as a team with a professor and other students. Each year the courses focus on a theme.

The Sisters of Mercy, founders of the university, believed that we are stewards of God's creation, so Salve Regina "encourages students to work for a world that is harmonious, just, and merciful." Students develop values of compassion, commitment, and service through their participation in the Feinstein Enriching America Program, which designs a community service learning project that matches a student's personal or career interest.

Students reap the benefits of small class sizes and faculty dedicated to undergraduate students. Janet Robinson, an alumnae and President and General Manager of the *New York Times* writes: "I will always treasure the atmosphere that surrounded me at Salve, for that is a quality that makes this university a wonderful haven for learning."

SAMFORD UNIVERSITY

Birmingham, Alabama

Total Undergraduate Enrollment: 2,645
Men: 974 Women: 1,671
Five-Year Graduation Rate: 68%

Tuition: $$
Room and Board: $
Residential Students: 65%

History Samford University was founded in 1841 in Perry County Alabama by a group of educational, economic, and Baptist leaders. Originally named Howard College in honor of John Howard, a British advocate of prison reform, it was later renamed for the Samford family, longtime benefactors.

Location The 180-acre beautifully wooded campus is located in suburban Birmingham, Alabama, the state's largest city, with abundant cultural and recreational opportunities. The state's largest shopping center is about 10 miles from the campus.

Top Programs of Study Business management, early childhood education, journalism

Arts and Sciences Art, Asian studies, athletic training, biochemistry, biology, chemistry, church music, classics, computer science, engineering, English, environmental science, environmental science and geographic information systems, exercise science, fitness and health promotion, French, general science, geography, German, graphic design, Greek, history, human development and family studies, instrumental music, interior design, international relations, journalism and mass communication, language and world trade, language arts, Latin, Latin American studies, marine science, mathematics, music, musical theater, nursing, nutrition and dietetics, organ, piano, philosophy, physics, political science, psychology, public administration, religion, sociology, social science, Spanish, speech communication, sports medicine, theater, theory/composition, voice

Business Accounting, management

Education Collaborative, early childhood, elementary, music, physical education, secondary, special

Pre-Professional Dentistry, engineering, law, medicine, optometry, pharmacy, veterinary medicine

Accredited Programs Allied health programs, business, dietetics and nutrition, education, interior design, law, music, nursing, theology

Special Programs Samford has a dual degree program in engineering with the University of Alabama, Auburn University, Washington University in St. Louis, and Mercer University. The Children's Learning Center has over 100 enrolled children and serves as a demonstration and laboratory school for the School of Education. The university has a Global Drug Information Center for pharmacy students and a Global Center that features interactive resources, including world population and demographic databases. Interdisciplinary majors are offered. There are study abroad, cooperative education, and internship opportunities. The BACHE program allows students to take courses at several colleges in Birmingham. The Christian Women's Leadership Center coordinates a minor in Christianity, Women, and Leadership Studies. There are Air Force and Army ROTC programs.

Facilities There are 62 buildings of Georgian-Colonial architecture, including a law building; a divinity school; a state-of-the-art science center, which includes a planetarium and a conservatory; a 2,700 seat concert hall; theater; recital hall; the Wright Fine Arts Center; and a radio station.

Transition to College Program Students can take a voluntary Horizons Freshman Adjustment Course taught by a highly trained, caring mentor, who helps students to make the necessary adjustments to college life.

Athletics NCAA I, Ohio Valley Conference

Men: Baseball, basketball, cross-country, football, golf, indoor track, tennis, track

Women: Basketball, cross-country, golf, indoor track, soccer, softball, tennis, track, volleyball

Student Life and Housing About 1,900 students can be accommodated in college housing. Forty-seven percent of the students are from Alabama, the majority from 41 other states, mostly the South, and 22 countries. Ethnicity: Caucasian— 90 percent. There are seven national fraternities and eight national sororities. All students may keep cars.

Accommodations for Students with Disabilities Reasonable accommodations are provided to students who provide current professional documentation of disabilities.

Financial Aid About 83 percent of freshmen receive aid. The average award was about $11,000.

Requirements for Admission SAT I or ACT scores and a college prep high school program. A campus visit is strongly recommended.

Application Although there is no formal admission deadline, applicants are encouraged to complete the process as soon as possible. Students may be admitted for the fall, spring, or summer semester.

International Students Students should allow a minimum of six months to complete all the necessary paperwork prior to admission. Required are official transcripts of all academic work, including mark sheets, examination results, certificates, diplomas, etc. If college credit has been earned at a foreign institution, applicants should submit certified copies of all academic work to the World Evaluation Service, requesting a course-by-course evaluation. A minimum TOEFL score of 550 paper or 213 computer is expected, as well as a financial affidavit of support.

Transfer Students Required is a 2.5 GPA on all college-level work taken at regionally accredited institutions, and only courses with a grade of C— or better will be considered for transfer. Students are required to earn at least 25 percent of the credits in each degree program from Samford. Also, a minimum of 15 credits in the major field must be earned at Samford. Required are official transcripts from each college attended and a letter of recommendation from a professor or adviser. If fewer than 24 credits have been earned, students must also meet the requirements of entering freshmen.

Admission Contact
Office of Admissions
Samford University
800 Lakeshore Drive
Birmingham, AL 35229
Phone: (800) 888-7218; (205) 726-3673
FAX: (205) 726-2171
E-mail: *admission@samford.edu*
Web: *www.samford.edu*

The Heart of the University In addition to its 2,700 undergraduate students, Samford artfully integrates 1,500 graduate students into its campus life, providing both with facilities and opportunities typically found at large universities. Samford is considered one of the best universities in the South as well as a "best buy." The university has a number of distinguished programs, including its education program, recognized by the U.S. Secretary of Education as a national model. Its wide array of undergraduate research opportunities for students is exemplified by Samford's large contingent traveling to the annual National Conference for Undergraduate Research, where students present papers to audiences of their academic peers. Stamford's debate program consistently ranks among the best in the nation. Samford's beautiful campus is graced with state-of-the-art facilities as well as graduate schools of law, pharmacy, and divinity. Several of its programs have earned national accreditation.

Students are offered an innovative curriculum called Co-nexus, which seeks to stimulate the mind and encourage enduring values. The curriculum works to help students see the interconnectedness of the arts and the humanities, while developing critical thinking skills and reasoning abilities—those qualities that are the desired outcomes of a liberal arts program. The curriculum is enhanced by a faculty recognized for its commitment to teaching excellence. In both 2000 and 2001, the Carnegie Foundation for the Advancement of Teaching named a Samford Professor as Professor of the Year. With moderate-sized classes, professors get to know their students and serve a mentor role.

There's a lot to do here, with over 100 academic and social organizations and a significant Greek life. The study abroad opportunities are wonderful, taking students to Spain, France, China, Hong Kong, Brazil, and Morocco. Students especially enjoy Samford's premier international program, which is housed in the heart of London's famous West End, within easy walking distance to some of the city's most famous cultural attractions.

At the heart of the university is a foundation of Christian values and belief, which is reflected in its mission statement: "We nurture persons—for God, for learning, forever." Values of integrity, goodness, and service are cultivated through a multitude of university ministries. Students can learn to preach or lead music in local Baptist churches across Alabama, visit weekly with nursing home residents, play basketball or cards with juvenile offenders, participate in a fellowship of Christian athletes, Habitat for Humanity, prayer groups, or spring break mission trips.

Samford is a quality Southern university, maintaining a comfortable-size population and still offering both undergraduate and graduate programs.

SEATTLE UNIVERSITY   Seattle, Washington

Total Undergraduate Enrollment: 3,700
Men: 1,500 Women: 2,200
Five-Year Graduation Rate: 57%

Tuition: $$$
Room and Board: $$$
Residential Students: 37%

History Seattle University is a Catholic Jesuit University, one of 28 in America, founded in 1891 as Seattle College. Later becoming a university, Seattle was the first Jesuit university to admit women.

Location The 46-acre attractively landscaped campus is located in Seattle, Washington, near the downtown section of the fourteenth largest metropolis in the nation.

Top Programs of Study Arts and sciences, accounting, engineering, nursing

Arts and Sciences Art history, biochemistry, biology, chemistry, civil engineering, communications, computer science, criminal justice, diagnostic ultrasound, drama, ecological studies, economics, electrical engineering, electrical and computer engineering, English/creative writing, environmental engineering, fine arts, French, general science, German, history, humanities, international studies, journalism, liberal studies, mathematics, mechanical engineering, medical technology, philosophy, physics, political science, psychology, public affairs, social work, sociology, Spanish, theology/religious studies, visual arts

Business Accounting, business administration, business economics, e-commerce/information systems, finance, international business, management, marketing

Education None

Pre-Professional Dentistry, law, medicine

Accredited Programs Allied health, business, chemistry, education, engineering, nursing

Special Programs There is a law school on campus. There are opportunities for study abroad, internships, and service. A Writers Series brings published authors to campus. There are several minors available, including cultural anthropology, music, and women's studies.

Facilities There are 27 buildings, many of which contain academic departments that have either had new or refurbished facilities built in the last few years. The Pigott Building is home to the Albers School of Business and Economics, with its high-tech teaching equipment and three-story Paccar Atrium. The School of Nursing is housed in the completely renovated Garrand Building, the 100-year-old birthplace of the university. The new student union is distinguished by its massive centerpiece atrium and fireplace and the Chapel of St. Ignatius is an award-winning structure. The middle of the campus is the Quad, featuring an open space resembling a Japanese rock garden, where a fountain provides soft background music. There are a radio station and the Kinsey Art Gallery.

Transition to College Program The Center for Student Success contacts faculty who teach freshmen and then provides help and support services for students who are having academic difficulty.

Athletics NCAA II, Northwest Conference of Independent Colleges, U.S. Collegiate Skiing Association

   Men: Basketball, cross-country, skiing (downhill), soccer, swimming, track

   Women: Basketball, cross-country, skiing (downhill), soccer, softball, track, volleyball

Student Life and Housing About 1,400 students can be accommodated in college housing, which includes single-sex and coed dorms. Priority is given to out-of-town students. Eighty-three percent of the students are from Washington, the remainder are from every state and 70 countries. Ethnicity: Caucasian—58 percent; Asian-American—16 percent; International—9 percent; Hispanic-American—6 percent; African-American—4 percent; Native-American—1 percent. There are no fraternities or sororities. All students may keep cars.

Accommodations for Student with Disabilities In compliance with section 504

Financial Aid About 89 percent of all freshmen receive aid. The average freshman award was about $16,000.

Requirements for Admission SAT I or ACT scores and a college prep high school program. Laboratory chemistry is required to be considered for the nursing program. Four years of math and both laboratory physics and chemistry are required for engineering program consideration.

Application Application deadlines are the following: February 1 for fall admission; November 1 for winter admission; February 1 for spring admission; and May 1 for summer admission.

International Students Students should submit applications six to nine months prior to the quarter in which they wish to enroll. Preferential application deadlines are as follows: Fall—February 15 (transfers March 1), Winter—September 1; Spring—December 1; Summer—February 1. Required are certified, official secondary and/or university transcripts, a TOEFL score, or a sufficiently high SAT or ACT score, which would be used to waive the TOEFL requirement. Students should also submit the international student declaration of finances form or an embassy letter indicating sponsorship.

Transfer Students Required are official copies of high school and college transcripts, a minimum GPA of 2.5, and at least a 2.75 GPA for transfer to the business and nursing programs. The final 45 credits must be taken at Seattle University.

Admission Contact
Office of Admissions
Seattle University
900 Broadway
Seattle, WA 98122-4340
Phone: (800) 426-7123; (206) 296-2000
FAX: (206) 296-5656
E-mail: *admission@seattle.edu*
Web: *www.seattle.edu*

The Heart of the University The heart of Seattle University is the city of Seattle, population 500,000, and one of the most progressive international cities in America. To a large degree, Seattle is the West Coast equivalent of what the East Coast city of Boston is to its colleges and universities. A dynamic city, Seattle is a major seaport and business center, the home of Boeing, Microsoft, Starbucks, and Pearl Jam. The city has six professional sports teams, music, theater, dance, movies, and an aquarium. Students can explore beaches and coastline and have a choice of three ski resorts within 45 minutes of campus. The city is considered an extension of the campus, not only for cultural and recreational opportunities, but for internships and class projects. The one caveat about Seattle is that the weather is damp. Compared to Northeastern cities that have more rainfall annually, Seattle has less rainfall but more days of it. However, because Seattle is such a safe clean city with so many resources, few students complain.

The university has a 60 percent commuter population, so it works creatively to establish a sense of community. For example, five spacious, comfortable Collegia centers are reserved for commuters as a place to study, eat, and relax with friends. The Collegia are furnished with living and study areas as well as small kitchens. Special activities are also scheduled to help commuters feel more connected to the university. All students are provided with several programs that match students with mentors in their fields of study. Students can also join the Undergraduate Student Research Association. Courses give high priority to students' working on projects and research using teams in order to facilitate students getting to know one another. Residence halls have a Jesuit moderator in each as well as two resident assistants on each floor to assist with the transition to college.

The university is considered one of the best comprehensive universities in the West, offering both the nation's first undergraduate program in environmental engineering and the first graduate program in software engineering. A core program of interdisciplinary courses provides students with an important foundation in liberal arts and sciences, where what students study in one class enhances what students learn in others. A major must be chosen by the end of the sophomore year, with focus on the major in the junior year. A senior synthesis course or project provides a capstone to the educational program. Throughout the program, students are encouraged to participate in collaborative projects with faculty as well as to conduct independent research.

Great emphasis is placed not only on educational excellence, but also on developing a sense of social justice through service learning. Many courses require students to commit to volunteer service and write or discuss their experiences in class.

Seattle University is unique in offering an education in the Jesuit tradition to an extraordinarily multicultural student population within an exciting city.

SHIPPENSBURG UNIVERSITY

Shippensburg, Pennsylvania

Total Undergraduate Enrollment: 6,600

Men: 3,040 Women: 3,560
Five-Year Graduation Rate: 58%

Tuition: In-state–$;
Out-of-state–$$
Room and Board: $
Residential Students: 38%

History Shippensburg University was founded in 1871 as the Cumberland Valley Normal School. It later became the State Teacher College of Pennsylvania and then Shippensburg State College. In 1983 the college was designated a university after graduate programs were approved.

Location The 200-acre campus is located in Shippensburg, Pennsylvania, a rural area 40 miles southwest of Harrisburg in the Cumberland Valley of south central Pennsylvania. The university is about two hours from Washington, D.C.

Top Programs of Study Elementary education, communication/journalism, criminal justice

Arts and Sciences Applied physics, art (including computer graphics), biology, communication/journalism, computer science, criminal justice, economics, English, French, geoenvironmental studies, geography, history, mathematics, medical technology, political science, physics, psychology, public administration, social work, sociology, Spanish, speech communication

Business Accounting, economics, finance, information management and analysis, information technology for business education, management (human resource, international), management information systems, marketing

Education Elementary, secondary

Pre-Professional Chiropractic, dentistry, law, medicine, optometry, pharmacy, physical therapy, podiatry, veterinary medicine

Accredited Programs Business, chemistry, counseling, education, social work

Special Programs The university offers allied health science cooperative programs in biotechnology, cytogenetic technology, cytotechnology, diagnostic imaging, nursing, occupational therapy, and physical therapy in conjunction with Thomas Jefferson University School of Allied Health Science in Philadelphia. There is a HEOP program for underprepared students from economically disadvantaged backgrounds. There are opportunities for independent study, internships, and study abroad. Students can also take courses for a semester at one of the other 13 universities in the Pennsylvania State System as a visiting student. The university offers child care on campus and has a Women's Center and a Multicultural Student Development Center.

Facilities There are 47 buildings, including the Lehman Memorial Library; the Seth Grove Stadium and Fieldhouse; Henderson Gymnasium; a student recreation center; the Franklin Science Center; Cumberland Student Union; the new Grove Hall College of Business; Memorial Auditorium; Hubert Art Center; a vertebrate museum, greenhouse, herbarium, and planetarium; buildings listed on the National Historic Register; student-run radio and TV stations; and an on-campus laboratory elementary school.

Transition to College Program Traditional orientation programs are offered prior to the beginning of the fall semester as well as in the summer. There is a special academic orientation for students who are undecided on a major area of study.

Athletics NCAA II, Pennsylvania State Athletic Conference

Men: Baseball, basketball, cross-country, football, lacrosse, soccer, swimming, wrestling

Women: Basketball, cheerleading, cross-country, field hockey, soccer, softball, swimming, tennis, track & field, volleyball

Student Life and Housing About 2,400 students can be accommodated in college housing. Ninety-three percent of the undergraduates are from Pennsylvania, the remainder are from 18 other states and 11 countries. Ethnicity: Caucasian—93 percent. There is 1 local and 13 national fraternities and 2 local and 6 national sororities. All students may keep cars.

Accommodations for Students with Disabilities In compliance with section 504

Financial Aid About 60 percent of all freshmen receive aid. The average freshman award was about $6,500.

Requirements for Admission SAT I or ACT results and a college prep high school program.

Application Freshmen are admitted fall and spring semesters. Application deadlines are open, and students are sent an admission decision on a rolling basis.

International Students Required are official copies of secondary and, if applicable, postsecondary work, with English translations if not in English; TOEFL results for students whose native language is not English; SAT scores for those who are native English speakers; and a financial support statement.

Transfer Students Required are official high school and college transcripts and SAT I or ACT scores. High school records and college entrance exams may be waived if the student has successfully completed 30 or more credits of college work. If admitted, the Dean of the college to which the student is admitted will determine the number of transferable credits. Students must take a minimum of 45 credits at Shippensburg. A policy allowing a seamless transfer exists for students with associate's degrees from Pennsylvania colleges or students in attendance at four-year Pennsylvania colleges. A 2.0 GPA is required, and only courses with an earned grade of D or higher can be transferred. Those students transferring from two-year institutions without the associate degree must have a 2.2 GPA.

Admission Contact

Office of Admissions
Shippensburg University
1871 Old Main Drive
Shippensburg, PA 17257-2299
Phone: (800) 822-8028; (717) 477-1231
FAX: (717) 477-4016
E-mail: *admiss@ship.edu*
Web: *www.ship.edu*

The Heart of the University Shippensburg University, or "Ship" as students refer to the university, is one of the largest schools included in this guide. The university offers students a great value for the low tuition, with graduates of its excellent programs in great demand. Students visiting the campus are initially impressed by its beauty and friendliness and later, as undergraduates, by its comfortable feel, challenging programs, and supportiveness. The average class size in "Ship's" lower division courses is 30, while in the upper division courses the average is 20. The results are stimulating classes, close relationships with faculty, and many opportunities for faculty to mentor. Nearly 90 percent of the faculty have earned the doctorate or highest degree in their fields, which is the highest percentage in the Pennsylvania State System of Higher Education. Just as important, many faculty have extensive real-life experience in the areas in which they teach, which makes them knowledgeable about the latest developments in their fields.

While students take a general education program designed to give them an exposure to a variety of disciplines and proficiency in critical thinking, speaking, writing, technology, and a cultural awareness, the heart of "Ship" is in its career focus. Ninety-six percent of its graduates are either working or in graduate school.

The College of Arts and Sciences seeks to involve students in collaborative research with faculty. One professor said: "There may be no Nobel Prize for my research. The benefit of the student—that's the prize." That attitude is instrumental to the success that students find at "Ship." For example, over its 21-year history the medical technology program has a 100 percent job placement rate! In computer science, students have a computer lab with 18 Sun Ultra 5 workstations for software engineering. Also, history majors intern at Gettysburg National Park, Old Bedford Village, and the Pennsylvania Historical and Museum Commission. "Ship" also has cooperative agreements with the Philadelphia College of Osteopathic Medicine, Temple University School of Podiatric Medicine, and New York Chiropractic College.

The Grove College of Business is one of the premier business schools in the Mid-Atlantic region, emphasizing teamwork, communication, computer skills, and internships. Students in the Investment Management Program manage a real-money portfolio, providing a real edge in the job market, where more than 90 percent of "Ship's" graduates work full time. Working with faculty members who are active as researchers and consultants to small business firms and major corporations, students are exposed to the latest developments in the business world. Every other year the college hosts a Career Expo with 40 firms participating.

The College of Education and Human Services graduates students who are in great demand. Education students have the luxury of a campus laboratory school and are observing and practicing in schools as early as freshman year. They also have a recruitment fair on campus each year. The NCATE accredited program was accepted on first review, an action reserved for

only the strongest programs. In addition, the nationally accredited program in social work offers senior year internships at women's shelters, mental health facilities, and senior centers. Criminal justice students gain practical experience in the juvenile justice system because the campus is home to the Center for Juvenile Justice Training and Research.

Although located in a rural setting, the university's 200 clubs and organizations, strong athletic programs, and proximity to Shippensburg—rated among the 100 best small towns in America—give students plenty to do, including the exploration of historical sites such as Gettysburg and activities for nature enthusiasts in five state parks and a section of the Appalachian Trail.

SIENA COLLEGE   Loudonville, New York

Total Undergraduate Enrollment: 2,900		Tuition: $$$	
Men: 1,400 Women: 1,500		Room and Board: $$$	
Five-Year Graduation Rate: 77%		Residential Students: 74%	

History Siena College was founded in 1937 by the Franscican Friars, at the invitation of Bishop Gibbons of Albany. The college was placed under the patronage of Saint Bernardine of Siena, the illustrious fifteenth-century Franciscan preacher.

Location The 155-acre campus is in Loudonville, New York, a suburb 2 miles north of Albany, the state capital.

Top Programs of Study Business, biology, psychology, political science

Arts and Sciences American studies, biochemistry, biology, classics, computer science, English, environmental studies, history, mathematics, modern languages, philosophy, physics, political science, psychology, religious studies, social work, sociology

Business Accounting, economics, finance, marketing, management

Education Secondary

Pre-Professional Dentistry, law, medicine, veterinary medicine

Accredited Programs Chemistry, social work

Special Programs There is a HEOP program for highly motivated economically and educationally disadvantaged students. There are study abroad opportunities, internships, and a Washington, D.C., semester. Certificate programs are offered in the following: health studies, with a track in health services administration and health and society; International Studies; foreign languages and business program; peace studies; and theater. There are a number of minors and multidisciplinary programs, such as the Convivium: Siena Center for Medieval and Early Modern Studies. There are several cooperative programs: engineering with Rensselaer and several other universities; environmental science/forestry with SUNY at Syracuse University; law school with Pace University and Western New England College; and an MBA program with

Clarkson University. There are also early assurance programs in dentistry, medicine, and optometry, as well as accelerated programs in optometry and podiatry. Several other special offerings include The Martin Luther King, Jr. and Coretta Scott King Lecture Series on Race and Nonviolent Social Change; the Reinhold Niebuhr Institute of Religion and Culture; A Family Business Institute; the Siena College Institute for Jewish–Christian Studies; and the Siena Research Institute.

Facilities There are 26 buildings, including a new science facility, the Fry Campus Center, the Office of Multicultural Affairs, the Marcelle Athletic Complex, a new library, and a radio station.

Transition to College Program The Foundations Sequence, mandated for all students, is an introduction to the intellectual life. Students meet in small classes with one professor for the entire year. Students look at important issues from a variety of perspectives, and there is a common set of readings for all students. The course emphasizes those skills and abilities important for academic success: careful reading, note taking, discussion, and writing. Field trips to various cultural and artistic sites are part of the program.

Athletics NCAA I, Metro Atlantic Athletic Conference

Men: Baseball, basketball, football (NCAA Div. I-AA), cross-country, golf, lacrosse, soccer, tennis

Women: Basketball, field hockey, golf, lacrosse, soccer, softball, swimming and diving, tennis, volleyball

Student Life and Housing About 2,200 students can be accommodated in college housing. Eighty-five percent of the students are from New York, the remainder from 24 other states and 8 countries. Ethnicity: Caucasian—90 percent. There are no fraternities or sororities. Upperclassmen may keep cars.

Accommodations for Students with Disabilities Students must register with the Office of Tutoring and Services for Students with Disabilities and pro-vide current documentation of the disability. The college provides reasonable accommodations to all students with disabilities and assistance in developing an individualized accommodation plan.

Financial Aid About 85 percent of all freshmen receive aid. The average freshman award was about $10,000.

Requirements for Admission SAT I or ACT results and a college prep high school program. A campus visit is strongly recommended.

Application Early Decision and Early Action applications are due December 1, with admission notification by January 1. Regular applications should be submitted in the fall but no later than March 1, with admission notification by March 15.

International Students In addition to the materials required for general admission, students must submit translated copies of secondary and/or college transcripts, a certificate of financial responsibility, and a TOEFL score no lower than 550, if the student does not have English as a native language.

Transfer Students Application deadlines are December 1 for spring semester, April 1 for summer semester, and June 1 for fall semester. Required are official high school and college transcripts, or GED transcript if the applicant has graduated within the last 10 years, a transfer recommendation form completed by an official from the student's last college attended, and SAT or ACT scores taken while in high school. Only C− grades and higher will be considered for transfer. A total of 90 credits can be transferred from a four-year college and 66 from a two-year college. A GPA of 2.5 is required, and students must complete a minimum of 30 credits at Siena and at least half of the major at Siena.

Admission Contact
Office of Admissions
Siena College
515 Loudon Road
Loudonville, NY 12211-1462
Phone: (888) AT-SIENA; (518) 783-2423

FAX: (518) 783-2436
E-mail: *admit@siena.edu*
Web: *www.siena.edu*

The Heart of the College Students love Siena. Just look at the high graduation rate. This is a friendly campus, with a strong athletic program and much to do at a modest tuition. Students really have fun here while they study a well-designed liberal arts program. Beginning with a year-long Foundations Sequence, students in the first semester study the interaction of nature, the person, and society; in the second semester, religious and secular world views and the American experience. Students begin to see the connection among disciplines and to approach information with analytical and questioning minds. These outcomes continue as students study a core curriculum, including courses in English, history, philosophy, religious studies, aesthetic perspectives and social sciences, and science and math. Siena is one of the few colleges or universities that admits what others don't: learning is not always easy and the most rewarding learning is sometimes very hard work. Moreover, Siena truly understands that a liberal arts program is studying something simply because you are fascinated by it. This is nowhere better illustrated than by the number of students and faculty collaborating on research, especially in the sciences.

The college location near Albany along with the student-centered focus of the college, the active Career Center, and small class size provide for many internship and employment opportunities. Students in the humanities and social sciences find employment with Smith Barney, the New York State Assembly, the Center for the Disabled, CBS, Thomas Publishing Company, and Paine Weber. Business students graduate to positions with Pepsi-Cola, Transamerica Financial Services, Albany Financial Group, and General Electric. Science students graduate to positions with Boston Biomedical Research, Milford Chemical, GE Corporate Research and Development, and Microsoft.

Siena also boasts outstanding pre-professional programs that have led to cooperative, accelerated, and early assurance programs with SUNY College of Medicine, the Boston University Goldman School of Dentistry, the Pennsylvania College of Optometry, Pace University Law School, and others. Siena takes pride in its 80 percent acceptance rate of candidates into medical schools.

The heart of the Siena experience is its Catholic Franciscan tradition that "knowledge must lead to good works." The Franciscan Center for Service and Advocacy serves as the college's primary vehicle for promoting service to the poor and marginalized.

SIMMONS COLLEGE   Boston, Massachusetts

Total Undergraduate Enrollment: 1,378
Men: 0 Women: 1,378
Five-Year Graduation Rate: 72%

Tuition: $$$$
Room and Board: $$$$
Residential Students: 58%

History Simmons College is a women's college founded in 1899. Boston businessman John Simmons noted in his will his intention of opening a college for women so that they may have the ability to "earn an independent living."

Location The 12-acre campus is located in Boston, Massachusetts, the nation's largest "college town."

Top Programs of Study Nursing, communications, psychology

Arts and Sciences Africana studies, art, arts administration, biochemistry, biology, chemistry, chemistry-management, communications, computer science, East Asian studies, economics, English, environmental science, French, graphic design, history, human services, information technology, international relations, mathematics, music, nursing, nutrition, pharmacy, philosophy, physical therapy, physics of materials, political science, psychobiology, psychology, public relations and marketing communications, society and health, sociology, Spanish

Business Finance, financial mathematics, management, management information systems, marketing, retail management

Education Early childhood, elementary, ESL, middle school, secondary, special

Pre-Professional Law, medicine

Accredited Programs Chemistry, nursing, nutrition, physical therapy, social work

Special Programs There are individualized majors, many internship opportunities, a Washington, D.C., semester, and many short-term study abroad programs supervised by Simmons faculty. The Excel Program is designed for students who are highly motivated but do not meet all of Simmons' standard admission requirements. It provides for the study of writing, math, and study skills in a four-week summer program. The Dorothea Lynde Dix Scholars Program welcomes students over the age of 23 to the college. Simmons is a member of the Colleges of the Fenway, sharing resources, student services, and cross-registration with five other colleges. Simmons also participates in an exchange program with Spelman College in Atlanta, Fisk University in Nashville, and Mills College in Oakland. There is an Army ROTC program. There is a five-year program in nutrition, a six-year program in pharmacy, a six-year program in physical therapy, and a dual degree program in becoming a physician's assistant with the Manchester College of Pharmacy and Health Services.

Facilities There are 26 buildings, including the Park Science Center; the Beatley Library; the state-of-the-art Holmes Center; Alumnae Hall, used for dances, parties, and performances; an art gallery; a TV studio; a nursing lab; a physical therapy motion lab; and a foreign language lab.

Transition to College Program Simmons offers a traditional orientation program.

Athletics NCAA III, Great Northeast Athletic Conference

   Women: Basketball, crew, field hockey, softball, swimming and diving, tennis, volleyball

Student Life and Housing About 1,000 students can be accommodated in college housing, which includes special-interest houses and is guaranteed for all four years. Sixty percent of the students are from Massachusetts, the remainder from 38 other states and 26 countries. Ethnicity: Caucasian—70 percent; African-American—7 percent; Asian-American—5 percent; Hispanic-American—4 percent; International—4 percent. There are no fraternities or sororities. No one may keep cars.

Accommodations for Students with Disabilities In compliance with section 504

Financial Aid About 90 percent of freshmen receive aid. The average freshman award was about $18,000.

Requirements for Admission SAT I or ACT scores and a college prep high school program. A campus interview is strongly recommended.

Application The Early Action deadline is December 1, with decision notification sent by January 20. Students not accepted in Early Action will automatically be reconsidered with the regular applicant pool. Regular application deadline is February 1, with decision notification by April 15.

International Students The preferred application deadline is February 1. Required are official secondary and, if applicable, postsecondary transcripts, documentation of financial support, minimum TOEFL scores of 560 paper and 220 computer-based if the student's native language is not English.

Transfer Students Entrance is for both the fall and spring semesters. Students who have earned a minimum of nine credits at another regionally accredited institution with a minimum course grade of C− are considered for transfer. Students must spend at least three semesters at Simmons and earn a minimum of 48 credits. Students interested in nursing, physical therapy, or physician's assistant programs should contact the office of admissions before applying. April 1 is the preferred application deadline. Students should submit official high school and college transcripts, SAT I or ACT scores, the latest midterm college report, a recommendation from a faculty member, and a letter of good standing from the academic dean.

Admission Contact

Office of Admissions
Simmons College
300 The Fenway
Boston, MA 02115-5898
Phone: (800) 345-8468; (617) 521-2051
FAX: (617) 521-3190
E-mail: *ugadm@simmons.edu*
Web: *www.simmons.edu*

The Heart of the College The heart of Simmons College is difficult to miss. Situated in Boston, one of America's greatest cities and the college student capital of America, with about 300,000 college students (that's about 20 percent of the Boston population) attending about 60 schools, 15 of which are within walking distance to Simmons, a Simmons education is a Boston education. While Simmons' neighborhood has much to offer in terms of clubs, athletic events, restaurants, theaters, museums, and galleries, the Boston subway, known as the T, can take students wherever they want to go, including the Esplanade—the 18-mile loop around the Charles River where students go biking, walking, running, and rollerblading; Newberry Street—eight blocks of trendy stores, restaurants, and cafes; Lansdowne Street's dance clubs; the European, cobblestoned North End; and, of course, Fenway Park—the home of the Boston Red Sox baseball team.

With Boston as a setting, Simmons is able to offer students plentiful wonderful internship and fieldwork opportunities. With guidance from faculty members, many Simmons students spend at least one semester working at a world-renowned hospital, museums, businesses, law firms, schools, health care organizations, government agencies, and nonprofit organizations, with many of these internships resulting in job offers upon graduation. Students studying the sciences do fieldwork projects of their choosing. The projects involve skills important for the marketplace as well: discipline, motivation, and innovative thinking.

The college's Boston location allows Simmons to easily blend career preparation within a liberal arts context. Use of technology, writing skills, and cultural understanding are all woven into a curriculum that explores living in a multicultural society, stresses foreign language competency, and explores modes of inquiry in the creative and performing arts, literature, science, sociology, history, and mathematics. Students devote about a third of their coursework to a major, and then complete their coursework with a "capstone" experience in an internship or independent research project.

A women's college consistently rated as one of the top colleges in the nation, Simmons offers its students the benefits of a small university—including several undergraduate-to-graduate programs that offer a seamless route to a master's degree—while maintaining an intimate supportive environment. Much of this is attributed to an accomplished, caring faulty, one of whom says: "The close-knit relationship between students and faculty is a reality at Simmons." Other faculty members praise Simmons' students for taking their education seriously and being eager to learn. The faculty is comprised not only of scholars but also working musicians, journalists, and physical therapists who bring great enthusiasm to the classroom and offer students plenty of personal attention. Students always point to the faculty as being the college's top asset.

The residence campus, with many lifestyle options, including smoke-free residences, quiet floors, commuter service floors, and an international residence, is just a short walk from the academic campus. The residence halls enclose a grassy, tree-lined quad and are situated in a distinguished neighborhood.

Students at Simmons have the best of both worlds: studying in a city where it's easy to meet guys from other colleges, yet receiving all the benefits of an exclusive women's education, one that celebrates women's lives and leadership. So many of the students cite how Simmons made them more confident and allowed then to believe in themselves. Denise Di Novi, alumnus and film producer of "Little Women" and "Edward Scissorhands," says: "I would not be who or what I am today if I had not come to Simmons College. The four-year respite here was where my voice became stronger, my opinions firmer, my dreams loftier."

SIMPSON COLLEGE   Indianola, Iowa

Total Undergraduate Enrollment: 1,351
Men: 590 Women: 761
Five-Year Graduation Rate: 65%

Tuition: $$$
Room and Board: $
Residential Students: 82%

History Simpson College was founded in 1860 by pioneer settlers of Indianola, Iowa, when the first session of the Western Conference of the Methodist Episcopal Church united to establish the Indianola Male and Female Seminary. Later, the college was renamed for Bishop Matthew Simpson, one of the leading statesmen and religious leaders of his time, who delivered the eulogy at President Lincoln's burial. The college maintains an affiliation with the United Methodist Church.

Location The 73-acre tree-lined campus is located in Indianola, Iowa (population 13,000), in a suburban area 12 miles south of Des Moines, the state capital. The campus is bordered on the north by one of the city's largest parks.

Top Programs of Study Biology, education, management

Arts and Sciences Art, athletic training, biochemistry, biology, chemistry, communication studies (corporate, journalism, rhetoric, and speech), computer information systems, computer science, criminal justice, economics, English, environmental science (with biology, chemistry, geology), French, German, history, international relations, mathematics, medical technology, music, music performance, philosophy, political science, religion, Russian studies, social work, sociology, Spanish, sports administration, theater arts, women's studies

Business Accounting, international management, management, marketing

Education Early childhood, elementary, secondary, music, physical education

Pre-Professional Dentistry, engineering, law, medicine, optometry, pharmacy, physical therapy, theology/ministry, veterinary medicine

Accredited Programs Music

Special Programs There is a Concerned Multicultural Students Organization. The Simpson Forum sponsors lectures, plays, films, and musical presentations. There is a Woodrow Wilson Visiting Fellows Program, opportunities for study abroad, a Washington, D.C., semester, and a United Nations semester. Simpson uses a 4-4-1 academic calendar: two four-month semesters and one three-week semester in May, consisting of one concentrated course. Simpson has a cooperative engineering program with Washington University in St. Louis.

Facilities There are 34 buildings, many situated around the campus quadrangle, including the Wallace Hall of Science, named to the National Register of Historic Places; the Robertson Music Center, including the new Salsburg Wing; the renovated and expanded Carver Science Hall, named after alumnus George Washington Carver; the renovated Brenton Student Center; the Art Center; Carse Fitness Hall; renovated Cowles-Hopper Athletic Complex; the Blank Performing Arts Center; and a radio station.

Transition to College Program In the First-Year Program, students select a Liberal Arts Seminar that will apply to other academic requirements. In addition to the regular course work, students attend special Forum events, workshops, community service, and career development activities. The course is taught by the student's adviser, who is personally concerned with each student's success.

Athletics NCAA III, Iowa Intercollegiate Athletic Conference

Men: Baseball, basketball, cross-country, football, golf, track & field, soccer, tennis, wrestling

Women: Basketball, cross-country, golf, track & field, soccer, softball, swimming, tennis, volleyball

Student Life and Housing About 1,000 students can be accommodated in college housing, which is guaranteed for all four years. Ninety-one percent of the students are from Iowa, the remainder are from 27 other states and 12 countries. Ethnicity: Caucasian—92 percent. There are one local and three national fraternities and four national sororities. All students may keep cars.

Accommodations for Students with Disabilities Students must present proper verification of disability to either the Student Development Office or Hawley Academic Resource Center. In addition, there are many academic support services available at the Resource Center.

Financial Aid About 98 percent of all students receive some form of aid. The average freshman award was about $16,000.

Requirements for Admission SAT I or ACT scores and a college prep high school program.

Application Application deadlines are open. Admission notification is made as soon as all information has been received and evaluated.

International Students Applications must be filed before May 1. Required are certified copies of original secondary and, if applicable, postsecondary records and certificates. TOEFL results are required as well as a financial statement attested to by the candidate's bank or other financial institution.

Transfer Students Required are evidence of good standing at the previous institution, official transcripts of high school and college work, SAT I or ACT results, or a GED equivalent. Courses with D or F grades are not transferable. Students from accredited two-year institutions with associate's degrees can transfer all credits if the GPA is 2.0 or higher.

Admission Contact
Office of Admissions
Simpson College
701 North C Street
Indianola, IA 50125
Phone: (800) 362-2454
FAX: (515) 961-1870
E-mail: *admiss@simpson.edu*
Web: *www.simpson.edu*

The Heart of the College Considered one of the top Midwestern liberal art colleges and a "best buy," Simpson can be considered "traditional" with its supportive faculty, well-designed liberal arts program, and internship opportunities. The Simpson community is a caring, nurturing one, providing a real sense of belonging and the opportunity to build strong personal relationships. The faculty members provide personal attention, are always accessible, are dedicated to quality education, and 87 percent have earned the highest degrees in their fields. With teaching and learning their priority, students and professors develop an easy rapport. The close community is fostered by many opportunities to establish friendships within the context of plenty of campus activities and organizations, a very strong athletic program, and an active religious life and community service. There are retreats, a drama troupe, musical ensembles, prayer groups, and campus worship (Protestant, Catholic, and nondenominational). The strongest community service groups are Habitat for Humanity and the Fellowship for Christian Athletes.

The liberal arts program is focused on the Cornerstone Studies, an interdisciplinary program of 40 credits from eight specific academic areas. Students learn about the Western tradition; natural sciences and scientific methods; social, political, and economic institutions; the humanities; and fine arts—a perspective that helps students to appreciate the contributions of minority groups in our culture and to study other cultures. Also, in the Senior Colloquium students address a significant topic from more than one perspective. Recent topics have been: "Values and Change: The Status of Women," and "Sport in Society." Simpson graduates are expected to write at an advanced college level and to show competency in math and foreign languages. Also, the arts are alive and well at Simpson, highlighted by a strong vocal and instrumental music tradition that has garnered much acclaim and numerous awards. Simpson graduates have successful careers with some of the nation's top opera companies.

The Simpson 4-4-1 academic calendar allows students to study abroad, intern, or study unique courses on campus during the May term. The college maintains a program in Schorndorf, Germany, where students can either study language and culture or intern at Daimler-Mercedez Benz and other international firms. Another popular international program is the Semester-in-London. On American soil, students have held internships with state senators, Chrysler Corporation, 3M Manufacturing, Pioneer Press in Chicago, television stations, Iowa Methodist Medical Center, and the Des Moines Chamber of Commerce.

Indianola offers students a friendly college town, with nearby Lake Ahquabi State Park offering opportunities for hiking, canoeing, fishing, and boating. Just 12 miles away, the state capital of Des Moines offers internships, art and science centers, a zoo, historic areas, and professional sports.

SOUTH DAKOTA STATE UNIVERSITY

Brookings, South Dakota

Total Undergraduate Enrollment: 6,300

Men: 3,300 Women: 3,000
Five-Year Graduation Rate: 52%

Tuition: In–state–$;
Out-of-state–$
Room and Board: $
Residential Students: 32%

History South Dakota State University was founded in 1881 by an act of the Territorial Legislature for "an Agricultural College for the Territory of Dakota to be established at Brookings." In 1889 a land-grant act provided 120,000 acres of land for the use and support of the Agricultural College. In 1964 the school officially became a university.

Location The 272-acre campus is located in Brookings, South Dakota (population 17,000), a small town about 50 miles north of Sioux Falls and 200 miles west of Minneapolis. The university is located on the eastern edge of the state, along the South Dakota–Minnesota border.

Top Programs of Study Nursing, sociology, animal science, engineering

Arts and Sciences Agricultural business, agricultural education, agricultural journalism, agricultural systems marketing, agriculture and resource management, agronomy, animal science, apparel merchandising, athletic training, biology, chemistry, civil and environmental engineering, clinical lab technology, communication studies and theater, computer science, construction science, consumer affairs, dairy manufacturing, dairy production, economics, electrical engineering technology, engineering physics, English, environmental management, French, general agriculture, geographic information sciences, geography, German, graphic design, health, physical education and recreation, health promotion, history, horticulture, hotel and food service management, human development and family studies, interior design, journalism, landscape design, Latin American area studies, liberal studies, manufacturing engineering, mathematics, mechanical engineering, microbiology, music, music education, music merchandising, nursing, nutrition and food science, park management, pharmacy, physics, psychology, public relations, range science, sociology, Spanish, visual arts

Business None

Education Art, career and technical, early childhood, family and consumer sciences, music, physical education, secondary

Pre-Professional Chiropractic, dentistry, law, medicine, ministry, mortuary science, occupational therapy, optometry, physical therapy, physician's assistant, veterinary medicine

Accredited Programs Agricultural systems technology, animal disease and diagnostic laboratory, athletic training, chemistry, dietetics, education, engineering, family and consumer sciences, journalism, music, pharmacy

Special Programs An associate's degree is offered in general studies. Aviation education is offered as a specialization, with students flying out of three airports to become certified. The university has many study abroad and internship opportunities, as well as a student exchange program that allows students to study for either a semester or a year at more than 150 other universities in the United States. There are Air Force and Army ROTC programs.

Facilities There are 325 buildings, including the new Yeager Journalism Building; the Northern Plains Biostress Lab; the Briggs Library; the Health, Physical Education, and Recreation Center; a campus art center; the Ritz Art Gallery; and the South Dakota Art Museum.

Transition to College Program The university offers a traditional orientation program.

Athletics NCAA II, North Central Conference

   Men: Baseball, basketball, cross-country, football, golf, indoor and outdoor track, swimming, tennis, wrestling

   Women: Basketball, cross-country, golf, indoor and outdoor track, soccer, softball, swimming, tennis, volleyball

Student Life and Housing About 3,000 students can be accommodated in college housing. Seventy-four percent of the students are from South Dakota, the remainder from 39 other states and 20 countries. Ethnicity: Caucasian—91 percent. There are six national fraternities and three national sororities. All students may keep cars.

Accommodations for Students with Disabilities Assistance is available for students with a wide range of disabilities. The Coordinator of Disabilities can be reached at (605) 688-6146 for information.

Financial Aid About 86 percent of all freshmen receive aid. The average freshman award was about $5,500.

Requirements for Admission Students are admitted if they have graduated in the top 60 percent of their class, or if they have a minimum ACT score of 18 or SAT I score of 870, or a GPA of at least 2.6, and they complete a college prep high school program.

Application Freshmen are admitted to all semesters. Application deadlines are open, with admission notification sent on a rolling basis.

International Students Required are official transcripts for all secondary and, if applicable, postsecondary education, TOEFL scores, a financial certification form, a 2.5 GPA, a syllabus from the transferring institution to determine course equivalency, or the courses will be evaluated by an independent credential evaluation service. If a student scores at least 600 on the TOEFL, then the Michigan Test of English Proficiency for non-native speakers of English will be waived.

Transfer Students Required are official college transcripts, a minimum of a 2.0 GPA, and good academic standing. Students seeking to enter the education program must have a 2.5 GPA, and admission to the professional programs in engineering, nursing, and pharmacy is on a competitive basis. Students with lower than a 2.0 GPA may be admitted on probation. Students with fewer than 12 college credits seeking to transfer into an associate's degree program must meet the regular entrance requirements. Those transfer students with more than 12 credits may transfer into an associate's degree program at the discretion of the university.

Home-Schooled Students Applicants must achieve a minimum ACT composite score of 18, a minimum ACT English subtest score of 18, a Math subtest score of 20 or above, and Social Studies/Reading and Science Reasoning subtest scores of 17 or above, or applicants can submit a GED with the total cumulative standard test scores for all five tests totaling 2250, with no standard score below 410.

Admission Contact

Office of Admissions
South Dakota State University
Box 2201
Brookings, SD 57007-0649
Phone: (800) 952-3541; (605) 688-4121
FAX: (605) 688-6891

E-mail: *sdsu_admissions@sdstate.edu*
Web: *www.sdstate.edu*

The Heart of the University South Dakota State University is one of the largest colleges selected for this guide that gives students a great range of majors and other choices, but still provides them with the personal attention typically received at small colleges. The university offers students a 30-credit thoughtful general education core, similar to the other carefully crafted core programs offered by the other colleges and universities selected for this guide; however, South Dakota's core includes one distinctive goal. As an institution that was founded as an agricultural college, the core curriculum promotes "land stewardship," requiring that students have an "understanding and appreciation for the role that land (soil, water, rock, organisms) plays in our society and our obligations as stewards of the land." While Agricultural and Biological Sciences represents one of the university's eight separate colleges, students also study within the following colleges on campus: General Studies, Arts and Sciences, Engineering, Education and Counseling, Family and Consumer Sciences, Nursing, and Pharmacy.

From the listing of colleges just provided, you can see that the heart of this university is about careers, and because of the quality of its programs—many of them nationally accredited—graduates do very well in the marketplace. A student-focused education gives students plenty of support, and South Dakota U. students get their fair share. The Career Counseling Center boasts a 95 percent placement rate over the last several years and provides resources and individual assistance. It's typical to have more than 2,000 individual job interviews set up during the year! The Career and Academic Planning Center forwards students' résumés to employers who have contacted the center in search of prospective employees. Also instrumental in the great placement rate is that internships are either required or strongly encouraged for every academic program. Opportunities for students to do real research is another factor. The Northern Plains Biostress Lab provides research opportunities to study the environmental stresses that affect plants, animals, and people, while the College of Agriculture and Biological Sciences has a premier program in research. The Center for Excellence in Technology offers nationally recognized programs in electrical engineering, construction management, and manufacturing engineering technology. The university's engineering students consistently rank in the upper 10–20 percent in the nation on the Fundamentals Exam, creating a strong demand for these students at Boeing, Burns & McDonnell, Chrysler, Daktronics, IBM, 3M, and other companies. The nursing program is a distinguished one, and the pharmacy program places 100 percent of its graduates.

These successful outcomes are almost ironic in that almost 25 percent of the freshman class comes to South Dakota State undecided about a major! That's what makes the College of General Studies the most popular freshman program on campus. The college is one of the few in the nation that specifically uses professional career planners to help students explore their interests and strengths to determine a major area of study. Students can take a career exploration course that is offered each semester. The college also offers advisers for the many pre-professional programs at the University.

The university offers students plenty to do, with 200 special interest and cultural organizations, Greek life, concerts, comedy nights, lectures, religious organizations, and more. There's a strong sports program, along with 4,000 students participating in intramurals. The atmosphere is friendly and casual, and the excellent theater productions, art exhibitions, and nationally renowned music program, engaging hundreds of students as performers, are successful in creating a healthy balance between play and career preparation.

SPELMAN COLLEGE   Atlanta, Georgia

Total Undergraduate Enrollment: 2,100
Men: 0 Women: 2,100
Five-Year Graduation Rate: 74%

Tuition: $$
Room and Board: $$$
Residential Students: 59%

History Spelman College was founded in 1881 by two missionaries from Boston, Sophia Packard and Harriet Giles, who were appalled at the lack of educational opportunity for black women. They opened a school in the basement of Atlanta's Baptist Church with $100. The first 11 pupils, 10 women and 1 girl, were mostly ex-slaves, determined to learn to read the Bible and write. The school relocated to a larger site and became the Atlanta Baptist Female Seminary. Later, through the generosity of John D. Rockefeller and his mother-in-law, Mrs. Lucy Henry Spelman, the name of the school was changed to Spelman Seminary in honor of the Spelman family, longtime activists in the anti-slavery move-

ment. In 1924 the school became Spelman College.

Location The 32-acre campus is located in Atlanta, Georgia, on the west side about a mile and-a-half from the downtown area.

Top Programs of Study Psychology, biology, English

Arts and Sciences Art, biochemistry, biology, chemistry, child development, comparative women's studies, computer information science, drama/dance, economics, engineering, environmental science, French, history, independent major, mathematics, music, natural sciences, philosophy, physics, political science, psychology, religion, sociology, sociology and anthropology, Spanish

Business A minor is offered in management and organization

Education Art, early childhood, health and physical education, music, secondary

Pre-Professional None

Accredited Programs Education, music

Special Programs The college offers a comprehensive student assessment program as part of its support services. There is a Phi Beta Kappa chapter. The Gateway Program offers mature learners an opportunity to begin or complete college studies. As a member of the Atlanta University Center Consortium, students have access to the resources of the other five participating institutions, including Columbia, Dartmouth, Auburn, and Georgia Institute of Technology. The college has a child development center and special minors in International Studies, Japan Studies, and Management and Organization. There are two special pre-freshman summer programs, one for students interested in pursuing a career in health/allied health professions, and the second for students intending to enter a scientific or technical career. There are study abroad, domestic, and international exchange programs.

Facilities There are 24 buildings, including the new Cosby Academic Center; the new Science Complex; and the renovation of McVicar Hall, which houses the Women's Health Center, the Office of Counseling Services, and living facilities for the resident nurses and students; the Rockefeller Fine Arts Building; the Manley College Center; and the historic administration building, Rockefeller Hall.

Transition to College Program Spelman offers a modified traditional orientation program, in which students spend their first two weeks on campus learning about Spelman's history and traditions, gather for student-led meetings, take placement exams, and meet professors. Students

can also audition for Glee Club, Dance Theater, and Jazz Ensemble and enjoy social activities. The capstone of the orientation is an induction ceremony followed by the opening convocation.

Athletics NCAA III, Conference of the Great South

Women: Basketball, cross-country, track & field, tennis, volleyball

Student Life and Housing About 1,200 students can be accommodated in college housing. Only 29 percent of the students are from Georgia, with the majority from 46 other states, mostly from the South, and 22 countries. Ethnicity: African-American—96 percent. There are four local and four national sororities. Upperclassmen may keep cars.

Accommodations for Students with Disabilities The Office of Disability Services coordinates and provides services for students who provide current documentation of their disability from a qualified health professional.

Financial Aid About 66 percent of all freshmen receive aid. The average freshman award was about $3,000.

Requirements for Admission Sat I or ACT scores and a college prep high school program.

Application First-year applicants are admitted for the fall semester only. The Early Action deadline is November 15, with decision notification by December 31. The regular admission deadline is February 1, with decision notification by April 1.

International Students In addition to the general requirements, students are asked to present a school-leaving certificate, and if English is not their native language, present a TOEFL score. Students must also complete a college declaration of finances form by December 31 of the year preceding the fall term in which they plan to enter.

Transfer Students The college will not admit students who have earned 90 or more credits. Applicants must be in good standing and eligible to return to their previous institutions. The following materials need to be submitted by February 1 for fall semester, and November 1 for spring semester: official transcripts from high school and all previous colleges, two recommendations from instructors (preferably in the applicant's intended major), and SAT I or ACT scores, if transferring with fewer than 30 credits. A minimum GPA of 2.0 is required. Courses with grades of C or better will be considered for transfer, provided that the courses were taken at a regionally accredited institution. The maximum number of credits transferable from two-year schools is 60.

Admission Contact
Office of Admissions
Spelman College
Packard Hall
350 Spelman Lane, SW
Atlanta, GA 30314-4399
Phone: (800) 982-2411; (404) 681-3643 x 2188
FAX: (404) 215-7788
E-mail: *admiss@spelman.edu*
Web: *www.spelman.edu*

The Heart of the College Spelman is one of only a select few colleges or universities with a predominantly African-American student population that has been chosen for this guide—and for many good reasons. Spelman captures its essence when it writes: "With its rich heritage and high standards, the college will continue to provide a first-rate liberal arts education for its students in an environment of excellence that is predicated upon a loyal scorn of second best." Spelman has a long history of graduating African-American women who assume leadership roles by providing them a quality education, instilling self-confidence, strength of character, a love of learning, a willingness to serve their communities, and commitment to making positive social change. Spelman's "sisterhood" is found in all walks of American life, reflective of the college's rating as one of the very best women's colleges and a "best buy" in college education.

Spelman prides itself on its focus on the liberal arts, sciences, and the fine arts, and its distinguished faculty, who act as caring mentors. The core curriculum reflects a rich array of courses in the humanities, fine arts, and social and natural sciences, plus required courses about the African Diaspora, International Studies, and Computer Literacy. The arts are also a source of great pride at Spelman, and the Spelman Art Museum is one of Atlanta's most acclaimed international galleries.

But behind this liberal arts program, there are some very distinctive things happening. First, Spelman brings to the campus, for six weeks prior to the start of their freshman year, students who have indicated interest in pursuing careers in medicine and other health-related fields, as well as those students who would like to pursue careers in science and technology. Students study mathematics, chemistry, biology, do library research, and improve critical thinking and problem-solving skills.

A second distinctive facet of the Spelman program is the comprehensive academic support program in place for students. Most noteworthy is an assessment of student learning and development program, which provides continuous feedback and guidance as students move through their years at Spelman. Each year several dimensions of a student's college life are assessed, whether by placement exam in freshman year or an identification of vocational interests in the sophomore year, a measurement of verbal skills in the junior year, or an assessment of student achievement in the student's major field of study. These assessments allow the student to identify strengths and weaknesses in academic and skill areas, as well as help to sharpen career objectives. This program is the most comprehensive one of its kind of all the institutions in this guide.

All of these programs lead to outstanding outcomes: In a recent year, Spelman had more African-American applicants accepted to medical school than Harvard, Emory, and Duke and was one of only six colleges to receive the

Model Institute for Excellence designation from both NASA and the National Science Foundation.

There's also plenty of fun at Spelman, which is one of the six institutions in Atlanta that constitute the Atlanta University Center, the world's largest consortium of historically black colleges. With joint registration and interconnecting walkways, joint college activities, Atlanta clubs, theaters, the Lenox Mall, and professional sports, the city of Atlanta provides a dynamic, youthful arena for Spelman students.

SPRING HILL COLLEGE Mobile, Alabama

Total Undergraduate Enrollment: 1,050
Men: 420 Women: 630
Five-Year Graduation Rate: 60%

Tuition: $$$
Room and Board: $$
Residential Students: 60%

History Spring Hill College was founded in 1830 by Bishop Michael Portier. At that time, Mobile, Alabama, had become, through successful French colonization, a focal point for commercial activity. Bishop Portier, recognizing the need for Catholic education in the Southeast, invited Fathers of the Society of Jesus (Jesuits) to take possession of a college he had constructed. Spring Hill is the oldest college in Alabama, the first Catholic college in the Southeast, and the third oldest Jesuit college in America.

Location The 400-acre campus is in a suburban area of Mobile, Alabama, near the Gulf Coast on elevated, beautiful grounds including 250 acres of woods. Mobile has a metropolitan area of almost 500,000 people.

Top Programs of Study Business and management, biology, communication arts

Arts and Sciences Art business, art studio, art therapy, biochemistry, biology, chemistry/chemistry-business, English, communication arts (concentration in advertising/radio and TV, journalism and media writing, public relations), engineering, environmental chemistry, general studies, graphic design, Hispanic studies, history, interdisciplinary humanities, international studies, mathematics (concentrations in actuarial/applied, computer analysis/pure), nursing, philosophy, political science, professional writing, psychology, theater, theology

Business Administration (concentrations in accounting, computer information systems, finance and economics, international business, management, marketing)

Education Early childhood, elementary, secondary

Pre-Professional Dentistry, engineering, law, medicine, occupational therapy, optometry, physical therapy, veterinary medicine

Accredited Programs Business, nursing

Special Programs Springhill offers a five-year BS/MBA Degree. The college offers a dual degree program in engineering with Auburn, University of Alabama, University of Florida, and Marquette University. There is a six-year cooperative program in physical/occupational therapy with Rockhurst University in Missouri. There are study abroad opportunities, a Washington, D.C., semester, and internships. The college also offers a leadership development program. There are Air Force and Army ROTC programs.

Facilities There are 32 buildings, many of them designated historic monuments, including the Administration Building and Solidarity Chapel. Yenni Hall, which houses the Division of Business and Management, was recently renovated and the Campus Center expanded. There are also the new Mitchell Theater and Outlaw Recreation

Center, new suite-based apartments, and the recently renovated Communication Arts and Physics Building. There are a radio station, the Eichold Art Gallery, and an 18-hole golf course.

Transition to College Program Student Academic Services offers both individual meetings with freshmen and a study skills course. There is also a seminar for transfer students.

Athletics NAIA, Gulf Coast Athletic Conference

Men: Baseball, basketball, cross-country, golf, soccer, swimming, tennis

Women: Basketball, cross-country, golf, soccer, softball, swimming, tennis, volleyball

Student Life and Housing About 800 students can be accommodated in college housing, which is guaranteed for all four years. Fifty-one percent of the students are from Alabama, the remainder from 33 other states and 10 countries. Ethnicity: Caucasian—76 percent; African-American—14 percent; Hispanic-American—4 percent. There are three local and two national fraternities and four national sororities. All students may keep cars.

Accommodations for Students with Disabilities The Coordinator of Academic Support Services is responsible for services for students with documented and self-disclosed disabilities.

Financial Aid About 90 percent of all freshmen receive aid. The average freshman award was about $15,500.

Requirements for Admission SAT I or ACT scores with a college prep high school program. Students are encouraged to visit the campus.

Application Freshmen are admitted fall, spring, and summer semesters. Applications should be submitted by July 1 for fall admission and December 15 for spring admission. Admission decisions are made on a rolling basis.

International Students In addition to meeting the requirements for freshmen or transfer admis-

sion, a minimum TOEFL score of 500 paper or 173 computer-based is required, or 82 on the Michigan Test. Students with lower scores may be admitted provisionally, taking courses in the Intensive English Language Institute until proficiency is achieved.

Transfer Students Students must submit official transcripts from each high school and college attended, official SAT I or ACT scores if the applicant has completed fewer than 20 credits, an evaluation of achievement and potential from the Registrar or Dean of Students from the last college attended, have a minimum of a 2.5 GPA, and must be in good academic standing at the last institution attended. Only grades of C or above are considered for transfer. A maximum of 64 credits may be transferred from two-year accredited institutions. A minimum of 24 of the last 30 credits must be taken at Spring Hill, along with 50 percent of the course work in the major.

Admission Contact
Office of Admissions
Spring Hill College
400 Dauphin Street
Mobile, AL 36608-1791
Phone: (800) 742-6704; (251) 380-3030
FAX: (251) 460-2186
E-mail: *admit@shc.edu*
Web: *www.shc.edu*

The Heart of the College In a spectacular setting, offering students a large metropolitan area as well as beaches a short distance away, the heart of the college is a reflection of the Jesuit tradition of Catholic higher education: a focus on educational excellence along with personal care, or, as the Jesuits are fond of calling it, "cura personalis"—a care for the spiritual, social, and intellectual growth of each student.

Considered one of the top institutions in the South and also a "best buy," the core curriculum, based in the liberal arts and sciences, sets Spring Hill apart from other colleges. This core comprises 54–60 credits and 18–20 courses, accounting for almost half of the graduation requirements. With courses spanning philosophy to computer science to fine arts, and with every student taking the core, students are able to interact with students from every major on campus, making for more interesting classes and bringing students together. And with a full-time faculty that includes 11 Jesuits, the professors are both demanding and supportive. The academic program and campus location within a large metropolitan area encourage 40 percent of the students to engage in internships.

The Jesuit mission "to educate students to become responsible leaders in service to others" is seen most abundantly in the many students who use Foley Community Service Center to locate volunteer service opportunities. Spring Hill students devote more than 10,000 hours to tutoring children in 10 inner-city middle schools in Mobile, organize and implement programs for mentally and emotionally challenged children, assist abused women and their children at a local shelter, or work with seniors in adult day health programs. The center also offers a limited number of scholarships in recognition of the impor-

tance of this work. As one student commented: "Service is at the very core of our human experience." The spiritual lives of students are also nourished by liturgies offered twice daily and three different levels of retreats.

The outcomes are very good, with 76 percent of graduates landing jobs shortly after graduation and 29 percent going on to graduate or professional schools. Also, since 1999, 100 percent of the nursing graduates are employed within three months of graduation. Spring Hill attributes this success especially to the liberal arts core, which creates flexible, adaptable, entrepreneurial, and well-rounded graduates, as well as to the Four-Year Career Success Plan implemented by both Career and Student Academic Services.

With more than 50 clubs, 65 percent of the students engaged in either varsity or intramural athletics, a free golf course right on campus, great weather, nearby beaches, the original Mardi Gras, and Mobile—an All-American City award winner—students have much to do and know how to have a good time.

STETSON UNIVERSITY   DeLand, Florida

Total Undergraduate Enrollment: 2,142
Men: 900 Women: 1,242
Five-Year Graduation Rate: 60%

Tuition: $$$
Room and Board: $$
Residential Students: 80%

History Stetson is Florida's first private university, founded in 1883 by Henry DeLand, a New York philanthropist, and named after its major benefactor, John Stetson, the hat manufacturer. Stetson University has always emphasized the importance of spiritual life and the quest for truth as part of its educational mission. Stetson has a historical relationship with the Christian community and the Baptist denominations, which shaped an inclusive institution comprised of students from diverse religious, ethnic, and cultural backgrounds.

Location Located in DeLand, Florida, 25 miles southwest from Daytona Beach and 35 miles from Orlando. The 170-acre campus of palm, oak, and pine trees, winding walkways, and fountains is listed on the National Register of Historic Places. Stetson's turn-of-the-century buildings have been modernized and updated, with a $9.5 million construction and renovation program recently completed. The College of Law is located in St. Petersburg.

Top Programs of Study Business administration, psychology, marketing

Arts and Sciences American studies, aquatic and marine biology, art studio, biochemistry, biology, communication studies, computer information systems, computer science, digital arts (art, music, computer science), economics, English, environmental science, French, geography, German, history, humanities, international studies, Latin American studies, mathematics, medical technology, music performance (orchestral instrument, piano/organ, voice, guitar), music theory and composition, philosophy, physics, political science, psychology, religious studies, Russian studies, social science, sociology, Spanish, sport and exercise science, theater arts

Business Accounting (public and private), computer information systems, economics, finance, international business, management, marketing, general business administration

Education Elementary, elementary/varying exceptionalities, music, secondary

Pre-Professional None

Accredited Programs Accounting, allied health, business, chemistry, education, law, music

Special Programs The digital arts program is the first one in the South. The aquatic and marine biology major has a focus on freshwater ecology. The University Values Council helps to lead faculty, students, and administrators in a conversation about values and commitment to action in key areas. Stetson is home to the first college-level Model Senate Program. Stetson also has an extensive internship program, including the Orlando Magic, CNN, Walt Disney World, PricewaterhouseCoopers, and overseas opportunities. The business courses provide much experience in making presentations, and the program includes the opportunity to study a foreign language. Stetson offers guaranteed admissions to Stetson's College of Law.

Facilities There are 62 buildings. Students studying environmental science or geology use Stetson's Gillespie Museum of Minerals, home to the South's most extensive mineral collection. The Pope and Margaret Duncan Art Gallery offer artwork from around the world. The Hollis Center has a student lounge, fitness/exercise room,

dance studio, NCAA-size basketball court, and swimming pool. The Mendy Stoll Tennis Center has six courts, with six more planned. The Wilson Athletic Center has an exercise physiology lab and sports medicine facility for students majoring in sports and exercise science.

Transition to College Program Stetson offers a six-week Early Start Program, open to all newly admitted first-year students, in which students can enroll in up to three summer courses before the beginning of the fall semester. It is especially recommended for students who want to strengthen their basic skills.

Stetson also offers the University Experience Program, which eases the first-year student into full university life. The courses are offered in the fall semester, earn college credit, and are taught by faculty and student mentors. For example, the Business School offers "How to Succeed in the Business School," and includes discussion of time management, study skills, and familiarity with campus offerings.

Students who have not declared a major are welcomed into the Discovery Program, which provides faculty advisers, a newsletter, and class visitations, all in an effort to help the student select a program of study.

Athletics NCAA Division I, Trans American Athletic Conference

Men: Baseball, basketball, crew, cross-country, golf, soccer, tennis

Women: Basketball, crew, cross-country, golf, soccer, softball, tennis, volleyball

Student Life and Housing About 1,500 students can be accommodated in campus housing, which is guaranteed for all four years. Seventy-four percent of students are from Florida, with the remainder from 43 other states and 48 countries. Ethnicity: Caucasian—82 percent; African-American—4 percent; Hispanic-American—5 percent; Asian—2 percent; International—7 percent. There are six sororities and seven fraternities. All students may keep cars.

Accommodations for Students with Disabilities Students who self-identify and provide appropriate documentation verifying a disability receive services.

Financial Aid About 96 percent of all freshmen receive aid. The average freshman award was about $19,000.

Requirements for Admission SAT I or ACT scores and a college prep high school program. Music students must satisfactorily complete an audition.

Application Applications should be submitted early in the fall semester of the senior year. Deadlines: fall—March 15; spring—January 1; summer—May 1. Transfer students should use the same dates.

International Students Students must meet regular admission requirements and demonstrate proficiency in English by scoring no less than 550 on the paper-based or 213 on the computer-based TOEFL.

Transfer Students Students must have completed a semester of academic work in good standing at an accredited college with a minimum GPA of 2.0. A 2.6 GPA and an interview are recommended. Of 120 credits, 45 must be completed at Stetson.

Admission Contact

Office of Admissions
Stetson University
421 N. Woodland Blvd.
Unit 8378
DeLand, FL 32720-3771
Phone: (800) 688-0101; (386) 822-7100
FAX: (386) 822-7112
E-mail: *admission@Stetson.edu*
Web: *www.Stetson.edu/admission*

The Heart of the University Stetson students love the vibrant quality of the college. Over 90 percent of the students are involved in campus activities. With more than 100 clubs, scholastic and honor societies, national sororities and fraternities, cultural events, and NCAA Division I sports events, the campus is jumping.

Stetson is also a college that appeals to student leaders—those who are and those who would like to be. There are many planned opportunities for developing leadership skills through courses, community involvement programs, and symposia with civic leaders.

The college enjoys its position as Florida's first private university and works hard to portray an image of also being Florida's premier university. Students are attracted to Stetson's continued emphasis on excellence in terms of its faculty, programs, emphasis on teaching, and class sizes, which are designed to engage the student. Students enjoy the highly interactive climate of the classrooms and the personal attention given by faculty. Stetson takes pride in pointing out that its graduates include senators, presidents of corporations, government officials, doctors, lawyers, and performing artists.

Students interested in music enjoy the luxury of a conservatory-quality education, with a six-to-one student-to-faculty ratio and opportunities to perform in high-quality orchestras, bands, choirs, and in fully staged operas and musical productions. And the program is for undergraduates only!

The heart of Stetson also involves a focus on values that will provide its students with a moral compass. The dignity, worth, and equality of all persons is emphasized, as well as the importance of community and social responsibility. Students at Stetson see these values in action on a daily basis and find these to be a meaningful part of their personal development. This focus on values has allowed the Institute for Christian Ethics to invite to campus such distinguished guests as Desmond Tutu of South Africa, former President Jimmy Carter, Nobel Peace Laureate Elie Weisel, and scientist Jane Goodall.

Stetson is also a racially and ethnically diverse community, with 18 percent of its students either non-Caucasian or international. The Stetson student sees this student body composition as a real plus, understanding that various cultural perspectives and traditions are a valuable part of their college education.

SUSQUEHANNA UNIVERSITY

Selinsgrove, Pennsylvania

Total Undergraduate Enrollment: 1,900
Men: 817 Women: 1,083
Five-Year Graduation Rate: 76%

Tuition: $$$$
Room and Board: $$
Residential Students: 80%

History Susquehanna University was founded in 1858 as the Missionary Institute of the Evangelical Lutheran Church. The school merged with Susquehanna Female College in 1873. In 1895 the school became a university.

Location The 210-acre campus is located in the small town of Selinsgrove, Pennsylvania, 50 miles north of Harrisburg, the state capital, three hours from Philadelphia, Washington, D.C., and New York City.

Top Programs of Study Business, communications, biology

Arts and Sciences Art, art history, biochemistry, biology, chemistry, communications/theater arts (concentrations in broadcasting, communication studies, corporate communications, journalism, mass communications, musical theater, public relations, speech communication, theater arts), computer science, economics, English, French, geological and environmental study, German, history, international studies, mathematics, music, philosophy, physics, political science, psychology, religion, sociology, Spanish, writing

Business Accounting, administration (concentrations in finance, global management, human resource management, marketing), information systems

Education Early childhood, elementary, secondary

Pre-Professional Dentistry, law, medicine, ministry, veterinary medicine

Accredited Programs Business, chemistry, education, music

Special Programs There are several interesting minors, including Film Studies, International Business and Foreign Language, Jewish Studies, and Music Technology. The university offers several cooperative degree programs: allied health with Thomas Jefferson University in Philadelphia; dentistry with Temple University School of Medicine; engineering with Penn State; and forestry and environmental management with Duke. There are dual majors and self-designed majors. The university also offers a United Nations semester and a Washington, D.C., semester, as well as internships in a Philadelphia Center and a Washington, D.C., Center. An accelerated degree option allows students to graduate in three years. The Adams Center for Law and Society focuses on the impact of the law on people and institutions. There is an Army ROTC program.

Facilities There are 52 buildings, mostly of Georgian architecture, spanning more than 140 years. Selinsgrove Hall, an administration building, is listed on the National Register of Historic Places, as is Siebert Hall, a multipurpose building. Renovations and expansion have taken place in Fisher Science Hall, which contains a greenhouse, an environmental chamber, and a nuclear magnetic resonance spectrometer, and Heilman Hall, home of the music and art programs. Affelbaum Hall is a high-tech center, with the renovated art studio providing studio space and a campus center housing the radio station, theater, and art gallery. The auditorium features a revolving stage, the new Sports and Fitness Complex, and the new Lombardo football and track stadium. The university also owns a 600-acre ecology laboratory. There are also TV studios and a child development center.

Transition to College Program Students are offered a series of presentations and activities to assist them in the development of personal habits that encourage physical, emotional, and intellectual well-being. Topics include study skills, stress management, substance abuse, nutrition, interpersonal communication, and appreciation of individual differences.

Athletics NCAA III, Middle Atlantic Conference

Men: Baseball, basketball, cross-country, football, golf, indoor track, lacrosse, soccer, swimming, tennis, track

Women: Basketball, cross-country, field hockey, indoor track, golf, lacrosse, soccer, softball, swimming, tennis, track, volleyball

Student Life and Housing About 1,500 students can be accommodated in college housing, which is guaranteed for all four years. Sixty percent of the students are from Pennsylvania, the remainder are from 28 other states and 15 countries. Ethnicity: Caucasian—92 percent. There are four national fraternities and four national sororities. All students may keep cars.

Accommodations for Students with Disabilities The university provides reasonable accommodations for students with disabilities documented by a medical professional within the last three years. The Director of Counseling serves as coordinator of such services, and students should meet with the Director as soon as possible to arrange for services.

Financial Aid About 58 percent of freshmen receive aid. The average freshman award was about $17,500.

Requirements for Admission Students who rank in the top fifth of their graduating classes in strong college prep high school programs have the option of submitting two graded writing samples in place of SAT I or ACT scores. A personal visit and interview are strongly recommended. Results of one or more SAT II exams, including English Composition are required.

Music applicants must audition, and writing students must submit a portfolio of their writing.

Application Freshmen are admitted to fall and spring semesters. The Early Decision deadline is December 15, with admission decision by January 15. Check with admissions office regarding regular application deadline.

International Students Required are three letters of recommendation, secondary course lists and examination results, a TOEFL score if English is not the student's native language, and the certificate of financial support. The SAT I is required of native English speakers, and SAT II Subject Test Scores are highly desirable.

Transfer Students July 1 is the deadline for fall admission, and December 1 for spring admission. Required are official transcripts of high school and, if applicable, college work, standardized test scores, a Dean's Transfer Evaluation Form completed by the Dean of the previous college, and an on-campus interview. Courses taken at regionally accredited institutions with a minimum grade of C− are considered for transfer. Associate's degree students will have their courses evaluated by the transfer coordinator to determine the number of credits to be transferred. Susquehanna has a formal dual admission agreement with Harrisburg Area Community College and articulation agreements with several community colleges.

Admission Contact
Office of Admissions
Susquehanna University
514 University Avenue
Selinsgrove, PA 17870-1040
Phone: (800) 326-9672; (570) 372-4260
FAX: (570) 372-2722
E-mail: *suadmiss@susqu.edu*
Web: *www.susqu.edu/admissions*

The Heart of the University Some college locations are not incredibly beautiful, exciting, or near metropolitan centers, and, as a result, colleges in these locations focus their attention on designing a beautiful campus, attractive buildings, state-of-the-art facilities, and wonderful academic and social programs. Susquehanna is one of these gems. Students are especially impressed with the flexibility provided to study double majors, self-designed majors, 48 minors, independent study, study abroad (taken by about 30 percent of the students), cooperative degree programs with major universities for Engineering, Environmental Management, and other majors, and an accelerated degree program. Colleges and small universities are supposed to be student-centered in their flexibility—but Susquehanna excels at this.

What is equally impressive is the highly qualified and talented faculty, who seem to be everywhere, establishing close relationships with students, making themselves accessible and easy to be with in so many different capacities: coaching the swim team; dining in the student cafeteria; leading a student research team; coaching the placekickers on the football team; leading a service learning trip to Appalachia or Central America.

With over 100 student organizations, students have plenty of fun and opportunities to assume leadership roles. Most impressive are the special service groups, students who share volunteer interests and live together in small Project House groups. Recognized for outstanding service by the White House, Project members have contributed the equivalent of 174 years of work since 1976! Overall, more than two-thirds of the students participate in volunteer service.

The Focus Program is another interesting one. Primarily intended for first- and second-year students, the intent is to broaden students' global perspectives early enough in their college years to have an impact on future study and career paths. Each program begins with an inter-disciplinary group of courses addressing issues central to a foreign country or region. Students then visit the country with Susquehanna faculty for a two-week cultural immersion during winter, spring, or summer break. Students, for example, have traveled to Australia and visited Sydney, the Great Barrier Reef, aboriginal sacred sites, and the Australian rain forest.

The programs in art, writing, and music help to create a rich cultural environment on campus. Team and independent research characterize the natural and social sciences, while the business program is nationally accredited and develops skills to thrive in a global economy with rapidly evolving technology. The core curriculum, required of all students, focuses on personal development, intellectual skills, writing and research, world populations, and the contemporary world.

It's not surprising that Susquehanna's graduates land jobs with impressive companies and organizations, and that 25 percent move on to graduate and professional schools.

TEXAS CHRISTIAN UNIVERSITY   **Fort Worth, Texas**

Total Undergraduate Enrollment: 6,400
Men: 2,460 Women: 3,940
Five-Year Graduation Rate: 65%

Tuition: $$$
Room and Board: $
Residential Students: 50%

History Texas Christian University was founded in 1873 and is affiliated with the Christian Church (Disciples of Christ). Progressive from its origins, the university was the first institution in the Southwest to educate both men and women.

Location The 300-acre campus is located in a suburban area in a residential section of Forth Worth, Texas, 45 minutes west of Dallas.

Top Programs of Study Business, biology, communications

Arts and Sciences Advertising/public relations, allied health professions (athletic training, pre-occupational therapy, pre-physician's assistant, pre-physical therapy), anthropology, art, astronomy, ballet, ballet and modern dance, biochemistry, biology, broadcast journalism, chemistry, computer information science, criminal justice, dietetics, economics, engineering (electrical, mechanical), English, environmental earth resources, environmental sciences, fashion merchandising, food management, French, general studies, geology, graphic design, habilitation of the deaf, health and fitness, history, interior design, international communications, international economics, international relations, journalism, kinesiology, Latin-American studies, liberal studies, mathematics, modern dance, movement science, music, neuroscience, nursing, nutrition, philosophy, physical education, physics, political science, psychology, radio–TV–film, religion, social work, sociology, Spanish, speech communication, speech-language pathology, theater, theater and television

Business Accounting, electronic business, entrepreneurial management, finance, finance/real estate, marketing

Education Art, early childhood, exceptional children, middle, secondary

Pre-Professional Dentistry, law, medicine, optometry, veterinary medicine

Accredited Programs Allied health education professions, business, dietetics and nutrition, engineering, journalism, music, social work, speech-language pathology

Special Programs Several business programs are available with an international emphasis. Students publish an award-winning newspaper and magazine. A certificate program is offered in ranch management. There are opportunities for study abroad, internships, service, and practicums. There are several doctoral programs offered at the graduate level. There are Air Force and Army ROTC programs.

Facilities There are 92 buildings, a blend of traditional and modern, including the Neely School of Business, which houses a "trading room"; the Walsh Center for the Performing Arts; a first-class library; two concert halls; a radio station; two television stations; an art gallery; a geological center for remote sensing; a nuclear magnetic resonance facility; a state-of-the-art electrical engineering lab; and an observatory. There is also a small lake on the campus.

Transition to College Program First-year students study Freshman Seminars, which are small classes taught by some of the university's best professors.

Athletics NCAA I-A, Western Athletic Conference

Men: Baseball, basketball, football, golf, soccer, swimming, tennis, track & field

Women: Basketball, cross-country, golf, riflery, soccer, tennis, track & field, swimming, volleyball

Student Life and Housing About 3,300 students can be accommodated in college housing, which is guaranteed for all four years. Seventy-three percent of the students are from Texas, the remainder are from every state and 76 countries. Ethnicity: Caucasian—78 percent; Hispanic-American—6 percent; International—4 percent; African-American—4 percent; Asian-American—2 percent. There are 1 local and 12 national fraternities and 3 local and 13 national sororities. All students may keep cars.

Accommodations for Students with Disabilities In compliance with section 504

Financial Aid About 70 percent of all freshmen receive aid.

Requirements for Admission SAT I & ACT scores and a college prep high school program.

Application The Early Notification deadline is November 15, with an admission decision made by January 1. Freshmen are admitted to all semesters. The fall application deadline is February 15.

International Students Students who do not have English as their primary language must take the TOEFL and score a minimum of 550. Students should also take the SAT I or ACT.

Transfer Students Required are official transcripts from high school and from each college attended, good academic standing, and submission of SAT I scores or ACT scores. If students have more than 24 transferable credits, the high school transcript and test scores are not required. Application deadlines are July 15 for the fall semester, December 15 for the spring semester, and May 1 for the summer.

Admission Contact

Office of Admissions
Texas Christian University
Box 297013
Fort Worth, TX 76129
Phone: (800) 828-3764; (817) 257-7490
FAX: (817) 257-7268
E-mail: *frogmail@tcu.edu*
Web: *www.tcu.edu*

The Heart of the University Although Texas Christian University is one of the largest schools in this guide, it is one of the friendliest of all. One upperclassman, recalling how nicely she was treated by upperclassmen when she was a freshman, commented: "I felt so welcomed!" With about 75 percent of the students from Texas, perhaps that friendly quality can be ascribed to that famous Southwestern hospitality. But make no mistake about it, "deep in the heart of Texas" is a university with a big heart and a friendliness and cooperation that permeate not only the whole campus but also its environs. Located in the city of Forth Worth, home of very fine museums, numerous other cultural and recreational opportunities, as well as American Airlines, Radio Shack, Pier One, and other large corporations, one student's comment is right on target: "It's not too big to be friendly."

Certainly the friendliness finds many avenues of expression as a result of the 200 clubs and organizations at TCU, ranging from the Horned Frog Marching Band to the Independent Film Society to the International Student Association. Also, with 25 Greek organizations, fraternities and sororities are another popular avenue of that expression of friendliness, but at TCU there is so much more to do that Greek life does not dominate the campus social scene. Of course, the athletic program is another vehicle for students to get together, and in the Southwest the TCU football team has a great history, with great fan support for this sport and the many others. Importantly, although TCU has a Christian affiliation, it is not an evangelical institution and religion is not a major factor on campus. In fact, the many religious clubs, from the Campus Crusade for Christ to Hillel (a Jewish association), function more to bring students together with common interests. A major common interest for about 25 percent of the students is travel abroad, and TCU has one of the truly outstanding study abroad programs in America.

The Neely School of Business is gaining a national reputation for its program in entrepreneurship. Its students welcome the global perspective of its programs and the internship opportunities provided by a location in one of the top business communities in America. Both of these factors are viewed as being instrumental to employment opportunities. The School of Communications, with programs in radio, TV, film, and journalism, offers students immediate hands-on experience at two fully operational TV studios, a radio station, and a daily newspaper. The College of Fine Arts is the first college in America to offer a degree in ballet. All of the programs enjoy excellent facilities, international visiting faculty, guest artists and performers, opportunities for students to perform internationally, and a close working relationship with visual and performing arts institutions in Fort Worth.

The faculty is proud of the rigorous—and in many cases—entertaining courses they offer in small interactive classes, using a variety of teaching styles. This is a faculty that, while fitting a teacher–scholar model, enjoys interaction with students, invites students to collaborate in research, and is caring and supportive, giving personal attention to students. Students respond well, with admiration and respect for their professors.

Blessed with a large endowment, TCU is able to provide all this at a moderate tuition, with many considering it to be a "best buy" institution.

TEXAS LUTHERAN UNIVERSITY

Seguin, Texas

Total Undergraduate Enrollment: 1,300
Men: 600 Women: 700
Five-Year Graduation Rate: 50%

Tuition: $$
Room and Board: $
Residential Students: 70%

History Texas Lutheran University was founded in Brenham, Texas, and is affiliated with the Evangelical Church of America. The university moved to Seguin in 1912.

Location The 196-acre campus is located in Seguin, Texas (population 23,000), 37 miles east of San Antonio and 450 miles south of Austin.

Top Programs of Study Business, education, biology

Arts and Sciences Applied science, art, biology, chemistry, communication studies, computer science, economics, English, history, international studies, kinesiology (coaching, exercise science, sport and fitness management), mathematics, music, philosophy, physics, political science, psychology, public history, social work, sociology (including criminal justice). Spanish studies, theater, theology (pre-seminary, youth ministry)

Business Accounting, administration (specializations in accounting, economics, finance, international business, management, marketing), management information systems

Education Elementary, physical education, secondary

Pre-Professional Dentistry, law, medicine, ministry, nursing, occupation therapy, pharmacy, physical therapy, veterinary medicine

Accredited Programs Business, social work

Special Programs There are a Mexican-American Studies Center, an International Student Exchange Program, and a Washington, D.C., semester. Several minors are offered. The Krost Life Enrichment Program seeks to promote a whole person approach to life and focuses on fitness and wellness. There are Air Force and Army ROTC.

Facilities There are 36 buildings, including the new Rinn Field House and state-of-the-art Grossman Fitness Center; the Blumberg Memorial Library; the Schueck Fine Arts Center; the Moody Science Building, which provides student research space; and the Jackson Auditorium, which seats 1,100 for student productions, major lectures, and the Mid-Texas Symphony.

Transition to College Program The university offers a traditional orientation program.

Athletics NCAA III, American Southwest Conference

  Men: Baseball, Basketball, football, golf, soccer, tennis

  Women: Basketball, cross-country, golf, soccer, softball, tennis, track, volleyball

Student Life and Housing About 1,000 students can be accommodated in college housing.

Ninety-two percent of the students are from Texas, the remainder are from 25 other states and 17 countries. Ethnicity: Caucasian—72 percent; Hispanic-American—17 percent; African-American—6 percent; Asian-American—2 percent. There are four local fraternities and four local sororities. All students may keep cars.

Accommodations for Students with Disabilities Students with recently documented disabilities should request reasonable accommodations through the Coordinator of the Office of the Americans with Disabilities Act, located in Alumni Student Center.

Financial Aid About 97 percent of all freshmen receive aid. The average freshman award was about $10,500.

Requirements for Admission SAT I or ACT scores with a college prep high school program.

Application Freshmen are admitted to all semesters. Applications should be filed by August 1 for fall admission, December 1 for spring admission, and May 1 for summer admission. Admission decisions are sent on a rolling basis.

International Students Required is a minimum TOEFL score of 550, or other sufficient documentation; official transcripts of all secondary and, if applicable, postsecondary work with English translation; and proof of financial solvency.

Transfer Students Students need to be in good standing at their previous colleges, submit official high school and college transcripts, and have a 2.25 GPA. Applicants with fewer than 15 credits will be evaluated under the requirements for regular freshman students.

Admission Contact
Office of Admissions
Texas Lutheran University
1000 West Court Street
Seguin, TX 78155-5999
Phone: (800) 771-8521; (830) 372-8050
FAX: (830) 372-8096
E-mail: *admission@tlu.edu*
Web: *www.tlu.edu*

The Heart of the University Considered one of the top liberal arts universities in the Southwest and a "best buy," Texas Lutheran gives students and their families extra value for their tuition dollars. Although students do not study a core curriculum, they are offered a strong liberal arts program, with nationally accredited programs in business and social work, and an excellent education program, in which faculty who were classroom teachers have designed a strong field-based program. Student research and important corporate-sponsored collaborative research with professors is commonplace, as well as exhibitions of student art work, field trips, and visiting artists and speakers such as Morris Dees, Co-Founder of the Southern Poverty Law Center; Robert McTeer, President of the Dallas Federal Reserve Bank; and artist Amy Freeman Lee.

Academics aside, the heart of the community is the student. This is a campus where the administrators and faculty actually help students move in! Here is a friendly community where there is a willingness on the part of every member to help. There's also an openness to new people and ideas that is so refreshing to faculty and students alike. One students says: "There really isn't just one type of person. Each is an individual—different, but at the same time alike in having a frame of mind of being accepted and open to everyone's ideas."

Texas Lutheran is also a place where faith is important. The university encourages each student to explore his or her deeper spirituality within a very open spiritual community. A faculty member comments: "So the sacred space here is everyone's space." Many of the students who come to campus are students who performed volunteer work in high school. At Texas Lutheran students are impressed with the university's mantra: "Discover something you're passionate about and use it to make the world a better place." Students do this through both student organizations that have a community service component and through the many Campus Ministry programs.

Students have meaningful and successful internship opportunities. One of the reasons is that course work emphasizes teamwork and collaboration and the second is that many of the professors have real-world experience. The result is that business students intern at Fortune 500 companies and science students intern in areas specific to their career goals.

The university takes great pride in the diversity of its student population and its International Program, where the study abroad opportunities are virtually limitless, both for students visiting foreign countries and for international students

studying at Texas Lutheran. Students remark about the significance of each in terms of their overall education.

But for the students, the heart of this close-knit community is created by caring, supportive faculty, who have students over for dinner, encourage students to travel abroad, take time to make phone calls for internship opportunities, and involve students in research and other aspects of their professional lives. These are quality mentors.

Nearby, the students have the vibrant, safe college town of Seguin, on the banks of the Guadalupe River. Only 35 minutes away is San Antonio, the eighth largest city in the United States, providing many cultural and recreational opportunities for students

UNIVERSITY OF INDIANAPOLIS

Indianapolis, Indiana

Total Undergraduate Enrollment: 2,858
Men: 958 Women: 1,900
Five-Year Graduation Rate: 58%

Tuition: $$$
Room and Board: $
Residential Students: 52%

History The University of Indianapolis was founded in 1902 by the members of the Church of the United Brethren in Christ. At first, the university was called Indiana Central University and had three divisions: the academy, which offered high school courses; the normal school, which provided a two-year program of teacher education; and the liberal arts college. After the first two divisions were phased out and additional professional programs were added the name was changed to the University of Indianapolis.

Location The 60-acre campus is located in a suburban area on the south side of Indianapolis, Indiana.

Top Programs of Study Business, education, nursing

Arts and Sciences Anthropology, archaelogy, art, art therapy, biology, biology/cell and molecular, chem-

istry, communication (concentrations include journalism, public relations, sport information), computer science, corrections, earth-space science, engineering (electrical and mechanical), English, environmental science, French, German, history, human biology, international relations, law enforcement, mathematics, medical technology, music, music performance, philosophy, physical education/sport administration, physics, political science, psychology, religion, social work, sociology, Spanish, studio art, theater, visual communication design

Business Accounting, administration, economics and finance, financial services, information systems, international business, management (concentrations in human resource management, production and operations management)

Education Athletic training, business, elementary, middle, physical education/exercise science, musical, secondary, visual arts, theater

Pre-Professional Dentistry, law, medical, occupational therapy, physical therapy, psychology, social work

Accredited Programs Business, education, music, nursing, occupational therapy, physical therapy, psychology, social work

Special Programs Associate's degree programs are offered in several areas, including corrections, nursing, pre-physical therapist assistant, and liberal arts. There are special internship opportunities in Washington, D.C. The university has a dual degree program in electrical and mechanical engineering with Purdue University. There is a program in medical technology in conjunction with Methodist Hospital and St. Francis Hospital and Health Clinics in Indianapolis. There is also a Create Your Own Major Program. The Lantz Center for Christian Vocations was established to help promote the integration of Christian spiritual formation into the curriculum. There are internships and study abroad programs, including "Odyssey in Athens," at a branch campus in Greece, as well as student exchange opportunities with several Asian institutions. Students may take courses at colleges that are part of a Consortium for Urban Education.

Facilities There are 13 buildings, including the Krannert Memorial Library, which houses the communications department and its state-of-the-art radio and television studios. Ransburg Auditorium features concerts and theater productions; the new Martin Hall houses programs in nursing, physical therapy, occupational therapy; the Lilly Science Hall has modernized science labs, an art gallery, and a planetarium.

Transition to College Program There are several First-Year programs designed to orient and connect first-year students to the university, including the New Student Experience and College Prep Workshop.

Athletics NCAA II, Great Lakes Valley Conference, Great Lakes Intercollegiate Athletic Conference

Men: Baseball, basketball, cross-country, football, golf, soccer, swimming, tennis, track & field

Women: Basketball, cross-country, golf, soccer, softball, swimming, tennis, track & field, volleyball

Student Life and Housing About 1,200 students can be accommodated in college housing, which is guaranteed for all four years. Eighty-five percent of the students are from Indiana, the remainder are from 17 other states and 61 countries. Ethnicity: Caucasian—79 percent; African-American—8 percent; International—6 percent. There are no fraternities or sororities. All students may keep cars.

Accommodations for Students with Disabilities The university provides a Structured Program. Students should contact the Vice President for Students Affairs to establish their needs and request accommodations.

Financial Aid About 82 percent of all freshmen receive aid. The average freshman award was about $13,000.

Requirements for Admission SAT I or ACT scores and a college prep high school program.

Application Freshmen are admitted to all semesters. Application deadlines are open, with an admission decision sent on a rolling basis.

International Students Students should typically meet the same requirements for admission as other students, with strong emphasis placed on the strength of the secondary school and, if applicable, college record. The SAT/ACT requirement may be waived for students who hold the General Certificate of Education, University of Cambridge Higher Education Certificate, or a comparable school certificate, and who have passed at least five or six examinations (one must be in English) at the "O" level and two at the "A" level. Typically a TOEFL minimum score of 500 is required, but may be waived for students who have substantial course work in English-speaking schools or universities, or for those students who have satisfactorily completed ESL programs. A statement of financial support is required.

Transfer Students Required are official high school and college transcripts, a C average in previous college work, and ACT or SAT scores, which are waived if the applicant has completed a minimum of 20 credits with a C average. Students who do not meet the grade requirement may be admitted on a conditional basis.

Admission Contact

Office of Admissions
University of Indianapolis
1400 East Hanna Avenue
Indianapolis, IN 46227-3697
Phone: (800) 232-8634; (317) 788-3216
FAX: (317) 788-3300
E-mail: *admissions@uindy.edu*
Web: *www.uindy.edu*

The Heart of the University The heart of the University of Indianapolis is the great diversity of student population, including an international population drawn from 60 countries that comes together and grows within a community of care and concern for the individual. The linchpin of this success is an excellent faculty teaching in small classes, with most senior faculty teaching freshmen as well as seniors. Professors come to the classroom with accomplished academic backgrounds, real-world experience, and actively pursue their scholarship so that students receive a cutting-edge education. Faculty members know their students personally, take time to chat with students, and provide help and support.

Although a comprehensive university, with many nationally accredited professional programs, the University of Indianapolis offers an excellent general education core grounded in the liberal arts and has an integrative approach showing the connections among several disciplines. The well-defined core is comprised of eight learning goals: critical thinking, historical consciousness, scientific method for the natural sciences, arts appreciation, cross-cultural understanding and global awareness, numerical liter-

acy, social inquiry, and values orientation and Judaic-Christian traditions.

To round out the students' academic experience, the university plans a significant lecture/performance series and students are required to attend a total of 10 events by the end of the junior year. Also, students are required to enroll in a three-week May term during either of their first two years. The May term consists of a course not offered during the regular semesters that has an interdisciplinary, creative, or innovative focus, with some involving national or international travel.

The Community Programs Center is designed to foster volunteer service among individual students as well as collaborative efforts between the university and the community. The center functions as a resource for students, faculty, and staff for locating interesting and diverse volunteer opportunities, service projects, funding sources, or information on service learning programs. Students may elect to have service hours documented on their transcripts, an indication of how the university views the significance of service as an integral part of an education.

The innovative Christian Vocations program offered by the Lantz Center provides faculty and staff who act as mentors and guides to students as they explore possible vocations of service, a program of Christian Exploration Courses, Christian Foundation Courses, and Service Learning Projects and Internships. The center also offers retreats, programs, and lectures.

A wonderful university–community service relationship is the Community Music Center, an extension of the Music Department housed in several Indianapolis schools. The program offers study and performance opportunities to people of all ages and stages of musical development. Numerous concerts and recitals are held at the university free of charge.

Graduates of the University of Indianapolis speak highly about the advantages offered by attending a university in a big city. These are not only advantages in terms of convenient field experiences, clinical opportunities, internships, and part-time work—all resources that provide an edge in the job market—but also the endless entertainment options, including clubs, the Indianapolis 500, professional sports, shopping, museums, theater, and much more. This adds to a vital campus activities program, including a strong athletic and intramural program, music ensembles, theater productions, and clubs and organizations.

UNIVERSITY OF MAINE AT FARMINGTON

Farmington, Maine

Total Undergraduate Enrollment: 2,395

Men: 792 Women: 1,603
Five-Year Graduation Rate: 50%

Tuition: In-state–$;
Out-of-state–$$
Room and Board: $
Residential Students: 40%

History The University of Maine at Farmington was established in 1863 as Maine's first public institution for higher education. Responding to the need for training better teachers, the university was founded as a teachers college in Farmington, which was connected by rail to the rest of Maine. Famous early graduates were the Stanley Brothers, inventors of the Stanley Steamer automobile, and John Stevens, engineer for the Panama Canal.

Location The 50-acre campus is in Farmington, Maine (population 7,500), a small town 38 miles northwest of Augusta, in the foothills of the mountains in western Maine.

Top Programs of Study Elementary education, psychology, interdisciplinary studies

Arts and Sciences Art, biology, community health education, computer science, creative writing, English, environmental planning and policy, environmental science, general studies, geography, geology/chemistry, geology/geography, history, individualized studies, international studies, mathematics, music/arts, philosophy/religion, political science/social science, psychology, rehabilitation services, sociology/anthropology, theater arts

Business Business/economics

Education Early childhood, early childhood special education, elementary, secondary, special education

Pre-Professional None

Accredited Programs Education

Special Programs Weekly forums showcase faculty research and creative work. The Visiting Writers Series hosts renowned writers who give public readings and visit classes in the Creative Writing Program. The university has four literary publications. There are interdisciplinary and individualized majors. There are several international study abroad opportunities. Twenty-one minors are offered, including Women's Studies and Nutrition. Certificate programs are offered in athletic coaching, exercise instruction, and ski industries. The campus is the home of Alice James Books, a respected poetry publisher. The university has its own nursery school. There are internships, practicums, and service learning opportunities.

Facilities There are 14 buildings, including the Mantor Library, a computer center, the Olsen Memorial Student Center, a new health and fitness center, a women's studies center, a student operated FM radio station, an art gallery, the Nordica Auditorium for musical performances, and a theater.

Transition to College Program The university offers a traditional orientation program.

Athletics NCAA, NAIA, Eastern College Athletic Conference, Maine Athletic Conference

Men: Baseball, basketball, cross-country, golf, soccer

Women: Basketball, cross-country, field hockey, soccer, softball, volleyball

Student Life and Housing About 900 students can be accommodated in college housing, which is guaranteed for all four years. Eighty-two percent of the students are from Maine, the remainder are from 32 other states and 17 countries. Ethnicity: Caucasian—95%. There are no fraternities or sororities. All students may keep cars.

Accommodations for Students with Disabilities To arrange for reasonable accommodations students need to contact the Coordinator of Academic Services for Students with Disabilities.

Financial Aid About 80 percent of all freshmen receive aid. The average freshman award was about $7,000.

Requirements for Admission A rank in the upper half of the graduating class of a college prep high school program. A campus visit and interview are recommended. While ACT and SAT scores are not required, students who wish to submit these are encouraged to do so.

Application Students are admitted to fall and spring semesters. Early Action applicants are notified in early January. Regular admission deadlines are open, with admission decisions made on a rolling basis.

International Students Required are official secondary and, if applicable, college transcripts with English translations, TOEFL scores if English is not the student's native language, and certification of finances.

Transfer Students Required are official high school and college transcripts with a minimum GPA of 2.0, and 2.5 for the School of Education, Health, and Rehabilitation. Course grades of C− or better that are taken outside of the University of Maine system are considered for transfer, while courses of D− or better taken within the system will be considered. Students must complete at least 30 credits at UMF, including 15 credits in their majors. There are transfer agreements with the University of Maine at Augusta and the Maine Technical Colleges. Applicants for Early Childhood Education and Elementary Education have February 1 as a fall admission deadline and October 1 for spring admission. Others should apply well before June 1 for fall and December 1 for spring admission.

Admission Contact
Office of Admissions
University of Maine at Farmington
246 Maine Street
Farmington, ME 04938-1994
Phone: (207) 778-7050
FAX: (207) 778-8182
E-mail: *umfadmit@maine.edu*
Web: *www.umf.maine.edu*

The Heart of the University The University of Maine at Farmington surprises people because of the small size of its student population and all the benefits of a true living–learning community that come with this size. Typically considered one of the best public liberal arts colleges in the Northeast, UMF's reputation attracted a growing number of applicants. Confronted with the dilemma of accepting significantly more students and thereby increasing the size of its student body, or keeping the student population a small one, thereby increasing the chances of retaining all those distinctive aspects that have garnered UMF a distinctive reputation—small classes, friendly atmosphere, faculty attention—the university decided to implement a flexible enrollment cap.

Historically a teachers college, UMF has about a third of its graduates pursuing teaching careers. What made UMF's programs distinctive—and still does—is the belief that a quality liberal arts background is integral for successful teaching. UMF's general education program provides freshmen with interdisciplinary courses in natural science, social science, health science, and English composition. Distribution requirements focus on developing breadth of knowledge in mathematics, fine arts, social science, natural science, and the humanities. And finally, students develop skills in presentation, writing, research, technology, and the ability to understand diverse cultures. Students then move on to their major areas of study, which involve two disciplines, such as Political Science/Social Science or Geology/Chemistry. Other students choose to create their own majors.

As with much of the atmosphere here, the faculty are informal and unpretentious, providing students with their first names and phone numbers. Professors enjoy being an active part of students' lives, sharing ideas, chatting, helping with an assignment. Faculty members also enjoy their students' work ethic and inquisitiveness, a combination that leads to student–faculty research projects.

The Farmington area is really into snow and the arts. Here you are near the world-class ski areas of Sugarbush and Sunday River. Snowboarders, hikers, and mountain bikers love the area. At the same time, the campus sits in the cultural center of the region, with an active local and campus community of poets, writers, artists, dancers, plays, concerts, book-signings, and art exhibits.

UNIVERSITY OF MINNESOTA AT MORRIS

Morris, Minnesota

Total Undergraduate Enrollment: 2,000

Men: 900 Women: 1,100
Five-Year Graduation Rate: 52%

Tuition: In-state–$;
Out-of-state–$$
Room and Board: $
Residential Students: 50%

History The University of Minnesota at Morris began as an American Indian boarding school operated for 22 years by the Sisters of Mercy and then by the federal government. In 1909 the campus was deeded by Congress to the State of Minnesota on the condition "that Indian pupils shall at all times be admitted to such school free of charge and on terms of equality with white pupils." In 1910 the West Central School of Agriculture offered a boarding school experience for rural youth under the auspices of the Univeristy of Minnesota. To meet changing educational needs, the school was phased out and, in 1960, the University of Minnesota at Morris was established as part of the state system of public higher education.

Location The 130-acre campus is located on a rolling prairie along the Pomme de Terre River adjacent to Morris, Minnesota (population 5,600), a small town 150 miles northwest of Minneapolis in west central Minnesota.

Top Programs of Study Biology, education, psychology

Arts and Sciences Anthropology, art history, biology, chemistry, computer science, economics, English, European studies, French, geology, German, history, Latin American area studies, liberal arts for the human services, mathematics, music, philosophy, physics, political science, psychology, social science, sociology, Spanish, speech communication, statistics, studio art, theater arts, women's studies

Business Management

Education Dance and theater arts, elementary, secondary, visual arts, vocal and instrumental music

Pre-Professional Dentistry, engineering, law, medicine, pharmacy, physical therapy, veterinary medicine

Accredited Programs Education

Special Programs The University of Minnesota has a consortium agreement, which allows students to attend another university within the consortium. The university is ranked among the most "computer-wired" schools in America. The Minority Student Program helps to meet the special concerns of ethnic minority students. The Commission on Women, Women's Resource Center, and Women of Color are organizations that promote the growth and development of women. There are two organizations that support gay, lesbian, bisexual, and transgender students. There is a Minority Mentorship Program. There are service learning, study abroad, and internship opportunities. A three-week May session is offered. Students can create their own interdisciplinary programs.

Facilities There are 36 buildings, a blend of modern and historic, which are situated around a pedestrian mall. The award-winning Humanities Fine Arts Center houses two theaters, a recital hall, a gallery, art studios, music rehearsal rooms, and two television studios. There are many other new and renovated facilities, including the Computing Services Center, the Student Center, a new science complex, and the new Regional Fitness Center.

Transition to College Program The university offers a traditional orientation program.

Athletics NCAA II, Northern Sun Intercollegiate Conference

   Men: Baseball, basketball, football, golf, tennis, indoor and outdoor track, wrestling

   Women: Basketball, cross-country, softball, golf, soccer, tennis, indoor and outdoor track, volleyball, wrestling

Student Life and Housing About 1,000 students can be accommodated in college housing. Sev-

enty-nine percent of the students are from Minnesota, the remainder are from 32 other states and 16 countries. Ethnicity: Caucasian—81 percent; Native-American—7 percent; African-American—5 percent; Asian-American—3 percent; Hispanic-American—2 percent. There are no fraternities or sororities. All students may keep cars.

Accommodations for Student with Disabilities The university offers a variety of accommodations and services through the Disability Services Office located in Briggs Library.

Financial Aid About 92 percent of all freshmen receive aid. The average freshman award was about $10,000.

Requirements for Admission SAT and ACT scores and a college prep high school program.

Application Freshmen are admitted to fall and spring semesters under three admission options: Early Decision applications should be filed by December 1, with admission decisions made by December 20; students file applications by February 1 and receive acceptance notification by February 15; students apply by March 15 and receive notification by April 1.

International Students Students must show evidence of exceptional academic achievement. Required are letters of reference from individuals under whom the applicant has studied, as well as good health and a minimum TOEFL score of 550 for students whose native language is not English.

Transfer Students Application deadlines are May 1 for fall and November 1 for spring, with notification upon receipt of all materials. Students are encouraged to talk with the transfer coordinator. Official college transcripts are required, and students with less than one year of college must submit a high school transcript and satisfy the regular freshman requirements. A minimum GPA of 2.5 is required from an accredited institution. Morris has a Minnesota Transfer Curriculum whereby students can transfer, as a package, the general education requirements taken at other Minnesota institutions.

Admission Contact

Office of Admissions
University of Minnesota—Morris
600 E. 4th Street
Morris, MN 56267-2199
Phone: (800) 992-8863; (320) 589-6035
FAX: (320) 589-1673
E-mail: *admisfa@mrs.umn.edu*
Web: *www.mrs.umn.edu*

The Heart of the University Considered one of the top national public liberal arts colleges as well as one of the best values in higher education, the Univerity of Minnesota at Morris has much to offer. What is unique about UMM is that it's a relatively small college that is part of the much larger state university system of the University of Minnesota, so students get the advantages of attending a small school as well as having the resources of a larger school. These resources include faculty who are held to high standards of teaching, research, and professional activity. The opportunities for universitywide academic and travel abroad scholarship, participation in an especially broad range of study abroad programs, and easy access to the entire university's library system. When the state university surveys its students, UMM receives the highest grades in more than 15 areas, including overall student satisfaction, quality of academic programs, quality of instruction, availability of instructors, job placement, and more. Added to this evaluation are outcomes showing that 80 percent of UMM alumni hold professional, technical, or managerial positions, over 45 percent eventually attend graduate school, and more than 67 percent remain in careers related to their academic

majors—significant indicators of UMM's excellent reputation.

Students love the openness of the campus community, the small town atmosphere, and the fact that courses are taught by professors and not graduate students. Many students are attracted to UMM because learning is more than a classroom activity. Here, students have the opportunity— and encouragement—to pursue academic interests outside the classroom. Students may work on independent research, but many choose to work with faculty in projects that have resulted in articles, presentation of papers at conferences, the staging of plays, art exhibitions, the development of computer software, and other fruits of collaboration. Several programs have been established to fund student–faculty collaborations: The Undergraduate Research Opportunity Program, the Morris Academic Partnership, and the Minority Mentorship Program.

The university has a wonderful study abroad program. The Center for International Programs and the International Study and Travel Center help students make the necessary arrangements, purchase Eurail passes, and obtain international student IDs and youth hostel passes. Through the University of Minnesota's Global Campus programs, students have study options in more than 50 countries.

Keeping in mind UMM's plains location and the tiny town of Morris, which offers little entertainment opportunity—except, of course, for the great outdoor opportunities typically enjoyed by winter enthusiasts—the UMM campus has had to develop a lively campus calendar, including a film series, concerts, speakers, and a popular performing arts series, as well as over 80 student clubs and organizations. As one student said; "There are tons of things to do on this campus!"

UNIVERSITY OF PITTSBURGH AT JOHNSTOWN

Johnstown, Pennsylvania

Total Undergraduate Enrollment: 3,150

Men: 1,500 Women: 1,650
Five-Year Graduation Rate: 58%

Tuition: In-state–$;
Out-of-state–$$$
Room and Board: $
Residential Students: 62%

History The University of Pittsburgh at Johnstown is part of the state-related University of Pittsburgh system, founded in 1927, which consists of four campuses.

Location The 650-acre campus is located in a suburb east of Johnstown, Pennsylvania (population 40,000), in a wooded setting 70 miles east of Pittsburgh, in southwest Pennsylvania. The campus is recognized as one of the most attractive in the East.

Top Programs of Study Natural sciences, business, education

Arts and Sciences Allied health (emergency medical services, respiratory care, surgical technology), biology, chemistry, civil engineering technology, communications, composite writing, computer science, creative writing, ecology, economics, electrical engineering technology, English literature, environmental studies, geography, geology, history, humanities, journalism, mathematics, mechanical engineering technology, natural sciences, political science, psychology, social sciences, sociology, technical theater, theater

Business Accounting, economics, finance/information systems management, marketing

Education: Elementary, secondary

Pre-Professional Clinical dietetics/nutrition, dentistry, health information management, law, medical technology, medicine, occupational therapy, optometry, physical therapy, pharmacy, seminary, veterinary medicine

Accredited Programs Engineering

Special Programs There are opportunities for internships, service, student-designed majors, cooperative education, study abroad, and double majors. Students may take courses at the schools that are part of the Pittsburgh Council of Higher Education. There are four associate's degree programs in health-related fields as well as several pre-health professional areas of study.

Facilities There are 28 buildings, including the Student Union, the Sport Center, Whalley Memorial Chapel, the Pasquerilla Performing Arts Center, the Zamur Aquatic Center, Owen Library, the Engineering and Science Building, an art gallery, a nature area, radio and television stations, and residence facilities, all wired for Internet access.

Transition to College Program In addition to an orientation class called "The College," which meets periodically throughout the student's first semester, there is a unique program, The Freshman Network, which provides information and advice on academic choices and strategies for academic success. Also, each freshman receives an Academic Source Book, which serves as an easy-to-use, accessible supplement to the college catalogue, containing outlines of each of the majors and programs at the university.

Athletics NCAA II, Independent Conference

    Men: Baseball, basketball, soccer, wrestling

    Women: Basketball, cross-country, track, volleyball

Student Life and Housing About 1,700 students can be accommodated in college housing, which includes special interest houses, and is guaranteed for all four years. Ninety-eight percent of the students are from Pennsylvania, the remainder from 12 other states. Ethnicity: Caucasian—96 percent. There are one local and three national fraternities and one local and four national sororities. All students may keep cars.

Accommodations for Students with Disabilities In compliance with section 504

Financial Aid About 81 percent of all freshmen receive aid. The average freshman award was about $6,500.

Requirements for Admission SAT I or ACT scores and a college prep high school program. For admission to the Engineering and Engineering Technology programs, students must have completed trigonometry as well as algebra, and the two lab sciences must be chemistry and physics. A campus visit and interview are encouraged.

Application Students are admitted for fall, spring, and summer semesters. Application deadlines are open, and students are notified of an admission decision on a rolling basis.

International Students Students whose first language is not English must score a minimum of 550 on the TOEFL. The SAT I may be required of some students.

Transfer Students Required are official high school and college transcripts from each institution attended. If the student is offered admission, a tentative transfer-credit evaluation will be provided following admission notification.

Admission Contact
Office of Admissions
University of Pittsburgh at Johnstown
157 Blockington Hall
450 Schoolhouse Road
Johnstown, PA 15904-9985
Phone: (800) 765-4875; (814) 269-7050
FAX: (814) 269-7044

E-mail: *upjadmit@pitt.edu*
Web: *www.upj.pitt.edu*

The Heart of the University The University of Pittsburgh is comprised of four separate campuses governed by one board of trustees and a chancellor, and serving a total of about 33,000 students. The campus at Johnstown is the only one of the four that meets the established criteria of this guide. As a "state-related" institution, UPJ's tuition is a bargain for the quality it delivers. Having the resources of a major university, yet having the personal appeal of a small college, UPJ is considered one of the best public comprehensive universities in the Mid-Atlantic area.

The largest and most significant programs are in Business, Biology, Education, and Engineering. The Business program provides a contemporary career-oriented curriculum, which includes a sequence of core courses in business, economics, mathematics, computer applications, information systems, and a broad group of social sciences. Students in the Biology program can choose from two options: a traditional concentration, which provides excellent preparation for entry into medical, dental, and other health-related fields, as well as graduate programs; or a Terrestrial Ecology concentration, which focuses on the evaluation and management of the environment. Both programs emphasize substantial laboratory work and/or field experiences. Facilities include faculty/student research laboratories, as well as sophisticated equipment (including equipment that would enable DNA sequencing research). UPJ offers teacher certification programs in both elementary and secondary education. After following a broad liberal arts curriculum, as well as student selected education courses, students typically apply for admission to one of the programs in the second term of the sophomore year. In addition to student teaching, there are many field-connected courses. All three Engineering Technology programs can be completed within four years at the Johnstown campus. If students elect to study Engineering they may do so at the Pittsburgh campus after one year at Johnstown. In addition to the excellent lab facilities in the Engineering and Science Building, the Mechanical Engineering Technology Program utilizes state-of-the-art facilities at Technologies Corporation in Johnstown.

The university has a wonderful relationship with the greater Johnstown community, which it has achieved in many ways. One significant way has been through the building of a new Performing Arts Center, a multipurpose arts space, which contains two theaters, a 1,000-seat proscenium mainstage, and a 200-seat studio theater. The center is the home of the Theater Department as well as the Southern Alleghenies Museum of Art. The center, as part of its schedule, offers a Family Fun Series as well as school performances, thereby helping to fulfill the center's mission of enriching the lives of both the UPJ family and the residents of the greater Johnstown community. Second, UPJ offers important associate's degrees, especially for those Johnstown residents currently working in the fields of Emergency Medical Services, Respiratory Care, and Surgical Technologist. These programs lead to certification and qualification to sit for registry or national exami-

nation. Also, the several pre-health professions programs lead to consistently high acceptance rates at professional schools.

Students love the excellent quality and variety of campus housing options. There are 5 two-story residence halls with impressive lobbies, high ceilings, working fireplaces, game rooms, and suite-like arrangements. There are small group lodges that can house a varsity team or other group that decides to live together. The Living/Learning Center combines 200 residence units with modern classroom/conference facilities and an in-house gym and fitness center. For upperclassmen there are townhouse apartments. Also, there is a 44-unit apartment complex just off campus.

The campus is alive with visual and performing arts, 70 clubs and organizations, 50 intramurals, and service groups. If that's not enough, the big city lights of Pittsburgh are about an hour away, with plenty of cultural activities, professional sports, and shopping. Also, skiers love the Johnstown area.

The campus president says: "I am most proud of the talent that exists throughout our university and the leadership that we provide to our community."

UNIVERSITY OF REDLANDS

Redlands, California

Total Undergraduate Enrollment: 2,100
Men: 900 Women: 1,200
Five-Year Graduation Rate: 63%

Tuition: $$$$
Room and Board: $$$$
Residential Students: 80%

History University of Redlands was founded in 1907 by American Baptists and today maintains an informal association with that denomination. The university is a liberal arts and sciences school and is named for the city in which it resides, which was named for its red soil.

Location The 140-acre tree-lined campus is located in Redlands, California (population 64,000), one hour's drive east of Los Angeles and coastal beaches. Overlooking the campus are the two highest mountains in Southern California.

Top Programs of Study Business, liberal studies and education, music

Arts and Sciences Art history, Asian studies, biochemistry and molecular biology, biology, chemistry, communicative disorders, computer science, creative writing, economics, English literature, environmental management, environmental science, environmental studies, French, German, government, history, international relations, Latin American studies, liberal studies, mathematics, music, philosophy, physics, psychology, race and ethnic studies, religious studies, sociology/anthropology, Spanish, studio art, theater arts, women's studies

Business Accounting, administration

Education Elementary, music, secondary

Pre-Professional Law, medicine

Accredited Programs Chemistry, communicative disorders, music

Special Programs There are opportunities for student-designed majors and many study abroad and internship opportunities. There is an alternative program within the College of Arts and Sciences. The university has a campus in Salzburg, Austria. There is a Phi Beta Kappa chapter.

Facilities There are 40 buildings including the Hunsaker University Center, the Aronacost Library, the Academic Computer Center, the Wallichs Theater, an art center, a new state-of-the-art fitness center, and the new Stauffer Center for Science and Mathematics. Residence halls are situated around an expansive quadrangle.

Transition to College Program All new students are required to take the First-Year Seminar during their first term. First-Year Seminars provide students with a close personal relationship with a faculty member who not only teaches the course but also serves as academic adviser and mentor to students, introducing them to college-level skills as well as assisting them in planning seminars that change each year. Seminars have included "The Rise of American Capitalism," "Shakespeare and Film," and "Ethics and the Scientific Method."

Athletics NCAA III, Southern California Intercollegiate Athletic Conference

Men: Baseball, basketball, cross country, football, golf, soccer, swimming, tennis, track, water polo

Women: Basketball, cross-country, lacrosse, softball, soccer, swimming, tennis, track, volleyball, water polo

Student Life and Housing About 1,500 students can be accommodated in college housing, which is guaranteed for all four years. Seventy-two per-

cent of the students are from California, the remainder from 45 other states and 33 countries. Ethnicity: Caucasian—62 percent; Hispanic-American—11 percent; Asian-American—6 percent; African-American—3 percent. There are seven local fraternities and five local sororities. All students may keep cars.

Accommodations for Students with Disabilities The university will make reasonable accommodations on an individual basis for the known physical and mental limitations of a qualified student.

Financial Aid About 82 percent of all freshmen receive aid. The average freshman award was about $17,500.

Requirements for Admission SAT I or ACT scores and a college prep high school program. A personal interview is strongly recommended.

Application Freshmen are admitted to all semesters. The Early Decision deadline is December 15. Regular admission applications should be submitted by February 1 for fall admission and January 1 for spring admission. Admission notification is made on a rolling basis.

International Students Required are two letters of recommendation, "certified true copies" of original secondary school records and certificates, an autobiographical essay, and a bank statement or certification of finances form. Students whose primary language is not English must achieve a minimum TOEFL of 550 paper and 213 computer-based scores. Successful completion of Level 109 at ELS Language Centers is accepted in lieu of TOEFL. Credentials should be filed by April 1 for fall admission and November 1 for spring admission.

Transfer Students A minimum GPA of 2.5 is required in at least 24 credits. If fewer than 24 credits have been completed, the student will be reviewed according to regular first-year standards. A maximum of 66 credits can be transferred from a two-year institution and 100 credits from a four-year college, but the last 32 credits must be taken at

Redlands. Two letters of recommendation and official high school and college transcripts are required. A personal interview is recommended.

Admission Contact
Office of Admissions
University of Redlands
1200 E. Colton Avenue
P.O. Box 3080
Redlands, CA 92373
Phone: (800) 455-5064; (909) 335-4074
FAX: (909) 335-4089
E-mail: *admissions@uor.edu*
Web: *www.redlands.edu*

The Heart of the University The University of Redlands has much to do with its location, being an hour's drive to green mountains, waterfalls, ocean beaches, and desert wilderness. Very few campuses can claim such an incredible location, which offers outdoor enthusiasts sunny skies to go hiking, mountain biking, swimming, or skiing. Students also have the big city attractions of Los Angeles, Hollywood, and San Diego. The city of Redlands has been rated as one of Southern California's five most livable cities. Visiting students are also impressed with the "laid back" atmosphere.

Typically rated as one of the best universities in the West, The University of Redlands could be characterized as innovative, courageous, "out-of-the-box," and actively concerned with the environment. Nearly 200 highly motivated students are enrolled in the Johnson Center for Integrative Studies, an alternative learning environment where students believe that they are responsible for their own educations and sign contracts with

professors that personalize the goals of the course for the student. Professors, in turn, provide extensive written evaluations instead of grades. In the second year, students create an individualized major. Much of this work is done within the context of a close-knit community.

Music is also one of Redland's greatest strengths, offering a conservatory-quality education, taught by full-time master teachers and adjunct professionals who perform throughout Southern California. The facilities and the opportunities for undergraduate musicians are impressive.

Redlands also offers one of the most extensive study abroad programs in the country, with more than 100 off-campus study opportunities. More than half of the students participate and spend either a semester, a January Interim, or even an entire year in another country.

The education program is excellent. Over the past decade, all of the students credentialed through Redlands have been offered jobs! There is also a strong writing program and hands-on science courses of incredible breadth.

Redlands offers a tight-knit community of talented teachers and diverse and engaging students. Faculty are from leading universities and teaching is their calling. They teach small classes, really get to know their students, are accessible, and encourage students to work with them on several projects. Students say that faculty members challenge them to try a broad range of things, encouraging them to think beyond the confines of their own disciplines.

At Redlands students tailor their educations to fit their interests and their futures.

UNIVERSITY OF THE PACIFIC Stockton, California

Total Undergraduate Enrollment: 3,233
Men: 1,350 Women: 1,883
Five-Year Graduation Rate: 64%

Tuition: $$$$
Room and Board: $$$
Residential Students: 62%

History The University of the Pacific was founded in 1851 by pioneer Methodist ministers as the first chartered institution of higher learning in California. Originally founded in Santa

Clara, the institution moved to College Park near San Jose in 1871, became coeducational, and then moved to Stockton in 1924. In 1961 the college became a university.

Location The 175-acre campus is in Stockton, California, 80 miles east of San Francisco and 40 miles south of Sacramento.

Top Programs of Study Business, biology, education

Arts and Sciences Applied music, art history, biochemistry, bioengineering, chemistry-biology, civil engineering, communication studies, computer engineering, electrical engineering, engineering management, engineering physics, English, environmental studies, film studies, gender studies, geology, geophysics, German, history, information systems, international relations, Japanese, liberal studies, mathematics, mechanical engineering, music composition, music education, music history, music management, music theory, organizational behavior, philosophy, physics, political science, psychology, religious studies, sociology, Spanish, speech-language pathology, sports management, sports medicine, sports pedagogy, theater arts

Business Accounting, arts and entertainment management, business law, entrepreneurship, finance, general business, industrial labor relations, international management, management information systems, management and human resources, marketing, real estate

Education Elementary, secondary

Pre-Professional Dentistry, law, pharmacy, speech-language pathology

Accredited Programs Business, education, engineering, music

Special Programs There are several accelerated professional programs: a three-year bachelor's degree in dental hygiene; a five-year bachelor's degree and MBA; a six-year bachelor's degree and law degree (JD); five-, six-, or seven-year den- tistry degrees (DDS); five-, six-, or seven-year doctor of pharmacy degrees; and a five-and-one-half year bachelor's degree and MS in speech–language pathology. There are opportunities for study abroad, cross-disciplinary majors and multidisciplinary majors, and a Washington, D.C., semester program. The library holds the complete papers, sketches, and writings of naturalist John Muir.

Facilities There are 98 buildings, complete with old brick buildings reminiscent of a New England campus, including the McCaffery Student Center; the Reynolds Art Gallery; the Baun Fitness Center; a public radio station; the Long Theater and the De Marcus Brown Studio; Bechtel International Center; Baun Hall, home of the School of Engineering and Computer Science; and the Morris Chapel.

Transition to College Program There is a traditional orientation program plus assigned student advisers who provide assistance with time management, taking lecture notes, and homework difficulties. In addition, student advisers work with an assigned faculty adviser in helping students with program planning, personal adjustment, and introducing students to the full range of campus services. Also, there are Mentor Seminars, taken by all freshmen, that are taught by an interdisciplinary team and result in supportive peer relationships.

Athletics NCAA I, Big West Conference

Men: Baseball, basketball, cheer and dance, swimming, tennis, volleyball, water polo

Women: Basketball, cheer and dance, cross-country, field hockey, soccer, softball, swimming, tennis, volleyball, water polo

Student Life and Housing About 2,000 students can be accommodated in college housing. Eighty percent of the students are from California, the remainder are from 20 other states and 50 countries. Ethnicity: Caucasian—51 percent; Asian-American—26 percent; Hispanic-American—10

percent; African-American—3 percent; International—3 percent. There are one local and five national fraternities and four national sororities. All students may keep cars.

Accommodations for Students with Disabilities
The university provides comprehensive services. To request accommodations, the Office of Services for Students with Disabilities must be provided with a medical or psychological evaluation or signed release authorizing the university to obtain documentation.

Financial Aid About 90 percent of all freshmen receive aid. The average freshman award was about $18,000.

Requirements for Admission SAT I or ACT scores and a college prep high school program. Students who have passed the GED Test or the High School Proficiency Exam will also be considered. Dental hygiene applicants must be interviewed, and music conservatory students must audition. A campus visit is recommended.

Application The Early Action deadline is December 1, with decision notification by January 15. Dental hygiene applicants must file by September 15 for spring semester and December 1 for fall semester. Regular applications are due by February 15, with decision notification on a rolling basis.

International Students Required are a minimum TOEFL score of 475 for students whose native language is not English, a detailed certification of finances, and official secondary and, if applicable, postsecondary transcripts.

Transfer Students If students would have qualified for admission as high school seniors, and are in good academic standing at the colleges in which they are currently enrolled, then they are generally eligible for admission, and there is no minimum number of credits required for transfer. If students would not have qualified for admission from high school, they may apply after completing at least one year of full-time study (30 or more credits) at another two- or four-year institution. The recommended minimum GPA is 2.5.

Admission Contact
Office of Admissions
University of the Pacific
3601 Pacific Avenue
Stockton, CA 95211
Phone: (800) 959-2867; (209) 946-2211
FAX: (209) 946-2413
E-mail: *admissions@usp.edu*
Web: *www.pacific.edu/admission*

The Heart of the University In keeping with the pioneering spirit and vision of those who settled the Old West, the heart of the University of the Pacific is its innovative programs. You know this is a special institution right from the start because it guarantees its freshmen that if they are unable to graduate in four years they will not pay any additional tuition! The general education programs—The Mentor Seminars and the Path Requirements—are taken by all undergraduates and are distinguished for their quality and innovativeness, comprising about one-third of a student's required course work. The Mentor Seminars are a series of three interdisciplinary courses, with the first two taken the freshman year. The first seminar focuses on "Timeless Issues: Where do humans come from? How do humans differ from one another? What is the good life?" Not only are faculty from different academic areas, but the students are intentionally grouped so that they represent different schools of the university, assuring a diversity of viewpoints. Students meet in small groups to discuss topics and write a series of short essays. In the second seminar, "Today's Decisions," students focus on public policy decisions that students may face during their lifetimes. Students sharpen their writing, speaking, discussion, and research skills, while at the same time generating friendships within each group. The last Mentor Seminar, "Ethical Applications of Knowledge," is taken in the senior year. The seminar focuses on moral decision-making strategies, and students explore the biography of a moral leader of their choice in order to study the strategies the leader used. The personalized part of the general education program, "The Path Requirement," allows students to design a personalized path comprised of courses selected from a set of approved lists to satisfy distribution requirements.

Another innovative program is the School of International Studies. Here is an entire school devoted to this discipline—one of only six in the United States, and the only one to use an interdisciplinary team teaching approach and require its students to study abroad. The School of Engineering and Computer Science offers a five-year degree in several engineering fields. All engineering students participate in a cooperative education program where they spend one year in a full-time, paid, practical experience with 1 or more of 100 engineering firms around the world and are paid an average of $2,500 per month. The School of Education has the luxury of its proximity to San Joaquin County—a community of 75 languages and 40 dialects to train its students. The placement rate of its graduates is nearly 100 percent.

Students say that this is a friendly campus with professors who love teaching and working with undergraduates. Many faculty members invite students to collaborate in projects and research. Faculty and staff are very accessible.

When you combine these innovative programs with the university's great location—near San Francisco, Lake Tahoe, the coastal redwoods, the 90 student organizations, and one of the most extensive study abroad programs in America, the University of the Pacific offers a gigantic education.

UNIVERSITY OF SCRANTON

Scranton, Pennsylvania

Total Undergraduate Enrollment: 4,060
Men: 1,722 Women: 2,338
Five-Year Graduation Rate: 77%

Tuition: $$$
Room and Board: $$$$
Residential Students: 47%

History The University of Scranton was founded in 1888 by Bishop William O'Hara. Originally named St. Thomas College, the university received its present name in 1938 and welcomed the Jesuit fathers in 1942. The university is listed on the Templeton Foundation's Honor Roll of Character-Building Colleges.

Location The beautiful 50-acre hillside campus is located overlooking Scranton, Pennsylvania (population 70,000), about 125 miles north of Philadelphia and about two-and-a-half hours from New York City.

Top Programs of Study Biology, elementary education, communication

Arts and Sciences Biochemistry, biology, biomathematics, biophysics, chemistry, chemistry/ business, chemistry/computers, classical languages, communication, computer engineering, computer science, criminal justice, economics, electrical engineering, electronic commerce, electronics/business, English, environmental science, exercise science, French, German, gerontology, health administration, history, human services, international studies, mathematics, media and information technology, medical technology, military science, modern languages, neuroscience, nursing, occupational therapy, philosophy, physical therapy, physics, political science, psychology, sociology, Spanish, theater, theology/religious studies

Business Accounting, accounting information systems, computer information systems, economics, enterprise management technology, finance, human resources studies, international business, international language/business, management, marketing, operations management

Education Early childhood, elementary, secondary, special education

Pre-Professional Engineering, law, medicine

Accredited Programs Business; computer science; education; nursing; physical therapy

Special Programs Several minors and concentrations are offered. The university's 4-1-4 academic calendar allows students to obtain a bachelor's degree in three years. Students can also earn a master's degree in several academic areas in five years, as well as a master's degree in four years in other academic areas. Students can study at 35 universities internationally or at one of the other 28 Jesuit American institutions during their junior year. There are several associate's degree and certificate programs, as well as internship and study abroad opportunities. The university is rated one of the most "computer-wired" colleges in America. There is an Air Force ROTC program.

Facilities There are 60 buildings, many of them new, including the Weinberg Library, four new townhouses with air-conditioned apartments, the Kania School of Management, and the Conference and Retreat Center at Chapman Lake, 20 minutes from campus. The university has built a staggering 22 new buildings and renovated 15 others in the last 20 years.

Transition to College Program The university offers a traditional orientation program.

Athletics NCAA III, Middle Atlantic States Collegiate Conference, Eastern College Athletic Conference

Men: Baseball, basketball, cross-country, golf, ice hockey, lacrosse, soccer, swimming, tennis

Women: Basketball, cross-country, field hockey, lacrosse, softball, swimming, tennis, volleyball

Student Life and Housing About 2,000 students can be accommodated in college housing, which is guaranteed for all four years. Fifty-two percent of the students are from Pennsylvania, the remainder from 26 states and 17 countries. Ethnicity: Caucasian—88 percent; Asian-American—2 percent; African-American—1 percent. There are no fraternities or sororities. Upperclassmen may keep cars.

Accommodations for Students with Disabilities Reasonable accommodations are provided by request through the Affirmative Action Office.

Financial Aid About 91 percent of all freshmen receive aid. The average freshman award was about $16,000.

Requirements for Admission SAT I or ACT scores with a college prep high school program.

Application Freshmen are admitted fall and spring semesters. Early Action applications should be filed by November 15. Regular admission applications should be filed by March 1 for fall admission, and December 15 for spring admission. Admission notification is sent on a rolling basis.

International Students A TOEFL score is required, but no minimum score is mandated. Instead, the test results are considered along with all other information. A certification of finances form must be completed.

Transfer Students Required are official transcripts from high schools and colleges attended, and SAT or ACT scores. The courses to be transferred must be from a regionally accredited institution and equivalent to courses offered at the University of Scranton. A GPA of 2.5 and certification of honorable dismissal from the previous college are also required. No credit will be given for courses with grades less than C.

Admission Contact
Office of Admissions
University of Scranton
Scranton, PA 18510-4699
Phone: (888) SCRANTON; (570) 941-7540
FAX: (570) 941-5928

E-mail: *admissions@scranton.edu*
Web: *www.scranton.edu*

The Heart of the University Overlooking the city of Scranton sits a gem: a university with new buildings and facilities and an academic program that puts it consistently among the top regional universities in the North and a "best buy" as well. The outcomes are great. Ninety-eight percent of the graduates are either employed, in graduate school, or volunteering on a full-time basis; nearly 90 percent of the graduates applying for law school are accepted; the acceptance rate of graduates into medical school and related schools is 88 percent. An impressive result for the Kania School of Management, over 1,000 Scranton alumni are CEO's of their organizations! A listing of employers who hired more than three Scranton graduates in a recent year included: PricewaterhouseCoopers, Lockheed Martin, Factset Research Systems, JP Morgan Chase, Vanguard, Eli Lilly, Fox Family, IBM, KPMG, Memorial Sloane Kettering, Goldman Sachs, and the Hospital of the University of Pennsylvania. Since 1972 the university has had 105 students awarded Fulbright Scholarships! The national accreditation of many of its professional programs demonstrates the quality of those programs and has a large impact on these outcomes.

The significant outcomes also demonstrate the advantages of an education that focuses on the whole student. Therefore, while achievement and leadership development are important, what really distinguishes the Jesuit tradition is the sense of community felt by University of Scranton students. As one CEO alumnus commented: "Academically, I would match this place against anywhere, but it is also a place people care about each other." When you look at the graduation rate of the school, you realize the benefits of creating and sustaining a supportive, nurturing, student-centered climate. Faculty come to Scranton to teach, to take an active interest in the lives of students, stimulate students to become life-long learners, and collaborate with students on research projects. The Faculty/Student Research Program gives students opportunities to do both routine tasks and sophisticated research. In a recent year, 138 students and one in five faculty members from 23 departments participated.

The university offers daily and Sunday liturgies and special campuswide liturgical celebrations. Students, faculty, and staff serve as musicians, readers, and Eucharistic ministers. There are retreats for prayer, reflection, and relaxation. The Collegiate Volunteers Office helped students contribute more than 140,000 hours of community service in a recent year.

With many clubs and organizations, a performing arts and distinguished lecture series, music and theater, a strong varsity athletic program, and a large intramural sports program, students have much to do on campus. Off campus, students have the Pocono Mountains, as well as ski resorts, a motor speedway, state parks, three museums, and professional sports.

UNIVERSITY OF TAMPA   **Tampa, Florida**

Total Undergraduate Enrollment: 3,730   Tuition: $$$
Men: 1,370 Women: 2,360   Room and Board: $$$
Five-Year Graduation Rate: 52%   Residential Students: 62%

History The University of Tampa, founded in 1931, is a private, comprehensive institution founded by the Tampa Chamber of Commerce.

Location The beautiful 85-acre campus is located in Tampa, Florida, along the banks of the Hillsborough River, with the Tampa Bay Area home to 2.3 million people.

Top Programs of Study Business, communication, biology and marine biology

Arts and Sciences Art, athletic training, biochemistry, biology, chemistry, communication, computer graphics, computer information systems, criminology, economics, English, environmental science, exercise science and sport studies, government and world affairs, graphic design, history, liberal studies, marine science, mathematical programming, mathematics, music, nursing performing arts, psychology, social sciences, sociology, Spanish, writing

Business Accounting, finance, international business, management, marketing, sports management

Education Elementary, secondary

Pre-Professional Allied health, dentistry, law, medicine, veterinary medicine

Accredited Programs There are certificate programs in art therapy, European studies, gerontology, and Latin American studies, and minors in several areas. There are also master's degree programs in business administration, nursing, and technology and innovation management.

Special Programs There are study abroad, internship, and service opportunities as well as a Washington, D.C., semester. The Elite Leadership Program teaches leadership skills, and the TECO Energy Center for Leadership studies the application of leadership principles in business organizations. There is an Army ROTC program.

Facilities The campus is a national historic landmark, with 39 buildings that include Plant Hall, a former luxury hotel of Moorish architecture that now serves as the main classroom and administration building; the American Language Academy; the Saunders Center for the Arts; the Jaeb Computer Center; the Dance Center; Ferman Music Center; the Henry Plant Museum; Sykes College of Business; the Falk Theater; the Marting Sports Center; the McNiff Fitness Center; the Scarfane/Hartley Gallery; and radio and television stations. Over the last few years, $100 million has been invested to modernize the university.

Transition to College Program The Gateways program not only introduces students to the university and teaches important skills that lead to college success, but also helps students explore career goals and gets students involved in an on-campus organization. Students see their Gateways instructor/adviser every week.

Athletics NCAA II, Sunshine State Conference

Men: Baseball, basketball, cross-country, golf, soccer, swimming, tennis

Women: Basketball, cross-country, rowing, softball, swimming, tennis, volleyball

Student Life and Housing About 2,000 students can be accommodated in college housing, which is guaranteed for all four years. Fifty percent of the students are from Florida, the remainder are from all states and 86 countries. Ethnicity: Caucasian—66 percent; Hispanic-American—9 percent; African-American—7 percent; International—5 percent. There are five national fraternities and seven national sororities. Upperclassmen may keep cars.

Accommodations for Students with Disabilities In compliance with section 504

Financial Aid About 87 percent of all students receive aid. The average freshman award was about $15,000.

Requirements for Admission SAT I and ACT results and a college prep high school program or GED results.

Application Freshmen are admitted to all semesters. Application deadlines are open.

International Students Required are official school transcripts or GED results, TOEFL results for those students who do not have English as a primary language, and evidence of financial support.

Transfer Students Students are considered transfer students if they have completed 17 or more college credits. Required are official high school and college transcripts from all schools attended.

Admission Contact
Office of Admissions
University of Tampa
401 West Kennedy Boulevard
Tampa, FL 33606-1490
Phone: (888) 646-2738; (813) 253-6211
FAX: (813) 253-6211
E-mail: *admissions@ut.edu*
Web: *www.ut.edu*

The Heart of the University With a multi-million dollar capital investment in buildings and facilities, the campus has been transformed into a state-of-the-art facility, with new buildings and air-conditioned residence halls. This campus transformation along with the wide array of academic programs reflects both the diverse student population and international population of the Tampa Bay area, a regional center of culture and commerce. With students representing every state in the Union and more than 80 countries, and with Tampa the home of Latin Americans, Asians, Africans, Caribbeans, and Europeans, the university represents a global village.

In this uniquely diverse community, students are involved in a number of cross-cultural experiences. Students can study abroad to develop language expertise, international business, European or Latin American studies, and more. There are also faculty-led study–travel courses. On campus, there are especially designed global issues courses, international guest speakers, a Model United Nations Program, and an American Language Academy for students needing to develop greater English proficiency. The Director of International Programs appreciates this international focus when he comments:

"Those who are equiped to participate in globalization will become effective players. Our job is to prepare you for such success."

Also, with over 600 business and community leaders, both local and international, affiliated with the university, students are provided valuable internships and networking opportunities.

The nationally accredited Sykes College of Business best represents the international focus of the academic programs. With close connections to the business community and a curriculum aligned with today's business realities, business students participate in the hands-on Strategies Analysis Program, a comprehensive analysis of a real-life business that concludes with students making recommendations to management. Also, a high-tech financial trading room where students manage their portfolio and investments uses Bloomburg real-time trading information.

A second major program is marine science, one of the first in the nation. Given the campus's location, with proximity to the Hillsborough River, Tampa Bay, the Gulf of Mexico, and the Florida Keys, no wonder 25 percent of all new freshmen are science majors.

Students love the talented, knowledgeable faculty members who make classrooms and discussions lively and interesting. Add to this the strong athletic program, beaches, professional sports, visual and performing arts centers, Disney and Universal Studios, and great weather—UT students are located where many students around the country travel as a vacation destination!

Considered a top Southern university, the university's graduates achieve excellent outcomes with most students employed or in graduate school within three months of graduation. Also, 95 percent of UT students who apply to medical, dental, or veterinary school are accepted.

UNIVERSITY OF VERMONT

Burlington, Vermont

Total Undergraduate Enrollment: 7,419

Men: 3,301 Women: 4,118
Five-Year Graduation Rate: 66%

Tuition: In-state–$;
Out-of-state–$$$
Room and Board: $$
Residential Students: 52%

History The University of Vermont was chartered in 1791. Ira Allen, who provided much of the initial funding and planning, is honored as UVM's founder.

Location The 425-acre campus is located in Burlington, Vermont (population 35,000), the state's largest city, which is 90 miles south of Montreal, Canada, 200 miles north of Boston, Massachusetts, and is on the shore of Lake Champlain, with magnificent views of the Adirondacks and Green Mountains.

Top Programs of Study Arts and sciences, agriculture and life sciences, business administration

Arts and Sciences Animal science (dairy production/farm management, equine science, general animal science), anthropology, area and international studies, art history, art studio, Asian studies, biochemical science, biological sciences, biology, biomedical technology, botany, Canadian studies, chemistry, civil engineering, classical civilization, communication sciences, community development and applied economics, computer science, computer science information systems, dietetics, economics, electrical engineering, engineering management, English, environmental sciences, European studies, family and consumer sciences education, forestry, French, geography, geology, German, Greek, history, human development and family studies, Latin, Latin American studies, mathematics, mechanical engineering, medical laboratory science, microbiology, molecular genetics, music, natural resources, nursing, nutrition and food services, philosophy, physics, plant and soil science, political science, psychology, radiation therapy, recreation management, religion, Russian,

Russian/East European Studies, social work, sociology, Spanish, statistics, sustainable landscape horticulture, theater, wildlife and fisheries, women's studies

Business Accounting, entrepreneurship, finance, human resources management, international management, management and the environment, management information systems, marketing, production and operations management

Education Art, music, early childhood, elementary, middle, physical education, secondary

Pre-Professional Dentistry, law, medicine, physical therapy, veterinary medicine

Accredited Programs Biomedical technologies, chemistry, dental hygiene, education, engineering, forestry, medicine, nursing, physical therapy, social work, speech-language pathology

Special Programs The university offers a seven-year program in veterinary medicine with Tufts University in Boston. The UVM College of Medicine is one of the oldest and most respected medical schools in the nation. The Lane Artists Series features a diversity of performing arts events. The Lawrence Debate Union provides opportunities for student debaters to compete across the nation. There is a Phi Beta Kappa chapter. There are individually designed majors and a semester-at-sea program. There is a dual program in dairy farm management with Vermont Technical College. There is also an Army ROTC program.

Facilities There are 118 buildings, many historic, including the Fleming Museum, housing a collection of 18,000 works; the Tyler Theater, visited by professional guest artists; the Merzer Horse

Farm, a laboratory for UVM students; TV and radio stations; four research farms; a lakeshore science center; an aquatic research ship; several libraries; the Rubenstein Ecosystem Science Center; and the new Health Sciences Complex.

Transition to College Program TREK, a week-long program just prior to the start of classes, sends groups out on mountain trails, waterways, and to community service sites, where good clean fun and work help to bond students. The "Teacher Adviser Program" places first-year arts and sciences students in small, interactive courses in which the teacher also serves as each student's adviser. There is also "Beginnings," a program for agriculture and life science students, which focuses on speaking and technology skills.

Athletics NCAA I, America East, Eastern College Athletic Conference

Men: Baseball, basketball, cross-country, golf, ice hockey, lacrosse, skiing, soccer, swimming and diving, tennis

Women: Basketball, cross-country, field hockey, ice hockey, track & field (indoor and outdoor), lacrosse, skiing, soccer, softball, swimming and diving, tennis

Student Life and Housing About 3,600 students can be accommodated in college housing. Only 39 percent of the students are from Vermont, the majority coming from all states, mostly the Northeast, and 37 countries. Ethnicity: Caucasian—92 percent. There are 10 national fraternities and 2 national sororities. Upperclassmen may keep cars.

Accommodations for Students with Disabilities The university provides comprehensive services with the submission of complete documentation of the disability.

Financial Aid About 62 percent of all freshmen receive aid. The average freshman award was about $15,000.

Requirements for Admission SAT I or ACT scores and a college prep high school program.

Music students must audition. Vermont residents are given priority.

Application The Early Decision and Early Action deadlines are November 1, with admission notification in late December. Deadline for regular admission is January 15, with notification in late March.

International Students Official secondary and, if applicable, postsecondary transcripts are required with English translations. First-year students must submit ACT or SAT scores. If English is not the first language, then a minimum TOEFL score of 550 paper or 213 computer is required. Also, certification of financial support is required.

Transfer Students The transfer application deadline is April 1, with notification on a rolling basis. Official transcripts of all previous high school and college work are required, and ACT or SAT scores are optional. If students have earned fewer than 30 college credits, the high school record is a major factor in a decision. Most successful transfer applicants have an overall GPA of 2.5. Out-of-state students require a 3.0 GPA.

Home-Schooled Students Students should contact the Associate Director of Admissions regarding specific information to include in the application.

Admission Contact
Office of Admissions
University of Vermont
194 South Prospect Street
Burlington, VT 05405-3596
Phone: (802) 656-3370
FAX: (802) 656-8611
E-mail: *admissions@uvm.edu*
Web: *www.uvm.edu*

The Heart of the University The University of Vermont, with about 7,000 full-time undergraduates, is one of the largest schools included in this guide. While it just meets our criteria for ceiling enrollment, the university is included for several excellent reasons. UVM is a comprehensive university offering more than 90 undergraduate programs and a vast array of resources for a major university. Yet UVM is also able to blend close faculty–student relationships typically found in the smaller institutions in this guide. The university is organized into nine distinct schools and a college, offering students a hands-on approach to their educations, including field experiences, research, and technology. Many programs incorporate field experiences at schools, businesses, government agencies, health clinics, and nature areas near Burlington. Students have many opportunities to collaborate with faculty in research, with almost $200,000 awarded to students in a recent year. Students in all majors— from English to engineering—find themselves developing web pages and researching data pages. A distinguished faculty, teaching in small classes, enjoys close interaction with students.

In the School of Arts and Sciences, where almost half of the undergraduates are enrolled, students select both a major and a minor and try out career interests through internships, independent research, and study abroad. During the first semester students can enroll in the Teacher–Adviser Program, which combines interactive courses with careful academic advisement. In the second semester, students can enroll in the Sophomore Transition and Engagement Program, which leads students from broad exposure across several disciplines to in-depth study in a particular field, most helpful to the more than one-third of the under-

graduates who come to UVM undecided about a major. In the College of Agriculture and Life Sciences students focus on field experiences and research, with animal science majors managing their own dairy herd and students conducting research and interning in agribusiness. The nationally accredited School of Business Administration graduates students to positions at IBM, XEROX, Fidelity, Liberty Mutual, General Electric, PricewaterhouseCoopers, Goldman Sachs, and others. Social work students are placed in agency settings in both their first and last years, along with a year-long field experience, while the nationally accredited education program finds its graduates highly desirable to school districts. IBM and NASA formally recognize the quality of the programs in engineering and mathematics. The range of clinical placements and facilities—including UVM's own College of Medicine—are unsurpassed at most institutions. UVM's School of Natural Resources, within minutes of a lake, mountains, forests, and wetlands, provides natural laboratories for students and research, while programs focusing on the environment are among UVM's most distinctive.

The safe city of Burlington provides a lively pedestrian mall along with department stores, bookstores, and a center for the performing arts. The countryside provides skiing, hiking, and bike trails, while Lake Champlain offers sailing and water sports. Students also have more than 80 clubs and organizations on campus, including social service activities that underscore UVM's proud tradition of liberal social activism.

VIRGINIA MILITARY INSTITUTE

Lexington, Virginia

Total Undergraduate Enrollment: 1,300

Tuition: In-state–$;
Out-of-state–$$$
Room and Board: $
Residential Students: 100%

Men: 1,205 Women: 95
Five-Year Graduation Rate: 64%

History Virginia Military Institute was founded in 1839, when a young Lexington attorney championed transforming an existing arsenal into a

military college so that its 20 soldiers—somewhat undisciplined—could pursue an education while protecting the arms. VMI is the nation's first state-supported military college. VMI combines the studies of a full college curriculum within a framework of military discipline.

Location The 134-acre campus is in Lexington, Virginia, a small town 50 miles north of Roanoke in the Shenandoah Valley of northwest Virginia, near the Blue Ridge Mountains.

Top Programs of Study History and international studies, business and economics, civil and mechanical engineering

Arts and Sciences Biology, chemistry, civil engineering, computer science, electrical engineering, English, history, international studies and political science, mathematics, mechanical engineering, modern languages and culture, physics, psychology

Business Business, economics

Education Secondary

Pre-Professional None

Accredited Programs Chemistry, engineering

Special Programs Students may declare a double major. There are international military academy exchange programs, semester/academic year abroad programs, summer abroad programs, international internships, and cultural exchanges and study tours. A minor in Environmental Leadership is offered in Civil Engineering. Students in Mechanical Engineering may take a concentration in Aerospace Engineering. There are Air Force, Army, Navy, and Marine ROTC programs.

Facilities There are 68 buildings, including the newly renovated Shipps Hall, the liberal arts building that houses 40 percent of faculty offices; Preston Library; Cormack Field House; a Learning Center; the Barracks, a four-story, newly renovated residence that houses the entire Corps of Cadets; two museums, including the VMI family album museum; an animal research facility; a language-learning laboratory; a research grade telescope and observatory; a nuclear-particle accelerator; and Lejeune Hall Activities Center.

Transition to College Program Affectionately referred to by students as the G.R.I.T. Seminar (goals, responsibility, initiative, and tenacity), this semester-long program helps students identify obstacles to their academic success and focuses on strategies for time management, effective note and test taking, and reading comprehension. Also, an academic adviser is assigned to teach new cadets, meeting every other week to discuss study habits and overall academic performance. Each adviser has responsibility for only seven cadets.

Athletics NCAA I, Big South Conference

Men: Baseball, basketball, cross-country, football, lacrosse, rifle, soccer, swimming, track (indoor and outdoor)

Women: Cross-country, rifle, track (indoor and outdoor)

Student Life and Housing About 1,400 students can be accommodated in college housing, which includes coed dorms and is guaranteed for all four years. All students live on campus. Fifty-one percent of the students are from Virginia, the remainder are from 45 other states and 20 countries. Ethnicity: Caucasian—83 percent; African-American—5 percent; Asian-American—4 percent; Hispanic-American—3 percent; International—3 percent. There are no fraternities or sororities. Upperclassmen may keep cars. Students live by an Honor Code.

Accommodations for Students with Disabilities The Miller Learning Center offers an integrated set of services to assist students. Students meet with the Disabilities Coordinator to design individualized support programs. The coordinator assists in securing approved classroom accommodations. The center also offers a cadet-led mentoring program for students with disabilities. Cadets who desire services should contact the Disabilities Coordinator at (540) 464-7765.

Financial Aid About 47 percent of all freshmen receive aid. The average freshman award was about $13,000.

Requirements for Admission SAT I or ACT scores and a college prep high school program. A one-page essay on a topic of the student's choice or a graded essay is recommended. Extracurricular activities and achievements are an important supplement to the application. A campus visit and interview are strongly recommended. A medical exam is required if the applicant is accepted.

Application New cadets are enrolled only at the beginning of each new semester in August. Early Decision applications may be made from September 1 through November 15, and regular decision applications may be submitted from September 1 through February 15.

International Students Applicants whose first language is not English must take the TOEFL and present evidence of adequate financial resources.

Transfer Students Students must not be younger than 16 or older than 22 years of age upon matriculation. At least two years of residence at VMI are required. Students should submit official high school transcripts and transcripts from accredited colleges. Students should have a minimum of a B average for all college work completed. Only grades of C or better will be considered for transfer. Students should also submit a college catalogue so that the VMI Admissions Committee can evaluate the course content. Transfer students enter VMI only in the fall semester.

Admission Contact

Office of Admissions
Virginia Military Institute
Lexington, VA 24450-0304
Phone: (800) 767-4207; (504) 464-7211
FAX: (540) 464-7746
E-mail: *admissions@vmi.edu*
Web: *www.vmi.edu*

The Heart of the Institute Virginia Military Institute is a very special place and offers a very distinctive education, based on the concept of the "citizen-soldier"—graduates who are able to take their places in civilian life but also prepared to respond as military leaders in times of national emergency. All students—called cadets—receive a first-class academic education along with participation in either the Air Force, Army, Marine, or Navy ROTC. So, in addition to receiving the bachelor's degree, about 35 percent of the cadets also receive a commission as a second lieutenant in their selected armed service, with 18 percent of the graduates making the military a career.

The academic programs are well respected, and VMI, because it has most of its graduates earning a degree in a liberal arts field, is classified in a liberal arts category. As a result, it is often considered one of the best public national liberal arts colleges in America. Noteworthy is VMI's encouragment of cadets to engage in collaborative research with faculty in all disciplines through its Undergraduate Research Initiative. Economics and Business majors have investment responsibility for a $200,000 fund. The engineering programs are very strong and nationally accredited, featuring a hands-on curriculum and the tackling of real-world engineering problems in capstone courses. The English and Fine Arts program brings important poets, novelists, critics, and artists to the "Post," as the campus is referred to. The English Society visits museums in Richmond and Washington, D.C., while the Music Society tours New York's operas and theaters. All civil engineering and computer science majors either have job offers or graduate school acceptances prior to graduation! Many of the history graduates enter graduate or law schools. VMI graduates can be found in careers ranging from operations managers for Lockheed to New York investment bankers, neurosurgeons, company presidents, college presidents (VMI has produced 35!), and generals or flag officers (VMI has produced 265!).

The VMI faculty have extraordinary roles to play. Not only are they engaged in research and scholarship, and have a primary role as teachers, they also provide continuous availability for academic support, advise student organizations, and serve as tactical officers in the barracks. To enhance the military atmosphere of the Post, all faculty wear uniforms. Faculty and staff are commissioned in the Virginia Militia.

The military system pervades all aspects of a cadet's life. In accordance with the provisions of the Code of Virginia, the cadets constitute a military corps, who live by the eternal values of integrity, loyalty, self-discipline, and self-reliance, as well as an Honor Code. These cadets are an ethnically, geographically, and socioeconomically diverse student population who live with classmates in barracks under a system of military

governance. Their schedule is rigorous, with 7:00 A.M. wake-up, classes, ROTC, and athletic activities, and study time designated after dinner. Athletics plays a large role, because physical well-being is given great emphasis. While a third of the students participate in intercollegiate athletics, others participate in intramurals and club sports.

VMI, boasting of graduates such as Stonewall Jackson and General George Marshall, is a college of great history and tradition, taking pride in the character of its graduates.

WAGNER COLLEGE

New York City, New York

Total Undergraduate Enrollment: 1,810
Men: 741 Women: 1,069
Five-Year Graduation Rate: 72%

Tuition: $$$$
Room and Board: $$$
Residential Students: 82%

History Wagner College was founded in 1883 in Rochester, New York, and was originally named the Rochester Lutheran Proseminary. Subsequently, the college was named in memory of George Wagner, whose father, John Wagner, donated funds for the purchase of the first campus. In 1918 Wagner College moved to Staten Island, New York City, onto the 38-acre estate of Sir Edward Cunard of the Cunard Shipping Lines. In 1930 the college became coeducational.

Location The 105-acre campus is located on a hilltop site in a suburban area 10 miles from Manhattan.

Top Programs of Study Business, education, psychology

Arts and Sciences Anthropology, art, arts administration, biology, biopsychology, chemistry (concentrations in biochemistry and chemical physics), computer science, economics, English, history, international affairs, mathematics, microbiology, music, nursing, physician's assistant, physics, political science, psychology, public policy and administration, sociology/anthropology (concentrations

in academic sociology, anthropology, criminal justice, family studies), Spanish, theater

Business Administration (concentrations in accounting, finance, marketing, management, international business)

Education Childhood, elementary, secondary, special, theater arts

Pre-Professional Chiropractic, dentistry, engineering, law, medical, ministry, optometry, pharmacy, podiatry, veterinary medicine

Accredited Programs Business, chemistry, nursing

Special Programs The college has a joint degree program in dentistry with New York University and a five-year master's program in accounting. There are several minors, including art history, dance, and journalism. There are study abroad and internship opportunities, as well as a Washington, D.C., program. The college also has a student exchange program with California Lutheran College in Thousand Oaks, California.

Facilities There are 18 buildings, including Campus Hall, which houses the Early Childhood Center; the Music and Performance Hall; a nursing lab; Cunard Hall, built in 1852; Harbor View Hall, a 15-story residence hall with panoramic views of lower Manhattan, New York Harbor, and the Verrazano Bridge; the Wagner College Theater; the Wagner Student Union; a planetarium; the Fischer Memorial Field, which has a new stadium; the new Spiro Sports Center; and an art gallery.

Transition to College Program Before attending the college, all freshmen are assigned to selected learning communities in thematically linked courses enrolling a common cohort of students. Every freshman is sent a *First Year Guide* booklet with a list of the first-year learning communities. Students are asked to send their preference of learning communities and other courses so that they can be preregistered. Students are linked to field experiences based on the themes of the learning communities, and each student takes a tutorial taught by his or her learning community professor. The tutorial emphasizes writing based upon the students' field experiences and readings.

Athletics NCAA I, Metro Atlantic Conference, Northeast Conference

Men: Baseball, basketball, football (Div. I-AA), golf, lacrosse, tennis, track/cross-country, wrestling

Women: Basketball, golf, lacrosse, soccer, softball, swimming, tennis, track/cross-country, volleyball, water polo

Student Life and Housing About 1,300 students can be accommodated in college housing, which is guaranteed for all four years. Sixty-nine percent of the students are from New York, the remainder are from 36 other states and 15 countries. Ethnicity: Caucasian—85 percent; African-American—5 percent; Hispanic-American—5 percent; Asian-American—3 percent; International—2 percent. There are four local and four national fraternities and one local and two national sororities. Upperclassmen may keep cars.

Accommodations for Students with Disabilities In compliance with section 504

Financial Aid About 71 percent of all freshmen receive aid. The average freshman award was about $13,000.

Requirements for Admission SAT I or ACT scores and a college prep high school program. An interview is strongly recommended. Physician's assistant candidates are selected after supplementary application and interviews.

Application Freshmen are admitted fall and spring semesters. The Early Decision deadline is December 1, with an admission decision by January 1.

International Students Required are a statement of financial support, two official copies of high school and, if applicable, college transcripts, with one copy in the original language of issue and the other a certified English translation. Students must also include a personal essay, letters of recommendation, and official test scores. A minimum TOEFL paper score of 500 or 213 computer-based is required. If a student has completed either two years of high school or college instruction in English, the SAT I test is highly recommended.

Transfer Students Official college transcripts are required from schools that are accredited institutions with the student in good academic standing. A maximum of 18 credits can be transferred by associate's degree applicants, and 27 credits by students from four-year institutions. Only courses in which a minimum grade of C was earned will be considered for transfer. The last nine credits of any degree must be earned at Wagner.

Admission Contact
Office of Admissions
Wagner College
One Campus Road
Staten Island, NY 10301
Phone: (800) 221-1010; (718) 390-3411

FAX: (718) 390-3105
E-Mail: *admissions@wagner.edu*
Web: *www.wagner.edu*

The Heart of the College Wagner College has come a long way from the years when its most recognized program was football. The last several years have seen wonderful progress designed and implemented at Wagner. Wagner has created an exceptionally innovative, experientially-based undergraduate curriculum that truly provides the linchpin that coalesces and highlights the college's strengths.

Under the Wagner Plan, students complete a liberal arts core program and a major, totaling 36 courses. As part of these requirements, students complete three learning communities, one in the first year, one during the intermediate years, and one in the senior year in the major. The Learning Communities are clusters of courses that are linked together by a single theme and that share a common set of students. The professors plan their LC courses with overlapping assignments, common readings, and joint problems, so that courses share some common ground. The Wagner Plan links the Learning Communities directly to field experience based on the theme of the Learning Community. The field placements are linked to Reflective Tutorials that emphasize writing skills, discussion, and linking field experiences directly to the course read-

ings. As seniors, students complete either a field-based internship or an original research project. An example of a first-year field experience was "The Tom's River Project," an in-depth, first-hand investigation of a serious health issue. An example of a senior field-experience could be an internship with Merrill Lynch or the Institute for Basic Research.

A chairman of a Board of Trustees and Wagner alumnus commented: "Proximity opened doors for me when I was a student and it continues to work for today's Wagner student body." Each year more than 1,000 Wagner students complete internships and field placements at such sites as the Museum of Modern Art, JP Morgan, Chase, NBC News, Paine Webber, and others. These internships, combined with the active and loyal Wagner alumni who take part in the college's Mentorship and Shadowing Programs, allow students to learn first-hand about career opportunities and provide for vital contacts that lead to jobs.

Manhattan is only a 25-minute ferry ride away and the college runs shuttle buses seven days a week. Back on campus, things are lively as well, with many clubs and organizations, Greek life, and excellent athletic and fitness facilities. If students want a study abroad experience, Wagner's affiliation with the Institute for the International Education of Students provides for study abroad in 22 cities around the world.

WARTBURG COLLEGE　　Waverly, Iowa

Total Undergraduate Enrollment: 1,700
Men: 725 Women: 975
Five-Year Graduation Rate: 70%

Tuition: $$$
Room and Board: $
Residential Students: 82%

History Wartburg College was founded in 1852 when a Bavarian pastor sent Georg Grosmann and five students to found a teachers' seminary in Saginaw, Michigan. The college moved several times before settling in Waverly, Iowa, in 1935. The college is named for the Wartburg Castle in Germany, which served as a refuge for Martin

Luther during the stormy days of the Reformation. There he completed a translation of the New Testament into the language of the common people. The college is affiliated with the Evangelical Lutheran Church in America. It is listed on the Templeton Foundation's Honor Roll of Character-Building Colleges.

Location The 118-acre campus is in Waverly, Iowa (population 10,000), a small town 15 miles north of Waterloo/Cedar Falls, a metropolitan area of 100,000.

Top Programs of Study Biology, business, education, communication arts

Arts and Sciences Art, biochemistry, biology, chemistry, church music, communication arts, communication design, communication studies (speech, theater), computer science, economics, engineering science, English, fitness management, history, international relations, mathematics, modern languages (French and French studies, German and German studies, Spanish and Spanish studies), music applied, music performance, music theory, philosophy, physics, political science, psychology, religion (campus ministry, parish education, urban ministry, youth and family ministry), social work, sociology, writing

Business Accounting, business administration (concentrations in finance, international business, management, marketing), computer information systems

Education Art, Christian Day School, early childhood, elementary, middle, music, physical education, secondary

Pre-Professional Dentistry, engineering, law, medicine, nursing, optometry, pharmacy, physical therapy, veterinary medicine

Accredited Programs Education, music, music therapy, social work

Special Programs There are interdepartmental and individualized majors as well as interdisciplinary minors and certification programs, including Leadership. There are cooperative programs in medical technology with several hospitals; occupational therapy with Washington University School of Occupational Therapy, St. Louis; and nursing with the University of Iowa College of Nursing. The college operates on a 4-4-1 academic calendar, offering a May semester. There are study abroad opportunities, internships, a Denver Center and a Washington, D.C., Center. The college is rated one of the nation's most computer-wired colleges. The Wartburg Institute for Leadership Education offers courses, workshops, mentoring, and community outreach projects.

Facilities There are 34 buildings, including the new Vogel Library, designed to foster collaboration among students, faculty, and librarians; the expanded and renovated Becker Hall of Science; the Fine Arts Center, which includes the Schmidt Art Gallery; the new McElroy Communication Arts Center; Old Main, which is listed on the National Register of Historic Places; the new Wartburg Chapel; the newly expanded and renovated Student Union; the new Watson-Hoover Stadium; and a new track. The nearby Lageschulte Prairie and Mullarky Woods are used for field studies and research. There are also student-run TV and radio stations and a student-run public relations agency.

Transition to College Program Wartburg offers a coordinated program that targets the needs of first-year students, beginning with orientation and then designing interactions with faculty help to orient students to expectations at Wartburg and support student success.

Athletics NCAA II, Iowa Intercollegiate Athletic Conference

Men: Baseball, basketball, cross-country, football, golf, soccer, tennis, track & field, wrestling

Women: Basketball, cross-country, golf, soccer, softball, tennis, track & field, volleyball

Student Life and Housing About 1,300 students can be accommodated in college housing, which is guaranteed for all four years. Seventy-six percent of the students are from Iowa, the remainder are from 26 other states and 36 countries. Ethnicity: Caucasian—89 percent; African-American—4 percent; International—4 percent; Asian-American—1 percent. There are no fraternities or sororities. All students may keep cars.

Accommodations for Students with Disabilities A recent evaluation made by a licensed psychologist or learning specialist should be presented to the Dean of Students in order to receive reasonable accommodations.

Financial Aid About 97 percent of all students receive aid. The average freshman award was about $14,000.

Requirements for Admission SAT I or ACT scores and a college prep high school program. A campus visit and interview are required. GED students are considered for admission if they have an average of 50 or above in the test composite, submit ACT or SAT scores (unless the student has been out of high school five years or more), and submit a high school transcript.

Application Freshmen are admitted fall and winter. Early Action applications should be filed by December 1, regular applications by August 1 for fall admission, and December 30 for winter admission. Admission notification is sent on a rolling basis.

International Students Required are official transcripts from secondary and, if applicable, postsecondary schools, and if the original documents are not in English, a certified English translation must be attached. A minimum TOEFL score of 550 is required. Students with scores in the 480–550 range will be placed in a Bridge Program that combines ESL and academic courses, all for academic credit; those who score in the 450–479 range must successfully complete the English for International Students Program before being admitted to a bachelor's degree program.

Transfer Students Official high school and college transcripts are required, including ACT or SAT scores, a written academic recommendation, and a personal interview. Courses with a minimum grade of C− are considered for transfer if taken at an accredited college. Students transferring from two-year institutions may transfer up to 22 credits.

Admission Contact
Office of Admissions
Wartburg College
100 Westbury Blvd.
Waverly, IA 50677
Phone: (800) 772-2085; (319) 352-8264
FAX: (319) 352-8579
E-mail: *admissions@wartburg.edu*
Web: *www.wartburg.edu*

The Heart of the College At this quality college in small town America, parents and students get a big bang for the dollar. Not only is Wartburg considered among the Midwest's best comprehensive colleges, it is also considered to have excellent science programs. With 82 percent of the students living on campus, Wartburg is truly a living–learning community, with a well-qualified and student-centered faculty, an advisement system that really tries to accommodate student needs, a strong varsity and intramural program that attracts 75 percent of the students, and clubs and organizations—activities that make this a fun campus—and numerous traditions that reflect the college's German heritage.

With students from many states and countries, Wartburg celebrates its diversity in many ways. One of its stated goals is "Wartburg students are educated to respect diversity and accept ambiguity within our society. . . ." Many student organizations and campus programs have an international focus. For example, a chapter of Amnesty International provides education regarding human rights violations around the world; Soujourners gives students who have returned from cultural immersions an opportunity to share and reflect on their experiences; and an Artist Series features artists and performing artists from around the world.

Music is big at Wartburg. Students participate in the Choirs, Wind Ensemble, Castle Singers, Jazz Band, and more. Visiting artists regularly teach master classes while they're on campus. World renowned opera star Simon Estes spends part of the year at Wartburg, working with students and speaking to classes.

The Wartburg Plan of Essential Education forms the basis for a liberally educated, ethically minded citizen. Students focus on thinking strategies, reasoning skills, fundamental literacies, health and wellness, faith and reflection, and a capstone course that helps students to synthesize their learning to address issues in their major. As a college of the Evangelical Church in America, Wartburg has a commitment to foster spiritual growth as well as intellectual growth and help students integrate the two. In the Wartburg Plan students take two religion/philosophy courses.

Wartburg students live their faith in a variety of ways. Campus ministry programs offer opportunities for service and fellowship. There are Bible study groups, Sunday services, half-hour chapels three times a week, and a Wednesday night Eucharist. Graduates report that they are active members of church congregations and more than 50 percent served in a church leadership role. However, because of the national diversity of the campus, Wartburg students learn much about other faiths. One student commented: "The faith community has been a big part of my college life. Meeting people of different faiths has broadened my perspective."

WASHINGTON COLLEGE   Chestertown, Maryland

Total Undergraduate Enrollment: 1,300
Men: 585 Women: 715
Five-Year Graduation Rate: 70%

Tuition: $$$$
Room and Board: $
Residential Students: 80%

History Washington College was founded in 1782 and named for none other than George Washington, who donated money and served on its board until he became President in 1789. It was the first chartered college in this new nation, and President Washington was well aware of the importance of an educated citizenry for a democratic government to thrive.

Location The 120-acre campus is located in Chestertown, Maryland, a small town on Maryland's Eastern Shore 75 miles from Baltimore, Philadelphia, and Washington, D.C.

Top Programs of Study English, business, psychology

Arts and Sciences American studies, anthropology, art, biology (concentration in biochemistry), chemistry, drama, economics, English, environmental studies, French studies, German studies, Hispanic studies, history, humanities, international literature and culture, mathematics and computer science, music, philosophy and religion, physics, political science, psychology (concentrations in clinical/counseling and neuroscience), sociology (concentration in social work)

Business Management

Education Elementary, secondary

Pre-Professional Law, medicine

Accredited Programs Chemistry

Special Programs There is a concentration in Chesapeake Regional Studies, a minor in creative writing, and several interdisciplinary minors. There are several dual degree programs offered: engineering with the University of Maryland; nursing with Johns Hopkins, the University of Delaware, and the University of Maryland; and pharmacy with the University of Maryland. Students can double major, do independent study, and design their own majors. There is a Model U.N. Program as well as internship and study abroad opportunities. There is a distinguished speakers series. The Starr Center for the Study of the American Experience is a forum for new scholarship about American history. The Center for the Environment and Society addresses difficult policy issues and promotes interdisciplinary approaches to problem solving.

Facilities There are 39 buildings. Smith Hall, named for the school's founder, is the main classroom building; Dunning Hall houses the sciences; the Casey Academic Center is the heart of campus activity. There are also the Miller Library, the Gibson Performing Arts Center, and the Larabee Arts Center for the visual arts. The O'Neill Literary House, a renovated Victorian building, is the focal point for literary activity. Recreational facilities include the Cain Athletic Center; Casey Swim Center; the Hynson Boating Park, featuring a waterfront pavilion for watching sailing and crew races; the Johnson Fitness Center; and a new tennis center. There are 12 new apartment-style residences.

Transition to College Program First-year students study CNW Seminar (community, nation, world), in which they are introduced to the political, social, artistic, economic, and environmental communities that exist in the Chesapeake Region. Students choose a community or nation seminar for the first semester and a world seminar for the second. Seminars include a focus on writing, the use of the computer, and research methodology.

Athletics NCAA III, the Centennial Conference

Men: Baseball, basketball, lacrosse, rowing, soccer, swimming, tennis

Women: Basketball, field hockey, lacrosse, rowing, soccer, softball, swimming, tennis, volleyball

Coeducational: Sailing

Student Life and Housing About 1,100 students can be accommodated in college housing, which includes special interest houses. Fifty-three percent of the students are from Maryland, the remainder from 37 other states and 38 countries. Ethnicity: Caucasian—84 percent; International—5 percent; African-American—3 percent; Asian-American—

2 percent. There are three national fraternities and three national sororities. All students may keep cars.

Accommodations for Students with Disabilities In order to obtain reasonable academic accommodations and/or variation in degree requirements, students must request these with appropriate supporting documentation submitted in writing to the Associate Dean, located in Bunting Hall.

Financial Aid About 80 percent of all freshmen receive aid. The average award was about $15,500.

Requirements for Admission SAT I or ACT scores and a college prep high school program. An interview is recommended. Those students who visit the college and meet with a member of the admissions staff are given preference in the admissions process.

Application Freshmen are admitted fall and spring semesters. The Early Decision deadline is November 15, with notification by December 15. The Early Action deadline is December 1, with admission notification by December 19. Regular applications should be filed by February 15.

International Students Appropriate academic transcripts should be submitted along with TOEFL results if English is not the applicant's first language. SAT I or ACT results are recommended.

Transfer Students Required are transcripts of all completed academic work, including an official secondary school transcript. It is advisable to consult with both the Admissions Office and the Registrar in order to obtain an accurate evaluation concerning transfer of academic credits. Students must complete a minimum of 56 credits at Washington College as well as the final eight courses. Students must also complete the senior obligation.

Home-Schooled Students Along with the application, applicants should submit SAT I or ACT scores, a transcript (or its equivalent) of academic coursework, one letter of recommendation, and interview on campus with a member of the admissions staff.

Admission Contact
Office of Admissions
Washington College
300 Washington Avenue
Chestertown, MD 21620-1197
Phone: (800) 422-1782
FAX: (410) 778-7287
E-mail: *adm-off@washcoll.edu*
Web: *www.washcoll.edu*

The Heart of the College As one of the leading national liberal arts colleges—and one with a generous financial aid program—Washington College makes a commitment to each student to provide an engaging, personalized, flexible education. Choices abound at this college. The First-Year Seminars offer students a most appealing variety of topics to explore, from "The History and Philosophy of Sports in America" to "Ethnic Identity in Literature and Film" to "It's Analytical, My Dear Watson!: An Introduction to Forensic Science." Students move to general education requirements, which allow them to choose courses in the liberal arts and sciences as well as one of many writing-intensive courses. Students then select a major and study that chosen academic area. They finally complete a "senior obligation"—a capstone experience that takes the form of a thesis, performance, or comprehensive exam.

The richness of the academic program is supplemented by a speakers series and a variety of campus activities, clubs, and organizations. Students can choose from speakers focused on environmental affairs, public policy, journalism, and national affairs, as well as writers, editors, and literary scholars. In addition, campus Honor Societies offer students choices in terms of programs related to academic majors, ranging from

archeological digs to essay contests to business networking. The creative arts program offers students a theme dorm for writers, artists, and performers who put on two creative projects each semester. Visiting writers and editors meet with students around the kitchen table in the O'Neill Literary House and the Writers Union, the largest club on campus, which sponsors a Wednesday series of informal talks as well as poetry readings and even provides grants to student editors who want to publish their own literary magazines. Some "quirky" clubs include The Royale Shakespeare Players, which enacts spoofs of Shakespearean plays, and the Early Music Concert, which performs music of the Middle Ages, Renaissance, and Baroque eras. Through service organizations, 65 percent of the students choose to volunteer with mentally challenged people, help preserve shorelines, tutor at-risk students, or work for Habitat for Humanity. Almost one-quarter of the students join a fraternity or a sorority, and almost 60 percent play a varsity, club, or intramural sport. Students have 33 international programs to choose from, including summer environmental programs in Equador, the Galapagos Islands, Desert Island in Maine, and Bermuda.

In what Washington College likes to call a "human-scaled community" of about 1,300 students, students actually choose those opportunities that are uniquely matched to them. At the same time, they are taught by a faculty of scholars and teachers that engages them in discussions in small classes and invites their participation in their research.

Students enjoy the historic and friendly charm of Chestertown on the Chester River, the natural beauty of the Chesapeake Bay region, and the proximity to the culture, recreation, and professional sports only 90 minutes away in Baltimore, Washington, D.C., and Philadelphia.

WASHINGTON & JEFFERSON COLLEGE

Washington, Pennsylvania

Total Undergraduate Enrollment: 1,250
Men: 648 Women: 602
Five-Year Graduation Rate: 78%

Tuition: $$$$
Room and Board: $$
Residential Students: 88%

History Washington & Jefferson, founded in 1781, is one of the oldest colleges in America. Actually established as three log cabin schools that evolved into two institutions only 10 miles apart that became rivals, and then merged in 1865 as the Civil War brought decreased enrollment and financial problems. The college became coeducational in 1969.

Location The 52-acre campus is located in Washington, Pennsylvania (population 15,000), a small town 27 miles southwest of Pittsburgh.

Top Programs of Study Education, accounting, business, psychology, pre-professional

Arts and Sciences Art, biochemistry, biology, chemistry, child development, economics, English, French, German, history, mathematics, music, philosophy, physics, political science, psychology, sociology, Spanish, theater

Business Accounting, administration, industrial chemistry and management, information technology leadership, international business

Education Art, elementary, secondary

Pre-Professional Dentistry, law, medicine, optometry, osteopathy, physical therapy, podiatry, veterinary medicine

Accredited Programs None

Special Programs Students may design an individualized thematic major. There are cooperative degree programs in the following: engineering with Case Western Reserve University and Washington University in St. Louis; law with Duquesne University and the University of Pittsburgh; and optometry and podiatry with Drexel University.

There are student exchange and study abroad programs and a Washington, D.C., semester. A January Intersession allows students to study abroad, pursue off-campus internships or independent study, or take a course not typically offered. There are also special programs in Human Resource Management; Entrepreneurial Studies; Mind, Brain and Behavior; and Environmental Studies. There are Air Force and Army ROTC programs.

Facilities There are 43 buildings, including the new Brunett Center, an academic facility with state-of-the-art technology and a Small Business Institute; the renovated Cameroon Stadium; radio stations; the Miller Library; the Olin Fine Arts Center with gallery and auditorium; the Rossin Campus Center; the Vilar Technology Center; a Wellness Center; and John McMillan Hall, the eighth oldest college building still in continuous use.

Transition to College Program All first-year students complete a Freshman Forum, a course and a set of related cultural and intellectual events (the "lyceum") designed to introduce students to the full range of the college's educational opportunities. Faculty members from across the college who serve as freshman advisers focus on a particular topic of general interest and offer related lectures and seminars. The "lyceum," which may consist of lectures, concerts, plays, and field trips to museums and galleries, is arranged to correlate with the chosen theme of the course.

Athletics NCAA III, President's Athletic Conference, Eastern Collegiate Athletic Conference

Men: Baseball, basketball, cross-country, football, golf, lacrosse, soccer, swimming and diving, tennis, track & field, water polo, wrestling

Women: Basketball, cross-country, field hockey, golf, soccer, softball, swimming and diving, tennis, track & field, volleyball, water polo

Student Life and Housing About 1,000 students can be accommodated in college housing, which is guaranteed for all four years. Eighty-four percent of the students are from Pennsylvania, the remainder are from 31 other states and one foreign country. Ethnicity: Caucasian—94 percent. There are eight national fraternities and four national sororities. All students may keep cars.

Accommodations for Students with Disabilities: In compliance with section 504

Financial Aid About 85 percent of all freshmen receive aid. The average freshman award was about $15,000.

Requirements for Admission SAT I or ACT scores with a college prep high school program.

Application Early Decision applications are due by December 1, with notification by December 15. Early Action applications are due by January 15, with notification by February 15. The regular application deadline is March 1, with notification by April 1.

International Students Required are official secondary and, if applicable, postsecondary transcripts in English, SAT I or ACT results if the student's native language is English, and TOEFL results if English is not the student's native language, diplomas, recommendations, and evidence of financial support.

Transfer Students Required are official transcripts from high school and accredited colleges attended, SAT or ACT scores, and a completed Transfer Student Clearance Form. A student must complete 18 courses at W & J to obtain a degree.

Admission Contact
Office of Admissions
Washington & Jefferson College
60 South Lincoln Street
Washington, PA 15301

Phone: (888) W-AND-JAY; (724) 223-6025
(FAX): 724-223-6534
E-mail: *admission@washjeff.edu*
Web: *www.washjeff.edu*

The Heart of the College Washington & Jefferson is considered a top liberal arts college and a "best buy." With a tradition of success that finds among W & J's 12,000 living alumni more than 1,500 medical professionals, more than 800 attorneys or judges, and more than 500 presidents or CEOs, it's obvious that something special happens at this college. Perhaps it's what one student described when she said: "W & J is a transforming experience. The college takes you from being an uncertain student to someone who's ready to take on the world." W & J accomplishes this transformation in several ways.

First, in the best liberal arts tradition, the college wants to develop students who are academically well-rounded, so all students take General Education Requirements in the arts, humanities, social sciences, natural sciences, and mathematics. In addition, W & J has an Open Major Policy, whereby students need not declare a major area of study until their junior year. This provides students with the encouragement to explore academically until they find their "passion." That's a term that's used a lot at W & J, because of a shared belief that personal happiness and success is achieved by doing something you are passionate about. The January Intersession is given special attention at W & J. During this time students can complete internships, take a month-long concentrated course, travel abroad, or conduct research.

Students cite the professors as being instrumental to their success. More than 90 percent of the faculty hold the highest degree in their field and have distinguished themselves as grant recipients and significant scholars. The small class sizes encourage dialogue rather than lecture, as well as close relationships with faculty. These are professors who set high expectations for students, inspire and support students to achieve these, and provide the necessary resources. This quality of support and accessibility is symbolized by W & J's president, who hosts frequent dinners and has an open door policy to his office. Students at W & J believe they have a great deal of influence in shaping their education.

There's much to do on this campus, nestled in the rolling, wooded hills, with more than 100 student clubs and organizations. Also, the Vilar Distinguished Artist Series has brought to campus internationally acclaimed performing artists

and the W & J Arts Series brings to campus more contemporary music. W & J takes great pride in a strong athletic program, including a football team that has won 14 championships in the last 15 years, and nationally ranked swimming and diving and water polo teams.

Then, of course, there's Pittsburgh, only 30 minutes away, offering professional sports, cultural opportunities, internships, and recreational activities in one of America's major cities.

WESTMINSTER COLLEGE

New Wilmington, Pennsylvania

Total Undergraduate Enrollment: 1,400
Men: 550 Women: 850
Five-Year Graduation Rate: 78%

Tuition: $$$
Room and Board: $
Residential Students: 88%

History Westminster College was founded in 1852 by members of the Associate Presbyterian Church. The first college catalogue stated that "no person will be refused admission on account of color, caste, or sex," making Westminster a pioneer in supporting nondiscrimination. For Westminster, the educated person is also one who has "ever-developing values and ideals identified in the Judeo-Christian tradition." The college is listed on the Templeton Foundation's Honor Roll of Character-Building Colleges.

Location The 300-acre campus is located in New Wilmington, Pennsylvania, a rural area 60 miles north of Pittsburgh in western Pennsylvania, 80 miles south of Erie, and 85 miles southeast of Cleveland.

Top Programs of Study Education, biology, business

Arts and Sciences Art (visual arts communications, general studio, visual arts technologies), biology, broadcast communications, chemistry, computer science, economics, English, environmental science, French, German, history, human resources/psychology, intercultural studies, international politics, Latin, mathematics, molecular biology, music, music

performance, music sacred, neuroscience, philosophy, physics, political science, psychology, public relations, religion, sociology (including criminal justice), Spanish, speech communication, theater

Business Accounting, business administration (concentrations in finance, health administration, human resources management, international business, marketing), computer information systems, financial economics, international business

Education Christian, elementary, music, secondary

Pre-Professional Dentistry, engineering, environmental science, health management systems, law, medicine, ministry, veterinary medicine

Accredited Programs Chemistry, music

Special Programs A cooperative engineering degree is offered with Case Western Reserve University, Penn State University, and Washington University in St. Louis. A dual law degree program is offered with Duquesne University. There are opportunities for interdisciplinary majors, double majors, minors, internships, and a Washington, D.C., semester. Students can also study in London at Regents College. The college is rated as one of America's most "computer-wired" colleges.

Facilities There are 22 buildings, a combination of old and new, including Old Main, a 1929 Gothic-style building, which houses Wallace Memorial Chapel and Thompson House, which is listed on the National Register of Historic Places. Other buildings include the renovated Thompson-Clark Hall; Patterson Hall, which houses a theater, art gallery, and an FM radio station; Memorial Field House and Natatorium; the Hoyt Science Resources Center, which houses a planetarium, observatory, electron microscope suite, and a pre-school facility; and the McGill Memorial Library. The Outdoor Laboratory for Biological and Environmental Science is used for courses and research in biology, environmental science, and chemistry and is comprised of three distinct areas: a research station, Britain Lake, and College Woods. There is also a cable TV station.

Transition to College Program The First-Year Program is comprised of three courses: an inquiry course that engages students with questions that have traditionally been at the center of a liberal arts education, writing, and oral communication.

Athletics NCAA III, President's Athletic Conference

Men: Baseball, basketball, cross-country, football, golf, swimming, soccer, tennis, track & field

Women: Basketball, cross-country, golf, swimming, soccer, softball, tennis, track & field, volleyball

Student Life and Housing About 1,100 students can be accommodated in college housing, which is guaranteed for all four years. Seventy-nine percent of the students are from Pennsylvania, the remainder from 23 other states and one foreign country. Ethnicity: Caucasian—97 percent. There are five national fraternities and five national sororities. All students may keep cars.

Accommodations for Students with Disabilities In compliance with Section 504

Financial Aid About 98 percent of all freshmen receive aid. The average freshman award was about $16,000.

Requirements for Admission SAT I or ACT scores and a college prep high school program.

Application Freshmen are admitted fall, winter, and spring semesters. Early Decision applications are due November 15, with admission notification by December 1. Regular application deadlines are open, with admission notification beginning December 1.

International Students Required are official secondary and, if applicable, postsecondary transcripts, a GPA of 3.0 (B), or a first division pass on the European University (o level) scale in courses that are college preparatory in nature. A minimum TOEFL score of 500 or Michigan Test score of 80 is required. SAT or ACT scores are required for those students who come from a country where English is the spoken language. Certification of financial resources is also required.

Transfer Students Required are official high school and college transcripts, with a college GPA of at least 2.5. No course grade lower than C − will be considered for transfer. Only credits taken at regionally accredited institutions will be considered. The student must be in good standing at their previous colleges. Westminster has transfer articulation agreements with several Pennsylvania colleges in order to facilitate transfer students, including Butler County C.C., Community College of Allegheny County, and the Pennsylvania State University—Shenango Campus.

Admission Contact
Office of Admissions
Westminster College
319 South Market Street
New Wilmington, PA 16172
Phone: (800) 942-8033; (724) 946-7100
FAX: (724) 946-6171
E-mail: *admis@westminster.edu*
Web: *www.westminster.edu*

The Heart of the College In a pastoral setting in western Pennsylvania, surrounded by wooded hills, farmlands, country roads, and streams, is one of the most successful national liberal arts colleges in the nation, especially in terms of graduation rate.

Many of the colleges in this guide have sought to offer a limited core of interdisciplinary courses to all students, usually in their first two years of study, but the Westminster Plan is distinct because its curriculum spans all four years. The faculty's purpose in creating the plan was to assure that all students possess a common base of knowledge and skills from a curriculum that would provide a broad spectrum of human accomplishments in the arts, social sciences, humanities, mathematics, and science. In the plan, students first study Inquiry courses exploring ethical, moral, and scientific questions in the liberal arts and sciences and focus on writing and oral communications. Students also study "cluster courses," which are linked together, taught by at least two different faculty members from two different disciplines to the same group of students. For example, one cluster course is studying "Changing Visions of Delinquency: Literature and Sociology," where students take an English course, "Adolescent Rebellion in Literature and Film," and a sociology course, "Juvenile Delinquency." The plan includes community service experiences within and outside the courses and a senior capstone course, typically consisting of a major individual project done under the guidance of a faculty mentor.

Throughout, a new telecommunications net-work is utilized to provide state-of-the-art voice, data, and video capabilities to students and faculty. The sophisticated technology requires Westminster students to focus on skills, collaboration, and problem-solving—attributes appreciated by prospective employers, as attested to by Westminster's 98 percent career and graduate school placement rate. Internships contribute to this success rate; 85 percent of students hold at least one before graduation, with the college offering internships in all majors.

The Christian heritage of the college has at its core those ideals exemplified by Jesus Christ, especially compassion and justice. Classes are small, and student–faculty interaction moves beyond academics, with a focus on the whole student's development. Students comment about the genuine care and kindness of students and the individual attention provided by faculty. Vespers are offered, as well as a special lecture series and an annual retreat.

Students have a busy extracurricular life with over 85 clubs and organizations, and one of the most successful small college athletic programs in the nation. A Celebrity Series brings Broadway musicals and entertainers of national acclaim to campus. There are several theater productions, a broad music program, and student-run cable TV and FM radio stations. With Pittsburgh just an hour away, students have the opportunity to watch professional sports, visit museums, and attend outdoor concerts.

WHITTIER COLLEGE   Whittier, California

Total Undergraduate Enrollment: 1,300
Men: 520 Women: 780
Five-Year Graduation Rate: 75%

Tuition: $$$$
Room and Board: $$$
Residential Students: 90%

History Whittier College was founded by the Religious Society of Friends (Quakers) in 1887, and takes great pride in its Quaker heritage.

Location The 95-acre campus is located in Whittier, California, in a suburban area 18 miles southeast of Los Angeles, in the foothills of the San Gabriel Mountains.

Top Programs of Study Business administration, English, political science, theater

Arts and Sciences Applied philosophy, art, biochemistry, biology, chemistry, economics, English, environmental science, French, history, mathematics, mathematics/business administration, music, philosophy, physical education and recreation, physics, political science, psychology, religious studies, social work, sociology, Spanish, theater arts

Business Administration

Education Early childhood, elementary

Pre-Professional Athletic training, dentistry, engineering, law, medicine, optometry, pharmacy, physical therapy, veterinary medicine

Accredited Programs Chemistry, social work

Special Programs There are interdisciplinary programs offered in Comparative Cultures, Women's Studies, and others. The college offers a cooperative engineering program with several universities and an accelerated program in the Whittier Law School. The residence halls use a "house" system with resident faculty masters living in the residence halls. The Whittier Scholars program allows students to design their own educational programs. The college has a specially designed writing program, a Center for Mexican-American Affairs, and a laboratory/demonstration school for kindergarten and primary grades.

Facilities There are 50 buildings, including the Wardman Library; the Shannon Center for the Performing Arts, which houses a 400-seat theater; the Erteszek Commputer Center; the Keck Foundation Image Processing Center; the GTE Language Resource Center; Dexter Student Center, which houses a radio station; Galbraith Athletics Complex; a law school; and the George Allen Fitness Center, a state-of-the-art facility.

Transition to College Program As part of Whitier's First-Year Mentor Program, each new student is assigned to a full-time faculty member who provides academic support and direction throughout the first year. It is the primary role of the faculty mentor to introduce the student to Whittier College and to further an understanding of its overall mission and the importance of a lib-

eral arts education. Mentors also help students become aware of the many resources available to them on campus.

Athletics NCAA III, Southern Intercollegiate Athletic Conference

Men: Baseball, basketball, cross-country, football, golf, lacrosse, soccer, swimming, tennis, track & field, water polo

Women: Basketball, cross-country, golf, lacrosse, soccer, softball, swimming, tennis, track & field, volleyball, water polo

Student Life and Housing About 2,000 students can be accommodated in college housing, which is guaranteed for all four years. Seventy-three percent of the students are from California, the remainder from 27 other states and 21 countries. Ethnicity: Caucasian—50 percent; Hispanic-American—30 percent; Asian-American—10 percent; African-American—5 percent; International—4 percent. There are four local fraternities and five local sororities. All students may keep cars.

Accommodations for Students with Disabilities In compliance with section 504

Financial Aid About 80 percent of all freshmen receive aid.

Requirements for Admission SAT I or ACT scores and a college prep high school program. A personal interview is recommended.

Application The Early Action deadline is December 1, with notification by December 30. The deadline for fall admission is February 1, and December 1 for spring admission. Admission decisions are mailed on a rolling basis.

International Students Required are official secondary and, if applicable, postsecondary transcripts, two academic recommendations, proof of attainment of a high school diploma, a certificate of finance, and minimum TOEFL results of 550 paper or 213 computer-based, if English is not the applicant's first language. Those who wish to have credits transferred must have their coursework evaluated by an external credit evaluation agency. Entrance is normally for the fall semester only.

Transfer Students Applicants must be in good standing at their previous fully accredited colleges. Required are a personal essay, high school and college transcripts, proof of attainment of the high school diploma (completion of the GED may be substituted if 30 transferable credits have been earned), and two academic recommendations. SAT or ACT scores are required if the candidate has not completed at least 30 transferable credits. A personal interview is recommended. A minimum course grade of C− is required to be considered for transfer. A maximum of 70 credits from a community college and a maximum of 90 credits from a four-year institution can be transferred.

Admission Contact
Office of Admissions
Whittier College
P.O. Box 634
Whittier, CA 90608-0634
Phone: (562) 907-4238
FAX: (562) 907-4870
E-mail: *admission@whittier.edu*
Web: *www.whittier.edu*

The Heart of the College Whittier College is one of the most ethnically diverse of all the schools in this guide, a diversity that sparks an incredibly energetic life on campus. The Quaker heritage provides the commitment to a diverse student population, tolerance of human differences, and a concern for the individual, but it is Whittier's superb faculty and curricula that make learning such a joy at this college. Professors love to "push the envelop" to provide students the greatest learning opportunities. For example, in "Advanced Fiction Writing," the professor brought to class eight different writers so that students could listen to them read their work and then discuss their writing. Professors are also innovative in how they present "paired courses," designed to overlap and converge. For example, students in "American Foreign Policy" do a computer-assisted simulation that requires them to make foreign policy decisions for the U.S. government, while in the "Recent United States History" course the same students learn a context for understanding U.S. policies.

The innovative tradition of Whittier is seen in its Scholars Program, where students, working with faculty advisers and their peers, design an individualized program for a liberal arts degree. Through interdisciplinary seminars, discussions, guest lecturers, study abroad, community service, and a Senior Project, the program sees students tackle significant and enduring questions and complete an important research effort. The Writing Program at Whittier receives great emphasis. Beginning with Freshmen Writing Seminars limited to 15 students and taught by faculty from all disciplines, it utilizes interesting seminar topics, such as "Wilderness Writing," and then moves to Writing Intensive courses that emphasize the process of writing. The third component is "writing across the curriculum," where students write in all courses, even science and math. Capping the program is the "paper-in-the-major," where students demonstrate their ability to communicate in writing their command of their subject areas. Expanding its innovation further, Whittier invites three senior professors, called "Faculty Masters," to reside in homes on campus where they regularly host special events. This innovation even extends to residence halls, which are part of a "house system" modeled after those established at Oxford and Cambridge Universities. At Whittier resident faculty masters and their families live adjacent to student residences. The "house system" is intended to extend the classroom learning experience with educational and social programs, such as lectures, dinners, and musical performances.

Whittier also offers study abroad programs in 20 countries and over 60 universities around the world. The college pioneered Denmark's International Study Program in 1959, where students in the Whittier-in-Copenhagen program spend their fall semester immersed in the Danish culture. The college offers internships in over 1,200 different sites, and faculty involve students in meaningful collaborative research. Whittier also prides itself on its strong lacrosse, women's basketball, and football teams. One senior said: "The happiest students here are those that are most involved. The only thing that isn't easily tolerated in our community is apathy."

Whittier offers shops, cafes, bookstores, nine movie theaters, and the sunshine and beaches of southern California. Is it any wonder that 45 percent of Whittier graduates want to continue their education in graduate school? The medical school acceptance rate is double the national average.

WHITWORTH COLLEGE   Spokane, Washington

Total Undergraduate Enrollment: 1,850
Men: 666 Women: 1,184
Five-Year Graduation Rate: 70%

Tuition: $$$
Room and Board: $$
Residential Students: 63%

History Whitworth College had its beginnings in 1853, when George Whitworth, an Ohio minister, set out with 50 families for the Western frontier to establish a college that would provide "a good English education and a thorough religious training." With only his family surviving the journey, Whitworth established Sumner Academy in 1883 in Sumner Village, and in 1890 the school was incorporated as Whitworth College, which later moved to Tacoma and finally found its present home in Spokane. The college is affiliated with the Presbyterian Church U.S.A. It is listed on the Templeton Foundation's Honor Roll of Character-Building Colleges.

Location The 200-acre wooded campus is in a suburban area only seven miles north of Spokane, Washington, a metropolitan area with a population of 400,000 people.

Top Programs of Study Education, business, psychology

Arts and Sciences American studies, art, arts administration, biology, chemistry, communication studies, computer science, cross-cultural studies, economics, English, French, history, international political economy, international studies, journalism, mathematics, music, nursing, peace studies, psychology, religion, sociol-ogy, Spanish, speech communication, sports medicine, theater

Business Accounting, international business, management

Education Art, elementary, music, secondary, special

Pre-Professional Dentistry, engineering, law, medicine, ministry, veterinary medicine

Accredited Programs Education, music, nursing

Special Programs The college uses a 4-1-4 calendar, offering students a January term for travel, internships, and on- and off-campus courses. There are opportunities for study abroad, international exchange programs, field studies, and independent study. The college has a cooperative program in engineering with Washington University in St. Louis, the University of Southern California, Columbia University, and Seattle Pacific University. There are minors in Leadership Studies and Women's Studies. There is an Army ROTC program.

Facilities There are 40 buildings, including the expanded Cowles Memorial Library; the renovated Aquatic Center; the 1,250-seat Cowles Auditorium; the remodeled Dixon Hall, the main classroom building; Hixson Union Building, the new student center; the recently renovated Johnson Science Center; the Koehler Art Gallery; the new Scotford Fitness Center; the Mudd Chapel; the recently remodeled Westminster Hall, with its beautiful courtyard; and a new athletics complex.

Transition to College Program The college offers a traditional orientation program.

Athletics NCAA III, Northwest Conference

Men: Baseball, basketball, cross-country, football, soccer, swimming, tennis, track

Women: Basketball, cross-country, soccer, softball, swimming, tennis, track & field, volleyball

Student Life and Housing About 1,000 students can be accommodated in college housing, which is guaranteed for all four years. Fifty-five percent of the students are from Washington, the remainder from 29 other states and 60 countries. Ethnicity: Caucasian—86 percent. There are no fraternities or sororities. All students may keep cars.

Accommodations for Students with Disabilities Legal documentation of disabilities is required for reasonable accommodations to be rendered. Students are required to request accommodations or auxiliary aids through the Educational Support Office in Career Services at least 16 weeks before classes, programs, or activities begin.

Financial Aid Ninety-three percent of all freshmen receive aid. The average freshman award was about $15,000.

Requirements for Admission SAT I or ACT scores and a college prep high school program. A campus visit and interview are recommended.

Application Freshmen are admitted fall, winter, and spring semesters. Early Action applications should be filed by November 30, with admission notification made by December 15. The preferred regular admission deadline is March 1.

International Students The preferred application deadline is June 1. Required are certification of financial resources, academic transcripts, certified English translations of all transcripts, and a minimum TOEFL score of 525 paper-based or 196 computer-based. Students who score 460–524 paper and 140–195 computer are accepted conditionally and will be granted regular admission upon completion of the Whitworth ESL Program.

Transfer Students Required are official transcripts of previous college work and a letter of recommendation. Students with fewer than 30 college credits are required to submit their high school transcripts. June 1 is the preferred application deadline for the fall. A maximum of 64 credits may be transferred from a two-year college. Only courses in which the student receives a grade of C− or better will be considered for transfer. Credits from Bible schools and nonaccredited colleges are evaluated on a course-by-course basis. Whitworth has special articulation agreements with Washington Community Colleges and North Idaho College. At least 32 credits must be completed at Whitworth.

Admission Contact
Office of Admissions
Whitworth College
300 West Hawthorne Rd.
Spokane, WA 99251
Phone: (800) 533-4668; (509) 777-1000
FAX: (509) 777-3758
E-mail: *admissions@whitworth.edu*
Web: *www.whitworth.edu*

The Heart of the College Whitworth College is considered one of the best colleges in the West as well as a "best buy." The college's mission is to provide "an education of the mind and the heart, equiping its graduates to honor God, follow Christ, and serve humanity. This mission is carried out by a community of Christian scholars committed to excellent teaching and to the integration of faith and learning." The faculty is accomplished, having received awards and grants, published books and articles, and engaged in significant research. But professors come to Whitworth to teach and mentor their students.

Included in the general education program is a Core, taken by all students and referred to as "the toughest courses you'll ever love." Taught by teams of Whitworth faculty, the Core is a series of three interdisciplinary courses that focus on three central paradigms that have shaped our lives and the world in which we live: Judeo-Christian worldviews, the rationalist tradition, and the scientific tradition.

Also, as part of the general education requirements, students must satisfy a multicultural studies requirement. This can be satisfied in several ways, the most interesting of which involves travel abroad or within the United States. In both January and May term semesters, students study under the direction of a Whitworth professor with opportunities to study the biological diversity of Baja, California, the people and cultures of the Holy Lands, the Spanish language in Mexico, jazz in Munich or Rome, or politics in South Africa. Domestically, education students visit Alaska, Hawaii, Idaho, and Louisiana to develop lessons for minority classrooms that encourage cultural diversity, visit San Francisco to study the arts, or participate in seminars with sports medicine specialists in Japan. Semester Abroad Programs include universities or colleges in China, France, Germany, Japan, Mexico, the Netherlands, South Korea, Thailand, and the United Kingdom. Two very interesting domestic Student Exchange Programs include Stillman College, an African-American College in Alabama, for students interested in African-American studies, and Sheldon Jackson College in Alaska for students interested in Native American history and culture.

The campus is located minutes from ski resorts, mountain lakes and rivers, and the pristine beauty that characterizes the Pacific Northwest. Also, the Spokane area offers an ideal climate and a friendly atmosphere, with many cultural and recreational opportunities, including shopping, movies, restaurants plays, concerts, and Riverfront Park.

WILLIAM JEWELL COLLEGE   Liberty, Missouri

Total Undergraduate Enrollment: 1,250
Men: 562 Women: 688
Five-Year Graduation Rate: 62%

Tuition: $$$
Room and Board: $
Residential Students: 75%

History William Jewell College was founded in 1849, and named in honor of Dr. William Jewell, a prominent physician, who rallied a coalition of Missouri Baptists and others to the cause of advancing higher education in Missouri. The college was one of the first four-year colleges located west of the Mississippi and became coeducational in 1921. The college is affiliated with the American Baptist Church U.S.A.

Location The 149-acre tree-lined campus is located in Liberty, Missouri, a residential area 15 miles northwest of Kansas City.

Top Programs of Study Business, sciences, education

Arts and Sciences Art, biochemistry, biology, chemistry, communication (concentrations in electronic media, organizational communication, speech education, theater), computer science, English, French, history, information systems, international relations, Japanese area studies, mathematics, mathematics with data processing emphasis, medical technology, music (concentrations in Church music, performance, theory), nursing, philosophy, physics, political science, psychology, religions, Spanish

Business Accounting, administration, international business/language

Education Early childhood, elementary, music, secondary, theater

Pre-Professional Dentistry, engineering, environmental management, forestry, law, medicine, ministry, occupational therapy, physical therapy

Accredited Programs Music, nursing

Special Programs There are study abroad opportunities, internships, and a Washington, D.C., internship. The Pryor Leadership Studies Program provides structured experiences to develop leadership skills. The Midwest Center for Service Learning and Women's Issues encourages students to learn and develop through community service. There are cooperative programs in engineering with Washington University, Columbia University, University of Missouri, and University of Kansas; forestry and environmental service with Duke; medial technology with North Kansas City Hospital; and occupational therapy with Washington University, St. Louis.

Facilities There are 23 buildings, evoking the charm of a classic East Coast liberal arts college. The buildings include Jewell Hall, the college's original structure listed in the National Register of Historic Places, which has recently been updated with new technology-friendly classrooms. The White Science Center is a state-of-the-art facility with advanced computer and science labs and a rooftop conservatory, Curry Library, an Olympic-size pool, the Pillsbury Music Center, Yates Student Union, and a new Greek housing complex.

Transition to College Program In addition to an Associate Dean of First-Year Experience, who meets with every freshman, students are assigned an upper classman who works as a mentor to 10 mentees. The mentees are contacted over the summer and work with the mentor in an orientation program right before classes begin. The transition is continued during the academic year by having freshmen take a general education course, "The Responsible Self," in which they read several seminal works.

Athletics NAIA, The Heart of America Athletic Conference

Men: Baseball, basketball, cross-country, football, golf, soccer, tennis, track, spirit squad

Women: Basketball, golf, softball, soccer, tennis, track, cross-country, volleyball, spirit squad

Student Life and Housing About 900 students can be accommodated in college housing, which is guaranteed for all four years. Eighty percent of the students are from Missouri, the remainder from 28 other states and 13 countries. Ethnicity: Caucasian—93 percent. There are four national fraternities and four national sororities. All students may keep cars.

Accommodations for Students with Disabilities In compliance with section 504

Financial Aid About 97 percent of all freshmen receive aid. The average freshman award was about $15,000.

Requirements for Admission Sat I or ACT scores and a college prep high school program.

Application Freshmen are admitted fall, spring, and summer semesters. Applications should be filed by March 15 for fall entry. Admission notification is sent on a rolling basis beginning September 1.

International Students Students whose primary language is not English must score a minimum of 550 on the paper-based TOEFL or take the MELAB. Students must also submit official secondary and, if applicable, postsecondary transcripts, as well as a declaration of finances.

Transfer Students An interview is recommended. Required are transcripts from high school (if student is transferring with fewer than 12 credits) and regionally accredited two- and four-year colleges, an optional essay, and a personal reference form. An overall GPA of 2.0 is required. At least 30 credits must be taken at William Jewell including at least 12 credits in the major to meet degree requirements.

Admission Contact
Office of Admissions
William Jewell College

500 College Hill
Liberty, MO 64068-1896
Phone: (800) 753-7009; (816) 781-7700, ext. 5137
FAX: (816) 415-5027
E-mail: *admission@william.jewell.edu*
Web: *www.jewell.edu*

The Heart of the College William Jewell College is a national liberal arts college, with special focus on leadership, service, and spiritual insight—all for a moderate cost. The Pryor Leadership Studies and Emerging Leaders program has garnered international attention for its success in developing leadership skills. During the two-year program, students first participate in an Introductory Seminar where students study leadership in different contexts and set goals for themselves. Students then participate in a 15-day long Outward Bound Experience, a Vocational Internship, a Volunteer Internship, and a Capstone Seminar where students create a leadership "legacy" and develop an action plan for continued leadership growth.

Service learning is a series of electives open to all students designed to encourage students to learn and develop through their active involvement in organized community service. Students may complete a certificate program by completing three courses: "Meeting Human Needs and Alleviating Suffering," "Strategies and Resources for Meeting Human Needs," and a "Service Learning Internship." Students also have an opportunity to participate in semester- or year-long service programs in Europe, South America, Mexico, Appalachia, and other areas. One student comments "In order to be an educated person you have to have a strong sense of service."

One aspect of the college's mission is "to be an institution loyal to the ideals of Christ, demonstrating a Christian philosophy for the whole of life. . . ." The Christian Student Ministries, a student-directed program, provides a comprehensive array of activities to fulfill that important aspect of William Jewell's mission. Students who have personal questions about faith feel comfortable asking any professor because, as one student commented: "People at Jewell recognize a spiritual dimension to life."

The innovative general education curriculum, "The Responsible Self," seeks to prepare students to be both successful and reflective citizens of a global community. Knowledge and skills are offered in an integrated core consisting of 38 credits, about one-third of the total credits required for graduation.

The college has a strong athletic and intramural program, over 70 clubs and organizations, a lecture series, and the nationally recognized Harriman Arts Program. This program brings to Kansas City's Music Hall and Folly Theatre acclaimed performers such as Luciano Pavarotti, Itzhak Perlman, Wynton Marsalis, Yo-Yo Ma, the American Ballet Theatre, the Alvin Ailey Dance Theater, and the Royal Shakespeare Company. All this at no cost to students!

William Jewell also offers excellent study abroad opportunities in Japan, Australia, and a one-semester program for accounting, business, or economics majors in Dijon, France, as well as other programs in Paris, Milan, Dublin, Vienna, and Madrid.

Downtown Kansas City is only 20 minutes away, offering a wonderful balance to the small town of Liberty. In Kansas City students are offered professional sports, performing arts, shopping, nightlife, major corporations, hospitals, and a large urban school district.

WINONA STATE UNIVERSITY

Winona, Minnesota

Total Undergraduate Enrollment: 7,500

Men: 3,000 Women: 4,500
Five-Year Graduation Rate: 68%

Tuition: In-state–$;
Out-of-state–$
Room and Board: $
Residential Students: 32%

History Winona State University was founded in 1858 as the first teacher preparation institution west of the Mississippi River. WSU is one of seven state universities that are part of the 34-member Minnesota State Colleges and Universities System. The university operates on three campuses: its original main campus and the west campus are located in the city of Winona; a nonresidential campus is located in Rochester, 45 miles to the west.

Location The 47-acre campus is located in Winona, Minnesota, a small city (population 29,000), 100 miles southeast of Minneapolis and St. Paul on the banks of the Mississippi River.

Top Programs of Study Education, nursing, communication

Arts and Sciences Allied health, art, biology, cardiopulmonary rehabilitation, cell and molecular biology, chemistry, communication studies, composite materials engineering, computer science, criminal justice, cytotechnology, ecology, economics, English, environmental science, French, geoscience, German, history, hydrogeology, law and society, marketing, mass communication, mathematics, medical technology, music, music business, nursing, paralegal, physics, political science, psychology, public administration, recreation and leisure studies, school and community health, social work, sociology, Spanish, sports medicine/athletic training, statistics, theater arts, therapeutic recreation, worksite health promotion

Business Accounting, administration, computer information systems, finance, human resources management, management information systems

Education Art, business, early childhood, elementary middle, special, physical education

Pre-Professional Dentistry, engineering, law, medicine, mortuary science, optometry, pharmacy, physical therapy, podiatry, veterinary medicine

Accredited Programs Athletic training, education, engineering, music, nursing, social work, theater

Special Programs The Maxwell Children's Center provides childcare services and educational programs for children of students, faculty, staff, and community. All entering students are required to lease a PC or Apple laptop computer for their years at WSU. There are minors in studio art, biochemistry, philosophy, international studies, and others.

Facilities There are 26 buildings, including a modern library, and all academic buildings are extensively wired for computer access. There are a performing arts center, a student center, and a fitness/wellness center.

Transition to College Program An orientation course is offered for in-coming first-year students, introducing them to services, activities, expectations, and opportunities at WSU. It provides them with the means to network with other students, faculty, and staff.

Athletics NCAA II, Northwestern Sun Intercollegiate Conference

Men: Baseball, basketball, cross-country, football, golf, tennis

Women: Basketball, cross-country, golf, gymnastics, soccer, softball, tennis, track & field, volleyball

Student Life and Housing About 2,000 students can be accommodated in college housing, which is guaranteed for all four years. Sixty percent of the students are from Minnesota, the remainder are from 40 states and 46 countries. Ethnicity: Caucasian—94 percent. There are three national fraternities and three national sororities. All students may keep cars.

Accommodations for Students with Disabilities Reasonable accommodations are made for students who provide proof of disability from a competent authority, as well as information regarding specific limitations for which accommodations are required.

Financial Aid About 82 percent of all freshmen receive aid. The average freshman award was about $3,500.

Requirements for Admission An SAT I score of 1,000 or above, or an ACT score of 21 or above, and a class rank in the top half of the class in a college prep high school program.

Application Freshmen are admitted fall and spring semesters. Application deadlines are open, with admission notification made on a rolling basis.

International Students Required are certified evaluations verifying completion of previous education studies, official mark sheets from all schools attended, a minimum paper TOEFL score of 500 and 173 computer-based, and proof of financial responsibility for the full course of study. WSU requires all non-native speakers of English to complete an on-campus English placement exam unless they transfer to WSU with English composition credits. The completed application should be submitted at least three months before the semester start.

Transfer Students Students are admitted if they have completed 24 transferable credits from a regionally accredited institution and have a minimum GPA of 2.4 for all colleges attended. Students may also be considered for admission if they have completed a minimum of 24 transferable credits with a GPA from 2.2 to 2.39. These students must visit the campus and interview with a transfer specialist. Students with fewer than 24 transferable credits must meet the regular freshman admission requirements.

Admission Contact
Office of Admissions
Winona State University
P.O. Box 5838
Winona, MN 55987
Phone: (800) DIAL-WSU; (507) 457-5100
FAX: (507) 457-5620
E-mail: *admissions@winona.edu*
Web: *www.winona.edu*

The Heart of the University Winona State University has strong academic programs and is considered a "best buy" in college education. Students are attracted to Winona for several important reasons. As part of the Minnesota University System, it has a larger student population than most of the schools in this guide; however, it remains midrange in size, attracting students from most states and many foreign countries. It provides breadth in every area of academic and student life, yet is small enough for students to develop close friendships.

Another reason for the popularity of WSU is its wonderful location. Situated in the heart of a small, safe, friendly town, Winona's location on the banks of the Mississippi provides natural beauty that is recognized by any visitor as a great boon for college students. In addition, the cultural and recreational attractions of Minneapolis and St. Paul are only two hours away.

The university focuses mainly on undergraduate education, with senior faculty teaching freshman courses, an innovative universitywide laptop computer program, and highly regarded programs in teacher education and nursing. Innovative programs include the first and only Composite Materials Engineering undergraduate major in America, and the work of students in the College of Business's Small Business Institute provides students with opportunities to apply skills to develop strategies and solutions for area small businesses.

Winona sees itself as "a community of learners dedicated to improving the world." To accomplish this the university is guided by what it refers to as "The Seven Principles for Good Practice in Undergraduate Education." First, there is an emphasis on student–faculty interaction, with faculty viewed as teachers first, working closely with students, collaborating on research, and planning internships. Second is a focus on learning as a team effort in classrooms, study groups, and across campus life. Third is making learning an active experience where students are engaged in discussion, internships, clinical experiences, and research. Fourth is giving students timely feedback regarding their performance. Fifth is helping students to manage their time so they can devote more time to the task of learning outside of the classroom. Sixth is a commitment to high expectations, both for faculty and students. The seventh principle encourages students to both respect and learn from the student diversity that is available to them.

The results of Winona's efforts have 89 percent of their graduates employed or pursuing advanced degrees soon after graduation. This success is explained by one student as having "an entire campus dedicated to seeing me succeed."

WINTHROP UNIVERSITY

Rock Hill, South Carolina

Total Undergraduate Enrollment: 4,300

Men: 1,300 Women: 3,000
Five-Year Graduation Rate: 55%

Tuition: In-state–$;
Out-of-state–$$
Room and Board: $
Residential Students: 50%

History Winthrop University, founded in 1886, is a state supported public university that has its origins as a women's college and teacher training institution.

Location The 418-acre tree-lined campus is located in Rock Hill, South Carolina, a small town 23 miles south of Charlotte, North Carolina.

Top Programs of Study Business, education, biology

Arts and Sciences Art, art history, chemistry, communication disorders, computer science, dance, English, environmental science, environmental studies, family and consumer sciences, French, history, human nutrition, integrated marketing communication, mass communication, mathematics, music, music performance, philosophy and religion, physical education (athletic training, fitness/wellness), political science (including public policy and administration), psychology, science

communication, social work, sociology (including criminology), Spanish, sports management, theater (design/technical, performance)

Business Administration (options include accounting, computer information systems, economics, entrepreneurship, finance, general business, health services management, international business, management, marketing)

Education Art, dance, early childhood, elementary, music, theater, physical education, special

Pre-Professional Dentistry, engineering, law, medicine, nursing, pharmacy, physical therapy, veterinary medicine

Accredited Programs Business, computer science, dance, dietetics, education, journalism and mass communication, music, social work, theater

Special Programs The university provides provisional admission through a LEAP program that provides academic support through the first semester. Winthrop participates in a Charlotte Consortium of 24 colleges/universities at which Winthrop students can register for courses. The university has a Distance Education Classroom that is fully interactive between the Winthrop College of Business and the remote site. Winthrop students host an annual Model United Nations event for high schoolers across the Southeast. There are opportunities for internships, cooperative education, study abroad, and domestic student exchange programs. Leadership Winthrop is offered as an eight-week, noncredit course that develops leadership skill. There are Army and Air Force ROTC programs.

Facilities There are 43 buildings. The campus is included in the National Register of Historic Places. Johnson Hall contains a 331-seat theater with excellent training and performance facilities; the renovated Rutledge Building and the Conservatory of Music serve the College of Visual and Performing Arts with gallery and performance space, studios, and labs; the Thurmond Building houses the College of Business Administration; Withers houses the Riley College of Education. The Life Sciences Building is the newest one, providing labs for biology and human nutrition. There is internet access from all buildings and residence halls. Other facilities include the library, Dinkins Student Center, Peabody Gym, a golf course, and Winthrop Lake. The university is also the home of the Macfeat Early Childhood Laboratory School.

Transition to College Program Traditional orientation sessions are offered in the summer for both students and family members. Also, peer mentors offer one-to-one help in adjusting to college life.

Athletics NCAA I, Big South Conference

Men: Baseball, basketball, cross-country, golf, indoor and outdoor track, soccer, tennis

Women: Basketball, cross-country, golf, indoor and outdoor track, softball, tennis, volleyball

Student Life and Housing About 2,400 students can be accommodated in college housing, which includes single-sex and coed dorms, and married student housing. Eighty-seven percent of the students are from South Carolina, with the remainder from 41 other states and 34 countries. Ethnicity: Caucasian—72 percent; African-American—24 percent. There are eight national fraternities and eight national sororities. All students may keep cars.

Accommodations for Students with Disabilities Appropriate accommodations are provided based on individual needs as assessed through documentation and an intake interview with the Conductor for Students with Disabilities.

Financial Aid About 50 percent of all freshmen receive aid. The average freshman award was about $3,000.

Requirements for Admission SAT I or ACT scores and a college prep high school program.

Application Freshmen are admitted to all sessions. Applications should be filed by May 1 for fall admission and December 14 for spring admission. Students are sent admission decisions on a rolling basis.

International Students Required are original or certified copies of official secondary school and, if applicable, postsecondary school transcripts with certified English translation, verification of English proficiency by testing a minimum TOEFL of 520 paper or 190 computer-based (there are also several other ways to verify English proficiency in lieu of the TOEFL), and certification of financial support.

Transfer Students Required are official copies of all course work from all institutions attended. Applicants must be in good standing at the last institution attended; students who have attempted 30 or more credits must have a minimum GPA of C; applicants with fewer than 30 credits must also submit their high school transcripts and SAT or ACT scores. Only courses graded at C or above and earned at a regionally accredited institution may be considered for transfer. A maximum of 65 credits may be transferred from a two-year college. Students must earn at least 31 credits at Winthrop. Application deadline for summer/fall is June 1.

Home-Schooled Students Students should submit transcripts (or other records of completed work) that show names of the completed courses, credit, and grades earned and an official copy of SAT or ACT scores. Students must complete the 20 high school courses that are prerequisites required by South Carolina. Letters of recommendation, an essay or personal statement, and/or a personal interview will also be considered if submitted.

Admission Contact
Office of Admissions
Winthrop University
Stewart House
Rock Hill, SC 29733
Phone: (800) 763-0230; (803) 323-2191
FAX: (803) 323-2137
E-mail: *admissions@winthrop*
Web: *www.winthrop.edu*

The Heart of the University The only institution in this guide that can boast 100 percent national accreditation of eligible degree programs, Winthrop is considered one of the best public universities in the South. Winthrop also offers a beautiful historic campus and multicultural student population.

The College of Business Administration has a talented faculty with real world experience and a personal interest in its students' achievements. Its work in mentoring is evident in the quality internships and co-op positions gained by students in such firms as Proctor and Gamble, Bank of America, Media Comm, Deloitte and Touche,

and Prudential Securities. Winthrop's distinguished history in teacher education is evident in the Riley College of Education's selection as one of four sites for the new Governor's School of Excellence in Teaching. Education students benefit from the college's collaboration with professional development schools as well as the Macfeat Early Childhood Laboratory School on campus. Students enjoy the experience gained from tutoring children as well as the abundant opportunities offered by the Instructional Technology Center to help prospective teachers learn how to construct Web pages and select appropriate software. The College of Visual and Performing Arts places Winthrop in an elite group of only six universities in America by having earned national accreditation in all of its programs.

As a university with a diverse student population, Winthrop supports a broad range of activities and organizations dedicated to the enrichment of minority students, including the Association of Ebonites, which sponsors cultural events, and the Ebonite Gospel Choir, which performs traditional and contemporary music on campus and throughout the region; eight historically black fraternities and sororities; and a publication that focuses on multicultural issues. Also, the university offers support for the unique needs of international students through its Office of International Students.

The more than 100 student groups keep students involved, and a very strong athletic program earns plenty of fan support. The campus includes a lake surrounded by a 325-acre recreational area that includes a golf course. Only a half hour from campus is Charlotte, North Carolina, where students can shop at malls, attend professional sporting events, visit a museum or theme park, and much more. Students also enjoy the variety of housing accommodations, all air-conditioned.

WITTENBERG UNIVERSITY

Springfield, Ohio

Total Undergraduate Enrollment: 2,140
Men: 920 Women: 1,220
Five-Year Graduation Rate: 72%

Tuition: $$$$
Room and Board: $$
Residential Students: 95%

History Wittenberg University was founded in 1845 by the English Evangelical Lutheran Synod of Ohio, with a mission to provide a classical education for the American frontier. The university is listed on the Templeton Foundation's Honor Roll of Character-Building Colleges.

Location The 100-acre campus is located in Springfield, Ohio (population 68,000), a suburban area 25 miles east of Dayton, 40 miles west of Columbus, and 72 miles northeast of Cincinnati, in southwestern Ohio.

Top Programs of Study Biology, management, education

Arts and Sciences American studies, art, biochemistry/molecular biology, biology, chemistry, communications, computer science, East Asian studies, economics, English, French, geography, geology, German, history, mathematics, music, philosophy, physics, political science, psychology, religion, Russian area studies, sociology, Spanish, theater and dance

Business Management (concentrations in accounting, finance, human resources, international business, marketing)

Education Early childhood, early childhood and special education, middle school

Pre-Professional Dentistry, law, medicine, nursing, optometry, physical therapy, theology, veterinary medicine

Accredited Programs None

Special Programs There are cooperative engineering programs with Washington University, Columbia University, Case Western Reserve University, and Georgia Institute of Technology. There is a cooperative nursing program with Johns Hopkins University, and an occupational therapy program with Washington University. There are opportunities for study abroad, internships, student-designed majors, double majors, course registration with colleges in the Southwest Ohio Consortium, and a Washington, D.C., semester. The Wittenberg Series of distinguished lectures and artistic events brings to the campus respected scholars and public figures as well as concerts and art exhibits. Foreign affairs specialists visit the campus through the Cincinnati Council on Foreign Affairs. There is a Model United Nations Program and a Black Culture House, a center for African-American culture, art, history, and music. There is also a Phi Beta Kappa chapter.

Facilities There are 35 buildings, including the modern Benham-Pence Student Center; Hollenbech Hall, a state-of-the-art academic building; and the newest building, Kress Science Center, with state-of-the-art labs. Myers Hall and Recitation Hall are on the National Register of Historic Places. There is also Krieg Hall, which houses the music facilities; Weaver Chapel; and the Thomas Library. Athletic facilities include a completely renovated football field and stadium, the new Albright Tennis Complex, a swimming pool, fitness center, and a gymnasium.

Transition to College Program Students take a first-semester Common Learning Course, which focuses on social issues and is taught by a professor who will serve as the class adviser. During the semester the professor not only teaches but also carefully notes each student's academic strengths and interests so that the professor can offer quality advisement for each student's education at Wittenberg and beyond.

Athletics NCAA III, North Coast Athletic Conference

Men: Baseball, basketball, cross-country, football, golf, indoor track, lacrosse, outdoor track, soccer, swimming and diving, tennis

Women: Basketball, cross-country, field hockey, golf, indoor track, lacrosse, outdoor track, soccer, softball, swimming and diving, tennis

Student Life and Housing About 1,200 students can be accommodated in college housing, which includes a variety of options and is guaranteed for all four years. Fifty-eight percent of the students are from Ohio, the remainder are from 40 other states and 24 countries. Ethnicity: Caucasian—85 percent; African-American—6 percent; International—2 percent; Hispanic-American—1 percent; Asian-American—1 percent. There are five national fraternities and seven national sororities. All students may keep cars.

Accommodations for Students with Disabilities In compliance with section 504

Financial Aid About 75 percent of all freshmen receive aid. The average freshman award was about $19,000.

Requirements for Admission SAT I or ACT scores and a college prep high school program. A campus visit and interview are highly encouraged.

Application The Early Decision application deadline is November 15, with decision notification by January 1. The Early Action Plan deadline is December 1, with decision notification by January 1. Applications submitted after the Early Action deadline will be considered for regular application, with decision notification made on a rolling basis.

International Students If English is not the student's primary language, students must score a minimum of 550 on the paper-based TOEFL or 230 on the computer version. Other applicants must submit SAT I scores. Students must also submit official secondary school and, if applicable, postsecondary transcripts, as well as a declaration of finances.

Transfer Students Required are official high school and college transcripts, an overall GPA of 2.25 or better from an accredited college/university, and being in good standing. An interview is recommended. Of 130 credits 75 must be completed at Wittenberg.

Admission Contact
Office of Admissions
Wittenberg University
Ward Street at North Wittenberg Avenue
P.O. Box 720
Springfield, OH 45501-0720
Phone: (800) 677-7558; (937) 327-6314
FAX: (937) 327-6379
E-mail: *Admission@witttenberg.edu*
Web: *www.wittenberg,edu*

The Heart of the University One of the top liberal arts universities in the nation, Wittenberg University is a close-knit community of living and learning on one of the most beautiful campuses. An accomplished faculty, who combine scholarship with excellent teaching, provides students with interesting courses and a caring, supportive accessibility. With a whopping 96 percent of the students residing on campus, the Wittenberg faculty and administration have the rarest of opportunities to design a comprehensive education—one that encompasses academics, extracurricular activities, and a residential life—that truly provides a "Wittenberg" education.

This is accomplished through the "Wittenberg Plan," a set of 16 learning goals that include not only those met through course competency and participation requirements, but also include the development of good writing and speaking skills, the ability to conduct research, an understanding of human behavior, as well as the role of diversity in American culture. By selecting from a broad range of courses across academic disciplines, students are able to fulfill most of these requirements. Wittenberg's education design includes off-campus learning, helping to assure that students "don't live in a bubble" during their years at the university. Important for future career opportunities, valuable internships are arranged, in which students can receive academic credit while gaining hands-on experience in a career-related setting. Also, through Wittenberg's Office of International Education, students are assisted with study and travel plans. More than 20 percent of the students travel abroad during their Wittenberg years. The importance of service at Wittenberg is demonstrated by the university's making it a requirement. Every student completes a non-credit service experience by volunteering at one of the many local agencies for children, the elderly, the environment, or the physically disabled, or by designing their own service projects.

Campus extracurricular life is rich and varied with over 125 clubs and organizations in which to participate. About 70 percent of the students participate in intramural sports, 30 percent in a very strong varsity program, and more in club sports like rugby and ice hockey. About 35 percent join a fraternity or sorority. There are several music groups which present a variety of concerts and recitals each year, a dance company, and several theater productions. Also, there are a variety of religious groups and services, both denominational and nondenominational. The Wittenberg planning board schedules lectures, art exhibits, concerts, dances, movies, and comedy acts. Wittenberg has also been thoughtful in terms of a residential living plan. During the first two years students live in residence halls in order to form close friendships. Students then move progressively to either university district housing, Greek houses, or townhouse-styled apartments.

This carefully designed Wittenberg education is supervised by a personal adviser who works with the student through all four years. The university offers a guarantee of graduation in four years. Students also have pre-professional advisers who bring special knowledge, personal contacts at many law and medical schools, and a sophisticated understanding of the admissions process, thereby increasing students' opportunities for admission to prominent law, medical, and professional schools.

The educational outcomes demonstrate the effectiveness of the Wittenberg Plan, with 100 percent of the teacher education students passing Ohio certification exams; about 70 percent eventually pursuing an advanced degree. The university ranks in the top 10 percent of private liberal arts and sciences colleges in the number of doctoral degrees earned by alumni.

XAVIER UNIVERSITY   Cincinnati, Ohio

Total Undergraduate Enrollment: 3,942
Men: 1,653 Women: 2,289
Five-Year Graduation Rate: 70%

Tuition: $$$
Room and Board: $$$
Residential Students: 48%

History Xavier University was established in 1831 as The Athenaeum, when Edward Fenwick, the first Bishop of Cincinnati, raised a two-story building near the cathedral in downtown Cincinnati to educate seminarians and other young men in the Ohio area. In 1840 the Jesuits were requested to assume leadership of the college, which was renamed St. Xavier College in honor of the Jesuit educator under whose patronage the college was originally placed. With continued growth, the college was moved to its present geographic location of Cincinnati in 1919, became a university in 1930, and coeducational in 1969.

Location The 125-acre beautifully landscaped campus is in a residential neighborhood five miles northeast of the center of Cincinnati, Ohio.

Top Programs of Study Business, biology/natural sciences, education

Arts and Sciences Applied biology (including environmental management and forestry), applied chemistry, applied physics, art, athletic training, biology, chemical science, chemistry, classical humanities, classics, communication arts, computer science, criminal justice, economics, English, fine arts, French, German, history, international affairs, Latin, mathematics, medical technology, music, natural science, nursing, occupational therapy, philosophy, physics, political science, psychology, social work, sociology, Spanish, sport management, sport marketing, theology

Business Accounting, entrepreneurial studies, finance, human resources, information systems, management, marketing

Education Early, middle, Montessori, music, physical education, secondary, special

Pre-Professional Dentistry, engineering, law, medicine, mortuary science, pharmacy

Accredited Programs Athletic training, business, chemistry, Montessori Education, nursing, occupational therapy, radiologic technology, social work

Special Programs Students can cross-register at other institutions that form the Greater Cincinnati Consortium of Colleges and Universities. An associate's degree is offered in radiologic technology. A dual degree program is offered with the University of Cincinnati, which grants admission to Xavier and UC's Medical School before students graduate from high school. There are study abroad, internship, and cooperative education opportunities. There are several minors offered, including Peace Studies, Art Studio, Corrections, and Information Technology. The Center for Commuter Services helps commuters stay connected to the campus. There is an Army ROTC program.

Facilities There are 66 buildings, including the new Gallagher Student Center, featuring a large four-story atrium and theater; the new Cintas Center, a multipurpose arena, conference, and banquet center; the McDonald observatory; and a new recreation park that includes tennis courts, an ecology trail, and a walking and jogging path; a new student apartment complex; and newly remodeled residence halls.

Transition to College Program Manresa is Xavier's campuswide effort to provide new students with a comprehensive introduction to life at Xavier. It is comprised of a balance of social, cultural, spiritual, and academic experiences that are designed to ease the transition to college life and introduce the extracurricula options at Xavier. Xavier also has a Freshman Focus that includes monitoring academic progress and coordinating the scheduling of first-semester classes.

Athletics NCAA I, Athletic 10 Conference

Men: Baseball, basketball, cross-country, golf, rifle, soccer, swimming, tennis

Women: Basketball, cross-country, golf, soccer, swimming, tennis, volleyball

Student Life and Housing About 2,000 students can be accommodated in college housing, which is guaranteed for all four years. Sixty-six percent of the students are from Ohio, the remainder are from 45 other states and 44 countries. Ethnicity: Caucasian—83 percent; African-American—9 percent; International—3 percent; Asian-American—2 percent. There are no fraternities or sororities. All students may keep cars.

Accommodations for Students with Disabilities In compliance with section 504

Financial Aid About 90 percent of all freshmen receive aid. The average freshman award was about $13,500.

Requirements for Admission SAT I or ACT scores and a college prep high school program.

Application Freshmen are admitted fall and spring semesters. Applications should be filed by February 16 for priority consideration for fall admission. Admission notification is sent on a rolling basis.

International Students Applicants must submit an English translation of a secondary school degree or the diploma/certificate of the highest academic degree earned, a TOEFL minimum score of 500 paper-based or 173 computer-based, a notarized certificate of financial responsibility, and official transcripts if the student is transferring from another college or university.

Transfer Students Students must have attended other regionally accredited institutions, submit credentials required of regular freshmen, and submit official transcripts from previous institutions. Students who have earned 30 or more credits are not required to submit ACT or SAT scores. Course grades of C or better are considered for transfer; at least one-half of the course requirements of the major and the last 30 credits must be completed at Xavier for all undergraduate degrees.

Home-Schooled Students Students with Home Schooling Diplomas must submit an application for admission, the appropriate documentation from state and/or national home schooling accrediting agencies, official transcripts, and ACT or SAT scores.

Admission Contact
Office of Admissions
Xavier University
3800 Victory Parkway
Cincinnati, OH 45207-5311
Phone: (877) 982-3648; (513) 745-3301
FAX: (513) 745-4319
E-mail: *xuadmit@xavier.edu*
Web: *www.xavier.edu*

The Heart of the University As with all Catholic institutions with a Jesuit tradition, Xavier's focus is on the integration of the intellectual, the moral, and the spiritual dimensions of its students. It succeeds very well in this mission with a core program that is the most comprehensive of all the Jesuit institutions and includes a 12-credit focus in ethics, religion, and society, as well as a cultural diversity course. The latter course makes great sense in that Xavier has a truly diverse student population, both ethnically and geographically. The university is very successful in creating a living–learning community that students find remarkably friendly and attentive, with a faculty whose first priority is teaching. A unique program is offered by the Center for Commuter Services. The university, with a 50 percent commuter population takes this extra step to cultivate a sense of community, keeping commuters connected to campus life through activities such as annual service projects, cookouts on the malls, and even complimentary breakfast during final exams.

The Jesuit focus on justice and a spiritual life is cultivated by offering students opportunities to work with the economically poor, both at home in Cincinnati as well as internationally in Nicaragua and Nepal. Students all work in Habitat for Humanity and Amnesty International, as well as tutor area children, volunteer in soup kitchens, run food drives, and coordinate neighborhood cleanups. Campus ministry offers students worship services, music ministry, and retreats.

But the heart of Xavier is its focus on getting students into careers. Unlike most of the schools in this guide, Xavier has a sizable graduate population, offering undergraduates opportunities for graduate work in education, nursing, business, health science administration, and criminal justice. With Cincinnati as a setting, many students come to Xavier because of the quality internships offered in every academic major, and cooperative education programs in which students can alternate between work and school on a daily basis or attend school full-time one semester then work full-time the next semester. The Professional Experience Program matches students with employers for part-time and summer jobs that are career related. The Community Service Jobs Program offers work–study students the opportunity to gain paid experience in human services fields. The alumni career advising service pairs students with locally employed alumni. Both pre-med and pre-law preceptorship programs provide students with partnerships and first-hand experience to help students prepare for medical and law schools. Education students have excellent resources, and health-care-related programs, such as athletic training, nursing, and occupational therapy, all have strong clinical components. Also, with Cincinnati the home of professional sports teams, sport management and sport marketing are two of the fastest growing majors. Communication arts students intern with major public relations and advertising firms as well as with 27 television and radio stations in the Cincinnati area. About 70 percent of business students complete a co-op internship at an area business.

Outcomes are very good, with nearly 400 companies requesting résumés from Xavier students each year, and graduates landing positions at employers such as Johnson and Johnson, General Electric, IBM, Coca Cola, Morgan Stanley, and PricewaterhouseCoopers. Nearly 70 percent of Xavier graduates who apply to law school are accepted, and more then 78 percent are accepted to medical school.

With new residence halls and over 90 percent of the students involved in the 100 clubs, organizations, and sports, students have much to do. Add to this the Greater Cincinnati area of 2 million people, and students have cultural and recreational opportunities, Fortune 500 companies, and temperate climate.

XAVIER UNIVERSITY OF LOUISIANA

New Orleans, Louisiana

Total Undergraduate Enrollment: 3,116
Men: 810 Women: 2,306
Five-Year Graduation Rate: 51%

Tuition: $$
Room and Board: $$
Residential Students: 40%

History Xavier University of Louisiana evolved from the coeducational secondary school that was founded by the Blessed Katharine Drexel and the Sisters of the Blessed Sacrament. The university was founded in 1915 in order to provide African-Americans with a Catholic higher education. Today, Xavier is the only historically black Catholic college in America.

Location The 29-acre campus is located in New Orleans, Louisiana, in an inner-city location.

Top Programs of Study Biology, pre-pharmacy, psychology

Arts and Sciences Art, biochemistry, biology, chemistry, environmental chemistry, computer science, computer engineering, English, French, history, mass communications, mathematics, microbiology, music, music performance, pharmacy, philosophy, physics, political science, psychology, sociology, Spanish, speech pathology, statistics, theology

Business Accounting, administration, computer information systems

Education Art, early childhood, elementary, health and physical education, music, special, speech pathology

Pre-Professional Dentistry, law, medicine, optometry, osteopathy, podiatry, veterinary medicine

Accredited Programs Chemistry, education, music, pharmacy

Special Programs There is a dual degree program in chemical engineering with the University of New Orleans, University of Maryland, University of Wisconsin, and other schools. Xavier also offers a Doctor of Pharmacy degree.

The Xavier University Family and Community Life Center offers several programs to help prevent and reduce violence among New Orleans' youth. The New Orleans Consortium allows cross-registration at Xavier, Loyola University, and Notre Dame Seminary. There is an accelerated MBA program with Tulane University and an accelerated pre-law and pre-health professions curricula. There is also a pre-medical early acceptance program with Tulane University. There are student exchange programs with Howard University and St. Michael's College in Vermont. There is a Center for Intercultural and International Programs and the McNair Project, which is designed to assist students interested in graduate study at the doctoral level. There is also a Center for Environmental Programs. There are study abroad, internship, and cooperative education opportunities. There are Air Force, Navy, and Army ROTC programs.

Facilities There are 34 buildings, which include two quadrangles, one formed by the distinctive limestone structure of the original campus buildings and the other formed by two more recent state-of-the-art constructions. There is a student center, a redesigned gymnasium, modern residence halls, the new Academic/Science Complex Addition, the Library Resource Center, and the Living Learning Center.

Transition to College Program Xavier offers a traditional orientation program.

Athletics NAIA, Gulf Coast Conference

   Men: Basketball, cross-country, tennis

   Women: Basketball, cross-country, tennis

Student Life and Housing About 1,000 students can be accommodated in campus housing. Only 38 percent of the students are from Louisiana, the majority from 37 other states, mostly Southern, and 35 countries. Ethnicity: African-American— 92 percent. There are four national fraternities and four national sororities. All students may keep cars.

Accommodations for Students with Disabilities In compliance with section 504

Financial Aid About 89 percent of all freshmen receive aid. The average freshman award was about $8,000.

Requirements for Admission SAT I or ACT scores and a college prep high school program.

Application Freshmen are admitted fall and spring semesters, with pharmacy students admitted in the fall only. The fall application deadline is March 1 and spring deadline is December 1.

International Students Required are official school records/transcripts, a letter of recommendation from a secondary school official, original certificate of national examination taken by the student, a notarized affidavit of support indicating who will pay the cost of attendance, and TOEFL results for students from non-English-speaking nations. All previous college work taken outside the United States must be evaluated by the Foreign Credential Education Service. Application deadlines are March 1 for summer and fall semesters, and September 1 for the spring semester.

Transfer Students Required are official copies of college transcripts from an appropriate university official at each institution attended, and the student must be in good standing. A résumé or statement of activities may be required to account for extended periods of nonenrollment. Additional requirements may apply for admission to the College of Pharmacy. Secondary school records and SAT or ACT scores may be required if the applicant has fewer than 20 transferable credits. Only C grades or better are considered for transfer. Not more than one-half of the credits required for the degree may be transferred from a community or junior college. At least 25 percent of course credit must be taken at Xavier, 18 credits of which must be in the major with a grade of C or better for each course.

Admission Contact
Office of Admissions
Xavier University of Louisiana

1 Drexel Drive
Box 132 C
New Orleans, LA 70125
Phone: (504) 483-7388
FAX: (504) 485-7941
E-mail: *apply@xula.edu*
Web: *www.xula.edu*

The Heart of the University Standing in the inner city of exciting New Orleans is the only Catholic African-American university in the nation. Xavier University attracts students who have great ambitions, for this is a university that both challenges and supports students. A famous student quote regarding a student's journey at Xavier captures the heart of the university: "Gradually, they saw away your cane, and you walk on your own." Starting with a core consisting of theology and philosophy, the arts and humanities, communications, history and the social sciences, mathematics, and the natural sciences, students are provided state-of-the-art technology and "model" professors to provide support in mastering course material, developing critical thinking skills, and self-confidence. Also, Xavier students in this very friendly community have developed a culture of tutoring and support, whereby more able students play leadership roles in study groups. Students have the benefit of a proactive program, GradStar/Excel, which prepares students for the rigors of graduate and professional schools. Xavier students also have the luxury of four fully staffed placement offices.

The results are fantastic. Over the past few years, Xavier has placed about 40 percent of its students in graduate schools, with pre-medical students enjoying an 80 percent acceptance rate at medical and dental schools throughout the country. The university has been designated a Model Institution for Excellence by the National Science Foundation, ranking nationally in the number of African-American undergraduates receiving degrees in the physical and health sciences. Xavier also ranks first in placing African-Americans into pharmacy schools and has educated about 25 percent of the 6,000 African-American pharmacists in the country. Xavier ranks first in the nation in placing African-American students in medical schools. Those students who have chosen other career paths have taken employment at places such as Shell Oil, the Environmental Protection Agency, Polaroid, Microsoft, and the Wall Street Journal and have also started their own businesses and pursued service-oriented careers.

Xavier's mission statement indicates that "the ultimate purpose of the university is the promotion of a more just and humane society." Therefore the success of the university is measured not only in the professional and leadership roles its graduates perform, but also in the degree of compassion it helps to cultivate in its students.

Although Xavier is best known for its science programs, there are also very strong programs in non-science areas. The education program is nationally accredited and typically has a 100 percent passing rate on the National Teacher Examination. The music program sends choral groups on an annual spring tour and has performed before the Pope in Rome's St. Peter's Basilica, and graduates have gone on to become teachers, recording artists, critics, and performers. The faculty in the growing creative writing program have received prestigious awards for their work.

With an abundance of food, music, festivals, art, the French Quarter, professional sports, a multicultural lifestyle, and opportunities for internships and cooperative education placements, New Orleans is the extended campus for Xavier students.

INFORMATION ON THE 150 GREAT COLLEGES ORGANIZED BY

GEOGRAPHICAL REGION

NEW ENGLAND

CONNECTICUT
Quinnipiac College
Sacred Heart University

MAINE
University of Maine
at Farmington

MASSACHUSETTS
Assumption College
Emmanuel College
Simmons College

NEW HAMPSHIRE
Keene State College
Saint Anselm College

RHODE ISLAND
Bryant College
Roger Williams University
Salve Regina University

VERMONT
Norwich University
Saint Michael's College
University of Vermont

MID-ATLANTIC

MARYLAND
McDaniel College
Mount Saint Mary's College
Washington College

NEW JERSEY
Rider University

NEW YORK
Alfred University
Canisius College

Elmira College
Hartwick College
Hobart and William Smith
Colleges
Iona College
LeMoyne College
Manhattan College
Marymount Manhattan
College
Mount Saint Mary College
Niagara University
Saint John Fisher College
Siena College
Wagner College

PENNSYLVANIA
Albright College
Bloomsburg University
DeSales University
Elizabethtown College
Geneva College
Juniata College
King's College
LaSalle University
Lebanon Valley College
Lycoming College
Marywood University
Mercyhurst College
Millersville University
Moravian College
Saint Vincent College
Shippensburg University
Susquehanna University
University of Pittsburgh
at Johnstown
University of Scranton
Washington & Jefferson
College
Westminster College

SOUTHEAST

FLORIDA
Stetson University
University of Tampa

GEORGIA
Berry College
Spelman College

NORTH CAROLINA
Elon University
Guilford College
High Point University
Lenoir-Rhyne College
Meredith College

SOUTH CAROLINA
The Citadel
Claflin University
Presbyterian College
Winthrop University

VIRGINIA
Bridgewater College
Eastern Mennonite University
Emory and Henry College
Hampden-Sydney College
Hampton University
Longwood College
Lynchburg College
Randolph-Macon College
Roanoke College
Virginia Military Institute

MIDWEST

ILLINOIS
Bradley University
Lake Forest College
Millikin University

STATE LOCATION

APPLICATIONS INVITED FROM HOME-SCHOOLED STUDENTS

Carson-Newman College, TN

College of Saint Benedict and Saint John's University, MN

College of Wooster, OH

Georgetown College, KY

Juniata College, PA

Lenoir-Rhyne College, NC

Loras College, IA

Lynchburg College, VA

Muskingum College, OH

Niagara University, NY

North Central College, IL

Ohio Northern University, OH

Oklahoma Baptist University, OK

Otterbein College, OH

Pacific University, OR

Saint Michael's College, VT

Salve Regina University, RI

South Dakota State University, SD

University of Vermont, VT

Washington College, MD

Winthrop University, SC

Xavier University, OH

SIZE OF UNDERGRADUATE POPULATION
(LISTED IN ALPHABETICAL ORDER)

901–1500 STUDENTS

Alma College, MI

Asbury College, KY

Birmingham—Southern University, AL

Blufton College, OH

Bridgewater College, VA

California Baptist University, CA

Carroll College, MT

Claflin University, SC

Coe College, IA

College of Mount St. Joseph, OH

Cornell College, IA

De Sales University, PA

Drury College, MO

Dordt College, IA

Eastern Mennonite University, VA

Elmira College, NY

Emmanuel College, MA

Emory & Henry College, VA

Franklin College, IN

Georgetown College, KY

Grace College, IN

Guilford College, NC

Hampden-Sydney College, VA

Hanover College, IN

Hartwick College, NY

Hastings College, NE

Hiram College, OH

Juniata College, PA

Lake Forest College, IL

Lenoir-Rhyne College, NC

Lycoming College, PA

Manchester College, IN

Marietta College, OH

Monmouth College, IL

Moravian College, PA

Northwestern College, IA

Norwich University, VT

Pacific University, OR

Presbyterian College, SC

Randolph-Macon College, VA

Saint Mary's University of Minnesota, MN

Saint Vincent College, PA

Simmons College, MA

Simpson College, IA

Spring Hill College, AL

Texas Lutheran University, TX

Virginia Military Institute, VA

Washington College, MD

Washington & Jefferson College, PA

Westminster College, PA

Whittier College, CA

William Jewell College, MO

1,501–3,000 STUDENTS

Albright College, PA

Alfred University, NY

Assumption College, MA

Augustana College, SD

Berry College, GA

Bethel College, MN

Biola University, CA

Bryant College, RI

California Lutheran University, CA

Carroll College, WI

Carson-Newman College, TN

Carthage College, WI

Central College, IA

The Citadel, SC
College of Saint Benedict & St. John's University, MN
College of Wooster, OH
Elizabethtown College, PA
Geneva College, PA
Hamline University, MN
High Point University, NC
Hobart and William Smith Colleges, NY
Iona College, NY
King's College, PA
Lebanon Valley College, PA
LeMoyne College, NY
Linfield College, OR
Loras College, IA
Lynchburg College, VA
Manhattan College, NY
Marymount Manhattan College, NY
Marywood University, PA
McDaniel College, MD
Meredith College, NC
Millikin University, IL
Mount Saint Mary College, NY
Mount Saint Mary's College, MD
Mount Union College, OH
Muskingum College, OH
Nebraska Wesleyan University, NE
Niagara University, NY
North Central College, IL
Ohio Northern University, OH

Oklahoma Baptist University, OK
Otterbein College, OH
Rider College, NJ
Roanoke College, VA
Roger Williams University, RI
Saint Anselm College, NH
Saint John Fisher College, NY
Saint Mary's College, IN
Saint Mary's College of California, CA
Saint Mary's University, TX
Saint Michael's College, VT
Saint Norbert College, WI
Salve Regina University, RI
Samford University, AL
Siena College, NY
Spelman College, GA
Stetson University, FL
Susquehanna University, PA
University of Indianapolis, IN
University of Maine at Farmington, ME
University of Minnesota at Morris, MN
University of Redlands, CA
Wagner College, NY
Wartburg College, IA
Whitworth College, WA
Wittenberg University, OH

3,001–6,000 STUDENTS
Bradley University, IL
Calvin College, MI

Canisius College, NY
Creighton University, NE
Elon University, NC
Hampton University, VA
High Point University, NC
Hope College, MI
John Carroll University, OH
Keene State College, NH
LaSalle University, PA
Longwood College, VA
Mercyhurst College, PA
Quinnipiac University, CT
Sacred Heart University, CT
Seattle University, WA
University of the Pacific, CA
University of Pittsburgh at Johnstown, PA
University of Scranton, PA
University of Tampa, FL
Winthrop University, SC
Xavier University, OH
Xavier University of Louisiana, LA

6,001–7,500 STUDENTS
Bloomsburg University, PA
Marquette University, WI
Millersville University, PA
Shippensburg University, PA
South Dakota State University, SD
Texas Christian University, TX
University of Vermont, VT
Winona State University, MN

LEVEL OF ADMISSION DIFFICULTY

LESS COMPETITIVE

These colleges and universities admit a very large percentage of students with below 1,000 on the SAT I and below 21 on the ACT. The grade-point averages of most students is a C or a 2.0–2.4. Also, these colleges usually admit more than 85 percent of their applicants.

California Lutheran University, CA

High Point University, NC

Norwich University, VT

University of Pittsburgh at Johnstown, PA

COMPETITIVE

These colleges and universities have a majority of students who score about 1,000 on the SAT I and between 21 and 23 on the ACT. The grade-point averages of many of the students are either a C, C+, or B−, or numerically, from a 2.0–2.9. These schools usually admit 75 percent to 85 percent of their applicants.

Albright College, PA
Alfred University, NY
Asbury College, KY
Assumption College, MA
Berry College, GA
Birmingham—Southern University, AL
Bloomsburg State University, PA
Blufton College, OH
Bridgewater College, VA
California Baptist University, CA
Canisius College, NY
Carroll College, MT
Carroll College, WI
Carson-Newman College, TN
Carthage College, WI
Central College, IA
The Citadel, SC
Claflin University, SC
College of Mount St. Joseph, OH
DeSales College, PA
Dordt College, IA

Emmanuel College, MA
Emory and Henry College, VA
Franklin College, IN
Geneva College, PA
Grace College, IN
Guilford College, NC
Hamline University, MN
Hampden-Sydney College, VA
Hampton College, VA
Hartwick College, NY
Hastings College, NE
Hope College, MI
Iona College, NY
Keene State College, NH
King's College, PA
LaSalle University, PA
LeMoyne College, NY
Lenoir–Rhyne College, NC
Longwood College, VA
Loras College, IA
Lycoming College, PA
Lynchburg College, VA
Manchester College, IN
Marietta College, OH
Marquette University, WI

Marywood University, PA
Mercyhurst College, PA
Meredith College, NC
Millikin University, IL
Monmouth College, IL
Mount Saint Mary's College, MD
Mount Saint Mary College, NY
Mount Union College, OH
Muskingum College, OH
Niagara University, NY
North Central College, IL
Northwestern College, IA
Otterbein College, OH
Pacific University, OR
Quinnipiac College, CT
Randolph-Macon College, VA
Rider College, NJ
Roger Williams University, RI
Saint Anselm College, NH
Saint John Fisher College, NY
Saint Mary's College of California, CA
Saint Mary's University, MN
Saint Mary's University, TX

Saint Norbert College, WI
Saint Vincent College, PA
Salve Regina, RI
Shippensburg University, PA
Simpson College, IA
South Dakota State University, SD
Spelman College, GA
Spring Hill College, AL

Texas Christian University, TX
Texas Lutheran University, TX
University of Indianapolis, IN
University of Maine at Farmington, ME
University of Scranton, PA
University of Tampa, FL
University of Vermont, VT
Virginia Military Institute, VA

Wagner College, NY
Westminster College, PA
Whittier College, CA
William Jewell College, MO
Winona State University, MN
Winthrop University, SC
Xavier University of Louisiana, LA
Xavier University, OH

VERY COMPETITIVE COLLEGES

These colleges and universities admit many students with B grade-point averages (3.0–3.4). Most of the students will have SAT I scores close to 1,050 or better and ACT scores from 24 to 26. These schools usually admit between 50 to 75 percent of their applicants.

Alma College, MI
Augustana College, SD
Bethel College, MN
Biola University, CA
Bradley University, IL
Bryant College, RI
Calvin College, MI
Coe College, IA
College of Saint Benedict & Saint John's University, MN
College of Wooster, OH
Cornell College, IA
Creighton University, NE
Drury College, MO
Eastern Mennonite University, VA
Elizabethtown College, PA
Elmira College, NY
Elon University, NC
Georgetown College, KY
Hanover College, IN

Hiram College, OH
Hobart and William Smith Colleges, NY
Juniata College, PA
John Carroll University, OH
Lake Forest College, IL
Lebanon Valley College, PA
Linfield College, OR
Manhattan College, NY
Marymount Manhattan College, NY
McDaniel College, MD
Millersville University, PA
Moravian College, PA
Nebraska Wesleyan University, NE
Ohio Northern University, OH
Oklahoma Baptist University, OK
Presbyterian College, SC

Roanoke College, VA
Sacred Heart University, CT
Saint Mary's College, IN
Saint Michael's College, VT
Samford University, AL
Seattle University, WA
Siena College, NY
Simmons College, MA
Stetson University, FL
Susquehanna University, PA
University of Minnesota at Morris, MN
University of the Pacific, CA
University of Redlands, CA
Wartburg College, IA
Washington College, MD
Washington & Jefferson College, PA
Whitworth College, WA
Wittenberg University, OH

ACCOMMODATIONS FOR LEARNING DISABLED STUDENTS

All colleges must comply with the mandates of section 504 of the Rehabilitation Act of 1973 and provide "reasonable" services and accommodations to students with learning disabilities when recent professional documentations of disabilities are presented and accommodations are requested by students. These services and accommodations cannot place the institution under financial or administrative burdens or alter the fundamental nature of the academic programs. Typical accommodations may include the following: the recording of classes, extending test time, a quiet room for test-taking, note takers, peer tutors, and the use of calculators and dictionaries during examinations.

Beyond this basic level of reasonable services and accommodations, some institutions provide either of two greater levels of services and accommodations. The next level is "comprehensive" services and accommodations, which include the basic level of services and accommodations and also include the following: learning disability specialists, professional tutors, priority registration, and, sometimes, a summer program of a few weeks' duration. The following institutions described in this guide provide this "comprehensive" level of services and accommodations:

Iona College, NY	Manhattan College, NY	Rider University, NJ
Lenoir-Rhyne College, NC	McDaniel College, MD	University of the Pacific, CA
Manchester College, IN	Norwich University, VT	University of Vermont, VT

The most extensive level of services and accommodations is provided within "structured" programs. These programs would include the "basic" and "comprehensive" services and also offer the following: a learning skills class, which includes instruction in college reading and writing skills, time management, and organizational skills; weekly meetings with the learning disabilities staff for planning and tutoring; a separate study workroom; special software programs; and no cap on the number of hours per week for services. These "structured" programs typically require a separate fee, ranging from $1,000 to $4,000 per year. Some institutions allow students to stay in the program for as long as they need or desire, and others permit students to choose only "basic" services and accommodations, thereby avoiding the additional cost of the "structured" program. The following institutions described in this guide provide "structured" programs:

College of Mount St. Joseph, OH	Mercyhurst College, PA	University of Indianapolis, IN
Loras College, IA	Muskingum College, OH	

ABOUT THE AUTHOR

John Palladino, Ed.D., holds a doctorate in education from Teachers College, Columbia University. He has done independent college admissions counseling for more than 20 years. Dr. Palladino has been a professor and administrator for 17 years at New York City metro-area colleges and universities. He has published articles, designed and provided staff development to schools, and is the creator of the Holistic Education Network for the Association of Supervision and Curriculum Development, the largest professional education association in the world.

Dr. Palladino can be contacted at Pal81@optonline.net.

13529023R00210